Abiud

Azor

Aliud filius Achim

Eliacim

Zorobabel

Achym

Sadoc

Salathiel

Nathan filiᵒ Eleazary

Eleazar

Jechonias

Jacobus

Josias

Luca criſti Joseph

Amon

Maria virgo

Joseph

Maria

THE NEW TESTAMENT OF OUR LORD
AND SAVIOUR JESUS CHRIST

The New Testament

OF OUR LORD AND SAVIOUR JESUS CHRIST

A NEW TRANSLATION

A Chanticleer Edition

published by

SHEED & WARD

NEW YORK · 1946

NIHIL OBSTAT

ARTHUR J. SCANLAN, S.T.D.

CENSOR LIBRORUM

IMPRIMATUR

✝FRANCIS J. SPELLMAN, D.D.

ARCHBISHOP, NEW YORK

New York, February 10, 1944

Fifth Printing of general edition
First Printing of illustrated edition

PRODUCED BY CHANTICLEER PRESS, INC.
MANUFACTURED IN THE UNITED STATES OF AMERICA

PREFACE

THIS translation of the New Testament was undertaken at the request of the Hierarchy of England and Wales, in 1939. In this edition, the old principle of beginning a new line of print with each new verse has been abandoned. The references are, however, given at the beginning of each verse.

The translator's thanks are due, not only to the Hierarchy, who have made it possible for the work to be carried through, but to many others who have taken a friendly interest in it. Above all to his Lordship the Bishop of Lancaster, Father Hugh Pope, O.P., S.T.M., D.S.S., the Revd. T. Bird, D.D., Ph.D., the Very Revd. Mgr. Barton, D.D., L.S.S., Consultor of the Pontifical Biblical Commission, the Revd. W. Brown, D.D., the Revd. J. A. O'Flynn, L.S.S., and Fathers Martindale and Corbishley, of the Society of Jesus; their criticisms, throughout, have been of the utmost value, and have had a greater influence on the present form of the text than they themselves can be induced to realize. Further acknowledgements are due to the Right Revd. H. Cogan, D.D., who contributed to the expenses of re-typing, to the Revd. Ivo Thomas, O.P., who gave an extra revision to the proofs, to Mr. Laurence Eyres, of Ampleforth, who was consulted on various classical points, and to the Sisters of the Assumption, who undertook the addressing of the labels.

In omnibus glorificetur Deus.

R. A. KNOX.

Aldenham Park, Bridgnorth,
Feast of St. Jerome, 1943.

NOTES CONCERNING THIS EDITION

This edition of Monsignor Knox's translation of the New Testament has been designed to bring to the reader an especially fine volume. The color illustrations were selected from museums and art galleries in the United States and England by Dr. Hans Tietze. The book was designed by Robert Haas, who also lettered the bookheadings and designed the end paper, binding, and bookjacket.

The chapter headings, slightly reduced, were taken from woodcuts used as chapter headings in the *Biblia Vulgar Historiata*, known by the name of its translator as the "Malermi" Bible. This is the earliest Italian translation of the Bible, printed in Venice in 1493 by Guilelmus Anima Mia. A copy is included in the Spencer Collection of the New York Public Library.

The initials are from the *Enneades ab orbe condito*, by Sabellicus, published in Venice in 1498 by Bernardinus Venetus de Vitalibus and Matthaeus Venetus. A copy of this book also is in the New York Public Library. The design of the endpaper is composed of a number of woodcuts representing the genealogy of Our Lord Jesus Christ, by Michael Pleydenwurff, from the "Nuremberg Chronicle," the first edition of which was printed in 1493 by Anton Koberger.

This book is set in 10 point Linotype Janson, the marginal notes in 6 point Old Style Italics. The following organizations have been engaged in its production: composition and plates, The William Byrd Press, Inc., Richmond, Virginia; text, The Ferris Printing Company, New York, N. Y.; color plates, Davis Delaney, Inc., New York, N. Y.; book jacket, The Ram Press, New York, N. Y.; binding, Charles H. Bohn and Company, Inc., New York, N. Y.

CONTENTS

ILLUSTRATIONS

THE NEW TESTAMENT OF OUR LORD
AND SAVIOUR JESUS CHRIST

THE HOLY GOSPEL OF JESUS CHRIST ACCORDING TO MATTHEW

Chapter One

A RECORD OF THE ANcestry from which Jesus Christ, the son of David, son of Abraham, was born. 2 Abraham was the father of Isaac, Isaac of Jacob, Jacob of Judas and his brethren; 3 Judas of Phares and Zara, by Thamar; Phares of Esron, Esron of Aram, 4 Aram of Aminadab, Aminadab of Naasson, Naasson of Salmon; 5 Salmon of Booz, by Rahab; Booz of Obed, by Ruth; Obed of Jesse; 6 and Jesse was the father of king David. And king David was the father of Solomon, by her that had been the wife of Urias. 7 Solomon was the father of Roboam, Roboam of Abia, Abia of Asa, 8 Asa of Josaphat, Josaphat of Joram, Joram of Ozias, 9 Ozias of Joatham, Joatham of Achaz, Achaz of Ezechias, 10 Ezechias of Manasses, Manasses of Amon, Amon of Josias; 11 and Josias was the father of Jechonias and his brethren, at the time of the removal to Babylon. 12 And after the removal to Babylon, Jechonias was the father of Salathiel, Salathiel of Zorobabel, 13 Zorobabel of Abiud, Abiud of Eliacim, Eliacim of Azor, 14 Azor of Sadoc, Sadoc of Achim, Achim of Eliud, 15 Eliud of Eleazar, Eleazar of Mathan, Mathan of Jacob, 16 and

v. 16. If this genealogy is compared with that given by St. Luke, iii. 23 and following, it is clear that one at least of the two Evangelists must have reckoned descent by adoption as sufficient to make our Lord the legal inheritor of Abraham's blessing and of David's Kingdom. It is therefore not surprising that both have traced his ancestry through his foster-father. It is a common opinion, derived from the Fathers, that St. Joseph and the Blessed Virgin were closely related.

I

Jacob was the father of Joseph, the husband of Mary; it was of her that Jesus was born, who is called Christ. 17 Thus there are fourteen generation in all from Abraham to David, fourteen from David to the captivity in Babylon, and fourteen from the captivity in Babylon to Christ.

18 And this was the manner of Christ's birth. His mother Mary was espoused to Joseph, but they had not yet come together, when she was found to be with child, by the power of the Holy Ghost. 19 Whereupon her husband Joseph (for he was a right-minded man, and would not have her put to open shame), was for sending her away in secret. 20 But hardly had this thought come to his mind, when an angel of the Lord appeared to him in a dream, and said, Joseph, son of David, do not be afraid to take thy wife Mary to thyself, for it is by the power of the Holy Ghost that she has conceived this child; 21 and she will bear a son, whom thou shalt call Jesus, for he is to save his people from their sins. 22 All this was so ordained to fulfill the word which the Lord spoke by his prophet: 23 Behold, the virgin shall be with child, and shall bear a son, and they shall call him Emmanuel, (which means God with us). 24 And Joseph awoke from sleep, and did as the angel of the Lord had bidden him, taking his wife to himself; 25 and he had not known her when she bore a son, her first-born, to whom he gave the name Jesus.

v. 23. Isaias vii. 14. 'The virgin' is a literal translation of the Hebrew; 'a virgin' would equally express the sense of the original prophecy.

v. 25. The text here is more literally rendered 'he knew her not till she bore a son'; but the Hebrew word represented by 'till' does not imply that the event which might have been expected did take place afterwards. (Cf. Genesis viii. 7, Psalm cix. 2, Daniel vi. 24, I Machabees v. 54.) So that this phrase does not impugn the perpetual virginity of our Lady. Nor is any such inference to be drawn when our Lord is called her 'first-born' Son, which refers to his position as redeemable under the old law (Luke ii. 23).

Chapter Two

JESUS WAS BORN AT Bethlehem, in Juda, in the days of king Herod. And thereupon certain wise men came out of the east to Jerusalem, 2 who asked, Where is he that has been born, the king of the Jews? We have seen his star out in the east, and we have come to worship him. 3 King Herod was troubled when he

2

heard it, and all Jerusalem with him; 4 so that he assembled all the chief priests and learned men among the people, and enquired of them where it was that Christ would be born. 5 And they told him, At Bethlehem in Juda; so it has been written by the prophet: 6 And thou, Bethlehem, of the land of Juda, art far from the least among the princes of Juda, for out of thee will arise a leader who is to be the shepherd of my people Israel. 7 Then, summoning the wise men in secret, Herod questioned them closely upon the time of the star's appearing. 8 And he sent them on their way to Bethlehem, saying to them, Go and enquire carefully for the child, and when you have found him, bring me back word, so that I too may come and worship him. 9 They obeyed the king and went on their journey; and all at once the star which they had seen in the east was there going before them, till at last it stood still over the place where the child was. 10 They, when they saw the star, were glad beyond measure; 11 and so, going into the dwelling, they found the child there, with his mother Mary, and fell down to worship him; and, opening their store of treasures, they offered him gifts, of gold and frankincense and myrrh. 12 Afterwards, because they had received a warning in a dream forbidding them to go back to Herod, they returned to their own country by a different way.

13 As soon as they had gone, an angel of the Lord appeared to Joseph in a dream, and said, Rise up, take with thee the child and his mother, and flee to Egypt; there remain, until I give thee word. For Herod will soon be making search for the child, to destroy him. 14 He rose up therefore, while it was still night, and took the child and his mother with him, and withdrew into Egypt, where he remained until the death of Herod, 15 in fulfilment of the word which the Lord spoke by his prophet, I called my son out of Egypt. 16 Meanwhile, when he found that the wise men had played him false, Herod was angry beyond measure; he sent and made away with all the male children in Bethlehem and in all its neighbourhood, of two years old and less, reckoning the time by the careful enquiry which he had made of the wise men. 17 It was then that the word spoken by the prophet Jeremy was fulfilled: 18 A voice was heard in Rama, lamentation and great mourning; it was Rachel weeping for her children, and she would not be comforted, because none is left. 19 But as soon as Herod was dead, an angel of the Lord appeared to Joseph in Egypt in a dream, 20 and said: Rise up, take with thee the child and his mother, and return to the land of Israel; for those who sought the child's life are dead.

v. 6. Micheas v. 2.

v. 15. Osee xi. 1.

v. 18. Jeremias xxxi. 15.

v. 23. No such prophecy has survived to us. But an obscure village is often regarded by its more important neighbours as typical of an unfashionable or provincial outlook; cf. John i. 46. The proph-

3

ecy (Is. liii. 3) that
our Lord would be
despised by men was
fulfilled when his con-
temporaries spoke of
him scornfully as 'a
prophet from Naza-
reth' (like our 'wise
men of Gotham').
Some think the word
should be, not Naza-
rene, but Nazirite;
cf. Gen. xlix. 26.

21 So he arose, and took the child and his mother with him, and came into the land of Israel. 22 But, when he heard that Archelaus was king in Judaea in the place of his father Herod, he was afraid to return there; and so, receiving a warning in a dream, he withdrew into the region of Galilee; 23 where he came to live in a town called Nazareth, in fulfilment of what was said by the prophets, He shall be called a Nazarene.

Chapter Three

vv. 1-17. Mark i. 1,
Luke iii. 1.
v. 3. Is. xl. 3.

IN THOSE DAYS JOHN the Baptist appeared, preaching in the wilderness of Judaea; 2 Repent, he said, the kingdom of heaven is at hand. 3 It was of him that the prophet Isaias spoke, when he said, There is a voice of one crying in the wilderness, Prepare the way of the Lord, straighten out his paths. 4 And he, John, wore a garment of camel's hair, and a leather girdle about his loins, and locusts and wild honey were his food. 5 Thereupon Jerusalem and all Judaea, and all those who dwelt round Jordan, went out to see him, 6 and he baptized them in the Jordan, while they confessed their sins. 7 Many of the Pharisees and of the Sadducees came to his baptizing; and when he saw these, he asked them, Who was it that taught you, brood of vipers, to flee from the vengeance that draws near? 8 Come, then, yield the acceptable fruit of repentance; 9 do not presume to say in your hearts, We have Abraham for our father; I tell you, God has power to raise up children to Abraham out of these very stones. 10 Already the axe has been put to the root of the trees, so that every tree which does not shew good fruit will be hewn down and cast into the fire. 11 As for me, I am baptizing you with water, for your repentance; but one is to come after me who is mightier than I, so that I am not worthy even to carry his shoes for him; he will baptize you with the Holy

v. 11. The baptism of
John did not confer
sanctifying grace; cf.
Acts xix. 1-6.

Ghost, and with fire. 12 He holds his winnowing-fan ready, to sweep his threshing-floor clean; he will gather the wheat into his barn, but the chaff he will consume with fire that can never be quenched.

13 Then Jesus came from Galilee and stood before John at the Jordan, to be baptized by him. 14 John would have restrained him; It is I, he said, that ought to be baptized by thee, and dost thou come to me instead? 15 But Jesus answered, Let it be so for the present; it is well that we should thus fulfil all due observance. Then John gave way to him. 16 So Jesus was baptized, and as he came straight up out of the water, suddenly heaven was opened, and he saw the Spirit of God coming down like a dove and resting upon him. 17 And with that, a voice came from heaven, which said, This is my beloved Son, in whom I am well pleased.

Chapter Four

AND NOW JESUS WAS led by the Spirit away into the wilderness, to be tempted there by the devil. 2 Forty days and forty nights he spent fasting, and at the end of them was hungry. 3 Then the tempter approached, and said to him, If thou art the Son of God, bid these stones turn into loaves of bread. 4 He answered, It is written, Man cannot live by bread only; there is life for him in all the words which proceed from the mouth of God. 5 Next, the devil took him into the holy city, and there set him down on the pinnacle of the temple, 6 saying to him, If thou art the Son of God, cast thyself down to earth; for it is written, He has given charge to his angels concerning thee, and they will hold thee up with their hands, lest thou shouldst chance to trip on a stone. 7 Jesus said to him, But it is further written, Thou shalt not put the Lord thy God to the proof. 8 Once more, the devil

vv. 1-11. Luke iv. 1.

v. 4. Deuteronomy viii. 3.

v. 6. Ps. xc. 11, 12.
v. 7. Deut. vi. 16. If our Lord had consented to cast himself down, he would have been testing God's loving care of him ('tempting Providence', as we say) by putting himself deliberately in danger.

took him to the top of an exceedingly high mountain, from which he shewed him all the kingdoms of the world and the glory of them, 9 and said, I will give thee all these if thou wilt fall down *v. 10. Deut. vi. 13.* and worship me. 10 Then Jesus said to him, Away with thee, Satan; it is written, Thou shalt worship the Lord thy God, and serve none but him. 11 Then the devil left him alone; and thereupon angels came and ministered to him.

12 After this, hearing of John's imprisonment, he withdrew into Galilee. 13 And now, forsaking the city of Nazareth, he came and settled down in Capharnaum, which is by the sea shore, in the country of Zabulon and Nephthalim, 14 in fulfilment of what was *v. 15. Is. ix. 1, 2.* said by the prophet Isaias: 15 The land of Zabulon and Nephthalim, on the sea road, beyond Jordan, the Galilee of the Gentiles! 16 The people that abode in darkness has seen a great light; for men abiding in a land where death overshadowed them, light has *vv. 17-22. Mark i. 14.* dawned. 17 From that time onwards, Jesus began to preach; Repent, he said, the kingdom of heaven is at hand.

18 And as he walked by the sea of Galilee, Jesus saw two brethren, Simon, who is called Peter, and his brother Andrew, casting a net into the sea, (for they were fishermen); 19 and he said to them, Come and follow me; I will make you into fishers of men. 20 And they dropped their nets immediately, and followed him. 21 Then he went further on, and saw two others that were brethren, James the son of Zebedee and his brother John; they were in the boat with their father Zebedee, repairing their nets, and he called them to him; 22 whereupon they dropped the nets and left their father immediately, and followed him.

23 So Jesus went about the whole of Galilee, teaching in their synagogues, preaching the gospel of the kingdom, and curing every kind of disease and infirmity among the people; 24 so that his fame spread throughout the whole of Syria, and they brought to him all those who were in affliction, distressed with pain and sickness of every sort, the possessed, the lunatics, the palsied; and he healed them. 25 And a great multitude followed him, from Galilee and Decapolis, Jerusalem and Judaea, and the country beyond Jordan.

Chapter Five

JESUS, WHEN HE SAW how great was their number, went up on to the mountain side; there he sat down, and his disciples came about him. 2 And he began speaking to them; this was the teaching he gave. 3 Blessed are the poor in spirit; the kingdom of heaven is theirs. 4 Blessed are the patient; they shall inherit the land. 5 Blessed are those who mourn; they shall be comforted. 6 Blessed are those who hunger and thirst for holiness; they shall have their fill. 7 Blessed are the merciful; they shall obtain mercy. 8 Blessed are the clean of heart; they shall see God. 9 Blessed are the peace-makers; they shall be counted the children of God. 10 Blessed are those who suffer persecution in the cause of right; the kingdom of heaven is theirs. 11 Blessed are you, when men revile you, and persecute you, and speak all manner of evil against you falsely, because of me. 12 Be glad and light-hearted, for a rich reward awaits you in heaven; so it was they persecuted the prophets who went before you. 13 You are the salt of the earth; if salt loses its taste, what is there left to give taste to it? There is no more to be done with it, but throw it out of doors for men to tread it under foot. 14 You are the light of the world; a city cannot be hidden if it is built on a mountain top. 15 A lamp is not lighted to be put away under a bushel measure; it is put on the lamp-stand, to give light to all the people of the house; 16 and your light must shine so brightly before men that they can see your good works, and glorify your Father who is in heaven.

17 Do not think that I have come to set aside the law and the prophets; I have not come to set them aside, but to bring them to perfection. 18 Believe me, heaven and earth must disappear sooner than that one jot, one flourish should disappear from the law; it must all be accomplished. 19 Whoever, then, sets aside one of these commandments, though it were the least, and teaches men to do the like, will be of least account in the kingdom of heaven; but the man who keeps them and teaches others to keep them will be accounted in the kingdom of heaven as the greatest.

vv. 3 and following. Many of the sayings recorded in these three chapters are also to be found in St. Luke, especially in chh. vi. and xii.

20 And I tell you, that if your justice does not give fuller measure than the justice of the scribes and Pharisees, you shall not enter into the kingdom of heaven. 21 You have heard that it was said to the men of old, Thou shalt do no murder; if a man commits murder he must answer for it before the court of justice. 22 But I tell you that any man who is angry with his brother must answer for it before the court of justice, and any man who says Raca to his brother must answer for it before the Council; and any man who says to his brother, Thou fool, must answer for it in hell fire. 23 If thou art bringing thy gift, then, before the altar, and rememberest there that thy brother has some ground of complaint against thee, 24 leave thy gift lying there before the altar, and go home; be reconciled with thy brother first, and then come back to offer thy gift. 25 If any man has a claim against thee, come to terms there and then, while thou art walking in the road with him; or else it may be that the claimant will hand thee over to the judge, and the judge to the officer, and so thou wilt be cast into prison. 26 Believe me, thou shalt not be set at liberty until thou hast paid the last farthing.

27 You have heard that it was said, Thou shalt not commit adultery. 28 But I tell you that he who casts his eyes on a woman so as to lust after her has already committed adultery with her in his heart. 29 If thy right eye is the occasion of thy falling into sin, pluck it out and cast it away from thee; better to lose one part of thy body than to have the whole cast into hell. 30 And if thy right hand is an occasion of falling, cut it off and cast it away from thee; better to lose one of thy limbs than to have thy whole body cast into hell. 31 It was said, too, Whoever will put away his wife must first give her a writ of separation. 32 But I tell you that the man who puts away his wife (setting aside the matter of unfaithfulness) makes an adulteress of her, and whoever marries her after she has been put away, commits adultery.

33 Again, you have heard that it was said to the men of old, Thou shalt not perjure thyself; thou shalt perform what thou hast sworn in the sight of the Lord. 34 But I tell you that you should not bind yourselves by any oath at all; not by heaven, for heaven is God's throne; 35 nor by earth, for earth is the footstool under his feet; nor by Jerusalem, for it is the city of the great king. 36 And thou shalt not swear by thy own head, for thou hast no power to turn a single hair of it white or black. 37 Let your word be Yes for Yes, and No for No; whatever goes beyond this, comes of evil. 38 You have heard that it was said, An eye for an eye and a tooth for a

v. 21. Exodus xx. 13.

vv. 31, 32. Deut. xxiv. 1. By the law of Moses, a husband might not turn his wife out of doors without giving her a certificate of freedom, which shewed that he had no further claim on her. Even so, our Lord teaches, the husband's behaviour is selfish, since the dismissed wife would be tempted to remarry, and thus become, in God's sight, an adulteress. The Greek word here translated 'setting aside' has commonly been taken as meaning 'unless she is unfaithful', but it can also be interpreted as meaning, 'whether she is unfaithful or not'. See further Matt. xix. 7-9, and note.

v. 33. Our Lord here condemns those Pharisaical evasions, which might make it lawful to perjure oneself as long as the oath was not taken directly in the name of God. Cf. Matt. xxiii. 16-22.

v. 38. Ex. xxi. 24, Leviticus xxiv. 20, Deut. xix. 21.

8

tooth. 39 But I tell you that you should not offer resistance to injury; if a man strikes thee on thy right cheek, turn the other cheek also towards him; 40 if he is ready to go to law with thee over thy coat, let him have it and thy cloak with it, 41 if he compels thee to attend him on a mile's journey, go two miles with him of thy own accord. 42 Give to him who asks, and if a man would borrow from thee, do not turn away.

43 You have heard that it was said, Thou shalt love thy neighbour and hate thy enemy. 44 But I tell you, Love your enemies, do good to those who hate you, pray for those who persecute and insult you, 45 that so you may be true sons of your Father in heaven, who makes his sun rise on the evil and equally on the good, his rain fall on the just and equally on the unjust. 46 If you love those who love you, what title have you to a reward? Will not the publicans do as much? 47 If you greet none but your brethren, what are you doing more than others? Will not the very heathen do as much? 48 But you are to be perfect, as your heavenly Father is perfect.

v. 43. Lev. xix. 18; where, however, nothing is said about hating enemies. This must have been a gloss put upon the text of the commandment.

Chapter Six

Be sure you do not perform your acts of piety before men, for them to watch; if you do that, you have no title to a reward from your Father who is in heaven. 2 Thus, when thou givest alms, do not sound a trumpet before thee, as the hypocrites do in synagogues and in streets, to win the esteem of men. Believe me, they have their reward already. 3 But when thou givest alms, thou shalt not so much as let thy left hand know what thy right hand is doing, 4 so secret is thy almsgiving to be; and then thy Father, who sees what is done in secret, will reward thee. 5 And when you pray, you are not to be like hypocrites, who love to stand praying in synagogues or at street corners, to be a mark for men's eyes; believe me, they have their reward already. 6 But when thou art praying, go into thy inner room and shut the door upon thyself, and so pray to thy Father in secret; and then thy Father, who sees what is done in secret, will reward thee.

v. 7. The very rare verb which our Lord uses here probably means 'to stammer', to 'hesitate'. The heathens used to address their gods by a series of titles, with the superstitious idea that the prayer would not be heard unless the right title was hit upon.

7 Moreover, when you are at prayer, do not use many phrases, like the heathens, who think to make themselves heard by their eloquence. 8 You are not to be like them; your heavenly Father knows well what your needs are before you ask him. 9 This, then, is to be your prayer, Our Father, who art in heaven, hallowed be thy name; 10 thy kingdom come; thy will be done, on earth as it is in heaven; 11 give us this day our daily bread; 12 and for-

v. 11. 'Daily'; the Latin here (but not in Luke xi. 2) coins the word supersubstantialis, which has sometimes been understood as a direct reference to the Holy Eucharist.

give us our trespasses, as we forgive them that trespass against us; 13 and lead us not into temptation, but deliver us from evil. Amen. 14 Your heavenly Father will forgive you your transgressions, if you forgive your fellow men theirs; 15 if you do not forgive them, your heavenly Father will not forgive your transgressions either.

16 Again, when you fast, do not shew it by gloomy looks, as the hypocrites do. They make their faces unsightly, so that men can see they are fasting; believe me, they have their reward already. 17 But do thou, at thy times of fasting, anoint thy head and wash thy face, 18 so that thy fast may not be known to men, but to thy Father who dwells in secret; and then thy Father, who sees what is done in secret, will reward thee.

19 Do not lay up treasure for yourselves on earth, where there is moth and rust to consume it, where there are thieves to break in and steal it; 20 lay up treasure for yourselves in heaven, where there is no moth or rust to consume it, no thieves to break in and steal. 21 Where your treasure-house is, there your heart is too. 22 The eye is the light of the whole body, so that if thy eye is clear, the whole of thy body will be lit up; 23 whereas if thy eye is diseased, the whole of thy body will be in darkness. And if the light which thou hast in thee is itself darkness, what of thy darkness? How deep will that be! 24 A man cannot be the slave of two masters at once; either he will hate the one and love the other, or he will devote himself to the one and despise the other. You must serve God or money; you cannot serve both.

25 I say to you, then, do not fret over your life, how to support it with food and drink; over your body, how to keep it clothed. Is not life itself a greater gift than food, the body than clothing?

v. 27. 'Height'; the Greek word here used can also mean 'length of life'; and some have thought that 'cubit' is used, by a metaphor, for a short space of time.

26 See how the birds of the air never sow, or reap, or gather grain into barns, and yet your heavenly Father feeds them; have you not an excellence beyond theirs? 27 Can any one of you, for all his

anxiety, add a cubit's growth to his height? 28 And why should you be anxious over clothing? See how the wild lilies grow; they do not toil or spin; 29 and yet I tell you that even Solomon in all his glory was not arrayed like one of these. 30 If God, then, so clothes the grasses of the field, which to-day live and will feed the oven to-morrow, will he not be much more ready to clothe you, men of little faith? 31 Do not fret, then, asking, What are we to eat? or What are we to drink? or How shall we find clothing? It is for the heathen to busy themselves over such things; 32 you have a Father in heaven who knows that you need them all. 33 Make it your first care to find the kingdom of God, and his approval, and all these things shall be yours without the asking. 34 Do not fret, then, over to-morrow; leave to-morrow to fret over its own needs; for to-day, to-day's troubles are enough.

Chapter Seven

Do NOT JUDGE OTHERS, or you yourselves will be judged. 2 As you have judged, so you will be judged, by the same rule; award shall be made you as you have made award, in the same measure. 3 How is it that thou canst see the speck of dust which is in thy brother's eye, and art not aware of the beam which is in thy own? 4 By what right wilt thou say to thy brother, Wait, let me rid thy eye of that speck, when there is a beam all the while in thy own? 5 Thou hypocrite, take the beam out of thy own eye first, and so thou shalt have clear sight to rid thy brother's of the speck.

6 You must not give that which is holy to dogs. Do not cast your pearls before swine, or the swine may trample them under foot, and then turn on you and tear you to pieces.

7 Ask, and the gift will come; seek, and you shall find; knock and the door shall be opened to you. 8 Everyone that asks, will receive;

11

that seeks, will find; that knocks, will have the door opened to him. 9 If any one of yourselves is asked by his son for bread, will he give him a stone? 10 If he is asked for a fish, will he give him a serpent instead? 11 Why then, if you, evil as you are, know well enough how to give your children what is good for them, is not your Father in heaven much more ready to give wholesome gifts to those who ask him?

12 Do to other men all that you would have them do to you; that is the law and the prophets.

13 Make your way in by the narrow gate. It is a broad gate and a wide road that leads on to perdition, and those who go in that way are many indeed; 14 but how small is the gate, how narrow the road that leads on to life, and how few there are that find it!

15 Be on your guard against false prophets, men who come to you in sheep's clothing, but are ravenous wolves within. 16 You will know them by the fruit they yield. Can grapes be plucked from briers, or figs from thistles? 17 So, indeed, any sound tree will bear good fruit, while any tree that is withered will bear fruit that is worthless; 18 that worthless fruit should come from a sound tree, or good fruit from a withered tree, is impossible. 19 Any tree which does not bear good fruit is cut down, and thrown into the fire. 20 I say therefore, it is by their fruit that you will know them. 21 The kingdom of heaven will not give entrance to every man who calls me Master, Master; only to the man that does the will of my Father who is in heaven. 22 There are many who will say to me, when that day comes, Master, Master, was it not in thy name we prophesied? Was it not in thy name that we performed many miracles? 23 Whereupon I will tell them openly, You were never friends of mine; depart from me, you that traffic in wrong-doing.

24 Whoever, then, hears these commandments of mine and carries them out, is like a wise man who built his house upon rocks; 25 and the rain fell and the floods came and the winds blew and beat upon that house, but it did not fall; it was founded upon rock. 26 But whoever hears these commandments of mine and does not carry them out is like a fool, who built his house upon sands; 27 and the rain fell and the floods came and the winds blew and beat upon that house, and it fell; and great was the fall of it.

28 Afterwards, when Jesus had finished these sayings, the multitudes found themselves amazed at his teaching. 29 For he taught them, not like their scribes and Pharisees, but like one who had authority.

Chapter Eight

A GREAT MULTITUDE followed him when he had come down from the mountain; 2 and now, a leper came and knelt before him, and said, Lord, if it be thy will, thou hast power to make me clean. 3 Jesus held out his hand and touched him, and said, It is my will; be thou made clean. Whereupon his leprosy was immediately cleansed. 4 Then Jesus said, Be sure thou dost not tell any man of it; rather go and shew thyself to the priest, and offer the gift which Moses ordained, to make the truth known to them.

5 As he entered Capharnaum, a centurion came to him, asking for his aid; 6 Lord, he said, I have a servant lying sick at my house, cruelly tormented with the palsy. 7 Jesus said to him, I will come and heal him. 8 But the centurion answered, Lord, I am not worthy to receive thee under my roof; my servant will be healed if thou wilt only speak a word of command. 9 I too know what it is to obey authority; I have soldiers under me, and I say, Go, to one man, and he goes, or, Come, to another, and he comes, or, Do this, to my servant, and he does it. 10 When he heard that, Jesus said to his followers in amazement, Believe me, I have not found faith like this, even in Israel. 11 And this I tell you, that there are many who will come from the east and from the west, and will take their places in the kingdom of God with Abraham and Isaac and Jacob, 12 while that kingdom's own sons are cast into the darkness without, where there will be weeping, and gnashing of teeth. 13 And to the centurion Jesus said, Go then; let it be done to thee as thy faith foretold. And at that hour his servant was healed.

14 And Jesus went into Peter's house, and found his wife's mother lying sick there with a fever. 15 He touched her hand, and the fever left her, so that she rose up and ministered to them. 16 And when evening came, they brought to him many persons who were possessed; and he cast out the evil spirits with his word, and healed all that were sick, 17 in fulfilment of the word spoken by Isaias the prophet, He took our infirmities upon himself, and bore our sicknesses.

vv. 2-4. Mark i. 40, Luke v. 12.

v. 4. Lev. xiv. 2.

vv. 5-13. Luke vii. 1.

vv. 14-17. Mark i. 30, Luke iv. 38.

v. 17. Is. liii. 4.

13

vv. 19-22. Luke ix. 57.

18 And now, seeing how great were the multitudes about him, he gave the word for crossing to the other side. 19 Whereupon one of the scribes came to him, and said, Master, I will follow thee wherever thou art going. 20 But Jesus told him, Foxes have holes, and the birds of the air their resting-places; the Son of Man has nowhere to lay his head. 21 And another of his disciples said to him, Lord, give me leave to go home and bury my father before I come. 22 But to him Jesus said, Do thou follow me, and leave the dead to bury their dead. 23 So he took ship, and his disciples followed him. 24 And suddenly a great storm arose on the sea, so that the waves rose high over the ship; but he lay asleep. 25 And his disciples came and roused him, crying, Lord, save us, we are sinking. 26 But Jesus said to them, Why are you faint-hearted, men of little faith? Then he rose up, and checked the winds, and the sea, and there was deep calm. 27 So that all asked in amazement, What kind of man is this, who is obeyed even by the winds and the sea? 28 So he reached the other shore, in the country of the Gerasenes; and here he was met by two possessed creatures who came out of the rock tombs, so exceedingly fierce that none could pass along that road. 29 And at once they cried aloud, Why dost thou meddle with us, Jesus, Son of God? Hast thou come here to torment us before the appointed time? 30 Some distance away, a great herd of swine was feeding; 31 and the devils asked a favour of him; If thou hast a mind to cast us out, they said, send us into the herd of swine. 32 He said to them, Away with you; and they came out and went into the herd of swine; and with that, all the herd rushed down the cliff into the sea, and perished in its waters. 33 The swineherds fled to the city, and there told all that had happened and the story of those who had been possessed. 34 And thereupon all the townspeople went out to meet Jesus; and when they found him, they entreated him to leave their country.

v. 22. Some think that the father was still alive, and the son wanted to defer his following of Christ until his father's death. Our Lord's answer is perhaps simply meant to imply that true life can only be found in following him.

vv. 23-34. Mark iv. 35, Luke viii. 22. Only St. Matthew mentions the second demoniac, who may have been a woman.

Chapter Nine

S O HE TOOK SHIP ACROSS
the sea, and came to his own city.
2 And now they brought before him a man who was palsied and
bed-ridden; whereupon Jesus, seeing their faith, said to the palsied
man, Son, take courage, thy sins are forgiven. 3 And at this, some
of the scribes said to themselves, He is talking blasphemously.
4 Jesus read their minds, and said, Why do you cherish wicked
thoughts in your hearts? 5 Tell me, which command is more lightly
given, to say to a man, Thy sins are forgiven, or to say, Rise up, and
walk? 6 And now, to convince you that the Son of Man has authority to forgive sins while he is on earth (here he spoke to the
palsied man), Rise up, take thy bed with thee, and go home. 7 And
he rose up, and went back to his house, 8 so that the multitudes
were filled with awe at seeing it, and praised God for giving such
powers to men.

9 As he passed further on his way, Jesus saw a man called Matthew sitting at work in the customs-house, and said to him, Follow
me; and Matthew rose from his place and followed him. 10 And
afterwards, when he was taking a meal in the house, many publicans
and sinners were to be found at table with him and his disciples.
11 The Pharisees saw this, and asked his disciples, How comes it
that your master eats with publicans and sinners? 12 Jesus heard it,
and said, It is not those who are in health that have need of the
physician, it is those who are sick. 13 Go home and find out
what the words mean, It is mercy that wins favour with me, not
sacrifice. I have come to call sinners, not the just.

14 Then John's disciples came to him, and asked, How is it that
thy disciples do not fast, when we and the Pharisees fast so often?
15 To them Jesus said, Can you expect the men of the bridegroom's
company to go mourning, while the bridegroom is still with them?
No, the days will come when the bridegroom is taken away from
them; then they will fast. 16 Nobody uses a piece of new cloth to
patch an old cloak; that would take away from the cloak all its pattern, and make the rent in it worse than before. 17 Nor is new

vv. 1-8. Mark ii. 1.

v. 5. 'Is more lightly
given', in the sense
that one who falsely
claims to cure disease
will (unlike the pre-
tender to spiritual
powers) be exposed
by failure.

vv. 9-13. Mark ii. 13,
Luke v. 27.

v. 13. Osee vi. 6.

vv. 14-17. Mark ii. 18,
Luke v. 33.

v. 16. 'All its pat-
tern', this is proba-
bly the sense of the
Latin; the Greek has,
'the new piece draws
away threads from
the old'.

15

wine put into old wineskins; if that is done, the skins burst, and there is the wine spilt and the skins spoiled. If the wine is new, it is put into fresh wineskins, and so both are kept safe.

vv. 18-26. Mark v. 22, Luke viii. 41. It seems likely that St. Matthew has here combined two separate appeals made by the ruler of the synagogue.

18 While he thus spoke to them, it chanced that one of the rulers came and knelt before him, and said, Lord, my daughter is this moment dead; come now and lay thy hand on her, and she will live. 19 So Jesus rose up and went after him, and so did his disciples. 20 And now a woman who for twelve years had been troubled with an issue of blood, came up behind him and touched the hem of his cloak; 21 she said to herself, If I can even touch the hem of his cloak, I shall be healed. 22 Jesus turned and caught sight of her; and he said, Have no fear, my daughter, thy faith has brought thee healing. And the woman recovered her health from that hour. 23 So Jesus came into the ruler's house, where he found mourners playing the flute, and the multitude, thronging noisily; 24 and he said, Make room there; the child is not dead, she is asleep; and they laughed aloud at him. 25 But when the multitude had been turned away, he went in and took the girl by the hand, and she rose up. 26 And the story of these doings spread abroad through all the country round.

27 As Jesus was passing further on his way, he was followed by two blind men, who cried aloud, Son of David, have pity on us. 28 These blind men came to him when he had gone into his lodging, and Jesus said to them, Have you the faith to believe that I can do this? And they said to him, Yes, Lord. 29 Thereupon, he touched their eyes, and said, Your faith shall not be disappointed. 30 Then their eyes were opened; and Jesus laid a strict charge on them, telling them, Be sure nobody hears of this. 31 But they had no sooner gone out than they talked of him in all the country round. 32 And it chanced that, as they were going, a dumb man was brought to him, possessed with a devil. 33 The devil was cast out, and the dumb man found speech; at which the multitudes were filled with amazement; Nothing like this, they said, was ever seen in Israel. 34 But the Pharisees said, It is the prince of the devils that enables him to cast the devils out.

35 So Jesus went about all their cities and villages, teaching in their synagogues, preaching the gospel of the kingdom, and curing every kind of disease and infirmity. 36 Yet still, when he looked at the multitudes, he was moved with pity for them, seeing them harried and abject, like sheep that have no shepherd. 37 Thereupon he said to his disciples, The harvest is plentiful enough, but the labourers are few; 38 you must ask the Lord to whom the harvest belongs to send labourers out for the harvesting.

Chapter Ten

SO HE CALLED HIS twelve disciples to him, and gave them authority to cast out unclean spirits, and to heal every kind of disease and infirmity. 2 These are the names of the twelve apostles; first, Simon, also called Peter, then his brother Andrew, 3 James the son of Zebedee and his brother John, Philip and Bartholomew, Thomas and Matthew the publican, James the son of Alphaeus, and Thaddaeus, 4 Simon the Cananean, and Judas Iscariot, the traitor.

vv. 1-4. Mark iii. 13, Luke vi. 13.

5 These twelve Jesus sent out; but first gave them their instructions; Do not go, he said, into the walks of the Gentiles, or enter any city of Samaria; 6 go rather to the lost sheep that belong to the house of Israel. 7 And preach as you go, telling them, The kingdom of heaven is at hand. 8 Heal the sick, raise the dead, cleanse the lepers, cast out devils: give as you have received the gift, without payment. 9 Do not provide gold or silver or copper to fill your purses, 10 nor a wallet for the journey, no second coat, no spare shoes or staff; the labourer has a right to his maintenance. 11 Whenever you enter a city or a village, find out who is worthy to be your host, and make your lodging there until you go away. 12 When you enter this house, you are to wish it well; 13 and so, if the house is worthy, your good wishes shall come down upon it; if unworthy, let them come back to you the way they went. 14 And wherever they will not receive you or listen to your words, shake off the dust from your feet as you leave that city or that house; 15 I promise you, it shall go less hard with the land of Sodom and Gomorrha at the day of judgement, than with that city.

vv. 5-42. Luke ix. 1 and x. 3.

16 Remember, I am sending you out to be like sheep among wolves; you must be wary, then, as serpents, and yet innocent as doves. 17 Do not put your trust in men; they will hand you over to courts of judgement, and scourge you in their synagogues; 18 yes, and you will be brought before governors and kings on my account, so that you can bear witness before them, and before the Gentiles. 19 Only, when they hand you over thus, do not consider

17

anxiously what you are to say or how you are to say it; words will be given you when the time comes; 20 it is not you who speak, it is the Spirit of your Father that speaks in you. 21 Brothers will be given up to execution by their brothers, and children by their fathers; children will rise up against their parents and will compass their deaths, 22 and you will be hated by all men because you bear my name; that man will be saved, who endures to the last. 23 Only, if they persecute you in one city, take refuge in another; I promise you, the Son of Man will come before your task with the cities of Israel is ended.

24 A disciple is no better than his master, a servant than his lord; 25 enough that the disciple should fare like his master, the servant like his lord. If they have cried Beelzebub at the master of the house, they will do it much more readily to the men of his household. 26 Do not, then, be afraid of them. What is veiled will all be revealed, what is hidden will all be known; 27 what I have said to you under cover of darkness, you are to utter in the light of day; what has been whispered in your ears, you are to proclaim on the house-tops. 28 And there is no need to fear those who kill the body, but have no means of killing the soul; fear him more, who has the power to ruin body and soul in hell. 29 Are not sparrows sold two for a penny? And yet it is impossible for one of them to fall to the ground without your heavenly Father's will. 30 And as for you, he takes every hair of your head into his reckoning. 31 Do not be afraid, then; you count for more than a host of sparrows. 32 And now, whoever acknowledges me before men, I too will acknowledge him before my Father who is in heaven; 33 and whoever disowns me before men, before my Father in heaven I too will disown him.

34 Do not imagine that I have come to bring peace to the earth; I have come to bring a sword, not peace. 35 I have come to set a man at variance with his father, and the daughter with her mother, and the daughter-in-law with her mother-in-law; 36 a man's enemies will be the people of his own house. 37 He is not worthy of me, that loves father or mother more; he is not worthy of me, that loves son or daughter more; 38 he is not worthy of me, that does not take up his cross and follow me. 39 He who secures his own life will lose it; it is the man who loses his life for my sake that will secure it. 40 He who gives you welcome, gives me welcome too; and he who gives me welcome gives welcome to him that sent me. 41 He who gives a prophet the welcome due to a prophet shall receive the reward given to prophets; and he who gives a just man

v. 39. 'Secures his life', by denying his faith under persecution, or otherwise making terms with the world at the expense of his own conscience.

the welcome due to a just man shall receive the reward given to just men. 42 And if a man gives so much as a draught of cold water to one of the least of these here, because he is a disciple of mine, I promise you, he shall not miss his reward.

Chapter Eleven

WHEN JESUS HAD DONE giving instructions to his twelve disciples, he left the place where he was, to teach and preach in their cities. 2 Now John had heard in his prison of Christ's doings, and he sent two of his disciples to him; 3 Is it thy coming that was foretold, he asked, or are we yet waiting for some other? 4 Jesus answered them, Go and tell John what your own ears and eyes have witnessed; 5 how the blind see, and the lame walk, how the lepers are made clean, and the deaf hear, how the dead are raised to life, and the poor have the gospel preached to them. 6 Blessed is the man who does not lose confidence in me.

7 As they went out, Jesus took occasion to speak of John to the multitudes; What was it, he asked, that you expected to see when you went out into the wilderness? Was it a reed trembling in the wind? 8 No, not that; what was it you went out to see? Was it a man clad in silk? You must look in kings' palaces for men that go clad in silk. 9 What was it, then, that you went out to see? A prophet? Yes, and something more, I tell you, than a prophet. 10 This is the man of whom it was written, Behold, I am sending before thee that angel of mine, who is to prepare thy way for thy coming. 11 Believe me, God has raised up no greater son of woman than John the Baptist; and yet to be least in the kingdom of heaven is to be greater than he. 12 Ever since John the Baptist's time, the kingdom of heaven has opened to force; and the forceful are even now making it their prize; 13 whereas all the prophets and the

vv. 2-19. Luke vii. 18.

v. 5. Is. xxxv. 5.

v. 10. Mal. iii. 1; where, however, our text reads, 'I am sending my messenger (or angel), who is to prepare the way before me'.

v. 11. St. John the Baptist, as the final product of the old Dispensation, is less than the least of those who enjoy the blessings of the new. Like the Patriarchs, he only looked forward to the world's redemption as something that lay in the future (verse 13) by the light of hope (Hebrews xi. 13), and died before its accomplishment (Matthew xiii. 17), instead of being able to press into the Kingdom of heaven like the common sort of Christians (verse 12).

law, before John's time, could only speak of things that were to come. 14 And this I tell you, if you will make room for it in your minds, that he is that Elias whose coming was prophesied. 15 Listen, you that have ears to hear with. 16 As for this generation, to what shall I compare it? It reminds me of those children who call out to their companions as they sit in the market-place, 17 and say, You would not dance when we piped to you, or beat the breast when we wept to you. 18 When John came, he would neither eat nor drink, and they say of him that he is possessed. 19 When the Son of Man came, he ate and drank with them, and of him they say, Here is a glutton; he loves wine; he is a friend of publicans and sinners. It is by her own children that wisdom is vindicated.

20 Thereupon he took occasion to reproach for their impenitence the cities in which he had done most of his miracles: 21 Woe to thee, Corozain, woe to thee, Bethsaida: Tyre and Sidon would have repented in sackcloth and ashes long ago, if the miracles done in you had been done there instead. 22 And I say this, that it shall go less hard with Tyre and Sidon at the day of judgement than with you. 23 And thou, Capharnaum, dost thou hope to be lifted up high as heaven? Thou shalt fall low as hell. Sodom itself, if the miracles done in thee had been done there, might have stood to this day. 24 And I say this, that it shall go less hard with the country of Sodom at the day of judgement than with thee.

25 At that time Jesus said openly, Father, who art Lord of heaven and earth, I give thee praise that thou hast hidden all this from the wise and the prudent, and revealed it to little children. 26 Be it so, Father, since this finds favour in thy sight. 27 My Father has entrusted everything into my hands; none knows the Son truly except the Father, and none knows the Father truly except the Son, and those to whom it is the Son's good pleasure to reveal him.

28 Come to me, all you that labour and are burdened; I will give you rest. 29 Take my yoke upon yourselves, and learn from me; I am gentle and humble of heart; and you shall find rest for your souls. 30 For my yoke is easy, and my burden is light.

Chapter Twelve

At this time, Jesus was walking through the corn-
fields on the sabbath day. And his disciples, who were hungry, fell
to plucking the ears of corn and eating them. 2 The Pharisees saw
this, and said to him, Look, thy disciples are doing a thing which it
is not lawful to do on the sabbath. 3 Whereupon he said to them,
Have you never read of what David did, when he and his followers
were hungry? 4 How he went into the tabernacle, and ate the
loaves set out there before God, although neither he nor his followers, nor anyone else except the priests had a right to eat them?
5 Or again, have you not read in the law that the priests violate the
sabbath rest in the temple, and none blames them? 6 And I tell you
there is one standing here who is greater than the temple. 7 If you
had found out what the words mean, It is mercy, not sacrifice, that
wins favour with me, you would not have passed judgement on the
guiltless. 8 The Son of Man has even the sabbath at his disposal.
9 So he went on his way, and afterwards came into their synagogue.
10 And here there was a man who had one of his hands withered;
and they asked Jesus whether it was lawful to do a work of healing
on the sabbath, so that they might have a charge to bring against
him. 11 But he answered, Is there a man among you that has a
sheep, who would not take hold of it and pull it out, if it should fall
into a pit on the sabbath? 12 And of what value is a sheep compared to a man? There is nothing unlawful, then, in doing a work of
mercy on the sabbath day. 13 And with that he said to the man,
Stretch out thy hand; and when he stretched it out, it was restored
to him as sound as the other.

14 Thereupon the Pharisees left the synagogue, and plotted together to make away with him. 15 Jesus was aware of this, and
withdrew from the place; great multitudes followed him, and he
healed all their diseases; 16 but he laid a strict charge on them
that they should not make him known. 17 This he did to fulfil the
word spoken by the prophet Isaias, 18 Behold, my servant, whom
I have chosen, my elect, with whom my soul is well pleased. I will

*vv. 1-14. Mark ii. 23,
Luke vi. 1.*

v. 3. I Kings xxi. 6.

v. 7. Osee vi. 6.

*v. 18. Is. xlii. 1. Our
Lord went into retire-
ment, lest it should
seem that he was de-
liberately provoking
the Pharisees to a
conflict.*

21

lay my spirit upon him, and he shall proclaim judgement among the Gentiles. 19 He will not protest and cry out; none shall hear his voice in the streets. 20 He will not snap the staff that is already crushed, or put out the wick that still smoulders, until the time comes when he crowns his judgement with victory. 21 And the Gentiles will put their trust in his name.

vv. 22-32. Mark iii. 22, Luke xi. 14.

22 Then they brought to him a man possessed, who was both blind and dumb; whom he cured, giving him both speech and sight. 23 The multitudes were filled with amazement; Can this, they asked, be no other than the Son of David? 24 But the Pharisees said, when they heard of it, It is only through the power of Beelzebub, the prince of the devils, that he casts the devils out. 25 Whereupon Jesus, who knew what was in their thoughts, said to them, No kingdom can be at war with itself without being laid waste; no city or household that is at war with itself can stand firm. 26 If it is Satan who casts Satan out, then Satan is at war with himself, and how is his kingdom to stand firm? 27 Again, if it is through Beelzebub that I cast out devils, by what means do your own sons cast them out? It is for these, then, to pronounce judgement on you. 28 But if, when I cast out devils, I do it through the Spirit of God, then it must be that the kingdom of God has already appeared among you. 29 How is anyone to gain entrance into the house of a strong man and plunder his goods without first making the strong man his prisoner? Then he can plunder his house at will. 30 He who is not with me, is against me; he who does not gather his store with me, scatters it abroad.

31 And now I tell you this; there is pardon for all the other sins and blasphemies of men, but not for blasphemy against the Holy Spirit.

v. 32. Blasphemy against the Holy Ghost is most commonly understood as resisting the known truth.

32 There is no one who blasphemes against the Son of Man but may find forgiveness; but for him who blasphemes against the Holy Spirit there is no forgiveness, either in this world or in the world to come. 33 Either tell us that the tree is sound and its fruit sound, or that the tree is withered and its fruit withered; the test of the tree is in its fruit. 34 Brood of vipers, how could you speak to good effect, wicked as you are? It is from the heart's overflow that the mouth speaks; 35 a good man utters good words from his store of goodness, the wicked man, from his store of wickedness, can utter nothing but what is evil. 36 And I say this, that in the day of judgement men will be brought to account for every thoughtless word they have spoken. 37 Thy words will be matter to acquit, or matter to condemn thee.

38 Hereupon some of the scribes and Pharisees answered him,

Master, may we see a sign from thee? 39 He answered them, The generation that asks for a sign is a wicked and unfaithful generation; the only sign that will be given it is the sign of the prophet Jonas. 40 Jonas was three days and three nights in the belly of the sea-beast, and the Son of Man will be three days and three nights in the heart of the earth. 41 The men of Nineve will rise up with this generation at the day of judgement, and will leave it without excuse; for they did penance when Jonas preached to them, and behold, a greater than Jonas is here. 42 The queen of the south will rise up with this generation at the day of judgement, and will leave it without excuse; for she came from the ends of the earth to hear the wisdom of Solomon, and behold, a greater than Solomon is here.

43 The unclean spirit, which has possessed a man and then goes out of him, walks about the desert looking for a resting-place, and finds none; 44 and it says, I will go back to my own dwelling, from which I came out. And it comes back, to find that dwelling empty, and swept out, and neatly set in order. 45 Thereupon, it goes away, and brings in seven other spirits more wicked than itself to bear it company, and together they enter in and settle down there; so that the last state of that man is worse than the first. So it shall fare with this wicked generation.

46 While he was still speaking to the multitude, it chanced that his mother and his brethren were standing without, desiring speech with him. 47 And someone told him, Here are thy mother and thy brethren standing without, looking for thee. 48 But he made answer to the man that brought him the news, Who is a mother, who are brethren, to me? 49 Then he stretched out his hand towards his disciples, and said, Here are my mother and my brethren! 50 If anyone does the will of my Father who is in heaven, he is my brother, and sister, and mother.

vv. 43-45. Luke xi. 24.

vv. 43-45. Our Lord perhaps means that the Jews, who had received the law and yet resisted the gospel, were in an even more unhappy state than the Gentiles, who had hitherto found no remedy against sin. He seems to warn us, that the soul which has received great graces and does not correspond with them will make the worst shipwreck of its fortunes.

vv. 46-50. Mark iii. 31, Luke viii. 19. Since it is impossible for anyone who holds the Catholic tradition to suppose that our Lord had brothers by blood, the most common opinion is that these 'brethren' were his cousins; a relationship for which the Jews had no separate name (cf. Gen. xxix. 12, Lev. x. 4). Our Lord here warns his fellow countrymen that they will not be reckoned as his 'brothers' unless they obey the will of their Father and his (cf. Matt. xxi. 28).

Chapter Thirteen

vv. 1-23. Mark iv. 1,
Luke viii. 4.

THAT DAY, LEAVING
the house, Jesus had sat down by
the sea shore, 2 and great multitudes gathered about him, so that he
went on board a ship and sat there instead, while the whole multitude remained standing on the beach. 3 And he spoke to them long,
in parables; Here, he began, is the sower gone out to sow. 4 And as
he sowed, there were grains that fell beside the path, so that all the
birds came and ate them up. 5 And others fell on rocky land, where
the soil was shallow; they sprang up all at once, because they had
not sunk deep in the ground; 6 but as soon as the sun rose they
were parched; they had taken no root, and so they withered away.
7 Some fell among briers, so that the briers grew up, and smothered
them. 8 But others fell where the soil was good, and these yielded
a harvest, some a hundredfold, some sixtyfold, some thirtyfold.
9 Listen, you that have ears to hear with.

10 And his disciples came to him, and said, Why dost thou
speak to them in parables? 11 Because, he answered, it is granted
to you to understand the secrets of God's kingdom, but not to these
others. 12 If a man is rich, gifts will be made to him, and his riches
will abound; if he is poor, even the little he has will be taken from
him. 13 And if I talk to them in parables, it is because, though they
have eyes, they cannot see, and though they have ears, they cannot
hear or understand. 14 Indeed, in them the prophecy of Isaias is
fulfilled, You will listen and listen, but for you there is no understanding; you will watch and watch, but for you there is no perceiving. 15 The heart of this people has become dull, their ears
are slow to listen, and they keep their eyes shut, so that they may
never see with those eyes, or hear with those ears, or understand
with that heart, and turn back to me, and win healing from me.

vv. 14, 15. Is. vi. 9.
Our Lord seems to
tone down the lan-
guage of this proph-
ecy, perhaps for fear
it might seem that the
failure of the Jews to
grasp his message was
due to some arbitrary
decree of heaven, not
to their own fault.

16 But blessed are your eyes, for they have sight; blessed are your
ears, for they have hearing. 17 And, believe me, there have been
many prophets and just men who have longed to see what you see,
and never saw it, to hear what you hear, and never heard it.

18 The parable of the sower, then, is for your hearing. 19 Wher-

24

ever a man hears the word by which the kingdom is preached, but does not grasp it, the evil one comes and carries off what was sown in his heart; his was the wayside sowing. 20 The man who took in the seed in rocky ground is the man who hears the word and at once entertains it gladly; 21 but there is no root in him, and he does not last long; no sooner does tribulation or persecution arise over the word, than his faith is shaken. 22 And the man who took in the seed in the midst of briers is the man who hears the word, but allows the cares of this world and the false charms of riches to stifle it, so that it remains fruitless. 23 Whereas the man who took in the seed in good soil is the man who both hears and grasps it; such men are fruitful, one grain yielding a hundredfold, one sixty-fold, one thirtyfold.

24 And he put before them another parable; Here is an image, he said, of the kingdom of heaven. There was a man who sowed his field with clean seed; 25 but while all the world was asleep, an enemy of his came and scattered tares among the wheat, and was gone. 26 So, when the blade had sprung up and come into ear, the tares, too, came to light; 27 and the farmer's men went to him and said, Sir, was it not clean seed thou didst sow in thy field? How comes it, then, that there are tares in it? 28 He said, An enemy has done it. And his men asked him, Wouldst thou then have us go and gather them up? 29 But he said, No; or perhaps while you are gathering the tares you will root up the wheat with them. 30 Leave them to grow side by side till harvest, and when harvest-time comes I will give the word to the reapers, Gather up the tares first, and tie them in bundles to be burned, and store the wheat in my barn.

31 Then he put before them another parable. The kingdom of heaven, he said, is like a grain of mustard seed, that a man has taken and sowed in his ground; 32 of all seeds, none is so little, but when it grows up it is greater than any garden herb; it grows into a tree, so that all the birds come and settle in its branches. 33 And he told them still another parable, The kingdom of heaven is like leaven, that a woman has taken and buried away in three measures of meal, enough to leaven the whole batch. 34 All this Jesus said to the multitude in parables, and would say it in parables only, 35 so ful- *v. 35. Ps. lxxvii. 2.* filling the words which were spoken by the prophet, I will speak my mind in parables, I will give utterance to things which have been kept secret from the beginning of the world.

36 Then he sent the multitude away, and went back into the house. There his disciples came to him, and said, Explain to us the parable of the tares in the field. 37 He answered, It is the Son of

Man that sows the good seed. 38 The field is the world, and the sons of the kingdom are the good seed; the sons of the wicked one are the tares. 39 The enemy that sowed them is the devil, and the end of the world is the harvest; it is reaped by the angels. 40 The tares were gathered together and burned in the fire, and so it will be when the world is brought to an end; 41 the Son of Man will give charge to his angels, and they will gather up all that gives offence in his kingdom, all those who do wickedly in it, 42 and will cast them into the furnace of fire, where there will be weeping, and gnashing of teeth. 43 Then, at last, the just will shine out, clear as the sun, in their Father's kingdom. Listen, you that have ears to hear with.

44 The kingdom of heaven is like a treasure hidden in a field; a man has found it and hidden it again, and now, for the joy it gives him, is going home to sell all that he has and buy that field. 45 Again, the kingdom of heaven is as if a trader were looking for rare pearls: 46 and now he has found one pearl of great cost, and has sold all that he had and bought it. 47 Again, the kingdom of heaven is like a net that was cast into the sea, and enclosed fish of every kind at once; 48 when it was full, the fishermen drew it up, and sat down on the beach, where they stored all that was worth keeping in their buckets, and threw the useless kind away. 49 So it will be when the world is brought to an end; the angels will go out and separate the wicked from the just, 50 and will cast them into the furnace of fire, where there will be weeping, and gnashing of teeth. 51 Have you grasped all this? Yes, Lord, they said to him.

v. 52. Perhaps in the sense that he must learn, on the principles laid down in the foregoing parables, the difference between the old Church of the Jews and the new Church of Christ.

vv. 54-58. Mark vi. 1, Luke iv. 16, John vi. 42.

52 And he said to them, Every scholar, then, whose learning is of the kingdom of heaven must be like a rich man, who knows how to bring both new and old things out of his treasure-house.

53 Afterwards, when he had finished these parables, Jesus journeyed on, 54 and came to his own country-side, where he taught them in their synagogue; so that they said in astonishment, How did he come by this wisdom, and these strange powers? 55 Is not this the carpenter's son, whose mother is called Mary, and his brethren James and Joseph and Simon and Judas? 56 And do not his sisters, all of them, live near us? How is it that all this has come to him? 57 And they had no confidence in him. But Jesus told them, It is only in his own country, in his own home, that a prophet goes unhonoured. 58 Nor did he do many miracles there, because of their unbelief.

Chapter Fourteen

At this time Herod, who ruled in that quarter, heard what was told of Jesus. 2 And he said to his men, This is no other vv. 1-12. Mark vi. 14, Luke ix. 7. than John the Baptist; he has risen from the dead, and that is why these powers are active in him. 3 For Herod himself had arrested John and put him in chains and thrown him into prison, for love of Herodias, his brother Philip's wife, 4 because John told him, It is wrong for thee to take her. 5 And he would willingly have put him to death, but was prevented by fear of the multitude, who looked upon John as a prophet. 6 Then, at the celebration of Herod's birthday, the daughter of Herodias danced before them all, and Herod was so well pleased with her 7 that he promised, on oath, to grant her whatever request she made. 8 She had been prompted beforehand by her mother; Give me, she said, the head of John the Baptist; give it me here on a dish. 9 And the king was stricken with remorse; but, out of respect for his oath and for those who sat with him at table, he granted her request, 10 and so had John beheaded in his prison. 11 His head was brought in on a dish, and given to the girl, and she carried it off to her mother. 12 But his disciples gained access to the body, which they took away and buried, and came to tell the news to Jesus.

13 Jesus, when he had heard it, took ship from the place where vv. 13-21. Mark vi. 31, Luke ix. 10, John vi. 3. he was, and withdrew into desert country, to be alone; but the multitudes from the towns heard of it, and followed him there by land. 14 So, when he disembarked, he found a great multitude there, and he took pity on them, and healed those who were sick. 15 And now it was evening, and his disciples came to him and said, This is a lonely place, and it is past the accustomed hour; give the multitudes leave to go into the villages and buy themselves food there. 16 But Jesus told them, There is no need for them to go away; it is for you to give them food to eat. 17 They answered, We have nothing with us, except five loaves and two fishes. 18 Bring them to me here, he said; 19 then he told the multitudes to sit down on the grass, and when the five loaves and the two fishes

were brought to him he looked up to heaven, blessed and broke the loaves, and gave them to his disciples; and the disciples gave them to the multitude. 20 All ate and had enough, and when they picked up what was left of the broken pieces they filled twelve baskets with them; 21 about five thousand men had eaten, not reckoning women and children.

vv. 22-27. Mark vi. 45.
22 As soon as this was done, he prevailed upon his disciples to take ship and cross to the other side before him, leaving him to send the multitudes home. 23 When he had finished sending them home, he went up by himself on to the hill side, to pray there; twilight had come, and he remained there alone. 24 Meanwhile the ship was already half-way across the sea, hard put to it by the waves, for the wind was against them. 25 And then, when the night had reached its fourth quarter, Jesus came to them, walking on the sea. 26 When they saw him walking on the sea, the disciples were terrified; they said, It is an apparition, and cried out for fear. 27 But all at once Jesus spoke to them; Take courage, he said, it is myself; do not be afraid. 28 And Peter answered him, Lord, if it is thyself, bid me come to thee over the water. 29 He said, Come; and Peter let himself down out of the ship and walked over the water to reach Jesus. 30 Then, seeing how strong the wind was, he lost courage and began to sink; whereupon he cried aloud, Lord, save me. 31 And Jesus at once stretched out his hand and caught hold of him, saying to him, Why didst thou hesitate, man of little faith? 32 So they went on board the ship, and thereupon the wind dropped. 33 And the ship's crew came and said, falling at his feet, Thou art indeed the Son of God.

vv. 34-36. Mark vi. 53.
34 When they had crossed, they reached the country of Genesar; 35 and the inhabitants of that place, recognizing him, sent into all the country round, and brought to him all those who were in affliction; 36 and they entreated him that they might be allowed to touch even the hem of his garments. And everyone who touched him was restored to health.

Chapter Fifteen

AFTER THIS, JESUS WAS approached by the scribes and Pharisees from Jerusalem, who asked: 2 Why is it that thy disciples violate the traditions of our ancestors? They do not wash their hands when they eat. 3 He answered them, Why is it that you yourselves violate the commandment of God with your traditions? 4 God has said, Honour thy father and thy mother; and again, He who curses his father or mother dies without hope of reprieve. 5 Whereas you say, If a man says to his father or mother, The offering which I make to God is all the advantage you will have from me, then father or mother can get no service from him. 6 So by these traditions of yours you have made God's law ineffectual. 7 You hypocrites, it was a true prophecy Isaias made of you, when he said, 8 This people does me honour with its lips, but its heart is far from me. 9 Their worship of me is vain, for the doctrines they teach are the commandments of men.

10 Then he gathered the multitude about him, and said to them, Listen to this, and grasp what it means. 11 It is not what goes into a man's mouth that makes him unclean; what makes a man unclean is what comes out of his mouth. 12 Thereupon his disciples came and said to him, Dost thou know that the Pharisees, when they heard thy saying, took it amiss? 13 He answered, There is no plant which my heavenly Father has not planted but will be rooted up. 14 Let them say what they will; they are blind men leading the blind, and when one blind man leads another, they will fall into the ditch together. 15 Peter answered him, Explain this parable to us. 16 What, he said, are you still without wits? 17 Do you not observe that any uncleanness which finds its way into a man's mouth travels down into his belly, and so is cast into the sewer; 18 whereas all that comes out of his mouth comes from the heart, and it is that which makes a man unclean? 19 It is from the heart that his wicked designs come, his sins of murder, adultery, fornication, theft, perjury and blasphemy. 20 It is these make a

vv. 1-31. Mark vii. 1.

v. 4. Ex. xx. 12, Deut. v. 16; Ex. xxi. 17, Lev. xx. 9, Proverbs xx. 20.

v. 5. There is much uncertainty about the text and the meaning here. But, since the Hebrews used the word 'honour' to imply a gift of money (cf. Ecclesiasticus xxxviii. 1, I Timothy v. 3) it is clear that our Lord refers to some shift by which sons were allowed to neglect the support of their parents. This was done, it appears, by a real or pretended consecration of themselves to God.

v. 8. Is. xxix. 13.

man unclean; he is not made unclean by eating without washing his hands.

21 After this, Jesus left those parts and withdrew into the neighbourhood of Tyre and Sidon. 22 And here a woman, a Chanaanite by birth, who came from that country, cried aloud, Have pity on me, Lord, thou son of David. My daughter is cruelly troubled by an evil spirit. 23 He gave her no word in answer; but his disciples came to him and pleaded with him; Rid us of her, they said, she is following us with her cries. 24 And he answered, My errand is only to the lost sheep that are of the house of Israel. 25 Then the woman came up and said, falling at his feet, Lord, help me. 26 He answered, It is not right to take the children's bread and throw it to the dogs. 27 Ah yes, Lord, she said; the dogs feed on the crumbs that fall from their masters' table. 28 And at that Jesus answered her, Woman, for this great faith of thine, let thy will be granted. And from that hour her daughter was cured.

29 Then Jesus left that country, and passed along the sea of Galilee, and went up into the mountain and sat down there. 30 Great multitudes came to him, bringing with them the lame, the blind, the deaf, the crippled, and many besides, whom they laid at his feet; and he healed them: 31 so that the multitudes were amazed to see the deaf hear, the cripples become whole, the lame walk, and the blind receive sight; and they praised the God of Israel for it.

vv. 32-39. Mark viii. 1. 32 But now Jesus called his disciples, and said, I am moved with pity for the multitude; it is three days now since they have been in attendance on me, and they have nothing to eat. I must not send them away fasting, or perhaps they will grow faint on their journey. 33 His disciples said to him, Where could we find loaves enough in a desert to feed such a multitude? 34 And Jesus asked them, How many loaves have you? Seven, they said, and a few small fishes. 35 Thereupon he bade the multitude sit down on the ground, 36 and he took the seven loaves and the fishes with them, and when he had blessed and broken he gave these to his disciples, and his disciples to the multitude. 37 And they all ate and had enough; and they took up what was left of the broken pieces, seven hampers full. 38 Four thousand men had eaten, not reckoning women and children. 39 And so, taking leave of the multitude, he went on board the ship, and crossed to the region of Magedan.

30

THE WEDDING OF THE BLESSED VIRGIN

NATIONAL GALLERY, LONDON

SIENESE SCHOOL
circa 1400

Chapter Sixteen

AND THE PHARISEES and Sadducees came and put him to the test, asking him to shew them a sign from heaven. 2 But he answered them, When evening comes, you say, It is fair weather, the sky is red; 3 or at sunrise, There will be a storm to-day, the sky is red and lowering. 4 You know, then, how to read the face of heaven; can you not read the signs of appointed times? It is a wicked and unfaithful generation that asks for a sign; the only sign that will be given to it is the sign of the prophet Jonas. And so he went on his way and left them.

vv. 1-2. Mark viii. 11.

5 And they crossed the sea, and his disciples found that they had forgotten to take bread with them. 6 So, when Jesus said to them, See that you have nothing to do with the leaven of the Pharisees and Sadducees, 7 they were anxious in their minds; We have brought no bread, they said. 8 Jesus knew it, and said to them, Men of little faith, what is this anxiety in your minds, that you have brought no bread with you? 9 Have you no wits even now, or have you forgotten the five thousand and their five loaves, and the number of baskets you filled? 10 Or the four thousand and their seven loaves, and the number of hampers you filled then? 11 How could you suppose that I was thinking of bread, when I said, Have nothing to do with the leaven of the Pharisees and Sadducees? 12 Then they understood that his warning was against the doctrine of the Pharisees and Sadducees, not against leavened bread.

13 Then Jesus came into the neighbourhood of Caesarea Philippi; and there he asked his disciples, What do men say of the Son of Man? Who do they think he is? 14 Some say John the Baptist, they told him, others Elias, others again, Jeremy or one of the prophets. 15 Jesus said to them, And what of you? Who do you say that I am? 16 Then Simon Peter answered, Thou art the Christ, the Son of the living God. 17 And Jesus answered him, Blessed art thou, Simon son of Jona; it is not flesh and blood, it is my Father in heaven that has revealed this to thee. 18 And I tell thee this in my turn, that thou art Peter, and it is upon this rock that I will

vv. 13-16. Mark viii. 27, Luke ix. 18.

31

build my church; and the gates of hell shall not prevail against it; 19 and I will give to thee the keys of the kingdom of heaven; and whatever thou shalt bind on earth shall be bound in heaven, and whatever thou shalt loose on earth shall be loosed in heaven. 20 Then he strictly forbade them to tell any man that he, Jesus, was the Christ.

vv. 20-28. Mark viii. 30, Luke ix. 21.

21 From that time onwards Jesus began to make it known to his disciples that he must go up to Jerusalem, and there, with much ill usage from the chief priests and elders and scribes, must be put to death, and rise again on the third day. 22 Whereupon Peter, drawing him to his side, began remonstrating with him; Never, Lord, he said; no such thing shall befall thee. 23 At which he turned round and said to Peter, Back, Satan; thou art a stone in my path; for these thoughts of thine are man's, not God's. 24 Jesus also said to his disciples, If any man has a mind to come my way, let him renounce self, and take up his cross, and follow me. 25 The man who tries to save his life shall lose it; it is the man who loses his life for my sake that will secure it. 26 How is a man the better for it, if he gains the whole world at the cost of losing his own soul? For a man's soul, what price can be high enough? 27 The Son of Man will come hereafter in his Father's glory with his angels about him, and he will recompense everyone, then, according to his works. 28 Believe me, there are those standing here who will not taste of death before they have seen the Son of Man coming in his kingdom.

Chapter Seventeen

SIX DAYS AFTERWARDS Jesus took Peter and James and

vv. 1-22. Mark ix. 1, Luke ix. 28.

his brother John with him, and led them up on to a high mountain where they were alone. 2 And he was transfigured in their presence, his face shining like the sun, and his garments becoming white as snow; 3 and all at once they had sight of Moses and Elias conversing with him. 4 Then Peter said aloud to Jesus, Lord, it is well that we should be here; if it pleases thee, let us make three arbours in this place, one for thee, one for Moses and one for Elias. 5 Even before he had finished speaking, a shining cloud overshadowed them. And now, there was a voice which said to them out of the cloud, This is my beloved Son, in whom I am well pleased; to him, then, listen. 6 The disciples, when they heard it, fell on their faces, overcome with fear; 7 but Jesus came near and roused them with his touch; Arise, he said, do not be afraid. 8 And they lifted up their eyes, and saw no man there but Jesus only.

9 And as they were coming down from the mountain, Jesus warned them, Do not tell anybody of what you have seen, until the Son of Man has risen from the dead. 10 And his disciples asked him, Tell us, why is it that the scribes say Elias must come before Christ? 11 He answered, Elias must needs come and restore all things as they were; 12 but I tell you this, that Elias has come already, and they did not recognize him, but misused him at their pleasure, just as the Son of Man is to suffer at their hands. 13 Then the disciples understood that he had been speaking to them of John the Baptist.

v. 12. See note on xi. 14 above.

14 When they reached the multitude, a man came up and knelt before him: Lord, he said, have pity on my son, who is a lunatic, and in great affliction; he will often throw himself into the fire, and often into water. 15 I brought him here to thy disciples, but they have not been able to cure him. 16 Jesus answered, Ah, faithless and misguided generation, how long must I be with you, how long must I bear with you? Bring him here before me. 17 And Jesus checked him with a word, and the devil came out of him; and from that hour the boy was cured. 18 Afterwards, when they were alone, the disciples came to Jesus and asked, Why was it that we could not cast it out? 19 Jesus said to them, Because you had no faith. I promise you, if you have faith, though it be but as a grain of mustard seed, you have only to say to this mountain, Remove from this place to that, and it will remove; nothing will be impossible to you. 20 But there is no way of casting out such spirits as this except by prayer and fasting.

21 While they were still together in Galilee, Jesus told them, The Son of Man is to be given up into the hands of men. 22 They will put him to death, and he will rise again on the third day. And they were overcome with sorrow.

33

23 And when they reached Capharnaum, the collectors of the Temple pence approached Peter, and asked, Does not your master pay the Temple pence? 24 Yes, he said. Soon afterwards he came into the house, and Jesus forestalled him; Simon, he said, tell us what thou thinkest; on whom do earthly kings impose customs and taxes, on their own sons, or on strangers? 25 On strangers, Peter told him; and Jesus said to him, Why then, the children go free. 26 But we will not hurt their consciences; go down to the sea, and cast thy hook; take out the first fish thou drawest up, and when thou hast opened its mouth thou wilt find a silver coin there; with this make payment to them for me and for thyself.

Chapter

Eighteen

vv. 1-5. Mark ix. 32, Luke ix. 46.

THE DISCIPLES CAME TO Jesus at this time and said, Tell us, who is greatest in the kingdom of heaven? 2 Whereupon Jesus called to his side a little child, to whom he gave a place in the midst of them, 3 and said, Believe me, unless you become like little children again, you shall not enter the kingdom of heaven. 4 He is greatest in the kingdom of heaven who will abase himself like this little child. 5 He who gives welcome to such a child as this in my name, gives welcome to me. 6 And if anyone hurts the conscience of one of these little ones, that believe in me, he had better have been drowned in the depths of the sea, with a millstone hung about his neck. 7 Woe to the world, for the hurt done to consciences! It must needs be that such hurt should come, but woe to the man through whom it comes! 8 If thy hand or thy foot is an occasion of falling to thee, cut it off and cast it away from thee; better for thee to enter into life crippled or lame, than to have two hands or two feet when thou art cast into eternal fire. 9 And if thy eye is an occasion of falling to thee, pluck it out and cast it away from thee; better for thee to enter into life with one eye, than to have two eyes when thou art cast into the fires of hell. 10 See to it that you do not treat one of these little ones with contempt; I tell you, they have angels of their own in heaven, that behold the face of my heavenly Father continually. 11 The Son of Man has come to save that which was lost. 12 Tell me this, if a man has a hundred sheep, and one of them has gone astray, does he not leave those ninety-nine others on the mountain side, and go out to look for the one that is straying? 13 And if, by good fortune, he finds it, he rejoices more, believe me, over that one, than over the ninety-nine which never strayed from him. 14 So too it is not your heavenly Father's pleasure that one of these little ones should be lost.

15 If thy brother does thee wrong, go at once and tax him with it, as a private matter between thee and him; and so, if he will listen to thee, thou hast won thy brother. 16 If he will not listen to thee, take with thee one or two more, that the whole matter may be certified by the voice of two or three witnesses. 17 If he will not listen to them, then speak of it to the church; and if he will not even listen to the church, then count him all one with the heathen and the publican. 18 I promise you, all that you bind on earth shall be bound in heaven, and all that you loose on earth shall be loosed in heaven. 19 And moreover I tell you, that if two of you agree over any request that you make on earth, it will be granted them by my Father who is in heaven. 20 Where two or three are gathered together in my name, I am there in the midst of them.

21 Then Peter came to him and asked, Lord, how often must I see my brother do me wrong, and still forgive him; as much as seven times? 22 Jesus said to him, I tell thee to forgive, not seven wrongs, but seventy times seven. 23 Here is an image of the kingdom of heaven; there was a king who resolved to enter into a reckoning with his servants, 24 and had scarcely begun the reckoning, when one was brought before him who was ten thousand talents in his debt. 25 He had no means of making payment; whereupon his master gave orders that he should be sold, with his wife and children and all that he had, and so the debt should be paid. 26 With that the servant fell at his feet and said, Have patience with me, and I will pay thee in full. 27 And his master, moved with pity for him, let the servant go and discharged him of his debt. 28 So the servant went out, and met with a fellow servant of his, who owed him a hundred pieces of silver; whereupon he caught hold of him and took him by the throat, and said, Pay me

v. 15. 'Does thee wrong', some of the best Greek manuscripts omit the word 'thee'.

35

all thou owest me. 29 His fellow servant went down on his knees in entreaty; Have patience with me, he said, and I will pay thee in full. 30 But the other refused; he went away and committed him to prison for such time as the debt was unpaid. 31 The rest of the servants were full of indignation when they saw this done, and went in to tell their master what had happened. 32 And so he was summoned by his master, who said to him, I remitted all that debt of thine, thou wicked servant, at thy entreaty; 33 was it not thy duty to have mercy on thy fellow servant, as I had mercy on thee? 34 And his master, in anger, gave him over to be tortured until the debt was paid. 35 It is thus that my heavenly Father will deal with you, if brother does not forgive brother with all his heart.

Chapter Nineteen

vv. 1-9. Mark x. 1; cf. Matt. v. 32, Luke xvi. 18, I Corinthians vii. 10.

v. 5. Gen. ii. 24.

v. 7. Deut. xxiv. 1.

v. 9. The apparent exception made here in connexion with unfaithfulness, not recognized in Mark or Luke, or by St. Paul, has been variously explained. It is to be observed in any case that our Lord is speaking of the man who puts away his innocent wife in order to marry another (this is often the force of the Hebrew 'and'). He considers the case of the guilty husband with the innocent wife, and that of the

AFTERWARDS, WHEN HE had finished saying all this, Jesus removed from Galilee and came into that part of Judaea which lies beyond the Jordan. 2 Great multitudes went with him, and he healed them there. 3 Then the Pharisees came to him, and put him to the test by asking, Is it right for a man to put away his wife, for whatever cause? 4 He answered, Have you never read, how he who created them, when they first came to be, created them male and female; and how he said, 5 A man, therefore, will leave his father and mother and will cling to his wife, and the two will become one flesh? 6 And so they are no longer two, they are one flesh; what God, then, has joined, let not man put asunder. 7 Why then, they said, did Moses enjoin that a man might give his wife a writ of separation, and then he might put her away? 8 He told them, It was to suit your hard hearts that Moses allowed you to put your wives away; it was not so at the beginning of things. 9 And I tell you that he who puts away his wife, not for any unfaithfulness of hers, and so marries another, commits adultery; and he too commits adultery, who marries her after she has been put away. 10 At this, his disciples said to him, If the case stands so between man and wife, it is better not to marry at all. 11 That conclusion, he said, cannot be taken in by everybody, but only by those who have the gift. 12 There are some eunuchs, who were so born from the mother's womb, some were made so by men, and some have made themselves so for love of the kingdom of heaven; take this in, you whose hearts are large enough for it.

innocent husband with the guilty wife; not that of the man who has a guilty wife and himself wants a change of partners. Thus it would be unsafe to infer that the husband has a right to re-marry.

v. 12. This verse evidently refers to those who have a vocation to celibacy.

13 Then they brought children to him, so that he might lay his hands on them in prayer; and his disciples rebuked them for it. 14 But Jesus said, Let the children be, do not keep them back from me; the kingdom of heaven belongs to such as these. 15 And so he laid his hands on them, and went on his way.

vv. 13-30. Mark x. 13, Luke xviii. 15.

16 And now a man came to him, and said, Master, who art so good, what good must I do to win eternal life? 17 He said to him, why dost thou come to me to ask of goodness? God is good, and he only. If thou hast a mind to enter into life, keep the commandments. 18 Which commandments? he asked. Jesus said, Thou shalt do no murder, Thou shalt not commit adultery, Thou shalt not steal, Thou shalt not bear false witness, 19 Honour thy father and thy mother, and, Thou shalt love thy neighbour as thyself. 20 I have kept all these, the young man told him, ever since I grew up; where is it that I am still wanting? 21 Jesus said to him, If thou hast a mind to be perfect, go home and sell all that belongs to thee; give it to the poor, and so the treasure thou hast shall be in heaven; then come back and follow me. 22 When he heard this, the young man went away sad at heart, for he had great possessions. 23 And Jesus said to his disciples, Believe me, a rich man will not enter God's kingdom easily. 24 And once again I tell you, it is easier for a camel to pass through a needle's eye, than for a man to enter the kingdom of heaven when he is rich. 25 At hearing this, the disciples were thrown into great bewilderment; Why then, they asked, who can be saved? 26 Jesus fastened his eyes on them, and said to them, Such a thing is impossible to man's powers, but to God all things are possible.

v. 18. Ex. xx. 13.

v. 21. Our Lord may simply have been testing the young man's resolution, or he may have been calling him to the special vocation of poverty. He does not make this demand of all, as we see in his treatment of Zacchaeus (Luke xix. 8).

27 Hereupon Peter took occasion to say, And what of us who have forsaken all, and followed thee; what is left for us? 28 Jesus said to them, I promise you, in the new birth, when the Son of Man sits on the throne of his glory, you also shall sit there on twelve thrones, you who have followed me, and shall be judges over the twelve tribes of Israel. 29 And every man that has forsaken home

or brothers, or sisters, or father, or mother, or wife, or children, or lands for my name's sake, shall receive his reward a hundredfold, and obtain everlasting life. 30 But many will be first that were last, and last that were first.

Chapter
Twenty

Here is an image of the kingdom of heaven; a rich man went out at daybreak to hire labourers for work in his vineyard; 2 and when he sent them out into his vineyard he agreed with the labourers on a silver piece for the day's wages. 3 About the third hour he came out again, and found others standing idle in the market-place; 4 and to these also he said, Away with you to the vineyard like the others; you shall have whatever payment is fair. 5 Away they went; and at noon, and once more at the ninth hour, he came out and did the like. 6 Yet he found others standing there when he came out at the eleventh hour; How is it, he said to them, that you are standing here, and have done nothing all the day? 7 They told him, It is because nobody has hired us; and he said, Away with you to the vineyard like the rest.

8 And now it was evening, and the owner of the vineyard said to his bailiff, Send for the workmen and pay them their wages, beginning with the last comers and going back to the first. 9 And so the men who were hired about the eleventh hour came forward, and each was paid a silver piece. 10 So that when the others came, who were hired first, they hoped to receive more. But they were paid a silver piece each, like their fellows. 11 And they were indignant with the rich man over their pay; 12 Here are these late-comers, they said, who have worked but one hour, and thou hast made no difference between them and us, who have borne the day's burden and the heat. 13 But he answered one of them thus; My friend, I

38

am not doing thee a wrong; did we not agree on a silver piece for thy wages? 14 Take what is thy due, and away with thee; it is my pleasure to give as much to this late-comer as thee. 15 Am I not free to use my money as I will? Must thou give me sour looks, because I am generous? 16 So it is that they shall be first who were last, and they shall be last who were first. Many are called, but few are chosen.

17 And now Jesus was going up to Jerusalem, and he took his twelve disciples aside on the way, and warned them, 18 Now we are going up to Jerusalem; and there the Son of Man will be given up into the hands of the chief priests and scribes, who will condemn him to death. 19 And these will give him up into the hands of the Gentiles, to be mocked and scourged and crucified; but on the third day he will rise again. 20 Thereupon the mother of the sons of Zebedee brought them to him, falling on her knees to make a request of him. 21 And when he asked her, What is thy will? she said to him, Here are my two sons; grant that in thy kingdom one may take his place on thy right and the other on thy left. 22 But Jesus answered, You do not know what it is you ask. Have you strength to drink of the cup I am to drink of? They said, We have. 23 And he told them, you shall indeed drink of my cup; but a place on my right hand or my left is not mine to give; it is for those for whom my Father has destined it. 24 The ten others were angry with the two brethren when they heard it; 25 but Jesus called them to him, and said, You know that, among the Gentiles, those who bear rule lord it over them, and great men vaunt their power over them; 26 with you it must be otherwise; 27 whoever would be a great man among you, must be your servant, and whoever has a mind to be first among you, must be your slave. 28 So it is that the Son of Man did not come to have service done him; he came to serve others, and to give his life as a ransom for the lives of many.

29 When they were leaving Jericho, there was a great multitude that followed him. 30 And there, by the road side, sat two blind folk, who heard of Jesus' passing by, and cried aloud, Lord, son of David, have pity on us. 31 The multitude rebuked them, bidding them be silent; but they cried out all the more, Son of David, Lord, have pity on us. 32 Then Jesus stopped, and called them to him; What would you have me do for you? he asked. 33 Lord, they said to him, we would have our eyes opened. 34 And Jesus, moved with compassion, touched their eyes, and immediately they recovered their sight, and followed after him.

vv. 17-19. Mark x. 32, Luke xviii. 31.

vv. 20-28. Mark x. 35.

vv. 29-34. Mark x. 46, Luke xviii. 35. Only one blind man is mentioned in these other accounts, perhaps because only one (Bartimaeus) was well known by name at the time when the gospels were written.

Chapter Twenty=one

vv. 1-9. Mark xi. 1,
Luke xix. 29, John
xii. 12. It appears
from these other ac-
counts that our Lord
rode on the colt, the
dam being brought so
as to make the colt
follow more easily.
The reading of the
manuscripts is uncer-
tain in verse 7.

v. 5. Zacharias ix. 9.

WHEN THEY WERE near Jerusalem, and had reached Bethphage, which is close to mount Olivet, Jesus sent two of his disciples on an errand; 2 Go into the village that faces you, he told them, and the first thing you will find there will be a she-ass tethered, and a foal at her side; untie them and bring them to me. 3 And if anyone speaks to you about it, tell him, The Lord has need of them, and he will let you have them without more ado. 4 All this was so ordained, to fulfil the word spoken by the prophet: 5 Tell the daughter of Sion, behold, thy king is coming to thee, humbly, riding on an ass, on a colt whose mother has borne the yoke. 6 The disciples went and did as Jesus told them; 7 they brought the she-ass and its colt, and saddled them with their garments, and bade Jesus mount. 8 Most of the multitude spread their garments along the way, while others strewed the way with branches cut down from the trees.

v. 9. Ps. cxvii. 26.

9 And the multitudes that went before him and that followed after him cried aloud, Hosanna for the son of David, blessed is he who comes in the name of the Lord, Hosanna in the heaven above. 10 When he reached Jerusalem, the whole city was in a stir; Who is this? they asked. 11 And the multitude answered, This is Jesus, the prophet from Nazareth, in Galilee.

vv. 12-13. Mark xi.
15, Luke xix. 45; cf.
John ii. 14.

v. 13. Is. lvi. 7 and
Jer. vii. 11.

12 Then Jesus went into the temple of God, and drove out from it all those who sold and bought there, and overthrew the tables of the bankers, and the chairs of the pigeon-sellers; 13 It is written, he told them, My house shall be known for a house of prayer, and you have made it into a den of thieves. 14 And there were blind and lame men who came up to him in the temple, and he healed them there. 15 The chief priests and scribes saw the miracles which he did, and the boys that cried aloud in the temple, Hosanna

v. 16. Ps. viii. 3.

for the son of David, and they were greatly angered at it. 16 Dost thou hear what these are saying? they asked. Yes, Jesus said to them, but have you never read the words, Thou hast made the lips of children, of infants at the breast, vocal with praise? 17 So he left them, and went out of the city to Bethany, where he made his lodging.

18 As he was returning to the city at daybreak, he was hungry: and, seeing a fig-tree by the road side, he went up to it, and found nothing but leaves on it. 19 And he said to it, Let no fruit ever grow on thee hereafter; whereupon the fig-tree withered away. 20 His disciples were amazed when they saw it; How suddenly it has withered away! they said. 21 Jesus answered them, I promise you, if you have faith, and do not hesitate, you will be able to do more than I have done over the fig-tree; if you say to this mountain, Remove, and be cast into the sea, it will come about. 22 If you will only believe, every gift you ask for in your prayer will be granted.

vv. 18-22. Mark xi. 12 and xi. 20. St. Mark tells us that it was not yet the season for figs; our Lord, then, did not expect to satisfy his hunger. He knew that the tree was barren, even of unripe fruit, and used it as a parable of the unfaithfulness which he found in the Jewish people.

23 Afterwards he came into the temple; and while he was teaching there, the chief priests and elders approached him, asking, What is the authority by which thou doest these things, and who gave thee this authority? 24 Jesus answered them, I too have a question to ask; if you can tell me the answer, I will tell you in return what is the authority by which I do these things. 25 Whence did John's baptism come, from heaven or from men? Whereupon they cast about in their minds; 26 If we tell him it was from heaven, they said, he will ask us, Then why did you not believe him? And if we say it was from men, we have reason to be afraid of the people; they all look upon John as a prophet. 27 And they answered Jesus, We cannot tell. He, in his turn, said, And you will not learn from me what is the authority by which I do these things. 28 But tell me what you think; there was a man who had two sons, and when he went up to the first, and said, Away with thee, my son, and work in my vineyard to-day, 29 he answered; Not I, but he relented afterwards and went. 30 Then he went up to the other, and said the like to him; and his answer was, I will, Sir; but he did not go. 31 Which of the two carried out his father's will? The first, they said. And Jesus said to them, Believe me, the publicans and the harlots are further on the road to God's kingdom than you. 32 John came among you following all due observance, but could win no belief from you; the publicans believed him, and the harlots, but even when you saw that, you would not relent, and believe him.

vv. 23-27. Mark xi. 27, Luke xx. 1.

33 Listen to another parable. There was a rich man who planted a vineyard; he walled it in, and dug a wine-press and built a tower in it, and then let it out to some vine-dressers, while he went on his travels. 34 When vintage-time drew near, he sent his own

vv. 33-46. Mark xii. 1, Luke xx. 9; cf. Is. vi. 1.

41

servants on an errand to the vine-dressers, to claim its revenues. 35 Whereupon the vine-dressers laid hands upon his servants; one they beat, one they killed outright, one they stoned. 36 And he sent other servants on a second errand, more than he had sent at first, but they were used no better. 37 After that, he sent his own son to them; They will have reverence, he said, for my son. 38 But when the vine-dressers found his son coming to them, they said among themselves, This is the heir; come, let us kill him, and seize upon the inheritance. 39 And they laid hands on him, thrust him out from the vineyard, and killed him. 40 And now, what will the owner of the vineyard do to those vine-dressers when he returns? 41 They said, He will bring those wretches to a wretched end, and will let out the vineyard to other vine-dressers, who will pay him his due when the season comes. 42 And Jesus said to them, Have you never read those words in the scriptures, The very stone which the builders rejected has become the chief stone at the corner; this is the Lord's doing, and it is marvellous in our eyes? 43 I tell you, then, that the kingdom of God will be taken away from you, and given to a people which yields the revenues that belong to it. 44 As for the stone, when a man falls against it, he will break his bones; when it falls upon him, it will scatter him like chaff. 45 The chief priests and the Pharisees saw clearly, when they heard his parables, that it was of themselves he was speaking, 46 and would gladly have laid hands on him, but they were afraid of the people, who looked upon him as a prophet.

v. 42. Ps. cxvii. 22, cf. Rom. ix. 33, I Peter ii. 7.

v. 44. St. Augustine explains that those who find a stumbling-block in Christ fall upon the stone; the stone falls upon them when he pronounces judgment.

Chapter
Twenty=two

AND JESUS ONCE MORE spoke to them in parables; 2 Here is an image, he said, of the kingdom of heaven; there was once a king, who held a marriage-feast for his son, 3 and sent

vv. 1-14. A similar parable is found in Luke xiv. 16.

out his servants with a summons to all those whom he had invited to the wedding; but they would not come. 4 Then he sent other servants with a fresh summons, bidding them tell those who had been invited, By this, I have prepared my feast, the oxen have been killed, and the fatlings, all is ready now; come to the wedding. 5 But still they paid no heed, and went off on other errands, one to his farm in the country, and another to his trading; 6 and the rest laid hands upon his servants, and insulted and killed them. 7 The king fell into a rage when he heard of it, and sent out his troops to put those murderers to death, and burn their city. 8 After this, he said to his servants, Here is the marriage-feast all ready, and those who had been invited have proved unworthy of it. 9 You must go out to the street corners, and invite all whom you find there to the wedding. 10 And his servants went out into the streets, where they mustered all they could find, rogues and honest men together; and so the wedding had its full tale of guests. 11 But when the king came in to look at the company, he saw a man there who had no wedding-garment on; 12 My friend, he said, how didst thou come to be here without a wedding-garment? And he made no reply. 13 Whereupon the king said to his servants, Bind him hand and foot, and cast him out into the darkness, where there shall be weeping, and gnashing of teeth. 14 Many are called, but few are chosen.

15 After this the Pharisees withdrew, and plotted together, to make him betray himself in his talk. 16 And they sent their own disciples to him, with those who were of Herod's party, and said, Master, we know well that thou art sincere, and teachest in all sincerity the way of God; that thou holdest no one in awe, making no distinction between man and man; 17 tell us, then, is it right to pay tribute to Caesar, or not? 18 Jesus saw their malice; Hypocrites, he said, why do you thus put me to the test? 19 Shew me the coinage in which the tribute is paid. So they brought him a silver piece, 20 and he asked them, Whose is this likeness? Whose name is inscribed on it? 21 Caesar's, they said; whereupon he answered, Why then, give back to Caesar what is Caesar's, and to God what is God's. 22 And they went away and left him in peace, full of admiration at his words.

23 On that day, too, he was approached with a question by the Sadducees, men who say that there is no resurrection; 24 Master, they said, Moses told us, If a man leaves no children when he dies, his brother shall marry the widow by right of kinship, and beget children in the dead brother's name. 25 We had seven brothers

v. 11. Some have suggested that wedding-garments were provided at the King's expense, but it is not certain that any such custom obtained. Like the foolish virgins (cf. xxv. 3), the man had neglected to make what preparations were in his power. It is the common opinion that the wedding-garment represents charity.

vv. 15-46. Mark xii. 13, Luke xx. 19.

v. 24. Deut. xxv. 5.

once in our country, of whom the first died, a married man with-out issue, bequeathing his wife to the second. 26 And the same befell the second brother, and then the third, and in the end all seven, 27 the woman dying last of all. 28 And now, when the dead rise again, which of the seven will be her husband, since she was wife to them all? 29 Jesus answered them, You are wrong; you do not understand the scriptures, or what is the power of God. 30 When the dead rise again, there is no marrying and giving in marriage; they are as the angels in heaven are. 31 But now, in the matter of the resurrection, did you never read what God himself said: 32 I am the God of Abraham, and the God of Isaac, and the God of Jacob? Yet it is of living men, not of dead men, that he is God. 33 This the multitude heard, and were amazed by his teach-ing.

v. 32. Ex. iii. 6.

34 And now the Pharisees, hearing how he had put the Saddu-cees to silence, met together; 35 and one of them, a lawyer, put a question to try him: 36 Master, which commandment in the law is the greatest? 37 Jesus said to him, Thou shalt love the Lord thy God with thy whole heart and thy whole soul and thy whole mind. 38 This is the greatest of the commandments, and the first. 39 And the second, its like, is this, Thou shalt love thy neighbour as thyself. 40 On these two commandments, all the law and the prophets depend. 41 Then, while the Pharisees were still gathered about him, Jesus asked them: 42 What is your opinion concern-ing Christ? 43 Whose son is he to be? They told him, David's. How is it then, said he, that David is moved by the Spirit to call him Master, when he says: 44 The Lord said to my Master, Sit on my right hand while I make thy enemies a footstool under thy feet? 45 David calls Christ his Master; how can he be also his son? 46 None could find a word to say in answer to him, nor did any-one dare, after that day, to try him with further questions.

v. 37. Deut. vi. 5.

v. 39. Lev. xix. 18.

v. 44. Ps. cix. 1.

Chapter Twenty=three

vv. 1-36. Much of this is also to be found in ch. xi. of St. Luke.

AFTER THIS, JESUS AD dressed himself to the multitudes, and to his disciples; 2 The scribes and Pharisees, he said, have established themselves in the place from which Moses used to teach; 3 do what they tell you, then, continue to observe what they tell you, but do not imitate their actions, for they tell you one thing and do another. 4 They fasten up packs too heavy to be borne, and lay them on men's shoulders; they themselves will not stir a finger to lift them. 5 They act, always, so as to be a mark for men's eyes. Boldly written are the texts they carry, and deep is the hem of their garments; 6 their heart is set on taking the chief places at table and the first seats in the synagogue, 7 and having their hands kissed in the market-place, and being called Rabbi among their fellow men. 8 You are not to claim the title of Rabbi; you have but one Master, and you are all brethren alike. 9 Nor are you to call any man on earth your father; you have but one Father, and he is in heaven. 10 Nor are you to be called teachers; you have one teacher, Christ. 11 Among you, the greatest of all is to be the servant of all; 12 the man who exalts himself will be humbled, and the man who humbles himself will be exalted.

13 Woe upon you, scribes and Pharisees, you hypocrites that shut the door of the kingdom of heaven in men's faces; you will neither enter yourselves, nor let others enter when they would. 14 Woe upon you, scribes and Pharisees, you hypocrites that swallow up the property of widows, under cover of your long prayers; your sentence will be all the heavier for that. 15 Woe upon you, scribes and Pharisees, you hypocrites that encompass sea and land to gain a single proselyte, and then make the proselyte twice as worthy of damnation as yourselves. 16 Woe upon you, blind leaders, who say, If a man swears by the temple, it goes for nothing; if he swears by the gold in the temple, his oath stands. 17 Blind fools, which is greater, the gold, or the temple that consecrates the gold? 18 And again, If a man swears by the altar it goes for nothing; if he swears by the gift on the altar, his oath stands. 19 Blind fools, which is greater, the gift, or the altar that

45

consecrates the gift? 20 The man who swears by the altar swears at the same time by all that is on it. 21 The man who swears by the temple swears at the same time by him who has made it his dwelling-place. 22 And the man who swears by heaven swears not only by God's throne, but by him who sits upon it.

23 Woe upon you, scribes and Pharisees, you hypocrites that will award to God his tithe, though it be of mint or dill or cummin, and have forgotten the weightier commandments of the law, justice, mercy, and honour; you did ill to forget one duty while you performed the other; 24 you blind leaders, that have a strainer for the gnat, and then swallow the camel! 25 Woe upon you, scribes and Pharisees, you hypocrites that scour the outward part of cup and dish, while all within is running with avarice and incontinence. 26 Scour the inside of cup and dish first, thou blind Pharisee, that so the outside, too, may become clean. 27 Woe upon you, scribes and Pharisees, you hypocrites that are like whitened sepulchres, fair in outward show, when they are full of dead men's bones and all manner of corruption within; 28 you too seem exact over your duties, outwardly, to men's eyes, while there is nothing within but hypocrisy and iniquity. 29 Woe upon you, scribes and Pharisees, you hypocrites that build up the tombs of the prophets and engrave the monuments of the just; 30 If we had lived in our fathers' times, you say, we would not have taken part in murdering the prophets. 31 Why then, you bear witness of your own ancestry; it was your fathers who slaughtered the prophets; 32 it is for you to complete your fathers' reckoning. 33 Serpents that you are, brood of vipers, how should you escape from the award of hell? 34 And now, behold, I am sending prophets and wise men and men of learning to preach to you; some of them you will put to death and crucify, some you will scourge in your synagogues, and persecute them from city to city; 35 so that you will make yourselves answerable for all the blood of just men that is shed on the earth, from the blood of the just Abel to the blood of Zacharias the son of Barachias, whom you slew between the temple and the altar. 36 Believe me, this generation shall be held answerable for all of it. 37 Jerusalem, Jerusalem, still murdering the prophets, and stoning the messengers that are sent to thee, how often have I been ready to gather thy children together, as a hen gathers her chickens under her wings; and thou didst refuse it! 38 Behold, your house is left to you, a house uninhabited. 39 Believe me, you shall see nothing of me henceforward, until the time when you will be saying, Blessed is he that comes in the name of the Lord.

v. 32. 'To complete your fathers' reckoning', by killing the Son of God, as their fathers had killed his prophets; cf. xxi. 38.

v. 35. See Gen. iv. 10, and II Paralipomenon xxiv. 20. Barachias will have been the name of some ancestor of Zacharias, son of Joiada; there can be no reference to the persons mentioned in Is. viii. 2, Zach. i. 1.

vv. 37-39. Luke xiii. 34.

THE ANNUNCIATION   ROGER VAN DER WEYDEN
circa 1400-1464

METROPOLITAN MUSEUM, NEW YORK

Chapter Twenty=four

THEN JESUS LEFT THE temple, and was going on his way, when his disciples came up to shew him the view of the temple building. 2 Do you see all this? he said to them. Believe me, there will not be a stone left on another in this place, it will all be thrown down. 3 Afterwards, while he was sitting down on mount Olivet, the disciples came to him privately, and said, Tell us, when will this be? And what sign will be given of thy coming, and of the world being brought to an end? 4 Jesus answered them, Take care that you do not allow anyone to deceive you. 5 Many will come making use of my name; they will say, I am Christ, and many will be deceived by it. 6 And you will hear tell of wars, and rumours of war; see to it that you are not disturbed in mind; such things must happen, but the end will not come yet. 7 Nation will rise in arms against nation, kingdom against kingdom, and there will be plagues and famines and earthquakes in this region or that; 8 but all this is but the beginning of travail. 9 In those days, men will give you up to persecution, and will put you to death; all the world will be hating you because you bear my name; 10 whereupon many will lose heart, will betray and hate one another. 11 Many false prophets will arise, and many will be deceived by them; 12 and the charity of most men will grow cold, as they see wickedness abound everywhere; 13 but that man will be saved who endures to the last. 14 This gospel of the kingdom must first be preached all over the world, so that all nations may hear the truth; only after that will the end come.

15 And now, when you see that which the prophet Daniel called the abomination of desolation, set up in the holy place (let him who reads this, recognize what it means), 16 then those who are in Judaea must take refuge in the mountains; 17 not going down to carry away anything from the house, if they are on the housetop; 18 not going back to pick up a cloak, if they are in the fields. 19 It will go hard with women who are with child, or have children at the breast, in those days; 20 and you must pray that

vv. 1-36. Mark xiii. 1, Luke xxi. 5.

v. 3. The question, When the Temple would be destroyed, is answered in the greater part, at least, of vv. 4-35. The question, When should the world be brought to an end, is chiefly answered in verse 36.

v. 15. Daniel ix. 27. The Evangelist here gives a hint to the reader, probably indicating that the sign mentioned by Daniel had been recognizably fulfilled when he wrote. But there is no certainty now what event he alludes to.

47

your flight may not be in the winter, or on the sabbath day, 21 for there will be distress then such as has not been since the beginning of the world, and can never be again. 22 There would have been no hope left for any human creature, if the number of those days had not been cut short; but those days will be cut short, for the sake of the elect. 23 At such a time, if a man tells you, See, here is Christ, or, See, he is there, do not believe him. 24 There will be false Christs and false prophets, who will rise up and shew great signs and wonders, so that if it were possible, even the elect would be deceived. 25 Mark well, I have given you warning of it. 26 If they tell you, then, See, he is here, in the desert, do not stir abroad; if they tell you, See, he is there, in hidden places, do not believe them; 27 when the Son of Man comes, it will be like the lightning that springs up from the east and flashes across to the west. 28 It is where the corpse lies that the eagles will gather.

29 Immediately after the distress of those days, the sun will be darkened, and the moon will refuse her light, and the stars will fall from heaven, and the powers of heaven will rock; 30 and then the sign of the Son of Man will be seen in heaven; then it is that all the tribes of the land will mourn, and they will see the Son of Man coming upon the clouds of heaven, with great power and glory; 31 and he will send out his angels with a loud blast of the trumpet, to gather his elect from the four winds, from one end of heaven to the other.

32 The fig-tree will teach you a parable; when its branch grows supple, and begins to put out leaves, you know that summer is near; 33 so you, when you see all this come about, are to know that it is near, at your very doors. 34 Believe me, this generation will not have passed, before all this is accomplished. 35 Though heaven and earth should pass away, my words will stand.

36 But as for that day and that hour you speak of, they are known to none, not even to the angels in heaven; only the Father knows them. 37 When the Son of Man comes, all will be as it was in the days of Noe; 38 in those days before the flood, they went on eating and drinking, marrying and giving in marriage, until the time when Noe entered the ark, 39 and they were taken unawares, when the flood came and drowned them all; so it will be at the coming of the Son of Man. 40 One man taken, one left, as they work together in the fields; 41 one woman taken, one left, as they grind together at the mill. 42 You must be on the watch, then, since you do not know the hour of your Lord's coming. 43 Be sure of this; if the master of the house had known at what time of

v. 28. Our Lord says that at the time when the false prophets arise, it will be easy to answer the question where the danger is coming from, just as it is easy for a man who sees dead carrion to prophesy where the birds will gather. 'Eagles' may be an allusion to the standards carried by the Roman armies.

v. 29. Such words as these were often used, by a metaphor, of the fall of kingdoms or dynasties; Is. xiii. 10, Ezechiel xxii. 7, Joel ii. 10, iii. 15.

v. 30. 'The land', or possibly 'the earth', but cf. Zach. xii. 12.

v. 31. 'Angels'; the Greek word used here might also mean 'messengers'.

vv. 42-51. Luke xii. 39.

48

night the thief was coming, he would have kept watch, and not allowed his house to be broken open. 44 And you too must stand ready; the Son of Man will come at an hour when you are not expecting him.

45 Which of you, then, is a faithful and wise servant, one whom his master will entrust with the care of the household, to give them their food at the appointed time? 46 Blessed is that servant who is found doing this when his lord comes; 47 I promise you, he will give him charge of all his goods. 48 But if that servant plays him false, and says in his heart, My lord is long in coming, 49 and so falls to beating his fellow servants, to eating and drinking with the drunkards, 50 then on some day when he expects nothing, at an hour when he is all unaware, his lord will come, 51 and will cut him off, and assign him his portion with the hypocrites; where there will be weeping, and gnashing of teeth.

Chapter Twenty=five

WHEN THAT DAY comes, the kingdom of heaven will be like ten virgins, who went to bring the bridegroom and his bride home, taking their lamps with them. 2 Five of these were foolish, and five were wise; 3 the five foolish, when they took their lamps, did not provide themselves with oil, 4 but those who were wise took oil in the vessels they carried, as well as the lamps. 5 The bridegroom was long in coming, so that they all grew drowsy, and fell asleep. 6 And at midnight the cry was raised, Behold, the bridegroom is on his way; go out to meet him. 7 Thereupon all these virgins awoke, and fell to trimming their lamps; 8 and now the foolish ones said to the wise, Share your oil with us, our lamps are burning low. 9 But the wise ones answered, How if there is not enough for us and for you? Better that

49

you should find your way to the merchants, and buy for yourselves. 10 And so, while they were away buying it, the bridegroom
came; those who stood ready escorted him to the wedding, and
the door was shut. 11 Afterwards those other virgins came, with
the cry, Lord, Lord, open to us. 12 And he answered, Believe me,
I do not recognize you. 13 Be on the watch, then; the day of it
and the hour of it are unknown to you.

vv. 14-30. A parable similar to this is found in Luke xix. 12.

14 So it was with a man who went on his travels; he called his
trusted servants to him and committed his money to their charge.
15 He gave five talents to one, two to another, and one to another,
according to their several abilities, and with that he set out on his
journey. 16 The man who had received five talents went and
traded with them, until he had made a profit of five talents more;
17 and in the same way he who had received two made a profit
of two. 18 Whereas he who had received but one went off and
made a hole in the ground, and there hid his master's money.
19 Long afterwards, the master of those servants came back, and
entered into a reckoning with them. 20 And so the man who had
received five talents came forward and brought him five talents
more; Lord, he said, it was five talents thou gavest me, see how I
have made a profit of five talents besides. 21 And his master said
to him, Well done, my good and faithful servant; since thou hast
been faithful over little things, I have great things to commit to
thy charge; come and share the joy of thy Lord. 22 Then came
the man who had received two talents; Lord, he said, it was two
talents thou gavest me; see how I have made a profit of two talents
besides. 23 And his master said to him, Well done, my good and
faithful servant; since thou hast been faithful over little things, I
have great things to commit to thy charge; come and share the joy
of thy Lord. 24 But when he who had received but one talent
came forward in his turn, he said, Lord, knowing thee for a hard
man, that reaps where he did not sow, and gathers in from fields he
never planted, 25 I took fright, and so went off and hid thy talent
in the earth; see now, thou hast received what is thine. 26 And
his lord answered him, Base and slothful servant, thou knewest
well that I reap where I did not sow, and gather in from fields I
never planted; 27 all the more was it thy part to lodge my money
with the bankers, so that I might have recovered it with interest
when I came. 28 Take the talent away from him, and give it to
him who has ten talents already. 29 Whenever a man is rich, gifts
will be made to him, and his riches will abound; if he is poor, even
what he accounts his own will be taken from him. 30 And now,

cast the unprofitable servant into the darkness without; where there shall be weeping, and gnashing of teeth.

31 When the Son of Man comes in his glory, and all the angels with him, he will sit down upon the throne of his glory, 32 and all nations will be gathered in his presence, where he will divide men one from the other, as the shepherd divides the sheep from the goats; 33 he will set the sheep on his right, and the goats on his left. 34 Then the King will say to those who are on his right hand, Come, you that have received a blessing from my Father, take possession of the kingdom which has been prepared for you since the foundation of the world. 35 For I was hungry, and you gave me food, thirsty, and you gave me drink; I was a stranger, and you brought me home, 36 naked, and you clothed me, sick, and you cared for me, a prisoner, and you came to me. 37 Whereupon the just will answer, Lord, when was it that we saw thee hungry, and fed thee, or thirsty, and gave thee drink? 38 When was it that we saw thee a stranger, and brought thee home, or naked, and clothed thee? 39 When was it that we saw thee sick or in prison and came to thee? 40 And the King will answer them, Believe me, when you did it to one of the least of my brethren here, you did it to me. 41 Then he will say to those who are on his left hand, in their turn, Go far from me, you that are accursed, into that eternal fire which has been prepared for the devil and his angels. 42 For I was hungry, and you never gave me food, I was thirsty, and you never gave me drink; 43 I was a stranger, and you did not bring me home, I was naked, and you did not clothe me, I was sick and in prison, and you did not care for me. 44 Whereupon they, in their turn, will answer, Lord, when was it that we saw thee hungry, or thirsty, or a stranger, or naked, or sick, or in prison, and did not minister to thee? 45 And he will answer them, Believe me, when you refused it to one of the least of my brethren here, you refused it to me. 46 And these shall pass on to eternal punishment, and the just to eternal life.

Chapter Twenty=six

vv. 1-5. Mark xiv. 1, Luke xxii. 1.

vv. 6-13. Mark xiv. 3, John xii. 1. According to St. John, this incident took place six days before the paschal feast.

vv. 14-25. Mark xiv. 12, Luke xxii. 3.

v. 17. We know from St. John (e.g. xviii. 28) that the 'first day of unleavened bread', that is, the paschal feast on the 14th day of the month Nisan, was kept by the Jews on the Friday that year. Possibly the Galileans had a different date, since it seems that the month was dated from the first night when the paschal moon was observed, and one cloudy night might falsify the reckoning. But the Greek Fathers understand St. Matthew here as calling Thursday 'the day before

AFTERWARDS, WHEN HE had made an end of saying all this, Jesus told his disciples: 2 You know that after two days the paschal feast is coming; it is then that the Son of Man must be given up to be crucified. 3 At this very time, the chief priests and the elders of the people gathered in the court of the high priest, whose name was Caiaphas; 4 and there they plotted to bring Jesus into their power by cunning, and put him to death. 5 Yet they still said, Not on the day of the feast, or perhaps there will be an uproar among the people. 6 But then, while Jesus was in the house of Simon the leper, at Bethany, 7 a woman came to him, with a pot of very precious ointment, and poured it over his head as he sat at table. 8 The disciples were indignant when they saw it: 9 What is the meaning of this waste? they asked. It would have been possible to sell this at a great price, and give alms to the poor. 10 This Jesus knew, and said to them, Why do you vex the woman? She did well to treat me so. 11 You have the poor among you always; I am not always among you. 12 When she poured this ointment over my body, she did it to prepare me for my burial; 13 and I promise you, in whatever part of the world this gospel is preached, the story of what she has done shall be told in its place, to preserve her memory. 14 And at that, one of the twelve, Judas who was called Iscariot, went to the chief priests 15 and asked them, What will you pay me for handing him over to you? Whereupon they laid down thirty pieces of silver. 16 And he, from that time onwards, looked about for an opportunity to betray him.

17 On the first of the days of unleavened bread the disciples came to Jesus and asked, Where wilt thou have us make ready for thee to eat the paschal meal? 18 And Jesus said, Go into the city, find such a man, and tell him, The Master says, My time is near; I and my disciples must keep the paschal feast at thy house. 19 The disciples did as Jesus bade them, and made all ready for the paschal meal there. 20 When evening came, he sat down with

his twelve disciples, 21 and, while they were at table, he said, Believe me, one of you is to betray me. 22 They were full of sorrow, and began to say, one after another, Lord, Is it I? 23 He answered, The man who has put his hand into the dish with me will betray me. 24 The Son of Man goes on his way, as the scripture foretells of him; but woe upon that man by whom the Son of Man is to be betrayed; better for that man if he had never been born. 25 Then Judas, he who was betraying him, said openly, Master, is it I? Jesus answered, Thy own lips have said it.

26 And while they were still at table, Jesus took bread, and blessed, and broke it, and gave it to his disciples, saying, Take, eat, this is my body. 27 Then he took a cup, and offered thanks, and gave it to them, saying, Drink, all of you, of this; 28 for this is my blood, of the new testament, shed for many, to the remission of sins. 29 And I tell you this, I shall not drink of this fruit of the vine again, until I drink it with you, new wine, in the kingdom of my Father. 30 And so they sang a hymn, and went out to mount Olivet. 31 After this, Jesus said to them, To-night you will all lose courage over me; for so it has been written, I will smite the shepherd, and the sheep of his flock will be scattered. 32 But I will go on before you into Galilee, when I have risen from the dead. 33 Peter answered him, Though all else should lose courage over thee, I will never lose mine. 34 Jesus said to him, Believe me, this night, before the cock crows, thou wilt thrice disown me. 35 Peter said to him, I will never disown thee, though I must lay down my life with thee. And all the rest of his disciples said the like.

36 So Jesus came, and they with him, to a plot of land called Gethsemani; and he said to his disciples, Sit down here, while I go in there and pray. 37 But he took Peter and the sons of Zebedee with him. And now he grew sorrowful and dismayed; 38 My soul, he said, is ready to die with sorrow; do you abide here, and watch with me. 39 When he had gone a little further, he fell upon his face in prayer, and said, My Father, if it is possible, let this chalice pass me by; only as thy will is, not as mine is. 40 Then he went back to his disciples, to find them asleep; and he said to Peter, Had you no strength, then, to watch with me even for an hour? 41 Watch and pray, that you may not enter into temptation; the spirit is willing enough, but the flesh is weak. 42 Then he went back again, and prayed a second time; and his prayer was, My Father, if this chalice may not pass me by, but I must drink it, then thy will be done. 43 And once more he found

the days of unleavened bread'. This would avoid any appearance of discrepancy. On such a view, it seems that our Lord deliberately anticipated the paschal meal by twenty-four hours; or we may suppose that the meal described in vv. 20 and following was not the meal mentioned in verse 19, but that of the night before it.

vv. 31-35. Mark xiv. 27, Luke xxii. 31, John xiii. 38.

v. 31. Zach. xiii. 7.

vv. 36-56. Mark xiv. 32, Luke xxii. 39, John xviii. 1.

53

his disciples asleep when he came to them, so heavy their eyelids were; 44 this time he went away without disturbing them, and made his third prayer, using the same words. 45 After that he returned to his disciples, and said to them, Sleep and take your rest hereafter; as I speak, the time draws near when the Son of Man is to be betrayed into the hands of sinners. 46 Rise up, let us go on our way; already, he that is to betray me is close at hand.

47 And all at once, while he was speaking, Judas, who was one of the twelve, came near; with him was a great multitude carrying swords and clubs, who had been sent by the chief priests and the elders of the people. 48 The traitor had appointed them a signal; It is none other, he told them, than the man whom I shall greet with a kiss; hold him fast. 49 No sooner, then, had he come near to Jesus than he said, Hail, Master, and kissed him. 50 Jesus said to him, My friend, on what errand hast thou come? Then they came forward and laid their hands on Jesus, and held him fast. 51 And at that, one of those who were with Jesus lifted a hand to draw his sword, and smote one of the high priest's servants with it, cutting off his ear. 52 Whereupon Jesus said to him, Put thy sword back into its place; all those who take up the sword will perish by the sword. 53 Dost thou doubt that if I call upon my Father, even now, he will send more than twelve legions of angels to my side? 54 But how, were it so, should the scriptures be fulfilled, which has prophesied that all must be as it is? 55 And Jesus said to the multitude at that hour, You have come out to my arrest with swords and clubs, as if I were a robber; and yet I used to sit teaching in the temple close to you, day after day, and you never laid hands on me. 56 All this was so ordained, to fulfil what was written by the prophets. And now all his disciples abandoned him, and fled. 57 And those who had arrested Jesus led him away into the presence of the high priest, Caiphas, where the scribes and the elders had assembled.

58 Yet Peter followed him at a long distance, as far as the high priest's palace; where he went in and sat among the servants, to see the end. 59 The chief priests and elders and all the Council tried to find false testimony against Jesus, such as would compass his death. 60 But they could find none, although many came forward falsely accusing him; until at last two false accusers came forward 61 who declared, This man said, I have power to destroy the temple of God and raise it again in three days. 62 Then the high priest stood up, and asked him, Hast thou no answer to make

v. 45. 'Hereafter'; some think this was said in irony, meaning 'from now on', but the sense may be 'sleep at some other time, not now'.

vv. 57-75. Mark xiv. 53, Luke xxii. 54, John xviii. 12.

v. 61. John ii. 19.

54

THE VISITATION   BARTHOLOMAEUS ZEITBLOM
circa 1450-1521

to the accusations these men bring against thee? 63 Jesus was silent; and the high priest said to him openly, I adjure thee by the living God to tell us whether thou art the Christ, the Son of God? 64 Jesus answered, Thy own lips have said it. And moreover I tell you this; you will see the Son of Man again, when he is seated at the right hand of God's power, and comes on the clouds of heaven. 65 At this, the high priest tore his garments, and said, He has blasphemed; what further need have we of witnesses? Mark well, you have heard his blasphemy for yourselves. 66 What is your finding? And they answered, The penalty is death. 67 Then they fell to spitting upon his face and buffeting him and smiting him on the cheek, 68 saying as they did so, Shew thyself a prophet, Christ; tell us who it is that smote thee.

69 Meanwhile, Peter sat in the court without; and there a maid-servant came up to him, and said, Thou too wast with Jesus the Galilean. 70 Whereupon he denied it before all the company; I do not know what thou meanest. 71 And he went out into the porch, where a second maidservant saw him, and said, to the bystanders, This man, too was with Jesus the Nazarene. 72 And he made denial again with an oath, I know nothing of the man. 73 But those who stood there came up to Peter soon afterwards, and said, It is certain that thou art one of them; even thy speech betrays thee. 74 And with that he fell to calling down curses on himself and swearing, I know nothing of the man; and thereupon the cock crew. 75 Then Peter remembered the word of Jesus, how he had said, Before the cock crows, thou wilt thrice disown me; and he went out, and wept bitterly.

Chapter Twenty-seven

A‌T DAYBREAK, ALL THE chief priests and elders of the people laid their plans for putting Jesus to death, 2 and they led him away in bonds, and gave him up to the governor, Pontius Pilate. 3 And now Judas, his betrayer, was full of remorse at seeing him condemned, so that he brought back to the chief priests and elders their thirty pieces of silver; 4 I have sinned, he told them, in betraying the blood of an innocent man. What is that to us? they said. It concerns thee only. 5 Whereupon he left them, throwing down the pieces of silver there in the temple, and went and hanged himself. 6 The chief priests, thus recovering the money, said, It must not be put in the treasury, since it is the price of blood; 7 and after consultation, they used it to buy the potter's field, as a burial place for strangers; 8 it is upon that account that the field has been called Haceldama, the field of blood, to this day. 9 And so the word was fulfilled which was spoken by the prophet Jeremy, when he said, And they took the thirty pieces of silver, the price of one who was appraised, for men of the race of Israel appraised him, 10 and bestowed them upon the potter's field, as the Lord had bidden me.

11 But Jesus stood before the governor. And the governor asked him, Art thou the king of the Jews? Jesus told him, Thy own lips have said it. 12 And when the chief priests and elders brought their accusation against him, he made no answer. 13 Then Pilate said to him, Dost thou not hear all the testimony they bring against thee? 14 But Jesus would not answer any of their charges, so that the governor was full of astonishment. 15 At the festival, the governor used to grant to the multitude the liberty of any one prisoner they should choose; 16 and there was one notable prisoner then in custody, whose name was Barabbas; 17 so, when they gathered about him, Pilate asked them, Whom shall I release? Barabbas, or Jesus who is called Christ? 18 He knew well that they had only given him up out of malice; 19 and even as he sat on the judgement seat, his wife had sent him a message, Do not

meddle with this innocent man; I dreamed to-day that I suffered much on his account. 20 But the chief priests and elders had persuaded the multitude to ask for Barabbas and have Jesus put to death; 21 and so, when the governor openly asked them, Which of the two would you have me release? they said, Barabbas. 22 Pilate said to them, What am I to do, then, with Jesus, who is called Christ? 23 They said, Let him be crucified. And when the governor said, Why, what wrong has he done? they cried louder than ever, Let him be crucified. 24 And so, finding that his good offices went for nothing, and the uproar only became worse, Pilate sent for water and washed his hands in full sight of the multitude, saying as he did so, I have no part in the death of this innocent man; it concerns you only. 25 And the whole people answered, His blood be upon us, and upon our children. 26 And with that he released Barabbas as they asked; Jesus he scourged, and gave him up to be crucified.

27 After this, the governor's soldiers took Jesus into the palace, and gathered the whole of their company about him. 28 First they stripped him, and arrayed him in a scarlet cloak; 29 then they put on his head a crown which they had woven out of thorns, and a rod in his right hand, and mocked him by kneeling down before him, and saying, Hail, king of the Jews. 30 And they spat upon him, and took the rod from him and beat him over the head with it. 31 At last they had done with mockery; stripping him of the scarlet cloak, they put his own garments on him, and led him away to be crucified. 32 As for his cross, they forced a man of Cyrene, Simon by name, whom they met on their way out, to carry it; 33 and so they reached a place called Golgotha, that is, the place named after a skull. 34 Here they offered him a draught of wine, mixed with gall, which he tasted, but would not drink, 35 and then crucified him, dividing his garments among them by casting lots.

36 There, then, they sat, keeping guard over him. 37 Over his head they set a written proclamation of his offence, This is Jesus, the king of the Jews; 38 and with him they crucified two thieves, one on his right and one on his left. 39 The passers-by blasphemed against him, tossing their heads; 40 Come now, they said, thou who wouldst destroy the temple and build it up in three days, rescue thyself; come down from that cross, if thou art the Son of God. The chief priests, with the scribes and elders, mocked him in the same way. 42 He saved others, they said, he cannot save himself. If he is the king of Israel, he has but to come down from

vv. 27-61. Mark xv. 20, Luke xxiii. 26, John xix. 17.

v. 35, Ps. xxi. 19.

v. 42. Wisdom ii. 18.

57

v. 43. Ps. xxi. 9.

v. 45. 'The earth', or
perhaps 'the land' of
Palestine.

v. 46. Ps. xxi. 2.

the cross, here and now, and we will believe in him. 43 He trusted in God; let God, if he favours him, succour him now; he told us, I am the Son of God. 44 Even the thieves who were crucified with him uttered the same taunts.

45 From the sixth hour onwards there was darkness over all the earth until the ninth hour; 46 and about the ninth hour Jesus cried out with a loud voice, Eli, Eli, lamma sabachthani? that is, My God, my God, why hast thou forsaken me? 47 Hearing this, some of those who stood by said, He is calling upon Elias: 48 and thereupon one of them ran to fetch a sponge, which he filled with vinegar and fixed upon a rod, and offered to let him drink; 49 the rest said, Wait, let us see whether Elias is to come and save him. 50 Then Jesus cried out again with a loud voice, and yielded up his spirit. 51 And all at once, the veil of the temple was torn this way and that from the top to the bottom, and the earth shook, and the rocks parted asunder; 52 and the graves were opened, and many bodies arose out of them, bodies of holy men gone to their rest: 53 who, after his rising again, left their graves and went into the holy city, where they were seen by many. 54 So that the centurion and those who kept guard over Jesus with him, when they perceived the earthquake and all that befell, were overcome with fear; No doubt, they said, but this was the Son of God.

55 Many women stood watching from far off; they had followed Jesus from Galilee, to minister to him; 56 among them were Mary Magdalen, and Mary the mother of James and Joseph, and the mother of the sons of Zebedee. 57 And now it was evening, and a man came forward, by name Joseph, a rich man from Arimathaea, who followed Jesus as a disciple like the rest; 58 he it was who approached Pilate, and asked to have the body of Jesus; whereupon Pilate ordered that the body should be given up. 59 Joseph took possession of the body, and wrapped it in a clean winding-sheet; then he buried it in a new grave, which he had fashioned for himself out of the rock, and left it there, rolling a great stone against the grave-door. 61 But there were two who sat on there opposite the tomb, Mary Magdalen and the other Mary with her.

62 Next day, the next after the day of preparation, the chief priests and the Pharisees gathered in Pilate's presence, 63 and said, Sir, we have recalled it to memory that this deceiver, while he yet lived, said, I am to rise again after three days. 64 Give orders, then, that his tomb shall be securely guarded until the third day; or perhaps his disciples will come and steal him away. If they should

then say to the people, He has risen from the dead, this last deceit will be more dangerous than the old. 65 Pilate said to them, You have guards; away with you, make it secure as you best know how. 66 And they went and made the tomb secure, putting a seal on the stone and setting a guard over it.

Chapter
Twenty=eight

ON THE NIGHT AFTER the sabbath, at the hour when dawn broke on the first day of the week, Mary Magdalen and the other Mary came near to contemplate the tomb. 2 And suddenly there was a great trembling of the earth, because an angel of the Lord came to the place, descending from heaven, and rolled away the stone and sat over it; 3 his face shone like lightning, and his garments were white as snow; 4 so that the guards trembled for fear of him, and were like dead men. 5 But the angel said openly to the women, You need not be afraid; I know well that you have come to look for Jesus of Nazareth, the man who was crucified. 6 He is not here; he has risen, as he told you. Come and see the place where the Lord was buried. 7 You must go in haste, and tell his disciples that he has risen from the dead; and now he is going on before you into Galilee, where you shall have sight of him. That is my message to you. 8 Whereupon they left the tomb, in fear and in great rejoicing, and ran to tell the news to his disciples. 9 And while they were on their way, all at once Jesus met them and said, All hail. With that, they came near to him, and clung to his feet, and worshipped him. 10 Then Jesus said to them, Do not be afraid; go and give word to my brethren to remove into Galilee; they shall see me there.

11 They had not finished their journey, when some of the guards reached the city, and told the chief priests of all that befell.

vv. 1-8. Mark xvi. 1, Luke xxiv. 1.

v. 1. 'The night after the sabbath', literally, in the Greek, 'late of the sabbath', which can bear the meaning 'too late for it to be the sabbath'. This interpretation must be the right one here, since it is clear that St. Matthew, like the other Evangelists, is speaking of early morning, not of the evening.

v. 2. The words 'of the earth' do not occur in the Greek; and it is possible that the 'trembling' here alluded to is that mentioned in verse 4.

v. 9. This encounter may be the same, or may have taken place nearly at the same time, as that recorded in John xx. 11-17.

12 These gathered with the elders to take counsel, and offered a rich bride to the soldiers; 13 Let this, they said, be your tale, His disciples came by night and stole him away, while we were asleep. 14 If this should come to the ears of the governor, we will satisfy him, and see that no harm comes to you. 15 The soldiers took the bribe, and did as they were instructed; and this is the tale which has gone abroad among the Jews, to this day.

16 And now the eleven disciples took their journey into Galilee, to the mountain where Jesus had bidden them meet him. 17 When they saw him there, they fell down to worship; though some were still doubtful. 18 But Jesus came near and spoke to them; All authority in heaven and on earth, he said, has been given to me; 19 you, therefore, must go out, making disciples of all nations, and baptizing them in the name of the Father, and of the Son, and of the Holy Ghost, 20 teaching them to observe all the commandments which I have given you. And behold I am with you all through the days that are coming, until the consummation of the world.

v. 17. 'Were still doubtful', probably in the sense that they did not recognize him while he was still at a distance (cf. John xxi. 7, 12, 13). Or it may mean that there were some (not of the apostles, but of those who followed them; I Cor. xv. 6), who had doubted until then.

THE HOLY ✠ OF GOSPEL JESUS CHRIST ACCORDING TO MARK

Chapter One

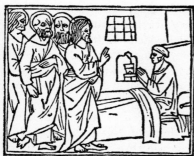

THE BEGINNING OF THE gospel of Jesus Christ, the Son of God. 2 It is written in the prophecy of Isaias, Behold, I am sending before thee that angel of mine who is to prepare thy way for thy coming; 3 there is a voice of one crying in the wilderness, Prepare the way of the Lord, straighten out his paths. 4 And so it was that John appeared in the wilderness baptizing, announcing a baptism whereby men repented, to have their sins forgiven. 5 And all the country of Judaea and all those who dwelt in Jerusalem went out to see him, and he baptized them in the river Jordan, while they confessed their sins. 6 John was clothed with a garment of camel's hair, and had a leather girdle about his loins, and he ate locusts and wild honey. 7 And thus he preached, One is to come after me who is mightier than I, so that I am not worthy to bend down and untie the strap of his shoes. 8 I have baptized you with water; he will baptize you with the Holy Ghost.

9 At this time, Jesus came from Nazareth, and was baptized by John in the Jordan. 10 And even as he came up out of the water he saw the heavens opened, and the Spirit, like a dove, coming

vv. 1-11. Matthew iii. 1, Luke iii. 1.

vv. 2-3. The second half of this prophecy is taken from Is. xl. 3; the first half is not from Isaias but from Malachy (iii. 1). St. Jerome suggests that St. Mark may have been using a catena of Old Testament prophecies, in which these two passages came together, and treated them as one, giving a reference only to the more important one.

down and resting upon him. 11 There was a voice, too, out of heaven, Thou art my beloved Son; in thee I am well pleased.

vv.12-15. Matthew iv. 1, Luke iv. 1.

12 Thereupon, the Spirit sent him out into the desert: 13 and in the desert he spent forty days and forty nights, tempted by the devil; there he lodged with the beasts, and there the angels ministered to him.

14 But when John had been put in prison, Jesus came into Galilee, preaching the gospel of God's kingdom: 15 The appointed time has come, he said, and the kingdom of God is near at hand; repent, and believe the gospel. 16 And as he passed along the sea

vv. 16-20. Matthew iv. 18.

of Galilee, he saw Simon and Simon's brother Andrew casting a net into the sea, (for they were fishermen); 17 Jesus said to them, Come and follow me; I will make you into fishers of men. 18 And they dropped their nets immediately, and followed him. 19 Then he went a little further, and saw James, the son of Zebedee, and his brother John; these too were in their boat, repairing their nets; 20 all at once he called them, and they, leaving their father Zebedee in the boat with the hired men, turned aside after him. 21 So they made their way to Capharnaum; here, as soon as the sabbath came, he went into the synagogue and taught; 22 and they were amazed by his teaching, for he sat there teaching them like one who had authority, not like the scribes. 23 And there, in the synagogue, was a man possessed by an unclean spirit, who cried aloud: 24 Why dost thou meddle with us, Jesus of Nazareth? Hast thou come to make an end of us? I recognize thee for what thou art, the Holy One of God. 25 Jesus spoke to him threateningly; Silence! he said; come out of him. 26 Then the unclean spirit threw him into a convulsion, and cried with a loud voice, and so came out of him. 27 All were full of astonishment; What can this be? they asked one another. What is this new teaching? See how he has authority to lay his commands even on the unclean spirits, and they obey him! 28 And the story of his doings at once spread through the whole region of Galilee.

vv. 29-34. Matthew viii. 14, Luke iv. 38.

29 As soon as they had left the synagogue, they came into Simon and Andrew's house; James and John were with them. 30 The mother of Simon's wife was lying sick there, with a fever, and they made haste to tell him of her; 31 whereupon he went close and took her by the hand, and lifted her up. And all at once the fever left her, and she began ministering to them. 32 And when it was evening and the sun went down, they brought to him all those who were afflicted, and those who were possessed by devils; 33 so that the whole city stood crowding there at the

door. 34 And he healed many that were afflicted with diseases of every sort, and cast out many devils; to the devils he would give no leave to speak, because they recognized him. 35 Then, at very early dawn, he left them, and went away to a lonely place, and began praying there. 36 Simon and his companions went in search of him: 37 and when they found him, they told him, All men are looking for thee. 38 And he said to them, Let us go to the next country towns, so that I can preach there too; it is for this I have come. 39 So he continued to preach in their synagogues, all through Galilee, and cast the devils out.

40 Then a leper came up to him, asking for his aid; he knelt at his feet and said, If it be thy will, thou hast power to make me clean. 41 Jesus was moved with pity; he held out his hand and touched him, and said, It is my will; be thou made clean. 42 And at the word, the leprosy all at once left him, and he was cleansed. 43 And he spoke to him threateningly, and sent him away there and then: 44 Be sure thou dost not speak of this at all, he said, to anyone; away with thee, shew thyself to the priest, and offer the gift for thy cleansing which Moses ordained, to make the truth known to them. 45 But he, as soon as he had gone away, began to talk publicly and spread the story round; so that Jesus could no longer go into any of the cities openly, but dwelt in lonely places apart; and still from every side they came to him.

vv. 40-45. Matthew viii. 1, Luke v. 12.

v. 44. Lev. xiv. 2.

Chapter Two

THEN, AFTER SOME DAYS, he went into Capharnaum again. 2 And as soon as word went round that he was in a house there, such a crowd gathered that there was no room left even in front of the door; and he preached the word to them. 3 And now they came to bring a palsied man to him, four of them carrying him

vv. 1-12. Matthew ix. 1.

63

at once; 4 and found they could not bring him close to, because of the multitude. So they stripped the tiles from the roof over the place where Jesus was, and made an opening; then they let down the bed on which the palsied man lay. 5 And Jesus, seeing their faith, said to the palsied man, Son, thy sins are forgiven. 6 But there were some of the scribes sitting there, who reasoned in their minds. 7 Why does he speak so? He is talking blasphemously. 8 Who can forgive sins but God, and God only? Jesus knew at once, in his spirit, of these secret thoughts of theirs, and said to them, Why do you reason thus in your minds? 9 Which command is more lightly given, to say to the palsied man, Thy sins are forgiven, or to say, Rise up, take thy bed with thee, and walk? 10 And now, to convince you that the Son of Man has authority to forgive sins while he is on earth (here he spoke to the palsied man): 11 I tell thee, rise up, take thy bed with thee, and go home. 12 And he rose up at once, and took his bed, and went out in full sight of them; so that all were astonished and gave praise to God; they said, We never saw the like.

13 Then he went out by the sea again; and all the multitude came to him, and he taught them there. 14 And as he passed further on, he saw Levi, the son of Alphaeus, sitting at work in the customs-house, and said to him, Follow me; and he rose up and followed him. 15 And afterwards, when he was taking a meal in his house, many publicans and sinners were at table with Jesus and his disciples; for there were many of these who followed him. 16 There upon the scribes and Pharisees, seeing him eat with publicans and sinners in his company, asked his disciples, How comes it that your master eats and drinks with publicans and sinners? 17 Jesus heard it, and said to them, It is not those who are in health that have need of the physician, it is those who are sick. I have come to call sinners, not the just.

18 John's disciples and the Pharisees used to fast at that time. And they came and said to him, How is it that thy disciples do not fast, when John's disciples and the Pharisees fast? 19 To them Jesus said, Can you expect the men of the bridegroom's company to go fasting, while the bridegroom is still with them? As long as they have the bridegroom with them, they cannot be expected to fast; 20 but the days will come when the bridegroom is taken away from them; then they will fast, when that day comes. 21 Nobody sews on a piece of new cloth to patch an old cloak; if that is done, the new piecing takes away threads from the old cloth, and makes the rent in it worse. 22 Nor does anybody put new wine

v. 9. See note on Matthew ix. 5.

vv. 14-22. Matthew ix. 9, Luke v. 27.
v. 14. This was clearly another name for St. Matthew, who introduces his more familiar name at this point (Matthew ix. 9).

64

into old wineskins; if that is done, the wine bursts the skins, and there is the wine spilt and the skins spoiled. New wine must be put into fresh wineskins.

23 It happened that he was walking through the corn-fields on the sabbath day; and his disciples fell to plucking the ears of corn as they went. 24 And the Pharisees said to him, Look, why are they doing what it is not lawful to do on the sabbath? 25 Whereupon he said to them, Have you never read of what David did, when he and his followers were hard put to it for hunger? 26 How he went into the tabernacle, when Abiathar was high priest, and ate the loaves set forth there before God, which only the priests may eat, and gave them, besides, to those who were with him? 27 And he told them, The sabbath was made for man, not man for the sabbath. 28 So that the Son of Man has even the sabbath at his disposal.

vv. 23-28. Matthew xii. 1, Luke vi. 1.

v. 25. I Kings xxi. 6.

Chapter Three

AND ONCE MORE HE went into a synagogue; and there was a man there who had one of his hands withered; 2 and they were watching him, to see whether he would do a work of healing on the sabbath, so that they might have a charge to bring against him. 3 So he said to the man who had his hand withered, Rise up, and come forward. 4 Then he said to them, Which is right, to do good on the sabbath day, or to do harm? To save life, or to make away with it? And they sat there in silence. 5 And he looked round on them in anger, grieved at the hardness of their hearts, and said to the man, Stretch out thy hand. He stretched it out, and his hand was restored to him.

vv. 1-6. Matthew xii. 9, Luke vi. 6.

6 Then the Pharisees went out, and at once began plotting with those who were of Herod's party to make away with him. 7 But

MARK

Jesus withdrew, with his disciples, towards the sea; and great crowds followed him, from Galilee, and from Judaea, 8 and from Jerusalem, and from Idumaea, and from beyond Jordan; and those who lived about Tyre and Sidon, hearing of all that he did, came in great numbers to him. 9 So he told his disciples to keep a boat ready at need because of the multitude, for fear they should press on him too close; 10 for he did many works of healing, so that all those who were visited with suffering thrust themselves upon him, to touch him. 11 The unclean spirits, too, whenever they saw him, used to fall at his feet and cry out, Thou art the Son of God; 12 and he would give them a strict charge not to make him known.

13 Then he went up on to the mountain side, and called to him those whom it pleased him to call; so these came to him, 14 and he appointed twelve to be his companions, and to go out preaching at his command, 15 with power to cure diseases and to cast out devils. 16 To Simon he gave the fresh name of Peter; 17 to James the son of Zebedee and his brother John, he gave the fresh name of Boanerges, that is, sons of thunder. 18 The others were Andrew, and Philip, and Bartholomew, and Matthew, and Thomas, and James the son of Alphaeus, and Thaddaeus, and Simon the Cananean; 19 and Judas Iscariot, the traitor.

20 And now they came into a house, and once more the multitude gathered so that they had no room even to sit and eat. 21 When word came to those who were nearest him, they went out to restrain him; they said, He must be mad. 22 And the scribes who had come down from Jerusalem said, He is possessed by Beelzebub; it is through the prince of the devils that he casts the devils out. 23 So he called them to him, and spoke to them in parables; How can it be Satan who casts Satan out? 24 Why, if a kingdom is at war with itself, that kingdom cannot stand firm, 25 and if a household is at war with itself, that household cannot stand firm; 26 if Satan, then, has risen up in arms against Satan, he is at war with himself; he cannot stand firm; his end has come. 27 No one can enter into a strong man's house and plunder his goods, without first making the strong man his prisoner; then he can plunder his house at will. 28 Believe me, there is pardon for all the other sins of mankind and the blasphemies they utter; 29 but if a man blasphemes against the Holy Spirit, there is no pardon for him in all eternity; he is guilty of a sin which is eternal. 30 This was because they were saying He has an unclean spirit.

31 Then his mother and his brethren came and sent a message

vv. 13-19. Matthew x. 1, Luke vi. 12.

v. 18. Thaddaeus (or Lebbaeus) must be identified with 'Judas, not Iscariot' (Luke vi. 16).

v. 21. It is uncertain what is meant by 'those who were nearest him'. Some think the Greek means that those who were with him in the house went out to restrain it (the crowd), saying that it must be mad. 'They said'; or perhaps, 'Men said.'

vv. 22-30. Matthew xii. 24, Luke xi. 15.

v. 29. See note on Matthew xii. 32.

vv. 31-35. Matthew xii. 46 (see note there), Luke viii. 19.

66

to him, calling him to them, while they stood without. 32 There was a multitude sitting round him when they told him, Behold, thy mother and thy brethren are without, looking for thee. 33 And he answered them, Who is a mother, who are brethren, to me? 34 Then he looked about at those who were sitting around him, and said, Here are my mother and my brethren! 35 If anyone does the will of God, he is my brother, and sister, and mother.

Chapter Four

THEN HE BEGAN TO teach by the sea side again; and a great multitude gathered before him, so that he went into a boat, and sat there on the sea, while all the multitude was on the land, at the sea's edge. 2 And he taught them for a long time, but in parables; Listen, his teaching began, 3 here is the sower gone out to sow. 4 And as he sowed, some grains chanced to fall beside the path, so that the birds came and ate them up. 5 And others fell on rocky land, where the soil was shallow; these sprang up all at once, because they had not sunk deep in the ground: 6 and when the sun rose they were parched; they had taken no root, and so they withered away. 7 Some fell among briers, so that the briers grew up and smothered them, and they gave no crop. 8 And others fell where the soil was good, and these sprouted and grew, and yielded a harvest; some of them thirtyfold, some sixtyfold, some a hundredfold. 9 Listen, he said, you that have ears to hear with.

10 When they could speak with him alone, the twelve who were with him asked the meaning of the parable. 11 And he said to them, It is granted to you to understand the secret of God's kingdom; for those others, who stand without, all is parable: 12 so they must watch and watch, yet never see, must listen and listen,

vv. 1-20. Matthew xiii. 1, Luke viii. 4.

v. 12. Is. vi. 9.

yet never understand, nor ever turn back, and have their sins forgiven them. 13 Then he said to them. You do not understand this parable? And are these the men who are to understand all parables? 14 What the sower sows is the word. 15 Those by the way side are those who have the word sown in them, but no sooner have they heard it than Satan comes, and takes away this word that was sown in their hearts. 16 In the same way, those who take in the seed in rocky ground are those who entertain the word with joy as soon as they hear it, 17 and yet have no root in themselves; they last for a time, but afterwards, when tribulation or persecution arises over the word, their faith is soon shaken. 18 And there are others who take in the seed in the midst of thorns; they are those who hear the word, 19 but allow the cares of this world and the deceitfulness of riches and their other appetites to smother the word, so that it remains fruitless. 20 And those who take in the seed in good soil are those who hear the word and welcome it and yield a harvest, one grain thirtyfold, one sixtyfold, one a hundredfold.

21 And he said to them, Is a lamp brought in to be put under a bushel measure, or under a bed, not in the lamp-stand? 22 What is hidden, is hidden only so that it may be revealed; what is kept secret, is kept secret only that it may come to light. 23 Listen, all you that have ears to hear with. 24 And he said to them, Look well what it is that you hear. The measure in which you give is the measure in which you will be repaid, and more will be given you besides. 25 If a man is rich, gifts will be made to him; if he is poor, even the little he has will be taken away from him.

26 And he said to them, The kingdom of heaven is like this; it is as if a man should sow a crop in his land, 27 and then go to sleep and wake again, night after night, day after day, while the crop sprouts and grows, without any knowledge of his. 28 So, of its own accord, the ground yields increase, first the blade, then the ear, then the perfect grain in the ear; 29 and when the fruit appears, then it is time for him to put in the sickle, because now the harvest is ripe.

vv. 30-34. Matthew xiii. 31, Luke xiii. 18.

30 And he said, What likeness can we find for the kingdom of God? To what image are we to compare it? 31 To a grain of mustard seed; when this is sown in the earth, no seed on earth is so little; 32 but, once sown, it shoots up and grows taller than any garden herb, putting out great branches, so that all the birds can come and settle under its shade. 33 And he used many parables of this kind, such as they could listen to easily, in preaching

the word to them; 34 to them he spoke only in parables, and made all plain to his disciples when they were alone.

35 That day, when evening came on, he said to them, Let us go across to the other side. 36 So they let the multitude go, and took him with them, just as he was, on the boat; there were other boats too with him. 37 And a great storm of wind arose, and drove the waves into the boat, so that the boat could hold no more. 38 Meanwhile, he was in the stern, asleep on the pillow there; and they roused him, crying, Master, art thou unconcerned? We are sinking. 39 So he rose up, and checked the wind, and said to the sea, Peace, be still. And the wind dropped, and there was deep calm. 40 Then he said to them, Why are you faint-hearted? Have you still no faith? And they were overcome with awe; Why, who is this, they said to one another, who is obeyed even by the winds and the sea?

vv. 35-40. Matthew viii. 23, Luke viii. 26.

Chapter Five

SO THEY CAME TO THE further shore of the sea, in the country of the Gerasenes. 2 And as soon as he had disembarked, a man possessed by an unclean spirit came out of the rock tombs to meet him. 3 This man made his dwelling among the tombs, and nobody could keep him bound any longer, even with chains. 4 He had been bound with fetters and chains often before, but had torn the chains apart and broken the fetters, and nobody had the strength to control him. 5 Thus he spent all his time, night and day, among the tombs and the hills, crying aloud and cutting himself with stones. 6 When he saw Jesus from far off, he ran up and fell at his feet, 7 and cried with a loud voice, Why dost thou meddle with me, Jesus, Son of the most high God? I adjure thee in God's name, do not torment me, 8 (for he was saying, Come out of the man, thou unclean spirit). 9 Then he asked him, What is

vv. 1-20. Matthew viii. 28, Luke viii. 26.

thy name? The spirit told him, My name is Legion; there are many of us, 10 and it was full of entreaties that he would not send them away out of the country. 11 There, at the foot of the mountain, was a great herd of swine feeding; 12 and the devils entreated him, Send us into the swine, let us make our lodging there. 13 With that, Jesus gave them leave; and the unclean spirits came out, and went into the swine; whereupon the herd rushed down at full speed into the sea, some two thousand in number, and the sea drowned them. 14 The swineherds fled, and told their news in the city and in the country-side; so that they came out to see what had befallen; 15 and when they reached Jesus, they found the possessed man sitting there, clothed and restored to his wits, and they were overcome with fear. 16 Then those who had seen it told them the story of the possessed man, and what had happened to the swine. 17 Whereupon they began entreating him to leave their country. 18 So he embarked on the boat; and as he did so the man who had been possessed was eager to go with him, 19 but Jesus would not give him leave; Go home to thy friends, he said, and tell them all that the Lord has done for thee, and what great mercy he shewed thee. 20 So he went back and began to spread word in Decapolis of what Jesus had done for him; and all wondered at it.

vv. 21-43. Matthew ix. 18 (see note there), Luke viii. 41.

21 So Jesus went back by boat across the sea, and a great multitude gathered about him; and while he was still by the sea, 22 one of the rulers of the synagogue came up, Jairus by name, and fell down at his feet when he saw him, 23 pleading for his aid. My daughter, he said, is at the point of death; come and lay thy hand on her, that so she may recover, and live. 24 So he turned aside with him, and a great multitude followed him, and pressed close upon him. 25 And now a woman who for twelve years had had an issue of blood, 26 and had undergone much from many physicians, spending all she had on them, and no better for it, but rather grown worse, 27 came up behind Jesus in the crowd (for she had been told of him), and touched his cloak; 28 If I can even touch his cloak, she said to herself, I shall be healed. 29 And immediately the source of the bleeding dried up, and she felt in her body that she had been cured of her affliction. 30 Jesus thereupon, inwardly aware of the power that had proceeded from him, turned back towards the multitude and asked, Who touched my garments? 31 His disciples said to him, Canst thou see the multitude pressing so close about thee, and ask, Who touched me? 32 But he looked round him to catch sight of the woman who had done this. 33 And now the woman, trembling with fear, since she recognized what

had befallen her, came and fell at his feet, and told him the whole truth. 34 Whereupon Jesus said to her, My daughter, thy faith has brought thee recovery; go in peace, and be rid of thy affliction.

35 While he was yet speaking, messengers came from the ruler's house to say, Thy daughter is dead; why dost thou trouble the Master any longer? 36 Jesus heard the word said, and told the ruler of the synagogue, No need to fear; thou hast only to believe. 37 And now he would not let anyone follow him, except Peter and James and James' brother John; 38 and so they came to the ruler's house, where he found a great stir, and much weeping and lamentation. 39 And he went in and said to them, What is this stir, this weeping? The child is not dead, she is asleep. 40 They laughed aloud at him; but he sent them all out, and, taking the child's father and mother and his own companions with him, went in to where the child lay. 41 Then he took hold of the child's hand, and said to her, Talitha, cumi, which means, Maiden, I say to thee, rise up. 42 And the girl stood up immediately, and began to walk; she was twelve years old. And they were beside themselves with wonder. 43 Then he laid a strict charge on them to let nobody hear of this, and ordered that she should be given something to eat.

Chapter Six

THEN HE LEFT THE place, and withdrew to his own country-side, his disciples following him. 2 Here, when the sabbath came, he began teaching in the synagogue, and many were astonished when they heard him; How did he come by all this? they asked. What is the meaning of this wisdom that has been given him, of all these wonderful works that are done by his hands? 3 Is not this the carpenter, the son of Mary, the brother of James

vv. 1-6. Matthew xiii. 54, Luke iv. 16, John vi. 42.

and Joseph and Judas and Simon? Do not his sisters live here near us? 4 And they had no confidence in him. Then Jesus said to them, It is only in his own country, in his own home, and among his own kindred, that a prophet goes unhonoured. 5 Nor could he do any wonderful works there, except that he laid his hands on a few who were sick, and cured them; 6 he was astonished at their unbelief. And so he went on round about the villages preaching.

vv. 7-13. Matthew x. 1, Luke ix. 1.

7 And now he called the twelve to him, and began sending them out, two and two, giving them authority over the unclean spirits. 8 And he gave them instructions to take a staff for their journey and nothing more; no wallet, no bread, no money for their purses; 9 to be shod with sandals, and not to wear a second coat. 10 You are to lodge, he told them, in the house you first enter, until you leave the place. 11 And wherever they give you no welcome and no hearing, shake off the dust from beneath your feet in witness against them. 12 So they went out and preached, bidding men repent; 13 they cast out many devils, and many who were sick they anointed with oil, and healed them.

vv. 14-30. Matthew xiv. 1, Luke ix. 7.

14 Then, as his name grew better known, king Herod came to hear of it. It is John the Baptist, he said, risen from the dead, and that is why these powers are active in him. 15 Others were saying, It is Elias, and others, It is a prophet like one of the old prophets; 16 but when Herod was told it, he declared, He has risen from the dead, John the Baptist, whom I beheaded. 17 Herod himself had sent and arrested John and put him in prison, in chains, for love of Herodias, his brother Philip's wife, whom he had married; 18 because John had told Herod, It is wrong for thee to take thy brother's wife. 19 Herodias was always plotting against him, and would willingly have murdered him, but could not, 20 because Herod was afraid of John, recognizing him for an upright and holy man; so that he kept him carefully, and followed his advice in many things, and was glad to listen to him. 21 And now came a fitting occasion, upon which Herod gave a birthday feast to his lords and officers, and to the chief men of Galilee. 22 Herodias' own daughter came in and danced, and gave such pleasure to Herod and his guests that the king said to the girl, Ask me for whatever thou wilt, and thou shalt have it; 23 he even bound himself by an oath, I will grant whatever request thou makest, though it were a half of my kingdom. 24 Thereupon she went out and said to her mother, What shall I ask for? 25 And she answered, The head of John the Baptist. With that, she hastened into the king's presence and made her request; My will is, she said, that thou shouldst give

v. 20. 'Follow his advice in many things'; some Greek manuscripts have, 'was much perplexed at what he heard from him'.

me the head of John the Baptist; give it me now, on a dish. 26 And the king was full of remorse, but out of respect to his oath and to those who sat with him at table, he would not disappoint her. 27 So he sent one of his guard with orders that the head should be brought on a dish. This soldier cut off his head in the prison, 28 and brought it on a dish, and gave it to the girl; and the girl gave it to her mother. 29 When John's disciples heard of it, they came and carried off his body, and laid it in a tomb.

30 And now the apostles came together again in the presence of Jesus, and told him of all they had done, and all the teaching they had given. 31 And he said to them, Come away into a quiet place *vv. 31-44. Matthew xiv. 15, Luke ix. 10,* by yourselves, and rest a little. For there were many coming and *John vi. 3.* going, and they scarcely had leisure even to eat. 32 So they took ship, and went to a lonely place by themselves. 33 But many saw them going, or came to know of it; gathering from all the cities, they hurried to the place by land, and were there before them. 34 So, when he disembarked, Jesus saw a great multitude there, and took pity on them, since they were like sheep that have no shepherd, and began to give them long instruction. 35 And when it was already late, his disciples came to him and said, This is a lonely place, and it is late already; 36 give them leave to go to the farms and villages round about, and buy themselves food there; they have nothing to eat. 37 But he answered them, It is for you to give them food to eat. Why then, they said to him, we must go and spend two hundred silver pieces buying bread to feed them. 38 He asked, How many loaves have you? Go and see. When they had found out, they told him, Five, and two fishes. 39 Then he told them all to sit down in companies on the green grass; 40 and they took their places in rows, by hundreds and fifties. 41 And he took the five loaves and the two fishes, and looked up to heaven, and blessed and broke the loaves, and gave these to his disciples to set before them, dividing the fishes, too, among them all. 42 All ate and had enough: 43 and when they took up the broken pieces, and what was left of the fishes, they filled twelve baskets with them. 44 The loaves had fed five thousand men.

45 As soon as this was done, he prevailed upon his disciples to *vv. 45-56. Matthew xiv. 22.* take ship and cross to Bethsaida, on the other side, before him, leaving him to send the multitude home. 46 And when he had taken leave of them, he went up on to the hill side, to pray there. 47 Twilight had already come, and the boat was half way across the sea, while he was on the shore alone. 48 And when the night

had reached its fourth quarter, seeing them hard put to it with rowing (for the wind was against them), he came to them, walking on the sea, and made as if to pass them by. 49 When they saw him walking on the sea, they thought it was an apparition, and cried aloud, 50 for all had seen him, and were full of dismay. But now he spoke to them; Take courage, he said, it is myself; do not be afraid. 51 So he came to them on board the boat, and thereupon the wind dropped. And they were astonished out of all measure; 52 they had not grasped the lesson of the loaves, so dulled were their hearts.

53 When they had crossed, they came to shore at Genesareth and moored there. 54 As soon as they had disembarked, he was recognized, 55 and they ran off into all the country round, and began bringing the sick after him, beds and all, wherever they heard he was. 56 And wherever he entered villages, or farmsteads, or towns, they used to lay the sick down in the open streets, and beg him to let them touch even the hem of his cloak; and all those who touched him recovered.

Chapter Seven

THEN THE PHARISEES and some of the scribes, who had

vv. 1-30. *Matthew* xv. 1.

come from Jerusalem, gathered round him; 2 and these found fault, because they saw that some of his disciples sat down to eat with their hands defiled, that is, unwashed. 3 For the Pharisees, and indeed all the Jews, holding to the tradition of their ancestors, never eat without washing their hands again and again; 4 they will not sit down to meat, coming from the market, without thorough cleansing; and there are many other customs which they hold to by tradition, purifying of cups and pitchers and pans and beds. 5 So the Pharisees and scribes asked him, Why do thy disciples eat with defiled hands, instead of following the tradition of our ancestors? 6 But he answered, You hypocrites, it was a true prophecy Isaias made of you, writing as he did, This people does me honour with its lips, but its heart is far from me; 7 their worship of me is vain, for the doctrines they teach are the commandments of men. 8 You leave God's commandment on one side, and hold to the tradition of man, the purifying of pitchers and cups, and many other like observances. 9 And he told them, You have quite defeated God's commandment, to establish your own tradition instead. 10 Moses said, Honour thy father and thy mother, and, He who curses father or mother dies without hope of reprieve. 11 But you say, Let a man tell his father or his mother, All the money out of which you might get help from me is now Corban (that is, an offering to God), 12 and then you will not let him do any more for father or mother. 13 With this and many like observances, you are making God's law ineffectual through the tradition you have handed down. 14 And he called the multitude to him, and said to them, Listen to me, all of you, and grasp this; 15 Nothing that finds its way into a man from outside can make him unclean; what makes a man unclean is what comes out of a man. 16 Listen, you that have ears to hear with.

17 When he had gone into the house, away from the multitude, his disciples asked him the meaning of the parable. 18 And he said to them, Are you still so slow of wit? Do you not observe that all the uncleanness which goes into a man has no means of defiling him, 19 because it travels, not into his heart, but into the belly, and so finds its way into the sewer? Thus he declared all meat to be clean, 20 and told them that what defiles a man is that which comes out of him. 21 For it is from within, from the hearts of men, that their wicked designs come, their sins of adultery, fornication, murder, 22 theft, covetousness, malice, deceit, lasciviousness, envy, blasphemy, pride and folly. 23 All these evils come from within, and it is these which make a man unclean.

24 After this, Jesus left those parts, and withdrew into the neighbourhood of Tyre and Sidon. There he went into a house, and did not wish anyone to know of it; but he could not go unrecognized, 25 for a woman came to hear of it, whose daughter was possessed by an unclean spirit, and she came in and fell at his feet. 26 This woman was a Gentile, a Syrophenician by race, and she begged him to cast the devil out of her daughter. 27 But he said to her, Let the children have their fill first; it is not right to take the children's bread and throw it to the dogs. 28 She an-

v. 6. Is. xxix. 13.

v. 10. Ex. xx. 12, Deut. v. 16.
v. 11. See note on Matthew xv. 5.

75

swered him, Ah, yes, Lord; the dogs eat of the crumbs the children leave, underneath the table. 29 And he said to her, In reward for this word of thine, back home with thee; the devil has left thy daughter. 30 And when she came back to her house, she found her daughter lying on the bed, and the devil gone.

31 Then he set out again from the region of Tyre, and came by way of Sidon to the sea of Galilee, right into the region of Decapolis. 32 And they brought to him a man who was deaf and dumb, with the prayer that he would lay his hand upon him. 33 And he took him aside out of the multitude; he put his fingers into his ears, and spat, and touched his tongue; 34 then he looked up to heaven, and sighed; Ephpheta, he said (that is, Be opened). 35 Whereupon his ears were opened, and the bond which tied his tongue was loosed and he talked plainly. 36 And he laid a strict charge on them, not to speak of it to anyone; but the more he charged them, the more widely they published it, 37 and were more than ever astonished; He has done well, they said, in all his doings; he has made the deaf hear, and the dumb speak.

Chapter Eight

vv. 1-9. Matthew xv.
32.

ONCE MORE, AT THIS time, the multitude had grown in numbers, and had nothing to eat. And he called his disciples to him, and said to them, 2 I am moved with pity for the multitude; it is three days now since they have been in attendance on me, and they have nothing to eat. 3 If I send them back to their homes fasting, they will grow faint on their journey; some of them have come from far off. 4 His disciples answered him, How could anyone find bread to feed them, here in the desert? 5 And he asked them, How many loaves have you? 6 Seven, they said. And he gave word to the multitude to sit down on the ground. Then he took the seven loaves, and when he had blessed and broken he gave these to his disciples to set before them; so they set them before the multitude. 7 And they had a few small fishes; these he blessed, and ordered that these, too, should be set before them; 8 and they ate, and had enough. When they picked up what was left of the broken pieces, it filled seven hampers; 9 about four thousand had eaten. And so he sent them home.

10 Thereupon he embarked, with his disciples, and went into the part round Dalmanutha. 11 Here the Pharisees came out and entered upon a dispute with him; to put him to the test, they asked him to shew them a sign from heaven. 12 And he sighed deeply in his spirit, and said, Why does this generation ask for a sign? Believe me, this generation shall have no sign given it. 13 And so he left them, and took ship again, and crossed to the further side.

14 They had forgotten to take bread with them, and had no more than one loaf in the boat; 15 and when he warned them, Look well, and avoid the leaven of the Pharisees, and the leaven of Herod, 16 they said anxiously to one another, We have brought no bread. 17 Jesus knew it, and said, what is this anxiety, that you have brought no bread with you? Have you no sense, no wits, even now? Is your heart still dull? 18 Have you eyes that cannot see, and ears that cannot hear; do you remember nothing? When I broke the five loaves among the five thousand, how many baskets full of broken pieces did you take up? They told him, Twelve. 20 And when I broke the seven loaves among the four thousand, how many hampers full of broken pieces did you take up then? And they told him, Seven. 21 Then he said to them, How is it that you still do not understand?

22 So they came to Bethsaida. And they brought to him a blind man, whom they entreated him to touch. 23 He took the blind man by the hand, and led him outside the village; then he spat into his eyes, and laid his hands on him, and asked him if he could see anything? 24 He looked up and said, I can see men as if they were trees, but walking. 25 Once more Jesus laid his hands upon his eyes, and he began to see right; and soon he recovered, so that he could see everything clearly. 26 Then he sent him back to his house; go home, he said, and if thou shouldst enter the village, do not tell anyone of it.

27 Then Jesus went with his disciples into the villages round Caesarea Philippi; and on the way he asked his disciples, Who do men say that I am? 28 They answered, John the Baptist, and others say Elias; others that thou art like one of the prophets.

vv. 11-21. Matthew xvi. 1.

vv. 27-39. Matthew xvi. 13, Luke ix. 18. St. Mark omits here the promises made to St. Peter, perhaps because St. Peter forbade it, out of humility; perhaps because writing (like St. Luke) at Rome he was unwilling to draw attention to the Apostle's prominence in the Church, for fear of persecution arising.

29 Then he said to them, And what of you? Who do you say that I am? Peter answered him, Thou art the Christ. 30 And he strictly charged them not to tell anyone about him. 31 And now he began to make it known to them that the Son of Man must be much ill-used, and be rejected by the elders and chief priests and scribes, and be put to death, and rise again after three days. 32 This he told them openly; whereupon Peter, drawing him to his side, fell to reproaching him. 33 But he turned about, and, seeing his disciples there, rebuked Peter; Back, Satan, he said, these thoughts of thine are man's, not God's. 34 And he called his diciples to him, and the multitude with them, and said to them, If any man has a mind to come my way, let him renounce self, and take up his cross, and follow me. 35 The man who tries to save his life will lose it; it is the man who loses his life for my sake and for the gospel's sake, that will save it. 36 How is a man the better for it, if he gains the whole world at the expense of losing his own soul? 37 For a man's soul, what price can be high enough? 38 If anyone is ashamed of acknowledging me and my words before this unfaithful and wicked generation, the Son of Man, when he comes in his father's glory with the holy angels, will be ashamed to acknowledge him. 39 Believe me, there are those standing here who will not taste of death before they have seen the kingdom of God present in all its power.

Chapter Nine

vv. 1-31. Matthew xvii. 1, Luke ix. 28.

SIX DAYS AFTERWARDS, Jesus took Peter and James and John with him, and led them up to a high mountain where they were alone by themselves; and he was transfigured in their presence. 2 His garments became bright, dazzling white like snow, white as no fuller here on earth could have made them. 3 And they had sight of Elias, with Moses; these two were conversing with Jesus. 4 Then Peter said aloud to Jesus, Master, it is well that we should be here; let us make three arbours, one for thee, and one for Moses, and one for Elias; 5 he did not know what to say, for they were overcome with fear. 6 And a cloud formed, overshadowing them; and from the cloud came a voice, which said, 7 This is my beloved Son; to him, then, listen. Then, on a sudden, they looked round them, and saw no one any more, but Jesus only with them.

8 And as they were coming down from the mountain, he warned them not to tell anyone what they had seen, until after the Son of Man had risen from the dead; 9 so they kept the matter to themselves, wondering what the words could mean, When he has risen from the dead. 10 And they asked him, Tell us, why do the Pharisees and scribes say Elias must come before Christ? 11 He answered them, Elias must needs come and restore all things as they were; and now, what is written of the Son of Man? That he must be much ill-used, and despised. 12 Elias too, I tell you, has already come, and they have misused him at their pleasure, as the scriptures tell of him.

v. 12. See note on Matthew xvii. 12.

13 When he reached his disciples, he found a great multitude gathered around them, and some of the scribes disputing with them. 14 The multitude, as soon as they saw him, were overcome with awe, and ran up to welcome him. 15 He asked them, What is the dispute you are holding among you? 16 And one of the multitude answered, Master, I have brought my son to thee; he is possessed by a dumb spirit, 17 and wherever it seizes on him, it tears him, and he foams at the mouth, and gnashes his teeth, and his strength is drained from him. And I bade thy disciples cast it out, but they were powerless. 18 And he answered them, Ah, faithless generation, how long must I be with you, how long must I bear with you? Bring him to me. 19 So they brought the boy to him; and the evil spirit, as soon as it saw him, threw the boy into a convulsion, so that he fell on the ground, writhing and foaming at the mouth. 20 And now Jesus asked the father, How long has this been happening to him? From childhood, he said; 21 and often it has thrown him into the fire, and into water, to make an end of him. Come, have pity on us, and help us if thou canst. 22 But Jesus said to him, If thou canst believe, to him who believes, everything is possible. 23 Whereupon the father of the boy cried aloud, in tears, Lord, I do believe; succour my unbelief. 24 And Jesus, seeing how the multitude was gathering round them, rebuked the unclean spirit; Thou dumb and deaf spirit, he said, it is

I that command thee; come out of him, and never enter into him again. 25 With that, crying aloud and throwing him into a violent convulsion, it came out of him, and he lay there like a corpse, so that many declared, He is dead. 26 But Jesus took hold of his hand, and raised him, and he stood up. 27 When he had gone into a house, and they were alone, the disciples asked him, Why was it that we could not cast it out? 28 And he told them, There is no way of casting out such spirits as this except by prayer and fasting.

29 Then they left those parts, and passed straight through Galilee, and he would not let anyone know of his passage; 30 he spent the time teaching his disciples, The Son of Man, he said, is to be given up into the hands of men. They will put him to death, and he will rise again on the third day. 31 But they could not understand his meaning, and were afraid to ask him. 32 So they came to Capharnaum, and there, when they were in the house, he asked them, What was the dispute you were holding on the way? 33 They said nothing, for they had been disputing among themselves which should be the greatest of them. 34 Then he sat down, and called the twelve to him, and said, If anyone has a mind to be the greatest, he must be the last of all, and the servant of all. 35 And he took a little child, and gave it a place in the midst of them; and he took it in his arms, and said to them: 36 Whoever welcomes such a child as this in my name, welcomes me; and whoever welcomes me, welcomes, not me, but him that sent me. 37 And John answered him, Master, we saw a man who does not follow in our company casting out devils in thy name, and we forbade him to do it. 38 But Jesus said, Forbid him no more; no one who does a miracle in my name will lightly speak evil of me. 39 The man who is not against you is on your side. 40 Why, if anyone gives you a cup of water to drink in my name, because you are Christ's, I promise you, he shall not miss his reward. 41 And if anyone hurts the conscience of one of these little ones, that believe in me, he had better have been cast into the sea, with a millstone about his neck. 42 If thy hand is an occasion of falling to thee, cut it off; better for thee to enter into life maimed, than to have two hands when thou goest into hell, into unquenchable fire; 43 the worm which eats them there never dies, the fire is never quenched. 44 And if thy foot is an occasion of falling to thee, cut it off; better for thee to enter into eternal life lame, than to have both feet when thou art cast into the unquenchable fire of hell; 45 the worm which eats them there never dies, the fire is never quenched. 46 And if thy eye is an occasion of falling, pluck it out; better for

thee to enter blind into the kingdom of God, than to have two eyes when thou art cast into the fire of hell; 47 the worm which eats them there never dies, the fire is never quenched. 48 Fire will be every man's seasoning; every victim must be seasoned with salt. 49 Salt is a good thing, but if the salt becomes tasteless, what will you use to season it with? You must have salt in yourselves, and keep peace among you.

Chapter Ten

REMOVING THENCE, HE entered the territory of Judaea which lies beyond the Jordan. Multitudes gathered round him once more; and once more he began to teach them, as his custom was. 2 Then the Pharisees came and put him to the test by asking him, whether it is right for a man to put away his wife. 3 He answered them, What command did Moses give you? 4 And they said, Moses left a man free to put his wife away, if he gave her a writ of separation. 5 Jesus answered them, It was to suit your hard hearts that Moses wrote such a command as that; 6 God, from the first days of creation, made them man and woman. 7 A man, therefore, will leave his father and mother and will cling to his wife, 8 and the two will become one flesh. Why then, since they are no longer two, but one flesh, 9 what God has joined, let not man put asunder. 10 And when they were in the house, his disciples asked him further about the same question. 11 Whereupon he told them, If a man puts away his wife and marries another, he behaves adulterously towards her; 12 and if a woman puts away her husband and marries another, she is an adulteress.

13 Then they brought children to him, asking him to touch them; and his disciples rebuked those who brought them. 14 But Jesus was indignant at seeing this; Let the children come to me, he said,

vv. 1-12. Matthew xix. 1; cf. Luke xvi. 18, Matthew v. 32, I Cor. vii. 10.

v. 4. Deut. xxiv. 1.

v. 7. Gen. ii. 24.

v. 11. See note on Matthew xix. 9.

vv. 13-31. Matthew xix. 13, Luke xviii. 15.

81

do not keep them back; the kingdom of God belongs to such as these. 15 I tell you truthfully, the man who does not welcome the kingdom of God like a child, will never enter into it. 16 And so he embraced them, laid his hands upon them, and blessed them.

17 Then he went out to continue his journey; and a man ran up and knelt down before him, asking him, Master, who art so good, what must I do to achieve eternal life? 18 Jesus said to him, Why dost thou call me good? None is good, except God only. 19 Thou knowest the commandments, Thou shalt not commit adultery, Thou shalt do no murder, Thou shalt not steal, Thou shalt not bear false witness, Thou shalt not wrong any man, Honour thy father and thy mother. 20 Master, he answered, I have kept all these ever since I grew up. 21 Then Jesus fastened his eyes on him, and conceived a love for him; In one thing, he said, thou art still wanting. Go home and sell all that belongs to thee; give it to the poor, and so the treasure thou hast shall be in heaven; then come back and follow me. 22 At this, his face fell, and he went away sorrowing, for he had great possessions. 23 And Jesus looked round, and said to his disciples, With what difficulty will those who have riches enter God's kingdom! 24 The disciples were amazed at his words; but Jesus gave them a second answer. My children, how hard it is for those who trust in riches to enter God's kingdom! 25 It is easier for a camel to pass through a needle's eye, than for a man to enter the kingdom of God when he is rich. 26 They were still more astonished; Why then, they said to themselves, who can be saved? 27 Jesus fastened his eyes on them, and said, Such things are impossible to man's powers, but not to God's; to God, all things are possible.

28 Hereupon Peter took occasion to say, What of us, who have forsaken all, and followed thee? 29 Jesus answered, I promise you, everyone who has forsaken home, or brothers, or sisters, or mother, or children, or lands for my sake and for the sake of the gospel, 30 will receive, now in this world, a hundred times their worth, houses, sisters, brothers, mothers, children and lands, but with persecution; and in the world to come he will receive everlasting life. 31 But many will be first that were last, and last that were first.

32 And now they were on the way going up to Jerusalem; and still Jesus led them on, while they were bewildered and followed him with faint hearts. Then once more he brought the twelve apostles to his side, and began to tell them what was to befall him: 33 Now, we are going up to Jerusalem; and there the Son of Man will be given up into the hands of the chief priests and scribes, who

v. 18. See note on Matthew xix. 17.

v. 19. Ex. xx. 13.

v. 21. See note on Matthew xix. 21.

vv. 32-34. Matthew xx. 17, Luke xviii. 31.

will condemn him to death; and these will give him up into the hands of the Gentiles, 34 who will mock him, and spit upon him, and scourge him, and kill him; but on the third day he will rise again.

35 Thereupon James and John, the sons of Zebedee, came to him and said, Master, we would have thee grant the request we are to make. 36 And he asked them, What would you have me do for you? 37 They said to him, Grant that one of us may take his place on thy right and the other on thy left, when thou art glorified. 38 But Jesus said to them, You do not know what it is you ask. Have you strength to drink of the cup I am to drink of, to be baptized with the baptism I am to be baptized with? 39 They said to him, We have. And Jesus told them, You shall indeed drink of the cup I am to drink of, and be baptized with the baptism I am to be baptized with; 40 but a place on my right hand or my left is not mine to give you; it is for those for whom it has been destined.

vv. 35-45. Matthew xx. 20.

41 The ten others grew indignant with James and John when they heard of it. 42 But Jesus called them to him, and said to them, You know that, among the Gentiles, those who claim to bear rule lord it over them, and those who are great among them make the most of the power they have. 43 With you it must be otherwise; whoever has a mind to be great among you, must be your servant, 44 and whoever has a mind to be first among you, must be your slave. 45 So it is that the Son of Man did not come to have service done him; he came to serve others, and to give his life as a ransom for the lives of many.

46 And now they reached Jericho. As he was leaving Jericho, with his disciples and with a great multitude, Bartimaeus, the blind man, Timaeus' son, was sitting there by the way side, begging. 47 And, hearing that this was Jesus of Nazareth, he fell to crying out, Jesus, son of David, have pity on me. 48 Many of them rebuked him and told him to be silent, but he cried out all the more, Son of David, have pity on me. 49 Jesus stopped, and bade them summon him; so they summoned the blind man; Take heart, they said, and rise up; he is summoning thee. 50 Whereupon he threw away his cloak and leapt to his feet, and so came to Jesus. 51 Then Jesus answered him, What wouldst thou have me do for thee? And the blind man said to him, Lord, give me back my sight. 52 Jesus said to him, Away home with thee; thy faith has brought thee recovery. And all at once he recovered his sight, and followed Jesus on his way.

vv. 46-52. Matthew xx. 29, Luke xviii. 35.

83

Chapter Eleven

vv. 1-10. Matthew
xxi. 1, Luke xix. 29,
John xii. 12.

W HEN THEY WERE AP
proaching Jerusalem, and Beth-
any, which is close to mount Olivet, he sent two of his disciples on
an errand: 2 Go into the village that faces you, he told them, and
the first thing you will find there upon entering will be a colt
tethered, one on which no man has ever ridden; untie it, and bring
it to me. 3 And if anyone asks you, Why are you doing that? tell
him, the Lord has need of it, and he will let you have it without
more ado. 4 So they went, and found the colt tethered before a
door at the entrance; and they untied it. 5 Some of the bystanders
asked them, What are you doing, untying the colt? 6 And they
answered them as Jesus had bidden, and were allowed to take it.
7 So they brought the colt to Jesus, and saddled it with their garments, and he mounted it. 8 Many of them spread their garments
in the way, and others strewed the way with leaves they had cut
down from the trees. 9 And those who went before him and followed after him cried aloud, Hosanna, 10 blessed is he who comes
in the name of the Lord; blessed is the kingdom of our father David
which is coming to us; Hosanna in heaven above. 11 So he came
to Jerusalem, and went into the temple, where he surveyed all that
was about him, and then, for the hour was already late, went out,
with the twelve, to Bethany.

vv. 12-24. Matthew
xxi. 12, Luke xix. 45.

v. 13. See note on
Matthew xxi. 18.

12 When they had left Bethany next day, he was hungry: 13 and,
observing a fig-tree some way off with its leaves out, he went up
to see if he could find anything on it. But when he reached it, he
found leaves and nothing else; it was not the right season for figs.
14 And he said to it aloud, in the hearing of his disciples; Let no
man ever eat fruit of thine hereafter. 15 So they came to Jerusalem.
And there Jesus went into the temple, and began driving out those
who sold and bought in the temple, and overthrew the tables of
the bankers, and the chairs of the pigeon-sellers; 16 nor would

v. 17. Is. lvi. 7, and
Jer. vii. 11.

he allow anyone to carry his wares through the temple. 17 And
this was the admonition he gave them, Is it not written, My house
shall be known among all the nations for a house of prayer? Where-

as you have made it into a den of thieves. 18 The chief priests and scribes heard of this, and looked for some means of making away with him; they were afraid of him, because all the multitude was so full of admiration at his teaching.

19 He left the city at evening, 20 and next morning, as they passed by, they saw the fig-tree withered from its roots. 21 Peter had not forgotten; Master, he said, look at the fig-tree which thou didst curse; it has withered away. 22 And Jesus answered them, Have faith in God. 23 I promise you, if anyone says to this mountain, Remove, and be cast into the sea, and has no hesitation in his heart, but is sure that what he says is to come about, his wish will be granted him. 24 I tell you, then, when you ask for anything in prayer, you have only to believe that it is yours, and it will be granted you. 25 When you stand praying, forgive whatever wrong any man has done you; so that your Father who is in heaven may forgive you your transgressions; 26 if you do not forgive, your Father who is in heaven will not forgive your transgressions either.

27 So they came back to Jerusalem. And as he was walking about in the temple, the chief priests and scribes and elders came to him 28 and asked him, What is the authority by which thou doest these things, and who gave thee this authority to do them? 29 Jesus answered them, I too have a question to ask; if you can tell me the answer, I will tell you in return what is the authority by which I do these things. 30 Whence did John's baptism come, from heaven or from men? 31 Whereupon they cast about in their minds; If we tell him it was from heaven, they said, he will ask us, Then why did you not believe him? 32 And if we say it was from men, we have reason to be afraid of the people; for the people all looked upon John as a prophet indeed. 33 And they answered Jesus, We cannot tell. Jesus answered them, And you will not learn from me what is the authority by which I do these things.

vv. 27-33. Matthew xxi. 23, Luke xx. 1.

Chapter Twelve

vv. 1-12. Matthew xxi.
33. Luke xx. 9; cf.
Is. v. 1.

THEN HE BEGAN TO speak to them in parables; There was a man who planted a vineyard, and put a wall round it, and dug a winepress and built a tower in it, and then let it out to some vine-dressers, while he went on his travels. 2 And when the season came, he sent one of his servants on an errand to the vine-dressers, to claim from the vine-dressers the revenue of his vineyard. 3 Whereupon they took him and beat him, and sent him away empty-handed. 4 Then he sent another servant on a second errand to them, and him too they beat over the head and used him outrageously. 5 He sent another, whom they killed; and many others, whom they beat or killed at their pleasure. 6 He had still one messenger left, his own well-beloved son; him he sent to them last of all; They will have reverence, he said, for my son. 7 But the vine-dressers said among themselves, This is the heir, come, let us kill him, and then his inheritance will be ours. 8 So they took him and killed him, and cast him out of the vineyard. 9 And now, what will the owner of the vineyard do? He will come, and make an end of those vine-dressers, and give his vineyard to others.

v. 10. Ps. cxvii. 22;
cf. Romans ix. 33,
I Peter ii. 7.

10 Why, have you not read this passage in the scriptures, The very stone which the builders rejected has become the chief stone at the corner; 11 this is the Lord's doing, and it is marvellous in our eyes? 12 This parable, they saw, was aimed at themselves, and they would gladly have laid hands on him, but they were afraid

vv. 13-37. Matthew
xxii. 15, Luke xx. 19.

of the multitude; so they went away and left him alone. 13 Then they sent some of the Pharisees to him, with those who were of Herod's party, to make him betray himself in his talk. 14 These came and said to him, Master, we know that thou art sincere; that thou holdest no one in awe, making no distinction between man and man, but teachest in all sincerity the way of God. Is it right that tribute should be paid to Caesar? Or should we refuse to pay it? 15 But he saw their treachery, and said to them, Why do you thus put me to the test? Bring me a silver piece, and let me look at it. 16 When they brought it, he asked them, Whose is this

THE NATIVITY   FRA ANGELICO
                                                            1387-1455

METROPOLITAN MUSEUM, NEW YORK

likeness? Whose name is inscribed on it? Caesar's, they said. 17 Whereupon Jesus answered them, Give back to Caesar what is Caesar's, and to God what is God's. And they were lost in admiration of him.

18 Then he was approached with a question by the Sadducees, men who say that there is no resurrection: 19 Master, they said, Moses prescribed for us that if a man's brother dies, leaving a widow behind him but no children, he, the brother, should marry the widow, and beget children in the dead brother's name. 20 There were seven brethren; the first married a wife, and died childless; 21 the second married her, and he too left no children, and so with the third; 22 all seven married her, without having children, and the woman died last of all. 23 And now, when the dead rise again, which of these will be her husband, since she was wife to all seven? 24 Jesus answered them, Is not this where you are wrong, that you do not understand the scriptures, or what is the power of God? 25 When the dead rise, there is no marrying or giving in marriage, they are as the angels in heaven are. 26 But as for the dead rising again, have you never read in the book of Moses how God spoke to him at the burning bush, and said, I am the God of Abraham, and the God of Isaac, and the God of Jacob? 27 Yet it is of living men, not of dead men, that he is the God; you are wrong, then, altogether. *v. 26. Ex. iii. 6.*

28 One of the scribes heard their dispute, and, finding that he answered to the purpose, came up and asked him, Which is the first commandment of all? 29 Jesus answered him, The first commandment of all is, Listen, Israel; there is no God but the Lord thy God; 30 and thou shalt love the Lord thy God with the love of thy whole heart, and thy whole soul, and thy whole mind, and thy whole strength. This is the first commandment, 31 and the second, its like, is this, Thou shalt love thy neighbour as thyself. There is no other commandment greater than these. 32 And the scribe said to him, Truly, Master, thou hast answered well; there is but one God, and no other beside him; 33 and to love him with the love of the whole heart, and the whole understanding, and the whole soul, and the whole strength, is a greater thing than all burnt offerings and sacrifices. 34 Then Jesus, seeing how wisely he had answered, said to him, Thou art not far from the kingdom of God. And after this, no one dared to try him with further questions. *v. 29. Deut. vi. 4.* *v. 31. Lev. xix. 18.*

35 Then Jesus said openly, still teaching in the temple. What do the scribes mean by saying that Christ is to be the son of David? 36 David himself was moved by the Holy Spirit to say, The Lord *v. 36. Ps. cix. 1.*

said to my Master, Sit on my right hand while I make thy enemies a footstool under thy feet. 37 Thus David himself calls Christ his Master; how can he be also his son? And the multitude at large listened to him readily. 38 This was part of the teaching he gave them, Beware of the scribes, who enjoy walking in long robes, and having their hands kissed in the market-place, 39 and the first seats in the synagogues, and the chief places at feasts; 40 who swallow up the property of widows, under cover of their long prayers; their sentence will be all the heavier for that.

41 As he was sitting opposite the treasury of the temple, Jesus watched the multitude throwing coins into the treasury, the many rich with their many offerings; 42 and there was one poor widow, who came and put in two mites, which make a farthing. 43 Thereupon he called his disciples to him, and said to them, Believe me, this poor widow has put in more than all those others who have put offerings into the treasury. 44 The others all gave out of what they had to spare; she, with so little to give, put in all that she had, her whole livelihood.

vv. 38-44. Luke xx. 45, xxi. 1.

Chapter Thirteen

AS HE WAS LEAVING the temple, one of his disciples said to him, Look, Master, what stones! What a fabric! 2 Jesus answered him, Do you see all this huge fabric? There will not be a stone of it left on another; it will all be thrown down. 3 So, when he was sitting down on mount Olivet, opposite the temple, Peter and James and John and Andrew asked him, now that they were alone: 4 Tell us, when will this be? And what sign will be given, when all this is soon to be accomplished? 5 Take care, Jesus began in answer, that you do not allow anyone to deceive you. 6 Many will come making use of my name; they will say, Here I am, and

vv. 1-33. Matthew xxiv. 1, Luke xxi. 5.

v. 4. See note on Matthew xxiv. 3.

many will be deceived by it. 7 When you hear tell of wars, and rumours of war, do not be disturbed in mind; such things must happen, but the end will not come yet. 8 Nation will rise in arms against nation, and kingdom against kingdom, there will be earthquakes in this region or that, there will be famines: all this is but the beginning of travail. 9 But you will have to think of yourselves; men will be giving you up to courts of justice, and scourging you in the synagogues, yes, and you will be brought before governors and kings on my account, so that you can bear witness to them; 10 the gospel must be preached to all nations before the end. 11 When they take you and hand you over thus, do not consider anxiously beforehand what you are to say; use what words are given you when the time comes; it is not you that speak, it is the Holy Spirit. 12 Brother will be given up to death by brother, and the son by his father; children will rise up against their parents, and will compass their deaths; 13 all the world will be hating you because you bear my name; but that man will be saved, who endures to the last.

14 And now, when you see the abomination of desolation standing where it should never stand (let him who reads this, recognize what it means), then those who are in Judaea must take refuge in the mountains; 15 not going down into the house, if they are on the house-top, or entering the house to carry anything away from it; not turning back, if they are in the fields, to pick up a cloak. 17 It will go hard with women who are with child, or have children at the breast, in those days. 18 And you must pray that your flight may not be in the winter; 19 for those will be days of distress, such as has not been since the beginning of creation till now, and can never be again. 20 There would have been no hope left for any human creature, if the Lord had not cut those days short; but he has cut the days short for the sake of the elect, whom he has chosen. 21 At such a time, if a man tells you, See, here is Christ, or, See, he is there, do not believe him. 22 There will be false Christs and false prophets who will rise up and shew signs and wonders, so that, if it were possible, even the elect would be deceived. 23 But you must be on your guard; hereby, I have given you warning of it all.

24 In those days, after this distress, the sun will be darkened, and the moon will refuse her light; 25 and the stars will be falling from heaven, and the powers that are in heaven will rock; 26 and then they will see the Son of Man coming upon the clouds, with great power and glory. 27 And then he will send out his angels,

v. 14. Daniel ix. 27; see note on Matthew xxiv. 15.

v. 24. See note on Matthew xxiv. 29.

v. 27. See note on Matthew xxiv. 31.

to gather his elect from the four winds, from earth's end to heaven's.
28 The fig-tree will teach you a parable; when its branch grows
supple, and begins to put out leaves, you know that summer is
near; 29 so you, when you see all this come about, are to know
that it is near, at your very doors. 30 Believe me, this generation
will not have passed, before all this is accomplished. 31 Though
heaven and earth should pass away, my words will stand.

32 But as for that day and that hour you speak of, they are
known to nobody, not even to the angels in heaven, not even to the
Son; only the Father knows them. 33 Look well to it; watch and
pray; you do not know when the time is to come. 34 It is as if a
man going on his travels had left his house, entrusting authority to
his servants, each of them to do his own work, and enjoining the
door-keeper to watch. 35 Be on the watch, then, since you do not
know when the master of the house is coming, at twilight, or midnight, or cockcrow, or dawn; 36 if not, he may come suddenly,
and find you asleep. And what I say to you, I say to all, Watch.

Chapter Fourteen

vv. 1-11. Matthew
xxvi. 1, Luke xxii. 1
(in part), John xii.
1 (in part).

IT WAS NOW TWO DAYS
to the paschal feast and the time
of unleavened bread; and the chief priests and scribes were trying
to bring Jesus into their power by cunning, and put him to death;
2 But not on the day of the feast, they said, or there may be an
uproar among the people. 3 And then, while he was in the house of
Simon the leper, at Bethany, sitting at table, a woman came in
with a pot of very precious spikenard ointment, which, first breaking the pot, she poured over his head. 4 There were some present
who were indignant when they saw it, and said among themselves,
What did she mean by wasting the ointment so? 5 This ointment
might have been sold for three hundred pieces of silver, and alms

90

might have been given to the poor. And they rebuked her angrily.
6 But Jesus said, Let her alone; why should you vex her? 7 She
did well to treat me so. You have the poor among you always, so
that you can do good to them when you will; I am not always
among you. 8 She has done what she could; she has anointed my
body beforehand to prepare it for burial. 9 I promise you, in whatever part of the world this gospel is preached, the story of what
she has done shall be told in its place, to preserve her memory.
10 Then Judas Iscariot, one of the twelve, went to the chief priests
and offered to betray him into their hands. 11 And they, listening
to him eagerly, promised him money; whereupon he looked about
for an opportunity to betray him.

12 On the first of the days of unleavened bread, the day on
which they killed the paschal victim, his disciples asked him, Where
wilt thou have us go and make ready for thee to eat the paschal
meal? 13 And he sent two of his disciples on this errand, Go into
the city, and there a man will meet you, carrying a jar of water;
you are to follow him, 14 and say to the owner of the house into
which he enters, the master says, Where is my room, in which I
am to eat the paschal meal with my disciples? 15 And he will shew
you a large upper room, furnished and prepared; it is there that
you are to make ready for us. 16 So the disciples left him and went
into the city, where they found all as he had told them, and so
made ready for the paschal meal. 17 When it was evening, he came
there with the twelve. 18 And as they sat at table and were eating,
Jesus said, Believe me, one of you, one who is eating with me, is to
betray me. 19 They began to ask him sorrowfully, each in turn,
Is it I? and then another, Is it I? 20 He told them, It is one of the
twelve, the man who puts his hand into the dish with me. 21 The
Son of Man goes on his way, as the scripture foretells of him;
but woe upon that man by whom the Son of Man is to be betrayed; better for that man if he had never been born.

22 And while they were still at table, Jesus took bread, and
blessed, and broke it, and gave it to them, saying, Take this; this
is my body. 23 Then he took a cup, and offered thanks, and gave
it to them, and they all drank of it. And he said, 24 This is my
blood of the new testament, shed for many. 25 I tell you truthfully,
I shall not drink of this fruit of the vine again, until the day when
I drink it with you, new wine, in the kingdom of God. 26 And so
they sang a hymn, and went out to mount Olivet. 27 And Jesus
said to them, To-night you will all lose courage over me; for so it
has been written, I will smite the shepherd, and the sheep will be

vv. 12-21. Matthew xxvi. 17 (see note there), Luke xxii. 7.

vv. 22-25. Matthew xxvi. 26, Luke xxii. 15, I Cor. xi. 23.

vv. 27-31. Matthew xxvi. 31, Luke xxii. 31, John xiii. 38.

v. 27. Zach. xiii. 7.

91

scattered. 28 But I will go on before you into Galilee, when I have risen from the dead. 29 Peter said to him, Though all else should lose courage over thee, I will never lose mine. 30 And Jesus said to him, Believe me, this night, before the second cock-crow, thou wilt thrice disown me. 31 But Peter insisted more than ever, I will not disown thee, though I must lay down my life with thee. And all of them said the like.

vv. 32-50. Matthew xxvi. 36, Luke xxii. 40, John xviii. 1.

32 So they came to a plot of land called Gethsemani; and he said to his disciples, Sit down here, while I go and pray. 33 But he took Peter and James and John with him. And now he grew dismayed and distressed: 34 My soul, he said to them, is ready to die with sorrow; do you abide here, and keep watch. 35 So he went forward a little, and fell on the ground, and prayed that if it were possible, the hour might pass him by: 36 Abba, Father, he said, all things are possible to thee; take away this chalice from before me; only as thy will is, not as mine is. 37 Then he went back, and found them asleep; and he said to Peter, Simon, art thou sleeping? 38 Hadst thou not strength to watch even for an hour? Watch and pray, that you may not enter into temptation; the spirit is willing enough, but the flesh is weak. 39 Then he went away and prayed again, using the same words. 40 And when he returned, once more he found them asleep, so heavy their eyelids were; and they did

v. 41. See note on Matthew xxvi. 45.

not know what answer to make to him. 41 When he came the third time, he said to them, Sleep and take your rest hereafter. Enough; the time has come; behold, the Son of Man is to be betrayed into the hands of sinners. 42 Rise up, let us go on our way; already, he that is to betray me is close at hand.

43 And thereupon, while he was yet speaking, Judas Iscariot, who was one of the twelve, came near; with him was a great multitude carrying swords and clubs, who had been sent by the chief priests and the scribes and the elders. 44 The traitor had appointed them a signal; It is none other, he said, than the man whom I shall greet with a kiss; hold him fast, and take him away under guard. 45 No sooner, then, had he come up than he went close to Jesus, saying, Hail, Master, and kissed him; 46 and with that they laid their hands on him, and held him fast. 47 And one of those who stood by drew his sword, and smote one of the high priest's servants with it, cutting off his ear. 48 Then Jesus said to them aloud, You have come out to my arrest with swords and clubs, as if I were a robber; 49 and yet I used to teach in the temple close to you, day after day, and you never laid hands on me. But the scriptures must be fulfilled. 50 And now all his disciples

abandoned him, and fled. 51 There was a young man there following him, who was wearing only a linen shirt on his bare body; and he, when they laid hold of him, 52 left the shirt in their hands, and ran away from them naked. 53 So they took Jesus into the presence of the high priest, and all the chief priests and elders and scribes were assembled about him.

vv. 53-72. Matthew xxvi. 57, Luke xxii. 54, John xviii. 12.

54 Yet Peter followed at a long distance, right into the high priest's palace, where he sat with the servants by the fire, to warm himself. 55 The high priest and all the council tried to find an accusation against Jesus, such as would compass his death, but they could find none; 56 many accused him falsely, but their accusations did not agree. 57 There were some who stood up and falsely accused him thus: 58 We heard him say, I will destroy this temple that is made by men's hands, and in three days I will build another, with no hand of man to help me. 59 But even so their accusations did not agree. 60 Then the high priest stood up, and asked Jesus, Hast thou no answer to the accusations these men bring against thee? 61 He was still silent, still did not answer; and the high priest questioned him again, Art thou the Christ, the Son of the blessed God? 62 Jesus said to him, I am. And you will see the Son of Man sitting at the right hand of God's power, and coming with the clouds of heaven. 63 At this, the high priest tore his garments, and said, What further need have we of witnesses? 64 You have heard his blasphemy for yourselves; what is your finding? And they all pronounced against him a sentence of death. 65 Then some of them fell to spitting upon him, and covering his face while they buffeted him and bade him prophesy; the servants, too, caught him blows on the cheek.

v. 58. John ii. 19.

v. 69. 'The maid', either the portress at the gate, or the same maid who had already challenged the Apostle at the fire; in the latter case, the discrepancy with St. Matthew (xxvi. 71) is, in the opinion of the Fathers, too slight to need apology.

66 Meanwhile, Peter was in the court without, and one of the maidservants of the high priest came by; 67 she saw Peter warming himself, and said, looking closely at him, Thou too wast with Jesus the Nazarene. 68 Whereupon he denied it; I know nothing of it, I do not understand what thou meanest. Then he went out into the porch; and the cock crew. 69 Again the maid looked at him, and said to the bystanders, This is one of them. 70 And again he denied it. Then, a little while afterwards, the bystanders said to Peter, It is certain that thou art one of them; why, thou art a Galilean. 71 And he fell to calling down curses on himself and swearing, I do not know the man you speak of. 72 Then came the second cock-crow; and Peter remembered the word Jesus had said to him, Before the second cock-crow thou wilt thrice deny me. And all at once he burst out weeping.

v. 72. The other Evangelists only mention one crowing of the cock; which is not wonderful, since it appears that the second crowing of the cock was regarded by the ancients as the time of cock-crow, that is the third division of the night (Mark xiii. 35): the first crowing had been an hour in advance of the time (Luke xxii. 59). The sense of the last three words of this chapter is not certain in the Greek; others render, 'when he thought upon it, he wept'.

93

Chapter Fifteen

*vv. 1-15 (in part).
Matthew xxvii. 11,
Luke xxiii. 2, John
xviii. 33.*

No SOONER HAD DAY broken, than the chief priests made their plans, with the elders and scribes and the whole council; they took Jesus away in bonds and gave him up to Pilate. 2 And Pilate asked him, Art thou the king of the Jews? He answered him, Thy own lips have said it. 3 And now the chief priests brought many accusations against him. 4 and Pilate questioned him again, Dost thou make no answer? See what a weight of accusation they bring against thee. 5 But Jesus still would not answer him, so that Pilate was full of astonishment. 6 At the festival, he used to grant them the liberty of any one prisoner they chose; 7 and the man they called Barabbas was then in custody, with the rebels who had been guilty of murder during the rebellion. 8 So, when the multitude came up towards him, and began to ask for the customary favour, 9 Pilate answered them, Would you have me release the king of the Jews? 10 He knew well that the chief priests had only given him up out of malice. 11 But the chief priests incited the multitude to ask for the release of Barabbas instead. 12 Once more Pilate answered them, What would you have me do, then, with the king of the Jews? 13 And they made a fresh cry of, Crucify him. 14 Why, Pilate said to them, what wrong has he done? But they cried all the more, Crucify him. 15 And so Pilate, determined to humour the multitude, released Barabbas as they asked; Jesus he scourged, and gave him up to be crucified.

*vv. 16-20. Matthew
xxvii. 27.*

16 Then the soldiers led him away into the court of the palace, and gathered there the whole of their company. 17 They arrayed him in a scarlet cloak, and put round his head a crown which they had woven out of thorns, 18 and fell to greeting him with, Hail, king of the Jews. 19 And they beat him over the head with a rod, and spat upon him, and bowed their knees in worship of him. 20 At last they had done with mockery; stripping him of the scarlet cloak, they put his own garments on him, and led him away to be cruci-

*vv. 21-47. Matthew
xxvii. 62, Luke xxiii.
26, John xix. 17.*

fied. 21 As for his cross, they forced a passer-by who was coming in from the country to carry it, one Simon of Cyrene, the father

THE ADORATION OF THE SHEPHERDS   GIORGIONE
1478-1510

NATIONAL GALLERY OF ART, WASHINGTON, D. C. (KRESS COLLECTION)

of Alexander and Rufus. 22 And so they took him to a place called Golgotha, which means, The place of a skull. 23 Here they offered him a draught of wine mixed with myrrh, which he would not take; 24 and then crucified him, dividing his garments among them by casting lots, to decide which should fall to each.

25 It was the third hour when they crucified him. 26 A proclamation of his offence was written up over him, The king of the Jews; 27 and with him they crucified two thieves, one on the right and the other on his left, 28 so fulfilling the words of scripture, And he was counted among the wrong-doers. 29 The passers-by blasphemed against him, shaking their heads; Come now, they said, thou who wouldst destroy the temple and build it up in three days, 30 come down from that cross, and rescue thyself. 31 In the same way, the chief priests and scribes said mockingly to one another, He saved others, he cannot save himself. 32 Let Christ, the king of Israel, come down from the cross, here and now, so that we can see it and believe in him. And the men who were crucified with him uttered taunts against him.

33 When the sixth hour came, there was darkness over all the earth until the ninth hour; 34 and at the ninth hour Jesus cried out with a loud voice, Eloi, Eloi, lama sabachthani? which means, My God, my God, why hast thou forsaken me? 35 Hearing this, some of those who stood by said, Why, he is calling upon Elias. 36 And thereupon one of them ran off to fill a sponge with vinegar, and fixed it on a rod, and offered to let him drink; Wait, he said, Let us see whether Elias is to come and save him. 37 Then Jesus gave a loud cry, and yielded up his spirit. 38 And the veil of the temple was torn this way and that, from the top to the bottom. 39 The centurion who stood in front of him, perceiving that he so yielded up his spirit with a cry, said, No doubt but this was the Son of God.

40 There were women there, who stood watching from far off; among them were Mary Magdalen, and Mary the mother of James the less and of Joseph, and Salome. 41 These used to follow him and minister to him when he was in Galilee, and there were many others who had come up with him to Jerusalem. 42 And now it was already evening; and because it was the day of preparation, that is, the day before the sabbath, 43 a rich councillor, named Joseph of Arimathea, one of those who waited for God's kingdom, boldly went to Pilate, and asked to have the body of Jesus. 44 Pilate, astonished that he should have died so soon, called the centurion to him, to ask if he was dead already, 45 and when he heard the

v. 25. It is generally thought that St. Mark is here treating the space between nine o'clock and noon as a single stretch of time, which he calls 'the third hour'; we are not, then, to suppose that our Lord was nailed to his cross at nine o'clock, and hung six hours upon it. If he was crucified at eleven, or even half-past eleven, it would still be during 'the third hour', in the sense that 'the sixth hour' had not yet begun (cf. v. 33 below). A further difficulty is raised upon the question of time by John xix. 14; see note there.
v. 28. Is. liii. 12.
v. 33. See note on Matthew xxvii. 45.
v. 34. Ps. xxi. 2.

v. 42. The body of a man who had been crucified must be taken down and buried before night-fall (Deut. xxi. 23). But here early action was necessary, because it was a Friday, and after six o'clock in the evening the sabbath would have begun, so that the work of burial would have become unlawful.

centurion's report, gave Joseph the body. 46 Joseph took him down, and wrapped him in a winding-sheet which he had bought, and laid him in a tomb cut out of the rock, rolling a stone against the door of the tomb. 47 Mary Magdalen, and Mary the mother of Joseph, saw where he had been laid.

Chapter

Sixteen

AND WHEN THE SAB bath was over, Mary Magdalen,

vv. 1-8. Matthew xxviii. 1, Luke xxiv. 1.

v. 2. See note on John xx. 1.

and Mary the mother of James, and Salome had bought spices, to come and anoint Jesus. 2 So they came to the tomb very early on the day after the sabbath, at sunrise. 3 And they began to question among themselves, Who is to roll the stone away for us from the door of the tomb? 4 Then they looked up, and saw that the stone, great as it was, had been rolled away already. 5 And they went into the tomb, and saw there, on the right, a young man seated, wearing a white robe; and they were dismayed. 6 But he said to them, No need to be dismayed; you have come to look for Jesus of Nazareth, who was crucified; he has risen again, he is not here. Here is the place where they laid him. 7 Go and tell Peter and the rest of his disciples that he is going before you into Galilee. 8 There you shall have sight of him, as he promised you. So they came out and ran away from the tomb, trembling and awe-struck, and said nothing to anyone, out of fear. 9 But he had risen again, at dawn on the first day of the week, and shewed himself first of all to Mary Magdalen, the woman out of whom he had cast seven devils. 10 She went and gave the news to those who had been of his company, where they mourned and wept; 11 and they, when they were told that he was alive and that she had seen him, could not believe it. 12 After that, he appeared in the form of a stranger to two of them as they were walking together, going out into the

v. 5. There were two angels according to St. Luke (xxiv. 4); perhaps ane of them was seen inside the tomb, the other outside (Matthew xxviii. 2), and the women may not have been agreed, whether it was the same angel they saw in both places.

v. 7. 'Peter and the rest of his disciples', literally 'his disciples and Peter', cf. Acts i. 14.

v. 8. That is, evidently, they said nothing to those whom they met on their way; if St. Mary Magdalen went on in front of the others, they will have passed St. Peter and St. John (John xx. 3).

vv. 9-20. It seems that the manuscripts of St.

country; 13 these went back and gave the news to the rest, but they did not believe them either.

14 Then at last he appeared to all eleven of them as they sat at table, and reproached them with their unbelief and their obstinacy of heart, in giving no credit to those who had seen him after he had risen. 15 And he said to them, Go out all over the world, and preach the gospel to the whole of creation; 16 he who believes and is baptized will be saved; he who refuses belief will be condemned. 17 Where believers go, these signs shall go with them; they will cast out devils in my name, they will speak in tongues that are strange to them; 18 they will take up serpents in their hands, and drink poisonous draughts without harm; they will lay their hands upon the sick and make them recover. 19 And so the Lord Jesus, when he had finished speaking to them, was taken up to heaven, and is seated now at the right hand of God; 20 and they went out and preached everywhere, the Lord aiding them, and attesting his word by the miracles that went with them.

Mark were mutilated at the end in very early times; the whole of this chapter being sometimes omitted (St. Jerome Ad Hedyb. q. 3). And in a few of our existing manuscripts these last twelve verses are wanting, which fact (together with the abruptness of their style) has made some critics think that they were added from another source. But they are evidently a primitive account, and there is no reason why we should not ascribe their inclusion here to St. Mark.

v. 9. John xx. 14.

v. 12. Luke xxiv. 13.

THE HOLY GOSPEL ✝ ACCORDING
OF JESUS CHRIST TO LUKE

Chapter One

MANY HAVE BEEN AT pains to set forth the history of what time has brought to fulfilment among us, 2 following the tradition of those first eye-witnesses who gave themselves up to the service of the word. 3 And I too, most noble Theophilus, have resolved to put the story in writing for thee as it befell, having first traced it carefully from its beginnings, 4 that thou mayst understand the instruction thou has already received, in all its certainty.

5 In the days when Herod was king of Judaea, there was a priest called Zachary, of Abia's turn of office, who had married a wife of Aaron's family, by name Elizabeth; 6 they were both well approved in God's sight, following all the commandments and observances of the Lord without reproach. 7 They had no child; Elizabeth was barren, and both were now well advanced in years. 8 He, then, as it happened, was doing a priest's duty before God in the order of his turn of office; 9 and had been chosen by lot, as was the custom among the priests, to go into the sanctuary of the Lord and burn incense there, 10 while the whole multitude of

v. 2. 'To the service of the word'; many of the early Fathers understood this to mean, that they were servants of the Word, that is of Christ. Such a rendering gives a better sense to the Greek; but it is not certain that this title was applied to our Lord by any writer earlier than St. John.
v. 5. Cf. I Paralip. xxiv. 19.

the people stood praying without, at the hour of sacrifice. 11 Suddenly he saw an angel of the Lord, standing at the right of the altar where incense was burnt. 12 Zachary was bewildered at the sight, and overcome with fear; 13 but the angel said, Zachary, do not be afraid; thy prayer has been heard, and thy wife Elizabeth is to bear thee a son, to whom thou shalt give the name of John. 11 Joy and gladness shall be thine, and many hearts shall rejoice over his birth, 15 for he is to be high in the Lord's favour; he is to drink neither wine nor strong drink; and from the time when he is yet a child in his mother's womb he shall be filled with the Holy Ghost. 16 He shall bring back many of the sons of Israel to the Lord their God, 17 ushering in his advent in the spirit and power of an Elias. He shall unite the hearts of all, the fathers with the children, and teach the disobedient the wisdom that makes men just, preparing for the Lord a people fit to receive him. 18 And Zachary said to the angel, By what sign am I to be assured of this? I am an old man now, and my wife is far advanced in age. 19 The angel answered, My name is Gabriel, and my place is in God's presence; I have been sent to speak with thee, and to bring thee this good news. 20 Behold, thou shalt be dumb, and have no power of speech, until the day when this is accomplished; and that, because thou hast not believed my promise, which shall in due time be fulfilled. 21 And now all the people were waiting for Zachary, and wondering that he delayed in the temple so long; 22 but he, when he came out, could speak no word to them; whereupon they made sure that he had seen some vision in the sanctuary. He could but stand there making signs to them, for he remained dumb.

23 And so, when the days of his ministry were at an end, he went back to his house. 24 It was after those days that his wife Elizabeth conceived, and for five months she dwelt retired; she said, 25 It is the Lord who has done this for me, visiting me at his own time, to take away my reproach among men.

26 When the sixth month came, God sent the angel Gabriel to a city of Galilee called Nazareth, 27 where a virgin dwelt, betrothed to a man of David's lineage; his name was Joseph, and the virgin's name was Mary. 28 Into her presence the angel came, and said, Hail, thou who art full of grace; the Lord is with thee; blessed art thou among women. 29 She was much perplexed at hearing him speak so, and cast about in her mind, what she was to make of such a greeting. 30 Then the angel said to her, Mary, do not be afraid; thou hast found favour in the sight of God. 31 And behold, thou shalt conceive in thy womb, and shalt bear a son, and shalt

v. 17. Mal. iii. 23.

v. 28. 'Blessed art thou among women'; these words are wanting here in some manuscripts. They are to be found in verse 42, below.

call him Jesus. 32 He shall be great, and men will know him for the Son of the most High; the Lord God will give him the throne of his father David, and he shall reign over the house of Jacob eternally; 33 his kingdom shall never have an end. 34 But Mary said to the angel, How can that be, since I have no knowledge of man? 35 And the angel answered her, The Holy Spirit will come upon thee, and the power of the most High will overshadow thee. Thus this holy offspring of thine shall be known for the Son of God. 36 See, moreover, how it fares with thy cousin Elizabeth; she is old, yet she too has conceived a son; she who was reproached with barrenness is now in her sixth month, 37 to prove that nothing can be impossible with God. 38 And Mary said, Behold the hand-maid of the Lord; let it be unto me according to thy word. And with that the angel left her.

39 In the days that followed, Mary rose up and went with all haste to a town of Juda, in the hill country 40 where Zachary dwelt; and there entering in she gave Elizabeth greeting. 41 No sooner had Elizabeth heard Mary's greeting, than the child leaped in her womb; and Elizabeth herself was filled with the Holy Ghost; 42 so that she cried out with a loud voice, Blessed art thou among women, and blessed is the fruit of thy womb. 43 How have I de-served to be thus visited by the mother of my Lord? 44 Why, as soon as ever the voice of thy greeting sounded in my ears, the child in my womb leaped for joy. 45 Blessed art thou for thy believing; the message that was brought to thee from the Lord shall have ful-filment.

46 And Mary said, My soul magnifies the Lord; 47 my spirit has found joy in God, who is my Saviour, 48 because he has looked graciously upon the lowliness of his handmaid. Behold, from this day forward all generations will count me blessed; 49 because he who is mighty, he whose name is holy, has wrought for me his won-ders. 50 He has mercy upon those who fear him, from generation to generation; 51 he has done valiantly with the strength of his arm, driving the proud astray in the conceit of their hearts; 52 he has put down the mighty from their seat, and exalted the lowly; 53 he has filled the hungry with good things, and sent the rich away empty-handed. 54 He has protected his servant Israel, keep-ing his merciful design in remembrance, 55 according to the promise which he made to our forefathers, Abraham and his pos-terity for evermore.

56 Mary returned home when she had been with her about three months; 57 meanwhile, Elizabeth's time had come for her child-

vv. 56-57. It is not certain whether the Blessed Virgin re-turned home before or after her cousin's delivery, since, by Greek usage, the verbs in verse 57 might have a pluperfect sense, 'she had brought forth a son.'

bearing, and she bore a son. 58 Her neighbours and her kinsfolk, hearing how wonderfully God had shewed his mercy to her, came to rejoice with her; 59 and now, when they assembled on the eighth day for the circumcision of the child, they were for calling him Zachary, because it was his father's name; 60 but his mother answered, No, he is to be called John. 61 And they said, There is none of thy kindred that is called by this name, 62 and began asking his father by signs, what name he would have him called by. 63 So he asked for a tablet, and wrote on it the words, His name is John; and they were all astonished. 64 Then, of a sudden, his lips and his tongue were unloosed, and he broke into speech, giving praise to God; 65 so that fear came upon all their neighbourhood, and there was none of these happenings but was noised abroad throughout all the hill country of Judaea. 66 All those who heard it laid it to heart; Why then, they asked, what will this boy grow to be? And indeed the hand of the Lord was with him.

67 Then his father Zachary was filled with the Holy Ghost, and spoke in prophecy: 68 Blessed be the Lord, the God of Israel; he has visited his people, and wrought their redemption. 69 He has raised up a sceptre of salvation for us among the posterity of his servant David, 70 according to the promise which he made by the lips of holy men that have been his prophets from the beginning; 71 salvation from our enemies, and from the hand of all those who hate us. 72 So he would carry out his merciful design towards our fathers, by remembering his holy covenant. 73 He had sworn an oath to our father Abraham, that he would enable us 74 to live without fear in his service, delivered from the hand of our enemies, 75 passing all our days in holiness, and approved in his sight. 76 And thou, my child, wilt be known for a prophet of the most High, going before the Lord, to clear his way for him; 77 thou wilt make known to his people the salvation that is to release them from their sins. 78 Such is the merciful kindness of our God, which has bidden him come to us, like a dawning from on high, 79 to give light to those who live in darkness, in the shadow of death, and to guide our feet into the way of peace.

80 And as the child grew, his spirit achieved strength, and he dwelt in the wilderness until the day when he was made manifest to Israel.

v. 62. *It would appear from this verse that Zachary became, not dumb only, but deaf; unless we understand that her kinsfolk made signs to him in private, for fear they should distress Elizabeth by their contradiction. Nothing is said of his being deaf in verse 64.*

v. 69. *'A sceptre'; literally 'a horn'. This was a common Hebrew metaphor for any means of defence, as for example in II Kings xxii. 3, but here the reference is perhaps rather to such passages as Dan. vii. 24.*

Chapter Two

IT HAPPENED THAT A decree went out at this time from the emperor Augustus, enjoining that the whole world should be registered; 2 this register was the one first made during the time when Cyrinus was governor of Syria. 3 All must go and give in their names, each in his own city; 4 and Joseph, being of David's clan and family, came up from the town of Nazareth, in Galilee, to David's city in Judaea, the city called Bethlehem, 5 to give in his name there. With him was his espoused wife Mary, who was then in her pregnancy; 6 and it was while they were still there that the time came for her delivery. She brought forth a son, her first-born, 7 whom she wrapped in his swaddling-clothes, and laid in a manger, because there was no room for them in the inn.

8 In the same country there were shepherds awake in the fields, keeping night-watches over their flocks. 9 And all at once an angel of the Lord came and stood by them, and the glory of the Lord shone about them, so that they were overcome with fear. 10 But the angel said to them, Do not be afraid; behold, I bring you good news of a great rejoicing for the whole people. 11 This day, in the city of David, a Saviour has been born for you, the Lord Christ himself. 12 This is the sign by which you are to know him; you will find a child still in swaddling-clothes, lying in a manger. 13 Then, on a sudden, a multitude of the heavenly army appeared to them at the angel's side, giving praise to God, 14 and saying, Glory to God in high heaven, and peace on earth to men that are God's friends.

15 When the angels had left them and gone back into heaven, the shepherds said to one another, Come, let us make our way to Bethlehem, and see for ourselves this happening which God has made known to us. 16 And so they went with all haste, and found Mary and Joseph there, with the child lying in the manger. 17 On seeing him, they discovered the truth of what had been told them about this child. 18 All those who heard it were full of amazement at the story which the shepherds told them; 19 but Mary treasured

v. 2. There is here an ambiguity in the Greek, and some have thought the sense to be, 'This was the register which was made before Cyrinus was governor of Syria'. (The same doubt arises in Matthew xxvi. 17.) This gives an excellent sense; St. Luke would be explaining that this was not the well-known census of the year 6 A.D., which led to an insurrection (Acts v. 37), but an earlier one. But the facts of Quirinius' career are not fully recorded.

v. 6. See note on Matthew i. 25.

v. 17. 'Discovered'; that is, to Mary and Joseph, according to the common usage of the Greek verb; the Latin, however, renders it as if the shepherds had discovered for themselves the truth of the angelic announcement.

up all these sayings, and reflected on them in her heart. 20 And the shepherds went home giving praise and glory to God, at seeing and hearing that all was as it had been told them.

21 When eight days had passed, and the boy must be circumcised, he was called Jesus, the name which the angel had given him before ever he was conceived in the womb. 22 And when the time had come for purification according to the law of Moses, they brought him up to Jerusalem, to present him before the Lord there. 23 It is written in God's law, that whatever male offspring opens the womb is to be reckoned sacred to the Lord; 24 and so they must offer in sacrifice for him, as God's law commanded, a pair of turtle-doves, or two young pigeons. 25 At this time there was a man named Simeon living in Jerusalem, an upright man of careful observance, who waited patiently for comfort to be brought to Israel. The Holy Spirit was upon him: 26 and by the Holy Spirit it had been revealed to him that he was not to meet death, until he had seen that Christ whom the Lord had anointed. 27 He now came, led by the Spirit, into the temple; and when the child Jesus was brought in by his parents, to perform the custom which the law enjoined concerning him, 28 Simeon too was able to take him in his arms. And he said, blessing God: 29 Ruler of all, now dost thou let thy servant go in peace, according to thy word; 30 for my own eyes have seen that saving power of thine 31 which thou hast prepared in the sight of all nations. 32 This is the light which shall give revelation to the Gentiles, this is the glory of thy people Israel. 33 The father and mother of the child were still wondering over all that was said of him, 34 when Simeon blessed them, and said to his mother Mary, Behold, this child is destined to bring about the fall of many and the rise of many in Israel; to be a sign which men will refuse to acknowledge 35 and so the thoughts of many hearts shall be made manifest; as for thy own soul, it shall have a sword to pierce it. 36 There was besides a prophetess named Anna, daughter to one Phanuel, of the tribe of Aser, (a woman greatly advanced in age, since she had lived with a husband for seven years after her maidenhood, 37 and had now been eighty-four years a widow) who abode continually in the temple night and day, serving God with fasting and prayer. 38 She too, at that very hour, came near to give God thanks, and spoke of the child to all that patiently waited for the deliverance of Israel. 39 And now, when all had been done that the law of the Lord required, they returned to Galilee, and to their own town of Nazareth.

v. 23. Ex. xiii. 2.
v. 24. Lev. xii. 8.

40 And so the child grew and came to his strength, full of wisdom; and the grace of God rested upon him. 41 Every year, his parents used to go up to Jerusalem at the paschal feast. 42 And when he was twelve years old, after going up to Jerusalem, as the custom was at the time of the feast, 43 and completing the days of its observance, they set about their return home. But the boy Jesus, unknown to his parents, continued his stay in Jerusalem. 44 And they, thinking that he was among their travelling companions, had gone a whole day's journey before they made enquiry for him among their kinsfolk and acquaintances. 45 When they could not find him, they made their way back to Jerusalem in search of him, 46 and it was only after three days that they found him. He was sitting in the temple, in the midst of those who taught there, listening to them and asking them questions; 47 and all those who heard him were in amazement at his quick understanding and at the answers he gave. 48 Seeing him there, they were full of wonder, and his mother said to him, My Son, why hast thou treated us so? Think, what anguish of mind thy father and I have endured, searching for thee. 49 But he asked them, What reason had you to search for me? Could you not tell that I must needs be in the place which belongs to my Father? 50 These words which he spoke to them were beyond their understanding; 51 but he went down with them on their journey to Nazareth, and lived there in subjection to them, while his mother kept in her heart the memory of all this. 52 And so Jesus advanced in wisdom with the years, and in favour both with God and with men.

v. 40. 'Grace'; or perhaps 'favour', as in v. 52, below.

v. 49. The phrase used is, 'in the things which are my Father's', and some would translate, 'about my Father's business'.

v. 52. Our Lord, as Man, acquired experimental knowledge of the world about him, like other men.

Chapter Three

v. 1. There is some
uncertainty about the
system on which the
Romans computed the
years of a given reign;
probably the fifteenth
year of Tiberius
would be 28 or 29
A.D. by our reckon-
ing.

v. 2. Caiphas was the
actual high priest;
Annas, who had been
deposed from that of-
fice, continued to ex-
ercise much influence.

vv. 3-22. Matthew iii.
1, Mark i. 1.

v. 4. Is. xl. 3.

IT WAS IN THE FIF teenth year of the emperor Tiberius' reign, when Pontius Pilate was governor of Judaea, when Herod was prince in Galilee, his brother Philip in the Ituraean and Trachonitid region, and Lysanias in Abilina, 2 in the high priesthood of Annas and Caiphas, that the word of God came upon John, the son of Zachary, in the desert. 3 And he went all over the country round Jordan, announcing a baptism whereby men repented, to have their sins forgiven: 4 as it is written in the book of the sayings of the prophet Isaias, There is a voice of one crying in the wilderness, Prepare the way of the Lord, straighten out his paths. 5 Every valley is to be bridged, and every mountain and hill levelled, and the windings are to be cut straight, and the rough paths made into smooth roads, 6 and all mankind is to see the saving power of God. 7 He said to the multitudes who came out to be baptized by him, Who was it that taught you, brood of vipers, to flee from the vengeance that draws near? 8 Come then, yield the acceptable fruit of repentance; do not think to say, We have Abraham for our father; I tell you, God has power to raise up children to Abraham out of these very stones. 9 Already the axe has been put to the root of the trees, so that every tree which does not shew good fruit will be hewn down and cast into the fire. 10 And the multitudes asked him, What is it, then, we are to do? 11 He answered them, The man who has two coats must share with the man who has none; and the man who has food to eat, must do the like. 12 The publicans, too, came to be baptized; Master, they said to him, what are we to do? 13 He told them, Do not go beyond the scale appointed you. 14 Even the soldiers on guard asked him, What of us? What are we to do? He said to them, Do not use men roughly, do not lay false information against them; be content with your pay.

v. 14. The soldiers
were perhaps those on
guard at the customs
houses; the tempta-
tions they are to re-
sist would be, in the
modern world, those
of the police.

15 And now the people was full of expectation; all had the same surmise in their hearts, whether John might not be the Christ. 16 But John gave them their answer by saying publicly, As for me,

106

I am baptizing you with water; but one is yet to come who is mightier than I, so that I am not worthy to untie the strap of his shoes. He will baptize you with the Holy Ghost and with fire. 17 He holds his winnowing-fan ready, to purge his threshing-floor clean; he will gather the wheat into his barn, but the chaff he will consume with fire that can never be quenched. 18 With these and many other warnings he gave his message to the people: 19 but when he rebuked prince Herod over his brother Philip's wife, and his shameful deeds, 20 Herod, to crown all, shut John up in prison. 21 It was while all the people were being baptized that Jesus was baptized too, and stood there praying. Suddenly heaven was opened, 22 and the Holy Spirit came down upon him in bodily form, like a dove, and a voice came from heaven, which said, Thou art my beloved Son, in thee I am well pleased.

23 Jesus himself had now reached the age of about thirty. He was, by repute, the son of Joseph, son of Heli, son of Mathat, 24 son of Levi, son of Melchi, son of Janne, son of Joseph, 25 son of Matthathias, son of Amos, son of Nahum, son of Hesli, son of Nagge, 26 son of Mahath, son of Matthathias, son of Semei, son of Joseph, son of Juda, 27 son of Joanna, son of Resa, son of Zorobabel, son of Salathiel, son of Neri, 28 son of Melchi, son of Addi, son of Cosan, son of Elmadam, son of Her, 29 son of Jesu, son of Eliezer, son of Jorim, son of Mathat, son of Levi, 30 son of Simeon, son of Juda, son of Joseph, son of Jona, son of Eliacim, 31 son of Melea, son of Menna, son of Matthatha, son of Nathan, son of David, 32 son of Jesse, son of Obed, son of Booz, son of Salmon, son of Naasson, 33 son of Aminadab, son of Aram, son of Esron, son of Phares, son of Juda, 34 son of Jacob, son of Isaac, son of Abraham, son of Thare, son of Nachor, 35 son of Sarug, son of Ragau, son of Phaleg, son of Heber, son of Sale, 36 son of Cainan, son of Arphaxad, son of Sem, son of Noe, son of Lamech, 37 son of Methusale, son of Henoch, son of Jared, son of Malaleel, son of Cainan, 38 son of Henos, son of Seth, son of Adam, who was the son of God.

vv. 23-38. See note on Matthew i. 16.

Chapter Four

vv. 1-13. Matthew iv.
1, Mark i. 12. We
have no means to de-
termine whether it is
St. Matthew or St.
Luke that has record-
ed the second and
third temptations in
their historical order.

v. 4. Deut. viii. 3.

v. 8. Deut. vi. 13.

v. 10. Ps. xc. 11, 12.

v. 12. Deut. vi. 16.
See note on Matthew
iv. 7.

v. 18. Is. xli. 1, 2.

JESUS RETURNED FROM the Jordan full of the Holy Spirit, and by the Spirit he was led on into the wilderness, 2 where he remained forty days, tempted by the devil. During those days he ate nothing, and when they were over, he was hungry. 3 Then the devil said to him, If thou art the Son of God, bid this stone turn into a loaf of bread. 4 Jesus answered him, It is written, Man cannot live by bread only; there is life for him in all the words that come from God. 5 And the devil led him up on to a high mountain, and shewed him all the kingdoms of the world in a moment of time; 6 I will give thee command, the devil said to him, over all these, and the glory that belongs to them; they have been made over to me, and I may give them to whomsoever I please; 7 come then, all shall be thine, if thou wilt fall down before me and worship. 8 Jesus answered him, It is written, Thou shalt worship the Lord thy God, to him only shalt thou do service. 9 And he led him to Jerusalem, and there set him down on the pinnacle of the temple; If thou art the Son of God, he said to him, cast thyself down from this to the earth; 10 for it is written, He shall give his angels charge concerning thee, to keep thee safe, 11 and they will hold thee up with their hands, lest thou shouldst chance to trip on a stone. 12 And Jesus answered him, We are told, Thou shalt not put the Lord thy God to the proof. 13 So the devil, when he had finished tempting him every way, left him in peace until the time should come.

14 And Jesus came back to Galilee with the power of the Spirit upon him; word of him went round through all the neighbouring country, 15 and he began to preach in their synagogues, so that his praise was on all men's lips. 16 Then he came to Nazareth, where he had been brought up; and he went into the synagogue there, as his custom was, on the sabbath day, and stood up to read. 17 The book given to him was the book of the prophet Isaias; so he opened it, and found the place where the words ran: 18 The Spirit of the Lord is upon me; he has anointed me, and sent me out

to preach the gospel to the poor, to restore the broken-hearted; to bid the prisoners go free, and the blind have sight; 19 to set the oppressed at liberty, to proclaim a year when men may find acceptance with the Lord. 20 Then he shut the book, and gave it back to the attendant, and sat down. All those who were in the synagogue fixed their eyes on him, 21 and thus he began speaking to them, This scripture which I have read in your hearing is to-day fulfilled. 22 All bore testimony to him, and were astonished at the gracious words which came from his mouth; Why, they said, is not this the son of Joseph? 23 Then he said to them, No doubt you will tell me, as the proverb says, Physician, heal thyself; do here in thy own country all that we have heard of thy doing at Capharnaum. 24 And he said, Believe me, no prophet finds acceptance in his own country. 25 Why, you may be sure of this, there were many widows among the people of Israel in the days of Elias, when a great famine came over all the land, after the heavens had remained shut for three years and six months, 26 but Elias was not sent to any of these. He was sent to a widow woman in Sarepta, which belongs to Sidon. 27 And there were many lepers among the people of Israel in the days of the prophet Eliseus; but it was none of them, it was Naaman the Syrian, who was made clean. 28 All those who were in the synagogue were full of indignation at hearing this; 29 they rose up and thrust him out of the city, and took him up to the brow of the hill on which their city was built, to throw him over it. 30 But he passed through the midst of them, and so went on his way.

31 Then he went down to Capharnaum, which is a city in Galilee, and began teaching them there on the sabbath; 32 and they were amazed by his teaching, such was the authority with which he spoke. 33 In the synagogue was a man who was possessed by an unclean spirit, that cried out with a loud voice: 34 Nay, why dost thou meddle with us, Jesus of Nazareth? Hast thou come to make an end of us? I recognize thee for what thou art, the Holy One of God. 35 Jesus rebuked it; Silence! he said; come out of him. Then the unclean spirit threw him into a convulsion before them all, and went out of him without doing him any injury. 36 Wonder fell upon them all, as they said to one another, What is this word of his? See how he has power and authority to lay his command on the unclean spirits, so that they come out! 37 And the story of his doings spread into every part of the country side.

38 So he rose up and left the synagogue, and went into Simon's

vv. 22-24. Matthew xiii. 34, Mark vi. 1, John vi. 42.

v. 25. III Kings xvii. 9.

v. 27. IV Kings v. 9.

vv. 31-37. Mark i. 21.

vv. 38-41. Matthew viii. 14, Mark i. 29.

house. The mother of Simon's wife was in the grip of a violent fever, and they entreated his aid for her. 39 He stood over her, and checked the fever, so that it left her; all at once she rose, and ministered to them. 40 And when the sun was going down, all those who had friends afflicted with diseases of any kind brought them to him: and he laid his hands upon each one of them, and healed them. 41 Many, too, had devils cast out of them, which cried aloud, Thou art the Son of God; but he rebuked them and would not have them speak, because they knew that he was the Christ. 42 Then, when day came, he went out and retired to a desert place. The multitude, who had set out in search of him and caught him up, would have kept him there, and not let him leave them. 43 But he told them, I must preach the gospel of God's kingdom to the other cities too; it is for this that I was sent. 44 And so he went on preaching in the synagogues of Galilee.

vv. 42-44. Mark i. 35.

Chapter Five

IT HAPPENED THAT HE was standing by the lake of Genesareth, at a time when the multitude was pressing close about him to hear the word of God; 2 and he saw two boats moored at the edge of the lake; the fishermen had gone ashore, and were washing their nets. 3 And he went on board one of the boats, which belonged to Simon, and asked him to stand off a little from the land; and so, sitting down, he began to teach the multitudes from the boat. 4 When he had finished speaking, he said to Simon, Stand out into the deep water, and let down your nets for a catch. 5 Simon answered him, Master, we have toiled all the night, and caught nothing; but at thy word I will let down the net. 6 And when they had done this, they took a great quantity of fish, so that the net was near breaking, 7 and they must needs

THE JOURNEY OF THE MAGI

STEFANO DI GIOVANNI SASSETTA
1392–1450

METROPOLITAN MUSEUM, NEW YORK

beckon to their partners who were in the other boat to come and help them. When these came, they filled both boats, so that they were ready to sink. 8 At seeing this, Simon Peter fell down and caught Jesus by the knees; Leave me to myself, Lord, he said; I am a sinner. 9 Such amazement had overcome both him and all his crew, at the catch of fish they had made; 10 so it was, too, with James and John, the sons of Zebedee, who were Simon's partners. But Jesus said to Simon, Do not be afraid; henceforth thou shalt be a fisher of men. 11 So, when they had brought their boats to land, they left all and followed him.

12 Afterwards, while he was in one of the cities, he came upon a man who was far gone in leprosy. When he saw Jesus, he fell on his face in entreaty; Lord, he said, if it be thy will, thou hast power to make me clean. 13 And he stretched out his hand, and touched him, and said, It is my will; be thou made clean. Whereupon all at once his leprosy passed from him. 14 And Jesus warned him not to tell anyone of it; Go and shew thyself to the priest, he said, and bring an offering for thy cleansing, as Moses commanded, to make the truth known to them. 15 But still the talk of him spread more and more, and great multitudes came together to listen to him, and be healed of their infirmities. 16 And he would steal away from them into the desert and pray there.

vv. 12-16. Matthew viii. 1, Mark i. 40.

v. 14. Lev. xiv. 2.

17 It chanced one day that he was teaching, and that some Pharisees and teachers of the law were sitting by, who had come from every village in Galilee, and Judaea, and Jerusalem; and the power of the Lord was there, to grant healing. 18 Just then, some men brought there on a bed one who was palsied, whom they tried to carry in and set down in Jesus' presence. 19 But, finding no way of carrying him in, because of the multitude, they went up on to the housetop, and let him down between the tiles, bed and all, into the clear space in front of Jesus. 20 And he, seeing their faith, said, Man, thy sins are forgiven thee. 21 Whereupon the Pharisees and scribes fell to reasoning thus, Who can this be, that he talks so blasphemously? 22 Who can forgive sins but God and God only? Jesus knew of these secret thoughts of theirs, and said to them openly, Why do you reason thus in your hearts? 23 Which command is more lightly given, to say, Thy sins are forgiven thee, or to say, Rise up and walk? 24 And now, to convince you that the Son of Man has power to forgive sins while he is on the earth (here he spoke to the palsied man), I tell thee, rise up, take thy bed with thee and go home. 25 And he rose up at once in full sight of them, took up his bedding, and went home, giving praise

vv. 17-38. Matthew ix. 1, Mark ii. 1.

v. 23. See note on Matthew ix. 5.

to God. 26 Astonishment came over them all, and they praised
God, full of awe; We have seen strange things, they said, to-day.
27 Then he went out, and caught sight of a publican, called
Levi, sitting at work in the customs-house, and said to him, Follow
me. 28 And he rose up, and left all behind, and followed him.
29 Then Levi made a great feast for him in his house, and there
was a crowded company of publicans and others who were their
fellow guests. 30 Whereupon the Pharisees and scribes complained
to his disciples, How comes it that you eat and drink with publicans and sinners? 31 But Jesus answered them, It is those who are
sick, not those who are in health, that have need of the physician.
32 I have not come to call the just; I have come to call sinners to
repentance. 33 Then they said to him, How is it that thy disciples
eat and drink, when John's disciples are always fasting and praying,
and the Pharisees' disciples too? 34 And he said to them, Can you
persuade the men of the bridegroom's company to fast, while the
bridegroom is still with them? 35 No, the days will come when
the bridegroom is taken away from them; then they will fast, when
that day comes. 36 And he told them this parable; Nobody uses a
piece taken from a new cloak to patch an old one; if that is done,
he will have torn the new cloak, and the piece taken from the new
will not match the old. 37 Nor does anybody put new wine into
old wineskins; if that is done, the new wine bursts the skins, and
there is the wine spilt and the skins spoiled. 38 If the wine is new,
it must be put into fresh wineskins, and so both are kept safe.
39 Nobody who has been drinking old wine calls all at once for
new; he will tell you, The old is better.

Chapter Six

IT HAPPENED THAT ON the next sabbath but one he was walking through the corn-fields; and his disciples were plucking the ears of corn and eating them, rubbing them between their hands. 2 And some of the Pharisees said to them, Why are you doing what it is not lawful to do on the sabbath? 3 Whereupon Jesus answered them, Why, have you never read of what David did, when he and his followers were hungry? 4 How he went into the tabernacle, and ate the loaves set forth there before God, and gave them to his followers, although it is not lawful for anyone except the priests to eat them? 5 And he told them, The Son of Man has even the sabbath at his disposal. 6 And on another sabbath day it happened that he went into the synagogue to teach, when there was a man there who had his right hand withered. 7 The scribes and Pharisees were watching him, to see whether he would restore health on the sabbath, so that they might have a charge to bring against him. 8 He knew their secret thoughts, and said to the man who had his hand withered, Rise up, and come forward; whereupon he rose to his feet. 9 Then Jesus said to them, I have a question to ask you; which is right, to do good on the sabbath day, or to do harm? To save life, or to make away with it? 10 And he looked round on them all, and said to him, Stretch out thy hand. And he did so, and his hand was restored to him. 11 And they were overcome with fury, debating with one another what they could do to Jesus.

12 It was at this time that he went out on to the mountain side, and passed the whole night offering prayer to God, 13 and when day dawned, he called his disciples to him, choosing out twelve of them; these he called his apostles. 14 Their names were, Simon, whom he also called Peter, his brother Andrew, James and John, Philip and Bartholomew, 15 Matthew and Thomas, James the son of Alphaeus, and Simon who is called the Zealot, 16 Jude the brother of James, and Judas Iscariot, the man who turned traitor. 17 With them he went down and stood on a level place; a multi-

vv. 1-5. Matthew xii. 1, Mark ii. 23.

v. 3. 1 Kings xxi. 6.

vv. 6-11. Matthew xii. 9, Mark iii. 1.

vv. 12-16. Matthew x. 1, Mark iii. 13.

v. 16. Judas brother of James, the author of the epistle, seems to have been also called Thaddaeus (Matthew x. 3, Mark iii. 18).

tude of his disciples was there, and a great gathering of the people from all Judaea, and Jerusalem, and the sea coast of Tyre and Sidon. 18 These had come there to listen to him, and to be healed of their diseases; and those who were troubled by unclean spirits were also cured; 19 so that all the multitude was eager to touch him, because power went out from him, and healed them all.

vv. 20-49. Many of the sayings recorded in these verses are also to be found in St. Matthew, especially v. 39, vii. 27.

20 Then he lifted up his eyes towards his disciples, and said; Blessed are you who are poor; the kingdom of God is yours. 21 Blessed are you who are hungry now; you will have your fill. 22 Blessed are you who weep now; you will laugh for joy. Blessed are you, when men hate you and cast you off and revile you, when they reject your name as something evil, for the Son of Man's sake. 23 When that day comes, rejoice and exult over it; for behold, a rich reward awaits you in heaven; their fathers treated the prophets no better. 24 But woe upon you who are rich; you have your comfort already. 25 Woe upon you who are filled full; you shall be hungry. Woe upon you who laugh now; you shall mourn and weep. 26 Woe upon you, when all men speak well of you; their fathers treated the false prophets no worse.

27 And now I say to you who are listening to me, Love your enemies, do good to those who hate you; 28 bless those who curse you, and pray for those who treat you insultingly. 29 If a man strikes thee on the cheek, offer him the other cheek too; if a man would take away thy cloak, do not grudge him thy coat along with it. 30 Give to every man who asks, and if a man takes what is thine, do not ask him to restore it. 31 As you would have men treat you, you are to treat them; no otherwise. 32 Why, what credit is it to you, if you love those who love you? Even sinners love those who love them. 33 What credit is it to you, if you do good to those who do good to you? Even sinners do as much. 34 What credit is it to you, if you lend to those from whom you expect repayment? Even sinners lend to sinners, to receive as much in exchange. 35 No, it is your enemies you must love, and do them good, and lend to them, without any hope of return; then your reward will be a rich one, and you will be true sons of the most High, generous like him towards the thankless and unjust.

36 Be merciful, then, as your Father is merciful. 37 Judge nobody, and you will not be judged; condemn nobody, and you will not be condemned; forgive, and you will be forgiven. 38 Give, and gifts will be yours; good measure, pressed down and shaken up and running over, will be poured into your lap; the measure you award to others is the measure that will be awarded to you.

39 And he told them this parable, Can one blind man lead another? Will not both fall into the ditch together?

40 A disciple is no better than his master; he will be fully perfect if he is as his master is.

41 How is it that thou canst see the speck of dust which is in thy brother's eye, and art not aware of the beam which is in thy own? 42 By what right wilt thou say to thy brother, Brother, let me rid thy eye of that speck, when thou canst not see the beam that is in thy own? Thou hypocrite, take the beam out of thy own eye first, and so thou shalt have clear sight to rid thy brother's of the speck.

43 There is no sound tree that will yield withered fruit, no withered tree that will yield sound fruit. 44 Each tree is known by its proper fruit; figs are not plucked from thorns, nor grapes gathered from brier bushes. 45 A good man utters what is good from his heart's store of goodness; the wicked man, from his heart's store of wickedness, can utter nothing but what is evil; it is from the heart's overflow that the mouth speaks.

46 How is it that you call me, Master, Master, and will not do what I bid you? 47 If anyone comes to me and listens to my commandments and carries them out, I will tell you what he is like; 48 he is like a man that would build a house, who dug, dug deep, and laid his foundation on rock. Then a flood came, and the river broke upon that house, but could not stir it; it was founded upon rock. 49 But the man who listens to what I say and does not carry it out is like a man who built his house in the earth without foundation; when the river broke upon it, it fell at once, and great was that house's ruin.

Chapter Seven

vv. 1-10. Matthew
viii. 5-13. St. Mat-
thew represents the
centurion as going to
our Lord personally,
and making no re-
quest that he should
come to his house. St.
Augustine and other
commentators explain
that the centurion
'approached' our Lord
only through his
friends. Others have
thought that the cen-
turion, perhaps anx-
ious at the delay, fol-
lowed up his two mes-
sages by coming out
to meet our Lord in
person.

WHEN HE HAD SAID his say in the hearing of the people, he went to Capharnaum. 2 There was a centurion that had a servant, very dear to him, who was then at the point of death; 3 and he, when he was told about Jesus, sent some of the elders of the Jews to him, asking him to come and heal his servant. 4 And these, presenting themselves before Jesus, began to make earnest appeal to him; He deserves, they said, to have this done for him; 5 he is a good friend to our race, and has built our synagogue for us at his own cost. 6 So Jesus set out in their company; and when he was already near the house, the centurion sent some friends to him; Do not put thyself to any trouble, Lord, he said; I am not worthy to receive thee under my roof. 7 That is why I did not presume to come to thee myself. My servant will be healed if thou wilt only speak a word of command. 8 I too know what it is to obey authority; I have soldiers under me, and I say, Go, to one man, and he goes, or, Come, to another, and he comes, or, Do this, to my servant, and he does it. 9 When he heard that, Jesus turned in amazement to the multitude which followed him, and said, Believe me, I have not found faith like this, even in Israel. 10 And the messengers, when they came back to the house, found the servant who had been sick fully recovered.

11 And now it happened that he was going into a city called Naim, attended by his disciples and by a great multitude of people. 12 And just as he drew near the gate of the city, a dead man was being carried out to his burial; the only son of his mother, and she was a widow; and a crowd of folk from the city went with her. 13 When the Lord saw her, he had pity on her, and said, Do not weep. 14 Then he went up and put his hand on the bier; and those who were carrying it stood still. And he said, Young man, I say to thee, rise up. 15 And the dead man sat up, and spoke; and Jesus gave him back to his mother. 16 They were all over-come with awe, and said, praising God, A great prophet has risen up among us; God has visited his people. 17 And this story of him

116

was noised abroad throughout the whole of Judaea and all the country round.

18 John was told of all this by his disciples. 19 And he summoned two of his disciples, and sent them to Jesus to ask, Is it thy coming that was foretold, or are we yet waiting for some other? 20 So they presented themselves before him, and said, John the Baptist has sent us to ask, Is it thy coming that was foretold, or are we yet waiting for some other? 21 At the very time of their visit, Jesus rid many of their diseases and afflictions and of evil spirits, and gave many that were blind the gift of sight. 22 Then he answered, Go and tell John what your own eyes and ears have witnessed; how the blind see, and the lame walk, and the lepers are made clean, and the deaf hear; how the dead are raised to life, and the poor have the gospel preached to them. 23 Blessed is he who does not lose confidence in me.

vv. 18-35. Matthew xi. 2; see notes there.

24 Then, when John's messengers had gone away, he took occasion to speak of John to the multitudes; What was it, he asked, that you expected to see when you went out into the wilderness? Was it a reed trembling in the wind? 25 No, not that; what was it you went out to see? Was it a man clad in silk? You must look in kings' palaces for men that go proudly dressed, and live in luxury. 26 What was it, then, that you went out to see? A prophet? Yes, and something more, I tell you, than a prophet. 27 This is the man of whom it is written, Behold, I am sending before thee that angel of mine who is to prepare thy way for thy coming. 28 I tell you, there is no greater than John the Baptist among all the sons of women; and yet to be least in the kingdom of heaven is to be greater than he. 29 It was the common folk who listened to him, and the publicans, that had given God his due, by receiving John's baptism, 30 whereas the Pharisees and lawyers, by refusing it, had frustrated God's plan for them. 31 And the Lord said, To what, then, shall I compare the men of this generation? What are they like? 32 They put me in mind of those children who call out to their companions as they sit in the market-place and say, You would not dance when we piped to you, you would not mourn when we wept to you. 33 When John came, he would neither eat nor drink, and you say, He is possessed. 34 When the Son of Man came, he ate and drank with you, and of him you say, Here is a glutton; he loves wine; he is a friend of publicans and sinners. 35 But wisdom is vindicated by all her children.

v. 27. Malachy iii. 1.

36 One of the Pharisees invited him to a meal; so he went into

the Pharisee's house and took his place at table. 37 And there was then a sinful woman in the city, who, hearing that he was at table in the Pharisee's house, brought a pot of ointment with her, 38 and took her place behind him at his feet, weeping; then she began washing his feet with her tears, and drying them with her hair, kissing his feet, and anointing them with the ointment. 39 His host, the Pharisee, saw it, and thought to himself, If this man were a prophet, he would know who this woman is that is touching him, and what kind of woman, a sinner. 40 But Jesus answered him thus, Simon, I have a word for thy hearing. Tell it me, Master, he said. 41 There was a creditor who had two debtors; one owed him five hundred pieces of silver, the other fifty; 42 they had no means of paying him, and he gave them both their discharge. 43 And now tell me, which of them loves him the more? I suppose, Simon answered, that it is the one who had the greater debt discharged. 44 And he said, Thou hast judged rightly. Then he turned towards the woman, and said to Simon, Dost thou see this woman? I came into thy house, and thou gavest me no water for my feet; she has washed my feet with her tears, and wiped them with her hair. 45 Thou gavest me no kiss of greeting; she has never ceased to kiss my feet since I entered; 46 thou didst not pour oil on my head; she has anointed my feet, and with ointment. 47 And so, I tell thee, if great sins have been forgiven her, she has also greatly loved. He loves little, who has little forgiven him. 48 Then he said to her, Thy sins are forgiven. 49 And his fellow guests thereupon thought to themselves, Who is this, that he even forgives sins? 50 But he told the woman, Thy faith has saved thee; go in peace.

v. 47. This may mean that the woman has shewn great love because she has been forgiven much, or that the woman has been forgiven much because she has shewn great love. The former interpretation seems to fit in with the parable which goes before, and with the sentence which immediately follows; the latter has the authority of the older commentators.

THE ADORATION OF THE MAGI   JEROME BOSCH
circa 1462-1516

METROPOLITAN MUSEUM, NEW YORK

Chapter Eight

vv. 4-15. Matthew xiii. 1, Mark iv. 1.

THEN FOLLOWED A TIME in which he went on journeying from one city or village to another, preaching and spreading the good news of God's kingdom. 2 With him were the twelve apostles, and certain women, whom he had freed from evil spirits and from sicknesses, Mary who is called Magdalen, who had had seven devils cast out of her, 3 and Joanna, the wife of Chusa, Herod's steward, and Susanna, and many others, who ministered to him with the means they had. 4 When a great multitude had gathered, and more came flocking to him out of the cities, he spoke to them in a parable. 5 Here is the sower gone out to sow his seed. And as he sowed, there were some grains that fell beside the path, so that they were trodden under foot, and the birds flew down and ate them. 6 And others fell on the rocks, where they withered as soon as they were up, because they had no moisture. 7 And some fell among briers, and the briers grew up with them and smothered them. 8 But others fell where the soil was good, and when these grew up they yielded a hundredfold. So saying, he cried aloud, Listen, you that have ears to hear with.

9 Then his disciples asked him what this parable meant. 10 And he told them, It is granted to you to understand the secret of God's kingdom; the rest must learn of it by parables, so that they can watch without seeing, and listen without understanding. 11 The parable means this; the seed is God's word. 12 Those by the way side hear the word, and then the devil comes and takes it away from their hearts, so that they cannot find faith and be saved. 13 Those on the rock, are those who entertain the word with joy as soon as they hear it, and yet have no roots; they last for a while, but in time of temptation they fall away. 14 And the grain that fell among the briers stands for those who hear it, and then, going on their way, are stifled by the cares, the riches, and the pleasures of life, and never reach maturity. 15 And the grain that fell in good soil stands for those who hear the word, and hold by it with a noble and generous heart, and endure, and yield a harvest.

16 Nobody lights a lamp, to hide it away in a jar or under a bed; it is put on a lamp-stand, so that all who come into the house can see its light. 17 What is covered up will all be revealed; what is hidden will all be made known, and come to light. 18 Look well, then, how you listen. If a man is rich, gifts will be made to him; if he is poor, he will lose even what he thinks his own.

vv. 19-22. Matthew xii. 46, Mark iii. 31; see note on Matthew xii. 46.

19 And his mother and brethren came to visit him, but could not reach him because of the multitude. 20 So word was given him, Thy mother and thy brethren are standing without, asking to see thee. 21 But he answered them, My mother and my brethren are those who hear the word of God, and keep it.

vv. 22-25. Matthew viii. 23, Mark iv. 35.

22 A day came when he and his disciples embarked on a boat; Let us cross to the other side of the lake, he said to them; and they began their voyage. 23 While they were sailing, he fell asleep. And now a storm of wind came down upon the lake, and they began to ship water perilously. 24 So they came and roused him, crying, Master, master, we are sinking. And he rose up, and checked both wind and wave, and there was calm. 25 Then he said to them, Where is your faith? And they were full of awe and astonishment, saying to one another, Why, who is this, who gives his command to wind and water, and is obeyed?

vv. 26-39. Matthew viii. 28, Mark v. 1.

26 So they came to land in the country of the Gerasenes, which is on the coast opposite Galilee; 27 and as he went ashore, he was met by a possessed man who for a long time had gone naked, and lived homeless among the tombs. 28 When he saw Jesus, he fell down before him, and cried with a loud voice, Why dost thou meddle with me, Jesus, Son of the most High God? I pray thee, do not torment me. 29 (For he was bidding the unclean spirit come out of the man.) Often, at times when it had seized upon him, the man had been bound, under guard, with chains and fetters, but still he would break his bonds, and the devil would drive him out into the wilderness. 30 Then Jesus asked him, What is thy name? And he said, Legion; for there were many devils that had entered into him. 31 And they entreated him not to bid them go back to the abyss. 32 There was a great herd of swine feeding on the mountain side, and the devils besought his leave to go into these instead; this leave he granted them. 33 So the devils left the man and entered into the swine; whereupon the herd rushed down the cliff into the lake, and were drowned. 34 The herdsmen fled when they saw it happen, and spread the news of it in the city and about the country-side; 35 so that they came out to see what had hap-

pened for themselves. When they reached Jesus, they found the man from whom the devils had been driven out sitting there, clothed and restored to his wits, at Jesus' feet; and they were terrified. 36 Those who had witnessed it told them how the possessed man had been delivered. 37 Then all the common folk of the country round Gerasa asked Jesus to leave them, such fear had gripped them; and he embarked on the boat and returned. 38 The man from whom the devils had been driven out asked leave to accompany him; but Jesus sent him away; 39 Go back home, he said, and make known all God's dealings with thee. So he went back, and published all over the city the news of the great things Jesus had done for him.

40 When Jesus returned, he found the multitude there to greet him; they had all been awaiting him. 41 And now a man named Jairus, who was a ruler of the synagogue, came and fell at Jesus' feet, imploring him to come to his house, 42 for he had an only daughter about twelve years old, who was dying. It happened that, as he went, the multitude pressed about him closely. 43 And a woman who for twelve years had had an issue of blood, and had spent all her money on doctors without finding one who could cure her, 44 came up behind and touched the hem of his cloak; and suddenly her issue of blood was stanched. 45 Then Jesus said, Who touched me? All disclaimed it; Master, said Peter and his companions, the multitudes are hemming thee in and crowding upon thee, and canst thou ask, Who touched me? 46 But Jesus said, Somebody touched me: I can tell that power has gone out from me. 47 And the woman, finding that there was no concealment, came forward trembling and fell at his feet, and so told him before all the people of her reason for touching him, and of her sudden cure. 48 And he said to her, My daughter, thy faith has brought thee recovery; go in peace.

49 While he was yet speaking, a messenger came to the ruler of the synagogue, to say, Thy daughter is dead; do not trouble the Master. 50 Jesus heard it, and said to him openly, Do not be afraid; thou hast only to believe, and she will recover. 51 When he reached the house, he would not let anyone come in with him, except Peter and James and John, and the child's father and mother. 52 All were weeping and bewailing her; There is no need to weep, he told them; she is not dead, she is asleep. 53 And they laughed aloud at him, well knowing that she was dead. 54 But he took her by the hand, and called aloud, Rise up, maiden, 55 and

vv. 40-56. Matthew ix. 18, Mark v. 21.

she rose up there and then with life restored to her. He ordered that she should be given something to eat, 56 and warned her parents, who were beside themselves with wonder, to let no one hear of what had befallen.

Chapter Nine

AND HE CALLED THE twelve apostles to him, and gave

vv. 1-5. Matthew x. 1, Mark vi. 7.

them power and authority over all devils, and to cure diseases, 2 sending them out to proclaim the kingdom of God, and to heal the sick. 3 He told them, Take nothing with you to use on your journey, staff or wallet or bread or money; you are not to have more than one coat apiece. 4 You are to lodge in the house you first enter, and not change your abode. 5 And wherever they deny you a welcome, as you leave the city, shake off the dust from your feet, in witness against them. 6 So they set out and passed through the villages, preaching the gospel and healing the sick wherever they went.

7 And Herod, who was prince in that quarter, heard of all his doings, 8 and did not know what to think, some telling him that John had risen from the dead, and some that Elias had appeared, and some that one of the old prophets had returned to life. 9 John, said Herod, I beheaded; who can this be, of whom I hear such reports? And he was eager to see him.

vv. 10-17. Matthew xiv. 13, Mark vi. 30, John vi. 1.

10 And now the apostles came back and told Jesus of all they had done. And he retired, taking them with him, to a desert place in the Bethsaida country, where they could be alone. 11 But the multitudes heard of it, and followed him; so he gave them welcome, and spoke to them of the kingdom of God, and cured those who were in need of healing. 12 And now the day began to wear on; and the twelve came and said to him, Give the multitudes leave to

122

go to the villages and farms round about, so that they can find lodging and food; we are in desert country here. 13 But he told them, It is for you to give them food to eat. We have no more, they said, than five loaves and two fishes, unless thou wouldst have us go ourselves and buy food for all this assembly. 14 About five thousand men were gathered there. So he said to his disciples, Make them sit down by companies of fifty; 15 and they did this, bidding all of them sit down. 16 Then he took the five loaves and the two fishes, and looked up to heaven, and blessed them, and broke, and gave them to his disciples, to set before the multitude. 17 All ate and had their fill, and when what they left over was picked up, it filled twelve baskets.

18 There was a time when he had gone apart to pray, and his disciples were with him; and he asked them, Who do the multitude say that I am? 19 They answered, John the Baptist; others say Elias, others, that one of the old prophets has returned to life. 20 Then he said to them, But who do you say that I am? And Peter answered, Thou art the Christ whom God has anointed. 21 And he laid a strict charge upon them, bidding them tell no one of it; 22 The Son of Man, he said, is to be much ill-used, and rejected by the elders and chief priests and scribes, and be put to death, and rise again on the third day. 23 And he said to all alike, If any man has a mind to come my way, let him renounce self, and take up his cross daily, and follow me. 24 He who tries to save his life will lose it; it is the man who loses his life for my sake, that will save it. 25 How is a man the better for gaining the whole world, if he loses himself, if he pays the forfeit of himself? 26 If anyone is ashamed of acknowledging me and my words, the Son of Man will be ashamed to acknowledge him, when he comes in his glory, with his Father and the holy angels to glorify him. 27 Believe me, there are those standing here who will not taste of death before they have seen the kingdom of God.

vv. 18-27. Matthew xvi. 13, Mark viii. 27.

28 It was about a week after all this was said, that he took Peter and John and James with him, and went up on to the mountain side to pray. 29 And even as he prayed, the fashion of his face was altered, and his garments became white and dazzling; 30 and two men appeared conversing with him, Moses and Elias, 31 seen now in glory; and they spoke of the death which he was to achieve at Jerusalem. 32 Meanwhile, Peter and his companions were sunk in sleep; and they awoke to see him in his glory, and the two men standing with him. 33 And, just as these were parting from him, Peter said to Jesus, Master, it is well that we should

vv. 28-43. Matthew xvii. 1, Mark ix. 1.

be here; let us make three arbours in this place, one for thee, and one for Moses, and one for Elias. 34 But he spoke at random: and even as he said it, a cloud formed, overshadowing them; they saw those others disappear into the cloud, and were terrified. 35 And a voice came from the cloud, This is my beloved Son; to him, then, listen. 36 And as the voice sounded, Jesus was discovered alone. They kept silence, and at the time said nothing of what they had seen to anybody.

37 It was on the next day that they came down from the mountain, and were met by a great multitude; 38 and now, from the midst of this multitude, a man cried out, I entreat thee, Master, look with favour upon my son; he is my only child. 39 There are times when a spirit seizes upon him, making him cry out suddenly, and throws him into a convulsion, foaming at the mouth; then it goes away, but only with a pang which lacerates him. 40 And I entreated thy disciples to cast it out, but they could not. 41 Jesus answered, Ah, faithless and misguided generation, how long must I be with you, how long must I bear with you? Bring thy son here. 42 And even as the boy was on his way, the devil threw him down in a convulsion. 43 But Jesus checked the unclean spirit, and cured the boy, and gave him to his father; 44 so that all were amazed at this great evidence of God's power. And while men were yet wondering at all that Jesus did, he said to his disciples, Remember this well. The Son of Man is soon to be betrayed into the hands of men. 45 But they could not understand what he said; it was hidden from them, so that they could not perceive the meaning of it; and they were afraid to ask him about this saying of his.

vv. 46-50. Matthew xviii. 1, Mark ix. 32.

46 And a question arose among them, which of them was the greatest. 47 Jesus, who saw what was occupying their thoughts, took hold of a little child and gave it a place beside him, 48 and said to them, He who welcomes this child in my name, welcomes me; and he who welcomes me welcomes him that sent me. He who is least in all your company is the greatest. 49 And John answered, Master, we saw a man who does not follow in our company casting out devils in thy name, and we forbade him to do it. 50 But Jesus said, Forbid him no more; the man who is not against you is on your side.

51 And now the time was drawing near for his taking away from the earth, and he turned his eyes stedfastly towards the way that led to Jerusalem. 52 And he sent messengers before him, who came into a Samaritan village, to make all in readiness. 53 But the

Samaritans refused to receive him, because his journey was in the direction of Jerusalem. 54 When they found this, two of his disciples, James and John, asked him, Lord, wouldst thou have us bid fire come down from heaven, and consume them? 55 But he turned and rebuked them, You do not understand, he said, what spirit it is you share. 56 The Son of Man has come to save men's lives, not to destroy them. And so they passed on to another village.

57 As they went on on their journey, a man said to him, I will follow thee wherever thou art going. 58 But Jesus told him, Foxes have holes, and the birds of the air their resting-places; the Son of Man has nowhere to lay his head. 59 To another he said, Follow me, and he answered, Lord, give me leave to go home and bury my father first. 60 But Jesus said to him, Leave the dead to bury their dead; it is for thee to go out and proclaim God's kingdom. 61 And there was yet another who said, Lord, I will follow thee, but first let me take leave of my friends. 62 To him Jesus said, No one who looks behind him, when he has once put his hand to the plough, is fitted for the kingdom of God.

v. 54. IV Kings i. 10. Many Greek manuscripts add, 'as Elias did'.

vv. 55, 56. Many Greek manuscripts have simply 'But he turned and rebuked them. And so they passed on to another village.' 'What spirit it is', perhaps in reference to IV Kings ii. 9, cf. v. 51 above.

vv. 57-60. Matthew viii. 19.

Chapter Ten

AFTER THIS, THE LORD appointed seventy-two others, and sent them before him, two and two, into all the cities and villages he himself was to visit. 2 The harvest, he told them, is plentiful enough, but the labourers are few; you must ask the Lord to whom the harvest belongs to send labourers out for the harvesting. 3 Go then, and remember, I am sending you out to be like lambs among wolves. 4 You are not to carry purse, or wallet, or shoes; you are to give no one greeting on your way. 5 When you enter a house, say first of all, Peace be to this house; 6 and if those who dwell there are men of good will, your good wishes shall come down upon it; if not, they will come back to you the way they went. 7 Remain in the same house, eating and drinking what they have to give you; the labourer has a right to his maintenance; do not move from one house to another. 8 When you enter a city, and they make you welcome, be content to eat the fare they offer you: 9 and heal those who are sick there; and tell them, The kingdom of God is close upon you. 10 But if you enter a city where they will not make you welcome, go out into their streets, and say, 11 We brush off in your faces the very dust from your city that has clung to our feet; and be sure of this, the kingdom of God is close at hand. 12 I tell you, it shall go less hard with Sodom at the day of judgement, than with that city. 13 Woe to thee, Corozain, woe to thee, Bethsaida! Tyre and Sidon would have repented long ago, humbling themselves with sackcloth and ashes, if the miracles done in you had been done there instead. 14 And indeed, it shall go less hard with Tyre and Sidon at the judgement, than with you. 15 And thou, Capharnaum, dost thou hope to be lifted up high as heaven? Thou shalt be brought low as hell. 16 He who listens to you, listens to me; he who despises you, despises me; and he who despises me, despises him that sent me.

17 And the seventy-two disciples came back full of rejoicing; Lord, they said, even the devils are made subject to us through thy name. 18 He said to them, I watched, while Satan was cast down like a lightning flash from heaven. 19 Behold, I have given you the right to trample on snakes and scorpions, and all the power of the enemy, and take no hurt from it. 20 But you, instead of rejoicing that the devils are made subject to you, should be rejoicing that your names are enrolled in heaven. 21 At this time, Jesus was filled with gladness by the Holy Spirit, and said, O Father, who art Lord of heaven and earth, I give thee praise that thou hast hidden all this from the wise and the prudent, and revealed it to little children. Be it so, Lord, since this finds favour in thy sight. 22 My Father has entrusted everything into my hands; none knows what the Son is, except the Father, and none knows what the Father is, except the Son, and those to whom it is the Son's good pleasure to reveal him. 23 Then, turning to his own disciples, he said, Blessed are the eyes that see what you see; 24 I tell you, there have been many prophets and kings who have longed to see what you see, and never saw it, to hear what you hear, and never heard it.

25 It happened once that a lawyer rose up, trying to put him to the test; Master, he said, what must I do to inherit eternal life? 26 Jesus asked him, What is it that is written in the law? What is thy reading of it? 27 And he answered, Thou shalt love the Lord thy God with the love of thy whole heart, and thy whole soul, and thy whole strength, and thy whole mind; and thy neighbour as thyself. 28 Thou hast answered right, he told him; do this, and thou shalt find life. 29 But he, to prove himself blameless, asked, And who is my neighbour? 30 Jesus gave him his answer; A man who was on his way down from Jerusalem to Jericho fell in with robbers, who stripped him and beat him, and went off leaving him half dead. 31 And a priest, who chanced to be going down by the same road, saw him there and passed by on the other side. 32 And a Levite who came there saw him, and passed by on the other side. 33 But a certain Samaritan, who was on his travels, saw him and took pity at the sight; 34 he went up to him and bound up his wounds, pouring oil and wine into them, and so mounted him upon his own beast and brought him to an inn, where he took care of him. 35 And next day he took out two silver pieces, which he gave to the inn-keeper, and said, Take care of him, and on my way home I will give thee whatever else is owing to thee for thy pains. 36 Which of these, thinkest thou, proved himself a neighbour to the man who had fallen in with robbers? 37 And he said, He that shewed mercy on him. Then Jesus said, Go thy way, and do thou likewise.

38 In one of the villages he entered during his journey, a woman called Martha entertained him in her house. 39 She had a sister called Mary; and Mary took her place at the Lord's feet, and listened to his words. 40 Martha was distracted by waiting on many needs; so she came to his side, and asked, Lord, art thou content that my sister should leave me to do the serving alone? Come, bid her help me. 41 Jesus answered her, Martha, Martha, how many cares and troubles thou hast! 42 But only one thing is necessary; and Mary has chosen for herself the best part of all, that which shall never be taken away from her.

v. 27. Deut. vi. 5, Lev. xix. 18.

Chapter Eleven

vv. 2-4, 9-13. Mat-thew vi. 9, vii. 7.

ONCE, WHEN HE HAD found a place to pray in, one of his disciples said to him, after his prayer was over, Lord, teach us how to pray, as John did for his disciples. 2 And he told them, When you pray, you are to say, Father, hallowed be thy name; thy kingdom come; 3 give us this day our daily bread; 4 and forgive us our sins; we too forgive all those who trespass against us; and lead us not into temptation. 5 Let us suppose that one of you has a friend, to whom he goes at dead of night, and asks him, Lend me three loaves of bread, neighbour; 6 a friend of mine has turned in to me after a journey, and I have nothing to offer him. 7 And suppose the other answers, from within doors, Do not put me to such trouble; the door is locked, my children and I are in bed; I cannot bestir myself to grant thy request. 8 I tell you, even if he will not bestir himself to grant it out of friendship, shameless asking will make him rise and give his friend all that he needs. 9 And I say the same to you; ask, and the gift will come, seek, and you shall find; knock, and the door shall be opened to you. 10 Everyone that asks, will receive, that seeks, will find, that knocks, will have the door opened to him. 11 Among yourselves, if a father is asked by his son for bread, will he give him a stone? Or for a fish, will he give him a snake instead of a fish? 12 Or if he is asked for an egg, will he give him a scorpion? 13 Why then, if you, evil as you are, know well enough how to give your children what is good for them, is not your Father much more ready to give, from heaven, his gracious Spirit to those who ask him?

vv. 14-22. Matthew xii. 22, Mark iii. 22.

14 He had just cast out a devil, which was dumb; and no sooner had the devil gone out than the dumb man found speech. The multitudes were filled with amazement; 15 but some of them said, It is through Beelzebub, the prince of the devils, that he casts the devils out, 16 while others, to put him to the test, would have him shew a sign out of heaven. 17 But he could read their thoughts, and said to them, No kingdom can be at war with itself without being brought to desolation, one house falling upon an-

other. 18 And how do you suppose that Satan's kingdom can stand firm if he is at war with himself, that you should accuse me of casting out devils through Beelzebub? 19 Again, if it is through Beelzebub that I cast out devils, by what means do your own sons cast them out? It is for these, then, to pronounce judgement on you. 20 But if, when I cast out devils, I do it through God's power, then it must be that the kingdom of God has suddenly appeared among you. 21 When a strong man, fully armed, mounts guard over his own palace, his goods are left in peace; 22 but when a man comes who is stronger still, he will take away all the armour that gave him confidence, and divide among others the spoils he has won. 23 He who is not with me, is against me; he who does not gather his store with me, scatters it abroad. 24 The unclean spirit which has possessed a man and then goes out of him, walks about the desert looking for a resting-place, and finds none; and it says, I will go back to my own dwelling, from which I came out. 25 And it comes back, to find that dwelling swept out, and neatly set in order. 26 Thereupon, it goes away and brings in seven other spirits more wicked than itself to bear it company, and together they enter in and settle down there; till the last state of that man is worse than the first. 27 When he spoke thus, a woman in the multitude said to him aloud, Blessed is the womb that bore thee, the breast which thou hast sucked. 28 And he answered, Shall we not say, Blessed are those who hear the word of God, and keep it?

vv. 24-32. Matthew xii. 38; see note on Matthew xii. 43.

v. 28. See note on Matthew xii. 46.

29 The multitudes gathered round him, and he began speaking to them thus; This is a wicked generation; it asks for a sign, and the only sign that will be given to it is the sign of the prophet Jonas. 30 Jonas was the sign given to the men of Nineve; the sign given to this generation will be the Son of Man. 31 The queen of the south will rise up with the men of this generation at the judgement, and will leave them without excuse; for she came from the ends of the earth to hear the wisdom of Solomon, and behold, a greater than Solomon is here. 32 The men of Nineve will rise up with this generation at the judgement, and will leave it without excuse; for they did penance when Jonas preached to them, and behold, a greater than Jonas is here.

vv. 31-32. I Paralip. ix. 1, Jonas i. 17.

33 Nobody lights a lamp, and then puts it away in a cellar or under a bushel measure; it is put on the lamp-stand, so that its light may be seen by all who come in. 34 Thy body has the eye for its lamp; and if thy eye is clear, the whole of thy body will be lit up; when it is diseased, the whole of thy body will be in darkness. 35 Take good care, then, that this principle of light which is in

thee is light, not darkness; 36 then, if thy whole body is in the light, with no part of it in darkness, it will all be lit up as if by a bright lamp enlightening thee.

37 At the time when he said this, one of the Pharisees invited him to his house for the mid-day meal; so he went in and sat down at table; 38 the Pharisee meanwhile was inwardly surmising, why he had not washed before his meal. 39 And the Lord said to him, You Pharisees are content to cleanse the outward part of cup and dish, while all within is running with avarice and wickedness. 40 Fools, did not he who made the outward part make the inward too? 41 Nay, you should give alms out of the store you have, and at once all that is yours becomes clean.

vv. 39-52. Matthew xxiii. 4.

42 Woe upon you, you Pharisees, that will award God his tithe, though it be of mint or rue or whatever herb you will, and leave on one side justice and the love of God; you do ill to forget one duty while you perform the other. 43 Woe upon you, you Pharisees, for loving the first seats in the synagogues, and to have your hands kissed in the market-place; 44 woe upon you, that are like hidden tombs which men walk over without knowing it.

45 And here one of the lawyers answered him; Master, he said, in speaking thus thou art bringing us too into contempt. 46 And he said, Woe upon you too, you lawyers, for loading men with packs too heavy to be borne, packs that you yourselves will not touch with one finger. 47 Woe upon you, for building up the tombs of the prophets, the same prophets who were murdered by your fathers; 48 sure witness that you approve what your fathers did, since you build tombs for the men they murdered. 49 Whereupon the wisdom of God warns you, I will send my prophets and my apostles to them, and there will be some they will kill and persecute; 50 so they will be answerable for all the blood of prophets that has been shed since the beginning of the world,

v. 51. See note on Matthew xxiii. 35.

51 from the blood of Abel to the blood of Zacharias, who was killed between the altar and the temple; yes, I tell you, this generation will be held answerable for it. 52 Woe upon you, you lawyers, for taking away with you the key of knowledge; you have neither entered yourselves, nor let others enter when they would.

53 As he said all this to them, the scribes and Pharisees resolved to hunt him down mercilessly and to browbeat him with a multitude of questions. 54 Thus they lay in wait for him, hoping to catch some word from his lips which would give them ground of accusation against him.

Chapter Twelve

<small>*vv. 1-12. Matthew x. 26.*</small>

AND NOW GREAT MUL titudes had gathered round him, so that they trod one another down; and he addressed himself first to his disciples; Have nothing to do with the leaven of the Pharisees, he said, it is all hypocrisy. 2 What is veiled will all be revealed, what is hidden will all be known; 3 what you have said in darkness, will be repeated in the light of day, what you have whispered in secret chambers, will be proclaimed on the housetops. 4 And I say this to you who are my friends, Do not be afraid of those who can kill the body, and after that can do no more. 5 I will tell you who it is you must fear; fear him who has power not only to kill but to cast a man into hell; him you must fear indeed. 6 Are not sparrows sold five for two pence? And yet not one of them is forgotten in God's sight. 7 As for you, he takes every hair of your head into his reckoning; do not be afraid, then; you count for more than a host of sparrows. 8 And I tell you this; whoever acknowledges me before men, will be acknowledged by the Son of Man in the presence of God's angels; 9 he who disowns me before men, will be disowned before God's angels. 10 There is no one who speaks a word against the Son of Man but may find forgiveness; there will be no forgiveness for the man who blasphemes against the Holy Spirit. 11 When they bring you to trial before synagogues, and magistrates, and officers, do not consider anxiously what you are to say, what defence to make or how to make it; 12 the Holy Spirit will instruct you when the time comes, what words to use.

<small>*v. 10. See note on Matthew xii. 32.*</small>

13 One of the multitude said to him, Master, bid my brother give me a share of our inheritance. 14 And he answered, Why, man, who has appointed me a judge to make awards between you? 15 Then he said to them, Look well and keep yourselves clear of all covetousness. A man's life does not consist in having more possessions than he needs. 16 And he told them a parable, There was a rich man whose lands yielded a heavy crop: 17 and he debated in his mind, What am I to do, with no room to store my

crops in? 18 Then he said, This is what I will do; I will pull down my barns, and build greater ones, and there I shall be able to store all my harvest and all the goods that are mine; 19 and then I will say to my soul, Come, soul, thou hast goods in plenty laid up for many years to come; take thy rest now, eat, drink, and make merry. 20 And God said, Thou fool, this night thou must render up thy soul; and who will be master now of all thou hast laid by? 21 Thus it is with the man who lays up treasure for himself, and has no credit with God.

vv. 22-31. Matthew vi. 25.

22 Then he said to his disciples, I say to you, then, do not fret over your life, how to support it with food, over your body, how to keep it clothed. 23 Life is a greater gift than food, the body than clothing; 24 see how the ravens never sow or reap, have neither storehouse nor barn, and yet God feeds them; have you not an excellence far beyond theirs? 25 Can any of you, for all his fretting, add a cubit's growth to his height? 26 And if you are powerless to do so small a thing, why do you fret about your other needs? 27 See how the lilies grow; they do not toil, or spin, and yet I tell you that even Solomon in all his glory was not arrayed like one of these. 28 If God, then, so clothes the grasses which live to-day in the fields and will feed the oven to-morrow, will he not be much more ready to clothe you, men of little faith? 29 You should not be asking, then, what you are to eat or drink, and living in suspense of mind; 30 it is for the heathen world to busy itself over such things; your Father knows well that you need them. 31 No, make it your first care to find the kingdom of God, and all these things shall be yours without the asking.

32 Do not be afraid, you, my little flock. Your Father has determined to give you his kingdom. 33 Sell what you have, and give alms, so providing yourselves with a purse that time cannot wear holes in, an inexhaustible treasure laid up in heaven, where no thief comes near, no moth consumes. 34 Where your treasure-house is, there your heart is too. 35 Your loins must be girt, and your lamps burning, 36 and you yourselves like men awaiting their master's return from a wedding-feast, so that they may open to him at once when he comes and knocks at the door. 37 Blessed are those servants, whom their master will find watching when he comes; I promise you, he will gird himself, and make them sit down to meat, and minister to them. 38 Whether he comes in the second quarter of the night or in the third, blessed are those servants if he finds them alert. 39 Be sure of this; if the master of

vv. 39-46. Matthew xxiv. 43.

the house had known at what time the thief was coming, he would have kept watch, and not allowed his house to be broken open. 40 You too, then, must stand ready; the Son of Man will come at an hour when you are not expecting him.

41 Hereupon Peter said to him, Lord, dost thou address this parable to us, or to all men? 42 And the Lord answered, Who, then, is a faithful and wise steward, one whom his master will entrust with the care of the household, to give them their allowance of food at the appointed time? 43 Blessed is that servant who is found doing this when his lord comes; 44 I promise you, he will give him charge of all his goods. 45 But if that servant says in his heart, My lord is long in coming, and falls to beating the men and the maids, eating and drinking himself drunk; 46 then on some day when he expects nothing, at an hour when he is all unaware, his lord will come, and will cut him off, and assign him his portion with the unfaithful. 47 Yet it is the servant who knew his Lord's will, and did not make ready for him, or do his will, that will have many strokes of the lash; 48 he who did not know of it, yet earned a beating, will have only a few. Much will be asked of the man to whom much has been given; more will be expected of him, because he was entrusted with more.

49 It is fire that I have come to spread over the earth, and what better wish can I have than that it should be kindled? 50 There is a baptism I must needs be baptized with, and how impatient am I for its accomplishment! 51 Do you think that I have come to bring peace on the earth? No, believe me, I have come to bring dissension. 52 Henceforward five in the same house will be found at variance, three against two and two against three; 53 the father will be at variance with his son, and the son with his father, the mother against her daughter, and the daughter against her mother, the mother-in-law against her daughter-in-law, and the daughter-in-law against her mother-in-law.

54 And he said to the multitudes, When you find a cloud rising out of the west, you say at once, There is rain coming, and so it does; 55 when you find the south-west wind blowing, you say, It will be hot, and so it is. 56 Poor fools, you know well enough how to interpret the face of land and sky; can you not interpret the times you live in? 57 Does not your own experience teach you to make the right decision? 58 If one has a claim against thee, and thou art going with him to the magistrate, then do thy utmost, while thou art still on the road, to be quit of his claim; or it may

vv. 51-53. Matthew x. 34.

vv. 54-56. Matthew xvi. 2.

v. 57. This verse seems to be a link between what went before and what follows. From the signs of their own times (our Lord's miracles, etc.), the Jews can satisfy themselves that the kingdom of God is at hand. Let them, then, use the same prudence in spiritual, as they would use in worldly affairs. Let them repent of their sins here and now, before punishment comes upon them, just as they would be anxious to settle out of court a law-suit which was likely to go against them. Cf. Matthew v. 25, 26.

be he will drag thee into the presence of the judge, and the judge will hand thee over to his officer, and the officer will cast thee into prison. 59 Be sure of this, thou wilt find no discharge from it until thou hast paid the last farthing.

Chapter Thirteen

At this very time there were some present that told him the story of those Galileans, whose blood Pilate had shed in the midst of their sacrifices. 2 And Jesus said in answer, Do you suppose, because this befell them, that these men were worse sinners than all else in Galilee? 3 I tell you it is not so; you will all perish as they did, if you do not repent. 4 What of those eighteen men on whom the tower fell in Siloe, and killed them; do you suppose that there was a heavier account against them, than against any others who then dwelt at Jerusalem? 5 I tell you it was not so; you will all perish as they did, if you do not repent.

6 And this was a parable he told them; There was a man that had a fig-tree planted in his vineyard, but when he came and looked for fruit on it, he could find none; 7 whereupon he said to his vine-dresser, See now, I have been coming to look for fruit on this fig-tree for three years, and cannot find any. Cut it down; why should it be a useless charge upon the land? 8 But he answered thus, Sir, let it stand this year too, so that I may have time to dig and put dung round it; 9 perhaps it will bear fruit; if not, it will be time to cut it down then.

10 There was a sabbath day on which he was preaching in one of their synagogues. 11 Here there was a woman who for eighteen years had suffered under some influence that disabled her; she was bent down, and could not lift her head straight. 12 Jesus saw her and called her to him; Woman, he said, thou art rid of thy in-

firmity. 13 Then he laid his hands on her, and immediately she was raised upright, and gave praise to God. 14 But the ruler of the synagogue, indignant that Jesus should heal them on the sabbath day, turned and said to the multitude, You have six days on which work is allowed; you should come and be healed on those days, not on the sabbath. 15 And the Lord gave him this answer, What, you hypocrites, is there any one of you that will not untie his ox or his ass from the stall and take them down to water, when it is the sabbath? 16 And here is this daughter of Abraham, whom Satan had kept bound these eighteen years past; was it wrong that she should be delivered on the sabbath day from bonds like these? 17 All his adversaries were put to shame by this saying of his, and the whole multitude rejoiced over the marvellous works he did.

18 He said, What is there that bears a likeness to the kingdom of heaven; what comparison shall I find for it? 19 It is like a grain of mustard seed, that a man has taken and planted in his garden, where it has thriven and grown into a great tree, and all the birds have come and settled in its branches. 20 And again, he said, What comparison shall I find for the kingdom of heaven? 21 It is like leaven, that a woman has taken and buried away in three measures of meal, enough to leaven the whole batch. *vv. 18-21. Matthew xiii. 31, Mark iv. 30.*

22 And so he went through the cities and villages teaching, and making his journey towards Jerusalem. 23 There was a man that said to him, Lord, is it only a few that are to be saved? Whereupon he said to them: 24 Fight your way in at the narrow door; I tell you, there are many who will try and will not be able to enter. 25 When the master of the house has gone in and has shut the door, you will fall to beating on the door as you stand without, and saying, Lord open to us. But this will be his answer, I know nothing of you, nor whence you come. 26 Thereupon you will fall to protesting, We have eaten and drunk in thy presence; thou hast taught in our streets. 27 But he will say, I tell you, I know nothing of you, nor whence you come; depart from me, you that traffic in iniquity. 28 Weeping shall be there, and gnashing of teeth, when you see Abraham and Isaac and Jacob and all the prophets within God's kingdom, while you yourselves are cast out. 29 Others will come from the east and the west, the north and the south, to take their ease in the kingdom of God. 30 And indeed, there are some who are last, and shall then be first, some who are first, and shall then be last.

31 It was on that day that some of the Pharisees came to him and said, Go elsewhere, and leave this place; Herod has a mind to

kill thee. 32 And he said to them, Go and tell that fox, Behold, to-day and to-morrow I am to continue casting out devils, and doing works of healing; it is on the third day that I am to reach my consummation. 33 But to-day and to-morrow and the next day I must go on my journeys; there is no room for a prophet to meet his death, except at Jerusalem. 34 Jerusalem, Jerusalem, still murdering the prophets, and stoning the messengers that are sent to thee, how often have I been ready to gather thy children to-gether, as a hen gathers her brood under her wings, and thou didst refuse it! 35 Behold, your house is left to you, a house unin-habited. I tell you, you shall see nothing of me until the time comes, when you will be saying, Blessed is he that comes in the name of the Lord.

Chapter Fourteen

THERE WAS A SABBATH day on which he was asked to take a meal with one of the chief Pharisees, and as he went into the house, they were watching him. 2 Here his eye was met by the sight of a man who had the dropsy. 3 Jesus asked the lawyers and Pharisees openly, Is healing allowed on the sabbath day? 4 Then, as they did not answer, he took the man by the hand, and sent him away healed. 5 And he turned on them, and said, Is there any one of you who will not pull out his ass or his ox immediately, if it falls into a pit on the sabbath? 6 To this they could make no answer. 7 He also had a parable for the guests who were invited, as he observed how they chose the chief places for themselves; he said to them: 8 When any man invites thee to a wedding, do not sit down in the chief place; he may have invited some guest whose rank is greater than thine. 9 If so, his host and thine will come and say to thee, Make room for this man; and so thou wilt find thyself taking, with a blush, the lowest place of all. 10 Rather, when thou art summoned, go straight to the lowest place and sit down there; so, when he who invited thee comes in, he will say, My friend, go higher than this; and then honour shall be thine before all that sit down in thy company. 11 Everyone who exalts himself shall be humbled, and he that humbles himself shall be exalted. 12 He said, moreover, to his host, When thou givest a dinner or a supper, do not ask thy neighbours to come, or thy brethren, or thy kindred, or thy friends who are rich; it may be they will send thee invitations in return, and so thou wilt be recompensed for thy pains. 13 Rather, when thou givest hospitality, invite poor men to come, the cripples, the lame, the blind: 14 so thou shalt win a blessing, for these cannot make thee any return; thy reward will come when the just rise again.

15 Hearing this, one of his fellow guests said to him, Blessed is the man who shall feast in the kingdom of God. 16 He answered him thus, There was a man that gave a great supper, and sent out many invitations. 17 And when the time came for his supper, he sent one of his own servants telling the invited guests to come, for all was now ready. 18 And all of them, with one accord, began making excuses. I have bought a farm, the first said to him, and I must needs go and look over it; I pray thee, count me excused. 19 And another said, I have bought five pair of oxen, and I am on my way to make trial of them; I pray thee, count me excused. 20 And another said, I have married a wife, and so I am unable to come. 21 The servant came back and told his master all this, whereupon the host fell into a rage, and said to his servant, Quick, go out into the streets and lanes of the city; bring in the poor, the cripples, the blind and the lame. 22 And when the servant told him, Sir, all has been done according to thy command, but there is room left still, 23 the master said to the servant, Go out into the highways and the hedgerows, and give them no choice but to come in, that so my house may be filled. 24 I tell you, none of those who were first invited shall taste of my supper.

vv. 16-24. A similar parable is found in Matthew xxii. 2.

25 Great multitudes bore him company on his way; to these he turned, and said: 26 If any man comes to me, without hating his father and mother and wife and children and brethren and sisters, yes, and his own life too, he can be no disciple of mine. 27 A man cannot be my disciple unless he takes up his own cross, and follows after me. 28 Consider, if one of you has a mind to build a tower, does he not first sit down and count the cost that must be paid, if he is to have enough to finish it? 29 Is he to lay the foundation,

and then find himself unable to complete the work, so that all who see it will fall to mocking him 30 and saying, Here is a man who began to build, and could not finish his building? 31 Or if a king is setting out to join battle with another king, does he not first sit down and deliberate, whether with his army of ten thousand he can meet the onset of one who has twenty thousand? 32 If he cannot, then, while the other is still at a distance, he despatches envoys to ask for conditions of peace. 33 And so it is with you; none of you can be my disciple if he does not take leave of all that he possesses. 34 Salt is a good thing; but if the salt itself becomes tasteless, what is there left to give taste to it? 35 It is of no use either to the soil or to the dung-heap; it will be thrown away altogether. Listen, you that have ears to hear with.

Chapter
Fifteen

WHEN THEY FOUND all the publicans and sinners coming to listen to him, 2 the Pharisees and scribes were indignant; Here is a man, they said, that entertains sinners, and eats with

vv. 3-7. Matthew xviii. 12.

them. 3 Whereupon he told them this parable: 4 If any of you owns a hundred sheep, and has lost one of them, does he not leave the other ninety-nine in the wilderness, and go after the one which is lost until he finds it? 5 And when he does find it, he sets it on his shoulders, rejoicing, 6 and so goes home, and calls his friends and his neighbours together; Rejoice with me, he says to them, I have found my sheep that was lost. 7 So it is, I tell you, in heaven; there will be more rejoicing over one sinner who repents, than over ninety-nine souls that are justified, and have no need of repentance. 8 Or if some woman has ten silver pieces by her, and has lost one of them, does she not light a lamp, and sweep the house, and search carefully until she finds it? 9 And when she does find it, she calls her friends and her neighbours together; Rejoice with me, she says, I have found the silver piece which I lost. 10 So it is, I tell you, with the angels of God; there is joy among them over one sinner that repents.

11 Then he said, There was a certain man who had two sons. 12 And the younger of these said to his father, Father, give me that portion of the estate which falls to me. So he divided his property between them. 13 Not many days afterwards, the younger son put together all that he had, and went on his travels to a far country, where he wasted his fortune in riotous living. 14 Then, when all was spent, a great famine arose in that country, and he found himself in want; 15 whereupon he went and attached himself to a citizen of that country, who put him on his farm, to feed swine. 16 He would have been glad to fill his belly with husks, such as the swine used to eat; but none was ready to give them to him. 17 Then he came to himself, and said, How many hired servants there are in my father's house, who have more bread than they can eat, and here am I perishing with hunger! 18 I will arise and go to my father, and say to him, Father, I have sinned against heaven, and before thee; 19 I am not worthy, now, to be called thy son; treat me as one of thy hired servants. 20 And he arose, and went on his way to his father. But, while he was still a long way off, his father saw him, and took pity on him; running up, he threw his arms round his neck and kissed him. 21 And when the son said, Father, I have sinned against heaven and before thee; I am not worthy, now, to be called thy son, 22 the father gave orders to his servants, Bring out the best robe, and clothe him in it; put a ring on his hand, and shoes on his feet. 23 Then bring out the calf that has been fattened, and kill it; let us eat, and make merry; 24 for my son here was dead, and has come to life again, was lost, and is found. And so they began their merry-making. 25 The elder son, meanwhile, was away on the farm; and on his way home, as he drew near the house, he heard music and dancing; 26 whereupon he called one of the servants and asked what all this meant. 27 He told him, Thy brother has come back, and thy father has killed the fattened calf, glad to have him restored safe and sound. 28 At this he fell into a rage, and would not go in. When his father came out and tried to win him over, 29 he answered his father thus, Think how many years I have lived as thy servant, never transgressing thy commands, and thou hast never made me a present of a kid, to make merry with my friends; 30 and now, when this son of thine has come home, one that has swallowed up

his patrimony in the company of harlots, thou hast killed the fattened calf in his honour. 31 He said to him, My son, thou art always at my side, and everything that I have is already thine; 32 but for this merry-making and rejoicing there was good reason; thy brother here was dead, and has come to life again; was lost, and is found.

Chapter Sixteen

vv. 1-9. The chief lesson of this parable seems to be that we should do service to God by giving alms to the poor, while we have still time for it. The steward was prudent in making himself friends before the audit of his accounts, while he had still money to do it; so we must give alms while life still lasts. It is doubtful whether we are meant to interpret the parable more closely than this.

AND HE SAID TO HIS DIS ciples, There was a rich man that had a steward, and a report came to him that this steward had wasted his goods. 2 Whereupon he sent for him, and said to him, What is this that I hear of thee? Give an account of thy stewardship, for thou canst not be my steward any longer. 3 At this, the steward said to himself, What am I to do, now that my master is taking my stewardship away from me? I have no strength to dig; I would be ashamed to beg for alms. 4 I see what I must do, so as to be welcomed into men's houses when I am dismissed from my stewardship. 5 Then he summoned his master's debtors one by one; and he said to the first, How much is it that thou owest my master? 6 A hundred firkins of oil, he said; and he told him, Here is thy bill; quick, sit down and write it as fifty. 7 Then he said to a second, And thou, how much dost thou owe? A hundred quarters of wheat, he said; and he told him, Here is thy bill, write it as eighty. 8 And this knavish steward was commended by his master for his prudence in what he had done; for indeed, the children of this world are more prudent after their own fashion than the children of the light. 9 And my counsel to you is, make use of your base wealth to win yourselves friends, who, when you leave it behind, will welcome you into eternal habitations. 10 He who is trustworthy over a little sum is trustworthy over a greater;

he who plays false over a little sum, plays false over a greater; 11 if you, then, could not be trusted to use the base riches you had, who will put the true riches in your keeping? 12 Who will give you property of your own, if you could not be trusted with what was only lent you?

13 No servant can be in the employment of two masters at once; either he will hate the one and love the other, or he will devote himself to the one and despise the other. You must serve God or money; you cannot serve both.

14 The Pharisees, who were fond of riches, heard all this, and poured scorn on him. 15 And he said to them, You are always courting the approval of men, but God sees your hearts; what is highly esteemed among men is an abomination in God's sight. 16 The law and the prophets lasted until John's time; since that time, it is the kingdom of heaven that has its preachers, and all who will, press their way into it. 17 And yet it is easier for heaven and earth to disappear than for one line of the law to perish. 18 Every man who puts away his wife and marries another is an adulterer, and he too is an adulterer, that marries a woman who has been put away.

19 There was a rich man once, that was clothed in purple and lawn, and feasted sumptuously every day. 20 And there was a beggar, called Lazarus, who lay at his gate, covered with sores, 21 wishing that he could be fed with the crumbs which fell from the rich man's table, but none was ready to give them to him; the very dogs came and licked his sores. 22 Time went on; the beggar died, and was carried by the angels to Abraham's bosom; the rich man died too, and found his grave in hell. 23 And there, in his suffering, he lifted up his eyes, and saw Abraham far off, and Lazarus in his bosom. 24 And he said, with a loud cry, Father Abraham, take pity on me; send Lazarus to dip the tip of his finger in water, and cool my tongue; I am tormented in this flame. 25 But Abraham said, My son, remember that thou didst receive thy good fortune in thy life-time, and Lazarus, no less, his ill fortune; now he is in comfort, thou in torment. 26 And, besides all this, there is a great gulf fixed between us and you, so that there is no passing from our side of it to you, no crossing over to us from yours. 27 Whereupon he said, Then, father, I pray thee send him to my own father's house; 28 for I have five brethren; let him give these a warning, so that they may not come, in their turn, into this place of suffering. 29 Abraham said to him, They have Moses and the prophets; let them listen to these. 30 They will not do

v. 22. The best Greek manuscripts include the words 'in hell' not in this sentence, but in the sentence which follows.

141

that, father Abraham, said he; but if a messenger comes to them from the dead, they will repent. 31 But he answered him, If they do not listen to Moses and the prophets, they will be unbelieving still, though one should rise from the dead.

Chapter Seventeen

AND HE SAID TO HIS DIS ciples, It is impossible that hurt should never be done to men's consciences; but woe betide the man who is the cause of it. 2 Better for him to have had a millstone tied about his neck, and to be cast into the sea, than to have hurt the conscience of one of these little ones. 3 Keep good watch over yourselves. As for thy brother, if he is in fault, tax him with it, and if he is sorry for it, forgive him; 4 nay, if he does thee wrong seven times in the day, and seven times in the day comes back to thee and says, I am sorry, thou shalt forgive him.

5 The apostles said to the Lord, Give us more faith. 6 And the Lord said, If you had faith, though it were as a grain of mustard seed, you might say to this mulberry tree, Uproot thyself and plant thyself in the sea, and it would obey you.

7 If any one of you had a servant following the plough, or herding the sheep, would he say to him, when he came back from the farm, Go and fall to at once? 8 Would he not say to him, Prepare my supper, and then gird thyself and wait upon me while I eat and drink; thou shalt eat and drink thyself afterwards? 9 Does he hold himself bound in gratitude to such a servant, for obeying his commands? 10 I do not think it of him; and you, in the same way, when you have done all that was commanded you, are to say, We are servants, and worthless; it was our duty to do what we have done.

11 A time came when he was on his way to Jerusalem, and was

passing between Samaria and Galilee; 12 and as he was going into a village, ten men that were lepers came towards him; they stood far off, 13 crying aloud, Jesus, Master, have pity on us. 14 He met them with the words, Go and shew yourselves to the priests; and thereupon, as they went, they were made clean. 15 One of them, finding that he was cured, came back, praising God aloud, 16 and threw himself at Jesus' feet with his face to the ground, to thank him; and this was a Samaritan. 17 Jesus answered, Were not all ten made clean? And the other nine, where are they? 18 Not one has come back to give God the praise, except this stranger. 19 And he said to him, Arise and go on thy way, thy faith has brought thee recovery.

20 Upon being asked by the Pharisees, when the kingdom of God was to come, he answered, The kingdom of God comes unwatched by men's eyes; 21 there will be no saying, See, it is here, or See, it is there; the kingdom of God is here, within you. 22 And to his own disciples he said, The time will come when you will long to enjoy, but for a day, the Son of Man's presence, and it will not be granted you. 23 Men will be saying to you, See, he is here, or See, he is there; do not turn aside and follow them; 24 the Son of Man, when his time comes, will be like the lightning which lightens from one border of heaven to the other. 25 But before that, he must undergo many sufferings, and be rejected by this generation. 26 In the days when the Son of Man comes, all will be as it was in the days of Noe; 27 they ate, they drank, they married and were given in marriage, until the day when Noe went into the ark, and the flood came and destroyed them all. 28 So it was, too, in the days of Lot; they ate, they drank, they bought and sold, they planted and built; 29 but on the day when Lot went out of Sodom, a rain of fire and brimstone came from heaven and destroyed them all. 30 And so it will be, in the day when the Son of Man is revealed. 31 In that day, if a man is on the housetop and his goods are in the house, let him not come down to take them with him; and if a man is in the fields, he too must beware of turning back. 32 Remember Lot's wife. 33 The man who tries to save his own life will lose it; it is the man who loses it that will keep it safe. 34 I tell you, on that night, where two men are sleeping in one bed, one will be taken and the other left; 35 one woman taken, one left, as they grind together at the mill, one man taken, one left, as they work together in the fields. 36 Then they answered him, Where, Lord? 37 And he told them, It is where the body lies that the eagles will gather.

v. 21. 'Within you'; the Greek might also mean, 'among you'.

v. 22. Some think this means, that in the time of persecution the Apostles will sigh for the glories of heaven; others, that they will look back with regret to the days when their Master was on earth.

vv. 23-37. Much of what is said here is found also in Matthew xxiv, and in Mark xiii.

143

Chapter Eighteen

AND HE TOLD THEM A parable, shewing them that they ought to pray continually, and never be discouraged. 2 There was a city once, he said, in which lived a judge who had no fear of God, no regard for man; 3 and there was a widow in this city who used to come before him and say, Give me redress against one who wrongs me. 4 For a time he refused; but then he said to himself, 5 Fear of God I have none, nor regard for man, but this widow wearies me; I will give her redress, or she will wear me down at last with her visits. 6 Listen, the Lord said, to the words of the unjust judge, 7 and tell me, will not God give redress to his elect, when they are crying out to him, day and night? Will he not be impatient with their wrongs? 8 I tell you, he will give them redress with all speed. But ah, when the Son of Man comes, will he find faith left on the earth?

9 There were some who had confidence in themselves, thinking they had won acceptance with God, and despised the rest of the world; to them he addressed this other parable: 10 Two men went up into the temple to pray; one was a Pharisee, the other a publican. 11 The Pharisee stood upright, and made this prayer in his heart, I thank thee, God, that I am not like the rest of men, who steal and cheat and commit adultery, or like this publican here; 12 for myself, I fast twice in the week, I give tithes of all that I possess. 13 And the publican stood far off; he would not even lift up his eyes towards heaven; he only beat his breast, and said, God, be merciful to me; I am a sinner. 14 I tell you, this man went back home higher in God's favour than the other; everyone who exalts himself will be humbled, and the man who humbles himself will be exalted.

vv. 15-30. Matthew xix. 13, Mark x. 13. 15 Then they brought little children to him, asking him to touch them. 16 The disciples saw them and rebuked them for it: but Jesus called the children to him, and said, Let them be, do not keep them back from me; the kingdom of God belongs to such as these. 17 Believe me, the man who does not accept the kingdom of God like a little child, will never enter into it. 18 And one of the rulers asked him, Master, who art so good, what must I do to win eternal life? 19 Jesus said to him, Why dost thou call me good? None is good, except God only. 20 Thou knowest the commandments, Thou shalt do no murder, Thou shalt not commit adultery, Thou shalt not steal, Thou shalt not bear false witness, Honour thy father and thy mother. 21 I have kept all these, he said, ever since I grew up. 22 When he heard that, Jesus said, In one thing thou art still wanting; sell all that belongs to thee, and give to the poor; so the treasure thou hast shall be in heaven; then come back and follow me. 23 The answer filled him with sadness, for he was very rich; 24 and Jesus, seeing his mournful look, said, With what difficulty will those who have riches enter God's kingdom! 25 It is easier for a camel to pass through a needle's eye, than for a man to enter the kingdom of God when he is rich. 26 But when he was asked by those who were listening to him, Why then, who can be saved? 27 he told them, What is impossible to man's powers is possible to God.

28 Hereupon Peter said, And what of us? we have forsaken all that was ours, and followed thee. 29 Jesus said to them, I promise you, everyone who has forsaken home, or parents, or brethren, or wife, or children for the sake of the kingdom of God, 30 will receive in this present world, many times their worth, and in the world to come, everlasting life.

31 Then he took the twelve apostles aside, and warned them, Now we are going up to Jerusalem, and all that has been written by the prophets about the Son of Man is to be accomplished. 32 He will be given up to the Gentiles, and mocked, and beaten, and spat upon; 33 they will scourge him, and then they will kill him; but on the third day he will rise again. 34 They could make nothing of all this; his meaning was hidden from them, so that they could not understand what he said.

35 When he came near Jericho, there was a blind man sitting there by the way side begging. 36 And he, hearing a multitude passing by, asked what it meant; 37 so they told him, that Jesus of Nazareth was going past. 38 Whereupon he cried out, Jesus, son of David, have pity on me. 39 Those who were in front rebuked him, and told him to be silent, but he cried out all the more, Son of David, have pity on me. 40 Then Jesus stopped, and gave orders that the man should be brought to him; and when he came close, he asked him, 41 What wouldst thou have me do for thee? Lord, he said, give me back my sight. 42 Jesus said to him, Receive

v. 20. Ex. xx. 12.

v. 22. See note on Matthew xix. 21.

vv. 31-33. Matthew xx. 17, Mark x. 32.

vv. 35-43. Matthew xx. 29, Mark x. 46. It would appear that St. Luke, in speaking of our Lord as drawing near Jericho, is only giving a vague indication of where the miracle took place, since the other Evangelists tell us that he met the blind man when he was leaving the city. It may be, however, that there is some confusion between the old city of Jericho, and that built by Herod the Great about two miles away.

thy sight; thy faith has brought thee recovery. 43 And at once the man recovered his sight, and followed him, glorifying God; all the people, too, gave praise to God at seeing it.

Chapter Nineteen

HE HAD ENTERED JERI cho, and was passing through it; 2 and here a rich man named Zacchaeus, the chief publican, 3 was trying to distinguish which was Jesus, but could not do so because of the multitude, being a man of small stature. 4 So he ran on in front, and climbed up into a sycamore tree, to catch sight of him, since he must needs pass that way. 5 Jesus, when he reached the place, looked up and saw him; Zacchaeus, he said, make haste and come down; I am to lodge to-day at thy house. 6 And he came down with all haste, and gladly made him welcome. 7 When they saw it, all took it amiss; He has gone in to lodge, they said, with one who is a sinner. 8 But Zacchaeus stood upright and said to the Lord, Here and now, Lord, I give half of what I have to the poor; and if I have wronged anyone in any way, I make restitution of it fourfold. 9 Jesus turned to him and said, To-day, salvation has been brought to this house; he too is a son of Abraham. 10 That is what the Son of man has come for, to search out and to save what was lost.

11 While they stood listening, he went on and told them a parable; this was because he had now nearly reached Jerusalem, and they supposed that the kingdom of God was to appear immediately. 12 He told them, then, There was a man of noble birth, who went away to a distant country, to have the royal title bestowed on him, and so return. 13 And he summoned ten of his servants, to whom he gave ten pounds, and said to them, Trade with this while I am away. 14 But his fellow citizens hated him, and

vv. 12-27. A similar parable is found in Matthew xxv. 14.

146

sent ambassadors after him to say, We will not have this man for our king. 15 Afterwards, when he came back as king, he sent for the servants to whom he had entrusted the money, to find out how much each of them had gained by his use of it. 16 The first came before him and said, Lord, thy pound has made ten pounds. 17 And he said to him, Well done, my true servant: since thou hast been faithful over a very little, thou shalt have authority over ten cities. 18 The second came and said, Lord, thy pound has made five pounds; 19 and to him he said, Thou too shalt have authority, over five cities. 20 Then another came and said, Lord, here is thy pound; I have kept it laid up in a handkerchief. 21 I was afraid of thee, knowing how exacting a man thou art; thou dost claim what thou didst never venture, dost reap what thou didst never sow. 22 Then he said to him, Thou false servant, I take thy judgement from thy own lips. Thou knewest that I was an exacting man, claiming what I never ventured and reaping what I never sowed; 23 then why didst thou not put my money into the bank, so that I might have recovered it with interest when I came? 24 Then he gave orders to those who stood by, Take the pound away from him, and give it to the man who has ten pounds. 25 (They said to him, Lord, he has ten pounds already.) 26 Nay, but I tell you, if ever a man is rich, gifts will be made to him, and his riches will abound; if he is poor, even the little he has will be taken from him. 27 But as for those enemies of mine, who refused to have me for their king, bring them here and kill them in my presence. 28 And when he had spoken thus, he went on his way, going up to Jerusalem.

29 After this, when he was approaching Bethphage and Bethany, close to the mountain which is called Olivet, he sent two of his disciples on an errand; 30 Go into the village that faces you, he told them, and as you enter it you will find a colt tethered there, one on which no man has yet ridden; untie it and bring it here. 31 And if anybody asks you, Why are you untying it? this must be your answer, the Lord has need of it. 32 So the two he had appointed went on their way, and found the colt standing there, just as he had told them. 33 As they were untying it, its owners asked them, Why are you untying the colt? 34 And they said, Because the Lord has need of it. 35 So they brought the colt to Jesus, and spread out their garments on it, and bade Jesus mount. 36 As he went, they strewed the road with their garments; 37 and when he drew near the descent of mount Olivet, the whole company of his disciples began rejoicing and praising God for all the miracles

vv. 29-38. Matthew xxi. 1, Mark xi. 1, John xii. 12.

they had seen. 38 Blessed is the king, they said, who comes in the name of the Lord; peace on earth, and glory in heaven above. 39 Some of the Pharisees who were among the multitude said to him, Master, rebuke thy disciples; 40 but he answered, I tell you, if they should keep silence, the stones will cry out instead.

41 And as he drew near, and caught sight of the city, he wept over it, and said: 42 Ah, if thou too couldst understand, above all in this day that is granted thee, the ways that can bring thee peace! As it is, they are hidden from thy sight. 43 The days will come upon thee when thy enemies will fence thee round about, and encircle thee, and press thee hard on every side, 44 and bring down in ruin both thee and thy children that are in thee, not leaving one stone of thee upon another; and all because thou didst not recognize the time of my visiting thee. 45 Then he went into the temple, and began driving out those who sold and bought there; 46 It is written, he told them, My house is a house of prayer; and you have made it into a den of thieves. 47 And he taught in the temple daily. The chief priests and scribes and the leading men among the people were eager to make away with him, 48 but they could not find any means to do it, because all the people hung upon his words.

vv. 45-48. Matthew xxi. 12, Mark xi. 15.

v. 46. Is. lvi. 7, Jer. vii. 11.

Chapter Twenty

vv. 1-8. Matthew xxi. 23, Mark xi. 27.

ONE DAY, AS HE taught the people and preached to them in the temple, the chief priests and scribes, with the elders, came up 2 and said to him, Tell us, What is the authority by which thou doest these things, and who gave thee this authority? 3 Jesus answered them, I too have a question to ask; you must tell me this, 4 Whence did John's baptism come, from heaven or from men? 5 Whereupon they cast about in their minds; If we tell him it was from heaven, they said, he will ask, Then why did you not believe him? 6 And if we say it was from men, all the people will be ready to stone us; they will have it that John was a prophet. 7 So they answered that they could not tell whence it came. 8 Jesus said to them, And you will not learn from me what is the authority by which I do these things.

9 And now he took occasion to tell the people this parable; There was a man who planted a vineyard, and let it out to some vine-dressers, while he went away to spend a long time abroad. 10 And when the season came, he sent one of his servants on an errand to the vine-dressers, bidding them pay him his share of the vineyard's revenues. Whereupon the vine-dressers beat him, and sent him away empty-handed. 11 Then he sent another servant; and him too they sent away empty-handed, beating him first, and insulting him. 12 Then he sent a third; and they drove him away wounded, like the others. 13 So the owner of the vineyard said, What am I to do? I will send my well-beloved son; perhaps they will have reverence for him. 14 But the vine-dressers, on seeing him, debated thus among themselves; This is the heir, let us kill him, so that his inheritance may pass into our hands. 15 And they thrust him out of the vineyard and killed him. And now, what will the owner of the vineyard do to them? 16 He will come and make an end of those vine-dressers, and give his vineyard to others. God forbid, they said, when they heard that. 17 But he fastened his eyes on them, and said, Why then, what is the meaning of those words which have been written, The very stone which the builders rejected has become the chief stone at the corner? 18 If ever a man falls against that stone, he will break his bones; if it falls upon him, it will grind him to powder.

vv. 9-19. Matthew xxi. 33, Mark xii. 2.

v. 17. Ps. cxvii. 22; cf. Rom. ix. 33, and I Pet. ii. 7.

v. 18. See note on Matthew xxi. 44.

19 At this, the chief priests and scribes would gladly have laid hands on him there and then, but they were afraid of the people. They saw clearly that this parable of his was aimed at them. 20 And so, watching for their opportunity, they sent agents of their own, who pretended to be men of honest purpose, to fasten on his words; then they would hand him over to the supreme authority of the governor. 21 These put a question to him; Master, they said, we know that thou art direct in thy talk and thy teaching; thou makest no distinction between man and man, but teachest the way of God in all sincerity. 22 Is it right that we should pay tribute to Caesar, or not? 23 And he, aware of their malice, said to them, Why do you thus put me to the test? 24 Shew me a silver piece. Whose likeness, whose name does it bear inscribed on

vv. 20-44. Matthew xxii. 15, Mark xii. 13.

it? When they answered, Caesar's, 25 he told them, Why then, give back to Caesar what is Caesar's, and to God what is God's. 26 And they said no more; they were full of admiration at his answer, finding no means of discrediting his words in the eyes of the people.

27 Then he was approached with a question by some of the Sadducees, men who deny the resurrection; 28 Master, they said, Moses prescribed for us, If a man has a married brother who dies without issue, the surviving brother must marry the widow, and beget children in the dead brother's name. 29 There were seven brethren, the first of whom married a wife, and died without issue. 30 So the next took her, and also died without issue, 31 then the third, and so with all the seven; they left no children when they died, 32 and the woman herself died last of all. 33 And now, when the dead rise again, which of these will be her husband, since she was wife to all seven? 34 Jesus told them, The children of this world marry and are given in marriage; 35 but those who are found worthy to attain that other world, and resurrection from the dead, take neither wife nor husband; 36 mortal no longer, they will be as the angels in heaven are, children of God, now that the resurrection has given them birth. 37 But as for the dead rising again, Moses himself has told you of it in the passage about the burning bush, where he calls the Lord the God of Abraham and the God of Isaac and the God of Jacob. 38 It is of living men, not of dead men, that he is the God; for him, all men are alive. 39 At this, some of the scribes answered, Master, thou hast spoken well; 40 no one dared to try him with further questions.

41 Then he said to them, What do they mean by saying that Christ is the son of David? 42 Why, David himself says in the book of Psalms, the Lord said to my Master, sit on my right hand 43 while I make thy enemies a footstool under thy feet. 44 Thus David calls Christ his Master; how can he also be his son? 45 And he said to his disciples, in the hearing of all the people: 46 Beware of the scribes, who enjoy walking in long robes, and love to have their hands kissed in the market-place, and to take the first seats in the synagogues, and the chief places at feasts; 47 who swallow up the property of widows, under cover of their long prayers; their sentence will be all the heavier for that.

v. 28. Deut. xxv. 5.

v. 37. Ex. iii. 6.

v. 42. Ps. cix. 1.

THE MASSACRE OF THE HOLY INNOCENTS   GIROLAMO MOCETTO
1458-1531(?)

NATIONAL GALLERY, LONDON

Chapter Twenty-one

AND HE LOOKED UP,
and saw the rich folk putting
their gifts into the treasury; 2 he saw also one poor widow, who
put in two mites. 3 Thereupon he said, Believe me, this poor widow
has put in more than all the others. 4 The others all made an
offering to God out of what they had to spare; she, with so little
to give, put in her whole livelihood.

vv. 1-33. Matthew xxiv. 1, Mark xiii. 1.

5 There were some who spoke to him of the temple, of the
noble masonry and the offerings which adorned it; to these he said,
6 The days will come when, of all this fabric you contemplate,
not one stone will be left on another; it will all be thrown down.
7 And they asked him, Master, when will this be? What sign will
be given, when it is soon to be accomplished? 8 Take care, he
said, that you do not allow anyone to deceive you. Many will
come making use of my name; they will say, Here I am, the time
is close at hand; do not turn aside after them. 9 And when you
hear of wars and revolts, do not be alarmed by it; such things must
happen first, but the end will not come all at once. 10 Then he
told them, Nation will rise in arms against nation, and kingdom
against kingdom; 11 there will be great earthquakes in this region
or that, and plagues and famines; and sights of terror and great
portents from heaven. 12 Before all this, men will be laying hands
on you and persecuting you; they will give you up to the synagogues, and to prison, and drag you into the presence of kings and
governors on my account; 13 that will be your opportunity for
making the truth known. 14 Resolve, then, not to prepare your
manner of answering beforehand; 15 I will give you such eloquence and such wisdom as all your adversaries shall not be able
to withstand, or to confute. 16 You will be given up by parents
and brethren and kinsmen and friends, and some of you will be
put to death; 17 all the world will be hating you because you bear
my name; 18 and yet no hair of your head shall perish. 19 It is
by endurance that you will secure possession of your souls.

20 But when you see Jerusalem surrounded by armies, be sure

that the time has come when she will be laid waste. 21 Then those who are in Judaea must take refuge in the mountains, those who are in the city itself withdrawing from it, and those who are in the country-side not making their way into it; 22 these will be days of vengeance, bringing fulfilment of all that has been written. 23 It will go hard with women who are with child, or have children at the breast, in those days; it will be a time of bitter distress all over the land, and retribution against this people. 24 They will be put to the sword, and led away into captivity all over the world; and Jerusalem will be trodden under the feet of the Gentiles, until the time granted to the Gentile nations has run out. 25 The sun and the moon and the stars will give portents, and on earth the nations will be in distress, bewildered by the roaring of the sea and of its waves; 26 men's hearts will be dried up with fear, as they await the troubles that are overtaking the whole world; the very powers of heaven will rock. 27 And then they will see the Son of Man coming in a cloud, with his full power and majesty.

28 When all this begins, look up, and lift up your heads; it means that the time draws near for your deliverance. 29 And he told them a parable; Look at the fig-tree, or any of the trees; 30 when they put out their fruit, you know by your own experience that summer is near. 31 Just so, when you see this happen, be sure that the kingdom of God is close at hand. 32 Believe me, this generation will not have passed, before all this is accomplished. 33 Though heaven and earth should pass away, my words will stand. 34 Only look well to yourselves; do not let your hearts grow dull with revelry and drunkenness and the affairs of this life, so that that day overtakes you unawares; 35 it will come like the springing of a trap on all those who dwell upon the face of the earth. 36 Keep watch, then, praying at all times, so that you may be found worthy to come safe through all that lies before you, and stand erect to meet the presence of the Son of Man.

37 Each day he went on teaching in the temple, and at night he lodged on the mountain which is called Olivet; 38 and all the people waited for him at early morning in the temple, to listen to him.

Chapter Twenty-two

And now the feast of unleavened bread, the paschal feast, as it is called, was drawing near. 2 The chief priests and scribes were still at a loss for some means of making away with him, frightened as they were of the people. 3 But now Satan found his way into the heart of Judas, who was also called Iscariot, one of the twelve, 4 and he went off and conferred with the chief priests and magistrates about the means to betray Jesus. 5 These gladly consented to pay him a sum of money; 6 so he promised to do it, and looked about for an opportunity to hand him over without any commotion.

vv. 1-23. Matthew xxvi. 1, Mark xiv. 1.

7 Then the day of unleavened bread came; on this day, the paschal victim must be killed; 8 and Jesus sent Peter and John on an errand; Go and make ready for us, he said, to eat the paschal meal. 9 When they asked him, Where wouldst thou have us make ready? 10 he said to them, Just as you are entering the city, you will be met by a man carrying a jar of water; follow him into the house to which he is going; 11 and there you will say to the owner of the house, The master sends word, Where is the room in which I am to eat the paschal meal with my disciples? 12 And he will shew you a large upper room, furnished; it is there that you are to make ready. 13 So they went, and found all as he had told them, and so made ready for the paschal meal. 14 And when the time came, he sat down with his twelve disciples.

15 And he said to them, I have longed and longed to share this paschal meal with you before my passion; 16 I tell you, I shall not eat it again, till it finds its fulfilment in the kingdom of God. 17 And he took a cup, and blessed it, and said, Take this and share it among you; I tell you, I shall not drink of the fruit of the vine again, till the kingdom of God has come. 19 Then he took bread, and blessed and broke it, and gave it to them, saying, This is my body, given for you; do this for a commemoration of me. 20 And so with the cup, when supper was ended, This cup, he

said, is the new testament, in my blood which is to be shed for you. 21 And now, the hand of my betrayer rests on this table, at my side. 22 The Son of Man goes on his way, for so it has been ordained; but woe upon that man by whom he is to be betrayed. 23 Thereupon they fell to surmising among themselves, which of them it was that would do this.

24 And there was rivalry between them over the question, which of them was to be accounted the greatest. 25 But he told them, The kings of the Gentiles lord it over them, and those who bear rule over them win the name of benefactors. 26 With you it is not to be so; no difference is to be made, among you, between the greatest and the youngest of all, between him who commands and him who serves. 27 Tell me, which is greater, the man who sits at table, or the man who serves him? Surely the man who sits at table; yet I am here among you as your servant.

28 You are the men who have kept to my side in my hours of trial: 29 and, as my Father has allotted a kingdom to me, so I allot to you 30 a place to eat and drink at my table in my kingdom; you shall sit on twelve thrones, judging the twelve tribes of Israel. 31 And the Lord said, Simon, Simon, behold, Satan has claimed power over you all, so that he can sift you like wheat: 32 but I have prayed for thee, that thy faith may not fail; when, after a while, thou hast come back to me, it is for thee to be the support of thy brethren. 33 Lord, said he, I am ready to bear thee company, though it were to prison or to death. 34 But he answered, I tell thee, Peter, by cock-crow this morning thou wilt thrice have denied knowledge of me. Then he said to them, 35 Did you go in want of anything, when I sent you out without purse, or wallet, or shoes? 36 They told him, Nothing; and he said, But now it is time for a man to take his purse with him, if he has one, and his wallet too; and to sell his cloak and buy a sword, if he has none.

v. 37. Is. liii. 12. Our Lord seems to suggest, in irony, that since he is to be apprehended like a robber, it is time that his companions should go armed like robbers, no longer in the peaceable manner of apostles.

vv. 39-53. Matthew xxvi. 36, Mark xiv. 32, John xviii. 1.

37 Believe me, one word has been written that has yet to find its fulfilment in me, And he was counted among the malefactors. Sure enough, all that has been written of me must be fulfilled. 38 See, Lord, they told him, here are two swords. And he said to them, That is enough.

39 And now he went out, as his custom was, to mount Olivet, his disciples following him. 40 When he reached the place, he said to them, Pray that you may not enter into temptation. 41 Then he parted from them, going a stone's throw off, and knelt down to pray; 42 Father, he said, if it pleases thee, take away this chalice from before me; only as thy will is, not as mine

is. 43 And he had sight of an angel from heaven, encouraging him. And now he was in an agony, and prayed still more earnestly; 44 his sweat fell to the ground like thick drops of blood. 45 When he rose from his prayer, he went back to his disciples, and found that they were sleeping, overwrought with sorrow. 46 How can you sleep? he asked. Rise up and pray, so that you may not enter into temptation.

47 Even as he spoke, a multitude came near; their guide was the man called Judas, one of the twelve, who came close to Jesus, to kiss him. 48 Jesus said to him, Judas, wouldst thou betray the Son of Man with a kiss? 49 Then those who were about him, seeing what would come of it, asked, Lord, shall we strike out with our swords? 50 And one of them struck a servant of the high priest, and cut off his right ear. 51 Jesus answered, Let them have their way in this. And he touched his ear, and healed him. 52 Then Jesus said to the chief priests and temple officers and elders who had come to find him, Have you come out with swords and clubs, as if I were a robber? 53 I was close to you in the temple, day after day, and you never laid hands on me. But your time has come now, and darkness has its will.

54 So they apprehended him, and led him away to the house of the high priest; and Peter followed at a long distance. 55 They had lit a fire in the midst of the court, and were sitting round it; and there Peter sat among them. 56 One of the maidservants, as she saw him sitting there in the firelight, looked closely at him and said, This is one of those who were with him. 57 And he disowned him; Woman, he said, I have no knowledge of him. 58 After a short while, another of the company said, when he caught sight of him, Thou too art one of them; and Peter said, Man, I am not. 59 Then there was an interval of about an hour, before another man insisted, It is the truth that this fellow was in his company; why, he is a Galilean. 60 Man, said Peter, I do not understand what thou meanest; and all at once, while the words were on his lips, the cock crew. 61 And the Lord turned, and looked at Peter; and Peter remembered what the Lord had said to him, Before cock-crow, thou wilt thrice disown me. 62 And Peter went out, and wept bitterly.

63 The men who held Jesus prisoner beat him and mocked him; 64 they blindfolded him and struck him on the face, and then questioned him, Come, prophesy; tell us who it is that smote thee. 65 And they used many other blasphemous words against him. 66 When day came, all the elders of the people, chief priests and

v. 51. Our Lord's words here are commonly interpreted as addressed to the apostles, in answer to their question (v. 49); some, however, think that they are addressed to his captors, who were already holding him, 'Release me for this once', that is, while he cured Malchus.

vv. 54-71. Matthew xxvi. 57, Mark xiv. 53, John xviii. 12. St. Luke describes the denial of St. Peter first of all, and then goes back to the condemnation of our Lord, not necessarily following the historical orders of events.

v. 58. This second challenge by the fireside is treated by St. Matthew and St. Mark as all one with the first; St. Luke does not record the encounter in the porch, which they interpret as the second denial (Matthew xxvi. 71, Mark xiv. 69).

vv. 63-64. It is possible that St. Luke, here again, has not narrated the facts in their historical order; it would seem from the account given by St. Matthew and St. Mark that our Lord was insulted only after his condemnation by the priests.

scribes, brought him before their council; If thou art the Christ, they said, tell us. 67 Why, he said, if I tell you, you will never believe me: 68 and if I ask you questions, I know you will not answer them, nor acquit me. 69 I will only tell you that a time is coming when the Son of Man will be seated in power at God's right hand. 70 And they all said, Thou art, then, the Son of God? He told them, Your own lips have said that I am. 71 And they said, What further need have we of witnesses? We have heard the words from his own mouth.

v. 70. This is a formula of assent, not a refusal to answer.

Chapter
Twenty=three

Then the whole assembly of them rose up and

vv. 1-25 (in part). Matthew xxvii. 11, Mark xv. 1, John xviii. 28. brought him before Pilate, 2 and there fell to accusing him; We have discovered, they said, that this man is subverting the loyalty of our people, forbids the payment of tribute to Caesar, and calls himself Christ the king. 3 And Pilate asked him, Art thou the king of the Jews? He answered him, Thy own lips have said it. 4 Pilate said to the chief priests and the multitudes, I cannot discover any fault in this man. 5 But they insisted, He rouses sedition among the people; he has gone round the whole of Judaea preaching, beginning in Galilee and ending here. 6 Pilate, upon the mention of Galilee, asked whether the man was a Galilean; 7 and learning that he belonged to Herod's jurisdiction, remitted his cause to Herod, who was also in Jerusalem at this time. 8 Herod was overjoyed at seeing Jesus; for a long time he had been eager to have sight of him, because he had heard so much of him, and now he hoped to witness some miracle of his. 9 He asked him many questions, but could get no answer from him, 10 although the chief priests and scribes stood there, loudly accusing him. 11 So

Herod and his attendants made a jest of him, arraying him in festal attire out of mockery, and sent him back to Pilate. 12 That day Herod and Pilate, who had hitherto been at enmity with one another, became friends.

13 And now Pilate summoned the chief priests, and the rulers, and the people, 14 and said to them, You have brought this man before me as one who seduces the people from their allegiance; I examined him in your presence, and could find no substance in any of the charges you bring against him; 15 nor could Herod, when I referred you to him. It is plain that he has done nothing which deserves death. 16 I will scourge him, and then he shall go free. 17 At the festival, he was obliged to grant them the liberty of one prisoner: 18 but the whole concourse raised the cry, Away with this man; we must have Barabbas released. 19 (Barabbas was a man who had been thrown into prison for raising a revolt in the city, and for murder.) 20 Once more Pilate spoke to them, offering to set Jesus at liberty; 21 but they continued to answer with shouts of, Crucify him, crucify him. 22 Then for the third time he said to them, Why, what wrong has he done? I can find no fault in him that deserves death; I will scourge him, and then he shall go free. 23 But they, with loud cries, insisted on their demand that he should be crucified; and their voices carried the day; 24 Pilate gave his assent that their request should be granted, 25 releasing the man of their choice who had been imprisoned for revolt and murder, while he handed Jesus over to their will.

26 As they led him off, they caught hold of a man called Simon of Cyrene, who was coming in from the country, and loaded him with the cross, so that he should carry it after Jesus. 27 Jesus was followed by a great multitude of the people, and also of women, who beat their breasts and mourned over him; 28 but he turned to them, and said, It is not for me that you should weep, daughters of Jerusalem; you should weep for yourselves and your children. 29 Behold, a time is coming when men will say, It is well for the barren, for the wombs that never bore children, and the breasts that never suckled them. 30 It is then that they will begin to say to the mountains, Fall on us, and to the hills, Cover us. 31 If it goes so hard with the tree that is still green, what will become of the tree that is already dried up? 32 Two others, who were criminals, were led off with him to be put to death. 33 And when they reached the place which is named after a skull, they crucified him there; and also the two criminals, one on his right and the other on

vv. 26-48 (in part). Matthew xxvii. 32, Mark xv. 21, John xix. 17.

v. 31. This verse is generally understood to mean, If crucifixion is the lot of the innocent, what punishment is to be expected by the guilty (that is, the Jews)?

his left. 34 Jesus meanwhile was saying, Father, forgive them; they do not know what it is they are doing. And they divided his garments among themselves by lot.

35 The people stood by, watching; and the rulers joined them in pouring scorn on him; He saved others, they said; if he is the Christ, God's chosen, let him save himself. 36 The soldiers, too, mocked him, when they came and offered him vinegar, 37 by saying, If thou art the king of the Jews, save thyself. 38 (A proclamation had been written up over him in Greek, Latin and Hebrew, This is the king of the Jews.) 39 And one of the two thieves who hung there fell to blaspheming against him; Save thyself, he said, and us too, if thou art the Christ. 40 But the other rebuked him; What, he said, hast thou no fear of God, when thou art undergoing the same sentence? 41 And we justly enough; we receive no more than the due reward of our deeds; but this man has done nothing amiss. 42 Then he said to Jesus, Lord, remember me when thou comest into thy kingdom. 43 And Jesus said to him, I promise thee, this day thou shalt be with me in Paradise.

44 It was about the sixth hour, and there was darkness over all the earth until the ninth hour. 45 The sun was darkened, and the veil of the temple was torn in the midst: 46 and Jesus said, crying with a loud voice, Father, into thy hands I commend my spirit; and yielded up his spirit as he said it. 47 And the centurion, when he saw what befell, gave glory to God; This, he said, was indeed a just man. 48 And the whole multitude of those who stood there watching it, when they saw the issue, went home beating their breasts.

49 All his acquaintances, with the women who had followed him from Galilee, watched while this happened, standing at a distance. 50 And now a man called Joseph came forward, one of the councillors, a good and upright man, 51 who had not taken part with the council and its doings; he was from Arimathea, a Jewish city, and was one of those who waited for the kingdom of God. 52 He it was who approached Pilate, and asked to have the body of Jesus. 53 This he took, and wrapped it in a winding-sheet, and laid it in a tomb fashioned out of the rock, in which no man had ever been buried. 54 It was the day of preparation; the next day was the sabbath. 55 And the women who had come with him from Galilee followed, and saw the tomb, and how his body was buried; 56 so they went back, and prepared spices and ointments, and while it was the sabbath they kept still, as the law commanded.

v. 47. See Matthew xxvii. 54, Mark xv. 29. St. Augustine suggests that the centurion did not recognize in our Lord the unique Son of God, but only 'a son of God' in the general sense in which 'a just man' would be the equivalent of that term; cf. Wisdom ii. 16. But it is possible that 'the Just One' was used in very early times as a cipher—used for "Son of God"; cf. Acts iii. 14, vii. 52, xxii. 14.

vv. 49-56. Matthew xxvii. 55, Mark xv. 40, John xix. 17.

THE PRESENTATION OF THE CHILD JESUS IN THE TEMPLE
GIOTTO
1266-1336

ISABELLA STEWART GARDNER MUSEUM, BOSTON

Chapter
Twenty=four

AND AT VERY EARLY dawn on the first day of the week they came to the tomb, bringing the spices they had pre-

pared: 2 and found the stone already rolled away from the door of the tomb. 3 They went into it, and could not find the body of the Lord Jesus. 4 They were still puzzling over this, when two men came and stood by them, in shining garments. 5 These said to them, as they bowed their faces to the earth in fear, Why are you seeking one who is alive, here among the dead? 6 He is not here, he has risen again; remember how he told you, while he was still in Galilee, 7 The Son of Man is to be given up into the hands of sinners, and to be crucified, and to rise again the third day. 8 Then they remembered what he had said, 9 and returned from the tomb bringing news of all this to the eleven apostles and to all the rest. 10 It was Mary Magdalen, and Joanna, and Mary the mother of James, who told the apostles this; 11 but to their minds the story seemed madness, and they could not believe it. 12 Only Peter rose up and ran to the tomb, where he looked in, and saw the grave-clothes lying by themselves, and went away full of sur- mise over what had befallen.

13 It was on the same day that two of them were walking to a village called Emmaus, sixty furlongs away from Jerusalem, 14 dis- cussing all that had happened. 15 They were still conversing and debating together, when Jesus himself drew near, and began to walk beside them; 16 but their eyes were held fast, so that they could not recognize him. 17 And he said to them, What talk is this you exchange between you as you go along, sad-faced? 18 And one of them, who was called Cleophas, answered him, What, art thou the only pilgrim in Jerusalem who has not heard of what has happened there in the last few days? 19 What happenings? he asked; and they said, About Jesus of Nazareth, a prophet whose words and acts had power with God, and with all the people; 20 how the chief priests, and our rulers, handed him over to be sentenced to death, and so crucified him. 21 For ourselves, we

vv. 1-9. Matthew xxviii. 1, Mark xvi. 1, John xx. 1.

v. 12. John xx. 3.

159

LUKE

had hoped that it was he who was to deliver Israel; but now, to crown it all, to-day is the third day since it befell. Some women, indeed, who belonged to our company, alarmed us; they had been at the tomb early in the morning 23 and could not find his body; whereupon they came back and told us that they had seen a vision of angels, who said that he was alive. 24 Some of those who were with us went to the tomb, and found that all was as the women had said, but of him they saw nothing.

v. 23. That the disciples do not mention the appearance of our Lord himself to the women (Matthew xxviii. 9) is perhaps due to their incredulity. (Mark xvi. 11).

25 Then he said to them, Too slow of wit, too dull of heart, to believe all those sayings of the prophets! 26 Was it not to be expected that the Christ should undergo these sufferings, and enter so into his glory? 27 Then, going back to Moses and the whole line of the prophets, he began to interpret the words used of himself by all the scriptures. 28 And now they were drawing near the village to which they were walking, and he made as if to go on further; 29 but they pressed him, Stay with us, they said; it is towards evening, and it is far on in the day. 30 So he went in to stay with them. And then, when he sat down at table with them, he took bread, and blessed, and broke it, and offered it to them; 31 whereupon their eyes were opened, and they recognized him; and with that, he disappeared from their sight. 32 And they said to one another, Were not our hearts burning within us when he spoke to us on the road, and when he made the scriptures plain to us? 33 Rising up there and then, they went back to Jerusalem, where they found the eleven apostles and their companions gathered

v. 34. I Cor. xv. 5.

together, 34 now saying, The Lord has indeed risen, and has appeared to Simon. 35 And they too told the story of their encounter in the road, and how they recognized him when he broke bread.

v. 36. John xx. 19.

36 While they were speaking of this, he himself stood in the midst of them, and said, Peace be upon you; it is myself, do not be afraid. 37 They cowered down, full of terror, thinking that they were seeing an apparition. 38 What, he said to them, are you dismayed? Whence come these surmises in your hearts? 39 Look at my hands and my feet, to be assured that it is myself; touch me, and look; a spirit has not flesh and bones, as you see that I have. 40 And as he spoke thus, he shewed them his hands and his feet. 41 Then, while they were still doubtful, and bewildered with joy, he asked them, Have you anything here to eat? 42 So they put before him a piece of roast fish, and a honeycomb; 43 and he took these and ate in their presence. 44 This is what I told you, he said, while I still walked in your company; how all that was written of

160

me in the law of Moses, and in the prophets, and in the psalms, must be fulfilled. 45 Then he enlightened their minds, to make them understand the scriptures; 46 So it was written, he told them, and so it was fitting that Christ should suffer, and should rise again from the dead on the third day; 47 and that repentance and remission of sins should be preached in his name to all nations, beginning at Jerusalem. 48 Of this, you are the witnesses. 49 And behold, I am sending down upon you the gift which was promised by my Father; you must wait in the city, until you are clothed with power from on high.

50 When he had led them out as far as Bethany, he lifted up his hands and blessed them; 51 and even as he blessed them he parted from them, and was carried up into heaven. 52 So they bowed down to worship him, and went back full of joy to Jerusalem, 53 where they spent their time continually in the temple, praising and blessing God.

vv. 46-53. St. Luke does not here mention the interval of forty days before the Ascension, although he certainly knew of it (Acts i. 3).

v. 49. Joel iii. 1.

THE HOLY GOSPEL OF ACCORDING TO JESUS CHRIST John

Chapter One

AT THE BEGINNING OF time the Word already was; and God had the Word abiding with him, and the Word was God. 2 He abode, at the beginning of time, with God. 3 It was through him that all things came into being, and without him came nothing that has come to be. 4 In him there was life, and that life was the light of men. 5 And the light shines in darkness, a darkness which was not able to master it.

6 A man appeared, sent from God, whose name was John. 7 He came for a witness, to bear witness of the light, so that through him all men might learn to believe. 8 He was not the Light; he was sent to bear witness to the light. 9 There is one who enlightens every soul born into the world; he was the true Light. 10 He, through whom the world was made, was in the world, and the world treated him as a stranger. 11 He came to what was his own, and they who were his own gave him no welcome. 12 But all those who did welcome him he empowered to become the children of God, all those who believe in his name; 13 their birth came, not from human stock, not from nature's

vv. 3, 4. Some divide these two sentences differently, and interpret thus: 'It was through him that all things came into being, and without him came nothing. What was in him was life, and that life was the light of men'.

v. 5. 'Master it' may be taken in the sense of overcoming it, or of understanding it.

v. 13. 'Their birth came'; several of the early Fathers seem to have used a text which read 'His birth came'.

163

will or man's, but from God. 14 And the Word was made flesh, and came to dwell among us; and we had sight of his glory, glory such as belongs to the Father's only-begotten Son, full of grace and truth. 15 We have John's witness to him; I told you, cried John, there was one coming after me who takes rank before me; he was when I was not. 16 We have all received something out of his abundance, grace answering to grace. 17 Through Moses the law was given to us; through Jesus Christ grace came to us, and truth. 18 No man has ever seen God; but now his only-begotten Son, who abides in the bosom of the Father, has himself become our interpreter.

v. 18. Some of the best manuscripts here read 'God, the only-begotten' instead of 'the only-begotten Son'.

19 This, then, was the testimony which John bore, when the Jews sent priests and Levites from Jerusalem, to ask him, Who art thou? 20 He admitted the truth, without concealment: admitted that he was not the Christ. 21 What then, they asked him, art thou Elias? Not Elias, he said. Art thou the prophet? And he answered, No. 22 So they said, Tell us who thou art, that we may give an answer to those who sent us; what account dost thou give of thyself? 23 And he told them, I am what the prophet Isaias spoke of, the voice of one crying in the wilderness, Straighten out the way of the Lord. 24 The Pharisees (for they were Pharisees who had come on this errand) 25 asked him, Why dost thou baptize, then, if thou thyself art not the Christ, nor Elias, nor the prophet? 26 John answered them, I am baptizing you with water; but there is one standing in your midst of whom you know nothing; 27 he it is, who, though he comes after me, takes rank before me. I am not worthy to untie the strap of his shoes. 28 All this happened in Bethany that is beyond Jordan, where John was baptizing.

v. 21. That is, the prophet whose coming was foretold by Moses in Deuteronomy xviii. 15-19.

vv. 23-28. Matthew iii. 1, Mark i. 1, Luke iii. 1.

v. 23. Is. xl. 3.

29 Next day, John saw Jesus coming towards him; and he said, Look, this is the Lamb of God; look, this is he who takes away the sin of the world. 30 It is of him that I said, One is coming after me who takes rank before me; he was when I was not. 31 I myself did not know who he was, although the very reason why I have come, with my baptism of water, is to make him known to Israel. 32 John also bore witness thus, I saw the Spirit coming down from heaven like a dove, and resting upon him. 33 Till then, I did not know him; but then I remembered what I had been told by the God who sent me to baptize with water. He told me, The man who will baptize with the Holy Spirit is the man on whom thou wilt see the Spirit come down and rest. 34 Now I have seen him, and have borne my witness that this is the Son of God.

35 The next day after this, John was standing there again, with two of his disciples; 36 and, watching Jesus as he walked by, he said, Look, this is the Lamb of God. 37 The two disciples heard him say it, and they followed Jesus. 38 Turning, and seeing them follow him, Jesus asked, What would you have of me? Rabbi, they said, (a word which means Master), where dost thou live? 39 He said to them, Come and see; so they went and saw where he lived, and they stayed with him all the rest of the day, from about the tenth hour onwards. 40 One of the two who had heard what John said, and followed him, was Andrew, the brother of Simon Peter. 41 He, first of all, found his own brother Simon, and told him, We have discovered the Messias (which means, the Christ), 42 and brought him to Jesus. Jesus looked at him closely, and said, Thou art Simon the son of Jona; thou shalt be called Cephas, (which means the same as Peter). 43 He was to remove into Galilee next day; and now he found Philip; to him Jesus said, Follow me. 44 This Philip came from Bethsaida, a fellow townsman of Andrew and Peter.

45 And Philip found Nathanael, and told him, We have discovered who it was Moses wrote of in his law, and the prophets too; it is Jesus the son of Joseph, from Nazareth. 46 When Nathanael asked him, Can anything that is good come from Nazareth? Philip said, Come and see. 47 Jesus saw Nathanael coming towards him, and said of him, Here comes one who belongs to the true Israel; there is no falsehood in him. 48 How dost thou know me? Nathanael asked; and Jesus answered him, I saw thee when thou wast under the fig-tree, before Philip called thee. 49 Then Nathanael answered him, Thou, Master, art the Son of God, thou art the King of Israel. 50 Jesus answered, What, believe because I told thee that I saw thee under the fig-tree? Thou shalt see greater things than that. 51 And he said to him, Believe me when I tell you this; you will see heaven opening, and the angels of God going up and coming down upon the Son of Man.

v. 41. 'First of all'; some have thought that the other disciple then called his brother St. John, who then called his brother St. James. But the contrast may be with verse 43 below.

v. 51. This is variously explained as referring to the Ascension, or to the Last Judgement.

Chapter Two

v. 4. 'Why dost thou
trouble me with that?'
The Greek here is am-
biguous; some would
interpret it, 'What
concern is that of
mine or of thine?',
but it is more proba-
bly to be understood
as a Hebrew idiom,
'What have I to do
with thee?', that is,
'Leave me alone, do
not interfere with
me', as in Matthew
viii. 29, and in many
passages of the Old
Testament. 'My time
has not come yet' is
understood by some
commentators as re-
ferring to his Passion;
others suppose that
the time had not yet
come for his perform-
ing this miracle, or
perhaps for perform-
ing a miracle in pub-
lic, since this was
witnessed only by a
few. 'Woman' was an
address used in the
ancient world without
any suggestion of dis-
respect.

v. 8. Our Lord is gen-
erally understood to
have turned the wa-
ter in the six water-
pots into wine. But,
since the verb here
used for 'to draw' ap-
plies more properly to
drawing from a well,
it is possible to sup-
pose that the water-
pots contained only
water throughout, and
that the wine came
from the well itself,
at the seventh time
of drawing.

vv. 15-17. Cf. Mat-
thew xxi. 12, Mark
xi. 15, Luke xix. 45;
but it would seem that
these passages refer
to a different occa-
sion.

v. 17. Ps. lxviii. 10.

TWO DAYS AFTER
wards, there was a wedding-
feast at Cana, in Galilee; and Jesus' mother was there. 2 Jesus himself, and his disciples, had also been invited to the wedding. 3 Here
the supply of wine failed; whereupon Jesus' mother said to him,
They have no wine left. 4 Jesus answered her, Nay, woman, why
dost thou trouble me with that? My time has not come yet. 5 And
his mother said to the servants, Do whatever he tells you. 6 There
were six waterpots standing there, as the Jewish custom of ceremonial washing demanded; they were of stone, and held two or
three firkins apiece. 7 And when Jesus said, Fill the waterpots
with water, they filled these up to the brim. 8 Then he said to
them, Now draw, and give a draught to the master of the feast.
So they gave it to him; 9 and the master of the feast tasted this
water, which had now been turned into wine. He did not know
whence it came; only the servants who had drawn the water knew
that. The master of the feast, then, called to the bridegroom, 10 and
said to him, It is ever the good wine that men set out first, and the
worse kind only when all have drunk deep; thou hast kept the good
wine till now. 11 So, in Cana of Galilee, Jesus began his miracles,
and made known the glory that was his, so that his disciples learned
to believe in him.

12 After this he went down to Capharnaum with his mother, his
brethren, and his disciples, not staying there many days.

13 And now the paschal feast which the Jews keep was drawing
near, so Jesus went up to Jerusalem. 14 And in the temple there
he found the merchants selling oxen and sheep and pigeons, and the
money-changers sitting at their trade. 15 So he made a kind of
whip out of cords, and drove them all, with their sheep and oxen,
out of the temple, spilling the bankers' coins and overthrowing
their tables; 16 and he said to the pigeon-sellers, Take these away,
do not turn my Father's house into a place of barter. 17 And his
disciples remembered how it is written, I am consumed with
jealousy for the honour of thy house. 18 Then the Jews answered

him, What sign canst thou show us as thy warrant for doing this? 19 Jesus answered them, Destroy this temple, and in three days I will raise it up again. 20 At which the Jews said, This temple took forty-six years to build; wilt thou raise it up in three days? 21 But the temple he was speaking of was his own body; 22 and when he had risen from the dead his disciples remembered his saying this, and learned to believe in the scriptures, and in the words Jesus had spoken.

v. 19. Matthew xxvi. 61, xxvii. 40, 63.

23 At this paschal season, while he was in Jerusalem for the feast, there were many who came to believe in his name, upon seeing the miracles which he did. 24 But Jesus would not give him his confidence; he had knowledge of them all, 25 and did not need assurances about any man, because he could read men's hearts.

Chapter Three

THERE WAS A MAN called Nicodemus, a Pharisee, and one of the rulers of the Jews, 2 who came to see Jesus by night; Master, he said to him, we know that thou hast come from God to teach us; no one, unless God were with him, could do the miracles which thou doest. 3 Jesus answered him, Believe me when I tell thee this; a man cannot see the kingdom of God without being born anew. 4 Why, Nicodemus asked him, how is it possible that a man should be born when he is already old? Can he enter a second time into his mother's womb, and so come to birth? 5 Jesus answered, Believe me, no man can enter into the kingdom of God unless birth comes to him from water, and from the Holy Spirit. 6 What is born by natural birth is a thing of nature, what is born by spiritual birth is a thing of spirit. 7 Do not be surprised, then, at my telling thee, You must be born anew. 8 The wind breathes where it will, and thou canst hear the sound of it, but knowest

v. 3. In the Greek, the word which Nico-demus understands as meaning 'anew' may have meant 'from above'.

v. 8. 'The wind'; this word in the Greek has three principal mean-

JOHN

Marginal notes:

ings, (i) a wind or breeze, (ii) the breath, (iii) spirit, and especially the Holy Spirit. The older commentators understood it here in the third sense, but it is difficult to see how it could be said to Nicodemus, 'thou hearest his voice'. By the moderns, it is generally understood of the wind. Maldonatus suggests that it may mean life, the breath of life, in living creatures and in man especially; the voice being conceived as the characteristic sign of life, because it is produced by the breath.

v. 11. 'You' in the plural seems to mean the Jews generally, of whose incredulity Nicodemus, at present, offers an example; 'we' in the plural is more difficult to account for, but it may be that our Lord is identifying his own preaching, by anticipation, with that of his apostles.

v. 13. 'But there is one who has come down': literally, 'except him who has come down': the same Hebrew idiom occurs in Apocalypse xxi. 27, and many other passages.

v. 14. Num. xxi. 9.

vv. 16-21. These verses, and possibly the three which go before them, may be regarded if we will as a comment by the Evangelist, not as part of our Lord's utterance to Nicodemus.

v. 17. 'To reject'; the word here used in the Greek may mean 'to judge' or 'to separate', and is perhaps used here with a certain play of sense upon the two meanings.

nothing of the way it came or the way it goes; so it is, when a man is born by the breath of the Spirit. 9 Nicodemus answered him, How can such things come to be? 10 What, answered Jesus, can such things be strange to thee, who art one of the teachers of Israel? 11 Believe me, we speak of what is known to us, and testify of what our eyes have seen, and still you will not accept our testimony. 12 You cannot trust me when I tell you of what passes on earth; how will you be able to trust me when I tell you of what passes in heaven? 13 No man has ever gone up into heaven; but there is one who has come down from heaven, the Son of Man, who dwells in heaven. 14 And this Son of Man must be lifted up, as the serpent was lifted up by Moses in the wilderness; 15 so that those who believe in him may not perish, but have eternal life.

16 God so loved the world, that he gave up his only-begotten Son, so that those who believe in him may not perish, but have eternal life. 17 When God sent his Son into the world, it was not to reject the world, but so that the world might find salvation through him. 18 For the man who believes in him, there is no rejection; the man who does not believe is already rejected; he has not found faith in the name of God's only-begotten Son. 19 Rejection lies in this, that when the light came into the world men preferred darkness to light; preferred it, because their doings were evil. 20 Anyone who acts shamefully hates the light, will not come into the light, for fear that his doings will be found out. 21 Whereas the man whose life is true comes to the light, so that his deeds may be seen for what they are, deeds done in God.

22 After this, Jesus and his disciples came into the land of Judaea, and there he remained with them, baptizing. 23 John was still baptizing, too, in Aenon, near Salim, where there was abundance of water; men went to him there to be baptized. 24 (It was only later that John was thrown into prison.) 25 John's disciples had had a dispute with the Jews, about purification, 26 and now they came to John, and told him, Master, there was one with thee on the other side of Jordan, to whom thou didst then bear testimony. We find that he is baptizing now, and all are flocking to him. 27 John answered, A man must be content to receive the gift which is given him from heaven, and nothing more. 28 You yourselves are my witnesses that I told you, I am not the Christ; I have been sent to go before him. 29 The bride is for the bridegroom; but the bridegroom's friend, who stands by and listens to him, rejoices too, rejoices at hearing the bridegroom's voice; and this joy is mine now

in full measure. 30 He must become more and more, I must become less and less.

31 He who comes from above is above all men's reach; the man who belongs to earth talks the language of earth, but one who comes from heaven must needs be beyond the reach of all; 32 he bears witness of things he has seen and heard, and nobody accepts his witness. 33 The man who does accept his witness has declared, once for all, that God cannot lie, 34 since the words spoken by him whom God has sent are God's own words; so boundless is the gift God makes of his Spirit. 35 The Father loves his Son, and so has given everything into his hands; 36 and he who believes in the Son possesses eternal life, whereas he who refuses to believe in the Son will never see life; God's displeasure hangs over him continually.

vv. 31-36. These verses may either be regarded as part of what St. John the Baptist said, or (perhaps more probably) as a comment by the Evangelist.

Chapter Four

AND NOW IT BECAME known to Jesus that the Pharisees had been told, Jesus is making more disciples and baptizing a greater number than John; 2 although it was his disciples who baptized, not Jesus himself. 3 So he left Judaea, and once more withdrew into Galilee. 4 And he was obliged to go by way of Samaria. 5 Thus he came to a Samaritan city called Sichar, close by the plot of ground which Jacob gave to his son Joseph; 6 and there was a well there called Jacob's well. There, then, Jesus sat down, tired after his journey, by the well; it was about noon. 7 And when a Samaritan woman came to draw water, Jesus said to her, Give me some to drink. 8 (His disciples were away in the city at this time, buying food.) 9 Whereupon the Samaritan woman said to him, How is it that thou, who art a Jew, dost ask me, a Samaritan,

v. 5. Gen. xlviii. 22, Josue xxiv. 22.

to give thee drink? (The Jews, you must know, have no dealings with the Samaritans.) 10 Jesus answered her, If thou knewest what it is God gives, and who this is that is saying to thee, Give me drink, it would have been for thee to ask him instead, and he would have given thee living water. 11 Sir, the woman said to him, thou hast no bucket, and the well is deep; how then canst thou provide living water? 12 Art thou a greater man than our father Jacob? It was he who gave us this well; he himself and his sons and his cattle have drunk out of it. 13 Jesus answered her, Anyone who drinks such water as this will be thirsty again afterwards; the man who drinks the water I give him will not know thirst any more. 14 The water I give him will be a spring of water within him, that flows continually to bring him everlasting life. 15 Then, Sir, said the woman, give me water such as that, so that I may never be thirsty and have to come here for water again.

16 At this, Jesus said to her, Go home, fetch thy husband, and come back here. 17 I have no husband, answered the woman; and Jesus told her, True enough, thou hast no husband. 18 Thou hast had five husbands, but the man who is with thee now is no husband of thine; thou hast told the truth over this. 19 The woman said to him, Sir, I perceive that thou art a prophet. 20 Well, it was our fathers' way to worship on this mountain, although you tell us that the place where men ought to worship is in Jerusalem. 21 Believe me, woman, Jesus said to her, the time is coming when you will not go to this mountain, nor yet to Jerusalem, to worship the Father. 22 You worship you cannot tell what, we worship knowing what it is we worship; salvation, after all, is to come from the Jews; 23 but the time is coming, nay, has already come, when true worshippers will worship the Father in spirit and in truth; such men as these the Father claims for his worshippers. 24 God is a spirit, and those who worship him must worship him in spirit and in truth. 25 Yes, said the woman, I know that Messias (that is, the Christ) is to come; and when he comes, he will tell us everything. 26 Jesus said to her, I, who speak to thee, am the Christ.

27 With that, his disciples came up, and were surprised to find him talking to the woman; but none of them asked, What meanest thou? or Why art thou talking to her? 28 And so the woman put down her waterpot, and went back to the city, to tell the folk there, 29 Come and have sight of a man who has told me all the story of my life; can this be the Christ? 30 So they left the city, and came out to find him. 31 Meanwhile, his disciples were urging him, Master, take some food. 32 But he told them, I have food to

eat of which you know nothing. 33 Whereupon his disciples said to one another, Can somebody have brought him food? 34 But Jesus said to them, My meat is to do the will of him who sent me, and to accomplish the task he gave me. 35 Is it not a saying of yours, It is four whole months before harvest comes? Why, lift up your eyes, I tell you, and look at the fields, they are white with the promise of harvest already. 36 The wages paid to him who reaps this harvest, the crop he gathers in, is eternal life, in which sower and reaper are to rejoice together. 37 And here the proverb fits, which is true enough, One man sows, and another reaps. 38 The harvest I have sent you out to reap is one on which you bestowed no labour; others have laboured, and it is their labours you have inherited. 39 Many of the Samaritans from that city came to believe in him through the woman's testimony, He told me all the story of my life. 40 And when they came out to him, the Samaritans urged him to stay with them, and he stayed two days there. 41 Many more of them came to believe through his preaching; 42 It is not through thy report, they told the woman, that we believe now; we have heard him for ourselves, and we recognize that he is indeed the Saviour of the world.

43 Then, after two days, he passed on and returned to Galilee. 44 Jesus himself bore witness that it is in his own country a prophet goes unhonoured. 45 And now, when he came into Galilee, the Galileans too made him welcome, because they had seen what he did in Jerusalem at the time of the feast; they had gone up to the feast like himself. 46 And so he came once more to Cana of Galilee, where he had turned the water into wine. And a nobleman, whose son was lying sick at Capharnaum, 47 hearing that Jesus had come from Judaea to Galilee, went to him and asked him to come down and heal his son, who was at the point of death. 48 Jesus said to him, You must see signs and miracles happen, or you will not believe. 49 Sir, the nobleman said to him, come down before my child dies. 50 Go back home, Jesus told him; thy son is to live. And the man began his journey home, putting his trust in the words Jesus had spoken to him; 51 and while he was still on his way down, his servants met him with the message that his son was still alive. 52 So he asked what time it had been when he felt easier; and they told him, He recovered from his fever yesterday, at the seventh hour. 53 The father recognized that it had happened at the very time when Jesus said to him, Thy son is to live; and he and all his household found faith. 54 Thus for the second time Jesus did a miracle upon his return from Judaea to Galilee.

v. 35. 'It is four whole months'; this may have been a proverb, meaning that there was no hurry, like our 'Rome was not built in a day'. Our Lord here rejects it (whereas he approves of another proverb in v. 37 below); it cannot be too soon to begin preaching his gospel.

v. 44. The bearing of this verse, which has been the subject of much dispute among commentators, is most simply explained if we understand it as meaning that our Lord had not yet won favour in his own country of Galilee (Cf. ii. 23, iv. 41).

Chapter Five

After this came a Jewish feast, for which Jesus went up to Jerusalem. 2 There is a pool in Jerusalem at the Sheep Gate, called in Hebrew Bethsaida, with five porches, 3 under which a multitude of diseased folk used to lie, the blind, the lame, the disabled, waiting for a disturbance of the water. 4 From time to time, an angel of the Lord came down upon the pool, and the water was stirred up; and the first man who stepped into the pool after the stirring of the water, recovered from whatever infirmity it was that oppressed him. 5 There was one man there who had been disabled for thirty-eight years. 6 Jesus saw him lying there, and knew that he had waited a long time; Hast thou a mind, he asked, to recover thy strength? 7 Sir, said the cripple, I have no one to let me down into the pool when the water is stirred; and while I am on my way, somebody else steps down before me. 8 Jesus said to him, Rise up, take up thy bed, and walk. 9 And all at once the man recovered his strength, and took up his bed, and walked. 10 That day, it was the sabbath: and the Jews said to the man who had been cured, It is the sabbath; it is not lawful for thee to carry thy bed. 11 He answered them, The man who gave me back my strength told me himself, Take up thy bed, and walk. 12 So they asked him, Who is this man who told thee, Take up thy bed, and walk? 13 The cripple who had been healed did not know who it was; Jesus had drawn aside from so crowded a place. 14 But afterwards when Jesus found him in the temple, and said to him, Behold, thou hast recovered thy strength; do not sin any more, for fear that worse should befall thee, 15 the man went back and told the Jews that it was Jesus who had restored his strength.

16 The Jews took occasion to rouse ill-will against Jesus for doing such things on the sabbath. 17 And Jesus answered them, My Father has never ceased working, and I too must be at work. 18 This made the Jews more determined than ever to make away with him, that he not only broke the sabbath, but spoke of God as his own Father, thereby treating himself as equal to God. 19 And

v. 4. This verse is omitted by some manuscripts.

172

Jesus answered them thus: Believe me when I tell you this, The Son cannot do anything at his own pleasure, he can only do what he sees his Father doing; what the Father does is what the Son does in his turn. 20 The Father loves the Son, and discloses to him all that he himself does. And he has greater doings yet to disclose to him, for your astonishment; 21 just as the Father bids the dead rise up and gives them life, so the Son gives life to whomsoever he will. 22 So it is with judgement; the Father, instead of passing judgement on any man himself, has left all judgement to the Son, 23 so that all may reverence the Son just as they reverence the Father; to deny reverence to the Son is to deny reverence to the Father who has sent him.

24 Believe me when I tell you this, the man who listens to my words, and puts his trust in him who sent me, enjoys eternal life; he does not meet with rejection, he has passed over already from death to life. 25 Believe me, the time is coming, nay, has already come, when the dead will listen to the voice of the Son of God, and those who listen to it will live. 26 As the Father has within him the gift of life, so he has granted to the Son that he too should have within him the gift of life, 27 and has also granted him power to execute judgement, since he is the Son of Man. 28 Do not be surprised at that; the time is coming, when all those who are in their graves will hear his voice 29 and will come out of them; those whose actions have been good, rising to new life, and those whose doings have been evil, rising to meet their sentence. 30 I cannot do anything on my own authority; I decide as I am bidden to decide, and my decision is never unjust, because I am consulting the will of him who sent me, not my own.

31 If I testify in my own behalf, that testimony of mine is worth nothing; 32 there is another who testifies to me, and I know well that the testimony he bears me is worthy of trust. 33 You yourselves sent a message to John, and he testified to the truth. 34 (Not that I depend on human testimony; it is for your own welfare that I say this.) 35 He, after all, was the lamp lit to show you the way, and there was a time when you were willing enough to sun yourselves in his light. 36 But the testimony I have is greater than John's; the actions which my Father has enabled me to achieve, those very actions which I perform, bear me witness that it is the Father who has sent me. 37 Nay, the Father who sent me has himself borne witness to me. You have always been deaf to his voice, blind to the vision of him, 38 and his word is not continually present in your hearts; that is why you will not trust one whom

v. 32. 'There is another'; some understand this of St. John the Baptist, but it is more commonly interpreted as applying to the Father; cf. v. 37.

v. 37. 'The vision of him'; if this is understood literally, it is hard to see how our Lord attaches any blame to the Jews for not seeing God (cf. i. 18 above); it is perhaps better to suppose that our Lord is reproaching them with a spiritual blindness towards all God's manifestations of himself.

v. 39. 'You pore over the scriptures'; the phrase was generally taken by the older commentators as a command, 'pore over the scriptures'; but this seems less appropriate to the context.

he has sent. 39 You pore over the scriptures, thinking to find eternal life in them (and indeed, it is of these I speak as bearing witness to me): 40 but you will not come to me, to find life. 41 I do not mean that I look for honour from men, 42 but that I can see you have no love of God in your hearts.

43 I have come in my Father's name, and you give me no welcome, although you will welcome some other, if he comes in his own name. 44 How should you learn to believe, you who are content to receive honour from one another, and are not ambitious for the honour which comes from him, who alone is God? 45 Do not suppose that it will be for me to accuse you before my Father; your accusation will come from Moses, the very man in whom you put your trust. 46 If you believed Moses, you would believe me; it was of me that he wrote. 47 But if you give no credence to his writings, how should you give credence to my words?

Chapter Six

vv. 1-15. Matthew xiv. 13, Mark vi. 30, Luke ix. 10.

AFTER THIS, JESUS RE tired across the sea of Galilee, or Tiberias, 2 and there was a great multitude following him; they had seen the miracles he performed over the sick. 3 So Jesus went up on to the hill side, and there sat down with his disciples. 4 It was nearly the time of the Jews' great feast, the paschal feast. 5 And now, lifting up his eyes and seeing that a great multitude had gathered round him, Jesus said to Philip, Whence are we to buy bread for these folk to eat? 6 In saying this, he was putting him to the test; he himself knew well enough what he meant to do. 7 Philip answered him, Two hundred silver pieces would not buy enough bread for them, even to give each a little. 8 One of his disciples (it was Andrew, Simon Peter's brother) said to him, 9 There is a boy here, who has five barley loaves and two fishes;

THE FLIGHT INTO EGYPT

GIOVANNI BELLINI
circa 1430-1516

NATIONAL GALLERY OF ART, WASHINGTON, D. C. (MELLON COLLECTION)

but what is that among so many? 10 Then Jesus said, Make the men sit down. There was no lack of grass where they were; so the men sat down, about five thousand in number. 11 And Jesus took the loaves, and gave thanks, and distributed them to the company, and a share of the fishes too, as much as they had a mind for. 12 Then, when they had all had enough, he told his disciples, Gather up the broken pieces that are left over, so that nothing may be wasted. 13 And when they gathered them up, they filled twelve baskets with the broken pieces left over by those who had eaten. 14 When they saw the miracle Jesus had done, these men began to say, Beyond doubt, this is the prophet who is to come into the world.

v. 14. Deut. xviii. 15.

15 Knowing, then, that they meant to come and carry him off, so as to make a king of him, Jesus once again withdrew on to the hill side all alone. 16 His disciples, when evening came on, went down to the lake, 17 and there, embarking on the boat, they began to cross the water to Capharnaum. Darkness had fallen, and Jesus had not yet come back to them. 18 Meanwhile there was a strong wind blowing, and the sea was beginning to grow rough. 19 And now they had rowed some twenty-five or thirty furlongs, when they saw Jesus walking on the sea, and already drawing near to the boat. 20 They were terrified: but he said to them, It is myself; do not be afraid. 21 Then they took him on board willingly enough; and all at once their boat reached the land they were making for.

vv. 16-21. Matthew xiv. 22, Mark vi. 45.

22 Next morning, the multitude was still waiting on the opposite shore. They had seen that there was only one boat there, and that Jesus did not embark with his disciples on this boat, but left his disciples to go back alone. 23 But now, since other boats from Tiberias had put in near the place where they ate the loaves when the Lord gave thanks over them, 24 the multitude, finding neither Jesus nor his disciples there, embarked on these boats in their turn, and went back to Capharnaum to look for Jesus. 25 And when they found that he had crossed the lake, they asked him, Master, when didst thou make thy way here? 26 Jesus answered them, Believe me, if you are looking for me now, it is not because of the miracles you have seen; it is because you were fed with the loaves, and had your fill. 27 You should not work to earn food which perishes in the using. Work to earn food which affords, continually, eternal life, such food as the Son of Man will give you; God, the Father, has authorized him. 28 What shall we do, then, they asked him, so as to work in God's service? 29 Jesus answered them, This is the service God asks of you, to believe in the Man whom he has sent.

JOHN

v. 30. Cf. Matthew xvi. 1.

v. 31. Ps. lxxvii. 24.

30 So they said to him, Why then, what miracle canst thou do? We must see it before we trust thee; what canst thou effect? 31 Our fathers had manna to eat in the desert; as the scripture says, He gave them bread out of heaven to eat. 32 Jesus said to them, Believe me when I tell you this; the bread that comes from heaven is not what Moses gave you. The real bread from heaven is given only by my Father. 33 God's gift of bread comes down from heaven and gives life to the whole world. 34 Then, Lord, they said, give us this bread all the while. 35 But Jesus told them, It is I who am the bread of life; he who comes to me will never be hungry, he who has faith in me will never know thirst. 36 (But you, as I have told you, though you have seen me, do not believe in me.) 37 All that the Father has entrusted to me will come to me, and him who comes to me I will never cast out. 38 It is the will of him who sent me, not my own will, that I have come down from heaven to do; 39 and he who sent me would have me keep without loss, and raise up at the last day, all he has entrusted to me. 40 Yes, this is the will of him who sent me, that all those who believe in the Son when they see him should enjoy eternal life; I am to raise them up at the last day.

v. 36. Our Lord is perhaps thinking, not of his immediate audience, but of the Jewish people in general; cf. v. 38 above.

41 The Jews were by now complaining of his saying, I am myself the bread which has come down from heaven. 42 Is not this Jesus, they said, the son of Joseph, whose father and mother are well known to us? What does he mean by saying, I have come down from heaven? 43 Jesus answered them, Do not whisper thus to one another. 44 Nobody can come to me without being attracted towards me by the Father who sent me, so that I can raise him up at the last day. 45 It is written in the book of the prophets, And they shall all have the Lord for their teacher; everyone who listens to the Father and learns, comes to me. 46 (Not that anyone has seen the Father, except him who comes from God; he alone has seen the Father.) 47 Believe me when I tell you this; the man who has faith in me enjoys eternal life. 48 It is I who am the bread of life. 49 Your fathers, who ate manna in the desert, died none the less; 50 the bread which comes down from heaven is such that he who eats of it never dies. 51 I myself am the living bread that has come down from heaven. 52 If anyone eats of this bread, he shall live for ever. And now, what is this bread which I am to give? It is my flesh, given for the life of the world.

v. 42. Matthew xiii. 55, Mark vi. 3.

v. 45. Is. liv. 13.

53 Then the Jews fell to disputing with one another, How can this man give us his flesh to eat? 54 Whereupon Jesus said to them, Believe me when I tell you this; you can have no life in yourselves,

176

unless you eat the flesh of the Son of Man, and drink his blood. 55 The man who eats my flesh and drinks my blood enjoys eternal life, and I will raise him up at the last day. 56 My flesh is real food, my blood is real drink. 57 He who eats my flesh, and drinks my blood, lives continually in me, and I in him. 58 As I live because of the Father, the living Father who has sent me, so he who eats me will live, in his turn, because of me. 59 Such is the bread which has come down from heaven; it is not as it was with your fathers, who ate manna and died none the less; the man who eats this bread will live eternally.

60 He said all this while he was teaching in the synagogue, at Capharnaum. 61 And there were many of his disciples who said, when they heard it, This is strange talk, who can be expected to listen to it? 62 But Jesus, inwardly aware that his disciples were complaining over it, said to them, Does this try your faith? 63 What will you make of it, if you see the Son of Man ascending to the place where he was before? 64 Only the spirit gives life; the flesh is of no avail; and the words I have been speaking to you are spirit, and life. 65 But there are some, even among you, who do not believe. Jesus knew from the first which were those who did not believe, and which of them was to betray him. 66 And he went on to say, That is what I meant when I told you that nobody can come to me unless he has received the gift from my Father. 67 After this, many of his disciples went back to their old ways, and walked no more in his company. 68 Whereupon Jesus said to the twelve, Would you, too, go away? 69 Simon Peter answered him, Lord, to whom should we go? Thy words are the words of eternal life; 70 we have learned to believe, and are assured that thou art the Christ, the Son of God. 71 Jesus answered them, Have I not chosen all twelve of you? And one of you is a devil. 72 He was speaking of Judas son of Simon, the Iscariot, who was one of the twelve, and was to betray him.

v. 64. If we understand 'the flesh' as referring to our Lord's flesh, we must suppose him to mean 'the flesh without spirit, without life', condemning the folly of those hearers who imagined that he had been speaking of his dead body in all that he said above. But it is possible to understand 'the flesh' in a different sense altogether, the sense in which it is contrasted, throughout the New Testament, with 'the spirit'. In this sense it denotes the natural as opposed to the supernatural man, and especially human wisdom as opposed to divine revelation (cf. viii. 15 below). The sentence will then mean, that the mystery of the Holy Eucharist must be approached by faith, not by human reasoning.

v. 70. The best Greek manuscripts have 'the Holy One of God' (as in Mark i. 24) instead of 'the Christ, the Son of God'.

Chapter Seven

AFTER THIS, JESUS WENT about in Galilee; he would not go about in Judaea, because the Jews had designs on his life. 2 And now one of the Jewish feasts, the feast of Tabernacles, was drawing near. 3 And his brethren said to him, This is no place for thee; go to Judaea, so that thy disciples also may see thy doings. 4 Nobody is content to act in secret, if he wishes to make himself known at large; if thou must needs act thus, show thyself before the world. 5 For even his brethren were without faith in him. 6 Whereupon Jesus said to them, My opportunity has not come yet. Your opportunity is always ready to hand; 7 the world cannot be expected to hate you, but it does hate me, because I denounce it for its evil doings. 8 It is for you to go up for the feast; I am not going up for the feast, because for me the time is not ripe yet. 9 And, saying so much to them, he stayed behind in Galilee.

10 But afterwards, when his brethren had gone up for the feast, he too went up, not publicly, but as if he would keep himself hidden. 11 The Jews were looking for him at the feast, and asked, Where can he be? 12 Among the crowd, there was much whispering about him; some said, He is a good man; No, said others, he leads the multitude astray. 13 But, for fear of the Jews, nobody dared to speak of him openly. 14 And it was not till the feast was half over that Jesus went up into the temple, and began to teach there. 15 The Jews were astonished; How does this man know how to read? they asked; he has never studied. 16 Jesus answered, The learning which I impart is not my own, it comes from him who sent me. 17 Anyone who is prepared to do his will, can tell for himself whether such learning comes from God, or whether I am delivering a message of my own. 18 The man who delivers a message of his own seeks to win credit for himself; when a man seeks to win credit for one who sent him, he tells the truth, there is no dishonesty in him. 19 Moses, for example; was it not Moses that gave you the law? And yet none of you keeps the law. 20 Why do you design to kill me? The multitude answered, Thou art

v. 2. Lev. xxiii. 34.

v. 3. For our Lord's 'brethren', see note on Matthew xii. 46. (It is perhaps noteworthy that in xiv. 22 St. Jude, who was one of them, raises exactly the same question which is raised by our Lord's brethren here.) Their suggestion that our Lord should go to Judaea in order to let his disciples see his miracles is difficult to understand, unless we suppose that they affected, perhaps in irony, to think that all his disciples in Galilee had deserted him (cf. vi. 67 above), and that he could only find followers now in Judaea.

v. 8. There is only an apparent inconsistency here between our Lord's statement, 'I am not going up for the feast', and his decision to go up to Jerusalem in verse 10. 'To go up for a feast' is clearly a technical expression for going up on pilgrimage, usually in company with a large party of neighbours (Luke ii. 44); whereas our Lord went to Jerusalem privately, and perhaps did not arrive till after the feast had begun.

possessed; who has a design to kill thee? 21 Jesus answered them, There is one action of mine which has astounded you all. 22 Listen to this; because Moses prescribed circumcision for you (not that it comes from Moses, it comes from the patriarchs), you are ready to circumcise a man on the sabbath day; 23 and if a man receives circumcision on the sabbath, so that the law of Moses may not be broken, have you any right to be indignant with me, for restoring a man's whole strength to him on the sabbath? 24 Be honest in your judgements, instead of judging by appearances.

25 At this, some of those who belonged to Jerusalem began to ask, Is not this the man they design to put to death? 26 Yet here he is, speaking publicly, and they have nothing to say to him. Can the rulers have made up their minds in earnest, that this is the Christ? 27 But then, we know this man's origins; when Christ appears, no one is to know whence he comes. 28 Whereupon Jesus cried aloud as he taught in the temple, You know me, and you know whence I come; but I have not come on my own errand, I was sent by one who has a right to send; and him you do not know. 29 I know him, because I come from him; it was he who sent me. 30 And now they were ready to seize him; but none of them laid hands on him; his time had not yet come. 31 And indeed, among the multitude there were many who learned to believe in him; they said, Can the Christ be expected to do more miracles at his coming than this man has done? 32 The Pharisees were told of these whispers about him among the multitude; and both chief priests and Pharisees sent officers to arrest him. 33 Then Jesus said, For a little while I am still with you, and then I am to go back to him who sent me. 34 You will look for me, but you will not be able to find me; you cannot reach the place where I am. 35 Whereupon the Jews said among themselves, Where can he mean to journey, that we should not be able to find him? Will he go to the Jews who are scattered about the Gentile world, and teach the Gentiles? 36 What can it mean, this saying of his, You will look for me, but you will not be able to find me; you cannot reach the place where I am?

37 On the last and greatest day of the feast Jesus stood there and cried aloud, If any man is thirsty, let him come to me, and drink; 38 yes, if a man believes in me, as the scripture says, Fountains of living water shall flow from his bosom. 39 He was speaking here of the Spirit, which was to be received by those who learned to believe in him; the Spirit which had not yet been given to men, because Jesus had not yet been raised to glory. 40 Some of the

v. 22. 'Listen to this'; literally, 'on this account'. The connexion of thought is not clear, but it seems as if our Lord must be referring back to vv. 18 and 19; the Jews recognize Moses as one who had a true mission from God, and on that account give the Mosaic rite of circumcision (Lev. xii. 3) precedence even over the Divine institution of the sabbath (Gen. ii. 3). Although indeed the rite of circumcision was older than Moses (Gen. xvii. 10).

v. 38. 'His bosom'; it is not clear whether this refers to the believer, or to our Lord himself; the old commentators are not agreed. In either case, it is impossible to trace these exact words in any passage of scripture as we have it; cf. however Is. xliv. 3, Zach. xiii. 1. Some would punctuate differently, with a full stop, instead of a comma, after 'believes in me'.

v. 40. Deut. xviii. 15.

multitude, on hearing these words, said, Beyond doubt this is the prophet. 41 Others said, This is the Christ; and others again, Is the Christ, then, to come from Galilee? 42 Has not the scripture told us that Christ is to come from the family of David, and from the village of Bethlehem, where David lived? 43 Thus there was a division of opinion about him among the multitude; 44 some of them would have seized him by violence, but no one laid hands on him.

v. 42. Mich. v. 2.

45 Meanwhile the officers had gone back to the chief priests and Pharisees, who asked them, Why have you not brought him here? 46 The officers answered, Nobody has ever spoken as this man speaks. 47 And the Pharisees answered, Have you, too, let yourselves be deceived? 48 Have any of the rulers come to believe in him yet, or of the Pharisees? 49 As for these common folk who have no knowledge of the law, a curse is on them. 50 Here Nicodemus, the same man who came to Jesus by night, who was one of their number, asked, 51 Is it the way of our law to judge a man without giving him a hearing first, and finding out what he is about? 52 They answered him, Art thou, too, from Galilee? Look in the scriptures; thou wilt find that Galilee does not breed prophets. 53 And they went back, each to his own home.

Chapter Eight

JESUS MEANWHILE went to the mount of Olives.

vv. 1-11. Many of the best Greek manuscripts omit this passage, together with verse 53 of ch. vii.

2 And at early morning he appeared again in the temple; all the common folk came to him, and he sat down there and began to teach them. 3 And now the scribes and Pharisees brought to him a woman who had been found committing adultery, and made her stand there in full view; 4 Master, they said, this woman has been caught in the act of adultery. 5 Moses, in his law, prescribed that

v. 5. Lev. xx. 10.

such persons should be stoned to death; what of thee? What is thy sentence? 6 They said this to put him to the test, hoping to find a charge to bring against him. But Jesus bent down, and began writing on the ground with his finger. 7. When he found that they continued to question him, he looked up and said to them, Whichever of you is free from sin shall cast the first stone at her. 8 Then he bent down again, and went on writing on the ground. 9 And they began to go out one by one, beginning with the eldest, till Jesus was left alone with the woman, still standing in full view. 10 Then Jesus looked up, and asked her, Woman, where are thy accusers? Has no one condemned thee? 11 No one, Lord, she said. And Jesus said to her, I will not condemn thee either. Go, and do not sin again henceforward.

12 And now once more Jesus spoke to them, I am the light of the world, he said. He who follows me can never walk in darkness; he will possess the light which is life. 13 Whereupon the Pharisees told him, Thou art testifying on thy own behalf, thy testimony is worth nothing. 14 Jesus answered them, My testimony is trustworthy, even when I testify on my own behalf; I know whence I have come, and where I am going; you do not know whence I have come, you do not know where I am going. 15 You set yourselves up to judge, after your earthly fashion; I do not set myself up to judge anybody. 16 And what if I should judge? My judgement is judgement indeed; it is not I alone, my Father who sent me is with me. 17 Just so it is prescribed in your law, The testimony of two men is trustworthy; 18 well, one is myself, testifying in my own behalf, and my Father who sent me testifies in my behalf too. 19 Hereupon they said to him, Where is this Father of thine? And Jesus answered, You have no knowledge, either of me or of my Father; had you knowledge of me, you would have knowledge of my Father as well. 20 All this Jesus said at the Treasury, while he was teaching in the temple; and no one seized him, because his time had not yet come.

21 And he said to them again, I am going away, and you will look for me, but you will have to die with your sins upon you; where I am going is where you cannot come. 22 At this, the Jews began to ask, Will he kill himself? Is that what he means by, Where I am going is where you cannot come? 23 But he went on to say, You belong to earth, I to heaven; you to this world, I to another. 24 That is why I have been telling you that you will die with your sins upon you; you will die with your sins upon you unless you come to believe that it is myself you look for. 25 Who

v. 24. 'It is myself you look for'; literally, 'It is myself', that is, 'I am the Christ', as in Mark xiii. 6; but here the elliptical phrase is helped out by verse 21 above, where our Lord has told the Jews that after his death they will be looking for him, i.e. looking for a Messias to deliver them.

v. 25. 'What, that I should be speaking to you at all?'; or perhaps, 'Why am I speaking to you at all?', though this is a more doubtful rendering of the Greek. Several other interpretations have been proposed, but none of them throws much light on a very obscure passage. The old translation 'The beginning, who also speak to you', only agrees with a reading which is not that of the best Latin manuscripts.

art thou, then? they asked. Jesus said to them, What, that I should be speaking to you at all? 26 There is much I could say of you, many judgements I could pass on you; but what I tell the world is only what I have learned from him who sent me, because he cannot deceive. 27 And they could not understand that he was calling God his Father. 28 Then Jesus said to them, When you have lifted up the Son of Man, you will recognize that it is myself you look for, and that I do not do anything on my own authority, but speak as my Father has instructed me to speak. 29 And he who sent me is with me; he has not left me all alone, since what I do is always what pleases him. 30 While he spoke thus, many of the Jews learned to believe in him.

31 And now Jesus said to those among the Jews who believed in him, If you continue faithful to my word, you are my disciples in earnest; 32 so you will come to know the truth, and the truth will set you free. 33 They answered him, We are of Abraham's breed, nobody ever enslaved us yet; what dost thou mean by saying, You shall become free? 34 And Jesus answered them, Believe me when I tell you this; everyone who acts sinfully is the slave of sin, 35 and the slave cannot make his home in the house for ever. To make his home in the house for ever, is for the Son. 36 Why then, if it is the Son who makes you free men, you will have freedom in earnest. 37 Yes, I know you are of Abraham's breed; yet you design to kill me, because my word does not find any place in you. 38 My words are what I have learned in the house of my Father, and your actions, it seems, are what you have learned in the school of your father. 39 Our father? they answered him; Abraham is our father. Jesus said to them, If you are Abraham's true children, it is for you to follow Abraham's example; 40 as it is, you are designing to kill me, who tell you the truth as I have heard it from God; this was not Abraham's way. 41 No, it is your father's example you follow. And now they said to him, We are no bastard children; God, and he only, is the Father we recognize. 42 Jesus told them, If you were children of God, you would welcome me gladly; it was from God I took my origin, from him I have come. I did not come on my own errand, it was he who sent me. 43 Why is it that you cannot understand the language I talk? It is because you have no ear for the message I bring. 44 You belong to your father, that is, the devil, and are eager to gratify the appetites which are your father's. He, from the first, was a murderer; and as for truth, he has never taken his stand upon that; there is no truth in him. When he utters falsehood, he is only uttering what is natural to him; he is all false,

v. 33. 'They answered'; some have understood this of the Jews who had come to believe in him (verse 31), but this seems contradicted by vv. 45, 46 below, and it is therefore best to understand the word 'they' of our Lord's Jewish audience in general.

182

THE CHILD JESUS IN THE TEMPLE   LUDOVICO MAZZOLINO
                                          1478-1528(?)

NATIONAL GALLERY, LONDON

and it was he who gave falsehood its birth. 45 And if you do not believe me, it is precisely because I am speaking the truth. 46 Can any of you convict me of sin? If not, why is it that you do not believe me when I tell you the truth? 47 The man who belongs to God listens to God's words; it is because you do not belong to God that you will not listen to me.

48 Hereupon the Jews answered him, We are right, surely, in saying that thou art a Samaritan, and art possessed? 49 I am not possessed, Jesus answered; it is because I reverence my Father that you have no reverence for me. 50 Not that I am looking to my own reputation; there is another who will look to it, and be the judge.

51 Believe me when I tell you this; if a man is true to my word, to all eternity he will never see death. 52 And the Jews said to him, Now we are certain that thou art possessed. What of Abraham and the prophets? They are dead; and thou sayest that a man will never taste death to all eternity, if he is true to thy word. 53 Art thou greater than our father Abraham? He is dead, and the prophets are dead. What dost thou claim to be? 54 If I should speak in my own honour, Jesus answered, such honour goes for nothing. Honour must come to me from my Father, from him whom you claim as your God: although you cannot recognize him. 55 But I have knowledge of him; if I should say I have not, I should be what you are, a liar. Yes, I have knowledge of him, and I am true to his word. 56 As for your father Abraham, his heart was proud to see the day of my coming; he saw, and rejoiced to see it. 57 Then the Jews asked him, Hast thou seen Abraham, thou, who art not yet fifty years old? 58 And Jesus said to them, Believe me, before ever Abraham came to be, I am. 59 Whereupon they took up stones to throw at him; but Jesus hid himself, and went out of the temple.

v. 56. It is uncertain whether our Lord means that Abraham 'saw' the coming of Christ merely in the sense that it was foretold to him (Gen. xxii. 18), or whether we are to suppose that he was granted some actual vision of the event, either in his life-time or after death.

v. 58. 'I am'; here our Lord seems explicitly to claim a Divine title, cf. Ex. iii. 14.

Chapter Nine

And JESUS SAW, AS HE passed on his way, a man who had been blind from his birth. 2 Whereupon his disciples asked him, Master, was this man guilty of sin, or was it his parents, that he should have been born blind? 3 Neither he nor his parents were guilty, Jesus answered; it was so that God's action might declare itself in him. 4 While daylight lasts, I must work in the service of him who sent me; the night is coming, when there is no working any more. 5 As long as I am in the world, I am the world's light. 6 With that, he spat on the ground, and made clay with the spittle; then he spread the clay on the man's eyes, 7 and said to him, Away with thee, and wash in the pool of Siloe (a word which means, Sent out). So he went and washed there, and came back with his sight restored. 8 And now the neighbours, and those who had been accustomed to see him begging, began to say, Is not this the man who used to sit here and beg? 9 Some said, This is the man; and others, No, but he looks like him. And he told them, Yes, I am the man. 10 How is it, then, they asked him, that thy eyes have been opened? 11 He answered, A man called Jesus made clay, and anointed my eyes with it, and said to me, Away with thee to the pool of Siloe and wash there. So I went there, and washed, and recovered my sight. 12 Where is he? they asked; and he said, I cannot tell.

13 And they brought him before the Pharisees, this man who had once been blind. 14 It was a sabbath day, you must know, when Jesus made clay and opened his eyes. 15 And so the Pharisees in their turn asked him how he had recovered his sight. Why, he said, he put clay on my eyes; and then I washed, and now I can see. 16 Whereupon some of the Pharisees said, This man can be no messenger from God; he does not observe the sabbath. Others asked, How can a man do miracles like this, and be a sinner? Thus there was a division of opinion among them. 17 And now they questioned the blind man again, What account dost thou give of him, that he should thus have opened thy eyes? Why, he said, he

v. 2. The disciples may not have known that the man was born blind; and the Greek may be interpreted as meaning, 'Did this man sin? or did his parents commit some sin, with the consequence that he was born blind?'

v. 4. The best Greek manuscripts read, 'we must work', not 'I must work'. If this reading is genuine, we must suppose that our Lord here associates his disciples with his own ministry; and indeed, he told them that they were the light of the world (Matthew v. 14.)

184

must be a prophet. 18 The Jews must send for the parents of the man who had recovered his sight, before they would believe his story that he had been blind, and that he had had his sight restored to him. 19 And they questioned them, Is this your son, who, you say, was born blind? How comes it, then, that he is now able to see? 20 His parents answered them, We can tell you that this is our son, and that he was blind when he was born; 21 we cannot tell how he is able to see now; we have no means of knowing who opened his eyes for him. Ask the man himself; he is of age; let him tell you his own story. 22 It was fear of the Jews that made his parents talk in this way; the Jews had by now come to an agreement that anyone who acknowledged Jesus as the Christ should be forbidden the synagogue; 23 that was why his parents said, He is of age, ask him himself.

24 So once more they summoned the man who had been blind. Give God the praise, they said; this man, to our knowledge, is a sinner. 25 Sinner or not, said the other, I cannot tell; all I know is that once I was blind, and, now I can see. 26 Then they asked him over again, What was it he did to thee? By what means did he open thy eyes? 27 And he answered them, I have told you already, and you would not listen to me. Why must you hear it over again? Would you too become his disciples? 28 Upon this, they covered him with abuse; Keep his discipleship for thyself, we are disciples of Moses. 29 We know for certain that God spoke to Moses; we know nothing of this man, or whence he comes. 30 Why, the man answered, here is matter for astonishment; here is a man that comes you cannot tell whence, and he has opened my eyes. 31 And yet we know for certain that God does not answer the prayers of sinners, it is only when a man is devout and does his will, that his prayer is answered. 32 That a man should open the eyes of one born blind is something unheard of since the world began. 33 No, if this man did not come from God, he would have no powers at all. 34 What, they answered, are we to have lessons from thee, all steeped in sin from thy birth? And they cast him out from their presence.

35 When Jesus heard that they had so cast him out, he went to find him, and asked him, Dost thou believe in the Son of God? 36 Tell me who he is, Lord, he answered, so that I can believe in him. 37 He is one whom thou hast seen, Jesus told him. It is he who is speaking to thee. 38 Then he said, I do believe, Lord, and fell down to worship him. 39 Hereupon Jesus said, I have come into this world so that a sentence may fall upon it, that those who

v. 35. 'The Son of God'; some Greek manuscripts read, 'The Son of Man', but it is clear from the context that, whichever title he used, our Lord was here identifying himself as the Christ.

v. 39. Our Lord's meaning (if we interpret it by v. 41 below) seems to be, that his coming into the world has the effect of enlightening those humble souls which are conscious of their own ignorance, and at the same time of involving those who think themselves wise and prudent (Matthew xi. 25) in worse blindness than ever. Cf. Apocalypse iii. 17, 18.

JOHN

are blind should see, and those who see should become blind. 40 Some of the Pharisees heard this, such as were in his company, and they asked him, Are we blind too? 41 If you were blind, Jesus told them, you would not be guilty. It is because you protest, We can see clearly, that you cannot be rid of your guilt.

Chapter Ten

BELIEVE ME WHEN I tell you this; the man who climbs into the sheepfold by some other way, instead of entering by the door, comes to steal and to plunder: 2 it is the shepherd who tends the sheep that comes in by the door. 3 At his coming the keeper of the door throws it open, and the sheep are attentive to his voice; and so he calls by name the sheep which belong to him, and leads them out with him. 4 When he has brought out all the sheep which belong to him, he walks in front of them, and the sheep follow him, recognizing his voice. 5 If a stranger comes, they run away from him instead of following him; they cannot recognize the voice of a stranger. 6 This was a parable which Jesus told them; and they could not understand what he meant to say to them. 7 So Jesus spoke to them again; Believe me, he said, it is I who am the door of the sheepfold. 8 Those others who have found their way in are all thieves and robbers; to these, the sheep paid no attention. 9 I am the door; a man will find salvation if he makes his way in through me; he will come and go at will, and find pasture. 10 The thief only comes to steal, to slaughter, to destroy; I have come so that they may have life, and have it more abundantly.

11 I am the good shepherd. The good shepherd lays down his life for his sheep, 12 whereas the hireling, who is no shepherd, and does not claim the sheep as his own, abandons the sheep and

v. 8. 'Those others' must not be taken as referring to the old prophets; our Lord says there are, not were, robbers, which shews he was thinking of religious leaders in his own time. These, he says, entered the sheep-fold unauthorized, instead of waiting until Christ, the Good Shepherd, should have opened that Door, which is also Christ.

186

takes to flight as soon as he sees the wolf coming, and so the wolf harries the sheep and scatters them. 13 The hireling, then, takes to flight because he is only a hireling, because he has no concern over the sheep. 14 I am the good shepherd; my sheep are known to me and know me; 15 just as I am known to my Father, and know him. And for these sheep I am laying down my life. 16 I have other sheep too, which do not belong to this fold; I must bring them in too; they will listen to my voice; so there will be one fold, and one shepherd. 17 This my Father loves in me, that I am laying down my life, to take it up again afterwards. 18 Nobody can rob me of it; I lay it down of my own accord. I am free to lay it down, free to take it up again; that is the charge which my Father has given me.

19 These words of his led to a fresh division of opinion among the Jews. 20 Many of them said, He must be possessed; he is a madman; why do you listen to him? 21 While others said, This is not the language of a man who is possessed by a devil. Has a devil power to open blind men's eyes? 22 And now the Dedication feast was taking place at Jerusalem, and it was winter; 23 and Jesus was walking about in the temple, in Solomon's porch. 24 So the Jews gathered round him, and said to him, How long wilt thou go on keeping us in suspense? If thou art the Christ, tell us openly. 25 Jesus answered them, I have told you, but you will not believe me. All that I do in my Father's name bears me testimony, 26 and still you will not believe me; that is because you are no sheep of mine. 27 My sheep listen to my voice, and I know them, and they follow me. 28 And I give them everlasting life, so that to all eternity they can never be lost; no one can tear them away from my hand. 29 This trust which my Father has committed to me is more precious than all else; no one can tear them away from the hand of my Father. 30 My Father and I are one.

31 At this, the Jews once again took up stones, to stone him with. 32 Jesus answered them, My Father has enabled me to do many deeds of mercy in your presence; for which of these are you stoning me? 33 It is not for any deed of mercy we are stoning thee, answered the Jews; it is for blasphemy; it is because thou, who art a man, dost pretend to be God. 34 Jesus answered them, Is it not written in your law, I have said, You are gods? 35 He gave the title of gods to those who had God's message sent to them; and we know that the words of scripture have binding force. 36 Why then, what of him whom God has sanctified and sent

v. 15. Some would translate, 'Just as I am known to my Father, so I know him', but this rendering seems less well suited to the context.
v. 16. 'One fold': the Greek here is more accurately rendered 'One flock'. Our Lord evidently refers to the Gentiles who would believe in him.

v. 22. I Machabees iv. 56.
v. 23. III. Kings vi. 3.

v. 29. Some Greek manuscripts read here 'My Father, who has committed this trust to me, is greater than all else'.

v. 34. Ps. lxxxi. 6. The judges of God's people are there called 'sons of God' and even 'gods'; which fact our Lord adduces as proof that 'Son of God' is not in itself a blasphemous title to adopt. But he shows that he claims it in a different sense, by insisting immediately afterwards that it is more applicable to the Word of God, than to those to whom the word of God was sent.

into the world? Will you call me a blasphemer, because I have told you I am the Son of God? 37 If you find that I do not act like the son of my Father, then put no trust in me; 38 but if I do, then let my actions convince you where I cannot; so you will recognize and learn to believe that the Father is in me, and I in him. 39 Thereupon once again they had a mind to seize him; but he escaped from their hands, 40 and went back to the other side of Jordan, to the place where John was when he first baptized. 41 There he waited, while many came out to see him. John, they said, never did a miracle, but all John told us about this man has proved true. 42 And many found faith in him there.

Chapter Eleven

THERE WAS A MAN called Lazarus, of Bethany, who had fallen sick. Bethany was the name of the village where Mary lived, with her sister Martha; 2 and this Mary, whose brother Lazarus had now fallen sick, was the woman who anointed the Lord with ointment and wiped his feet with her hair. 3 The sisters sent a message to him, to say, Lord, he whom thou lovest lies here sick. 4 And Jesus said, on hearing it, The end of this sickness is not death; it is meant for God's honour, to bring honour to the Son of God. 5 Jesus loved Martha, and her sister, and Lazarus. 6 At the time, then, after hearing the news, he waited for two days in the place where he was; 7 and then, after that interval, he said to his disciples, Let us go back into Judaea. 8 Master, his disciples said to him, the Jews were but now threatening to stone thee; art thou for Judaea again? 9 Jesus answered, Are there not just twelve hours of daylight? A man can walk in the day-time without stumbling, with this world's light to see by; 10 he only stumbles if he walks by night, because then the light

v. 2. Since St. John only mentions this incident in the chapter which follows, this verse perhaps implies that he assumed his readers to be familiar with the other gospels. (Matthew xxvi. 6, Mark xiv. 3.) Cf. also Luke vii. 36 sqq.

v. 9. The most probable explanation of this allegory is that our Lord compares the predestined length of his own life-time with the hours of daylight; there is no danger for him in Judaea yet, because the hour of darkness (Luke xxii. 53) has not yet come. Cf. ix. 4 above.

cannot reach him. 11 So much he said, and then he told them, Our friend Lazarus is at rest now; I am going there to awake him. 12 But, Lord, the disciples said to him, if he is rested, his life will be saved. 13 Jesus had been telling them of his death; but they supposed he meant the rest which comes with sleep. 14 So now Jesus told them openly, Lazarus is dead. 15 And for your sakes, I am glad I was not there; it will help you to believe. But come, let us make our way to him. 16 Thereupon Thomas, who is also called Didymus, said to his fellow disciples, Let us go too, and be killed along with him.

17 When Jesus arrived, he found that Lazarus had already been four days in the grave. 18 Since Bethany was near Jerusalem, about fifteen furlongs away, 19 many of the Jews had gone out there to comfort Martha and Mary over the loss of their brother. 20 Martha, when she heard that Jesus had come, went out to meet him, while Mary sat on in the house. 21 Lord, said Martha to Jesus, if thou hadst been here, my brother would not have died; 22 and I know well that even now God will grant whatever thou wilt ask of him. 23 Thy brother, Jesus said to her, will rise again. 24 Martha said to him, I know well enough that he will rise again at the resurrection, when the last day comes. 25 Jesus said to her, I am the resurrection and life; he who believes in me, though he is dead, will live on, 26 and whoever has life, and has faith in me, to all eternity cannot die. 27 Dost thou believe this? Yes, Lord, she told him, I have learned to believe that thou art the Christ; thou art the Son of the living God; it is for thy coming the world has waited. 28 And with that she went back and called her sister Mary aside; The Master is here, she said, and bids thee come. 29 She rose up at once on hearing it, and went to him. 30 (Jesus had not yet reached the village; he was still at the place where Martha had gone out to meet him.) 31 And so the Jews who were in the house with Mary, comforting her, when they saw how quickly she rose up and went out, followed her; She has gone to the grave, they said, to weep there.

32 So Mary reached the place where Jesus was; and when she saw him, she fell at his feet; Lord, she said, if thou hadst been here, my brother would not have died. 33 And Jesus, when he saw her in tears, and the tears of the Jews who accompanied her, sighed deeply, and distressed himself over it; 34 Where have you buried him? he asked. Lord, they said to him, come and see. 35 Then Jesus wept. 36 See, said the Jews, how he loved him; 37 and some of them asked, Could not he, who opened the blind

man's eyes, have prevented this man's death? 38 So Jesus, once more sighing to himself, came to the tomb; it was a cave, and a stone had been put over the mouth of it. 39 Take away the stone, Jesus told them. And Martha, the dead man's sister, said to him, Lord, the air is foul by now; he has been four days dead. 40 Why, Jesus said to her, have I not told thee that if thou hast faith, thou wilt see God glorified? 41 So they took the stone away; and Jesus lifted his eyes to heaven, Father, he said, I thank thee for hearing my prayer. 42 For myself, I know that thou hearest me at all times, but I say this for the sake of the multitude which is standing round, that they may learn to believe it is thou who hast sent me. 43 And with that he cried in a loud voice, Come out, Lazarus, to my side. 44 Whereupon the dead man came out, his feet and hands tied with linen strips, and his face muffled in a veil. Loose him, said Jesus, and let him go free.

45 Many of these Jews who had visited Martha and Mary, and seen what Jesus did, learned to believe in him, 46 but some went off to the Pharisees, and reported to them all Jesus had done. 47 So the chief priests and Pharisees summoned a council; What are we about? they said. This man is performing many miracles, 48 and if we leave him to his own devices, he will find credit everywhere. Then the Romans will come, and make an end of our city and our race. 49 And one of them, Caiphas, who held the high priesthood in that year, said to them, You have no perception at all; 50 you do not reflect that it is best for us if one man is put to death for the sake of the people, to save a whole nation from destruction. 51 It was not of his own impulse that he said this; holding the high priesthood as he did in that year, he was able to prophesy that Jesus was to die for the sake of the nation; 52 and not only for that nation's sake, but so as to bring together into one all God's children, scattered far and wide. 53 From that day forward, then, they plotted his death; 54 and Jesus no longer went about openly among the Jews, but retired to a city called Ephrem, in the country which borders on the desert, and waited there with his disciples. 55 The paschal feast which the Jews keep was now close at hand, and there were many from the country who went up to Jerusalem to purify themselves before paschal time began; 56 so they looked out for Jesus, and said to one another as they stood there in the temple, What is your way of it? Will he come up to the feast? And the chief priests and Pharisees had given orders that anyone who knew where he was should report it to them, so that they could arrest him.

v. 49. The Jewish high priests were not elected annually, but held the office for life. The Romans were continually interfering to make changes in the high-priestly succession, and St. John may be thinking of a slightly later period. He may however mean, that Caiphas was high priest in that all-important year which witnessed the world's redemption; or possibly that in this year Caiphas still held the office, from which he was in fact deposed by the Romans not many years afterwards.

Chapter Twelve

<small>S</small>IX DAYS BEFORE THE paschal feast, Jesus went to Bethany. Bethany was the home of Lazarus, the dead man whom Jesus raised to life. 2 And a feast was made for him there, at which Martha was waiting at table, while Lazarus was one of his fellow guests. 3 And now Mary brought in a pound of pure spikenard ointment, which was very precious, and poured it over Jesus' feet, wiping his feet with her hair; the whole house was scented with the ointment. 4 One of his disciples, the same Judas Iscariot who was to betray him, said when he saw it, 5 Why should not this ointment have been sold? It would have fetched two hundred silver pieces, and alms might have been given to the poor. 6 He said this, not from any concern for the poor, but because he was a thief; he kept the common purse, and took what was put into it. 7 And Jesus said, Let her alone; enough that she should keep it for the day when my body is prepared for burial. 8 You have the poor among you always; I am not always among you.

9 A great number of the Jews heard that he was there and went out there, not only on account of Jesus, but so as to have sight of Lazarus, whom he raised from the dead; 10 and the chief priests made a plot against Lazarus' life too, 11 because so many of the Jews, on his account, were beginning to go off and find faith in Jesus. 12 Next day, a great multitude of those who had come up for the feast, hearing that Jesus was coming into Jerusalem, 13 took palm branches with them and went out to meet him, crying aloud, Hosanna, blessed is he who comes in the name of the Lord, blessed is the king of Israel. 14 And Jesus took an ass's foal, and mounted on it; so it is written, 15 Do not be afraid, daughter of Sion; behold, thy king is coming to thee, riding on an ass's colt. 16 The disciples did not understand all this at the time; only after Jesus had attained his glory did they remember what they had done, and how it fulfilled the words written of him. 17 There were many who had been with him, when he called

vv. 1-8. Matthew xxvi. 6, Mark xiv. 3.

vv. 12-16. Matthew xxi. 1, Mark xi. 1, Luke xix. 29.

v. 15. Zach. ix. 9.

191

JOHN

Lazarus out of the tomb and raised him to life, and these too bore witness of him. 18 Indeed, that was why the multitude went out to meet him, because they had heard of his performing this miracle. 19 And the Pharisees said to one another, Do you see how vain are your efforts? Look, the whole world has turned aside to follow him.

20 And there were certain Gentiles, among those that had come up to worship at the feast, 21 who approached Philip, the man from Bethsaida in Galilee, and made a request of him; Sir, they said, we desire to see Jesus. 22 Philip came and told Andrew, and together Andrew and Philip went and told Jesus. 23 And Jesus answered them thus, The time has come now for the Son of Man to achieve his glory. 24 Believe me when I tell you this; a grain of wheat must fall into the ground and die, or else it remains nothing more than a grain of wheat; but if it dies, then it yields rich fruit. 25 He who loves his life will lose it; he who is an enemy to his own life in this world will keep it, so as to live eternally. 26 If anyone is to be my servant, he must follow my way; so shall my servant too be where I am. If anyone serves me, my Father will do him honour.

v. 27. Ps. vi. 4. 'I will say'; some understand this as a question, 'Shall I say?'

27 And now my soul is distressed. What am I to say? I will say, Father, save me from undergoing this hour of trial; and yet, I have only reached this hour of trial that I might undergo it. 28 Father, make thy name known. And at this, a voice came from heaven, I have made it known, and will yet make it known. 29 Thereupon the multitude which stood listening declared that it had thundered; but some of them said, An angel has spoken to him. 30 Jesus answered, It was for your sake, not for mine, that this utterance was made. 31 Sentence is now being passed on this world; now is the time when the prince of this world is to be cast out. 32 Yes, if only I am lifted up from the earth, I will attract all men to myself. 33 (In saying this, he prophesied the death he was to die.)

v. 34. Dan. vii. 14.

34 The multitude answered him, We have been told, out of the law, that Christ is to remain undisturbed for ever; what dost thou mean by saying that the Son of Man must be lifted up? What Son of Man is this? 35 And Jesus said to them, The light is among you still, but only for a short time. Finish your journey while you still have the light, for fear darkness should overtake you; he who journeys in darkness cannot tell which way he is going. 36 While you still have the light, have faith in the light,

192

that so you may become children of the light. So much Jesus told them, and then went away, and was lost to their view.

37 Such great miracles he did in their presence, and still they did not believe in him; 38 this was in fulfilment of the words spoken by the prophet Isaias, Lord, is there anyone who has believed our message, to whom the power of God has been made known? 39 So it was that they could not believe; and indeed, Isaias has said elsewhere: 40 He has blinded their eyes, and hardened their heart, so that they could not see with those eyes, and understand with that heart, and turn back to me, and win healing from me. 41 Isaias said this, as one who had seen his glory; it was of him that he spoke. 42 There were, for all that, many of the rulers who had learned to believe in him; but they would not profess it because of the Pharisees, afraid of being forbidden the synagogue. 43 They valued their credit with men higher than their credit with God.

44 And Jesus cried out, If a man believes in me, it is in him who sent me, not in me, that he believes; 45 to see me is to see him who sent me. 46 I have come into the world as a light, so that all those who believe in me may continue no longer in darkness. 47 If a man hears my words, and does not keep true to them, I do not pass sentence on him; I have come to save the world, not to pass sentence on the world. 48 The man who makes me of no account, and does not accept my words, has a judge appointed to try him; it is the message I have uttered that will be his judge at the last day. 49 And this, because it is not on my own authority that I have spoken; it was my Father who sent me that commanded me what words I was to say, what message I was to utter. 50 And I know well that what he commands is eternal life; everything then, which I utter, I utter as my Father has bidden me.

v. 38. Is. liii. 2. 'The power'; literally 'the arm' of the Lord.

v. 40. Is. vi. 9.

Chapter Thirteen

BEFORE THE PASCHAL feast began, Jesus already knew that the time had come for his passage from this world to the Father. He still loved those who were his own, whom he was leaving in the world, and he would give them the uttermost proof of his love. 2 Supper was over, and the devil had already put it into the heart of Judas, son of Simon, the Iscariot, to betray him. 3 Jesus knew well that the Father had left everything in his hands; knew it was from God that he came, and to God that he went. 4 And now, rising from supper, he laid his garments aside, took a towel, and put it about him; 5 and then he poured water into the basin, and began to wash the feet of his disciples, wiping them with the towel that girded him. 6 So, when he came to Simon Peter, Peter asked him, Lord, is it for thee to wash my feet? 7 Jesus answered him, It is not for thee to know, now, what I am doing; but thou wilt understand it afterwards. 8 Peter said to him, I will never let thee wash my feet; and Jesus answered him, If I do not wash thee, it means thou hast no companionship with me. 9 Then, Lord, said Peter, wash my hands and my head too, not only my feet. 10 But Jesus told him, A man who has bathed does not need to do more than wash the stains from his feet; he is clean all over. 11 And you are clean now; only, not all of you. He knew who his betrayer was; that is why he said, You are not all clean.

12 Then, when he had finished washing their feet and put on his garments, he sat down again, and said to them, Do you understand what it is I have done to you? 13 You hail me as the Master, and the Lord; and you are right, it is what I am. 14 Why then, if I have washed your feet, I who am the Master and the Lord, you in your turn ought to wash each other's feet; 15 I have been setting you an example, which will teach you in your turn to do what I have done for you. 16 Believe me, no slave can be greater than his master, no apostle greater than he by whom he

v. 10. The best interpretation of this passage seems to be that of St. Cyprian, that the washing of feet symbolizes sacramental absolution. He who has once been baptized can need no second baptism, but he may need absolution from post-baptismal sin, which is compared here to the incidental stains of travel. Since Judas had been baptized, and had his feet washed, he remains 'unclean' because in his case the washing of feet has taken no effect.

194

was sent. 17 Now that you know this, blessed are you if you perform it. 18 I am not thinking of all of you when I say this, I know who are the men I have chosen; well, it remains for the passage in scripture to be fulfilled, The man who shared my bread has lifted his heel to trip me up. 19 I am telling you this now, before it happens, so that when it happens you may believe it was written of me.

20 Believe me when I tell you this; the man who welcomes one whom I send, welcomes me; and the man who welcomes me, welcomes him who sent me.

21 After saying so much, Jesus bore witness to the distress he felt in his heart; Believe me, he said, believe me, one of you is to betray me. 22 And the disciples looked at one another, at a loss to know which of them he meant. 23 Jesus had one disciple, whom he loved, who was now sitting with his head against Jesus' breast; 24 to him, therefore, Simon Peter made a sign, and asked him, Who is it he means? 25 And he, leaning his head back upon Jesus' breast, asked him, Lord, who is it? 26 Jesus answered, It is the man to whom I give this piece of bread which I am dipping in the dish. Then he dipped the bread, and gave it to Judas the son of Simon, the Iscariot. 27 The morsel once given, Satan entered into him; and Jesus said to him, Be quick on thy errand. 28 None of those who sat there could understand the drift of what he said; 29 some of them thought, since Judas kept the common purse, that Jesus was saying to him, Go and buy what we need for the feast, or bidding him give some alms to the poor. 30 He, as soon as he received the morsel, had gone out; and now it was night.

31 When he had gone out, Jesus said, Now the Son of Man has achieved his glory, and in his glory God is exalted. 32 Since, in his glory, God is exalted, it is for God to exalt him in his own glory, and exalt him without delay. 33 It is only for a short time that I am with you, my children. You will look for me, and now I have to tell you what I once told the Jews, you cannot reach the place where I am. 34 I have a new commandment to give you, that you are to love one another; that your love for one another is to be like the love I have borne you. 35 The mark by which all men will know you for my disciples will be the love you bear one another. 36 Simon Peter said to him, Lord, where art thou going? Jesus answered him, I am going where thou canst not follow me now, but shalt follow me afterwards. 37 Lord,

v. 18. Ps. xl. 10.

v. 19. 'You may believe it was written of me'; literally, 'you may believe that it is myself', as in viii. 24 above. Here, as there, the sense is plainly, 'that I am the Christ'; but it has to be inferred, here as there, from the context, and the context seems to imply that our Lord is the Christ inasmuch as he is the person in whom David's prophecy is fulfilled.

vv. 21-30. Matthew xxvi. 21, Mark xiv. 18.

v. 23. The ancients did not sit as we do over meals, but reclined, leaning on the left elbow. In this verse, we are simply told that St. John, lying at our Lord's right, found his head nearly at a level with his breast; in verse 25 he leans back to speak to him, with his head actually resting upon it. That St. Peter should have had to communicate by signs probably means that he was sitting on the further side of our Lord, that is, in the place of honour at his left.

v. 33. Cf. vii. 34, viii. 21 above.

Peter said to him, why cannot I follow thee now? I am ready to lay down my life for thy sake. 38 Thou art ready, answered Jesus, to lay down thy life for my sake? Believe me, by cock-crow thou wilt thrice disown me.

Chapter Fourteen

v. 2. 'Should I have said to you'; cf. x. 4, xii. 26 above. Some commentators take the words as a statement, 'I would have said to you', which is difficult to reconcile with the verse which immediately follows; others would translate, 'I would have told you, because'; but this is a doubtful rendering of the Greek, and seems wanting in relevance. Our Lord's thought appears to be, 'there are places waiting in heaven for others besides myself, as you may infer from my saying that I am going to prepare a home for you'.

DO NOT LET YOUR heart be distressed; as you have faith in God, have faith in me. 2 There are many dwelling-places in my Father's house; otherwise, should I have said to you, I am going away to prepare a home for you? 3 And though I do go away, to prepare you a home, I am coming back; and then I will take you to myself, so that you too may be where I am. 4 And now you know where it is I am going; and you know the way there. 5 Thomas said to him, But, Lord, we do not know where thou art going; how are we to know the way there? 6 Jesus said to him, I am the way; I am truth and life; nobody can come to the Father, except through me. 7 If you had learned to recognize me, you would have learned to recognize my Father too. From now onwards you are to recognize him; you have seen him. 8 At this, Philip said to him, Lord, let us see the Father; that is all we ask. 9 What, Philip, Jesus said to him, here am I, who have been all this while in your company; hast thou not learned to recognize me yet? Whoever has seen me, has seen the Father; what dost thou mean by saying, Let us see the Father? 10 Do you not believe that I am in the Father, and the Father is in me? The words I speak to you are not my own words; and the Father, who dwells continually in me, achieves in me his own acts of power. 11 If you cannot trust my word, when I tell you that I am in the Father, and the Father is in me, 12 let these powerful acts themselves be my warrant. Believe me when I tell you this; the man

v. 10. The manuscripts here have 'Dost thou not believe'.

196

who has learned to believe in me will be able to do what I do; nay, he will be able to do greater things yet. 13 It is to my Father I am going: and whatever request you make of the Father in my name, I will grant, so that through the Son the Father may be glorified; 14 every request you make of me in my own name, I myself will grant it to you.

15 If you have any love for me, you must keep the commandments which I give you; 16 and then I will ask the Father, and he will give you another to befriend you, one who is to dwell continually with you for ever. 17 It is the truth-giving Spirit, for whom the world can find no room, because it cannot see him, cannot recognize him. But you are to recognize him; he will be continually at your side, nay, he will be in you. 18 I will not leave you friendless; I am coming to you. 19 It is only a little while now, before the world is to see me no more; but you can see me, because I live on, and you too will have life. 20 When that day comes, you will learn for yourselves that I am in my Father, and you are in me, and I am in you. 21 The man who loves me is the man who keeps the commandments he has from me; and he who loves me will win my Father's love, and I too will love him, and will reveal myself to him. 22 Here Judas, not the Iscariot, said to him, Lord, how comes it that thou wilt only reveal thyself to us, and not to the world? 23 Jesus answered him, If a man has any love for me, he will be true to my word; and then he will win my Father's love, and we will both come to him, and make our continual abode with him; 24 whereas the man who has no love for me, lets my sayings pass him by. And this word, which you have been hearing from me, comes not from me, but from my Father who sent me.

25 So much converse I have held with you, still at your side. 26 He who is to befriend you, the Holy Spirit, whom the Father will send on my account, will in his turn make everything plain, and recall to your minds everything I have said to you.

27 Peace is my bequest to you, and the peace which I give you is mine to give; I do not give peace as the world gives it. Do not let your heart be distressed, or play the coward. 28 You have heard me say that I am going away and coming back to you. If you really loved me, you would be glad to hear that I am on my way to my Father; my Father has greater power than I. 29 I have told you of this before it happens, so that when it happens you may learn to believe. 30 I have no longer much time for converse with you; one is coming, who has power over the world, but no

v. 13. The words 'of the Father' are not found in the manuscripts.

v. 14. Some Greek manuscripts omit 'of me'.

v. 16. 'To befriend you'; the Greek word here used is 'the Paraclete', which means, properly, an advocate called in to defend one who is defending an action at law. It is clear from Matthew x. 20 that this office is fulfilled by the Holy Spirit; but the reference in this and the following chapters suggest that the title indicates a more general manner of assistance.

v. 30. 'One who has power'; that is, the devil; cf. xii. 31 above.

v. 31. Some think that after announcing his departure our Lord still lingered talking to the apostles; others, that they left the Cenacle at this point, and that

the words recorded
in the three chapters
which follow were
spoken on the way to
Gethsemani.

hold over me. 31 No, but the world must be convinced that I love the Father, and act only as the Father has commanded me to act. Rise up, we must be going on our way.

Chapter
Fifteen

I AM THE TRUE VINE, and it is my Father who tends it. 2 The branch that yields no fruit in me, he cuts away; the branch that does yield fruit, he trims clean, so that it may yield more fruit. 3 You, through the message I have preached to you, are clean already; you have only to live on in me, and I will live on in you. 4 The branch that does not live on in the vine can yield no fruit of itself; no more can you, if you do not live on in me. 5 I am the vine, you are its branches; if a man lives on in me, and I in him, then he will yield abundant fruit; separated from me, you have no power to do anything. 6 If a man does not live on in me, he can only be like the branch that is cast off and withers away; such a branch is picked up and thrown into the fire, to burn there. 7 As long as you live on in me, and my words live on in you, you will be able to make what request you will, and have it granted. 8 My Father's name has been glorified, if you yield abundant fruit, and prove yourselves my disciples. 9 I have bestowed my love upon you, just as my Father has bestowed his love upon me; live on, then, in my love. 10 You will live on in my love, if you keep my commandments, just as it is by keeping my Father's commandments that I live on in his love.

11 All this I have told you, so that my joy may be yours, and the measure of your joy may be filled up. 12 This is my commandment, that you should love one another, as I have loved you. 13 This is the greatest love a man can show, that he should lay down his life for his friends; 14 and you, if you do all that I

198

command you, are my friends. 15 I do not speak of you any more as my servants; a servant is one who does not understand what his master is about, whereas I have made known to you all that my Father has told me; and so I have called you my friends. 16 It was not you that chose me, it was I that chose you. The task I have appointed you is to go out and bear fruit, fruit which will endure; so that every request you make of the Father in my name may be granted you. 17 These are the directions I give you, that you should love one another.

18 If the world hates you, be sure that it hated me before it it learned to hate you. 19 If you belonged to the world, the world would know you for its own and love you; it is because you do not belong to the world, because I have singled you out from the midst of the world, that the world hates you. 20 Do not forget what I said to you, No servant can be greater than his master. They will persecute you just as they have persecuted me; they will pay the same attention to your words as to mine. 21 And they will treat you thus because you bear my name; they have no knowledge of him who sent me. 22 If I had not come and given them my message, they would not have been in fault; as it is, their fault can find no excuse. 23 To hate me is to hate my Father too. 24 If I had not done what no one else ever did in their midst they would not have been in fault; as it is, they have hated, with open eyes, both me and my Father. 25 And all this, in fulfilment of the saying which is written in their law, They hated me without cause. 26 Well, when the truth-giving Spirit, who proceeds from the Father, has come to befriend you, he whom I will send to you from the Father's side, he will bear witness of what I was; 27 and you too are to be my witnesses, you who from the first have been in my company.

v. 17. Our Lord seems to refer to his one commandment of love as if it were in itself a series of commandments, in place of those given on Sinai. Some, however, would translate, 'I am giving you all these directions (contained in the foregoing verses) in order that you may learn to love one another'.

v. 20. 'They will pay the same attention'; that is, none. Some would render 'they will keep a watch upon your words' (cf. Luke xi. 53, 54); but this would be contrary to St. John's use of language.

v. 25. Ps. xxxiv. 19, lviii. 5.

Chapter Sixteen

I HAVE TOLD YOU THIS, so that your faith may not be taken unawares. 2 They will forbid you the synagogue; nay, the time is coming when anyone who puts you to death will claim that he is performing an act of worship to God; 3 such things they will do to you, because they have no knowledge of the Father, or of me. 4 And I have told you this, so that when the time comes for it to happen, you may remember that I told you of it. If I did not tell you of it from the first, it was because I was to be still in your company. 5 Now, I am going back to him who sent me. None of you is asking me, Where is it thou art going? 6 so full are your hearts with sorrow at my telling you this. 7 And yet I can say truly that it is better for you I should go away; he who is to befriend you will not come to you unless I do go, but if only I make my way there, I will send him to you. 8 He will come, and it will be for him to prove the world wrong, about sin, and about rightness of heart, and about judging. 9 About sin; they have not found belief in me. 10 About rightness of heart; I am going back to my Father, and you are not to see me any more. 11 About judging; he who rules this world has had sentence passed on him already. 12 I have still much to say to you, but it is beyond your reach as yet. 13 It will be for him, the truth-giving Spirit, when he comes, to guide you into all truth. He will not utter a message of his own; he will utter the message that has been given to him; and he will make plain to you what is still to come. 14 And he will bring honour to me, because it is from me that he will derive what he makes plain to you. 15 I say that he will derive from me what he makes plain to you, because all that belongs to the Father belongs to me.

16 After a little while, you will see me no longer; and again after a little while you will have sight of me, because I am going back to the Father. 17 Upon this, some of his disciples said to one another, What does this mean, that he is saying to us, After a little while, you will see me no longer, and again after a little

v. 5. 'None of you is asking me'; that is, any longer; St. Peter had asked this question (xiii. 36), but now it would appear that the disciples have lost their interest in our Lord's movements, and given themselves up to useless sorrowing over his departure.

v. 11. 'He who rules'; that is, the devil, as in x. 4. 30.

vv. 13-15. The teaching office of the Holy Spirit does not consist in imparting to the Church the knowledge of hitherto unknown doctrines, in addition to the deposit of faith, but in making our knowledge of doctrines already revealed fuller and more precise; all that he 'makes plain' to us is derived from the teaching (not all of it recorded in the gospels, cf. Acts i. 3) given by our Lord to his apostles while he was on earth.

vv. 16-19. 'You will see me no longer'; according to most

while you will have sight of me? And then, Because I am going back to my Father? 18 What is this little while he speaks of? they asked. We cannot understand what he means by it. 19 Jesus, knowing that they were eager to question him, said to them, You are wondering among yourselves over what I have been saying, After a little while you will see me no longer, and again after a little while you will have sight of me. 20 Believe me when I tell you this, you will weep and lament while the world rejoices; you will be distressed, but your distress shall be turned into joy. 21 A woman in childbirth feels distress, because now her time has come; but when she has borne her child, she does not remember the distress any longer, so glad is she that a man has been born into the world. 22 So it is with you, you are distressed now; but one day I will see you again, and then your hearts will be glad; and your gladness will be one which nobody can take away from you. 23 When that day comes, you will not need to ask anything of me. Believe me, you have only to make any request of the Father in my name, and he will grant it to you. 24 Until now, you have not been making any requests in my name; make them, and they will be granted, to bring you gladness in full measure.

25 I have been telling you this in parable; now comes the hour when I will talk to you in parables no longer, but tell you openly about the Father. 26 At the time I speak of, you will make your requests in my name; and there is no need for me to tell you that I will ask the Father to grant them to you, 27 because the Father himself is your friend, since you have become my friends, and have learned to believe that I came from God. 28 It was from the Father I came out, when I entered the world, and now I am leaving the world, and going on my way to the Father. 29 Hereupon his disciples said to him, Why, now thou art speaking openly enough; this is no parable thou art uttering. 30 Now we can be sure that thou knowest all things, not needing to wait till thou art asked; this gives us faith that thou wast sent by God. 31 You have faith now? Jesus answered. 32 Behold, the time is coming, nay, has already come, when you are to be scattered, each of you taking his own path, and to leave me alone. And yet I am not alone, because the Father is with me. 33 I have said this to you, so that in me you may find peace. In the world, you will only find tribulation; but take courage, I have overcome the world.

commentators, this refers to the Ascension. 'You will have sight of me'; there is less agreement about the reference here, which is variously attributed to the time of the Holy Spirit's coming, that of the apostles' death, and that of the general Resurrection. The first of these interpretations would seem to fit in best with the context.

v. 23. 'To ask anything'; the Greek word here used may mean either to ask a question, or to ask a favour. The Latin seems to give it the latter meaning here, as in verse 26 below; in verse 30 below, according to the Latin, it means 'to ask a question', as in verse 19 above.

v. 32. Cf. III Kings xxii. 17, Is. liii. 6, Matthew xxvi. 31.

201

Chapter Seventeen

THUS JESUS SPOKE TO them, and then, lifting up his eyes to heaven, he said, Father, the time has come; give glory now to thy Son, that thy Son may give the glory to thee. 2 Thou hast put him in authority over all mankind, to bring eternal life to all those thou hast entrusted to him. 3 Eternal life is knowing thee, who art the only true God, and Jesus Christ, whom thou hast sent. 4 I have exalted thy glory on earth, by achieving the task which thou gavest me to do; 5 now, Father, do thou exalt me at thy own side, in that glory which I had with thee before the world began. 6 I have made thy name known to the men whom thou hast entrusted to me, chosen out of the world. They belonged to thee, and have become mine through thy gift, and they have kept true to thy word. 7 Now they have learned to recognize all the gifts thou gavest me as coming from thee; 8 I have given them the message which thou gavest to me, and they, receiving it, recognized it for truth that I came from thee, and found faith to believe that it was thou who didst send me. 9 It is for these I pray; I am not praying for the world, but for those whom thou hast entrusted to me; they belong to thee, 10 as all I have is thine, and all thou hast is mine; and in them my glory is achieved.

v. 11. 'Thy gift to me'; some of the Greek manuscripts refer this to the Father's name, some to the Apostles.
v. 12. The reference is perhaps to Ps. cviii. 8, as in Acts i. 20.

11 I am remaining in the world no longer, but they remain in the world, while I am on my way to thee. Holy Father, keep them true to thy name, thy gift to me, that they may be one, as we are one. 12 As long as I was with them, it was for me to keep them true to thy name; and I have watched over them, so that only one has been lost, he whom perdition claims for its own, in fulfilment of the scripture. 13 But now I am coming to thee; and while I am still in the world I am telling them this, so that my joy may be theirs, and reach its full measure in them. 14 I have given them thy message, and the world has nothing but hatred for them, because they do not belong to the world, as I, too, do not belong to the world. 15 I am not asking that thou shouldst take them out of the world, but that thou shouldst keep them clear

of what is evil. 16 They do not belong to the world, as I, too, do not belong to the world; 17 keep them holy, then, through the truth; it is thy word that is truth. 18 Thou hast sent me into the world on thy errand, and I have sent them into the world on my errand; 19 and I dedicate myself for their sakes, that they too may be dedicated through the truth.

20 It is not only for them that I pray; I pray for those who are to find faith in me through their words; 21 that they may all be one; that they too may be one in us, as thou Father, art in me, and I in thee; so that the world may come to believe that it is thou who hast sent me. 22 And I have given them the privilege which thou gavest to me, that they should all be one, as we are one; 23 that while thou art in me, I may be in them, and so they may be perfectly made one. So let the world know that it is thou who hast sent me, and that thou hast bestowed thy love upon them, as thou hast bestowed it upon me. 24 This, Father, is my desire, that all those whom thou hast entrusted to me may be with me where I am, so as to see my glory, thy gift made to me, in that love which thou didst bestow upon me before the foundation of the world. 25 Father, thou art just; the world has never acknowledged thee, but I have acknowledged thee, and these men have acknowledged that thou didst send me. 26 I have revealed, and will reveal, thy name to them; so that the love thou hast bestowed upon me may dwell in them, and I, too, may dwell in them.

Chapter Eighteen

ALL THIS JESUS SAID, and now, with his disciples, he went out across the Cedron valley. Here there was a garden, into which he and his disciples went. 2 Judas, his betrayer, knew

vv. 1-27. Matthew xxvi. 36, Mark xiv. 32, Luke xxii. 39.

the place well; Jesus and his disciples had often forgathered in it. 3 There, then, Judas came, accompanied by the guard, and officers sent by the chief priests and Pharisees, with lanterns and torches and weapons. 4 So Jesus, knowing well what was to befall him, went out to meet them; Who is it, he asked, you are looking for? 5 Jesus of Nazareth, they answered; and he told them, I am Jesus of Nazareth. And there was Judas, his betrayer, standing in their company. 6 When he said to them, I am Jesus of Nazareth, they all shrank back, and fell to the ground. 7 So, once more, Jesus asked them, Who is it you are looking for? and when they said, Jesus of Nazareth, 8 he answered, I have told you already that I am Jesus. If I am the man you are looking for, let these others go free. 9 Thus he would make good the words he had spoken to them, I have not lost any of those whom thou hast entrusted to me. 10 Then Simon Peter, who had a sword, drew it, and struck the high priest's servant, cutting off his right ear; Malchus was the name of the servant. 11 Whereupon Jesus said to Peter, Put thy sword back into its sheath. Am I not to drink that cup which my Father himself has appointed for me?

12 And now the guard, with their captain, and the Jewish officers arrested Jesus and pinioned him. 13 They led him off, in the first instance, to Annas, father-in-law of Caiphas, who held the high priesthood in that year. 14 (It was this Caiphas who had given it as his advice to the Jews, that it was best to put one man to death for the sake of the people.) 15 Simon Peter followed Jesus, with another disciple; this disciple was acquainted with the high priest, and went into the high priest's court with Jesus, 16 while Peter stood at the door without. Afterwards the other disciple, who was the high priest's acquaintance, went out and spoke to the door-keeper, and so brought Peter in. 17 This maidservant who kept the door asked Peter, Art thou another of this man's disciples? and he said, Not I. 18 It was cold, and the servants and officers had made a charcoal fire, and stood there warming themselves; there Peter stood too, warming himself with the rest.

19 And now the high priest questioned Jesus about his disciples, and about his teaching. 20 Jesus answered, I have spoken openly before the world; my teaching has been given in the synagogue and in the temple, where all the Jews forgather; nothing that I have said was said in secret. 21 Why dost thou question me? Ask those who listened to me what my words were; they know well enough what I said. 22 When he spoke thus, one of the

v. 9. See xvii. 12 above.

v. 15. Some Greek manuscripts read 'the other disciple'; which has given rise to the conjecture that St. John is referring to himself. But St. Augustine warns us that we should assert nothing rashly on this point.

v. 17. This interview with the maidservant upon St. Peter's first admission to the palace is not reckoned by the other Evangelists among his three denials. See note on Luke xxii. 58.

officers, who was standing by, struck Jesus on the cheek; Is this, he said, how thou makest answer to the high priest? 23 If there was harm in what I said, Jesus answered, tell us what was harmful in it; if not, why dost thou strike me? 24 Annas, you must know, had sent him on, still bound, to the high priest Caiphas.

25 Meanwhile Simon Peter stood there, and warmed himself. So they asked him, Art thou, too, one of his disciples? And he denied it; Not I, he said. 26 Why, said one of the high priest's servants, a kinsman of the man whose ear Peter had cut off, did I not see thee with him in the garden? 27 Whereupon Peter denied again; and immediately the cock crew.

28 And now they led Jesus away from the house of Caiphas to the governor's palace. It was morning, and they would not enter the palace themselves; there was the paschal meal to be eaten, and they must not incur defilement. 29 And so Pilate went to meet them without; What charge, he asked, do you bring against this man? 30 They answered, we would not have given him up to thee, if he had not been a malefactor. 31 Take him yourselves, Pilate said to them, and judge him according to your own law. Whereupon the Jews said to him, We have no power to put any man to death. 32 (This was in fulfilment of the words Jesus had spoken when he prophesied what death he was to die.) 33 So Pilate went back into the palace, and summoned Jesus; Art thou the king of the Jews? he asked. 34 Dost thou say this of thy own accord, Jesus answered, or is it what others have told thee of me? 35 And Pilate answered, Am I a Jew? It is thy own nation, and its chief priests, who have given thee up to me. What offence hast thou committed? 36 My kingdom, said Jesus, does not belong to this world. If my kingdom were one which belonged to this world, my servants would be fighting, to prevent my falling into the hands of the Jews; but no, my kingdom does not take its origin here. 37 Thou art a king, then? Pilate asked. And Jesus answered, It is thy own lips that have called me a king. What I was born for, what I came into the world for, is to bear witness of the truth. Whoever belongs to the truth, listens to my voice. 38 Pilate said to him, What is truth? And with that he went back to the Jews again, and told them, I can find no fault in him. 39 You have a custom of demanding that I should release one prisoner at paschal time; would you have me release the king of the Jews? 40 Whereupon they all made a fresh outcry; Barabbas, they said, not this man. Barabbas was a robber.

v. 24. It is evident that verses 15-23 refer to what happened when our Lord was arraigned before Caiphas, not before Annas. A very few among the early authorities consequently put verse 24 immediately after verse 13. But it is more likely that verse 24 is simply a delayed foot-note. St. John, who wrote his gospel as a very old man, often gives details about names, times and places as a kind of afterthought; cf. i. 24, 39, iv. 8, v. 9, vi. 23, vii. 45, ix. 14, xi. 5, and verse 5 above.
vv. 28-40. Matthew xxvii. 1, Mark xv. 1, Luke xxiii. 1.

v. 32. See Matthew xx. 19 and elsewhere.

Chapter Nineteen

vv. 1-42. Matthew
xxvii. 27, Mark xv.
18, Luke xxiii. 33.

THEN PILATE TOOK Jesus and scourged him. 2 And the soldiers put on his head a crown which they had woven out of thorns, and dressed him in a scarlet cloak; 3 they would come up to him and say, Hail, king of the Jews, and then strike him on the face. 4 And now Pilate went out again, and said, See, I am bringing him out to you, to show that I cannot find any fault in him. 5 Then, as Jesus came out, still wearing the crown of thorns and the scarlet cloak, he said to them, See, here is the man. 6 When the chief priests and their officers saw him, they cried out, Crucify him, crucify him. Take him yourselves, said Pilate, and crucify him; I cannot find any fault in him. 7 The Jews answered, We have our own law, and by our law he ought to die, for pretending to be the Son of God. 8 When Pilate heard this said, he was more afraid than ever; 9 going back into the palace, he asked Jesus, Whence hast thou come? But Jesus gave him no answer. 10 What, said Pilate, hast thou no word for me? Dost thou not know that I have power to crucify thee, and power to release thee? 11 Jesus answered, Thou wouldst not have any power over me at all, if it had not been given thee from above. That is why the man who gave me up to thee is more guilty yet. 12 After this, Pilate was for releasing him, but the Jews went on crying out, Thou art no friend to Caesar, if thou dost release him; the man who pretends to be a king is Caesar's rival. 13 When Pilate heard them speak thus, he brought Jesus out, and sat down on the judgement seat, in a place which is called Lithostrotos; its Hebrew name is Gabbatha. 14 It was now about the sixth hour, on the eve of the paschal feast. See, he said to the Jews, here is your king. 15 But they cried out, Away with him, away with him, crucify him. What, Pilate said to them, shall I crucify your king? We have no king, the chief priests answered, except Caesar. 16 Thereupon he gave Jesus up into their hands, to be crucified: and they, once he was in their hands, led him away.

17 So Jesus went out, carrying his own cross, to the place

v. 11. St. Augustine
seems to give the
clearest account of
the meaning here;
namely that Pilate
exercised, as the del-
egate of Caesar, an
authority given him
from above, and con-
sented to a miscar-
riage of justice only
through fear of of-
fending that author-
ity (cf. verse 12).
He is therefore less
guilty than the man
who handed our Lord
over to him; this
may mean either Ju-
das or Caiphas.

v. 13. Lithostrótos,
in Greek, means pav-
ed with stone; the
meaning of Gabbatha
is uncertain.

v. 14. 'About the
sixth hour'; that is
to say, getting on to-
wards noon; see note
on Mark xv. 25.

named after a skull; its Hebrew name is Golgotha. 18 There they crucified him, and with him two others, one on each side with Jesus in the midst. 19 And Pilate wrote out a proclamation, which he put on the cross; it ran, Jesus of Nazareth, the king of the Jews. 20 This proclamation was read by many of the Jews, since the place where Jesus was crucified was close to the city; it was written in Hebrew, Greek, and Latin. 21 And the Jewish chief priests said to Pilate, Thou shouldst not write, The king of the Jews; thou shouldst write, This man said, I am the king of the Jews. 22 Pilate's answer was, What I have written, I have written. 23 The soldiers, when they had crucified Jesus, took up his garments, which they divided into four shares, one share for each soldier. They took up his cloak, too, which was without seam, woven from the top throughout; 24 so they said to one another, Better not to tear it; let us cast lots to decide whose it shall be. This was in fulfilment of the passage in scripture which says, They divide my spoils among them; cast lots for my clothing. So it was, then, that the soldiers occupied themselves; 25 and meanwhile his mother, and his mother's sister, Mary the wife of Cleophas, and Mary Magdalen, had taken their stand beside the cross of Jesus. 26 And Jesus, seeing his mother there, and the disciple, too, whom he loved, standing by, said to his mother, Woman, this is thy son. 27 Then he said to the disciple, This is thy mother. And from that hour the disciple took her into his own keeping.

28 And now Jesus knew well that all was achieved which the scripture demanded for its accomplishment; and he said, I am thirsty. 29 There was a jar there full of vinegar; so they filled a sponge with the vinegar and put it on a stick of hyssop, and brought it close to his mouth. 30 Jesus drank the vinegar, and said, It is achieved. Then he bowed his head, and yielded up his spirit.

31 The Jews would not let the bodies remain crucified on the sabbath, because that sabbath day was a solemn one; and since it was now the eve, they asked Pilate that the bodies might have their legs broken, and be taken away. 32 And so the soldiers came and broke the legs both of the one and of the other that were crucified with him; 33 but when they came to Jesus, and found him already dead, they did not break his legs, 34 but one of the soldiers opened his side with a spear; and immediately blood and water flowed out. 35 He who saw it has borne his witness; and his witness is worthy of trust. He tells what he knows to be the truth, that you, like him, may learn to believe. 36 This was so

v. 24. Ps. xxi. 19.

v. 25. It is not clear here whether three women are alluded to, or four. It seems unlikely that our Lady should have had a sister of the same name, but it is possible that she was in fact a cousin or sister-in-law. Mary of Cleophas is probably the same as Mary the mother of James and Joseph (Matthew xxvii. 56).

v. 28. This verse may also be construed, 'Jesus knew well that all was achieved, and he said, I am thirsty, in order that the scripture might be accomplished'. In that case, the reference is to Ps. lxviii. 22.

v. 36. Ex. xii. 46, Ps. xxxiii. 21.

v. 37. Zach. xii. 10.

ordained to fulfil what is written, You shall not break a single bone of his. 37 And again, another passage in scripture says, They will look upon the man whom they have pierced.

38 After this Joseph of Arimathea, who was a disciple of Jesus, but in secret, for fear of the Jews, asked Pilate to let him take away the body of Jesus. Pilate gave him leave; so he came and took Jesus' body away; 39 and with him was Nicodemus, the same who made his first visit to Jesus by night; he brought with him a mixture of myrrh and aloes, of about a hundred pounds' weight. 40 They took Jesus' body, then, and wrapped it in winding-cloths with the spices; that is how the Jews prepare a body for burial. 41 In the same quarter where he was crucified there was a garden, with a new tomb in it, one in which no man had ever yet been buried. 42 Here, since the tomb was close at hand, they laid Jesus, because of the Jewish feast on the morrow.

v. 42. 'Because of the Jewish feast'; St. John seems to imply that the burial was only provisional, allowing for the possibility of a reinterment later on.

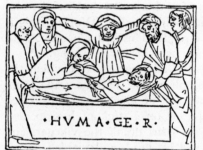

·HVM A·GE·R·

Chapter Twenty

v. 1. This seems to be the same visit as that recorded in Matthew xxviii. 1, Mark xvi. 1, Luke xxiv. 1; that Mary Magdalen was not alone, is implied by the words 'we cannot tell' in v. 2. St. Mark tells us that the women came to the tomb at sunrise; it seems therefore that St. John must have dated their visit from the moment, some time earlier, when they began their preparations for the journey.

EARLY IN THE MORNING on the first day of the week, while it was still dark, Mary Magdalen went to the tomb, and found the stone moved away from the tomb door. 2 So she came running to Simon Peter, and that other disciple, whom Jesus loved; They have carried the Lord away from the tomb, she said to them, and we cannot tell where they have taken him. 3 Upon this, Peter and the other disciple both set out, and made their way to the tomb; 4 they began running side by side, but the other disciple outran Peter, and reached the tomb first. 5 He looked in and saw the linen cloths lying there, but he did not go in. 6 Simon Peter, coming up after him, went into the tomb and saw the linen cloths lying there, 7 and also the veil which had been put over Jesus' head, not lying with the linen cloths, but still wrapped round and round in a place by itself. 8 Then the other disciple, who had reached the tomb first, also went in, and saw this, and learned to believe. 9 They had not yet mastered what was written of him, that he was to rise from the dead. 10 The disciples went back home; 11 but Mary stood without before the tomb, weeping. And she bent down, still weeping, and looked into the tomb; 12 and saw two angels clothed in white sitting there, one at the head, and the other at the feet, where the body of Jesus had lain. 13 They said to her, Woman, why art thou weeping? Because they have carried away my Lord, she said, and I cannot tell where they have taken him. 14 Saying this, she turned round, and saw Jesus standing there, without knowing that it was Jesus. 15 Woman, Jesus said to her, why art thou weeping? For whom art thou searching? She supposed that it must be the gardener, and said to him, If it is thou, Sir, that hast carried him off, tell me where thou hast put him, and I will take him away. 16 Jesus said to her, Mary. And she turned and said to him, Rabboni (which is the Hebrew for Master). 17 Then Jesus said, Do not cling to me thus; I have not yet gone up to my Father's side. Return to my brethren, and tell them this; I am going up to him who is my Father and your Father, who is my God and your God.

18 So Mary Magdalen brought news to the disciples, of how she had seen the Lord, and he had spoken thus to her. 19 And now it was evening on the same day, the first day of the week; for fear of the Jews, the disciples had locked the doors of the room in which they had assembled; and Jesus came, and stood there in their midst; Peace be upon you, he said. 20 And with that, he shewed them his hands and his side. Thus the disciples saw the Lord, and were glad. 21 Once more Jesus said to them, Peace be upon you; I came upon an errand from my Father, and now I am sending you out in my turn. 22 With that, he breathed on them, and said to them, Receive the Holy Spirit; 23 when you forgive men's sins, they are forgiven, when you hold them bound, they are held bound.

24 There was one of the twelve, Thomas, who is also called Didymus, who was not with them when Jesus came. 25 And when the other disciples told him, We have seen the Lord, he said to them, Until I have seen the mark of the nails on his hands, until I have put my finger into the mark of the nails, and put my hand into his side, you will never make me believe. 26 So, eight days afterwards, once more the disciples were within, and Thomas was with them; and the doors were locked. Jesus came and stood there in their midst; Peace be upon you, he said. 27 Then he

vv. 11-14. This appearance of the angels cannot be the same as that recorded by the other Evangelists. On the other hand, the appearance of our Lord to St. Mary Magdalen may be the same as that recorded in Matthew xxviii. 9; or the other women may have seen our Lord somewhat later. St. Mark records the appearance to St. Mary Magdalen, xvi. 9.

vv. 19-23. Mark xvi. 14, Luke xxiv. 36.

said to Thomas, Let me have thy finger; see, here are my hands. Let me have thy hand; put it into my side. Cease thy doubting, and believe. 28 Thomas answered, Thou art my Lord and my God. 29 And Jesus said to him, Thou hast learned to believe, Thomas, because thou hast seen me. Blessed are those who have not seen, and yet have learned to believe.

30 There are many other miracles Jesus did in the presence of his disciples, which are not written down in this book; 31 so much has been written down, that you may learn to believe Jesus is the Christ, the Son of God, and so believing find life through his name.

Chapter
Twenty=one

JESUS APPEARED TO HIS disciples again afterwards, at the sea of Tiberias, and this is how he appeared to them. 2 Simon Peter was there, and with him were Thomas, who is also called Didymus, and Nathanael, from Cana of Galilee, and the sons of Zebedee, and two more of his disciples. 3 Simon Peter told them, I am going out fishing; and they said, We, too, will go with thee. So they went out and embarked on the boat; and all that night they caught nothing. 4 But when morning came, there was Jesus standing on the shore; only the disciples did not know that it was Jesus. 5 Have you caught anything, friends, Jesus asked them, to season your bread with? And when they answered No, 6 he said to them, Cast to the right of the boat, and you will have a catch. So they cast the net, and found before long they had no strength to haul it in, such a shoal of fish was in it. 7 Whereupon the disciple whom Jesus loved said to Peter, It is the Lord. And Simon Peter, hearing him say that it was the

Lord, girded up the fisherman's coat, which was all he wore, and sprang into the sea. 8 The other disciples followed in the boat (they were not far from land, only some hundred yards away), dragging their catch in the net behind them. 9 So they went ashore, and found a charcoal fire made there, with fish and bread cooking on it. 10 Bring some of the fish you have just caught, Jesus said to them: and Simon Peter, going on board, hauled in the net to land. 11 It was loaded with great fish, a hundred and fifty three of them; and with all that number the net had not broken. 12 When Jesus said to them, Come and break your fast, none of the disciples ventured to ask him, Who art thou? knowing well that it was the Lord. 13 So Jesus came up and took bread, which he gave to them, and fish as well. 14 Thus Jesus appeared to his disciples a third time after his rising from the dead.

15 And when they had eaten, Jesus said to Simon Peter, Simon, son of John, dost thou care for me more than these others? Yes, Lord, he told him, thou knowest well that I love thee. And he said to him, Feed my lambs. 16 And again, a second time, he asked him, Simon, son of John, dost thou care for me? Yes, Lord, he told him, thou knowest well that I love thee. He said to him, Tend my shearlings. 17 Then he asked him a third question, Simon, son of John, dost thou love me? Peter was deeply moved when he was asked a third time, Dost thou love me? and said to him, Lord, thou knowest all things; thou canst tell that I love thee. Jesus said to him, Feed my sheep. 18 Believe me when I tell thee this; as a young man, thou wouldst gird thyself and walk where thou hadst the will to go, but when thou hast grown old, another shall gird thee, and carry thee where thou goest, not of thy own will. 19 So much he told him, prophesying the death by which he was to glorify God; and with that he said to him, Follow me. 20 Peter turned, and saw the disciple whom Jesus loved following him; the same who leaned back on his breast at supper and asked, Who is it that is to betray thee? 21 Seeing him, Peter asked Jesus, And what of this man, Lord? 22 Jesus said to him, If it is my will that he should wait till I come, what is it to thee? Do thou follow me. 23 That was why the story went round among the brethren that this disciple was not to die. But Jesus did not say, He is not to die; he said, If it is my will that he should wait till I come, what is it to thee? 24 It is the same disciple that bears witness of all this and has written the story of it; and

v. 12. It would seem that our Lord made himself strange to his apostles here, as he did to the two disciples on the road to Emmaus (Luke xxiv. 16, Mark xvi. 12); yet the miracle, or something else about his manner of action, convinced them from the first that it was he and no other. We are perhaps meant to understand that they 'recognized him when he broke bread', as in Luke xxiv. 35.

v. 16. Some of the Greek manuscripts here have 'my sheep', others 'my little sheep'; it would seem that the second reading was accepted by the Latin, which translates 'lambs', here as in verse 15. Probably our Lord meant yearling sheep, which would need to be tended, that is, led out to pasture, with greater care than the others.

211

we know well that his witness is truthful. 25 There is much else besides that Jesus did; if all of it were put in writing, I do not think the world itself would contain the books which would have to be written.

The ACTS OF THE APOSTLES

Chapter One

THE FIRST BOOK WHICH
I wrote, Theophilus, was con-
cerned with all that Jesus set out to do and teach, 2 until the day
came when he was taken up into heaven. He then laid a charge, by
the power of the Holy Spirit, on the apostles whom he had chosen.
3 He had shewn them by many proofs that he was still alive, after
his passion; throughout the course of forty days he had been appearing to them, and telling them about the kingdom of God;
4 and now he gave them orders, as he shared a meal with them, not
to leave Jerusalem, but to wait there for the fulfilment of the
Father's promise. You have heard it, he said, from my own lips;
5 John's baptism, I told you, was with water, but there is a baptism
with the Holy Spirit which you are to receive, not many days from
this.

6 And his companions asked him, Lord, dost thou mean to restore
the dominion to Israel here and now? 7 But he told them, It is not
for you to know the times and seasons which the Father has fixed
by his own authority. 8 Enough for you, that the Holy Spirit will
come upon you, and you will receive strength from him; you are
to be my witnesses in Jerusalem and throughout Judaea, in Samaria,

*v. 1. St. Luke says
'the first', not 'the
former', which has
made some commen-
tators think that he
intended to write
three books altogeth-
er, but this inference
is uncertain.*

*vv. 6-9. Mark xvi.
19, Luke xxiv. 50.*

213

yes, and to the ends of the earth. 9 When he had said this, they saw him lifted up, and a cloud caught him away from their sight. 10 And as they strained their eyes towards heaven, to watch his journey, all at once two men in white garments were standing at their side. 11 Men of Galilee, they said, why do you stand here looking heavenwards? He who has been taken from you into heaven, this same Jesus, will come back in the same fashion, just as you have watched him going into heaven. 12 Then, from the mountain which is called Olivet, they went back to Jerusalem; the distance from Jerusalem is not great, a sabbath day's journey. 13 Coming in, they went up into the upper room where they dwelt, Peter and John, James and Andrew, Philip and Thomas, Bartholomew and Matthew, James the son of Alphaeus and Simon the Zealot, and Judas the brother of James. 14 All these, with one mind, gave themselves up to prayer, together with Mary the mother of Jesus, and the rest of the women and his brethren.

15 At this time, Peter stood up and spoke before all the brethren; a company of about a hundred and twenty were gathered there. 16 Brethren, he said, there is a prophecy in scripture that must needs be fulfilled; that which the Holy Spirit made, by the lips of David, about Judas, who shewed the way to the men that arrested Jesus. 17 Judas was counted among our number, and had been given a share in this ministry of ours. 18 (With the price of his treachery, this man came into possession of a field; and afterwards, when he fell from a height, and his belly burst open, so that he was disembowelled, 19 all Jerusalem heard of it, and the field came to be called, in their language, Haceldama, that is, the Field of Blood.) Well, in the book of Psalms the words are written, Let their camping-place be deserted, and let no man be found to dwell in it. And again, Let another take over his office. 21 There are men who have walked in our company all through the time when the Lord Jesus came and went among us, 22 from the time when John used to baptize to the day when he, Jesus, was taken from us. One of these ought to be added to our number as a witness of his resurrection. 23 So they named two of them, Joseph called Barsabbas, who had been given the fresh name of Justus, and Matthias. 24 And they offered this prayer, Lord, who knowest the hearts of all men, shew us which of these two thou hast chosen 25 to take his place in this work of apostleship, from which Judas has fallen away, and gone to the place which belonged to him. 26 They gave them lots; and the lot fell upon Matthias, and he took rank with the eleven apostles.

v. 14. See note on Mark xvi. 7.

vv. 18-19. These words may be part of St. Peter's speech, but are more easily understood as a note by the author. From a comparison of them with Matthew xxvii. 5 and following, it must be inferred that Judas attempted to hang himself by jumping over the edge of a precipice, and that the rope broke or slipped with the result here described.

v. 20. Ps. lxviii. 26, cviii. 8.

214

THE BAPTISM OF CHRIST

GIOVANNI BARONZIO
active around 1344-45

NATIONAL GALLERY OF ART, WASHINGTON, D. C. (KRESS COLLECTION)

Chapter Two

WHEN THE DAY OF Pentecost came round, while they were all gathered together in unity of purpose, 2 all at once a sound came from heaven like that of a strong wind blowing, and filled the whole house where they were sitting. 3 Then appeared to them what seemed to be tongues of fire, which parted and came to rest on each of them; 4 and they were all filled with the Holy Spirit, and began to speak in strange languages, as the Spirit gave utterance to each. 5 Among those who were dwelling in Jerusalem at this time were devout Jews from every country under heaven; 6 so, when the noise of this went abroad, the crowd which gathered was in bewilderment; each man severally heard them speak in his own language. 7 And they were all beside themselves with astonishment; Are they not all Galileans speaking? they asked. 8 How is it that each of us hears them talking his own native tongue? 9 There are Parthians among us, and Medes, and Elamites; our homes are in Mesopotamia, or Judaea, or Cappadocia; in Pontus or Asia, 10 Phrygia or Pamphylia, Egypt or the parts of Libya round Cyrene; some of us are visitors from Rome, some of us are Jews and others proselytes; 11 there are Cretans among us too, and Arabians; and each has been hearing them tell of God's wonders in his own language. 12 So they were all beside themselves with perplexity, and asked one another, What can this mean? 13 There were others who said, mockingly, They have had their fill of new wine.

14 But Peter, with the eleven apostles at his side, stood there and raised his voice to speak to them; Men of Judaea, he said, and all you who are dwelling in Jerusalem, I must tell you this; listen to what I have to say. 15 These men are not drunk, as you suppose; it is only the third hour of the day. 16 This is what was foretold by the prophet Joel: 17 In the last times, God says, I will pour out my spirit upon all mankind, and your sons and daughters will be prophets. Your young men shall see visions, and your old men shall dream dreams; 18 and I will pour out my spirit in those days

v. 4. 'Strange', or, according to some Latin manuscripts, 'various' languages.

v. 5. It is not clear whether the people here mentioned were Jews who had been born abroad but now lived in Jerusalem, or Jews from abroad who were staying in Jerusalem for the feast. They were in any case bi-lingual, being conversant with the native speech, or perhaps with the various Greek dialects, spoken in the countries to which they belonged.

v. 9. It is not certain in what sense the word 'Judaea' is here used; some have thought that it was written by an early copyist in mistake for 'Lydia', or some other distant province.

v. 17. Joel ii. 28.

215

upon my servants and handmaids, so that they will prophesy. 19 I will shew wonders in heaven above, and signs on the earth beneath, v. 20. The Hebrew has 'terrible' instead of 'glorious'. blood and fire and whirling smoke; 20 the sun will be turned into darkness and the moon into blood, before the day of the Lord comes, great and glorious. 21 And then everyone who calls on the name of the Lord shall be saved. 22 Men of Israel, listen to this. Jesus of Nazareth was a man duly accredited to you from God; such were the miracles and wonders and signs which God did through him in your midst, as you yourselves well know. 23 This man you have put to death; by God's fixed design and foreknowledge, he was betrayed to you, and you, through the hands of sinful men, have cruelly murdered him. 24 But God raised him up again, releasing him from the pangs of death; it was impossible that death v. 25. Ps. xv. 8. should have the mastery over him. 25 It is in his person that David says, Always I can keep the Lord within sight; always he is at my right hand, to make me stand firm. 26 So there is gladness in my heart, and rejoicing on my lips; my body, too, shall rest in confidence 27 that thou wilt not leave my soul in the place of death, or allow thy faithful servant to see corruption. 28 Thou hast shewn me the way of life; thou wilt make me full of gladness in thy presence. 29 My brethren, I can say this to you about the patriarch David without fear of contradiction, that he did die, and was buried, and his tomb is among us to this day. 30 But he was a prophet, and he knew God had promised him on oath that he would set the sons of his body upon his throne; 31 it was of the Christ he said, foreseeing his resurrection, that he was not left in the place of death, and that his body did not see corruption. 32 God, then, has raised up this man, Jesus, from the dead; we are all witnesses of it. 33 And now, exalted at God's right hand, he has claimed from his Father his promise to bestow the Holy Spirit; and he has poured out that Spirit, as you can see and hear for yourselves. v. 34. Ps. cix. 1. 34 David never went up to heaven, and yet David has told us, The Lord said to my Master, Sit on my right hand, 35 while I make thy enemies a footstool under thy feet. 36 Let it be known, then, beyond doubt, to all the house of Israel, that God has made him Master and Christ, this Jesus whom you crucified.

37 When they heard this, their consciences were stung; and they asked Peter and his fellow apostles, Brethren, what must we do? 38 Repent, Peter said to them, and be baptized, every one of you, in the name of Jesus Christ, to have your sins forgiven; then you will receive the gift of the Holy Spirit. 39 This promise is for you and for your children, and for all those, however far away, whom

the Lord our God calls to himself. 40 And he used many more words besides, urgently appealing to them; Save yourselves, he said, from this false-minded generation. 41 So all those who had taken his words to heart were baptized, and about three thousand souls were won for the Lord that day. 42 These occupied themselves continually with the apostles' teaching, their fellowship in the breaking of bread, and the fixed times of prayer, 43 and every soul was struck with awe, so many were the wonders and signs performed by the apostles in Jerusalem. 44 All the faithful held together, and shared all they had, 45 selling their possessions and their means of livelihood, so as to distribute to all, as each had need. 46 They persevered with one accord, day by day, in the Temple worship, and, as they broke bread in this house or that, took their share of food with gladness and simplicity of heart, 47 praising God, and winning favour with all the people. And each day the Lord added to their fellowship others that were to be saved.

v. 42. The Greek has 'the apostles' teaching and fellowship, and the breaking of bread, and (the) prayers'.

Chapter Three

PETER AND JOHN WERE going up to the temple at the ninth hour, which is an hour of prayer, 2 when a man was carried by who had been lame from birth. Every day he was put down at what is called the Beautiful Gate of the temple, so that he could beg alms from the temple visitors. 3 And he asked Peter and John, as he saw them on their way into the temple, if he might have alms from them. 4 Peter fastened his eyes on him, as John did too, and said, Turn towards us; 5 and he looked at them attentively, hoping that something would be given him. 6 Then Peter said to him, Silver and gold are not mine to give, I give thee what I can. In the name of Jesus Christ of Nazareth, rise up and walk. 7 So, taking him by his right hand, he lifted him up; and with that, strength came to his feet and ankles; 8 he sprang up, and began walking, and went into the temple with them, walking, and leaping, and giving praise to God. 9 All the people, as they saw him walking and praising God, 10 recognized him for the man who used to sit begging at the Beautiful Gate of the temple, and were full of wonder and bewilderment at what had befallen him. 11 And he would not let go of Peter and John, so that all the crowd gathered about them in what is called Solomon's Porch, beside themselves with wonder.

12 Peter, when he saw it, addressed himself to the people; Men of Israel, he said, why does this astonish you? Why do you fasten your eyes on us, as if we had enabled him to walk through some power or virtue of our own? 13 It is the God of Abraham and Isaac and Jacob, the God of our forefathers, who has thus brought honour to his Son Jesus. You gave him up, and disowned him in the presence of Pilate, when Pilate's voice was for setting him free. 14 You disowned the holy, the just, and asked for the pardon of a murderer, 15 while you killed the author of life. But God has raised him up again from the dead, and we are here to bear witness of it. 16 Here is a man you all know by sight, who has put his faith in that name, and that name has brought him strength; it is the faith which comes through Jesus that has restored him to full health in the sight of you all. 17 Come then, brethren, I know that you, like your rulers, acted in ignorance; 18 but God has fulfilled in this way what was foretold by all the prophets about the sufferings of his Christ. 19 Repent, then, and turn back to him, to have your sins effaced, 20 against the day when the Lord sees fit to refresh our hearts. Then he will send out Jesus Christ, who has now been made known to you, 21 but must have his dwelling-place in heaven until the time when all is restored anew, the time which God has spoken of by his holy prophets from the beginning. 22 Thus, Moses said, The Lord your God will raise up for you a prophet like myself, from among your own brethren; to him, to every word of his, you must listen. 23 It is ordained that everyone who will not listen to the voice of that prophet shall be lost to his people. 24 And all the prophets who spoke to you, from Samuel onwards, have foretold those days. 25 You are the heirs of the prophets, and of the covenant which God made with our fathers, when he said to Abraham, Every race on earth shall receive a blessing through thy posterity. 26 It is to you first of all that God has sent his Son, whom he raised up from the dead to bring you a blessing, to turn away every one of you from his sins.

v. 20. 'Against the day when'; the Greek here may mean 'in order that the time may come', or possibly, 'when the time comes'. The Latin, apparently by an error, has 'in order that when the time comes', which spoils the grammar of the sentence.

v. 23. Deut. xviii. 15.

Chapter Four

BEFORE THEY HAD FIN
ished speaking to the crowd, they
were interrupted by the chief priests, the temple superintendent,
and the Sadducees. 2 These, indignant at their teaching the multitude and proclaiming the resurrection of Jesus from the dead, 3 laid
hands on them, and put them in prison (for it was already evening)
until the next day. 4 (Meanwhile, many of those who had listened
to their preaching had joined the believers, so that their numbers
had now risen to five thousand men.) 5 On the next day, there
was a gathering of the rulers and elders and scribes in Jerusalem;
6 the high priest Annas was there, and Caiphas, and John, and
Alexander, and all those who belonged to the high-priestly family.
7 And they had Peter and John brought into their presence, and
asked them, By what power, in whose name, have such men as you
done this? 8 Then Peter was filled with the Holy Spirit, and said
to them, Rulers of the people, elders of Israel, listen to me. 9 If it
is over kindness done to a cripple, and the means by which he has
been restored, that we are called in question, 10 here is news for
you and for the whole people of Israel. You crucified Jesus Christ,
the Nazarene, and God raised him from the dead; it is through his
name that this man stands before you restored. 11 He is that stone,
rejected by you, the builders, that has become the chief stone at
the corner. 12 Salvation is not to be found elsewhere; this alone
of all the names under heaven has been appointed to men as the one
by which we must needs be saved.

13 Seeing the boldness of Peter and John, and discovering that
they were simple men, without learning, they were astonished,
and recognized them now as having been in Jesus' company.
14 They could find no answer to make, with the man who had been
healed standing there beside them; 15 so they ordered them out of
the council-chamber, and conferred together. 16 What are we to
do with these men? they asked. It is commonly known among all
the people of Jerusalem that a notable miracle has been done by
their means, and we are powerless to deny it. 17 But the news must
not spread any further; we must deter them by threats from

v. 6. It was Caiphas,
not Annas, who was
high priest at this
time; but St. Luke
seems to have re-
garded Annas as
somehow associated
with his son-in-law
in the exercise of
the office; cf. Luke
iii. 2.

v. 8. Cf. Matthew
x. 20.

v. 11. Ps. cxvii. 22.
Cf. Matthew xxi. 42,
I Peter ii. 7.

preaching to anybody in this man's name again. 18 So they called them in, and warned them not to utter a word or give any teaching in the name of Jesus. 19 At this, Peter and John answered them, Judge for yourselves whether it would be right for us, in the sight of God, to listen to your voice instead of God's. 20 It is impossible for us to refrain from speaking of what we have seen and heard. 21 And they, after threatening them further, let them go; they could find no means of punishing them, because all the people were exclaiming at the astonishing circumstances of what had befallen; 22 the man in whom this miracle of healing had taken place was more than forty years old.

23 Now that they were set free, they went back to their company, and told them all the chief priests and elders had said. 24 And they, when they heard it, uttered prayer to God with one accord; Ruler of all, thou art the maker of heaven and earth and the sea, and all that is in them. 25 Thou hast said through thy holy Spirit, by the lips of thy servant David, our father, What means this turmoil among the nations; why do the peoples cherish vain dreams? 26 See how the kings of the earth stand in array, how its rulers make common cause, against the Lord and his Christ. 27 True enough, in this city of ours, Herod and Pontius Pilate, with the Gentiles and the people of Israel to aid them, made common cause against thy holy servant Jesus, 28 so accomplishing all that thy power and wisdom had decreed. 29 Look down upon their threats, Lord, now as of old; enable thy servants to preach thy word confidently, 30 by stretching out thy hand to heal; and let signs and miracles be performed in the name of Jesus, thy holy Son. 31 When they had finished praying, the place in which they had gathered rocked to and fro, and they were all filled with the Holy Spirit, and began to preach the word of God with confidence.

32 There was one heart and soul in all the company of believers; none of them called any of his possessions his own, everything was shared in common. 33 Great was the power with which the apostles testified to the resurrection of our Lord Jesus Christ, and great was the grace that rested on them all. 34 None of them was destitute; all those who owned farms or houses used to sell them, and bring the price of what they had sold 35 to lay it at the apostles' feet, so that each could have what share of it he needed. 36 There was a Levite called Joseph, a Cypriot by birth, to whom the apostle gave the fresh name of Barnabas, which means, the man of encouragement; 37 he had an estate, which he sold, and brought the purchase-money to lay it at the apostles' feet.

v. 21. 'Exclaiming at the astonishing circumstances of'; the Greek manuscripts have 'praising God over'.

v. 25. Ps. ii. 1.

Chapter Five

BUT THERE WAS A MAN called Ananias who, with his wife Sapphira, sold an estate, 2 and kept back some of the money, with his wife's knowledge, only bringing a part of it to lay at the feet of the apostles. 3 Whereupon Peter said, Ananias, how is it that Satan has taken possession of thy heart, bidding thee defraud the Holy Spirit by keeping back some of the money that was paid thee for the land? 4 Unsold, the property was thine; after the sale, the money was at thy disposal; what has put it into thy heart so to act? It is God, not man, thou hast defrauded. 5 At these words, Ananias fell down and died; and a great fear came upon all those who heard it. 6 So the young men rose up and took him up, and carried him out to burial. 7 It was about three hours later that his wife came in, knowing nothing of what had happened; 8 and Peter said to her, Tell me, woman, was it for so much that you sold the estate? Yes, she said, for so much. 9 Then Peter said to her, What is this conspiracy between you, to put the Spirit of the Lord to the test? Even now I hear at the door the footsteps of those who have been burying thy husband; they will carry thee out too. 10 And all at once she fell at his feet and died; so that when the young men came in they found her a corpse, and carried her out to bury her with her husband. 11 Great fear came upon the church and upon all who heard the story. 12 And there were many signs and miracles done by the apostles before the people. 13 They used to gather with one accord in Solomon's porch. No one else dared to join them, (although the people held them in high honour, 14 and the number of those who believed in the Lord, both men and women, still increased), 15 but they used to bring sick folk into the streets, and lay them down there on beds and pallets, in the hope that even the shadow of Peter might fall upon one of them here and there, as he passed by, and so they would be healed of their infirmities. 16 From neighbouring cities, too, the common people flocked to Jerusalem, bringing with them the sick and those who were troubled by unclean spirits; and all of them were cured.

vv. 13-15. It cannot be decided with certainty whether 'no one else' refers to other Christians or to those outside the Church, and what was the fear which kept them at a distance.

221

17 This roused the high priest and those who thought with him, that is, the party of the Sadducees. 18 Full of indignation, they arrested the apostles and shut them up in the common gaol. 19 But, in the night, an angel of the Lord came and opened the prison doors, and led them out; 20 Go, he said, and take your stand in the temple; preach fully to the people the message of true life. 21 So, at his word, they went into the temple at dawn, and began preaching. Meanwhile the high priest and his followers met, and summoned the Council, with all the elders of the Jewish people; and they sent to the prison-house to have them brought in. 22 When they came to look in the prison, the officers could not find them there; so they went back and reported, 23 We found the prison-house locked up with all due care, and the guards at their posts before the door; but when we opened it there was no one to be found within. 24 At hearing this, the temple superintendent and the chief priests were at a loss to know what had become of them; 25 until an eye-witness told them, The men you put in prison are standing in the temple, teaching the people there. 26 So the superintendent and his officers went and fetched them, using no violence, because they were afraid of being stoned by the people; 27 and they brought them in and bade them stand before the Council, where the high priest questioned them. 28 We warned you in set terms, he said, not to preach in this man's name, and you have filled all Jerusalem with your preaching; you are determined to lay this man's death at our door. 29 Peter and the other apostles answered, God has more right to be obeyed than men. 30 It was the God of our fathers that raised up Jesus, the man you hung on a gibbet to die. 31 It is God that has raised him up to his own right hand, as the prince and Saviour who is to bring Israel repentance, and remission of sins. 32 Of this, we are witnesses; we and the Holy Spirit God gives to all those who obey him.

33 On hearing this they were cut to the quick, and designed to kill them. 34 But now one of the Pharisees in the Council, a lawyer named Gamaliel, who was held in esteem by all the people, rose and bade them send the apostles out for a little; 35 then he said to them, Men of Israel, think well what you mean to do with these men. 36 There was Theodas, who appeared in days gone by and claimed to be someone of importance, and was supported by about four hundred men; he was killed, and all his followers were dispersed, and came to nothing. 37 And after him Judas the Galilean appeared in the days of the registration; he persuaded the people to rebel under his leadership, but he too perished, and all his fol-

v. 20. 'True life'; literally 'this life', but such a translation would imply that 'life' referred to a way of living, whereas the Greek word used applies to a principle of life, namely, the principle of supernatural life which is implanted in us by baptism.

v. 36. This Theodas cannot be the same as the Theudas mentioned by Josephus (Ant. xx. v. 1) as having revolted under Cuspius Fadus (A.D. 44-46) unless Josephus has made an error over dates.

222

THE CALLING OF ST. PETER AND ST. ANDREW   DUCCIO DI BUONINSEGNA
active 1278-1319

NATIONAL GALLERY OF ART, WASHINGTON, D. C. (KRESS COLLECTION)

lowers were scattered. 38 And my advice is still the same; have nothing to do with these men, let them be. If this is man's design or man's undertaking, it will be overthrown; 39 if it is God's, you will have no power to overthrow it. You would not willingly be found fighting against God. And they fell in with his opinion; 40 so they sent for the apostles and, after scourging them, let them go with a warning that they were not on any account to preach in the name of Jesus. 41 And they left the presence of the Council, rejoicing that they had been found worthy to suffer indignity for the sake of Jesus' name. 42 And every day, both in the temple and from house to house, their teaching and their preaching was continually of Jesus Christ.

Chapter Six

 T this time, as the number of the disciples increased, complaints were brought against those who spoke Hebrew by those who spoke Greek; their widows, they said, were neglected in the daily administration of relief. 2 So the twelve called together the general body of the disciples, and said, It is too much that we should have to forgo preaching God's word, and bestow our care upon tables. 3 Come then, brethren, you must find among you seven men who are well spoken of, full of the Holy Spirit and of wisdom, for us to put in charge of this business, 4 while we devote ourselves to prayer, and to the ministry of preaching. 5 This advice found favour with all the assembly; and they chose Stephen, a man who was full of faith and of the Holy Spirit, Philip, Prochorus, Nicanor, Timon, Parmenas, and Nicolas, who was a proselyte from Antioch. 6 These they presented to the apostles, who laid their hands on them with prayer.

v. 1. 'Those who spoke Greek'; that is, Jews who had been brought up outside Palestine, and Gentiles who had become proselytes to the Jewish religion, and afterwards Christians.

7 By now the word of God was gaining influence, and the number of disciples in Jerusalem was greatly increasing; many of the priests had given their allegiance to the faith. 8 And Stephen, full of grace and power, performed great miracles and signs among the people. 9 There were those who came forward to debate with him, some of the synagogue of the Freedmen (as it is called), and

v. 9. 'The Freedmen'; according to some Greek manuscripts, 'the Libyans'.

223

v. 10. Some Latin
manuscripts have 'the
Spirit with which he
spoke', which is the
natural (though not
the only possible)
rendering of the
Greek.

of the Cyreneans and Alexandrians, and of those who came from Cilicia and Asia; 10 but they were no match for Stephen's wisdom, and for the Spirit which then gave utterance. 11 Thereupon they employed agents to say they had heard him speaking blasphemously of Moses, and of God. 12 Having thus roused the feelings of the people, and of the elders and scribes, they set upon him and carried him off, and so brought him before the Council. 13 There they put forward false witnesses, who declared, This man is never tired of uttering insults against the holy place, and the law. 14 We have heard him say that the Nazarene, Jesus, will destroy this place, and will alter the traditions which Moses handed down to us. 15 And all those who sat there in the Council fastened their eyes on him, and saw his face looking like the face of an angel.

Chapter Seven

THEN THE HIGH PRIEST asked, Are these charges true? 2 And he answered, Brethren and fathers, listen to me. When the God of glory appeared to our father Abraham, it was while he was still in Mesopotamia, before he took up his dwelling in Charan.

v. 3. Gen. xii. 1.

3 Leave thy country, he said, and thy kindred, and come to the land to which I direct thee. 4 So it was that he left the country of the Chaldeans, and lived in Charan; it was only after his father's death that he was bidden to remove thence into this land where you now dwell. 5 There, God gave him no inheritance, not so much as a foot's space; he only promised the possession of it to him and to his posterity after him, although at this time he had no child.

vv. 6, 7. Gen. xv.
13; perhaps with a
reminiscence of Ex.
iii. 12 added at the
end.

6 And this is what God told him, that his descendants would live as strangers in a foreign land, where they would be enslaved and ill-used for four hundred years. 7 But I will pass judgement, the Lord said, on the nation which enslaves them; and at last they will

escape, and settle down to worship me here. 8 Then he made a covenant with Abraham, the covenant that ordained circumcision. So it was that he became the father of Isaac, whom he circumcised seven days afterwards, and Isaac of Jacob, and Jacob of the twelve patriarchs.

9 The patriarchs, out of jealousy, sold Joseph as a slave, to be taken to Egypt. In Egypt, God was with him; 10 he rescued him from all his afflictions, and won him favour and a name for wisdom with Pharao, king of Egypt, who made him ruler over Egypt and over all the royal household. 11 And now a famine came upon all Egypt and Chanaan, cruelly afflicting them, till our fathers could procure no food. 12 So Jacob, hearing that there was corn in Egypt, sent out our fathers on their first journey; 13 and on their second journey Joseph made himself known to them, and Pharao learned about Joseph's kindred. 14 Then Joseph sent for his father Jacob, and for his family, seventy-five souls in all; 15 and Jacob went down into Egypt, where he and our fathers died. 16 They were removed afterwards to Sichem; and it was in the grave which Abraham had bought for a sum of money from the sons of Hemor, the man of Sichem, that they were buried.

17 And when the time drew near for the fulfilment of the promise which God had made to Abraham, the people had increased and multiplied in Egypt. 18 And now a new king arose in Egypt, one who knew nothing of Joseph; 19 this king dealt treacherously with our race, using them so ill that they exposed their children, instead of rearing them. 20 It was at this time that Moses was born, and, finding favour with God, was brought up in his father's house for three months; 21 then, when he had been exposed, he was rescued by Pharao's daughter, who adopted him as her son. 22 Thus Moses was well trained in all the learning of the Egyptians; he was vigorous, too, in speech and in act. 23 And now, when he had reached forty years of age, it came into his mind to visit his brethren, the children of Israel. 24 When he saw one of them being unjustly used, he came to the rescue and avenged the man who was wronged, by killing the Egyptian. 25 He expected them to understand, but they could not understand, that he was the means by which God was to bring them deliverance. 26 Next day, he came in sight when two of them were quarrelling, and tried to restore peace between them; Sirs, he said, you are brethren; why do you inflict injury on one another? 27 Whereupon the man who was doing his neighbour a wrong thrust him aside, asking, Who made thee a ruler and a judge over us? 28 Art thou ready

v. 16. There is a discrepancy between this account and that given in Genesis, which suggests either that St. Stephen's memory played him false in the course of an extempore speech, or that there was some early corruption in the text. According to Gen. l. 13, Jacob was buried in the grave bought by Abraham at Hebron, not at Sichem. Joseph was buried at Sichem (Josue xxiv. 32).

to kill me, as thou didst kill the Egyptian yesterday? 29 And at that Moses fled, and lived as an exile in the land of Madian; it was there that two sons were born to him.

vv. 30-34. Ex. ii. 2 and following.

30 Forty years later, a vision came to him in the wilderness of mount Sinai; a bush had caught fire; and an angel was standing among the flames. 31 Moses saw it, and was astonished at the sight; and as he drew near to look, the voice of the Lord came to him, 32 I am the God of thy fathers, of Abraham, and Isaac, and Jacob. And Moses did not dare to look close; fear made him tremble. 33 Then the Lord said to him, Take the shoes off thy feet; the place on which thou standest is holy ground. 34 The affliction of my people in Egypt is before my eyes continually; I have heard their lamenting, and have come down to deliver them. Come now, I have an errand for thee in Egypt. 35 It was this same Moses, the man whom they had disowned, and asked him Who made thee a ruler and a judge over us? that God sent to be their ruler and their deliverer, helped by the angel whom he saw there at the bush. 36 He it was who led them out, performing wonders and signs in Egypt, and at the Red Sea, and in the wilderness, over a space of forty years.

v. 37. Deut. xviii. 15.

37 It was this Moses who said to the children of Israel, The Lord your God will raise up for you a prophet like myself, from among your own brethren; to him you must listen. 38 He it was who took part with the angel that spoke to him on mount Sinai, and with our fathers, at the meeting in the desert. There he received words of life to hand on to us; 39 and yet our fathers would not give him obedience. They disowned him; they turned their thoughts towards Egypt, 40 and said to Aaron, Make us gods, to lead our march; as for this Moses, who brought us out of the land of Egypt, there is no saying what has become of him. 41 So they fashioned a calf at this time, making offerings to an idol, and keeping holiday over the works of their own hands. Whereupon God turned away from them, 42 and gave them over to the worship of all the host of heaven; so it is written in the book of the prophets, Is it true that you brought me victims and sacrifices, you sons of Israel, for forty years in the wilderness? 43 You carried about the tent of Moloch, and the star of your god Rempham, and worshipped them, images of your own fashioning. And now I will send you into exile on the further side of Babylon.

v. 40. Ex. xxxii. 1.

vv. 42, 43. Amos v. 25, where, however, there is a difference of reading in the Hebrew. St. Stephen quotes from the Septuagint, but has substituted 'Babylon' for 'Damascus' in the original.

44 In the wilderness, our fathers had the tabernacle with them, to remind them of God's covenant; he who spoke to Moses bade him fashion it after the model which had been shewn him. 45 And when

God dispossessed the Gentiles, to make room for our fathers' coming, our fathers under Josue brought this tabernacle, as an heirloom, into the land which they conquered. So it was until the time of David. 46 David, who had won favour in God's sight, longed to devise a resting-place for the God of Israel, 47 but in the end it was Solomon that built the house for him. 48 Yet we are not to think that the most High dwells in temples made by men's hands; the prophet says: 49 Heaven is my throne, and earth is the footstool under my feet. What home will you build for me, says the Lord, what place can be my resting-place? 50 Was it not my hands that made all this?

vv. 49, 50. Is. lxvi. 1.

51 Stiff-necked race, your heart and ears still uncircumcised, you are for ever resisting the Holy Spirit, just as your fathers did. 52 There was not one of the prophets they did not persecute; it was death to foretell the coming of that just man, whom you in these times have betrayed and murdered; 53 you, who received the law dictated by angels, and did not keep it.

54 At hearing this, they were cut to the heart, and began to gnash their teeth at him. 55 But he, full of the Holy Spirit, fastened his eyes on heaven, and saw there the glory of God, and Jesus standing at God's right hand; I see heaven opening, he said, and the Son of Man standing at the right hand of God. 56 Then they cried aloud, and put their fingers into their ears; with one accord they fell upon him, 57 thrust him out of the city, and stoned him. And the witnesses put down their clothes at the feet of a young man named Saul. 58 Thus they stoned Stephen; he, meanwhile, was praying; Lord Jesus, he said, receive my spirit; 59 and then, kneeling down, he cried aloud, Lord, do not count this sin against them. And with that, he fell asleep in the Lord.

Saul was one of those who gave their voices for his murder.

Chapter Eight

HE church in Jerusalem was much persecuted at this time, and all except the apostles were scattered about over the country-side of Judaea and Samaria. 2 Stephen was buried by devout men, who mourned greatly over him. 3 Saul, meanwhile, was making havoc of the church; he made his way into house after house, carrying men and women off and committing them to prison.

4 Those who had been driven away spread the gospel as they went from place to place; 5 and Philip, who had gone down to one of the cities of Samaria, preached Christ there. 6 The multitude listened with general accord to what Philip said, as their own eyes and ears witnessed the miracles he did. 7 There were many possessed by unclean spirits, and these came out, crying aloud; 8 many, too, were healed of the palsy, and of lameness, 9 and there was great rejoicing in that city. And there was a man called Simon, who had been in the city before Philip came there, misleading the people of Samaria with sorcery, and pretending to have great powers, 10 so that high and low hung upon his words; This, they said, is an angel called the great angel of God. 11 Long misled by his sorceries, they continued to pay attention to him, 12 until Philip came and preached to them about God's kingdom. Then they found faith and were baptized, men and women alike, in the name of Jesus Christ; 13 and Simon, who had found faith and been baptized with the rest, kept close to Philip's side; he was astonished by the great miracles and signs he saw happening.

14 And now the apostles at Jerusalem, hearing that Samaria had received the word of God, sent Peter and John to visit them. 15 So these two came down and prayed for them, that they might receive the Holy Spirit, 16 who had not, as yet, come down on any of them; they had received nothing so far except baptism in the name of the Lord Jesus. 17 Then the apostles began to lay their hands on them, so that the Holy Spirit was given them, 18 and Simon, seeing that the Holy Spirit was granted through the imposition of the apostles' hands, offered them money; 19 Let me too, he said, have such powers that when I lay my hands on anyone he will receive the Holy Spirit. 20 Whereupon Peter said to him, Take thy wealth with thee to perdition, thou who hast told thyself that

God's free gift can be bought with money. 21 There is no share, no part for thee in these doings; thy heart is not true in the sight of God. 22 Repent of this baseness of thine, and pray to God, in the hope of finding pardon for the thought which thy heart has conceived. 23 I see plainly that a bitter poison has taken hold of thee; thou art the bondsman of iniquity. 24 And Simon answered, Pray for me to the Lord, that none of this harm you have spoken of may fall upon me.

25 So, when they had borne their full witness and preached the word of the Lord, they began their journey back to Jerusalem, carrying the gospel into many Samaritan villages. 26 Meanwhile, Philip was commanded by an angel of the Lord, Rise up, and go south to meet the road which leads from Jerusalem to Gaza, out in the desert. 27 So he rose up and went; and found there an Ethiopian. This man was a eunuch, a courtier of Candace, queen of Ethiopia, and had charge of all her wealth; he had been up to worship at Jerusalem, 28 and was now on his way home, driving along in his chariot and reading the prophet Isaias. 29 The Spirit said to Philip, Go up to that chariot and keep close by it. 30 And Philip, as he ran up, heard him reading the prophet Isaias, and asked, Canst thou understand what thou art reading? 31 How could I, said he, without someone to guide me? And he entreated Philip to come up and sit beside him. 32 The passage of scripture which he was reading was this; He was led away like a sheep to be slaughtered; like a lamb that is dumb before its shearer, he would not open his mouth. 33 He was brought low, and all his rights taken away; who shall tell the story of his age? His life is being cut off from the earth. 34 And the eunuch turned to Philip, and said, Tell me, about whom does the prophet say this? 35 Himself, or some other man? Then Philip began speaking, and preached to him about Jesus, taking this passage as his theme. 36 As they went on their way, they came to a piece of water, and the eunuch said, See, there is water here; why may I not be baptized? 37 Philip said, If thou dost believe with all thy heart, thou mayest. And he answered, I believe that Jesus Christ is the Son of God. 38 So he had the chariot stopped, and both of them, Philip and the eunuch, went down into the water, and Philip baptized him there. 39 But when they came up from the water, Philip was carried off by the spirit of the Lord, and the eunuch did not see him any longer; he went on his way rejoicing. 40 As for Philip, he was next heard of at Azotus; and from there he went preaching all round the villages, until he reached Caesarea.

v. 26. Some have supposed that it was the road, not Gaza itself, which was 'deserted'; but it is possible that the old Gaza, destroyed in B.C. 96, is here distinguished from the new Gaza, built in B.C. 58, and destroyed in A.D. 65.

vv. 32, 33. Is. liii. 7. The Hebrew differs in several points from the text of the Septuagint, which is here quoted. Nor is the meaning of the Greek here beyond dispute; some would render 'his condemnation' instead of 'his rights', and 'his posterity' instead of 'his age'.

v. 37. This verse is wanting in some of the Greek, and also in some of the Latin manuscripts.

Chapter Nine

SAUL, WITH EVERY breath he drew, still threatened the disciples of the Lord with massacre; and now he went to the high priest 2 and asked him for letters of commendation to the synagogues at Damascus, so that he could arrest all those he found there, men and women, who belonged to the way, and bring them back to Jerusalem. 3 Then, on his journey, when he was nearly at Damascus, a light from heaven shone suddenly about him. 4 He fell to the ground, and heard a voice saying to him, Saul, Saul, why dost thou persecute me? 5 Who art thou, Lord? he asked. And he said, I am Jesus, whom Saul persecutes. This is a thankless task of thine, kicking against the goad. 6 And he, dazed and trembling, asked, Lord, what wilt thou have me do? Then the Lord said to him, Rise up, and go into the city, and there thou shalt be told what thy work is. 7 His companions stood in bewilderment, hearing the voice speak, but not seeing anyone. 8 When he rose from the ground he could see nothing, although his eyes were open, and they had to lead him by the hand, to take him into Damascus. 9 Here for three days he remained without sight, and neither ate nor drank.

10 There was, in Damascus, a disciple named Ananias; to him the Lord called in a vision, Ananias. Here I am, Lord, he answered. 11 And the Lord said to him, Rise up and go to the road called Straight Street; and enquire at the house of Judas for a man of Tarsus, named Saul. 12 Even now he is at his prayers: and he has had a vision of a man called Ananias coming in and laying hands on him, to cure him of blindness. 13 At this, Ananias answered, Lord, many have told me about this man, and all the hurt he has done to thy saints at Jerusalem; 14 and he has come here with authority from the chief priests to imprison all those who call upon thy name. 15 But the Lord said to him, Go on thy errand; this is a man I have chosen to be the instrument for bringing my name before the heathen and their rulers, and before the people of Israel too. 16 I have yet to tell him, how much suffering he will

v. 2. 'The way'; that is, the Christian profession.

vv. 5, 6. The words from 'This is a thankless task . . .' to '. . . the Lord said to him' are omitted by all the Greek and some Latin manuscripts.

v. 7. 'Hearing the voice speak', but not hearing what was said. This is made clear in xxii. 9 below, where 'to hear' is used in the sense of 'to understand', as in I Cor. xiv. 2.

have to undergo for my name's sake. 17 So Ananias set out; and as soon as he came into the house he laid his hands upon him, and said, Brother Saul, I have been sent by that Lord Jesus who appeared to thee on thy way as thou camest here; thou art to recover thy sight, and be filled with the Holy Spirit. 18 And with that, a kind of film fell away from his eyes, and his sight was recovered. He rose up, and was baptized; 19 and now, when he had taken food, his strength returned to him. For some days he lived with the disciples at Damascus, 20 and from the first, in the synagogues, he preached that Jesus was the Son of God. 21 All those who heard it were amazed; Why, they said, is not this the man who brought ruin on all those who invoked this name, when he was in Jerusalem; the man who came here for the very purpose of arresting such people and presenting them to the chief priests? 22 But Saul was inspired with ever greater strength, and silenced the Jews who lived at Damascus by shewing them clearly that this was the Christ.

23 So many days passed, and then the Jews plotted against his life. 24 Saul was aware of the plot; and, since they kept watch over the gates, day and night, to make an end of him, 25 the disciples contrived to let him down by night along the face of the wall, lowering him to the ground in a hamper. 26 So he reached Jerusalem, where he tried to attach himself to the disciples; but they could not believe he was a true disciple, and all avoided his company. 27 Whereupon Barnabas took him by the hand and brought him in to the apostles, telling them how, on his journey, he had seen the Lord and had speech with him, and how at Damascus he had spoken boldly in the name of Jesus. 28 So he came and went in their company at Jerusalem, and spoke boldly in the name of the Lord. 29 He preached, besides, to the Jews who talked Greek, and disputed with them, till they set about trying to take his life. 30 As soon as they heard of this, the brethren took him down to Caesarea, and put him on his way to Tarsus.

31 Meanwhile, all through Judaea and Galilee and Samaria, the church enjoyed peace and became firmly established, guided by the fear of God and filled with encouragement by the Holy Spirit. 32 And now Peter, as he visited the saints everywhere, came down to see those who dwelt at Lydda. 33 There he found a man called Aeneas, who had not left his bed for eight years, being palsied. 34 And Peter said to him, Aeneas, Jesus Christ sends thee healing; rise up, and make thy bed; whereupon he rose up at once. 35 All those who dwelt at Lydda and Saron came to see him, and their hearts turned to the Lord. 36 And there was a disciple at Joppa

v. 23. It would appear from Galatians i. 16-18, that the 'days' here mentioned covers a period of three years, during part of which St. Paul was in retirement in Arabia.

v. 29. Some manuscripts of the Latin give the sense 'He preached, besides, to the Gentiles, and disputed with the Jews who talked Greek'.

v. 31. 'Filled with the encouragement'; the Greek seems rather to mean, 'grew (in numbers) through the encouragement' of the Holy Spirit.

called Tabitha, which means the same as Dorcas, a gazelle. She abounded in acts of charity and in almsdeeds; 37 and it so happened that at this time she fell sick, and died, and they washed the body and laid it in an upper room. 38 Since Lydda was close to Joppa, the disciples, hearing that Peter was there, sent two men to find him; Come to us, they urged him, without delay. 39 So Peter rose and went with them; and when he came there they took him into the upper room, where all the widows stood round him in tears, shewing him the coats and cloaks which Dorcas used to make while she was among them. 40 Peter sent them all out, and went on his knees to pray; then, turning to the body, he said, Tabitha, rise up; and she opened her eyes and looked at Peter, and sat up on the bed. 41 So he gave her his hand, and raised her to her feet; and then, calling in the saints and the widows, he shewed her to them alive. 42 This became known all over Joppa, and many learned to believe in the Lord. 43 He stayed in Joppa a number of days after this, lodging with a tanner whose name was Simon.

Chapter Ten

HERE was, at Caesarea, a centurion named Cornelius, belonging to what is called the Italian cohort, 2 a pious man who worshipped the true God, like all his household, gave alms freely to the people, and prayed to God continually. 3 He, about the ninth hour of the day, had a vision, in which he clearly saw an angel of God come in and address him by his name. 4 What is it, Lord? he asked, gazing at him in terror. And he answered, Thy prayers and almsdeeds are recorded on high in God's sight. 5 And now he would have thee send men to Joppa, to bring here one Simon, who is surnamed Peter; 6 he lodges with a tanner, called Simon, whose house is close to the sea; thou wilt learn from him what thou hast to do. 7 So the angel visitor left him, and thereupon he summoned two of his servants, and one of the soldiers who were in attendance on him, a man of piety; 8 he told them all that had passed, and sent them on their way to Joppa.

9 Next day, while these were on their journey and were drawing

v. 2. Cornelius was one of those Gentiles who, without adopting the rite of circumcision, conformed to the Jewish religion in general; he was not a proselyte in the full sense.

v. 6. The last ten words of this verse are omitted in the Greek manuscripts.

near the city, Peter went up to the housetop about noon, to pray there. 10 He was hungry, and waiting for a meal; and while they were preparing it, he fell into a trance. 11 He saw heaven opening, and a bundle, like a great sheet, let down by its four corners on to the earth; 12 in it were all kinds of four-footed beasts, and things that creep on the earth, and all the birds of heaven. 13 And a voice came to him, Rise up, Peter, lay about thee and eat. 14 It cannot be, Lord, answered Peter; never in my life have I eaten anything profane, anything unclean. 15 Then the voice came to him a second time, It is not for thee to call anything profane, which God has made clean. 16 Three times this happened, and then the bundle was drawn up again into heaven. 17 Peter was still puzzling in his mind over the meaning of his vision, when Cornelius' messengers, who had now found their way to Simon's house, were seen standing at the gate; 18 where they called out and asked if Simon, who was also called Peter, lodged there. 19 To Peter, as he was turning over the vision in his mind, the Spirit said, Here are three men asking for thee; 20 rise and go down, and accompany them without misgiving; it is I who have sent them. 21 So Peter went down to the men; Here I am, he said, the man you are looking for; what is your errand? 22 The centurion Cornelius, they said, a man who worships the true God and keeps his law, as all the Jewish people will testify, has received a revelation from one of the holy angels; he was to have thee brought to his house, and listen to what thou wouldst say. 23 Thereupon Peter bade them come in, and made them welcome; and next day he set out with them, accompanied by some of the brethren from Joppa.

24 The day after that, they reached Caesarea, where Cornelius was awaiting them; he had gathered his kinsmen and his closest friends about him. 25 And as soon as Peter had entered, he was met by Cornelius, who fell at his feet and did reverence to him; 26 but Peter raised him; Stand up, he said, I am a man like thyself. 27 So he went in, still conversing with him, and found a great company assembled. 28 You know well enough, he told them, that a Jew is contaminated if he consorts with one of another race, or visits him; but God has been shewing me that we ought not to speak of any man as profane or unclean; 29 and so, when I was sent for, I came without demur. Tell me then, why you have sent for me. 30 And Cornelius said, Three days ago, at this very time, I was making my afternoon prayer in my house, when suddenly I saw a man standing before me, in white clothes, 31 who said to me, Cornelius, thy prayer has been heard, thy almsdeeds have won

v. 14. St. Peter seems to have interpreted the command as a direction to satisfy his hunger indiscriminately, although some of the creatures he saw were unclean according to the Mosaic law.

v. 30. Some manuscripts imply that Cornelius was fasting until three in the afternoon, the time of his vision.

v. 32. Some manu-
scripts add, at the
end of this verse,
'and he, when he
comes, will speak to
thee.'

remembrance in God's sight. 32 Thou art to send to Joppa, and summon thence that Simon who is also called Peter; he is lodging with a tanner called Simon, close to the sea. 33 I lost no time, therefore, in sending for thee, and thou last done me a favour in coming. Now thou seest us assembled in thy presence, ready to listen to whatever charge the Lord has given thee.

34 Thereupon Peter began speaking; I see clearly enough, he said, that God makes no distinction between man and man; 35 he welcomes anybody, whatever his race, who fears him and does what piety demands. 36 God has sent his word to the sons of Israel, giving them news of peace through Jesus Christ, who is Lord of all. 37 You have heard the story, a story which ran through the whole of Judaea, though it began in Galilee, after the baptism which John proclaimed; 38 about Jesus of Nazareth, how God anointed him with the Holy Spirit and with power, so that he went about doing good, and curing all those who were under the devil's tyranny, with God at his side. 39 We are witnesses of all he did in the country of the Jews, and in Jerusalem. And they killed him, hanging him on a gibbet; 40 but on the third day God raised him up again, and granted the clear sight of him, 41 not to the people at large, but to us, the witnesses whom God had appointed beforehand; we ate and drank in his company after his rising from the dead. 42 And he gave us a commission to preach to the people, and to bear witness that he, and none other, has been chosen by God to judge the living and the dead. 43 All the prophets bear him this testimony, that every-one who has faith in him is to find remission of sins through his name.

v. 44. This is the
only occasion on
which we hear of the
Holy Spirit being
granted to those who,
although they had
the desire of baptism,
had not yet received
that sacrament. It
seems that the early
Church needed spe-
cial encouragement
before it adopted the
practice of receiving
as converts those who
did not conform to
the full law of Moses.

44 Before Peter had finished speaking to them thus, the Holy Spirit fell on all those who were listening to his message. 45 The faithful who had come over with Peter, holding to the tradition of circumcision as they did, were astonished to find that the free gift of the Holy Spirit could be lavished upon the Gentiles, 46 whom they heard speaking with tongues, and proclaiming the greatness of God. 47 Then Peter said openly, Who will grudge us the water for baptizing these men, that have received the Holy Spirit just as we did? 48 And he gave orders that they should be baptized in the name of the Lord Jesus Christ. And after this, they asked him to stay on some days with them.

Chapter Eleven

AND NOW THE APOS tles and brethren in Judaea were told how the word of God had been given to the Gentiles. 2 And when Peter came up to Jerusalem, those who held to the tradition of circumcision found fault with him; 3 Why didst thou pay a visit, they asked, to men who are uncircumcised, and eat with them? 4 Whereupon Peter told them the story point by point from the beginning; 5 I was in the city of Joppa, he said, at my prayers, when I fell into a trance and saw a vision. A bundle, like a great sheet, came down from heaven, lowered by the four corners, till it reached me. 6 I looked closely to find out what it was, and there I saw four-footed creatures of earth, and wild beasts, and creeping things, and the birds that fly in heaven. 7 And I heard a voice saying to me, Rise up, Peter, lay about thee and eat. 8 So I answered, It cannot be, Lord; nothing profane or unclean has ever crossed my lips. 9 And a second utterance came from heaven in answer, It is not for thee to call anything profane, which God has made clean. 10 Three times this happened, and then all was drawn up again into heaven. 11 And at that very moment three men appeared at the door of the house where I was, with a message to me from Caesarea. 12 The Spirit bade me accompany them without misgiving; so these six brethren came with me, and together we entered the man's home. 13 There he told us how he had had a vision of an angel in his house; this angel stood before him, and said, Send to Joppa, and bid Simon, who is also called Peter, come to thee. 14 He will have such a message for thee as will bring salvation to thee and to all thy household. 15 And then, when I had set about speaking to them, the Holy Spirit fell upon them, just as it was with us at the beginning. 16 Then I was reminded of what the Lord said to us, John's baptism was with water, but there is a baptism with the Holy Spirit which you are to receive. 17 And now, if God has made them the same free gift, which he made to us when faith in the Lord Jesus had gone before it, who was I, what power had I, to stay God's hand? 18 At these words, they

v. 16. See i. 5 above.

235

A C T S

were content, and gave glory to God; Why then, they said, it seems God has granted life-giving repentance of heart to the Gentiles too.

19 Meanwhile, those who had been dispersed owing to the persecution that was raised over Stephen had travelled as far away as Phoenice and Cyprus and Antioch, without preaching the word to anyone except the Jews. 20 But there were some of them, men of Cyprus and Cyrene, who, when they found their way to Antioch, spoke to the Greeks as well, preaching the Lord Jesus to them. 21 And the Lord's power went with them, so that a great number learned to believe, and turned to the Lord. 22 The story of this came to the ears of the Church at Jerusalem, and they sent Barnabas on a mission to Antioch. 23 When he came there and saw what grace God was bestowing on them, he was full of joy, and encouraged them all to remain true to the Lord with steady purpose of heart, 24 like the good man he was, full of the Holy Spirit, full of faith; a great multitude was thus won over to the Lord. 25 He went on to Tarsus, to look for Saul, and when he found him, brought him back to Antioch. 26 For a whole year after this they were made welcome in the Church there, teaching a great multitude. And Antioch was the first place in which the disciples were called Christians.

27 At this time, some prophets from Jerusalem visited Antioch; 28 and one of these, Agabus by name, stood up and prophesied through the Spirit that a great famine was to come upon the whole world, as it did in the reign of the emperor Claudius. 29 Thereupon it was decided that each of the disciples should contribute according to his means, to send relief to the brethren who lived in Judaea. 30 And so they did; and in sending it to the presbyters they entrusted it to the hands of Barnabas and Saul.

v. 20. We are not told that these Greeks were distinguished, like Cornelius, even by a partial observance of the Jewish law, and it seems probable that here, for the first time, the gospel was preached generally to heathens.

vv. 28-30. See note on Gal. ii. 1-10. Claudius was emperor A.D. 41-54.

Chapter Twelve

IT WAS AT THIS SAME time that Herod exerted his authority to persecute some of those who belonged to the Church. 2 James, the brother of John, he beheaded, 3 and then, finding that this was acceptable to the Jews, he went further, and laid hands on Peter too. It was the time of unleavened bread; 4 and he imprisoned Peter, after arresting him, with a guard of four soldiers, relieved four times a day; when paschal-time was over, he would bring him out in the presence of the people. 5 Peter, then, was well guarded in prison, but there was a continual stream of prayer going up to God from the Church on his behalf. 6 And now the day was coming when Herod was to bring him out; that night, Peter was sleeping with two chains on him, between two soldiers, and there were warders at the door guarding his prison. 7 Suddenly an angel of the Lord stood over him, and a light shone in his cell. He smote Peter on the side, to rouse him; Quick, he said, rise up; and thereupon the chains fell from his hands. 8 Then the angel said to him, Gird thyself up, and put on thy shoes; and, when he had done this, Throw thy cloak over thee, and follow me. 9 So he followed him out, unaware that what the angel had done for him was true; he thought he was seeing a vision. 10 Thus they passed one party of guards, then a second, and reached the iron gate which leads out into the city; this opened for them of its own accord. They came out, and as soon as they had passed on up one street, the angel left him.

11 At this, Peter came to himself. Now I can tell for certain, he said, that the Lord has sent his angel, to deliver me out of Herod's hands, and from all that the people of the Jews hoped to see. 12 After some thought, he made for the house belonging to Mary the mother of John, also called Mark. Here many had gathered for prayer; 13 a girl named Rhoda came to answer, when he knocked at the porch door, 14 and she, recognizing Peter's voice, was too overjoyed to open the gate for him; she ran in, and told them that Peter was standing at the gate. 15 Thou art mad, they told her,

but she still insisted that it was so; and then they said, It must be his guardian angel. 16 Meanwhile, Peter went on knocking; so they opened, and found him there, and stood astonished. 17 Calling for silence by a gesture of his hand, he told them how the Lord had delivered him from prison; Give news of this, he said, to James and the rest of the brethren. And so he left them, and went elsewhere.

18 When day broke, there was a great to-do among the soldiers, to know what had become of Peter. 19 Herod, after searching for him without avail, questioned the warders and had them punished. Then he went down from Judaea to Caesarea, and spent his time there. 20 He was much out of humour with the people of Tyre and Sidon; and these, since their country depended on the king's country for its supplies, waited upon him by common consent, and tried (by winning over Blastus, the royal chamberlain), to make their peace. 21 So, on an appointed day, Herod put on his royal finery and sat down on a raised dais to harangue them; 22 whereupon the people cried out in applause, It is no man, it is a god that speaks. 23 And immediately the angel of the Lord smote him, for not referring the glory to God; and he was eaten up by worms, and so died.

And still the word of God grew strong and spread wide. 24 Barnabas and Saul returned from Jerusalem, their mission of relief fulfilled, and took John, also called Mark, in their company.

Chapter Thirteen

THE CHURCH AT ANTIOCH had as its prophets and teachers Barnabas, and Simon who was called Niger, and Lucius of Cyrene, and Manahen, foster-brother of Herod the tetrarch, and Saul. 2 These were offering worship to God and fasting, when the Holy Spirit said, I must have Barnabas and Saul dedicated to

SALOME ASKING FOR THE HEAD OF ST. JOHN THE BAPTIST

GIOVANNI DI PAOLO
active 1423-1482

COURTESY OF THE ART INSTITUTE OF CHICAGO

the work to which I have called them. 3 Thereupon they fasted
and prayed and laid their hands on them, and so took leave of them.
4 And they, sent on their travels by the Holy Spirit, went down to
Seleucia, and from there took ship for Cyprus. 5 So they reached
Salamis, where they preached God's word in the Jewish synagogues; they had John, too, to help them. 6 And when they had
been through the whole island up to Paphos, they encountered
there a magician who claimed to be a prophet, a Jew named Bar-
jesus. 7 He was in the company of the governor, Sergius Paulus, a
man of good sense, who had sent for Barnabas and Saul and asked
if he might hear the word of God. 8 and Elymas, the magician
(that is what his name means when translated), opposed them, trying to turn the governor away from the faith. 9 Then Saul, whose
other name is Paul, filled with the Holy Spirit, fastened his eyes
on him, 10 and said; Child of the devil, versed in all trickery and
cunning, enemy of all honest dealing, wilt thou never have done
with trying to twist the straight paths of the Lord? 11 See, then,
if the hand of the Lord does not fall upon thee now. Thou shalt
become blind, and see the sun no more for a while. At this, a dark
mist fell upon him, and he had to go about looking for someone to
lead him by the hand. 12 And now the governor, seeing what had
happened, and overcome with awe at the Lord's teaching, learned
to believe.

13 After this Paul and his companions took ship from Paphos
and made for Perge in Pamphylia; here John left them, and went
back to Jerusalem. 14 They passed on from Perge, and reached
Pisidian Antioch, where they went and took their seats in the
synagogue on the sabbath day. 15 When the reading from the
law and the prophets was finished, the rulers of the synagogue sent
a message to them to say, Brethren, if you have in your hearts any
word of encouragement for the people, let us hear it. 16 Then
Paul stood up, and made a gesture with his hand to claim audience.
Listen, he said, men of Israel, and all you who worship the true
God. 17 The God of this people of Israel chose out our fathers,
and made his people great at the time when they were strangers in
the land of Egypt, stretching out his arm to deliver them from it.
18 For forty years he bore with their hard hearts in the wilderness;
19 then he overthrew seven nations in the land of Chanaan, whose
lands he gave them for an inheritance. 20 By now, some four
hundred and fifty years had passed; and after this he appointed
judges over them, up to the time of the prophet Samuel. 21 Then
they asked for a king, and God gave them Saul, son of Cis, a man

v. 8. 'The magician'
is a translation, not
of Bar-Jesus, but of
Elymas, a name which
Bar-Jesus had adopt-
ed.

v. 9. The name of
Paul is here men-
tioned for the first
time, probably be-
cause it was the
name he used when
travelling in Gentile
countries.

v. 16. 'You who wor-
ship the true God',
that is, Gentile ad-
herents of the Jewish
faith, like Cornelius
(x. 2).

v. 20. St. Paul is
probably reckoning
as four hundred and
fifty years the space
of time between the
patriarchs and Josue.
Some early authori-
ties give a different
reading, according to
which the space of
four hundred and
fifty years is reck-
oned between Josue
and Samuel.

239

v. 22. I Kings xiii.
14.

of the tribe of Benjamin, who reigned forty years; 22 but afterwards dispossessed him, and raised up David to be their king. To him, he gave this testimony, I have found in David, son of Jesse, a man after my own heart, who will accomplish all that is my will.

23 It is out of this man's posterity, according to the promise made to him, that God has brought us a Saviour, Jesus. 24 John had prepared the way for his coming, by proclaiming a baptism in which all the people of Israel was to repent; 25 but John himself, when he was coming to the end of his life's course, told them, I am not what you suspect me to be; look rather for one who comes after me; I am not worthy to untie the shoes on his feet. 26 Brethren, you who are sons of Abraham, and you others who fear God, this message of salvation is sent to you. 27 The people at Jerusalem, like their rulers, did not recognize Jesus for what he was; unwittingly they fulfilled, by condemning him, those utterances of the prophets which they had heard read, sabbath after sabbath. 28 And although they could find no capital charge against him, they petitioned Pilate for his death. 29 So, when they had fulfilled all that had been written about him, they took him down from the cross and laid him in a tomb.

30 And, on the third day, God raised him from the dead. 31 He was seen, over a space of many days, by the men who had come up with him from Galilee to Jerusalem; it is they who now bear witness of him before the people. 32 And this is the message we

v. 33. 'For our posterity'; a few early authorities have 'for us, their children'. The quotation is from Ps. ii. 7.
v. 34. Is. lv. 3.

preach to you; there was a promise made to our forefathers, 33 and this promise God has redeemed for our posterity, by raising Jesus to life. Thus, it is written in the second Psalm, Thou art my son; I have begotten thee this day. 34 And this is how he describes raising him from the dead, never to return to corruption again, I

v. 35. Ps. xv. 10. Cf. St. Peter's argument in Acts ii. 27.

will grant you the privileges I have promised to David; 35 to which purpose he says in another psalm, Thou wilt not allow thy faithful servant to see corruption. 36 David saw corruption; he served God's purpose in his own generation, and then fell asleep, and rested with his fathers; 37 but he whom God raised to life saw no corruption at all. 38 Here is news for you, then, brethren; remission of your sins is offered to you through him. There are claims from which you could not be acquitted by the law of Moses, 39 and whoever believes in Jesus is quit of all these. 40 Be-

v. 41. Habacuc i. 5; there are some differences in the Hebrew.

ware, then, of incurring the prophets' rebuke; 41 Look upon this, you scornful souls, and lose yourselves in astonishment. Such wonders I am doing in your days, that if a man told you the story you would not believe him.

42 As they left, they were implored to preach the same message there on the next sabbath. 43 And when the synagogue broke up, many Jews and many who worshipped the true God as proselytes followed Paul and Barnabas; and they preached to them, urging them to be true to the grace of God. 44 On the following sabbath almost all the city had assembled to hear God's word. 45 The Jews, when they saw these crowds, were full of indignation, and began to argue blasphemously against all that Paul said. 46 Whereupon Paul and Barnabas told them roundly, We were bound to preach God's word to you first; but now, since you reject it, since you declare yourselves unfit for eternal life, be it so; we will turn our thoughts to the Gentiles. 47 This, after all, is the *v. 47. Is. xlix. 6.* charge the Lord has given us, I have appointed thee to be a light for the Gentiles, that thou mayst bring salvation to the ends of the earth. 48 The Gentiles were rejoiced to hear this, and praised the word of the Lord; and they found faith, all those of them who were destined to eternal life. 49 And the word of the Lord spread far and wide all through the country. 50 But the Jews used influence with such women of fashion as worshipped the true God, and with the leading men in the city, setting on foot a persecution against Paul and Barnabas and driving them out of their territory; 51 so they shook off the dust from their feet as they left them, and went on to Iconium. 52 The disciples, meanwhile, were filled with rejoicing, and with the Holy Spirit.

Chapter Fourteen

WHILE THEY WERE AT Iconium, they went into the Jewish synagogue together, and preached in such a way that a great number both of Jews and of Greeks found faith, 2 although the Jews who would not believe stirred up trouble among the Gentiles and poisoned their minds against the brethren. 3 For a long time, then, they remained there, speaking boldly in the Lord's name, while he attested the preaching of his grace by allowing signs and wonders to be performed by their means; 4 the common folk of the city were divided in opinion, some taking part with the Jews, and some with the apostles. 5 Then, when both Gentiles and Jews, in concert with their rulers, made a movement to assault and stone them, 6 they thought it best to take refuge in the Lycaonian cities, Lystra and Derbe, and the country round them; and they preached the gospel there. 7 There was a lame man sitting at Lystra, crippled from birth, so that he had never walked, 8 who listened to Paul's preaching; and Paul, looking closely at him, and seeing that there was saving faith in him, 9 said aloud, Stand upright on thy feet; whereupon he sprang up, and began to walk. 10 The multitudes, seeing what Paul had done, cried out in the Lycaonian dialect, It is the gods, who have come down to us in human shape. 11 They called Barnabas Jupiter, and Paul Mercury, because he was the chief speaker; 12 and the priest of Jupiter, Defender of the City, brought out bulls and wreaths to the gates, eager, like the multitude, to do sacrifice.

13 The apostles tore their garments when they heard of it; and both Barnabas and Paul ran out among the multitude, crying aloud: 14 Sirs, why are you doing all this? We too are mortal men like yourselves; the whole burden of our preaching is that you must turn away from follies like this to the worship of the living God, who made sky and earth and sea and all that is in them. 15 In the ages that are past, he has allowed Gentile folk everywhere to follow their own devices; 16 yet even so he has not left us without some proof of what he is; it is his bounty that grants us rain from heaven, and the seasons which give birth to our crops, so that we have nourishment and comfort to our heart's desire. 17 With words like this they persuaded the people, not easily, to refrain from offering sacrifice to them.

18 But some of the Jews from Antioch and Iconium had followed them; these won over the multitude to their side, and they stoned Paul and dragged him out of the city, leaving him there for dead. 19 But the disciples formed a ring about him, and soon he rose up and went back into the city; next day he left, with Barnabas, for Derbe. 20 In that city too they preached, and made many disciples; then they returned to Lystra, Iconium and Antioch, 21 where they fortified the spirits of the disciples, encouraging them to be true to the faith, and telling them that we cannot enter

the kingdom of heaven without many trials. 22 Then, with fasting and prayer, they appointed presbyters for them in each of the churches, and commended them to the care of the Lord in whom they had learned to believe. 23 So they passed through Pisidia, and reached Pamphylia. 24 They preached the word of the Lord in Perge, and went down to Attalia, 25 taking ship there for Antioch, where they had been committed to God's grace for the work they had now achieved. 26 On their arrival, they called the Church together, and told the story of all God had done to aid them, and how, through faith, he had left a door open for the Gentiles. 27 And they stayed there a considerable time with the disciples.

Chapter
Fifteen

BUT NOW SOME VISItors came down from Judaea, who began to tell the brethren, You cannot be saved without being circumcised according to the tradition of Moses. 2 Paul and Barnabas were drawn into a great controversy with them; and it was decided that Paul and Barnabas and certain of the rest should go up to see the apostles and presbyters in Jerusalem about this question. 3 So the Church saw them on their way, and they passed through Phoenice and Samaria, relating how the Gentiles were turning to God, and so brought great rejoicing to all the brethren. 4 When they reached Jerusalem, they were welcomed by the Church, and by the apostles and presbyters; and they told them of all that God had done to aid them. 5 But some believers who belonged to the party of the Pharisees came forward and declared, They must be circumcised; we must call upon them to keep the law of Moses.

6 When the apostles and presbyters assembled to decide about

v. 2. 'Of the rest'; or perhaps 'of the other party'.

243

ACTS

this matter 7 there was much disputing over it, until Peter rose and said to them, Brethren, you know well enough how from early days it has been God's choice that the Gentiles should hear the message of the gospel from my lips, and so learn to believe. 8 God, who can read men's hearts, has assured them of his favour by giving the Holy Spirit to them as to us. 9 He would not make any difference between us and them; he had removed all the uncleanness from their hearts when he gave them faith. 10 How is it, then, that you would now call God in question, by putting a yoke on the necks of the disciples, such as we and our fathers have been too weak to bear? 11 It is by the grace of our Lord Jesus Christ that we hope to be saved, and they no less. 12 Then the whole company kept silence, and listened to Barnabas and Paul describing all the signs and wonders God had performed among the Gentiles by their means.

13 And when they had finished speaking, James answered thus, Listen, brethren, to what I have to say. 14 Simon has told us, how for the first time God has looked with favour on the Gentiles, and chosen from among them a people dedicated to his name. 15 This is in agreement with the words of the prophets, where it is written: 16 Afterwards, I will come back, and build up again David's tabernacle that has fallen; I will build up its ruins, and raise it afresh; 17 so that all the rest of mankind may find the Lord, all those Gentiles among whom my name is named, says the Lord, who is the doer of all this. 18 God has known from all eternity what he does to-day. 19 And so I give my voice for sparing the consciences of those Gentiles who have found their way to God; 20 only writing to bid them abstain from what is contaminated by idolatry, from fornication, and from meat which has been strangled or has the blood in it. 21 As for Moses, ever since the earliest times he has been read, sabbath after sabbath, in the synagogues, and has preachers in every city to expound him.

22 Thereupon it was resolved by the apostles and presbyters, with the agreement of the whole Church, to choose out some of their own number and despatch them to Antioch with Paul and Barnabas; namely, Judas who was called Barsabas, and Silas, who were leading men among the brethren. 23 And they sent, by their hands, this message in writing; To the Gentile brethren in Antioch, Syria and Cilicia, their brethren the apostles and presbyters send greeting. 24 We hear that some of our number who visited you have disquieted you by what they said, unsettling your consciences, although we had given them no such commission 25 and

v. 10. 'Tempting God' is generally used of one who challenges God to prove his power by working a miracle; here it must be understood in a less precise sense of shewing distrust, by taking no notice of the signs he has already given. 'Been too weak to bear', in the sense, apparently, that the Law of Moses was in fact ill kept; cf. vii. 53 above.

vv. 16-17. Amos ix. 11, 12. The Hebrew, as we have it, does not agree with the quotation St. James here makes from the Greek Septuagint.

v. 18. The end of this verse is wanting in some manuscripts; according to this reading, it is necessary to connect what remains of v. 18 with v. 17, 'says the Lord, who makes this known from all eternity'. If v. 18 stands in full, it is not part of the quotation, but a reflection by St. James that God's inclusion of the Gentiles in his Church does not imply any change in his eternal decrees.

v. 21. There is much difference of opinion about the bearing of this verse on the argument. Perhaps it is simplest to take it as meaning, that the Church has no need to keep alive the custom of circumcision, since there are Jewish synagogues everywhere to hand down the tradition of the Mosaic law. Or the sense may be, that it

244

therefore, meeting together with common purpose of heart, we have resolved to send you chosen messengers, in company with our well-beloved Barnabas and Paul, 26 men who have staked their lives for the name of our Lord Jesus Christ. 27 We have given this commission to Judas and Silas, who will confirm the message by word of mouth. 28 It is the Holy Spirit's pleasure and ours that no burden should be laid upon you beyond these, which cannot be avoided; 29 you are to abstain from what is sacrificed to idols, from blood-meat and meat which has been strangled, and from fornication. If you keep away from such things, you will have done your part. Farewell.

was not advisable to abrogate all the ceremonial precepts of the old law, as long as its continued recitation in the synagogue gave them prominence.

30 So they took their leave and went down to Antioch, where they called the multitude together and delivered the letter to them; 31 and they, upon reading it, were rejoiced at this encouragement. 32 Judas and Silas, for they were prophets too, said much to encourage the brethren and establish their faith; 33 they stayed there for some time before the brethren let them go home, in peace, to those who had sent them. 34 But Silas had a mind to remain there; so Judas went back alone to Jerusalem. 35 Paul and Barnabas waited at Antioch, teaching and preaching God's word, with many others to help them; 36 and then, after some days, Paul said to Barnabas, Let us go back and visit the brethren in all the cities where we have preached the word of the Lord, to see how they are doing. 37 And Barnabas was for taking John, also called Mark, with them. 38 But Paul said, here was a man who left them when they reached Pamphylia, and took no part with them in the work; it was not right to admit such a man to their company. 39 So sharp was their disagreement, that they separated from each other; Barnabas took Mark with him, and sailed off to Cyprus, 40 while Paul chose Silas for his companion and went on his journey, commended by the brethren to the Lord's grace. 41 And he travelled all through Syria and Cilicia, establishing the churches in the faith, and bidding them observe the commands which the apostles and presbyters had given.

v. 34. Some of the Latin manuscripts, following the Greek, omit either the whole of this verse or the second half of it.

v. 41. The Greek manuscripts and a few of the Latin omit the second half of this verse, from 'and bidding them' onwards.

Chapter Sixteen

So he reached Derbe, and Lystra. Here he met a disciple, named Timothy, son of a believer who was a Jewess and a Gentile father. 2 He was well spoken of by the brethren at Lystra and Iconium, and Paul resolved to take him as a companion on his journey. 3 But he was careful to circumcise him; he was thinking of the Jews living in those parts, who all knew that Timothy's father was a Gentile. 4 As they passed from city to city, they recommended to their observance the decree laid down by the apostles and presbyters at Jerusalem. 5 They found the churches firmly established in the faith, and their numbers daily increasing. 6 Thus they passed through Phrygia and the Galatian country; the Holy Spirit prevented them from preaching the word in Asia. 7 Then, when they had come as far as Mysia on their journey, they planned to enter Bithynia; but the Spirit of Jesus would not allow it. 8 So they crossed Mysia, and went down to the sea at Troas.

9 Here Paul saw a vision in the night; a certain Macedonian stood by him in entreaty, and said, Come over into Macedonia, and help us. 10 That vision once seen, we were eager to sail for Macedonia; we concluded that God had called us there to preach to them. 11 So we put out from Troas, made a straight course to Samothrace, and next day to Neapolis. 12 Thence we reached Philippi, which is a Roman colony and the chief city in that part of Macedonia; in this city we remained for some days, conferring together. 13 On the sabbath day we went out beyond the city gates, by the river side, a meeting-place, we were told, for prayer; and we sat down and preached to the women who had assembled there. 14 One of those who were listening was a woman called Lydia, a purple-seller from the city of Thyatira, and a worshipper of the true God; and the Lord opened her heart, so that she was attentive to Paul's preaching. 15 She was baptized, with all her household; and she was urgent with us; Now you have decided that I have faith in the Lord, she said, come to my house and lodge

vv. 6, 7. If the apostles went, by way of Galatia, into Phrygia proper, they would pass on from there into Bithynia without coming anywhere near Mysia. Some commentators, therefore, would translate in v. 6, 'they passed through the Phrygio-Galatic region', that is, the country round Pisidian Antioch which Paul had visited already on his previous journey. The Greek has, 'the Phrygian and Galatian country'.

v. 10. It is evident from this verse that St. Luke himself joined St. Paul about the time when he reached Troas.

v. 12. 'Conferring together'; this appears to be the meaning of the Latin. The Greek, however, has simply 'passing the time'.

246

THE BEHEADING OF ST. JOHN THE BAPTIST   LUCAS VAN LEYDEN
                                                  1494-1533

COURTESY OF THE JOHNSON COLLECTION, PHILADELPHIA

there; and she would take no denial. 16 And now, as we were on our way to the place of prayer, we chanced to meet a girl who was possessed by a divining spirit; her predictions brought in large profits to her masters. 17 This girl used to follow behind Paul and the rest of us, crying out, These men are the servants of the most high God; they are proclaiming to us the way of salvation. 18 And when she had done this for a number of days, Paul was distressed by it; he turned round and said to the spirit, I command thee to come out of her, in the name of our Lord Jesus Christ; and there and then it came out of her.

19 Her masters, who saw that all their hopes of profit had vanished, took hold of Paul and Silas and dragged them off to justice in the market-place. 20 When they brought them before the magistrates, they said, These men, Jews by origin, are disturbing the peace of our city; 21 they are recommending customs which it is impossible for us, as Roman citizens, to admit or to observe. 22 The crowd gathered round, to join in the accusation; and the magistrates, tearing their clothes off them, gave orders that they should be beaten; 23 then, when they had inflicted many lashes on them, put them in prison, and bade the gaoler keep them in safe custody. 24 Thus instructed, he put them in the inner ward, and secured their feet in the stocks. 25 At midnight, Paul and Silas were at their prayers, praising God, while the prisoners listened to them. 26 And all at once there was a violent earthquake, so that the foundations of the prison rocked; whereupon every door opened, and every man's chains were undone. 27 The gaoler, who had been awakened, saw the prison doors open, and drew his sword as if to kill himself, thinking the prisoners had escaped; 28 but Paul cried with a loud voice, Do no hurt to thyself; we are all here. 29 And so, when he had called for a light, he came running in and fell at the feet of Paul and Silas, all trembling; 30 Sirs, he asked, as he led them out, what am I to do, to save myself? 31 Have faith, they said to him, in the Lord Jesus; there lies salvation for thee, and for thy household. 32 Then they preached the word of the Lord to him, and to all that were in his house; 33 and he, there and then, at dead of night, took them away to wash their wounds, and without delay he and all his were baptized. 34 So he led them to his home, where he put food before them, and he and all his household made rejoicing at having found faith in God.

35 When day came, the magistrates sent their officers to say, Those men are to be discharged. 36 And the gaoler reported the

message to Paul; The magistrates have sent ordering your discharge; it is time you should come out, and go on your way in peace. 37 But Paul said to them, What, have they beaten us in public, without trial, Roman citizens as we are, and sent us to prison, and now would they let us out secretly? That will not serve; they must come here themselves, 38 and fetch us out in person. When the officers gave this message to the magistrates, they were alarmed by this talk of Roman citizenship; 39 so they came and pleaded with them, urging them, as they brought them out, to leave the city. 40 On leaving the prison, they went to Lydia's house, where they saw the brethren and gave them encouragement; then they set out on their journey.

v. 37. Cf. 25 xxii. below.

Chapter Seventeen

THEY continued their journey through Amphipolis and Apollonia, and so reached Thessalonica. Here the Jews had a synagogue, 2 and Paul, as his custom was, paid them a visit there. Over a space of three sabbaths he reasoned with them out of the scriptures, 3 expounding these and bringing proofs from them that the sufferings of Christ and his rising from the dead were foreordained; the Christ, he said, is none other than the Jesus whom I am preaching to you. 4 Some of them were convinced, and threw in their lot with Paul and Silas; a great number of those Gentiles who worshipped the true God, and not a few of the leading women. 5 The Jews were indignant at this, and they found confederates among the riff-raff of the market-place, to make a disturbance and throw the city into an uproar. Then they made a sudden descent on Jason's house, in the hope of bringing Paul and Silas out into the presence of the people; 6 but, as they could not find them, they dragged Jason and some of the brethren before the city council, crying out, Here they are, the men who are turning the state upside down; they have come here too; 7 and Jason has given them hospitality. All these folk defy the edicts of Caesar; they say there is another king, one Jesus. 8 Both the crowd and the city council took alarm at hearing this, 9 and they demanded bail from

v. 5. Jason was perhaps a person well known in the early Church, since his name is thus introduced without further explanation. It is not certain whether he was the Jason mentioned in Rom. xvi. 21, then living at Rome, where the Acts were probably written.

v. 6. 'Turning the state upside down'; rather, according to the Greek, 'the world', but through the early corruption of one letter in certain Latin manuscripts the Vulgate text reads, 'the city'.

Jason and the others before they would let them go. 10 Thereupon the brethren sent Paul and Silas away by night to Beroea; where, as soon as they arrived, they made their way to the Jewish synagogue. 11 These were of a better breed than the Thessalonians; they welcomed the word with all eagerness, and examined the scriptures, day after day, to find out whether all this was true; 12 so that many of them learned to believe, as certain Greek women of fashion did, and not a few of the men as well. 13 But now some of the Thessalonian Jews, hearing that the word of God had been preached by Paul at Beroea too, came on there, to upset and disturb the minds of the multitude; 14 whereupon the brethren sent Paul away, to continue his journey up to the coast; Silas and Timothy remained there still.

15 Those who were escorting Paul on his journey saw him as far as Athens, and then left him, with instructions for Silas and Timothy to rejoin him as soon as possible. 16 And while Paul was waiting for them in Athens, his heart was moved within him to find the city so much given over to idolatry, 17 and he reasoned, not only in the synagogue with Jews and worshippers of the true God, but in the market-place, with all he met. 18 He encountered philosophers, Stoics and Epicureans, some of whom asked, What can his drift be, this dabbler? while others said, He would appear to be proclaiming strange gods; because he had preached to them about Jesus and Resurrection. 19 So they took him by the sleeve and led him up to the Areopagus; May we ask, they said, what this new teaching is thou art delivering? 20 Thou dost introduce terms which are strange to our ears; pray let us know what may be the meaning of it. 21 (No townsman of Athens, or stranger visiting it, has time for anything else than saying something new, or hearing it said.)

22 So Paul stood up in full view of the Areopagus, and said, Men of Athens, wherever I look I find you scrupulously religious. 23 Why, in examining your monuments as I passed by them, I found among others an altar which bore the inscription, To the unknown God. And it is this unknown object of your devotion that I am revealing to you. 24 The God who made the world and all that is in it, that God who is Lord of heaven and earth, does not dwell in temples that our hands have made; 25 no human handicraft can do him service, as if he stood in need of anything, he, who gives to all of us life and breath and all we have. 26 It is he who has made, of one single stock, all the nations that were to dwell over the whole face of the earth. And he has given to each

v. 14. Beroea is close to the sea, and a long way from Athens. It is possible that St. Paul started out, following the line of his previous journey, for Dyrrhachium on the West Coast of Greece, but for some reason had to change his plans (Rom. xv. 19, 22).

v. 18. 'This dabbler'; the Greek word means properly a bird which picks up seeds, and so became a term of contempt for a lounger who picks up gossip. The Latin translators, apparently not understanding this, invented a rendering, 'the seed-word man', which St. Augustine interprets as meaning 'one who sows the Word'.

v. 26. It is not clear whether these 'cycles' are seasons of the year (cf. xiv. 16 above), or decisive moments in history; nor whether the 'limits' are geographical boundaries, or periods set to the enjoyment by this or that nation of its possessions.

the cycles it was to pass through and the fixed limits of its habitation, 27 leaving them to search for God; would they somehow grope their way towards him? Would they find him? And yet, after all, he is not far from any one of us; 28 it is in him that we live, and move, and have our being; thus, some of your own poets have told us, For indeed, we are his children. 29 Why then, if we are the children of God, we must not imagine that the divine nature can be represented in gold, or silver, or stone, carved by man's art and thought. 30 God has shut his eyes to these passing follies of ours; now, he calls upon all men, everywhere, to repent, 31 because he has fixed a day when he will pronounce just judgement on the whole world. And the man whom he has appointed for that end he has accredited to all of us, by raising him up from the dead.

32 When resurrection from the dead was mentioned, some mocked, while others said, We must hear more from thee about this. So Paul went away from among them. 33 But there were men who attached themselves to him and learned to believe, among them Dionysius the Areopagite; and so did a woman called Damaris, and others with them.

Chapter
Eighteen

PAUL LEFT ATHENS after this, and went to Corinth. 2 Here he met a Jew named Aquila, born in Pontus, who, with his wife Priscilla, had lately come from Italy, when Claudius decreed that all Jews should leave Rome. 3 He paid them a visit: then, since they were brothers of the same craft (both were tent-makers) he stayed and worked with them. 4 Every sabbath he held a disputation in the synagogue, trying to convince both Jews and Greeks by confronting them with the name of the Lord Jesus.

5 Just at the time when Silas and Timothy arrived from Macedonia, Paul was much occupied with preaching, while he bore witness to the Jews that Jesus was the Christ. 6 But they set their faces against it and talked blasphemy, until he shook the dust out of his garments, and said to them, Your blood be upon your own heads; I am clear of it; I will go to the Gentiles henceforward. 7 So he left them, and went to the house of one Titius Justus, a worshipper of the true God, who lived next door to the synagogue. 8 But Crispus, the ruler of the synagogue, learned to believe in the Lord, and so did all his household; and by now many of the Corinthians listened and found faith, and were baptized. 9 And the Lord said to Paul in a vision at night, Do not be afraid, speak out, and refuse to be silenced; 10 I am with thee, and none shall come near to do thee harm; I have a great following in this city. 11 So he remained there a year and six months, preaching the word of God among them.

12 Then, when Gallio was proconsul of Achaia, the Jews made a concerted attack on Paul, and dragged him before the judgement seat. 13 This fellow, they said, is persuading men to worship God in a manner the law forbids. 14 Paul was just opening his mouth to speak, when Gallio said to the Jews, It would be only right for me to listen to you Jews with patience, if we had here some wrong done, or some malicious contrivance, 15 but the questions you raise are a matter of words and names, of the law which holds good among yourselves. You must see to it; I have no mind to try such cases. 16 And he drove them away from the judgement seat. 17 Thereupon there was a general onslaught upon Sosthenes, the ruler of the synagogue, who was beaten before the judgement seat; but all this caused Gallio no concern.

18 Paul stayed on many days yet, then took leave of the brethren and sailed off to Syria; before he left Cenchrae he shaved his head, since he was under a vow. 19 He took Priscilla and Aquila with him, but left them behind when he reached Ephesus. He himself went to the synagogue and reasoned with the Jews, 20 who asked him to make a longer stay. But he would not consent; 21 he said, as he took leave of them, I will come back to you again, if it is God's will, and departed from Ephesus by sea. 22 On landing at Caesarea, he went up from there to greet the church, then went down again to Antioch, 23 where he spent some time; he left it to make an orderly progress through the Galatian and Phrygian country, where he established all the disciples in the faith.

24 Meanwhile a Jewish visitor came to Ephesus, Apollo by

v. 17. It is not clear whether Sosthenes was a Christian who was beaten by the Jews or, perhaps more probably, a Jew who was beaten by the Gentiles. The same name appears in I Cor. i. 1.
v. 18. Num. vi. 9.

v. 23. This may refer either to the countries of Phrygia and Galatia, or to the district which could be indifferently described as Phrygian or Galatian (see note on xvi. 6 above).

251

v. 25. 'The way of
the Lord' is perhaps
not to be understood
here of the Christian
religion, but of that
way which was pre-
pared for the Lord
by St. John the Bap-
tist (Matthew iii. 3).

name; he was born in Alexandria, and was an eloquent man, well grounded in the scriptures. 25 He had had instruction in the way of the Lord; and, with a spirit full of zeal, used to preach and teach about the life of Jesus accurately enough, although he knew of no baptism except that of John. 26 So he began to speak out boldly in the synagogue, whereupon Priscilla and Aquila, who had been listening, made friends with him, and explained the way of God to him more particularly. 27 He was meaning to continue his journey into Achaia; in this the brethren encouraged him, and wrote asking the disciples there to welcome him. His visit was a welcome reinforcement to the believers; 28 he spared no pains to refute the Jews publicly, proving from the scriptures that Jesus was the Christ.

Chapter Nineteen

T was while Apollo was away at Corinth that Paul finished his journey through the inland country, and came to Ephesus. He met some disciples there 2 and asked them, Was the Holy Spirit given to you, when you learned to believe? Why, they said, nobody even mentioned to us the existence of a Holy Spirit. 3 What baptism, then, did you receive? Paul asked; and they said, John's baptism. 4 So Paul told them, John baptized to bring men to repentance; but he bade the people have faith in one who was to come after him, that is, in Jesus. 5 On hearing this, they received baptism in the name of the Lord Jesus; 6 and when Paul laid his hands upon them, the Holy Spirit came down on them, and they spoke with tongues, and prophesied. 7 In all, these men were about twelve in number.

8 And now he went into the synagogue, and for three months spoke boldly there, reasoning with them and trying to convince them about the kingdom of God; 9 but since there were some who hardened their hearts and refused belief, discrediting the way of the Lord in the eyes of the multitude, he left them, and withdrew his own disciples, holding disputations daily in the school of a certain Tyrannus. 10 This lasted for two years, so that the

Lord's word came to the ears of all those who lived in Asia, both Jews and Greeks. 11 And God did miracles through Paul's hands that were beyond all wont; 12 so much so, that when hand-kerchiefs or aprons which had touched his body were taken to the sick, they got rid of their diseases, and evil spirits were driven out. 13 Some of the wandering Jewish exorcists took it upon themselves to invoke the name of the Lord Jesus over those who were possessed by evil spirits, with the words, I conjure you in the name of Jesus, the name that is preached by Paul. 14 Among these were the seven sons of Sceva, one of the Jewish chief priests. 15 And the evil spirit answered, Jesus I recognize, Paul I know well enough; but you, what are you? 16 And with that, the man who was possessed by the evil spirit ran at them and got the better of them, defying the power of both; so that they fled from the house naked and wounded. 17 This came to the ears of every Jew and Greek living in Ephesus; fear fell upon them all, and the name of the Lord Jesus was held in great honour. 18 Many believers came forward, confessing their evil practices and giving a full account of them; 19 and a number of those who followed magic arts made their books into a heap and burned them in public: the value of these was reckoned up, and proved to be fifty thousand silver pieces. 20 So, irresistibly, the word of the Lord spread and prevailed.

21 When all this was over, the thought in Paul's heart was to go to Jerusalem, first travelling through Macedonia and Achaia; When I have been there, he said, I must go on and see Rome. 22 And he sent on two of those who ministered to him, Timothy and Erastus, into Macedonia, but waited for a while himself in Asia. 23 It was just at this time that the way of the Lord was the cause of a notable disturbance. 24 There was a silversmith called Demetrius, who used to make silver models of Diana's temple, and so gave plentiful employment to the craftsmen. 25 And now he called a meeting of these, and of the workmen who were in the same trade, and spoke thus, Friends, you all know that our prosperity depends upon this business of ours. 26 And you can see and hear for yourselves that this Paul has persuaded a whole multitude to change their allegiance, not only at Ephesus but over most of Asia, by telling them that gods made by men's hands are no gods at all. 27 It is not only that we are in danger of finding this work of ours discredited. The temple of the great goddess Diana will count for nothing, she will be shorn of her greatness, the goddess whom Asia and all the world reveres. 28 At these

vv. 14-16. If we assume, with the best manuscripts, that we are to read 'seven' in verse 14 and 'both' in verse 16, it is difficult to see how the two verses can be reconciled; unless we are to understand that the possessed man defied the power of both names, those of Jesus and Paul. (In a fragment which dates from the second century A.D., we find 'both' used for 'all'.)

words, they were all overcome with rage, and began to shout, Great is Diana of Ephesus. 29 Their uproar filled the whole city, as they ran by common consent into the theatre, carrying with them Gaius and Aristarchus, who were companions of Paul from Macedonia. 30 When Paul had a mind to shew himself before the people, his disciples tried to prevent it: 31 and some of the delegates of Asia, who were his friends, sent a message to him, imploring him not to risk his life in the theatre.

32 Meanwhile some cried this, some that; the meeting was all in confusion, and most of them could not tell what had brought them together. 33 The Jews thrust Alexander forward, and some of the crowd brought him down with them; so Alexander made a gesture with his hand, and tried to give an account of himself before the people; 34 but as soon as they found out that he was a Jew, a single cry came from every mouth, and for some two hours they kept on shouting, Great is Diana of Ephesus. 35 Then the town clerk restored quiet among the crowd; Ephesians, he said, as if there were anyone who does not know that the city of Ephesus is the acolyte of the great Diana, and of the image which is Jupiter's offspring! 36 Since this is beyond dispute, you had best be quiet, and do nothing rashly. 37 These men you have brought here have not robbed the temples; they have not used blasphemous language about your goddess. 38 And if Demetrius and his fellow craftsmen have any charge to bring against them, why, we have court days, we have proconsuls; let the two parties go to law. 39 If, on the other hand, you have any further question to raise, it can be settled by lawful assembly. 40 We may easily be called to account for to-day's proceedings, and there is no grievance which will enable us to account for this riot. 41 With these words he broke up the meeting.

v. 33. Here, as in xviii. 17, it is not clear whether the Jew mentioned was a Christian or not; but it seems the name must have been one which St. Luke's readers would be expected to recognize without introduction (cf. xvii. 6). It is not likely that this is the Alexander mentioned in I Tim. i. 20, II Tim. iv. 14.

Chapter Twenty

WHEN THE TUMULT was over, Paul summoned his disciples, to rally their spirits and bid them farewell, and set out on his journey into Macedonia. 2 He passed through all that region, and gave them much encouragement; then he entered Greece. 3 When he had stayed three months there, he was meaning to take ship for Syria; but, finding that the Jews were plotting against him, he resolved to go back again through Macedonia. 4 He was accompanied as far as Asia by Sopater, son of Pyrrhus, from Beroea, Aristarchus and Secundus from Thessalonica, Gaius from Derbe, Timothy, and two friends from Asia, Tychicus and Trophimus. 5 These went on first, and waited for us at Troas. 6 As soon as the time of unleavened bread was over, we set sail from Philippi, and took five days to reach them at Troas, where we spent seven days. 7 When the new week began, we had met for the breaking of bread, and Paul was preaching to them; he meant to leave them next day, and he continued speaking till midnight. 8 There were many lamps burning in the upper room where we had met; 9 and a young man called Eutychus, who was sitting in the embrasure of the window, was overcome by deep sleep. As Paul still went on preaching, sleep weighed him down, and he fell from the third storey to the ground, where he was taken up dead. 10 Paul went down, bent over him, and embraced him; then he said, Do not disturb yourselves; his life is yet in him. 11 And so he went up again and broke bread and ate; afterwards he talked with them for some time until dawn came, when he left. 12 And the boy was taken home alive, to their great comfort.

13 For ourselves, we took ship and sailed to Assos, where we were to take Paul on board; he had arranged this, because he himself meant to go across by land. 14 So at Assos we met him, and took him on board, and journeyed to Mitylene. 15 Sailing thence, we reached a point opposite Chios the following day; on the next, we put in at Samos, and arrived on the third at Miletus. 16 Paul had made up his mind to sail past Ephesus, for fear of having to

v. 7. 'When the new week began'; literally 'on the first day of the week'; but evidently, since the Jewish sabbath ended at six in the evening, the scene here described took place on the Saturday, not on the Sunday night.

255

waste time in Asia; he was eager, if he found it possible, to keep the day of Pentecost at Jerusalem. 17 From Miletus he sent a message to Ephesus, summoning the presbyters of the church there. 18 And when they had come out to him and gathered round him, he said to them, It is within your knowledge, how I have lived among you, since the first day when I set foot in Asia, 19 serving the Lord in all humility, not without tears over the trials which beset me, through the plots of the Jews; 20 and how I have never failed you, when there was any need of preaching to you, or teaching you, whether publicly or house by house. 21 I have proclaimed both to Jew and to Greek repentance before God and faith in our Lord Jesus Christ.

22 Now, a prisoner in spirit, I am going up to Jerusalem, knowing nothing of what is to befall me there; 23 only, as I go on from city to city, the Holy Spirit assures me that at Jerusalem bondage and affliction await me. 24 I care nothing for all that; I do not count my life precious compared with my work, which is to finish the course I run, the task of preaching which the Lord Jesus has given me, in proclaiming the good news of God's grace. 25 Here, then, I stand, well knowing that you will not see my face again; you, among whom I came and went, preaching the kingdom of God. 26 And I ask you to bear me witness to-day that I have no man's blood on my hands; 27 I have never shrunk from revealing to you the whole of God's plan. 28 Keep watch, then, over yourselves, and over God's Church, in which the Holy Spirit has made you bishops; you are to be the shepherds of that flock which he won for himself at the price of his own blood. 29 I know well that ravening wolves will come among you when I am gone, and will not spare the flock; 30 there will be men among your own number who wll come forward with a false message, and find disciples to follow them. 31 Be on the watch, then; do not forget the three years I spent, instructing every one of you continually, and with tears. 32 Now, as then, I commend you to God, and to his gracious word, that can build you up and give you your allotted place among the saints everywhere. 33 I have never asked for silver or gold or clothing from any man; 34 you will bear me out, that these hands of mine have sufficed for all that I and my companions needed. 35 Always I have tried to shew you that it is our duty so to work, and be the support of the weak, remembering the words spoken by the Lord Jesus himself, It is more blessed to give than to receive. 36 When he had said this, he knelt down and prayed with them all. 37 They all wept abundantly, and em-

v. 24. The text here is very confused; and the Latin rendering would be literally translated, 'I do not count my life more precious than myself, as long as I can finish my course'; the Greek sense is probably, 'I do not count my life precious to myself, as long as I can finish my course.'

v. 25. It seems likely, from several references in the epistles, that St. Paul was at Ephesus again after the end of his first captivity. If so, it is clear that he speaks here only of human probabilities, not foreseeing his release; all he knew by revelation was that he was to be imprisoned (v. 23 above).

v. 35. This saying of our Lord's has not been recorded in any of the four gospels.

braced Paul and kissed him, 38 grieving most over what he had said about never seeing his face again. And so they escorted him to the ship.

Chapter Twenty=one

WHEN WE TORE OUR selves away from them, and at last put out to sea, we made a straight course, sailing to Cos, and next day to Rhodes, and thence to Patara. 2 There, finding a ship crossing to Phoenice, we went on board and set sail. 3 We sighted Cyprus, but passed it on our left, and held on for Syria, where we landed at Tyre, the port for which the vessel had shipped her cargo. 4 Here we enquired for the brethren, and made a stay of seven days with them; they, by revelation, warned Paul not to go up to Jerusalem, 5 but when the time came to an end, we left them and continued our journey. All of them, with their wives and children, escorted us until we were out of the city; and so we knelt down on the beach to pray; 6 then, when farewells had been made on either side, we went on board the ship, while they returned home. 7 The end of our voyage brought us from Tyre to Ptolemais, where we greeted the brethren and stayed one day with them; 8 the day after, we left them and arrived at Caesarea, where we went to the house of Philip the evangelist, one of the seven, and lodged with him. 9 He had four daughters, who possessed the gift of prophecy. 10 During our stay of several days there, a prophet named Agabus came down from Judaea. 11 When he visited us, he took up Paul's girdle, and bound his own hands and feet with it; then he said, Thus speaks the Holy Spirit, The man to whom this girdle belongs will be bound, like this, by the Jews at Jerusalem, and given over into the hands of the Gentiles. 12 At hearing this, both we and our

v. 8. Cf. vi. 5 above.

v. 10. Cf. xi. 28 above.

257

hosts implored Paul not to go up to Jerusalem. 13 To which he answered, What do you mean by lamenting, and crushing my spirits? I am ready to meet prison and death as well in Jerusalem for the name of the Lord Jesus. 14 Finding that he would not take our advice, we composed ourselves, and said, The Lord's will be done.

15 When the time came to an end, we made all ready, and went up to Jerusalem. 16 Some of the brethren from Caesarea went with us, to take us to the house of a Cypriot called Mnason, one of the first disciples, with whom we were to lodge. 17 When we reached Jerusalem, the brethren received us with joy. 18 The next day Paul took us with him to see James; all the presbyters had gathered; 19 and he greeted them, and told them point by point of all that God had done among the Gentiles through his ministry. 20 They praised God for the news he gave, and said, Brother, thou canst see for thyself how many thousands of the Jews have learned to believe, and they are all zealous supporters of the law. 21 And this is what has come to their ears about thee; that thou dost teach the Jews in Gentile parts to break away from the law of Moses, telling them not to circumcise their children, and not to follow the tradition. 22 What will happen? Why, a multitude of them will assuredly gather round thee, hearing that thou hast come. 23 Follow our advice, then, in this; we have four men here who are under a vow; 24 if thou wilt take these with thee, and join in their purification and defray the cost for the shaving of their heads, then all will see clearly that the report they have heard about thee has no substance, and that thou dost follow the observances of the law like other men. 25 As for the Gentile believers, we have already written to them; we laid it down that they must abstain from what is sacrificed to idols, and from blood-meat and meat which has been strangled, and from fornication.

26 So, next day, Paul took the men with him, and began going to the temple, publicly fulfilling the days of purification, until the time came for each to have sacrifice made on his behalf. 27 And when the seven days were all but at an end, the Jews from Asia saw him in the temple. Whereupon they threw the whole multitude into an uproar, and laid hands on him, crying out; 28 Men of Israel, come to the rescue; here is the man who goes about everywhere, teaching everybody to despise our people, and our law, and this place. He has brought Gentiles into the temple, too, profaning these sacred precincts. 29 They had seen Trophimus, who was from Ephesus, in the city with him, and it

v. 24. Num. vi. 9. It was the custom for richer Jews to pay for the sacrifices offered by the poor on such occasions; and St. Paul, though he asserted the freedom of the Gentiles, himself conformed to such Jewish usages, cf. I Cor. ix. 20.

was he whom they suspected Paul of introducing into the temple.
30 The whole city was in a commotion, and the common folk ran
up from all sides. They seized Paul and dragged him out of the
temple, upon which the gates were shut; 31 and they were preparing to kill him, when word came to the captain of the garrison
that the whole of Jerusalem was in an uproar. 32 He at once summoned his troops, with their officers, and swept down upon them;
and at the sight of the captain with his troops they left off beating
Paul.

33 The captain came up and arrested him, giving orders that
he should be bound with a double chain; then he asked who he
was, and what he had done. 34 But some of the crowd were
shouting this and some that, and it was impossible to find out
the truth amidst the clamour; so he gave orders that Paul should
be taken to the soldiers' quarters. 35 When he reached the steps,
he had to be carried by the soldiers because of the crowd's violence;
36 a rabble of the common people kept following behind, with
cries of, Put him to death. 37 And just as he was being taken
into the soldiers' quarters, Paul asked the centurion, May I have
a word with thee? At which he said, What, canst thou talk Greek?
38 Thou art not, then, that Egyptian, that raised a band of four
thousand cutthroats, some time back, and led them out into the
wilderness? 39 I am a Jew, said Paul, a citizen of Tarsus in
Cilicia, no mean city; my request of thee is that thou wouldst let
me speak to the people. 40 And so, having obtained his leave, Paul
stood there on the steps, and made a gesture with his hand to the
people. There was deep silence, and he began addressing himself
to them in Hebrew.

v. 40. 'Hebrew'; that is, probably, the Aramaic spoken by the Jews of that time.

259

Chapter Twenty=two

RETHREN and fathers, listen to the defence I am putting before you. 2 (And now they gave him even better audience, finding that he spoke to them in Hebrew.) 3 I am a Jew, born at Tarsus in Cilicia and brought up in this city; I was trained, under Gamaliel, in exact knowledge of our ancestral law, as jealous for the honour of the law as you are, all of you, to-day. 4 I persecuted this way to the death, putting men and women in chains and handing them over to the prisons. 5 The chief priests and all the elders will bear me out in that; it was from them that I was carrying letters to their brethren, when I was on my way to Damascus, to make fresh prisoners there and bring them to Jerusalem for punishment. 6 While I was on my journey, not far from Damascus, about mid-day, this befell me; all at once a great light from heaven shone about me, 7 and I fell to the ground, and heard a voice saying to me, Saul, Saul, why dost thou persecute me? 8 Who art thou, Lord? I answered. And he said to me, I am Jesus of Nazareth, whom Saul persecutes. 9 My companions saw the light, but could not catch the voice of him who spoke to me. 10 Then I said, What must I do, Lord? And the Lord said to me, Rise up, and go into Damascus; there thou shalt be told of all the work that is destined for thee. 11 The glory of that light had blinded me, and my companions were leading me by the hand when I came into Damascus. 12 There a certain Ananias, a man well known among his Jewish neighbours for his pious observance of the law, 13 came and stood beside me, and said, Brother Saul, look up and see. And at that instant I looked up into his face. 14 Then he said to me, The God of our fathers has made choice of thee to know his will, to have sight of him who is Just, and hear speech from his lips; 15 and what thou hast seen and heard, thou shalt testify before all men. 16 Come then, why art thou wasting time? Rise up, and receive baptism, washing away thy sins at the invocation of his name. 17 Afterwards, when I had gone back to Jerusalem, and was at prayer in the temple, I fell into a trance, 18 and saw the Lord there speaking to me; Make haste, he said, leave Jerusalem with all speed; they will not accept thy witness of me here. 19 But, Lord, I said, it is within their own knowledge, how I used to imprison those who believed in thee, and scourge them in the synagogues; 20 and when the blood of Stephen, thy martyr, was shed, I too stood by and gave my consent, and watched over the garments of those who slew him. 21 And he said to me, Go on thy way; I mean to send thee on a distant errand, to the Gentiles.

22 Up to this point, they listened to his speech; but then they cried aloud, Away with such a fellow from the earth; it is a disgrace that he should live. 23 So, when he saw them raising shouts and throwing down their garments and flinging dust into the air, 24 the captain had Paul taken into the soldiers' quarters, telling them to examine him under the lash; thus he would find out the cause of the outcry against him. 25 And they had already tied Paul down with thongs, when he said to the centurion who was in charge, Have you the right to scourge a man, when he is a Roman citizen, and has not been sentenced? 26 The centurion, as soon as he heard this, went to the captain and told him of it, What art thou about? he said. This man is a Roman citizen. 27 So the captain came and asked him, What is this? Thou art a Roman citizen? Yes, he said. 28 Why, answered the captain, it cost me a heavy sum to win this privilege. Ah, said Paul, but I am a citizen by birth. 29 Upon this, the men who were to have put him to the question moved away from him; and the captain himself was alarmed, to find out that this was a Roman citizen, and he had put him in bonds. 30 So, the next day, determined to discover the truth about the charge the Jews were bringing against him, he released him, summoned a meeting of the chief priests and the whole Council, and brought Paul down to confront them with him.

Chapter Twenty-three

v. 5. It seems likely that St. Paul, looking round the Council to see what faces he could recognize, heard the high priest's interruption without seeing who the speaker was.

PAUL FASTENED HIS eyes on the Council, and said, Brethren, all my life I have behaved myself with full loyalty of conscience towards God. 2 At this, the high priest Ananias bade those who were standing near smite him on the mouth. 3 Then Paul said to him, It is God that will smite thee, for the whitened wall thou art; thou art sitting there to judge me according to the law, and wilt thou break the law by ordering them to smite me? 4 What, said the bystanders, wouldst thou insult God's high priest? 5 And Paul said, Brethren, I could not tell that it was the high priest; to be sure, it is written, Thou shalt not speak ill of him who rules thy people. 6 And now, finding that there were two factions among them, one of the Sadducees and the other of the Pharisees, Paul cried out in the Council, Brethren, I am a Pharisee, and my fathers were Pharisees before me. And I am standing on my trial because I am one who hopes for the resurrection of the dead. 7 When he said this, a dissension arose between the Pharisees and the Sadducees and the assembly was in two minds. 8 The Sadducees will have it that there is no resurrection, that there are no angels or spirits, whereas the Pharisees believe in both. 9 So that a great clamour followed; and some of the Pharisees came forward to protest; We cannot find any fault in this man, they said. Perhaps he has had a message from a spirit, or an angel. 10 Then dissension rose high; and the captain, who was afraid that they would tear Paul in pieces, ordered his troops to come down and rescue Paul from their midst, and bring him safe to the soldiers' quarters.

11 On the next night, the Lord came to his side, and told him, Do not lose heart; thou hast done with bearing me witness in Jerusalem, and now thou must carry the same witness to Rome. 12 When day came, the Jews held a conclave, and bound themselves under a solemn curse that they would not eat or drink until they had killed Paul; 13 more than forty of them joined in this conspiracy. 14 So they went to the chief priests and elders, and told them, We have bound ourselves under a solemn curse not to

take food until we have killed Paul. 15 Your part, then, is to signify to the captain your wish and the Council's, that he would bring him down before you, as if you meant to examine his cause more precisely; and we are ready to make away with him before he reaches you. 16 Paul's sister had a son who heard of this ambush being laid; and he went to the soldiers' quarters and gave news of it to Paul. 17 Whereupon Paul had one of the centurions brought to him, and said, Take this young man to the captain; he has news to give him. 18 So he bade him follow, and took him to the captain; The prisoner, Paul, he said, had me summoned and asked me to take this young man into thy presence; he has a message for thee. 19 And the captain, taking him by the hand and drawing him aside, asked, What is the news thou bringest me? 20 The Jews, he said, have formed this design; they will ask thee to bring Paul down before the Council to-morrow, as if they meant to examine his cause more precisely. 21 Do not listen to them; some of them will be lying in ambush for him, more than forty in number. They have sworn not to eat or drink until they have made away with him; even now they are in readiness, only waiting for thy consent.

22 Thereupon the captain dismissed the young man, warning him not to let anyone know that he had revealed this secret to him. 23 Then he summoned two of the centurions, and told them, You are to have two hundred men from the cohort ready to march to Caesarea, with seventy horsemen and two hundred spearmen; they will set out at the third hour of the night. 24 And you must provide beasts, so that they can mount Paul and take him safely to the governor, Felix. 25 (He was afraid that the Jews might seize on Paul and kill him; and that he himself might be falsely accused of taking a bribe from them.) 26 He also wrote a letter, with these contents: Claudius Lysias, to his excellency Felix, the governor, sends greeting. 27 Here is a man whom the Jews seized, and set about killing him; but I came up with my men and rescued him, learning that he was a Roman citizen. 28 Since I had a mind to discover what complaint it was they had against him, I took him down into the presence of their Council; 29 but I found that the accusation was concerned with disputes about their own law, and that he was charged with nothing that deserved death or imprisonment. 30 And now, since I have information of a plot which they have laid against him, I am sending him to thee, telling his accusers at the same time that they must plead their cause before thee. Farewell.

v. 25. This verse is wanting in the majority of manuscripts.

31 The soldiers, obeying their orders, took Paul with them, and conducted him, travelling all night, to Antipatris. 32 Next day they left the horsemen to accompany him, and went back to their quarters. 33 The horsemen, upon reaching Caesarea, delivered the letter to the governor, and brought Paul, too, into his presence. 34 So the governor read the letter, asked from what province he came, and was told, From Cilicia; 35 then he said, I will give thee a hearing when thy accusers, too, are present. And he gave orders that he should be kept safe in Herod's palace.

Chapter Twenty=four

FIVE DAYS LATER THE high priest Ananias came down, accompanied by some of the elders and by an advocate named Tertullus; these appeared before the governor against Paul. 2 So, when Paul had been summoned, Tertullus began his indictment thus, Such is the peace thou hast enabled us to enjoy, so many wrongs have been righted for us through thy wisdom, 3 that always and everywhere, most noble Felix, we are ready to acknowledge it with grateful hearts. 4 But I must not weary thee with more of this; what we ask of thy courtesy is no more than a brief audience. 5 Here is a man who is known to us as a pestilent mover of sedition among Jews all over the world, a ringleader of the sect of the Nazarenes, 6 who has not scrupled to attempt a violation of the temple. We arrested him, and had intended to try him according to our own law, 7 when the captain, Lysias, came and took him out of our hands, with great violence, 8 and insisted that his accusers must appear before thee. Interrogate him thyself, and thou wilt be able to learn the truth about all the accusations we bring against him. 9 And the Jews, for their part, supported the indictment, alleging that all this was the truth.

vv. 6-8. The words 'and had intended to try him according to our own law', 'and insisted that his accusers must appear before thee', are wanting in some manuscripts; others omit the intervening words as well, so that the passage reads 'We arrested him; interrogate him, and thou wilt be able to learn

10 Then the governor made a sign to bid Paul speak, and he answered, I am the more emboldened to make my defence, because I know well that thou hast been a judge over this nation for many years. 11 Thou hast the means of assuring thyself that it is only twelve days since I came up to Jerusalem, to worship there. 12 They have never found me raising controversy, or bringing a crowd together, either in the temple, or in the synagogues, 13 or in the open city; nor can they produce any proof of the charges they bring against me. 14 But this I admit to thee, that in worshipping God, my Father, I follow what we call the way, and they call a sect. I put my trust in all that is written in the law and the prophets, 15 sharing before God the hope they have too, that the dead will rise again, both just and unjust. 16 To that end I, like them, am at pains to keep my conscience clear of offence towards God or man, at all times. 17 After some years' absence I came up to bring alms to the men of my own race, and certain offerings. 18 It was when I had just made these offerings and had been purified in the temple, that I was found there, no crowd about me, no rioting, by whom? 19 By some Jews from Asia, who ought to be here, standing in thy presence, if they had any quarrel with me. 20 In default of that, it is for those who are here to give their own account of what blame they found in me, when I stood before the Council; 21 unless it were over one single utterance, when I cried out, standing there among them, If I am on my trial before you to-day, it is because of the resurrection of the dead.

22 Felix, who had full information about this way, reserved judgement; I will give you a hearing, he said, when Lysias, the captain, has come down here. 23 And he gave orders to the centurion that Paul was to be kept safely, but left at his ease, and that any of his friends should be given liberty to minister to him. 24 And some days afterwards, when Felix was there with his wife Drusilla, who was a Jewess, he sent for Paul, and listened to his message about faith in Jesus Christ. 25 When he spoke of justice, and continence, and of the judgement that is to come, Felix was terrified; No more of this for the present, he said, I will send for thee when I can find leisure. 26 At the same time, he hoped that Paul would offer him a bribe, and for that reason sent for him often, and courted his company. 27 So two years passed; then Porcius Festus came as successor to Felix; and Felix, who wished to ingratiate himself with the Jews, left Paul in prison.

the truth about all the accusation we bring against him'. As the text stands, it is not quite certain whether Felix is asked to interrogate St. Paul, or Claudius Lysias; probably the former (but cf. v. 22 below).

v. 26. Some manuscripts read 'would offer him a bribe for his release', which is evidently the meaning of the passage.

Chapter Twenty=five

ND Festus, three days after entering his province, went up from Caesarea to Jerusalem. 2 Here the high priest and the leaders of the Jews put before him their case against Paul, and were urgent with him, 3 asking as a favour, that he would summon Paul to Jerusalem; meanwhile they were preparing an ambush, so as to make away with him on the journey. 4 But Festus answered that Paul was in safe keeping at Caesarea; he himself would be removing there as soon as possible; 5 Let those of you who are men of influence, he said, travel down with me, and bring your charges against this man, if you have anything against him. 6 So, when he had spent a week with them, or ten days at most, he went down to Caesarea; and next day, sitting on the judgement seat, he gave orders for Paul to be brought in. 7 When he appeared, there were the Jews who had come down from Jerusalem, standing round him and bringing many grave accusations against him, which they could not prove; 8 while Paul said in his defence, I have committed no crime against the Jewish law, or against the temple, or against Caesar. 9 But Festus had a mind to ingratiate himself with the Jews, so he answered Paul thus, Art thou ready to go up to Jerusalem, and meet these charges before me there? 10 Upon which Paul said, I am standing at Caesar's judgement seat, where I have a right to be tried. As for the Jews, I have done them no wrong, as thou knowest well enough. 11 If I am guilty, if I have done something which deserves death, I do not ask for reprieve; if their charges are without substance, no one has a right to make them a present of my life. I appeal to Caesar. 12 Then Festus conferred with his council, and answered, Hast thou appealed to Caesar? To Caesar thou shalt go.

13 Some days later, king Agrippa and Bernice came to Caesarea, to give Festus their greeting, 14 and, since he was spending several days there, Festus put Paul's case before the king; There is a man here, he said, whom Felix left behind him in prison; 15 and when I went to Jerusalem the chief priests and elders of the Jews denounced him to me, asking for his condemnation. 16 I replied that it is not the Roman custom to pronounce a condemnation, until the accused man has been confronted with his accusers, and

been given the opportunity to clear himself of the charge. 17 So they came here with me, and I did not keep them waiting; the next day, sitting on the judgement seat, I gave orders for the man to be brought in. 18 His accusers, as they stood round him, could not tax him with any criminal offence, such as I had expected; 19 their controversies with him were concerned with scruples of their own, and with a dead man called Jesus, whom Paul declared to be alive. 20 For myself, I hesitated to enter upon the discussion of such matters; so I asked whether he was willing to go to Jerusalem, and meet these charges there. 21 Upon which Paul appealed to have his case reserved for the emperor's cognizance; and I gave orders that he should be kept safe until I can send him to Caesar. 22 Then Agrippa said to Festus, I have often wished, myself, to hear this man speak. Thou shalt hear him, said he, to-morrow.

23 So, on the next day, Agrippa and Bernice came with great pomp, and made their entry into the hall of judgement, attended by the captains and all the eminent persons of the city; and Paul, at Festus' command, was brought in. 24 Then Festus said, King Agrippa, and all you who are present, you see before you a man over whom the whole Jewish body has been petitioning me, not only here but at Jerusalem, crying out that he must not be allowed to live a day longer. 25 For myself, I was satisfied that he had not done anything deserving of death; but, since he has appealed to the emperor, I have thought it best to send him, 26 and now, writing to my sovereign lord, I have no clear account to give of him. 27 That is why I have brought him before you, and before thee especially, king Agrippa, so that the examination may afford material for my letter. 28 It would be unreasonable, I conceive, to remit a prisoner for trial without putting on record the charges that lie against him.

Chapter Twenty=six

THEN Agrippa said to Paul, Thou art free to give an account of thyself. 2 And Paul, stretching out his hand, began his defence: King Agrippa, I count myself fortunate to-day, to be defending myself against all the accusations of the Jews in thy presence. 3 No one is more familiar than thou with the customs of the Jews, and their controversies; and this makes me bold to ask thee for a patient audience. 4 What my life was like when boyhood was over, spent from the first among my own people and in Jerusalem, all the Jews know; 5 their earliest memory of me, would they but admit it, is of one who lived according to the strictest tradition of observance we have, a Pharisee. 6 And if I stand here on my trial, it is for my hope of the promise God made to our fathers. 7 Our twelve tribes worship him ceaselessly, night and day, in the hope of attaining that promise; and this is the hope, my lord king, for which the Jews call me to account. 8 Why should it be beyond the belief of men such as thou art, that God should raise the dead?

9 Well then, I thought it my duty to defy, in many ways, the name of Jesus the Nazarene. 10 And that is what I did, at Jerusalem; it was I, under powers granted me by the chief priests, who shut up many of the faithful in prison; and when they were done to death, I raised my voice against them. 11 Often have I tried to force them into blaspheming, by inflicting punishment on them in one synagogue after another; nay, so unmeasured was my rage against them that I used to go to foreign cities to persecute them. 12 It was on such an errand that I was making my way to Damascus, with powers delegated to me by the chief priests, 13 when, journeying at mid-day, I saw, my lord king, a light from heaven, surpassing the brightness of the sun, which shone about me and

v. 14. They all fell to the ground at the first shock of the apparition, but the others soon regained their feet (ix. 7 above).

my companions. 14 We all fell to the ground, and I heard a voice which said to me, in Hebrew, Saul, Saul, why dost thou persecute me? This is a thankless task of thine, kicking against the goad. 15 Who art thou, Lord? I asked. And the Lord said, I am Jesus, whom Saul persecutes. 16 Rise up, and stand on thy feet; I have shewn myself to thee, that I may single thee out to serve me, as the witness of this vision thou hast had, and other visions thou wilt have of me. 17 I will be thy deliverer from the hands of thy people, and of the Gentiles, to whom I am now sending thee. 18 Thou shalt open their eyes, and turn them from darkness to light, from the power of Satan to God, so that they may receive, through faith in me, remission of their sins and an inheritance among the saints.

19 Whereupon, king Agrippa, I did not shew myself disobedient to the heavenly vision. 20 First to those in Damascus, then in Jerusalem, then to all the country of Judaea, then to the heathen, I preached repentance, bidding them turn to God, and so act as befits men who are penitent. 21 That is why the Jews, when they caught me in the temple, tried to murder me. 22 But, thanks to God's help, I still stand here to-day, bearing my witness to small and great alike. Yet there is nothing in my message which goes beyond what the prophets spoke of, and Moses spoke of, as things to come; 23 a suffering Christ, and one who should shew light to his people and to the Gentiles by being the first to rise from the dead.

24 When Paul had proceeded so far with his defence, Festus said in a loud voice, Paul, thou art mad; they are driving thee to madness, these long studies of thine. 25 But Paul answered, No, most noble Festus, I am not mad; the message which I utter is sober truth. 26 The king knows about all this well enough; that is why I speak with such confidence in his presence. None of this, I am sure, is news to him; it was not in some secret corner that all this happened. 27 Dost thou believe the prophets, king Agrippa? I am well assured thou dost believe them. 28 At this, Agrippa said to Paul, Thou wouldst have me turn Christian with very little ado. 29 Why, said Paul, it would be my prayer to God that, whether it were with much ado or little, both thou and all those who are listening to me to-day should become just such as I am, but for these chains. 30 Then the king rose, and so did the governor, and Bernice, and all those who sat there with them. 31 When they had retired, they said to one another, This man is guilty of no fault that deserves death or imprisonment. 32 And Agrippa said to Festus, If he had not appealed to Caesar, this man might have been set at liberty.

v. 28. Some commentators have thought that Agrippa said, whether sarcastically or in earnest, 'Thou dost almost persuade me to turn Christian'; but the Greek has rather the sense, 'Thou art trying to persuade me to be a Christian with very little effort (from thyself)', or perhaps 'at very short notice'.

v. 29. 'But for these chains'; the Greek may mean, 'these chains notwithstanding'.

Chapter Twenty-seven

AND NOW WORD WAS given for the voyage to Italy, Paul being handed over, with some other prisoners, to a centurion called Julius, who belonged to the Augustan cohort. 2 We embarked on a boat from Adrumetum which was bound for the Asiatic ports, and set sail; the Macedonian, Aristarchus, from Thessalonica, was with us. 3 Next day we put in at Sidon; and here Julius shewed Paul courtesy by allowing him to visit his friends and be cared for. 4 Then, setting sail, we coasted under the lee of Cyprus, to avoid contrary winds, 5 but made a straight course over the open sea that lies off Cilicia and Pamphylia, and so reached Lystra, in Lycia. 6 There the centurion found a boat from Alexandria which was sailing for Italy, and put us on board. 7 We had a slow voyage for many days after this; we made Gnidus with difficulty, and then, with the wind beating us back, had to sail under the lee of Crete by way of Salmone. 8 Here we were hard put to it to coast along as far as a place called Fair Havens, near the city of Thalassa. 9 Much time had now been wasted, and sailing had become dangerous; the fast was already over; and Paul bade them make the best of it. 10 Sirs, he said, I can see plainly that there is no sailing now, without injury and great loss, not only of our freight and of the vessel, but of our own lives too.

11 The centurion, however, paid more attention to the helmsman and the master than to Paul's advice. 12 The harbour was not well placed for wintering in; so that more of them gave their voices for sailing further still, in the hope of making Phoenice and wintering there; it is a harbour in Crete, which faces in the direction of the South-west and North-west winds. 13 A light breeze was now blowing from the South, so that they thought they had achieved their purpose, and coasted along Crete, leaving their anchorage at Assos. 14 But it was not long before a gale of wind struck the ship, the wind called Euraquilo; 15 she was carried out of her course, and could make no head against the wind, so we

v. 5. We have no other record of a port called Lystra on the Lycian coast; the well known name of Myra is given instead by most manuscripts, but this may be a mere correction.

v. 8. Thalassa; a better reading is Lasea.

v. 9. The fast was the day of expiation, occurring about the time of the equinoctial gales.

v. 10. St. Paul here is not prophesying; he is using maxims of common prudence.

v. 12. 'In the direction of'; this probably means not 'in the teeth of', but 'down along the course of', so that the harbour would face North-east and South-east, as the modern Loutro does.

v. 13. No port called Assos is known to have existed in Crete; the Latin interpreters seem to have mistaken for a proper name the Greek word, 'close in'.

v. 14. Euraquilo, that is, the North-east wind.

gave up and let her drive. 16 We now ran under the lee of an island named Cauda, where we contrived, with difficulty, to secure the ship's boat. 17 When it had been hoisted aboard, they strengthened the ship by passing ropes round her; then, for fear of being driven on to the Syrtis sands, they let down the sea-anchor, and so drifted. 18 On the next day, so violently were we tossed about in the gale, they lightened ship, 19 and on the third, they deliberately threw the spare tackle overboard.

20 For several days we saw nothing of the sun or the stars, and a heavy gale pressed us hard, so that we had lost, by now, all hope of surviving: and we were much in want of food. 21 And now Paul stood up in their presence, and said, Sirs, you should have taken my advice; if you had not put out from Crete, you would have saved all this injury and damage. 22 But I would not have you lose courage, even now; there is to be no loss of life among you, only of the ship. 23 An angel stood before me last night, sent by the God to whom I belong, the God whom I serve, 24 and said, Have no fear, Paul, thou art to stand in Caesar's presence; and behold, God has granted thee the safety of all thy fellow voyagers. 25 Have courage, then, sirs; I trust in God, believing that all will fall out as he has told me. 26 Only we are to be cast up on an island. 27 On the fourteenth night, as we drifted about in the Adriatic sea, the crew began to suspect, about midnight, that we were nearing land; 28 so they took soundings, and made it twenty fathom; then they sounded again a short distance away, and made it fifteen fathom. 29 Afraid, therefore, that we might be cast ashore on some rocky coast, they let down four anchors from the stern, and fell to wishing it were day. 30 And now the sailors had a mind to abandon the ship, and lowered the boat into the sea, pretending that they meant to lay out anchors from the bows. 31 But Paul told the centurion and the soldiers, These must stay on board, or there is no hope left for you; 32 whereupon the soldiers cut the boat's ropes away and let it drop.

33 As day began to break, Paul entreated them all to take some food; To-day, he said, is the fourteenth day you have been in suspense, and all that time gone hungry, neglecting to eat; 34 pray take some food, then; it will make for your preservation; not a hair of anyone's head is to be lost. 35 And with that he took bread, and gave thanks to God before them all, and broke it, and began to eat. 36 Thereupon they all found courage, and themselves took a meal. 37 The whole number of souls on board was

v. 17. 'The sea-anchor'; literally 'the instrument'. It appears that the ancients sometimes dragged a heavy plank behind their ships, to retard their speed in a gale, and this seems to be the intention of the Latin rendering; some would translate the Greek 'lowering the sails', but this precaution must surely have been taken earlier.

v. 27. The Adriatic sea, that is, the central Mediterranean in general.

two hundred and seventy six. 38 So all ate till they were content; and afterwards they began to lighten the ship, throwing the corn into the sea.

39 When day broke, they found that the coast was strange to them. But they sighted a bay with a sloping beach, and made up their minds, if it should be possible, to run the ship ashore there. 40 They lifted the anchors and trusted themselves to the mercy of the sea, at the same time unlashing the tiller; then they hoisted the foresail to the breeze, and held on for the shore. 41 But now, finding they were running into a cross sea, they grounded the ship where they were. The bows, which were stuck fast, felt no movement, but the stern began falling to pieces under the violence of the waves. 42 Whereupon the soldiers would have killed the prisoners, for fear that any of them should dive overboard and escape, 43 but the centurion balked them of their will, because he had a mind to keep Paul safe. He gave orders that those who could swim should go overboard first, and make their way to land; 44 of the rest, some were ferried across on planks, and some on the ship's wreckage. So it was that all reached land in safety.

v. 40. It is not certain which of the sails is meant by the word here used.

Chapter
Twenty=eight

WHEN WE WERE SAFE on land, we found that the island was called Melita. The kindness which the natives shewed to us was beyond the ordinary; 2 they welcomed us all by making a fire for us, because rain was coming on, and it was cold. 3 Paul had collected a bundle of faggots and had just put them on the fire, when a viper, coming out to escape the heat, fastened on his hand; 4 and the natives, when they saw the beast coiled round his hand, said to one another, This must be some murderer; he

v. 3. There are no poisonous snakes in Malta to-day; if this was true in St. Paul's time, it is not difficult to suppose that this viper may have come over in, and escaped from, one of the African grain-ships.

has been rescued from the sea, but divine vengeance would not let him live. 5 He, meanwhile, shook the beast into the fire, and was none the worse. 6 They still waited to see him swell up, or fall down dead on a sudden; but when they had waited a long time, and found that there was nothing amiss with him, they changed their minds, and declared that he must be a god. 7 Among the estates in that part were some which belonged to the leading citizen of the island, a man named Publius, who took us in and for three days entertained us hospitably; 8 and it so happened that Publius' father had taken to his bed, laid up with fever and dysentery. Paul, who had gone to visit him, laid his hands upon him with prayer, and healed him; 9 whereupon all the other folk in the island who were suffering from infirmities came to him and found a cure. 10 These paid us great honour, and when we embarked they loaded us with all the supplies we needed.

11 It was at the end of three months that we sailed, in a ship from Alexandria which had wintered at the island; its sign was Castor and Pollux. 12 We put in at Syracuse, where we waited for three days; 13 then we coasted round the further shore, and so arrived at Rhegium. When we had spent a day there, a South wind came on, and we made Puteoli on the second day out. 14 Here we found some brethren, who prevailed on us to stay with them for a week. And so we ended our journey at Rome. 15 The brethren there, who had heard our story, came out as far as Appius' Forum, and on to the Three Taverns, to meet us; Paul gave thanks to God and took courage when he saw them.

16 Once we were in Rome, Paul was allowed to have his own residence, which he shared with the soldier who guarded him. 17 It was three days later that he called a meeting of the leading men among the Jews. When they had assembled, he told them, Brethren, I am one who has done nothing to the prejudice of our people, or of our ancestral customs; yet, in Jerusalem, they handed me over to the Romans as a prisoner. 18 These, when they had examined me, had a mind to release me, since no capital charge lay against me; 19 but the Jews cried out against it, and I was forced to appeal to Caesar, though it is not as if I had any fault to find with my own nation. 20 That is why I have asked for the opportunity of seeing you and speaking to you. It is because I hope as Israel hopes, that I wear this chain. 21 At this they said to him, We have not received any letter about thee from Judaea, nor has any of the brethren come here with any ill report or hard

words about thee. 22 We ask nothing better than to hear what thy opinions are; all we know of this sect is, that it is everywhere decried.

23 So they made an appointment with him, and met him at his lodging in great numbers. And he bore his testimony and told them about the kingdom of God, trying to convince them from Moses and the prophets of what Jesus was, from dawn till dusk. 24 Some were convinced by his words, others refused belief; 25 and they took their leave still at variance among themselves, but not till Paul had spoken one last word, It was a true utterance the Holy Spirit made to our fathers through the prophet Isaias: 26 Go to this people, and tell them, You will listen and listen, but for you there is no understanding; you will watch and watch, but for you there is no perceiving. 27 The heart of this people has become dull, their ears are slow to listen, and they keep their eyes shut, so that they may never see with those eyes, or hear with those ears, or understand with that heart, and turn back to me, and win healing from me. 28 Take notice, then, that this message of salvation has been sent by God to the Gentiles, and they, at least, will listen to it.

29 So much he told the Jews, and then they left him, with much dissension among themselves. 30 And for two whole years he lived in a lodging hired at his own expense, and welcomed all who came to visit him, 31 proclaiming God's kingdom, and teaching them the truths which concern our Lord Jesus Christ, boldly enough, without let or hindrance.

vv. 26, 27. Is. vi. 9.

v. 29. This verse is wanting in some manuscripts.

THE EPISTLE OF THE BLESSED APOSTLE PAUL TO THE ROMANS

Chapter One

IT IS PAUL WHO WRITES; a servant of Jesus Christ, called to be his apostle, and set apart to preach the gospel of God. 2 That gospel, promised long ago by means of his prophets in the holy scriptures, 3 tells us of his Son, descended, in respect of his human birth, from the line of David, 4 but, in respect of the sanctified spirit that was his, marked out miraculously as the Son of God by his resurrection from the dead; our Lord Jesus Christ. 5 It is through him we have received the grace of apostleship; all over the world, men must be taught to honour his name by paying him the homage of their faith, 6 and you among them, you, who are called to belong to Jesus Christ. 7 I wish to all those at Rome whom God loves and has called to be holy, grace and peace from God our Father, and from the Lord Jesus Christ. 8 And first, I offer thanks to my God through Jesus Christ for all of you, you whose faith is so renowned throughout the world. 9 The God to whom I address the inner worship of my heart, while I preach the gospel of his Son, is my witness how constantly I make mention of you, 10 never failing to ask, when I am at my prayers, that somehow, in God's Providence, I may be granted at last an opportunity of visiting you. 11 I long to see you, in the hope that I may have some spiritual gift to share with you, so as to strengthen your resolve; 12 or rather, so that the faith we find in each other, you and I, may be an encouragement to you and to me as well. 13 I should be sorry, brethren, if you were left in doubt that (although hitherto I have always been prevented) I have often planned to visit you, and to be able to claim some harvest among you, as I can among the Gentiles elsewhere. 14 I have the same duty to all, Greek and barbarian, learned and simple; 15 and for my own part I am eager to preach the gospel to you in Rome as I have to others. 16 I am not ashamed of this gospel. It is an instrument of God's power, that brings salvation to all who believe in it, Jew first and then Greek. 17 It reveals God's way of justifying us, faith first and last; as the scripture says, It is faith that brings life to the just man.

18 God's anger is being revealed from heaven; his anger against the impiety and wrong-doing of the men whose wrong-doing denies his truth its full scope. 19 The knowledge of God is clear to their minds; God himself has made it clear to them; 20 from the foundations of the world men have caught sight of his invisible nature, his eternal power and his divineness, as they are known through his creatures. Thus there is no excuse for them; 21 although they had the knowledge of God, they did not honour him or give thanks to him as God; they became fantastic in their notions, and their senseless hearts grew benighted; 22 they, who claimed to be so wise, turned fools, 23 and exchanged the glory of the imperishable God for representations of perishable man, of bird and beast and reptile. 24 That is why God abandoned their lustful hearts to filthy practices of dishonouring their own bodies among themselves. 25 They had exchanged God's truth for a lie, reverencing and worshipping the creature in preference to the Creator (blessed is he for ever, Amen); 26 and, in return, God abandoned them to passions which brought dishonour to themselves. Their women exchanged natural for unnatural intercourse; 27 and the men, on their side, giving up natural intercourse with women, were burnt up with desire for each other; men practising vileness with their fellow men. Thus they have received a fitting retribution for their false belief.

28 And as they scorned to keep God in their view, so God has abandoned them to a frame of mind worthy of all scorn, that prompts them to disgraceful acts. 29 They are versed in every

v. 17. Habacuc ii. 4. It is not certain whether the expression 'faith first and last' (literally 'from faith to faith') implies a progress from belief in the Old Testament prophecies to belief in our Lord, or a progress from the act of faith by which we become Christians to the spirit of faith in which, as Christians, we ought to live.

vv. 18-27. Many of the considerations here brought forward are to be found in Wisdom, ch. xiii. It is not clear, in verse 18, whether the heathen are blamed for 'holding the truth and yet sinning', or for 'hindering the truth by means of their sin'.

kind of injustice, knavery, impurity, avarice, and ill-will; spiteful, murderous, contentious, deceitful, depraved, backbiters, slanderers, God's enemies; 30 insolent, haughty, vainglorious; inventive in wickedness, disobedient to their parents; 31 without prudence, without honour, without love, without loyalty, without pity. 32 Yet, with the just decree of God before their minds, they never grasped the truth that those who so live are deserving of death; not only those who commit such acts, but those who countenance such a manner of living.

v. 32. The words 'they never grasped the truth' are not found in the best Greek manuscripts; these read, at the end of the verse, 'they not only commit such acts, but countenance those who commit them.'

Chapter Two

 O, friend, if thou canst see thy neighbour's faults, no excuse is left thee, whoever thou art; in blaming him, thou dost own thyself guilty, since thou, for all thy blame, livest the same life as he. 2 We know that God passes unerring judgement upon such lives; 3 and dost thou, friend, think to escape God's judgement, thou who dost blame men for living thus, and art guilty of the same acts thyself? 4 Or is it that thou art presuming on that abundant kindness of his, which bears with thee and waits for thee? Dost thou not know that God's kindness is inviting thee to repent? 5 Whereas thou, by the stubborn impenitence of thy heart, dost continue to store up retribution for thyself against the day of retribution, when God will reveal the justice of his judgements. 6 He will award to every man what his acts have deserved; 7 eternal life to those who have striven for glory, and honour, and immortality, by perseverance in doing good; 8 the retribution of his anger to those who are contumacious, rebelling against truth and paying homage to wickedness.

v. 1. 'Whoever thou art' probably implies that verses 1-16 are addressed both to Jews and to Gentiles.

9 There will be affliction then and distress for every human soul that has practised wickedness, the Jew in the first instance, but the Gentile too; 10 there will be glory and honour and peace for everyone who has done good, the Jew in the first instance, but the Gentile too. 11 There are no human preferences with God. 12 Those who have been sinners without regard to the law will be doomed without regard to the law; those who have

been sinners with the law for their rule will be judged with the law for their rule. 13 To have heard the law read out is no claim to acceptance with God; it is those who obey the law that will be justified. 14 As for the Gentiles, though they have no law to guide them, there are times when they carry out the precepts of the law unbidden, finding in their own natures a rule to guide them, in default of any other rule; 15 and this shews that the obligations of the law are written in their hearts; their conscience utters its own testimony, and when they dispute with one another they find themselves condemning this, approving that. 16 And there will be a day when God (according to the gospel I preach) will pass judgement, through Jesus Christ, on the hidden thoughts of men.

17 Thou claimest Jewish blood; thou reliest on the law; God is all thy boast; 18 thou canst tell what is his will, discern what things are of moment, because the law has taught thee. 19 Thou hast confidence in thyself as one who leads the blind, a light to their darkness; 20 admonishing the fool, instructing the simple, because in the law thou hast the incarnation of all knowledge and all truth. 21 Tell me, then, thou who teachest others, hast thou no lesson for thyself? Is it a thief that preaches against stealing, 22 an adulterer that forbids adultery? Dost thou rob temples, thou, who shrinkest from the touch of an idol? 23 Thy boast is in the law; wilt thou break the law, to God's dishonour? 24 The name of God says the scripture, has become a reproach among the Gentiles, because of you.

v. 24. Ezechiel xxxvi. 23.

25 Circumcision, to be sure, is of value, so long as thou keepest the law; but if thou breakest the law, thy circumcision has lost its effect. 26 And if one who has never been circumcised observes the conditions of the law, does it not follow that he, though uncircumcised, will be reckoned as one who is circumcised? 27 That he, who keeps the law, though uncircumcised in body, will be able to pass judgement on thee, who breakest the law, though circumcised according to the letter of it? 28 To be a Jew is not to be a Jew outwardly; to be circumcised is not to be circumcised outwardly, in the flesh. 29 He is a Jew indeed who is one inwardly; true circumcision is achieved in the heart, according to the spirit, not the letter of the law, for God's, not for man's approval.

278

THE TRANSFIGURATION OF CHRIST

DUCCIO DI BUONINSEGNA
active 1278-1319

NATIONAL GALLERY, LONDON

Chapter Three

F what use is it, then, to be a Jew? What value was there in circumcision? 2 Much, I answer, in every respect; chiefly because the Jews had the words of God entrusted to them. 3 Some, to be sure, shewed unfaithfulness on their side; but can we suppose that unfaithfulness on their part will dispense God from his promise? 4 It is not to be thought of; God must prove true to his word, though all men should play him false; so it is written, Thy dealings were just, and if thou art called in question, thou hast right on thy side. 5 Thus our fault only serves to bring God's integrity to light. (Does that mean that God does wrong in punishing us for it? 6 Impossible again, even according to our human standards; that would mean that God has no right to judge the world; 7 it would mean that because my deceitfulness has promoted God's glory by giving scope to his truthfulness, I on my side do not deserve to be condemned as a sinner. 8 If so, why should we not do evil so that good may come of it? That is what we are accused of preaching by some of our detractors; and their condemnation of it is just.)

9 Well then, has either side the advantage? In no way. Jews and Gentiles, as we have before alleged, are alike convicted of sin. 10 Thus, it is written, There is not an innocent man among them, no, not one. 11 There is nobody who reflects, and searches for God; 12 all alike are on the wrong course, all are wasted lives; not one of them acts honourably, no, not one. 13 Their mouths are gaping tombs, they use their tongues to flatter. Under their lips the venom of asps is hidden. 14 Their talk overflows with curses and calumny. 15 They run hot-foot to shed blood; 16 havoc and ruin follow in their path; 17 the way of peace is unknown to them. 18 They do not keep the fear of God before their eyes. 19 So the law says, and we know that the words of the law are meant for the law's own subjects; it is determined that no one shall have anything to say for himself, that the whole world shall own itself liable to God's judgements. 20 No human creature can become acceptable in his sight by observing the law; what the law does is to give us the full consciousness of sin.

21 But, in these days, God's way of justification has at last been brought to light; one which was attested by the law and the

v. 4. Ps. l. 6.

v. 9. 'Has either side the advantage?'; the Greek word here may mean 'Do we excel them?' or 'Are we excelled by them?' Nor are commentators agreed whether 'we' refers to the Jews or to the Gentiles. But the general sense remains clear.
vv. 10-12. Ps. xiii. 2, 3.
v. 13. Ps. v. 11, Ps. cxxxix. 4.
v. 14. Ps. ix (second part). 7.
vv. 15-17. Is. lix. 7, 8.
v. 18. Ps. xxxv. 2.
v. 19. 'The law' seems to be used here, as often, for the Old Testament generally.

279

prophets, but stands apart from the law; 22 God's way of justification through faith in Jesus Christ, meant for everybody and sent down upon everybody without distinction, if he has faith. 23 All alike have sinned, all alike are unworthy of God's praise. 24 And justification comes to us as a free gift from his grace, through our redemption in Jesus Christ. 25 God has offered him to us as a means of reconciliation, in virtue of faith, ransoming us with his blood. Thus God has vindicated his own holiness, shewing us why he overlooked our former sins 26 in the days of his forbearance; and he has also vindicated the holiness of Jesus Christ, here and now, as one who is himself holy, and imparts holiness to those who take their stand upon faith in him. 27 What has become, then, of thy pride? No room has been left for it. On what principle? The principle which depends on observances? No, the principle which depends on faith; 28 our contention is, that a man is justified by faith apart from the observances of the law. 29 Is God the God of the Jews only? Is he not the God of the Gentiles too? Of the Gentiles too, assuredly; 30 there is only one God, who will justify the circumcised man if he learns to believe, and the Gentile because he believes.

31 Does that mean that we are using faith to rob the law of its force? No, we are setting the law on its right footing.

v. 23. 'God's praise'; some translate 'the glory of God', but it seems commonly simplest to understand the words here as in John xii. 43, as referring to the praise which God bestows.

v. 26. The Greek text here can be, and commonly is, translated thus: 'he has also vindicated his (God's) holiness, here and now, as one who is himself holy, and imparts holiness to those who take their stand upon faith in Jesus Christ'. The other interpretation is, apparently, that of the Latin translators.

v. 31. As in verse 19 above, 'the law' seems to indicate the Old Testament generally, since the considerations here introduced relate to the story of Abraham.

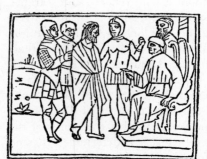

Chapter Four

WHAT, FOR INSTANCE, shall we say of Abraham, our forefather by human descent? What kind of blessing did he win? 2 If it was by observances that Abraham attained his justification, he, to be sure, has something to be proud of. But it was not so in God's sight; 3 what does the scripture tell us? Abraham put his faith in God, and it was reckoned virtue in him. 4 The reward

v. 3. Gen. xv. 6.

given to one who works to earn it is not reckoned as a favour, it is reckoned as his due. 5 When a man's faith is reckoned virtue in him, according to God's gracious plan, it is not because of anything he does; it is because he has faith, faith in the God who makes a just man of the sinner. 6 So, too, David pronounces his blessing on the man whom God accepts, without any mention of observances: 7 Blessed are those who have all their faults forgiven, all their transgressions buried away; 8 blessed is the man who is not a sinner in the Lord's reckoning. 9 This blessing, then, does it fall only on those who are circumcised, or on the uncircumcised as well? We saw that Abraham's faith was reckoned virtue in him. 10 And in what state of things was that reckoning made? Was he circumcised or uncircumcised at the time? Uncircumcised, not circumcised yet. 11 Circumcision was only given to him as a token; as the seal of that justification which came to him through his faith while he was still uncircumcised. And thus he is the father of all those who, still uncircumcised, have the faith that will be reckoned virtue in them too. 12 Meanwhile, he is the father of those who are circumcised, as long as they do not merely take their stand on circumcision, but follow in the steps of that faith which he, our father Abraham, had before circumcision began.

13 It was not through obedience to the law, but through faith justifying them, that Abraham and his posterity were promised the inheritance of the world. 14 If it is only those who obey the law that receive the inheritance, then his faith was ill founded, and the promise has been annulled. 15 (The effect of the law is only to bring God's displeasure upon us; it is only where there is a law that transgression becomes possible.) 16 The inheritance, then, must come through faith (and so by free gift); thus the promise is made good to all Abraham's posterity, not only that posterity of his which keeps the law, but that which imitates his faith. We are all Abraham's children; 17 and so it was written of him, I have made thee the father of many nations. We are his children in the sight of God, in whom he put his faith, who can raise the dead to life, and send his call to that which has no being, as if it already were.

18 Abraham, then, believed, hoping against hope; and thus became the father of many nations; Like these, he was told, thy posterity shall be. 19 There was no wavering in his faith; he gave no thought to the want of life in his own body, though he was nearly a hundred years old at the time, nor to the deadness of Sara's womb; 20 he shewed no hesitation or doubt at God's promise, but drew strength from his faith, confessing God's power, 21 fully con-

v. 5. 'According to God's gracious plan'; these words do not appear in the Greek manuscripts.

v. 7. Ps. xxxi. 1.

v. 10. Gen. xii. 2, and elsewhere; circumcision is first mentioned in Gen. xvii. 10.

v. 13. None of the promises recorded in Genesis would appear to justify this assertion literally; but it seems likely that Jewish tradition, from a comparison of Gen. xii. 3, xv. 5, and so on, interpreted them in the sense of world-wide diffusion. This promise of world-inheritance, St. Paul argues, has not been kept, if by Abraham's posterity we mean only the Jews; it remains to be fulfilled, therefore, in the Church of Christ, which is Abraham's posterity in a spiritual sense.

v. 18. Gen. xv. 5.

vinced that God was able to perform what he had promised. 22 This, then, was reckoned virtue in him; 23 and the words, It was reckoned virtue in him, were not written of him only: they were written of us too. 24 It will be reckoned virtue in us, if we believe in God as having raised our Lord Jesus Christ from the dead: 25 handed over to death for our sins, and raised to life for our justification.

Chapter Five

NCE justified, then, on the ground of our faith, let us enjoy peace with God through our Lord Jesus Christ, 2 as it was through him that we have obtained access, by faith, to that grace in which we stand. We are confident in the hope of attaining glory as the sons of God; 3 nay, we are confident even over our afflictions, knowing well that affliction gives rise to endurance, 4 and endurance gives proof of our faith, and a proved faith gives ground for hope. 5 Nor does this hope delude us; the love of God has been poured out in our hearts by the Holy Spirit, whom we have received. 6 Were that hope vain, why did Christ, in his own appointed time, undergo death for us sinners, while we were still powerless to help ourselves? 7 It is hard enough to find anyone who will die on behalf of a just man, although perhaps there may be those who will face death for one so deserving. 8 But here, as if God meant to prove how well he loves us, it was while we were still sinners 9 that Christ, in his own appointed time, died for us. All the more surely, then, now that we have found justification through his blood, shall we be saved, through him, from God's displeasure. 10 Enemies of God, we were reconciled to him through his Son's death; reconciled to him, we are surer than ever of finding salvation in his Son's life. 11 And, what is more, we can boast of God's protection; always through our Lord Jesus Christ, since it is through him that we have attained our reconciliation.

12 It was through one man that guilt came into the world; and, since death came owing to guilt, death was handed on to all mankind by one man. (All alike were guilty men; 13 there was guilt

v. 1. Some Greek manuscripts have 'we enjoy' for 'let us enjoy.'

v. 12. 'All alike were guilty'; some would translate 'In him (Adam) all had sinned'.

v. 13. The sense seems to be, that those who lived be-

in the world before ever the law of Moses was given. Now, it is only where there is a law to transgress that guilt is imputed, 14 and yet we see death reigning in the world from Adam's time to the time of Moses, over men who were not themselves guilty of transgressing a law, as Adam was.) In this, Adam was the type of him who was to come. 15 Only, the grace which came to us was out of all proportion to the fault. If this one man's fault brought death on a whole multitude, all the more lavish was God's grace, shewn to a whole multitude, that free gift he made us in the grace brought by one man, Jesus Christ. 16 The extent of the gift is not as if it followed a single guilty act; the sentence which brought us condemnation arose out of one man's action, whereas the pardon that brings us acquittal arises out of a multitude of faults. 17 And if death began its reign through one man, owing to one man's fault, more fruitful still is the grace, the gift of justification, which bids men enjoy a reign of life through one man, Jesus Christ.

18 Well then, one man commits a fault, and it brings condemnation upon all; one man makes amends, and it brings to all justification, that is, life. 19 A multitude will become acceptable to God through one man's obedience, just as a multitude, through one man's disobedience, became guilty. 20 The law intervened, only to amplify our fault; but, as our fault was amplified, grace has been more amply bestowed than ever; 21 that so, where guilt held its reign of death, justifying grace should reign instead, to bring us eternal life through Jesus Christ our Lord.

tween Adam's time and that of Moses, whatever their sins were, incurred no guilt of disobedience, there being no (revealed) law to disobey. Death is the penalty of disobedience; and the fact that death came to Adam's immediate descendants must therefore be attributed to Adam's disobedience, not to their own. St. Paul must not be understood as meaning that men are not responsible for their actions where they have no revealed law to guide them; cf. ii. 15 above.

Chapter Six

DOES it follow that we ought to go on sinning, to give still more occasion for grace? 2 God forbid. We have died, once for all, to sin; can we breathe its air again? 3 You know well enough that we who were taken up into Christ by baptism have been taken up, all of us, into his death. 4 In our baptism, we have been buried with him, died like him, that so, just as Christ was raised up by his Father's power from the dead, we too might live and move in a new kind of existence. 5 We have to be closely fitted into the pattern of his

vv. 1-5. Here, as in Colossians ii. 12, St. Paul thinks of baptism not as washing us from our sins, but as burying us to our sins. Baptism (which

283

then suggested the idea of total immersion) mystically identifies us with our Lord's passage through the tomb. (Cf. I Cor. x. 2.)

v. 6. 'The living power of our guilt'; literally, 'the body of guilt'. Some think that this means our bodies, considered as the instruments of sin; but this does not seem to follow the line of St. Paul's allegory.

v. 7. This probably introduces a maxim of ordinary human law; namely, that no criminal action lies against a man when he is already dead. Cf. vii. 1, below.

v. 10. Christ died to sin, in the sense that the burden of human sins which he freely took upon himself demanded, as of right, his death, but now, having undergone that sentence, he has satisfied all the obligations which his condescension brought upon him.

v. 17. Some would translate, 'You accepted obedience with all your hearts to the pattern of teaching which was handed on to you'.

v. 19. 'Nature is still strong in you'; probably in the sense that they are not yet sufficiently advanced in spirituality to be able to understand St. Paul unless he uses crude metaphors.

resurrection, as we have been into the pattern of his death; 6 we have to be sure of this, that our former nature has been crucified with him, and the living power of our guilt annihilated, so that we are the slaves of guilt no longer. 7 Guilt makes no more claim on a man who is dead. 8 And if we have died with Christ, we have faith to believe that we shall share his life. 9 We know that Christ, now he has risen from the dead, cannot die any more; death has no more power over him; 10 the death he died was a death, once for all, to sin; the life he now lives is a life that looks towards God. 11 And you, too, must think of yourselves as dead to sin, and alive with a life that looks towards God, through Christ Jesus our Lord.

12 You must not, then, allow sin to tyrannize over your perishable bodies, to make you subject to its appetites. 13 You must not make your bodily powers over to sin, to be the instruments of harm; make yourselves over to God, as men who have been dead and come to life again; make your bodily powers over to God, to be the instruments of right-doing. 14 Sin will not be able to play the master over you any longer; you serve grace now, not the law. 15 And if it is grace, not the law, we serve, are we therefore to fall into sin? God forbid. 16 You know well enough that wherever you give a slave's consent, you prove yourselves the slaves of that master; slaves of sin, marked out for death, or slaves of obedience, marked out for justification. 17 And you, thanks be to God, although you were the slaves of sin once, accepted obedience with all your hearts, true to the pattern of teaching to which you are now engaged. 18 Thus you escaped from the bondage of sin, and became the slaves of right-doing instead. 19 I am speaking in the language of common life, because nature is still strong in you. Just as you once made over your natural powers as slaves to impurity and wickedness, till all was wickedness, you must now make over your natural powers as slaves to right-doing, till all is sanctified. 20 At the time when you were the slaves of sin, right-doing had no claim upon you. 21 And what harvest were you then reaping, from acts which now make you blush? Their reward is death. 22 Now that you are free from the claims of sin, and have become God's slaves instead, you have a harvest in your sanctification, and your reward is eternal life. 23 Sin offers death, for wages; God offers us eternal life as a free gift, through Christ Jesus our Lord.

Chapter Seven

You MUST SURELY BE aware, brethren (I am speaking to men who have some knowledge of law) that legal claims are only binding on a man so long as he is alive. 2 A married woman, for instance, is bound by law to her husband while he lives; if she is widowed, she is quit of her husband's claim on her; 3 she will be held an adulteress if she gives herself to another man during her husband's lifetime, but once he is dead she is quit of his claim, and can give herself to another man without adultery. 4 Well, brethren, you too have undergone death, as far as the law is concerned, in the person of Christ crucified, so that you now belong to another, to him who rose from the dead. We yield increase to God, 5 whereas, when we were merely our natural selves, the sinful passions to which the law bound us worked on our natural powers, so as to yield increase only to death. 6 Now we are quit of the claim which death had on us, so that we can do service in a new manner, according to the spirit, not according to the letter as of old.

7 Does this mean that law and guilt are the same thing? God forbid we should say that. But it was only the law that gave me my knowledge of sin; I should not even have known concupiscence for what it is, if the law had not told me, Thou shalt not covet. 8 But the sense of sin, with the law's ban for its foothold, produced in me every sort of concupiscence. Without the law, the sense of sin is a dead thing. 9 At first, without the law, I was alive; then, when the law came with its ban, the sense of sin found new life, and with that, I died. 10 The ban, which was meant to bring life, proved death to me; 11 the sense of sin, with the law's ban for its foothold, caught me unawares, and by that means killed me. 12 The law, to be sure, is something holy; the ban is holy, and right, and good. 13 A good thing, and did it prove death to me? God forbid we should say that. No, it was sin that produced death in me, using this good thing to make itself appear as sin indeed, sin made more sinful than ever by the ban imposed on it.

v. 4. Literally, 'You were put to death ... through the body of Christ'.

v. 6. 'Quit of the claim which death had upon us'; this is the intention of the Latin. The Greek manuscripts have 'We are quit of the law's claim, since we have died in (or 'to') that which hitherto held us bound'.

vv. 7-25. Commentators are not agreed, whether St. Paul is giving us his own experience in this matter, or is dramatically representing the experience of mankind under his own person. There is a further doubt, whether what is here said should be understood only of man unregenerate, or equally of souls regenerated by grace, in which concupiscence nevertheless persists. St. Paul's main contention, in any case, appears to be that we cast no aspersions on the holiness of the Mosaic law, when we describe it as powerless to save us. The very struggles which our moral experience entails are proof that the law is holy, since our conscience continues to approve of it even when we are disobeying our consciences by yielding to sin.

14 The law, as we know, is something spiritual; I am a thing of flesh and blood, sold into the slavery of sin. 15 My own actions bewilder me; what I do is not what I wish to do, but something which I hate. 16 Why then, if what I do is something I have no wish to do, I thereby admit that the law is worthy of all honour; 17 meanwhile, my action does not come from me, but from the sinful principle that dwells in me. 18 Of this I am certain, that no principle of good dwells in me, that is, in my natural self; praiseworthy intentions are always ready to hand, but I cannot find my way to the performance of them; 19 it is not the good my will prefers, but the evil my will disapproves, that I find myself doing. 20 And if what I do is something I have not the will to do, it cannot be I that bring it about, it must be the sinful principle that

v. 21. 'This, then, is what I find about the law, that' . . . etc. Others would render, 'I discover, then, this principle, that' . . . etc. But this would be very doubtful Greek.

dwells in me. 21 This, then, is what I find about the law, that evil is close at my side, when my will is to do what is praiseworthy. 22 Inwardly, I applaud God's disposition, 23 but I observe another disposition in my lower self, which raises war against the disposition of my conscience, and so I am handed over as a captive to that disposition towards sin which my lower self contains. 24 Pitiable

v. 25. Most Greek manuscripts have 'Thanks be to God', instead of 'Nothing else than the grace of God'; their meaning is evidently the same.

creature that I am, who is to set me free from a nature thus doomed to death? 25 Nothing else than the grace of God, through Jesus Christ our Lord. If I am left to myself, my conscience is at God's disposition, but my natural powers are at the disposition of sin.

Chapter Eight

WELL THEN, NO JUDGE ment stands now against those who live in Christ Jesus, not following the ways of flesh and blood. 2 The spiritual principle of life has set me free, in Jesus Christ, from the principle of sin and of death. 3 There was something the law could not do, because flesh and blood could not lend it the power;

THE LAST SUPPER   SCHOOL OF AMIENS
around 1480

COURTESY OF THE ART INSTITUTE OF CHICAGO

and this God has done, by sending us his own Son, in the fashion of our guilty nature, to make amends for our guilt. He has signed the death-warrant of sin in our nature, 4 so that we should be fully quit of the law's claim, we, who follow the ways of the spirit, not the ways of flesh and blood. 5 To live the life of nature is to think the thoughts of nature; to live the life of the spirit is to think the thoughts of the spirit; 6 and natural wisdom brings only death, whereas the wisdom of the spirit brings life and peace. 7 That is because natural wisdom is at enmity with God, not submitting itself to his law; it is impossible that it should. 8 Those who live the life of nature cannot be acceptable to God; 9 but you live the life of the spirit, not the life of nature; that is, if the Spirit of God dwells in you. A man cannot belong to Christ unless he has the Spirit of Christ. 10 But if Christ lives in you, then although the body be a dead thing in virtue of our guilt, the spirit is a living thing, by virtue of our justification. 11 And if the spirit of him who raised up Jesus from the dead dwells in you, he who raised up Jesus Christ from the dead will give life to your perishable bodies too, for the sake of his Spirit who dwells in you.

12 Thus, brethren, nature has no longer any claim upon us, that we should live a life of nature. 13 If you live a life of nature, you are marked out for death; if you mortify the ways of nature through the power of the Spirit, you will have life. 14 Those who follow the leading of God's Spirit are all God's sons; 15 the spirit you have now received is not, as of old, a spirit of slavery, to govern you by fear; it is the spirit of adoption, which makes us cry out, Abba, Father. 16 The Spirit himself thus assures our spirit, that we are children of God; 17 and if we are his children, then we are his heirs too; heirs of God, sharing the inheritance of Christ; only we must share his sufferings, if we are to share his glory.

18 Not that I count these present sufferings as the measure of that glory which is to be revealed in us. 19 If creation is full of expectancy, that is because it is waiting for the sons of God to be made known. 20 Created nature has been condemned to frustration; not for some deliberate fault of its own, but for the sake of him who so condemned it, with a hope to look forward to; 21 namely, that nature in its turn will be set free from the tyranny of corruption, to share in the glorious freedom of God's sons. 22 The whole of nature, as we know, groans in a common travail all the while. 23 And not only do we see that, but we ourselves do the same; we ourselves, although we have already begun to reap our spiritual harvest, groan in our hearts, waiting for that adoption

v. 10. 'Although the body be a dead thing'; this may refer either to physical death (v. 12 above), or to the mortifications inflicted on the body during life (vi. 2 above).

v. 13. 'The ways of nature'; many Greek manuscripts have 'the activities of the body'.

vv. 18-22. The word here translated 'creation' or 'created nature' probably means creation as a whole. St. Paul, with something of a poetic outlook, sees the struggle for survival in nature as a proof of its dumb aspiration towards that more perfect creation which is to come; the agony of its frustrated striving is the birth-pang of a new order (cf. Matthew xxiv. 8, John xvi. 21). Others interpret 'creation' as referring to human nature; in which case 'we ourselves' in verse 23 must be understood of the apostles, or of Christians as opposed to those who live according to nature.

v. 20. 'Him who so condemned it'; this is ordinarily understood of God, but it is hard to see the force of this interpretation. It is perhaps better to take it of Adam, as St. Chrysostom does.

which is the ransoming of our bodies from their slavery. 24 It must be so, since our salvation is founded upon the hope of something. Hope would not be hope at all if its object were in view; how could a man still hope for something which he sees? 25 And if we are hoping for something still unseen, then we need endurance to wait for it. 26 Only, as before, the Spirit comes to the aid of our weakness; when we do not know what prayer to offer, to pray as we ought, the Spirit himself intercedes for us, with groans beyond all utterance: 27 and God, who can read our hearts, knows well what the Spirit's intent is; for indeed it is according to the mind of God that he makes intercession for the saints.

28 Meanwhile, we are well assured that everything helps to secure the good of those who love God, those whom he has called in fulfilment of his design. 29 All those who from the first were known to him, he has destined from the first to be moulded into the image of his Son, who is thus to become the eldest-born among many brethren. 30 So predestined, he called them; so called, he justified them; so justified, he glorified them. 31 When that is said, what follows? Who can be our adversary, if God is on our side? 32 He did not even spare his own Son, but gave him up for us all; and must not that gift be accompanied by the gift of all else? 33 Who will come forward to accuse God's elect, when God acquits us? 34 Who will pass sentence against us, when Jesus Christ, who died, nay, has risen again, and sits at the right hand of God, is pleading for us? 35 Who will separate us from the love of Christ? Will affliction, or distress, or persecution, or hunger, or nakedness, or peril, or the sword? 36 For thy sake, says the scripture, we face death at every moment, reckoned no better than sheep marked down for slaughter. 37 Yet in all this we are conquerors, through him who has granted us his love. 38 Of this I am fully persuaded; neither death nor life, no angels or principalities or powers, neither what is present nor what is to come, no force whatever, 39 neither the height above us nor the depth beneath us, nor any other created thing, will be able to separate us from the love of God, which comes to us in Christ Jesus our Lord.

v. 26. 'As before'; that is, as in verse 16 above.

v. 28. Some Greek manuscripts read 'God helps in every way to secure the good of those who love God'. 'In fulfilment of his design'; the Greek fathers, however, interpret, 'in accordance with their wills'.

v. 36. Ps. xliii. 22.

Chapter Nine

I AM NOT DECEIVING you, I am telling you the truth in Christ's name, with the full assurance of a conscience enlightened by the Holy Spirit, 2 when I tell you of the great sorrow, the continual anguish I feel in my heart, 3 and how it has ever been my wish that I myself might be doomed to separation from Christ, if that would benefit my brethren, my own kinsmen by race. 4 They are Israelites, adopted as God's sons; the visible presence, and the covenant, and the giving of the law, and the Temple worship, and the promises, are their inheritance; 5 the patriarchs belong to them, and theirs is the human stock from which Christ came; Christ, who rules as God over all things, blessed for ever, Amen. 6 And yet it is not as if God's promise had failed of its effect. Not all those who are sprung from Israel are truly Israelites; 7 not all the posterity of Abraham are Abraham's children; it is through Isaac, he was told, that thy posterity shall be traced. 8 That is to say, God's sonship is not for all those who are Abraham's children by natural descent; it is only the children given to him as the result of God's promise that are to be counted as his posterity. 9 It was a promise God made, when he said, When this season comes round again, I will visit thee, and Sara shall have a son. 10 And not only she, but Rebecca too received a promise, when she bore two sons to the same husband, our father Isaac. 11 They had not yet been born; they had done nothing, good or evil; and already,'so that God's purpose might stand out clearly as his own choice, with no action of theirs to account for it, nothing but his will, from whom the call came, 12 she was told, The elder is to be the servant of the younger. 13 So it is that we read, I have been a friend to Jacob, and an enemy to Esau.

14 What does this mean? That God acts unjustly? That is not to be thought of. 15 I will shew pity, he tells Moses, on those whom I pity; I will shew mercy where I am merciful; 16 the effect comes, then, from God's mercy, not from man's will, or man's alacrity. 17 Pharao, too, is told in scripture, This is the

v. 3. St. Paul only says that he would be prepared to sacrifice his own salvation conditionally (i.e., if God sanctioned, and were prepared to accept, such offers of substitution); not absolutely (since we are bound to desire our own salvation).

v. 5. 'Christ, who rules as God'; some commentators would translate, 'Blessed be God who is above all things, for ever', making this a distinct sentence; but they have not been able to suggest any plausible grounds for the intrusion of this irrelevant apostrophe, and the order of words in the Greek makes it almost impossible.

vv. 11-23. St. Paul is speaking here, not of predestination to eternal life, but of that first grace, entirely gratuitous, which leads men to Christ.

v. 12. Gen. xxv. 23.

v. 13. Mal. i. 2.

vv. 15-18. Some commentators have understood these verses as part of the objection made by the imaginary critic whom St. Paul is answering; they are more often taken as part of St. Paul's own assertion.

v. 15. Ex. xxxiii. 19.

v. 17. 'I have made thee what thou art',

289

very reason why I have made thee what thou art, so as to give proof, in thee, of my power, and to let my name be known all over the earth. 18 Thus he shews mercy where it is his will, and where it is his will he hardens men's hearts. 19 Hereupon thou wilt ask, If that is so, how can he find fault with us, since there is no resisting his will? 20 Nay, but who art thou, friend, to bandy words with God? Is the pot to ask the potter, Why hast thou fashioned me thus? 21 Is not the potter free to do what he wills with the clay, using the same lump to make two objects, one for noble and one for ignoble use? 22 It may be that God has borne, long and patiently, with those who are the objects of his vengeance, fit only for destruction, meaning to give proof of that vengeance, and display his power at last; 23 meaning also to display, in those who are the objects of his mercy, how rich is the glory he bestows, that glory for which he has destined them.

24 We are the objects of his mercy; we, whom he has called, Jews and Gentiles alike. 25 That is what he says in the book of Osee, Those who were no people of mine, I will call my people; she who was unpitied and unloved shall be loved and pitied. 26 In places where they used to be told, You are no people of mine, they will be called, now, sons of the living God. 27 And, where Israel is concerned, Isaias cries out, The number of the sons of Israel may be like the sand of the sea, but it is a remnant that will be left; 28 the Lord is making up his reckoning and cutting it short in his justice; it is a short reckoning that he will make upon earth. 29 So Isaias had said earlier on, If the Lord of Hosts had not left us a stock to breed from, we should have been like Sodom, we should have gone the way of Gomorrah. 30 What do we conclude, then? Why, that the Gentiles, who never aimed at justifying themselves, attained justification, that justification which comes of faith; 31 whereas the Israelites aimed at a disposition which should justify them, and never reached it. 32 Why was this? Because they hoped to derive their justification from observance, not from faith. They tripped on the stone which trips men's feet; 33 so we read in scripture, Behold, I am setting down in Sion one who is a stone to trip men's feet, a boulder to catch them unawares; those who believe in him will not be disappointed.

Chapter Ten

BRETHREN, they have all the good will of my heart, all my prayers to God, for their salvation. 2 That they are jealous for God's honour, I can testify; but it is with imperfect understanding. 3 They did not recognize God's way of justification, and so they tried to institute a way of their own, instead of submitting to his. 4 Christ has superseded the law, bringing justification to anyone who will believe. 5 The account which Moses gives of that justification which comes from the law, is that a man will find life in its commandments if he observes them. 6 But the justification which comes from faith makes a different claim; Do not say, Who will scale heaven for us? (as if we had to bring Christ down to earth), 7 or, Who will go down into the depth for us? (as if we had to bring Christ back from the dead). 8 No, says the scripture, the message is close to thy hand, it is on thy lips, it is in thy heart; meaning by that the message of faith, which we preach. 9 Thou canst find salvation, if thou wilt use thy lips to confess that Jesus is the Lord, and thy heart to believe that God has raised him up from the dead. 10 The heart has only to believe, if we are to be justified; the lips have only to make confession, if we are to be saved. 11 That is what the scripture says, Anyone who believes in him will not be disappointed.

12 There is no distinction made here between Jew and Gentile; all alike have one Lord, and he has enough and to spare for all those who call upon him. 13 Every one who calls upon the name of the Lord will be saved. 14 Only, how are they to call upon him until they have learned to believe in him? And how are they to believe in him, until they listen to him? And how can they listen, without a preacher to listen to? 15 And how can there be preachers, unless preachers are sent on their errand? So we read in scripture, How welcome is the coming of those who tell of peace, who tell of good news. 16 True, there are some who have not obeyed the call of the gospel; so Isaias says, Lord, who has given us a faithful hearing? 17 (See how faith comes from hearing; and hearing through Christ's word.) 18 But, tell me, did the news never come to them? Why, yes; the utterance fills every land, the message reaches the ends of the world. 19 And, tell me, was

v. 5. Lev. xviii. 5.

vv. 6-8. Deut. xxx. 12. In the Hebrew, the second question is 'Who shall cross the sea?' The sense of the passage is, in any case, that no heroic efforts are needed to find God's law; this St. Paul here applies to the grace of the gospel, which Christ brought down from heaven (and back from the grave) to us, without any effort of our own to find it.

v. 11. Is. xxviii. 16.

v. 13. Joel ii. 32.

v. 15. Is. lii. 7.

v. 16. Is. liii. 1.
v. 17. This verse has here been printed as a parenthesis, because the sense of verse 18 evidently follows closely on that of verse 16, 'True, they did not obey the call of the gospel, but this does not mean that they did not hear it'.
v. 18. Ps. xviii. 5.
v. 19. Deut. xxxii. 21.

not Israel warned of it? Why, there is a saying that goes back to Moses, I will make them jealous of a nation that is no nation at all; I will put rivalry between them and a nation which has never learnt wisdom. 20 And Isaias speaks out boldly, Those who never looked for me have found me; I have made myself known to those who never asked for word of me; 21 and he says of Israel, I have stretched out my hands all day to a people that refuses obedience, and cries out against me.

vv. 20, 21. Is. lxv. 1.

Chapter Eleven

ELL me, then, has God disowned his people? That is not to be thought of. Why, I am an Israelite myself, descended from Abraham; Benjamin is my tribe. 2 No, God has not disowned the people which, from the first, he recognized as his. Do you not remember what scripture tells us about Elias? The complaint, I mean, which he made before God about Israel: 3 Lord, they have killed thy prophets, and overthrown thy altars; I am the only one left, and my life, too, is threatened. 4 And what does the divine revelation tell him? There are seven thousand men I have kept true to myself, with knees that never bowed to Baal. 5 So it is in our time; a remnant has remained true; grace has chosen it. 6 And if it is due to grace, then it is not due to observance of the law; if it were, grace would be no grace at all. 7 What does it mean, then? Why, that Israel has missed its mark; only this chosen remnant has attained it, while the rest were blinded; 8 so we read in scripture, God has numbed their senses, given them unseeing eyes and deaf ears, to this day. 9 David, too, says, Let their feasting be turned into a trap, a snare, a spring to recoil upon them; 10 let their eyes be dim, so that they cannot see, keep their backs bowed down continually. 11 Tell me, then, have they stumbled so as to fall altogether? God forbid; the result of their false step has been to bring the Gentiles salvation, and the result of that must be to rouse the Jews to emulate them. 12 Why then, if their false step has enriched the world, if the Gentiles have been enriched by their default, what must we expect, when it is made good? (I am speaking

vv. 3, 4. III. Kings xix. 10, 18.

v. 7. 'Blinded'; the Greek word, here and in v. 25 below, implies rather that they became callous, insensible.
v. 8. Is. vi. 9, xxi. 10.
vv. 9, 10. Ps. lxviii. 23.

v. 12. The words here printed in brackets are usually taken as referring only to what follows; but the

292

now to you Gentiles.) 13 As long as my apostolate is to the Gentiles, I mean to make much of my office, 14 in the hope of stirring up my own flesh and blood to emulation, and saving some of them. 15 If the losing of them has meant a world reconciled to God, what can the winning of them mean, but life risen from the dead?

16 When the first loaf is consecrated, the whole batch is consecrated with it; so, when the root is consecrated, the branches are consecrated too. 17 The branches have been thinned out, and thou, a wild olive, hast been grafted in among them; sharest, with them, the root and the richness of the true olive. 18 That is no reason why thou shouldst boast thyself better than the branches; remember, in thy mood of boastfulness, that thou owest life to the root, not the root to thee. 19 Branches were cut away, thou wilt tell me, so that I might be grafted in. 20 True enough, but it was for want of faith that they were cut away, and it is only faith that keeps thee where thou art; thou hast no reason for pride, rather for fear; 21 God was unforgiving with the branches that were native to the tree, what if he should find occasion to be unforgiving with thee too? 22 There is graciousness, then, in God, and there is also severity. His severity is for those who have fallen away, his graciousness is for thee, only so long as thou dost continue in his grace; if not, thou too shalt be pruned away. 23 Just so they too will be grafted in, if they do not continue in their unbelief; to graft them in afresh is not beyond God's power. 24 Indeed, it was against nature when thou wast grafted on to the true olive's stock, thou, who wert native to the wild olive; it will be all the easier for him to graft these natural branches on to their own parent stock.

25 I must not fail, brethren, to make this revelation known to you; or else you might have too good a conceit of yourselves. Blindness has fallen upon a part of Israel, but only until the tale of the Gentile nations is complete; 26 then the whole of Israel will find salvation, as we read in scripture, A deliverer shall come from Sion, to rid Jacob of his unfaithfulness; 27 and this shall be the fulfilment of my covenant with them, when I take away their sins. 28 In the preaching of the gospel, God rejects them, to make room for you; but in his elective purpose he still welcomes them, for the sake of their fathers; 29 God does not repent of the gifts he makes, or of the calls he issues. 30 You were once rebels, until through their rebellion you obtained pardon; 31 they are rebels now, obtaining pardon for you, only to be pardoned in their turn.

whole passage from verse 11 onwards seems to be addressed to the Gentile reader.

v. 15. 'Life risen from the dead'; many commentators understand this as meaning that the return of the Jews to Christ will be the signal for the second Coming. But if St. Paul had had this in his mind, he would have been more likely to say 'the resurrection of the dead' than to use this unwonted formula.

v. 16. Num. xv. 20. The olive tree here represents the Jewish people, and its 'root' is generally understood of the patriarchs.

vv. 26, 27. Is. lix. 20, xxvii. 9.

293

32 Thus God has abandoned all men to their rebellion, only to include them all in his pardon.

33 How deep is the mine of God's wisdom, of his knowledge; how inscrutable are his judgements, how undiscoverable his ways! 34 Who has ever understood the Lord's thoughts, or been his counsellor? 35 Who ever was the first to give, and so earned his favours? 36 All things find in him their origin, their impulse, the centre of their being; to him be glory throughout all ages, Amen.

v. 34. Is. xl. 13.

v. 35. Job xli. 2.

v. 36. 'The centre of their being'. in the Greek, 'their goal'.

Chapter Twelve

AND now, brethren, I appeal to you by God's mercies to offer up your bodies as a living sacrifice, consecrated to God and worthy of his acceptance; this is the worship due from you as rational creatures. 2 And you must not not fall in with the manners of this world; there must be an inward change, a remaking of your minds, so that you can satisfy yourselves what is God's will, the good thing, the desirable thing, the perfect thing. 3 Thus, in virtue of the grace that is given me, I warn every man who is of your company not to think highly of himself, beyond his just estimation, but to have a sober esteem of himself, according to the measure of faith which God has apportioned to each. 4 Each of us has one body, with many different parts, and not all these parts have the same function; 5 just so we, though many in number, form one body in Christ, and each acts as the counterpart of another. 6 The spiritual gifts we have differ, according to the special grace which has been assigned to each. If a man is a prophet, let him prophesy as far as the measure of his faith will let him. 7 The administrator must be content with his administration, the teacher, with his work of teaching, the preacher, with his preaching. 8 Each must perform his own task well; giving alms with generosity, exercising authority with anxious care, or doing works of mercy smilingly.

9 Your love must be a sincere love; you must hold what is evil in abomination, fix all your desire upon what is good. 10 Be affectionate towards each other, as the love of brothers demands, eager to give one another precedence. 11 I would see you un-

v. 1. 'Your bodies', that is, 'yourselves'; but perhaps, for the benefit of the uncircumcised Gentiles, St. Paul is specially careful to insist on the need of consecrating our .bodily powers to God.

v. 6. 'As far as the measure of his faith will let him'; this has commonly been rendered 'according to the rule of faith', but neither the Greek nor the Latin text justifies this interpretation. The sense is determined by verse 3 above.

v. 7. 'The administrator'; the word here used is the technical term for a deacon, but the meaning of it here is probably more general.

wearied in activity, aglow with the Spirit, waiting like slaves upon the Lord; 12 buoyed up by hope, patient in affliction, persevering in prayer; 13 providing generously for the needs of the saints, giving the stranger a loving welcome. 14 Bestow a blessing on those who persecute you; a blessing, not a curse. 15 Rejoice with those who rejoice, mourn with the mourner. 16 Live in harmony of mind, falling in with the opinions of common folk, instead of following conceited thoughts; never give yourselves airs of wisdom.

17 Do not repay injury with injury; study your behaviour in the world's sight as well as in God's. 18 Keep peace with all men, where it is possible, for your part. 19 Do not avenge yourselves, beloved; allow retribution to run its course; so we read in scripture, Vengeance is for me, I will repay, says the Lord. 20 Rather, feed thy enemy if he is hungry, give him drink if he is thirsty; by doing this, thou wilt heap coals of fire upon his head. 21 Do not be disarmed by malice; disarm malice with kindness.

v. 16. 'Fall in with the opinions of common folk'; some would render 'be content with a humble position'; but it does not appear how the verb can have this meaning.

v. 17. The words 'as well as in God's' are wanting in most Greek manuscripts.

v. 19. Deut. xxxii. 35. For 'allow retribution to run its course' others would prefer to translate, 'make way before the anger' (of your opponent), or 'give space for your anger' (to simmer down). v. 20. Prov. xxv. 21. St. Augustine and other commentators tell us that the coals of fire are a metaphorical description of the shame and remorse which our enemy feels at our kind usage of him. v. 21. If we avenge ourselves, we Christians are converted to the enemy's point of view, instead of converting him to ours.

Chapter Thirteen

E VERY SOUL MUST BE submissive to its lawful superiors; authority comes from God only, and all authorities that hold sway are of his ordinance. 2 Thus the man who opposes authority is a rebel against the ordinance of God, and rebels secure their own condemnation. 3 A good conscience has no need to go in fear of the magistrate, as a bad conscience does. If thou wouldst be free from the fear of authority, do right, and thou shalt win its approval; 4 the magistrate is God's minister, working for thy good. Only if thou dost wrong, needst thou be afraid; it is not for nothing that he bears the sword; he is God's minister still, to inflict punishment on the wrong-doer. 5 Thou must needs, then, be submissive, not only for fear of punishment, but in conscience. 6 It is for this same reason that you pay taxes; magistrates are in God's service, and must give all their time to it. 7 Pay every man, then, his due; taxes, if it be taxes, customs, if it be customs; respect and honour, if it be respect and honour. 8 Do not let anybody have a claim upon you, except the claim which binds us to love one another. 9 The man who loves his neighbour has done all that the law demands. (All the commandments, Thou shalt not commit adultery, Thou shalt do no murder, Thou shalt not steal, Thou shalt not covet, and the rest, are resumed in this one saying, Thou shalt love thy neighbour as thyself.) 10 Love of our neighbour refrains from doing harm of any kind; that is why it fulfils all the demands of the law.

11 Meanwhile, make no mistake about the age we live in; already it is high time for us to awake out of our sleep; our salvation is closer to us now than when we first learned to believe. 12 The night is far on its course; day draws near. Let us abandon the ways of darkness, and put on the armour of light. 13 Let us pass our time honourably, as by the light of day, not in revelling and drunkenness, not in lust and wantonness, not in quarrels and rivalries. 14 Rather, arm yourselves with the Lord Jesus Christ; spend no more thought on nature and nature's appetites.

v. 8. 'Do not let anybody have a claim on you' etc.; this is usually explained as meaning, that we are to be diligent in paying off our debts, except that debt of mutual love, which can never be paid off, but always urges. In view of what immediately follows, it seems likely St. Paul also means, that we shall seldom have scruples of conscience over the obligations of human justice, if we live by the law of Divine love.

v. 9. Ex. xx. 13-17. Lev. xix. 18.

v. 11. The connexion of this passage with what goes before is only general; it is more closely related to what follows, viz. the anxiety of St. Paul over the want of unity among Christians at Rome.

Chapter Fourteen

 IND room among you for a man of over-delicate conscience, without arguing about his scruples. 2 Another man can, in conscience, eat what he will; one who is scrupulous must be content with vegetable fare. 3 Let not the first, over his meat, mock at him who does not eat it, or the second, while he abstains, pass judgement on him who eats it. God, after all, has found room for him. 4 Who art thou, to pass judgement on the servant of another? Whether he keeps his feet or falls, concerns none but his master. And keep his feet he

v. 1. 'A man of over-delicate conscience'; literally, one who is 'weak in faith'. But the context of this whole chapter makes it clear that

will; God is well able to give him a sure footing. 5 One man makes a distinction between this day and that; another regards all days alike; let either rest fully content in his own opinion. 6 He who observes the day, observes it in the Lord's honour. Just so, he who eats does so in the Lord's honour; he gives thanks to God for it; and he who abstains from eating, abstains in the Lord's honour, and he too thanks God. 7 None of us lives as his own master, and none of us dies as his own master. 8 While we live, we live as the Lord's servants, when we die, we die as the Lord's servants; in life and in death, we belong to the Lord. 9 That was why Christ died and lived again; he would be Lord both of the dead and of the living. 10 And who art thou, to pass judgement on thy brother? Who art thou, to mock at thy brother? We shall all stand, one day, before the judgement seat of Christ; 11 (so we read in scripture, As I live, says the Lord, there is no knee but shall bend before me, no tongue but shall pay homage to God); 12 and so each of us will have to give an account of himself before God. 13 Let us cease, then, to lay down rules for one another, and make this rule for ourselves instead, not to trip up or entangle a brother's conscience.

14 This is my assurance, this is what my conscience tells me in the name of our Lord Jesus, that there is nothing which is unclean in itself; it is only when a man believes a thing to be unclean that it becomes unclean for him. 15 And if thy brother's peace of mind is disturbed over food, it is because thou art neglecting to follow the rule of charity. Here is a soul for which Christ died; it is not for thee to bring it to perdition with the food thou eatest. 16 We must not allow that which is a good thing for us to be brought into disrepute. 17 The kingdom of God is not a matter of eating or drinking this or that; it means rightness of heart, finding our peace and our joy in the Holy Spirit. 18 Such is the badge of Christ's service which wins acceptance with God, and the good opinion of our fellow men. 19 Let our aim, then, be peace, and strengthening one another's faith. 20 It is not for thee to destroy God's work for the sake of a mouthful of food. Nothing is unclean; yet it goes ill with the man who eats to the hurt of his own conscience. 21 Thou dost well if thou refusest to eat meat, or to drink wine, or to do anything in which thy brother can find an occasion of sin, a cause for scandal or scruple. 22 Thou hast a good conscience? Keep it a matter between thyself and God; he is fortunate, who can make his own choice without self-questioning.

St. Paul is using the word 'faith' in a special sense, corresponding to what we mean by 'conscience'. Accordingly, the word 'weak' must be interpreted in the sense which St. Paul sometimes gives it, of 'scrupulous', 'easily scandalized'; cf. II Cor. xi. 29.

v. 2. The close connexion between this and the chapter which follows is proof that St. Paul is still dealing with disputes between Jewish and Gentile converts, as such. It is clear, then, that the weaker brother who refuses to eat meat does so, not on any vegetarian principles (since the ordinary Jew had none), but either (i) because the meat put before him has not been killed in the Jewish fashion (cf. Acts xv. 20), or (ii) because he is afraid that the meat put before him may have been offered in sacrifice to idols (cf. I Cor. x. 25, and viii. throughout).

v. 4. 'Falls'; that is, incurs condemnation, as in I Cor. x. 12.

v. 5. This evidently refers to the keeping of certain Jewish festivals and fasts, which were not enjoined upon Gentile Christians. 'Rest fully content in his own opinion'; the Greek may also mean, 'have a clear conviction in his own mind'.

v. 11. Is. xlv. 24.

vv. 14 and following. St. Paul here forbids the Gentile Christians to exercise any kind of pressure upon their Jewish brethren, over food, etc., which would cause them to act against their own conscience out of human respect. It is not clear that he meant the Gentiles to abstain from food which they thought lawful, for fear of scandalizing Jewish Christians who might be watching.

v. 16. 'That which is

a good thing for us'; namely, freedom from scruple in matters of food and drink. This is St. Anselm's interpretation; others

23 He who hesitates, and eats none the less, is self-condemned; he acts in bad conscience, and wherever there is bad conscience, there is sin.

have understood the words 'our good thing' as referring to the Christian faith generally. *v. 21.* This is more likely to be a general assertion of the importance of avoiding scandal (cf. I Cor. viii. 13) than a direction given to the Roman Christians in these special circumstances. *v. 23.* 'Wherever there is bad conscience, there is sin'; literally, 'Whatever does not proceed from faith, is sin'. This has been understood by many writers from St. Augustine onwards as meaning that all the actions of the heathen have the nature of sin. But such an interpretation is quite wide of the present context; it is plain that here, as in the rest of the chapter, St. Paul uses the word 'faith' where we should use the word 'conscience'.

Chapter Fifteen

O, we who are bold in our confidence ought to bear with the scruples of those who are timorous; not to insist on having our own way. 2 Each of us ought to give way to his neighbour, where it serves a good purpose by building up his faith. 3 Christ, after all, would

v. 3. Ps. lxviii. 10. not have everything his own way; Was it not uttered against thee, says the scripture, the reproach I bore? 4 (See how all the words written long ago were written for our instruction; we were to derive hope from that message of endurance and courage which the scriptures bring us.) 5 May God, the author of all endurance and all encouragement, enable you to be all of one mind according to the mind of Christ Jesus, 6 so that you may all have but one heart and one mouth, to glorify God, the Father of our Lord Jesus Christ. 7 You must befriend one another, as Christ has befriended you, for God's honour. 8 I would remind those who are circumcised, that Christ came to relieve their needs; God's fidelity

v. 9. Ps. xvii. 50. demanded it; he must make good his promises to our fathers. 9 And I would remind the Gentiles to praise God for his mercy. So we read in scripture, I will give thanks to thee for this, and sing of

v. 10. Deut. xxxii. 43.
v. 11. Ps. cxvi. 1. thy praise, in the midst of the Gentiles; 10 and again it says, You too, Gentiles, rejoice with his own people; 11 and again, Praise the Lord, all you Gentiles; let all the nations of the world do him

v. 12. Is. xi. 10. honour; 12 and once more Isaias says, A root shall spring from Jesse, one who shall rise up to rule the Gentiles; the Gentiles, in him, shall find hope.

13 May God, the author of our hope, fill you with all joy and peace in your believing; so that you may have hope in abundance,

through the power of the Holy Spirit. 14 It is not that I have any doubt of you, my brethren; I know that you are full of good will, knowing all you need to know, so that you can give advice to one another if need be; 15 and yet I have written to you, here and there, somewhat freely, by way of refreshing your memory. So much I owe to the grace which God has given me, 16 in making me a priest of Jesus Christ for the Gentiles, with God's gospel for my priestly charge, to make the Gentiles an offering worthy of acceptance, consecrated by the Holy Spirit. 17 I have, then, through Christ Jesus, some reason for confidence in God's sight. 18 It is not for me to give you any account of what Christ has done through agents other than myself to secure the submission of the Gentiles, by word and action, 19 in virtue of wonders and signs, done in the power of the Holy Spirit. My own work has been to complete the preaching of Christ's gospel, in a wide sweep from Jerusalem as far as Illyricum. 20 It has been a point of honour with me to preach the gospel thus, never in places where Christ's name was already known; I would not build on the foundation another man had laid, 21 but follow the rule of scripture, He shall be seen by those who had had no tidings of him, he shall be made known to those who had never heard of him.

22 This was the chief reason which prevented me from visiting you; it has kept me back until now. 23 But now I can find no further scope in these countries, and I have been eager, these many years past, to find my way to you; 24 as soon, then, as I can set out on my journey to Spain, I hope to see you in passing; and you shall put me on my way, when you have done something to gratify this longing of mine. 25 As I write, I am making a journey to Jerusalem, with an errand of relief to the saints there. 26 You must know that Macedonia and Achaia have thought fit to give those saints at Jerusalem who are in need some share of their wealth; 27 they have thought fit to do it, I say, and indeed, they are in their debt. The Gentiles, if they have been allowed to share their spiritual gifts, are bound to contribute to their temporal needs in return. 28 When that is done, and I have seen this revenue safely in their hands, you shall be a stage on my journey to Spain; 29 and I am well assured that when I visit you, I shall be able to visit you in the fulness of Christ's blessing. 30 Only, brethren, I entreat you by our Lord Jesus Christ, and by the love of the Holy Spirit, to give me the help of your prayers to God on my behalf. 31 Pray that I may be kept safe from those who reject the faith in Judaea, and that my mission to Jerusalem may be well received

v. 18. 'Christ has done through agents other than myself', literally 'Christ has not done through me'. The verse is usually interpreted as if St. Paul meant, 'I will not tell you about anything except what Christ has done through me'; but this is not what St. Paul says. He says that it would be impertinent in him to tell the Romans what God has done in the way of reconciling the Gentiles through means other than his own. The miracles, therefore, referred to in the next verse were not performed by St. Paul, but by other Christian missionaries.

v. 19. St. Paul, in his humility, represents his own part in the work of the Church as 'filling up' the gospel, that is, filling in the gaps left by other missionaries. This has led him to take a wide sweep, as far as Illyricum, avoiding Asia and Bithynia (Acts vxi. 6, 7), and other countries already evangelized (cf. I Peter i. 1); his principle has been not to build on the foundations laid by other apostles, and that is why he has not visited Rome yet.

v. 21. Is. lii. 15.

by the saints there; 32 so that I may reach you, God willing, glad at heart, and make holiday with you. 33 May God, the author of peace, be with you all, Amen.

Chapter Sixteen

I commend our sister Phoebe to you; she has devoted her services to the church at Cenchrae. 2 Make her welcome in the Lord as saints should, and help her in any business where she needs your help; she has been a good friend to many, myself among them. 3 My greetings to Prisca and Aquila, who have worked at my side in the service of Christ Jesus, 4 and put their heads on the block to save my life; not only I but all the churches of the Gentiles have reason to be grateful to them. 5 My greetings, also, to the congregation which meets at their house; to my dear Epaenetus, the first offering Asia made to Christ, 6 and to Mary, who has spent so much labour on you. 7 My greetings to Andronicus and Junias, kinsmen and fellow prisoners of mine, who have won repute among the apostles that were in Christ's service before me. 8 My greetings to Amplias, whom I love so well in the Lord; 9 to Urbanus, who helped our work in Christ's cause, and to my dear Stachys; 10 to Apelles, a man tried in Christ's service; 11 and those of Aristobulus' household; to my kinsman Herodion, and to such of Narcissus' household as belong to the Lord. 12 My greetings to Tryphaena and Tryphosa, who have worked for the Lord so well; and dear Persis, too; she has been long in the Lord's service. 13 My greetings to Rufus, a chosen servant of the Lord, and his mother, who has been a mother to me; 14 to Asyncritus, Phlegon, Hermas, Patrobas, Hermes, and the brethren who are with them; 15 to Philologus and Julia, Nereus and his sister, Olympias, and all the saints who are of their company. 16 Greet one another with the kiss of saints; all the churches of Christ send you their greeting.

17 Brethren, I entreat you to keep a watch on those who are causing dissension and doing hurt to consciences, without regard to the teaching which has been given you; avoid their company. 18 Such men are no servants of Christ our Lord; their own hungry

v. 3. Cf. Acts xviii. 2. Prisca and Aquila, we are there told, had left Rome because of Claudius' edict expelling the Jews; and it seems probable that the other persons to whom St. Paul sends his greeting were also, for the most part, Jews who had met St. Paul in Asia or Greece, upon the same occasion.

v. 7. Commentators are not agreed whether the word 'kinsmen' means relatives of St. Paul, or merely fellow Jews, as in ix. 3 above. But the former explanation seems more likely, if only because several others among the persons addressed must have been of Jewish race; Aquila certainly, and Mary presumably. See last note.

v. 13. This Rufus may be the person mentioned in Mark xv. 21.

bellies are their masters; but guileless hearts are deceived by their flattering talk and their pious greetings. 19 You are renowned all over the world for your loyalty to the gospel, and I am proud of you; but I would wish to see you circumspect where there is a good end to be served, innocent only of harmful intent. 20 So God, who is the author of peace, will crush Satan under your feet before long. May the grace of our Lord Jesus Christ be with you.

21 Timothy, who works at my side, sends you his greeting; so do my kinsmen, Lucius and Jason and Sosipater. 22 (I, Tertius, who have committed this letter to paper, greet you in the name of the Lord.) 23 Greetings to you from my host, Caius, and from all the church; from Erastus, treasurer of the city, and your brother Quartus. 24 May the grace of our Lord Jesus Christ be with you all, Amen.

25 There is one who is able to set your feet firmly in the path of that gospel which I preach, when I herald Jesus Christ; a gospel which reveals the mystery, hidden from us through countless ages, 26 but now made plain, through what the prophets have written, and published, at the eternal God's command, to all the nations, so as to win the homage of their faith. 27 To him, to God who alone is wise, glory be given from age to age, through Jesus Christ, Amen.

v. 20. In mentioning Satan, St. Paul probably thinks of him as typified by those adversaries who were disturbing the peace of the Roman Church.

v. 23. 'And from all the church'; this, according to most manuscripts, should read, 'who is the host, too, of the whole church'.

THE AGONY IN THE GARDEN   RAPHAEL
                                                           1483-1520

METROPOLITAN MUSEUM, NEW YORK

THE FIRST EPISTLE OF THE BLESSED APOSTLE PAUL TO THE CORINTHIANS

Chapter One

PAUL, WHOM THE WILL of God has called to be an apostle of Jesus Christ, and Sosthenes, who is their brother, 2 send greeting to the church of God at Corinth, to those who have been sanctified in Jesus Christ, and called to be holy; with all those who invoke the name of our Lord Jesus Christ, in every dependency of theirs, and so of ours. 3 Grace and peace be yours from God, who is our Father, and from the Lord Jesus Christ. 4 I give thanks to my God continually in your name for that grace of God which has been bestowed upon you in Jesus Christ; 5 that you have become rich, through him, in every way, in eloquence and in knowledge of every sort; 6 so fully has the message of Christ established itself among you. 7 And now there is no gift in which you are still lacking; you have only to look forward to the revealing of our Lord Jesus Christ. 8 He will strengthen your resolution to the last, so that no charge will lie against you on the day when our Lord Jesus Christ comes. 9 The God, who has called you into the fellowship of his Son, Jesus Christ our Lord, is faithful to his promise.

v. 2. The sense appears to be, that St. Paul sends greeting to the Christians, not only in Corinth itself, but in the other towns of the province of Achaia (cf. II Cor. i. 1), which were politically dependent on it. These, it appears, had derived their knowledge of the gospel from it, and so ultimately from the preaching of St. Paul. That he associates Sosthenes with himself in this greeting, makes it probable that we should identify him with the person mentioned in Acts xviii. 17.

10 Only I entreat you, brethren, as you love the name of our Lord Jesus Christ, use, all of you, the same language. There must be no divisions among you; you must be restored to unity of mind and purpose. 11 The account I have of you, my brethren, from Chloe's household, is that there are dissensions among you; 12 each of you, I mean, has a cry of his own, I am for Paul, I am for Apollo, I am for Cephas, I am for Christ. 13 What, has Christ been divided up? Was it Paul that was crucified for you? Was it in Paul's name that you were baptized? 14 Thank God I did not baptize any of you except Crispus and Gaius; 15 so that no one can say it was in my name you were baptized. 16 (Yes, and I did baptize the household of Stephanas; I do not know that I baptized anyone else.)

17 Christ did not send me to baptize; he sent me to preach the gospel; not with an orator's cleverness, for so the cross of Christ might be robbed of its force. 18 To those who court their own ruin, the message of the cross is but folly; to us, who are on the way to salvation, it is the evidence of God's power. 19 So we read in scripture, I will confound the wisdom of wise men, disappoint the calculations of the prudent. 20 What has become of the wise men, the scribes, the philosophers of this age we live in? Must we not say that God has turned our worldly wisdom to folly? 21 When God shewed us his wisdom, the world, with all its wisdom, could not find its way to God; and now God would use a foolish thing, our preaching, to save those who will believe in it. 22 Here are the Jews asking for signs and wonders, here are the Greeks intent on their philosophy; 23 but what we preach is Christ crucified; to the Jews, a discouragement, to the Gentiles, mere folly; 24 but to us who have been called, Jew and Gentile alike, Christ the power of God, Christ the wisdom of God. 25 So much wiser than men is God's foolishness; so much stronger than men is God's weakness. 26 Consider, brethren, the circumstances of your own calling; not many of you are wise, in the world's fashion, not many powerful, not many well born. 27 No, God has chosen what the world holds foolish, so as to abash the wise, God has chosen what the world holds weak, so as to abash the strong. 28 God has chosen what the world holds base and contemptible, nay, has chosen what is nothing, so as to bring to nothing what is now in being; 29 no human creature was to have any ground for boasting, in the presence of God. 30 It is from him that you take your origin, through Christ Jesus, whom God gave us to be all our wisdom, our justification, our sanctification, and our atone-

vv. 17 and following. It is probable that St. Paul is thinking, here, of the comparatively small success which his preaching had in Athens, just before he went to Corinth (Acts xvii). It is possible, also, that some of the Corinthians had contrasted his preaching unfavourably with the eloquence of Apollo (cf. Acts xviii. 24-28).
v. 19. Is. xxix. 14.
v. 21. 'When God shewed us his wisdom', etc. Others understand this sentence as meaning, 'God's wisdom had decreed that the world, with all its wisdom, should not find its way to God.'

v. 27. 'What the world holds foolish', etc.; literally, 'the foolish things of the world' etc.

ment; 31 so that the scripture might be fulfilled, If anyone boasts, *v. 31. Jer. ix. 23.*
let him make his boast in the Lord.

Chapter Two

O it was, brethren, that when I came to you and preached Christ's message to you, I did so without any high pretensions to eloquence, or to philosophy. 2 I had no thought of bringing you any other knowledge than that of Jesus Christ, and of him as crucified. 3 It was with distrust of myself, full of anxious fear, that I approached you; *v. 3. 'Distrust of my-myself'; some would understand this word rather of physical infirmity.*
4 my preaching, my message depended on no persuasive language, devised by human wisdom, but rather on the proof I gave you of spiritual power; 5 God's power, not man's wisdom, was to be the foundation of your faith.

6 There is, to be sure, a wisdom which we make known among those who are fully grounded; but it is not the wisdom of this world, or of this world's rulers, whose power is to be abrogated. 7 What we make known is the wisdom of God, his secret, kept hidden till now; so, before the ages, God had decreed, reserving glory for us. 8 (None of the rulers of this world could read his secret, or they would not have crucified him to whom all glory belongs.) 9 So we read of, Things no eye has seen, no ear has heard, *v. 9. The words St. Paul uses here seem to be a reminiscence of Is. lxiv. 4.*
no human heart conceived, the welcome God has prepared for those who love him. 10 To us, then, God has made a revelation of it through his Spirit; there is no depth in God's nature so deep that the Spirit cannot find it out. 11 Who else can know a man's thoughts, except the man's own spirit that is within him? So no one else can know God's thoughts, but the Spirit of God. 12 And what *v. 13. 'Matching what is spiritual with what is spiritual'; others would translate 'interpreting what is spiritual for those who are spiritual'.*
we have received is no spirit of worldly wisdom; it is the Spirit that comes from God, to make us understand God's gifts to us; 13 gifts which we make known, not in such words as human wisdom teaches, but in words taught us by the Spirit, matching what is spiritual with what is spiritual. 14 Mere man with his natural gifts *v. 15. This does not mean that the 'spiritual man' need pay no attention to human criticisms of his conduct, but that the wisdom communicated to him is not to be judged by the world's standards.*
cannot take in the thoughts of God's Spirit; they seem mere folly to him, and he cannot grasp them, because they demand a scrutiny which is spiritual. 15 Whereas the man who has spiritual gifts can

v. 16. Is. xl. 13. It will be noticed how clearly, in using this quotation, St. Paul assumes the Divinity of Christ.

scrutinize everything, without being subject, himself, to any other man's scrutiny. 16 Who has entered into the mind of the Lord, so as to be able to instruct him? And Christ's mind is ours.

Chapter Three

ND when I preached to you, I had to approach you as men with natural, not with spiritual thoughts. You were little children in Christ's nursery, 2 and I gave you milk, not meat; you were not strong enough for it. You are not strong enough for it even now; nature still lives in you. 3 Do not these rivalries, these dissensions among you shew that nature is still alive, that you are guided by human standards? 4 When one of you says, I am for Paul, and another, I am for Apollo, are not these human thoughts? Why, what is Apollo, what is Paul? 5 Only the ministers of the God in whom your faith rests, who have brought that faith to each of you in the measure God granted. 6 It was for me to plant the seed, for Apollo to water it, but it was God who gave the increase. 7 And if so, the man who plants, the man who waters, count for nothing; God is everything, since it is he who gives the increase. 8 This man plants, that man waters; it is all one. And yet either will receive his own wages, in proportion to his own work. 9 You are a field of God's tilling, a structure of God's design; and we are only his assistants.

10 With what grace God has bestowed on me, I have laid a foundation as a careful architect should; it is left for someone else to build upon it. Only, whoever builds on it must be careful how he builds. 11 The foundation which has been laid is the only one which anybody can lay; I mean Jesus Christ. 12 But on this foundation different men will build in gold, silver, precious stones, wood, grass, or straw, 13 and each man's workmanship will be plainly seen. It is the day of the Lord that will disclose it, since that day is to reveal itself in fire, and fire will test the quality of each man's workmanship. 14 He will receive a reward, if the building he has added on stands firm; 15 if it is burnt up, he will be the loser; and

v. 5. This is the sense of the Latin; the Greek has, 'Only serving - men, who have brought you faith, brought it to each of you in the measure God granted'.

vv. 10-15. In its immediate reference, this passage seems to imply that we cannot decide yet how much good the influence of any Christian teacher (e.g. Apollo) has done; it is only at the last day that such things will be made known to us. (Cf. iv. 5, below.) But it has always been understood as having a wider application; each one of us is building upon the foundation of Christian faith which has been laid in him, and the merits or demerits of his building will be made known only at his judgement. At the same time, we are to recognize that many whose actions in this

yet he himself will be saved, though only as men are saved by passing through fire.

16 Do you not understand that you are God's temple, and that God's Spirit has his dwelling in you? 17 If anybody desecrates the temple of God, God will bring him to ruin. It is a holy thing, this temple of God which is nothing other than yourselves. 18 You must not deceive yourselves, any of you, about this. If any of you thinks he is wise, after the fashion of his fellow men, he must turn himself into a fool, so as to be truly wise. 19 This world's wisdom, with God, is but folly. So we read in scripture, I will entrap the wise with their own cunning. 20 And again, The Lord knows the thoughts of the wise, and how empty they are. 21 Nobody, therefore, should repose his confidence in men. 22 Everything is for you, whether it be Paul, or Apollo, or Cephas, or the world, or life, or death, or the present, or the future; it is all for you, 23 and you for Christ, and Christ for God.

world have had little value, will themselves escape condemnation, though only by passing through the fires of Purgatory.

vv. 16, 17. Here St. Paul, though keeping to the same metaphor, turns to a different subject; the position of those who destroy the unity of the Church by schism. Thus he returns to his main theme, the dissensions among the Christians at Corinth.

v. 19. Job v. 13.

v. 20. Ps. xciii. 11.

v. 22. 'Everything is for you'; that is, you must not say, 'I am for Paul', and 'I am for Apollo', and 'I am for Cephas'; Paul and Apollo and Cephas, like all God's gifts, exist for you.

Chapter Four

THAT IS HOW WE ought to be regarded, as Christ's servants, and stewards of God's mysteries. 2 And this is what we look for in choosing a steward; we must find one who is trustworthy. 3 Yet for myself, I make little account of your scrutiny, or of any human audit-day; I am not even at pains to scrutinize my own conduct. 4 My conscience does not, in fact, reproach me; but that is not where my justification lies; it is the Lord's scrutiny I must undergo. 5 You do ill, therefore, to pass judgement prematurely, before the Lord's coming; he will bring to light what is hidden in darkness, and reveal the secrets of men's hearts; then each of us will receive his due award from God.

v. 6. St. Paul apparently means that all he has been saying (about the account which Christian teachers will have to give of themselves) is intended as a warning to the heads of the rival factions in Corinth. Out of charity, he does not mention these by name, but uses his own name and that of Apollo to illustrate what he has been saying. 'Not to go beyond what is laid down for you' must have been a proverbial expres-

6 All this, brethren, I have applied to myself and to Apollo, but it is meant for you. The lesson you must learn from our example is, not to go beyond what is laid down for you, one man slighting another out of partiality for someone else. 7 After all, friend, who is it that gives thee this pre-eminence? What powers hast thou, that did not come to thee by gift? And if they came to thee by gift, why dost thou boast of them, as if there were no gift in question?

8 Well, you are already fully content; already you have grown rich; already you have come into your kingdom, without waiting for help from us. Would that you had come into your kingdom indeed; then we should be sharing it with you. 9 As it is, it seems as if God had destined us, his apostles, to be in the lowest place of all, like men under sentence of death; such a spectacle do we present to the whole creation, men and angels alike. 10 We are fools for Christ's sake, you are so wise; we are so helpless, you so stout of heart; you are held in honour, while we are despised. 11 Still, as I write, we go hungry and thirsty and naked; we are mishandled, we have no home to settle in, 12 we are hard put to it, working with our own hands. Men revile us, and we answer with a blessing, persecute us, and we make the best of it, 13 speak ill of us, and we fall to entreaty. We are still the world's refuse; everybody thinks himself well rid of us. 14 I am not writing this to shame you; you are my dearly loved children, and I would bring you to a better mind. 15 Yes, you may have ten thousand schoolmasters in Christ, but not more than one father; it was I that begot you in Jesus Christ, when I preached the gospel to you. 16 Follow my example, then, I entreat you, as I follow Christ's.

17 That is why I have sent Timothy to you, a faithful and dearly loved son of mine in the Lord; he will remind you of the path I tread in Christ Jesus, the lessons I give to all churches alike. 18 Some of you have grown contemptuous, thinking that I would never come to visit you. 19 But I shall be coming to see you soon, if the Lord is willing, and then I will test, not the fine words of those who hold me in contempt, but the powers they can shew. 20 It is power that builds up the kingdom of God, not words. 21 Choose, then; am I to come to you rod in hand, or lovingly, in a spirit of forbearance?

308

Chapter Five

WHY, THERE ARE RE ports of incontinence among you, and such incontinence as is not practised even among the heathen; a man taking to himself his father's wife. 2 And you, it seems, have been contumacious over it, instead of deploring it, and expelling the man who has been guilty of such a deed from your company. 3 For myself, though I am not with you in person, I am with you in spirit; and, so present with you, I have already passed sentence on the man who has acted thus. 4 Call an assembly, at which I will be present in spirit, with all the power of our Lord Jesus Christ, 5 and so, in the name of our Lord Jesus Christ, hand over the person named to Satan, for the overthrow of his corrupt nature, so that his spirit may find salvation in the day of our Lord Jesus Christ. 6 This good conceit of yourselves is ill grounded. Have you never been told that a little leaven is enough to leaven the whole batch? 7 Rid yourselves of the leaven which remains over, so that you may be a new mixture, still uncontaminated as you are. Has not Christ been sacrificed for us, our paschal victim? 8 Let us keep the feast, then, not with the leaven of yesterday, that was all vice and mischief, but with unleavened bread, with purity and honesty of intent.

9 In the letter I wrote to you, I told you to avoid the company of fornicators; 10 not meaning everyone in the world around you who is debauched, or a miser, or an extortioner, or an idolater; to do that, you would have to cut yourselves off from the world altogether. 11 No, my letter meant that if anyone who is counted among the brethren is debauched, or a miser, or an idolater, or bitter of speech, or a drunkard, or an extortioner, you must avoid his company; you must not even sit at table with him. 12 Why should I claim jurisdiction over those who are without? No, it is for you to pass judgement within your own number, 13 leaving God to judge those who are without. Banish, then, the offender from your company.

vv. 3-5. Either St. Paul directs the Corinthians to meet, as if in his presence, and condemn the delinquent; or he has already passed sentence, as if in the presence of the Corinthian assembly, and he is only calling upon them to give the sentence its effect. In either case, the authority of the apostle is strongly emphasized. The punishment inflicted is evidently that of excommunication; and some commentators think that the effect of this was to be physical harm (such as disease) inflicted by Satan on the offender. But this is not certain; St. Paul alludes to the destruction or overthrow, not of the body (corpus), but of the flesh (caro), by which he commonly means the natural (as opposed to the spiritual) principle in man.

v. 7. Ex. xii. 15; during the days of unleavened bread, the Jews were not allowed to have any leaven at all in their houses. It is probable that St. Paul wrote his letter, or expected it to be received, about Eastertide (Cf. xvi. 8, below).

309

Chapter Six

v. 4. 'You would do better', etc.; some commentators translate, 'You are appointing as your judges men who have no position at all in the Church', that is, the heathen.

v. 12. 'I am free to do what I will'; this phrase is repeated below (x. 23), and looks as if it were a catchword, perhaps a quotation from St. Paul's own lips, by which the Gentiles reminded themselves of their freedom from the ceremonial obligations of the Jewish law. There seems to have been reason to fear that some of the Corinthians were in danger of holding themselves dispensed from its moral obligations as well. The Apostles in Acts xv. 29 were apparently guarding against a similar misconception when they wrote to the Christians of Syria and Cilicia. 'Abdicate my own liberty'; that is, become enslaved to vicious habits.

v. 13. It seems unlikely that there is any reference here to the sin of gluttony. St. Paul is citing the prohibition of certain foods by the Mosaic law as an instance of those ceremonial obligations which are morally indifferent, and therefore not binding upon Gentile converts to the Church. Such regulations, he says, refer only to the temporal order of things, and have no significance for eternity; with the moral law it is otherwise.

v. 16. Gen. ii. 24.

RE you prepared to go to law before a profane court, when one of you has a quarrel with another, instead of bringing it before the saints? 2 You know well enough that it is the saints who will pass judgement on the world; and if a world is to abide your judgement, are you unfit to take cognisance of trifling matters? 3 You have been told that we shall sit in judgement on angels; how much more, then, over the things of common life? 4 You would do better to appoint the most insignificant of your own number as judges, when you have these common quarrels to decide. 5 That I say to humble you. What, have you really not a single man among you wise enough to decide a claim brought by his own brother? 6 Must two brethren go to law over it, and before a profane court? 7 And indeed, it is a defect in you at the best of times, that you should have quarrels among you at all. How is it that you do not prefer to put up with wrong, prefer to suffer loss? 8 Instead of that you commit wrong, you inflict loss, and at a brother's expense. 9 Yet you know well enough that wrong-doers will not inherit God's kingdom. Make no mistake about it; it is not the debauched, the idolaters, the adulterous, 10 it is not the effeminate, the sinners against nature, the misers, the drunkards, the bitter of speech, the extortioners that will inherit the kingdom of God. 11 That is what some of you once were; but now you have been washed clean, now you have been sanctified, now you have been justified in the name of the Lord Jesus, by the Spirit of the God we serve.

12 I am free to do what I will; yes, but not everything can be done without harm. I am free to do what I will, but I must not abdicate my own liberty. 13 Food is meant for our animal nature, and our animal nature claims its food; true enough, but then, God will bring both one and the other to an end. But your bodies are not meant for debauchery, they are meant for the Lord, and the Lord claims your bodies. 14 And God, just as he has raised our Lord from the dead, by his great power will raise us up too. 15 Have you never been told that your bodies belong to the body of Christ? And am I to take what belongs to Christ and make it one with a harlot? God forbid. 16 Or did you never hear that the man who unites himself to a harlot becomes one body with her?

THE SCOURGING OF CHRIST

BERNARDO DADDI
active 1320-1348

NATIONAL GALLERY OF ART, WASHINGTON, D. C. (KRESS COLLECTION)

The two, we are told, will become one flesh. 17 Whereas the man who unites himself to the Lord becomes one spirit with him. 18 Keep clear, then, of debauchery. Any other sin a man commits, leaves the body untouched, but the fornicator is committing a crime against his own body. 19 Surely you know that your bodies are the shrines of the Holy Spirit, who dwells in you. And he is God's gift to you, so that you are no longer your own masters. 20 A great price was paid to ransom you; glorify God by making your bodies the shrines of his presence.

v. 18. 'Leaves the body untouched'; literally, 'is outside the body'. Evidently other sins, that of gluttony, for example, are concerned with the use of our bodily powers, but they do not strike directly at the sanctity of the body, as fornication does.

v. 20. 'Glorify God', etc.; in the Greek, this sentence reads 'Glorify God in your bodies'. The Latin rendering, 'carry God about in your bodies', is probably due to an error in the text.

Chapter Seven

As FOR THE QUESTIONS raised in your letter; a man does well to abstain from all commerce with women. 2 But, to avoid the danger of fornication, let every man keep his own wife, and every woman her own husband. 3 Let every man give his wife what is her due, and every woman do the same by her husband; 4 he, not she, claims the right over her body, as she, not he, claims the right over his. 5 Do not starve one another, unless perhaps you do so for a time, by mutual consent, to have more freedom for prayer; come together again, or Satan will tempt you, weak as you are. 6 I say this by way of concession; I am not imposing a rule on you. 7 I wish you were all in the same state as myself; but each of us has his own endowment from God, one to live in this way, another in that. 8 To the unmarried, and to the widows, I would say that they will do well to remain in the same state as myself, 9 but if they have not the gift of continence, let them marry; better to marry than to feel the heat of passion. 10 For those who have married already, the precept holds which is the Lord's precept, not mine; the wife is not to leave her husband,

v. 10. Matthew v. 32, xix. 3, Mark x. 11, Luke xvi. 18.

311

11 (if she has left him, she must either remain unmarried, or go back to her own husband again), and the husband is not to put away his wife.

12 To those others, I give my own instructions, not the Lord's. If any of the brethren has a wife, not a believer, who is well content to live with him, there is no reason why he should put her away, 13 nor is there any reason for a woman to part with her husband, not a believer, if he is content to live with her. 14 The unbelieving husband has shared in his wife's consecration, and the unbelieving wife has shared in the consecration of one who is a brother. Were it otherwise, their offspring would be born under a stain, whereas in fact it is holy. 15 On the other hand, if the unbelieving partner is for separating, let them separate; in such a case, the brother or the sister is under no compulsion. It is in a spirit of peace that God's call has come to us. 16 There is no knowing whether thou, the wife, wilt save thy husband, whether thou, the husband, wilt save thy wife. 17 No, the part which God has assigned, the vocation which God has bestowed, is to be the rule in each case. That is the direction which I am giving all through the churches. 18 If a man is already circumcised when he is called, he is not to disguise it; if he is uncircumcised, he is not to undergo circumcision. 19 There is no virtue either in circumcision or in the want of it; it is keeping the commandments of God that signifies. 20 Everyone has his own vocation, in which he has been called; let him keep to it. 21 Hast thou been called as a slave? Do not let it trouble thee; and if thou hast the means to become free, make all the more use of thy opportunity. 22 If a slave is called to enter Christ's service, he is Christ's freedman; just as the free man, when he is called, becomes the slave of Christ. 23 A price was paid to redeem you; do not enslave yourselves to human masters. 24 Each of you is to remain, brethren, in the condition in which he was called.

25 About virgins, I have no command from the Lord; but I give you my opinion, as one who is, under the Lord's mercy, a true counsellor. 26 This, then, I hold to be the best counsel in such times of stress, that this is the best condition for man to be in. 27 Art thou yoked to a wife? Then, do not go about to free thyself. Art thou free of wedlock? Then do not go about to find a wife. 28 Not that thou dost commit sin if thou marriest; nor, if she marries, has the virgin committed sin. It is only that those who do so will meet with outward distress. But I leave you your freedom. 29 Only, brethren, I would say this; the time is drawing to an end; nothing remains, but for those who have wives to behave as though

v. 14. The baptism of wife or husband is here conceived as doing away with whatever defilement a heathen marriage brings with it. It is not to be understood that either the heathen partner or the children receive sanctifying grace as the result of the union.

v. 15. 'In a spirit of peace'; so that the Christian partner is not bound to live in the restless atmosphere of a divided household.

v. 16. Commentators are not agreed, whether St. Paul means that the Christian partner is free to go away, as having little chance of winning the other's conversion, or that the Christian partner is justified in going on as before, as having some hope of winning the other's conversion.

v. 21. 'All the more use of thy opportunity'; that is, according to some, the opportunity of gaining freedom. Others understand it of the opportunity to show patience in a servile condition, although the opportunity of gaining freedom is present; this view perhaps fits in better with the preceding verse, and with the general context.

v. 22. This direction is probably meant in the general sense, that we should think of Christ's service as having a higher claim on us than any human obligation.

v. 26. 'This is the best condition'; that is, virginity. Others have thought the phrase means 'Your present condition is the best' (whichever it is).

v. 28. 'I leave you your freedom'; liter-

312

they had none; 30 those who weep must forget their tears, and those who rejoice their rejoicing, and those who buy must renounce possession; 31 and those who take advantage of what the world offers must not take full advantage of it; the fashion of this world is soon to pass away. 32 And I would have you free from concern. He who is unmarried is concerned with God's claim, asking how he is to please God; 33 whereas the married man is concerned with the world's claim, asking how he is to please his wife; and thus he is at issue with himself. 34 So a woman who is free of wedlock, or a virgin, is concerned with the Lord's claim, intent on holiness, bodily and spiritual; whereas the married woman is concerned with the world's claim, asking how she is to please her husband.

35 I am thinking of your own interest when I say this. It is not that I would hold you in a leash; I am thinking of what is suitable for you, and how you may best attend on the Lord without distraction. 36 And if anyone considers that he is behaving unsuitably towards the girl who is in his charge, on the ground that she is now past her prime, and there is no way of avoiding it, why, let him please himself; there is nothing sinful in it; let her marry. 37 Whereas, if a man remains fixed in his resolution, and makes up his mind to keep the girl who is in his charge unwed, although there is no necessity for it, and he is free to choose for himself, such a man is well advised. 38 Thus, a man is well advised to give his ward in marriage, and still better advised not to give her in marriage. 39 As for a wife, she is yoked to her husband as long as he lives; if her husband is dead, she is free to marry anyone she will, so long as she marries in the Lord. 40 But more blessed is she, if she remains as she is, in my judgement; and I, too, claim to have the Spirit of God.

Chapter Eight

ND now about meat that has been used in idolatrous worship. We all know, to be sure, what is the truth about it; but knowledge only breeds self-conceit, it is charity that binds the building together. 2 If anybody claims to have superior knowledge, it means that he has not yet attained the knowledge which is true knowledge; 3 it is only when a man loves God that God acknowledges him. 4 About meat, then, used in idolatrous worship, we can be sure of this, that a false god has no existence in the order of things; there is one God, and there can be no other. 5 Whatever gods may be spoken of as existing in heaven or on earth (and there are many such gods, many such lords), 6 for us there is only one God, the Father who is the origin of all things, and the end of our being; only one Lord, Jesus Christ, the creator of all things, who is our way to him. 7 But it is not everybody who has this knowledge; there are those who still think of such meat, while they eat it, as something belonging to idolatrous worship, with the thought of the false god in their minds; their conscience is not easy, and so incurs guilt. 8 And it is not what we eat that gives us our standing in God's sight; we gain nothing by eating, lose nothing by abstaining; 9 it is for you to see that the liberty you allow yourselves does not prove a snare to doubtful consciences. 10 If any of them sees one who is better instructed sitting down to eat in the temple of a false god, will not his conscience, all uneasy as it is, be emboldened to approve of eating idolatrously? 11 And thus, through thy enlightenment, the doubting soul will be lost; thy brother, for whose sake Christ died. 12 When you thus sin against your brethren, by injuring their doubtful consciences, you sin against Christ. 13 Why then, if a mouthful of food is an occasion of sin to my brother, I will abstain from flesh meat perpetually, rather than be the occasion of my brother's sin.

v. 6. 'Who is our way to him'; this can also be rendered, 'And our creator too', but it is hard to see why St. Paul should have thought the addition necessary. He seems rather to be saying, 'We draw our origin from the Father by way of Christ as Creator; and we must tend back to the Father by way of Christ as Mediator'.

v. 7. This is in apparent contradiction with v. 1, where it is said that all Christians have the knowledge in question. Possibly the doubtful consciences to which St. Paul refers are those of heathens who are beginning to be attracted towards the faith, yet still retain a half-belief in their false gods. Or possibly 'we all' in verse 1 refers to the Gentile Christians, and the doubtful consciences are those of Jewish Christians, who still feel themselves bound by the rule laid down in

Acts xv. 29; in which case the position here is much the same as that considered in Romans xiv. The principle, in either case, is that a man is bound to follow his own conscience, and we must sometimes abstain from what our own conscience finds harmless, lest our example should give scandal to one whose conscience is differently formed. 'With the thought of the false god in their minds'; some manuscripts in the Greek read 'through being accustomed to (the worship of) false gods'.

314

Chapter Nine

A M I not free to do as I will? Am I not an apostle, have I not seen our Lord Jesus Christ? Are not you yourselves my achievement in the Lord? 2 To others I may not be an apostle, but to you at least I am; why, you are the sign-manual of my apostleship in the Lord. 3 This is the answer I make to those who call me in question. 4 Have we not a right to be provided with food and drink; 5 nay, have we not the right to travel about with a woman who is a sister, as the other apostles do, as the Lord's brethren do, and Cephas? 6 Must I and Barnabas, alone among them, be forbidden to do as much? 7 Why, what soldier ever fought at his own expense? Who would plant a vineyard, and not live on its fruits, or tend a flock, and not live on the milk which the flock yields? 8 This is not a plea of man's invention; the law declares it. 9 When we read in the law of Moses, Thou shalt not muzzle the ox that treads out the corn, must we suppose that God is making provision for oxen? 10 Is it not clear that he says it for our sakes? For our sakes it was laid down that the ploughman has a right to plough, and the thrasher to thrash, with the expectation of sharing in the crop. 11 Here are we, who have sown in you a spiritual harvest; is it much to ask, that we should reap from you a temporal harvest in return? 12 If others claim a share of such rights over you, have not we a better claim still? And yet we have never availed ourselves of those rights; we bear every hardship, sooner than hinder the preaching of Christ's gospel. 13 You know, surely, that those who do the temple's work live on the temple's revenues; that those who preside at the altar share the altar's offerings. 14 And so it is that the Lord has bidden the heralds of the gospel live by preaching the gospel. 15 Yet I have not availed myself of any such right.

I am not writing thus in the hope of being treated otherwise; I would rather die than have this boast taken from me. 16 When I preach the gospel, I take no credit for that; I act under constraint; it would go hard with me indeed if I did not preach the gospel. 17 I can claim a reward for what I do of my own choice; but when I act under constraint, I am only executing a commission. 18 What title have I, then, to a reward? Why, that when I preach the gospel I should preach the gospel free of charge, not making

v. 1. 'Am I not free to do as I will?' St. Paul here alludes to the principle laid down in vi. 12 and x. 23. He is free to take stipends if he will, but he abstains for fear of giving scandal; the Corinthians, too, must be careful not to give scandal.

v. 3. 'This' probably refers, not to what follows, but to what has gone before; when St. Paul's apostleship is challenged, he points to the Corinthian church as the proof of it.

v. 5. 'Woman' may also be translated 'wife'; and that may be the sense intended. We know that St. Peter was married, and his wife, if she was still alive, may have travelled with him on his missionary journeys. But it is not impossible that he, or other apostles, may have been cared for by pious women, as our Lord himself was (Luke viii. 3). 'Sister' does not imply any relationship, physical or spiritual; it only means that the woman was a Christian. St. Paul is not claiming credit here for avoiding the society of women; he only claims credit for living at his own expense, when other apostles supported not only themselves, but the women who waited on their needs, out of offerings made by the faithful. 'The Lord's brethren'; see on Matthew xii. 46.

v. 8. Deut. xxv. 4.

v. 12. This verse ex-

315

plains the connexion of the present passage with what has gone before. St. Paul cites his own thoughtfulness in the matter of accepting stipends, by way of encouraging the Corinthians to shew a similar thoughtfulness in sparing the consciences of the weaker brethren. We ought to forego some of our rights, he says, so as not to hinder the preaching of Christ's gospel.

vv. 17, 18. 'I can claim a reward', literally, 'I have a reward'; 'what title have I to a reward?', literally, 'what reward have I?' The word 'reward' is thus used in the sense of something which entitles one to a reward in Matthew v. 46 and vi. 1; no other meaning appears to suit the context here. St. Paul takes no credit to himself for preaching, since he is only fulfilling an express command (Luke xvii.

full use of the rights which gospel preaching gives me. 19 Thus nobody has any claim on me, and yet I have made myself everybody's slave, to win more souls. 20 With the Jews I lived like a Jew, to win the Jews; 21 with those who keep the law, as one who keeps the law (though the law had no claim on me), to win those who kept the law; with those who are free of the law, like one free of the law (not that I recognized no divine law, but it was the law of Christ that bound me), to win those who were free of the law. 22 With the scrupulous, I behaved myself like one who is scrupulous, to win the scrupulous. I have been everything by turns to everybody, to bring everybody salvation.

23 All that I do, I do for the sake of the gospel promises, to win myself a share in them. 24 You know well enough that when men run in a race, the race is for all, but the prize for one; run, then, for victory. 25 Every athlete must keep all his appetites under control; and he does it to win a crown that fades, whereas ours is imperishable. 26 So I do not run my course like a man in doubt of his goal; I do not fight my battle like a man who wastes his blows on the air. 27 I buffet my own body, and make it my slave; or I, who have preached to others, may myself be rejected as worthless.

10); he does, however, take credit to himself for preaching Christ free of charge, since he does this 'of his own choice'. vv. 23 and following. Here St. Paul alters the bearing of his argument. So far, he has been urging the Corinthians to abstain from the contact of idolatry for fear of giving scandal. Now he begins urging them to abstain from it for fear of a relapse into heathen ways. He prefaces this part of the argument by telling them that he himself does not regard his own salvation as assured; it calls for watchfulness. v. 27. 'Rejected', probably in the sense of being a competitor disqualified in a race; the word 'preached' might also be rendered 'been a herald', with the same reference.

Chapter Ten

vv. 1-12. The Jews, St. Paul argues, were figuratively baptized when they were hidden by the fiery cloud (Ex. xiv. 20) and passed through

LET ME REMIND YOU, brethren, of this. Our fathers were hidden, all of them, under the cloud, and found a path, all of them, through the sea; 2 all alike, in the cloud and in the sea, were baptized into Moses' fellowship. 3 They all ate the same prophetic food, 4 and all drank the same prophetic drink, watered by the same prophetic rock which bore them company, the rock that was Christ. 5 And for all that, God was ill pleased with most of them; see how they were laid low in the wilderness. 6 It is we that were foreshadowed in these events. We were not to set our hearts, as some of them set their hearts, on forbidden things. 7 You were not to turn idolatrous, as some of them did; so we read, The people sat down to eat and drink, and rose up to take their pleasure. 8 We were not to commit fornication, as some of them committed fornication, when twenty-three thousand of them were killed in one day. 9 We were not to try the patience of Christ, as some of them tried it, the men who were slain by the serpents; 10 nor were you to complain, as some of them complained, till the destroying angel slew them. 11 When all this happened to them, it was a symbol; the record of it was written as a warning to us, in whom history has reached its fulfilment; 12 and it means that he who thinks he stands firmly should beware of a fall. 13 I pray that no temptation may come upon you that is beyond man's strength. Not that God will play you false; he will not allow you to be tempted beyond your powers. With the temptation itself, he will ordain the issue of it, and enable you to hold your own.

14 Keep far away, then, my well beloved, from idolatry. I am speaking to you as men of good sense; weigh my words for yourselves. 16 We have a cup that we bless; is not this cup we bless a participation in Christ's blood? Is not the bread we break a participation in Christ's body? 17 The one bread makes us one body, though we are many in number; the same bread is shared by all. 18 Or look at Israel, God's people by nature; do not those who eat their sacrifices associate themselves with the altar of sacrifice? 19 I am not suggesting that anything can really be sacrificed to a false god, or that a false god has any existence; 20 I mean that when the heathen offer sacrifice they are really offering it to evil spirits and not to a God at all. I have no mind to see you associating yourselves with evil spirits. 21 To drink the Lord's cup, and yet to drink the cup of evil spirits, to share the Lord's feast, and to share the feast of evil spirits, is impossible for you. 22 Are we, then, to provoke the Lord to jealousy? Have we powers greater than his?

I am free to do what I will; yes, but not everything can be done without harm. 23 I am free to do what I will, but some things disedify. 24 Each of you ought to study the well-being of others, not his own. 25 When things are sold in the open market, then

the Red Sea, as we are mystically associated by baptism with the passage of Christ through the tomb (Rom. vi. 2-4, Col. iii. 3). They became, figuratively, communicants when they ate the bread of angels, the manna, and were nourished from the riven rock (Ex. xvii. 6), as we are sacramentally nourished from the riven side of Christ (John xix. 34). Baptized communicants, in this figurative sense, they nevertheless fell away from God and incurred his anger. The Corinthians, then, must not think that they, as baptized communicants, are proof against every temptation; they must avoid the occasions of sin, especially that of idolatry.

v. 3. 'Prophetic'; literally, 'spiritual'. The sense may be merely that of 'supernatural', but it seems more likely that St. Paul is regarding the manna, the water, and the rock as types of things to come; cf. Apoc. xi. 8.

v. 4. St. Paul is no doubt alluding to a Jewish legend, according to which the rock from which the water came was enabled, by a miracle, to accompany the wanderings of the Israelites; he means, perhaps, to attribute this abiding presence to the thing signified rather than to the rock itself.

v. 7. Ex. xxxii. 6.
v. 8. Num. xxv. 1-9.
v. 9. Num. xxi. 6. The Greek manuscripts read 'the Lord', not 'Christ'.
v. 10. Num. xiv. 36.
v. 13. According to St. Basil, St. Paul here looks forward to the persecutions which were soon to bring Christians into grave danger of consenting to idolatry. 'I pray that no temptation may befall you'; the Greek here has, 'So far, no temptation has befallen you'.
v. 17. The beginning of this verse may al-

so be translated, 'For we are one bread, one body, though many in number'.
v. 26. Ps. xxiii. 1.
vv. 29, 30. It is probable that St. Paul means, 'Keep your own interior liberty of conscience, although you abstain out of charity; one man's conscience cannot be the rule for another's'. He may, however, mean, 'Is it worth while to use your own liberty at the price of incurring censure from others?'
v. 30. The Greek here may mean, 'Grace lets me eat this food', that is, the liberty of the Gospel, as opposed to the strictness of the Jewish law. 'For saying grace over it';

you may eat them, without making any enquiries to satisfy your consciences; 26 this world, as we know, and all that is in it belongs to the Lord. 27 If some unbeliever invites you to his table, and you consent to go, then you need not ask questions to satisfy your consciences, you may eat whatever is put before you. 28 But if someone says to you, This has been used in idolatrous worship, then, for the sake of your informant, you must refuse to eat; it is a matter of conscience; 29 his conscience, I mean, not yours. There is no reason why I should let my freedom be called in question by another man's conscience. 30 I can eat such food and be grateful for it; why should I incur reproach for saying grace over it? 31 In eating, in drinking, in all that you do, do everything as for God's glory. 32 Give no offence to Jew, or to Greek, or to God's church. 33 That is my own rule, to satisfy all alike, studying the general welfare rather than my own, so as to win their salvation.

in the Greek, 'for that over which I say grace'. It is to be observed that the Gospel liberty of which St. Paul speaks justified the faithful in eating the food offered them without asking questions, but did not justify them in frequenting feasts held in honour of heathen deities, which is the situation contemplated in verses 16 to 22, as in viii. 10.

Chapter Eleven

vv. 3-16. It is not clear why St. Paul here appears to regulate the conditions under which women may undertake public utterances, when in xiv. 34 below he lays it down that women are not to speak openly in the Christian assembly. If we suppose, as some authors do, that Christian women wore a heavy veil in front of their faces, such as was used in Eastern countries, the difficulty disappears; in forbidding women to speak unveiled the Apostle is forbidding

FOLLOW my example, then, as I follow the example of Christ. 2 I must needs praise you for your constant memory of me, for upholding your traditions just as I handed them on to you. 3 And here is something you must know. The head to which a wife is united is her husband, just as the head to which every man is united is Christ; so, too, the head to which Christ is united is God. 4 And whereas any man who keeps his head covered when he prays or utters prophecy brings shame upon his head, 5 a woman brings shame upon her head if she uncovers it to pray or prophesy; she is no better than the woman who has her head shaved. 6 If a woman would go without a veil, why does she not cut her hair short too? If she admits that a woman is disgraced when her hair is cut short or shaved, then let her go veiled. 7 A man has no need to veil his head; he is God's image, the pride of his creation, whereas the wife is the pride of her husband. 8 (The woman takes her origin from the man, not the man from the woman; 9 and indeed, it was not man that was created for woman's sake, but woman for man's.) 10 And for that reason the woman ought to have authority over her head, for the angels' sake. 11 (Not that, in the Lord's service, man has his place apart from woman, or woman hers apart from man; 12 if woman takes her origin from man, man equally comes to birth through woman. And indeed all things have their origin in God.) 13 Judge for yourselves; is it fitting that a woman should offer prayer to God unveiled? 14 Does not nature itself teach you that, whereas it is a disgrace to a man to wear his hair long, 15 when a woman grows her hair long, it is an added grace to her? That is because her hair has been given her to take the place of a veil. 16 And if anyone is prepared to argue the matter, he must know that no such custom is found among us, or in any of God's churches.

17 And here is a warning I have for you. I can give you no praise for holding your assemblies in a way that does harm, not good. 18 From the first, when you meet in church, there are divisions among you; so I hear, and in some measure believe it. 19 Parties there must needs be among you, so that those who are true metal may be distinguished from the rest. 20 And when you assemble together, there is no opportunity to eat a supper of the Lord; 21 each comer hastens to eat the supper he has brought for himself, so that one man goes hungry, while another has drunk deep. 22 Have you no homes to eat and drink in, that you should shew contempt to God's church, and shame the poor? Praise you? There is no room for praise here. 23 The tradition which I received from the Lord, and handed on to you, is that the Lord Jesus, on the night when he was being betrayed, took bread, 24 and gave thanks, and broke it, and said, Take, eat; this is my body, given up for you. Do this for a commemoration of me. 25 And so with the cup, when supper was ended, This cup, he said, is the new testament, in my blood. Do this, whenever you drink it, for a commemoration of me. 26 So it is the Lord's death that you are heralding, whenever you eat this bread and drink this cup, until he comes; 27 and therefore, if anyone eats this bread or drinks this cup of the Lord unworthily, he will be held to account for the Lord's body and blood. 28 A man must examine himself first, and then eat of that bread and drink of that cup; 29 he is eating and drinking damnation to himself if he eats and drinks unworthily, not recognizing the Lord's body for what it is. 30 That is why many of your number want strength and health, and not a few have died. 31 If we recognized our own fault, we should not incur

them to speak at all. Others suggest that the prohibition here applies, not to formal assemblies for worship, but for occasional meetings in private houses.

v. 3. Cf. Eph. v. 24.

vv. 4, 5. 'To bring shame upon one's head' should probably be understood in a double sense; that of treating one's own body with disrespect, and that of disloyalty to one's own spiritual head; the man muffling himself up, as if he were ashamed of Christ to whom he prays, the woman shewing her face in public, and so infringing the rights of her husband.

v. 5. It appears that a woman's head was sometimes shaved close by way of branding her as having been guilty of incontinence. This may be the meaning here, or it may refer to shameless women in Corinthian society who shaved their heads to look like men.

v. 8. The reference here is probably not to Gen. ii. 21, but to the facts of physical generation; cf. v. 12 below.

v. 10. This verse, which is here literally rendered, remains very obscure, in spite of the commentators. The word translated 'authority' may mean authority, or power to do things, or (most commonly in this epistle) liberty of choice. If we understand that the wife ought to wear on her head a symbol of her husband's authority over her, we satisfy the sense, but give a very strained interpretation of the Greek. If we understand that the wife has power over her own head, liberty to dispose of it as she likes, the Greek is satisfied, but the whole sense of the context is ignored. Some think that St. Paul is here giving a literal translation of a Hebrew word meaning 'veil', derived from a verb *which means 'to control'; but it is hard to see why he should have done so. Most commentators understand 'for the angels' sake' as meaning that the angels join with us in worship, and therefore we must be careful to shew all possible reverence in*

these judgements; 32 as it is, the Lord judges us and chastises us, so that we may not incur, as this world incurs, damnation. 33 So, brethren, when you assemble to eat together, wait for one another; 34 those who are hungry had best eat at home, for fear that your meeting should bring you condemnation. The other questions I will settle when I come.

church; some think that St. Paul is citing the example of those angels who veil their faces before the presence of God (Is. vi. 2). vv. 17-34. It is clear that the early Christians met (not literally in a church, for there were then no dedicated buildings) for an agape or love-feast, followed by celebration of the Holy Eucharist. This should have been a common meal, to which all contributed; instead of which a rich Corinthian would eat the food he himself had brought, while his poorer neighbour came late (verse 33) so as not to disclose his poverty. This exclusiveness and want of charity meant that when the Eucharist was finally celebrated many of the faithful were in bad dispositions. v. 24. The words 'take, eat' are omitted in most Greek and in some Latin manuscripts. v. 29. The word 'unworthily' is wanting in some of the best Greek manuscripts. v. 30. 'Have died'; literally, 'have fallen asleep.'

Chapter Twelve

AND now about spiritual gifts; I would not willingly leave you in doubt about these. 2 While you were still heathen, as you can remember well enough, you let yourselves be led away wherever men would lead you, to worship false gods that gave no utterance. 3 That is why I am telling you of this. Just as no one can be speaking through God's Spirit if he calls Jesus accursed, so it is only through the Holy Spirit that anyone can say, Jesus is the Lord; 4 and yet there are different kinds of gifts, though it is the same Spirit who gives them, 5 just as there are different kinds of service, though it is the same Lord we serve, 6 and different manifestations of power, though it is the same God who manifests his power everywhere in all of us. 7 The revelation of the Spirit is imparted to each, to make the best advantage of it. 8 One learns to speak with wisdom, by the power of the Spirit, another to speak with knowledge, with the same Spirit for his rule; 9 one, through the same Spirit, is given faith; another, through the same Spirit, powers of healing; 10 one can perform miracles, one can prophesy, another can test the spirit of the prophets; one can speak in different tongues, another can interpret the tongues; 11 but all this is the work of one and the same Spirit, who distributes his gifts as he will to each severally.

12 A man's body is all one, though it has a number of different organs; and all this multitude of organs goes to make up one body;

so it is with Christ. 13 We too, all of us, have been baptized into a single body by the power of a single Spirit, Jews and Greeks, slaves and free men alike; we have all been given drink at a single source, the one Spirit. 14 The body, after all, consists not of one organ but of many; 15 if the foot should say, I am not the hand, and therefore I do not belong to the body, does it belong to the body any the less for that?_ 16 If the ear should say, I am not the eye, and therefore I do not belong to the body, does it belong to the body any the less for that? 17 Where would the power of hearing be, if the body were all eye? Or the power of smell, if the body were all ear? 18 As it is, God has given each one of them its own position in the body, as he would. 19 If the whole were one single organ, what would become of the body? 20 Instead of that, we have a multitude of organs, and one body. 21 The eye cannot say to the hand, I have no need of thee, or the head to the feet, I have no need of you. 22 On the contrary, it is those parts of our body which seem most contemptible that are necessary to it; 23 what seems base in our bodies, we surround with special honour, treating with special seemliness that which is unseemly in us, 24 whereas that which is seemly in us has no need of it. Thus God has established a harmony in the body, giving special honour to that which needed it most. 25 There was to be no want of unity in the body; all the different parts of it were to make each other's welfare their common care. 26 If one part is suffering, all the rest suffer with it; if one part is treated with honour, all the rest find pleasure in it. 27 And you are Christ's body, organs of it depending upon each other. 28 God has given us different positions in the church; apostles first, then prophets, and thirdly teachers; then come miraculous powers, then gifts of healing, works of mercy, the management of affairs, speaking with different tongues, and interpreting prophecy. 29 Are all of us apostles, all prophets, all teachers? 30 Have all miraculous powers, or gifts of healing? Can all speak with tongues, can all interpret?

31 Prize the best gifts of heaven. Meanwhile, I can shew you a way which is better than any other.

v. 13. 'We have all been given drink'; St. Paul is probably referring to the rock which gave out water to the Israelites in the wilderness, cf. x. 4 above. It is not certain which of the Sacraments he is alluding to.

v. 27. There is doubt in this verse both about the text and about the exact rendering of it, but the context seems to make it clear that the general sense is that given here.

v. 31. Charity is itself a gift, and, if it is contrasted with other spiritual gifts, overshadows them all.

Chapter Thirteen

v. 2. Cf. Matthew
xxi. 21.

v. 3. Some Greek
manuscripts have 'in
order to boast of it'
instead of 'to be
burnt at the stake'.

v. 5. 'Never inso-
lent'; the Latin word
used here means 'am-
bitious', but the
Greek original has
rather the sense of
'indecorous'.

I MAY SPEAK WITH every tongue that men and angels use; yet, if I lack charity, I am no better than echoing bronze, or the clash of cymbals. 2 I may have powers of prophecy, no secret hidden from me, no knowledge too deep for me; I may have utter faith, so that I can move mountains; yet if I lack charity, I count for nothing. 3 I may give away all that I have, to feed the poor; I may give myself up to be burnt at the stake; if I lack charity, it goes for nothing. 4 Charity is patient, is kind; charity feels no envy; charity is never perverse or proud, 5 never insolent; does not claim its rights, cannot be provoked, does not brood over an injury; 6 takes no pleasure in wrongdoing, but rejoices at the victory of truth; 7 sustains, believes, hopes, endures, to the last. 8 The time will come when we shall outgrow prophecy, when speaking with tongues will come to an end, when knowledge will be swept away; we shall never have finished with charity. 9 Our knowledge, our prophecy, are only glimpses of the truth; 10 and these glimpses will be swept away when the time of fulfilment comes. 11 (Just so, when I was a child, I talked like a child, I had the intelligence, the thoughts of a child; since I became a man, I have outgrown childish ways.) 12 At present, we are looking at a confused reflection in a mirror; then, we shall see face to face; now, I have only glimpses of knowledge; then, I shall recognize God as he has recognized me. 13 Meanwhile, faith, hope and charity persist, all three; but the greatest of them all is charity.

v. 13. St. Irenaeus
and Tertullian, fol-
lowed by some mod-
ern authors, under-
stand this as mean-
ing that all three the-
ological virtues will
persist in heaven;
but this interpreta-
tion would be irrele-
vant to the present
context.

Chapter Fourteen

AKE charity your aim, the spiritual gifts your aspiration; and, by preference, the gift of prophecy. 2 The man who talks in a strange tongue is talking to God, not to men; nobody understands him, he is holding mysterious converse with his own spirit; 3 whereas the prophet speaks to edify, to encourage, to comfort his fellow men. 4 By talking in a strange tongue, a man may strengthen his own faith; by prophesying he can strengthen the faith of the church. 5 I would gladly see you all speaking with strange tongues, but I would rather you should prophesy, because the prophet ranks higher than the man who speaks with strange tongues. It would be different if he could translate them, to strengthen the faith of the church; 6 but as things are, brethren, what good can I do you by coming and talking to you in strange languages, instead of addressing you with a revelation, or a manifestation of inner knowledge, or a prophecy, or words of instruction? 7 Senseless things may be vocal, a flute, for example, or a harp; but even with these, there must be distinctions between the sounds they give, or how can we recognize what melody flute or harp is playing? 8 If a trumpet, for that matter, gives out an uncertain note, who will arm himself for battle? 9 So it is with you, how can it be known what your message is, if you speak in a language whose accents cannot be understood? Your words will fall on empty air. 10 No doubt all these different languages exist somewhere in the world, and each of them has its significance; 11 but if I cannot understand what the language means, the effect is that I am a foreigner to the man who is speaking, and he is a foreigner to me. 12 So the case stands with you. Since you have set your hearts on spiritual gifts, ask for them in abundant measure, but only so as to strengthen the faith of the church; 13 the man who can speak in a strange tongue should pray for the power to interpret them.

14 If I use a strange tongue when I offer prayer, my spirit is praying, but my mind reaps no advantage from it. 15 What, then, is my drift? Why, I mean to use mind as well as spirit when I offer prayer, use mind as well as spirit when I sing psalms. 16 If thou dost pronounce a blessing in this spiritual fashion, how can one who takes his place among the uninstructed say Amen to thy thanks-

v. 16. 'One who takes his place among the uninstructed'; probably in the literal sense of sitting in a

323

particular part of the church. It would seem likely, from a comparison with verse 23, that the uninstructed are the catechumens, as opposed to the baptized Christians. The words 'blessing' and 'thanksgiving' are sometimes used in connexion with the Holy Eucharist, but we can hardly suppose that they have this sense here.

v. 18. The Greek here has 'I can speak with tongues more than any of you'; the Latin 'I can speak with the tongues of all of you'.

v. 21. Is. xxviii. 11; the form of the quotation differs considerably from the Septuagint text.

vv. 22-25. The sequence of thought here is difficult; perhaps St. Paul means that an outsider might be impressed by hearing one Christian speaking in a language he had never learned, but would only be disgusted by a babel of competing voices. Prophecy, on the other hand, is primarily meant to edify believers; but even an unbeliever might be impressed by finding several people who could read the secrets of his heart.

giving? He cannot tell what thou art saying. 17 Thou, true enough, art duly giving thanks, but the other's faith is not strengthened. 18 Thank God, I can speak any of the tongues you use; 19 but in the church, I would rather speak five words which my mind utters, for your instruction, than ten thousand in a strange tongue. 20 Brethren, do not be content to think childish thoughts; keep the innocence of children, with the thoughts of grown men. 21 We read in the law, I will speak to this people with an unknown tongue, with the lips of strangers, and even so they will not listen to me, says the Lord. 22 thus talking with a strange tongue is a sign given to unbelievers, not to the faithful; whereas prophecy is meant for the faithful, not for unbelievers. 23 And now, what will happen if the uninstructed or the unbelievers come in when the whole church has met together, and find everyone speaking with strange tongues at once? Will they not say you are mad? 24 Whereas, if some unbeliever or some uninstructed person comes in when all alike are prophesying, everyone will read his thoughts, everyone will scrutinize him, 25 all that is kept hidden in his heart will be revealed; and so he will fall on his face and worship God, publicly confessing that God is indeed among you.

26 What am I urging, then, brethren? Why, when you meet together, each of you with a psalm to sing, or some doctrine to impart, or a revelation to give, or ready to speak in strange tongues, or to interpret them, see that all is done to your spiritual advantage. 27 If there is speaking with strange tongues, do not let more than two speak, or three at the most; let each take his turn, with someone to interpret for him, 28 and if he can find nobody to interpret, let him be silent in the church, conversing with his own spirit and with God. 29 As for the prophets, let two or three of them speak, while the rest sit in judgement on their prophecies. 30 If some revelation comes to another who is sitting by, let him who spoke first keep silence; 31 there is room for you all to prophesy one by one, so that the whole company may receive instruction and comfort; 32 and it is for the prophets to exercise control over their own spiritual gifts. 33 God is the author of peace, not of disorder; such is the teaching I give in all the churches of the saints. 34 And women are to be silent in the churches; utterance is not permitted to them; let them keep their rank, as the law tells them: 35 if they have any question to raise, let them ask their husbands at home. That a woman should make her voice heard in the church is not seemly. 36 Tell me, was it from you that God's word was sent out? Are you the only people it has reached? 37 If any-

v. 33. 'Such is the teaching I give in all the churches'; according to most Greek manuscripts, the sense is rather 'all the churches of the saints give proof of it'.

324

body claims to be a prophet, or to have spiritual gifts, let him prove it by recognizing that this message of mine to you is God's commandment. 38 If he does not recognize it, he himself shall receive no recognition. 39 Set your hearts, then, brethren, on prophesying; and as for speaking with strange tongues, do not interfere with it. 40 Only let us have everything done suitably, and with right order.

v. 38. 'He himself shall receive no recognition', possibly in the congregation, but more probably in the sight of God (cf. xiii. 12 above). Some Greek manuscripts read 'let him go on in his ignorance'.

Chapter Fifteen

ERE, brethren, is an account of the gospel I preached to you. It was this that was handed on to you; upon this your faith rests; 2 through this (if you keep in mind the tenor of its preaching) you are in the way of salvation; unless indeed your belief was ill founded. 3 The chief message I handed on to you, as it was handed on to me, was that Christ, as the scriptures had foretold, died for our sins; 4 that he was buried, and then, as the scriptures had foretold, rose again on the third day. 5 That he was seen by Cephas, then by the eleven apostles, 6 and afterwards by more than five hundred of the brethren at once, most of whom are alive at this day, though some have gone to their rest. 7 Then he was seen by James, then by all the apostles; 8 and last of all, I too saw him, like the last child, that comes to birth unexpectedly. 9 Of all the apostles, I am the least; nay, I am not fit to be called an apostle, since there was a time when I persecuted the church of God; 10 only, by God's grace, I am what I am, and the grace he has shewn me has not been without fruit; I have worked harder than all of them, or rather, it was not I, but the grace of God working with me. 11 That is our preaching, mine or theirs as you will; that is the faith which has come to you.

12 If what we preach about Christ, then, is that he rose from the dead, how is it that some of you say the dead do not rise again? 13 If the dead do not rise, then Christ has not risen either; 14 and if Christ has not risen, then our preaching is groundless, and your faith, too, is groundless. 15 Worse still, we are convicted of giving false testimony about God; we bore God witness that he had raised

v. 2. 'Unless indeed your belief was ill founded'; some commentators take this as meaning 'Unless your belief has been ineffectual', i.e. 'has not succeeded in forming a true Christian character.'

v. 8. St. Paul compares himself to a child born prematurely; hence it is difficult to see how there can be any allusion to the comparative lateness of our Lord's appearance to him. He seems to be thinking rather of the sudden, catastrophic manner in which grace came to him. Others think that he compares himself, out of humility, to a child born physically weak.

Christ up from the dead, and he has not raised him up, if it is true that the dead do not rise again. 16 If the dead, I say, do not rise, then Christ has not risen either; 17 and if Christ has not risen, all your faith is a delusion; you are back in your sins. 18 It follows, too, that those who have gone to their rest in Christ have been lost. 19 If the hope we have learned to repose in Christ belongs to this world only, then we are unhappy beyond all other men. 20 But no, Christ has risen from the dead, the first fruits of all those who have fallen asleep, 21 a man had brought us death, and a man should bring us resurrection from the dead; 22 just as all have died with Adam, so with Christ all will be brought to life. 23 But each must rise in his own rank; Christ is the first fruits, and after him follow those who belong to him, those who have put their trust in his return. 24 Full completion comes after that, when he places his kingship in the hands of God, his Father, having first dispossessed every other sort of rule, authority, and power; 25 his reign, as we know, must continue until he has put all his enemies under his feet, 26 and the last of those enemies to be dispossessed is death. God has put all things in subjection under his feet; that is, 27 all things have been made subject to him, except indeed that power which made them his subjects. 28 And when that subjection is complete, then the Son himself will become subject to the power which made all things his subjects, so that God may be all in all.

29 Tell me, what can be the use of being baptized for the dead, if the dead do not rise again? Why should anyone be baptized for them? 30 Why do we, for that matter, face peril hour after hour? 31 I swear to you, brethren, by all the pride I take in you in the name of our Lord Jesus Christ, that death is daily at my side. 32 When I fought against beasts at Ephesus with all my strength, of what use was it, if the dead do not rise again? Let us eat and drink, since we must die to-morrow. 33 Do not be led into such errors; bad company, they say, can corrupt noble minds. 34 Come back to your senses, like right-minded men, and sin no longer; there are some, I say it to your shame, who lack the knowledge of God.

35 But perhaps someone will ask, How can the dead rise up? What kind of body will they be wearing when they appear? 36 Poor fool, when thou sowest seed in the ground, it must die before it can be brought to life; 37 and what thou sowest is not the full body that is one day to be, it is only bare grain, of wheat, it may be, or some other crop, 38 it is for God to embody it according to his will, each grain in the body that belongs to it. 39 Nature is not all one; men have one nature, the beasts another.

v. 23. 'Those who have put their trust in his return'; most Greek manuscripts have simply 'when he comes'.

vv. 23-26. Probably three stages in the Resurrection are here given, (i) that of our Lord himself, (ii) that of the predestined, or perhaps only that of predestined persons who are still alive at the second Coming, (iii) that of the rest of mankind, implied in verse 26.

v. 29. There may be an allusion to the practice of vicarious baptism on behalf of those who had died unchristened, which is known to have existed (though only amongst heretics) in the second century A.D. The other explanations which have been suggested are only conjectures.

v. 32. Others would render, 'If it was from human motives that I fought against beasts at Ephesus, of what use was it? If the dead do not rise again, let us eat and drink', etc. 'Fighting against beasts' is generally understood of withstanding bitter human persecution. Cf. Is. xxii. 13.

v. 33. 'Bad company', etc.; this was a heathen proverb, which is to be found in the works of the poet Menander.

326

the birds another, the fishes another; 40 so, too, there are bodies that belong to earth and bodies that belong to heaven; and heavenly bodies have one kind of beauty, earthly bodies another. 41 The sun has its own beauty, the moon has hers, the stars have theirs, one star even differs from another in its beauty. 42 So it is with the resurrection of the dead. What is sown corruptible, rises incorruptible; 43 what is sown unhonoured, rises in glory; what is sown in weakness, is raised in power; 44 what is sown a natural body, rises a spiritual body. If there is such a thing as a natural body, there must be a spiritual body too. 45 Mankind begins with the Adam who became, as scripture tells us, a living soul; it is fulfilled in the Adam who has become a life-giving spirit. 46 It was not the principle of spiritual life that came first; natural life came first, then spiritual life; 47 the man who came first came from earth, fashioned of dust, the man who came afterwards came from heaven, and his fashion is heavenly. 48 The nature of that earth-born man is shared by his earthly sons, the nature of the heaven-born man, by his heavenly sons; 49 and it remains for us, who once bore the stamp of earth, to bear the stamp of heaven. 50 What I mean, brethren, is this; the kingdom of God cannot be enjoyed by flesh and blood; the principle of corruption cannot share a life which is incorruptible.

51 Here is a secret I will make known to you; we shall all rise again, but not all of us will undergo the change I speak of. 52 It will happen in a moment, in the twinkling of an eye, when the last trumpet sounds; the trumpet will sound, and the dead will rise again, free from corruption, and we shall find ourselves changed, 53 this corruptible nature of ours must be clothed with incorruptible life, this mortal nature with immortality. 54 Then, when this corruptible nature wears its incorruptible garment, this mortal nature its immortality, the saying of scripture will come true, Death is swallowed up in victory. 55 Where then, death, is thy victory; where, death, is thy sting? 56 It is sin that gives death its sting, just as it is the law that gives sin its power; 57 thanks be to God, then, who gives us victory through our Lord Jesus Christ. 58 Stand firm, then, my beloved brethren, immovable in your resolve, doing your full share continually in the task the Lord has given you, since you know that your labour in the Lord's service cannot be spent in vain.

v. 45. Gen. ii. 7.
v. 49. 'It remains for us to bear'; the Greek texts here are divided between 'we shall bear' (in heaven) and 'let us bear' (presumably on earth); the Latin versions follow the second reading.
v. 50. 'Flesh and blood', that is, flesh and blood as we know it here, under earthly conditions. That St. Paul taught the continuity of the Resurrection body with the body which is the soul's partner on earth, is evident from the comparison he uses in verses 36-38 above.
v. 51. The Greek manuscripts are here strangely divided; some read the text given here, but there is better support for the reading 'We shall not all fall asleep, but we shall all be changed'. The sense in that case would be, that those of the elect who are still alive at the Day of Judgement will pass into a heavenly existence without undergoing death. According to the text here given, which is that of the Latin versions, the sense is rather that all men will die, but only the elect will be glorified after death. Owing to this textual doubt, the generally received view that those who are alive at the Second Coming will experience physical death is not certain, but only a more probable opinion.

v. 52. 'We shall find ourselves changed'; St. Paul, it seems, writing as a living man to living men, identifies them and himself with those who will be alive at the time of the Second Coming.   v. 54. Is. xxv. 8.   v. 55. Osee xiii. 14. The text here agrees with the Greek Septuagint, but not with the Hebrew.

Chapter Sixteen

An ND NOW ABOUT THE collection which is being made for the saints; follow the plan which I have prescribed for the Galatian churches. 2 Each of you should put aside, on the first day of the week, what he can afford to spare, and save it up, so that there may be no need for a collection at the time of my visit; 3 and when I am with you I will despatch your envoys, with letters of recommendation from you, to convey your charity to Jerusalem. 4 If I find it worth while to make the journey myself, they shall travel with me. 5 I shall be coming to you as soon as I have made the round of Macedonia (I mean to go round Macedonia), 6 and perhaps stay with you or even pass the winter with you; it will be for you to put me on my way to my next stage, whatever it be. 7 This is no occasion for a mere passing visit to you; I hope to spend some time with you, if the Lord will let me. 8 Till Pentecost, I shall be staying at Ephesus; 9 a great opportunity lies open to me, plain to view, and strong forces oppose me. 10 If Timothy comes, be sure to make him free of your company; he is doing the Lord's work as I am. 11 He is not to be treated with disrespect; put him on his way in peace so that he reaches me safely; I am awaiting him here with the brethren. 12 As for our brother Apollo, you may be sure I have urged him strongly to accompany the brethren on their journey to you; but no, he will not consent to visit you yet, he will come when he has leisure.

13 Be on the watch, stand firm in the faith, play the man, be full of courage. 14 And let everything you do be done in a spirit of charity.

15 This appeal, brethren, I must make to you. You know that the household of Stephanas, Fortunatus, and Achaicus was the first offering Achaia gave; you know how they have devoted themselves to supplying the needs of the saints; 16 you must shew deference to such persons, to everyone who shares in the labours of our ministry. 17 I am glad that Stephanas and Fortunatus and Achaicus

v. 5. Cf. Acts xx. 1.

v. 15. The words 'Fortunatus and Achaicus' are not given in the best Greek manuscripts.

328

are here; they have made up for your absence, 18 bringing relief to my mind as well as yours. Such men deserve your recognition. 19 A greeting to you from all the churches of Asia, and many greetings, in the Lord's name, from Aquila and Priscilla, as well as the church in their household; it is with them I am lodging. 20 All the brethren greet you; greet one another with the kiss of saints. 21 I send you my greetings in my own handwriting, PAUL. 22 If there is anyone who has no love for the Lord, let him be held accursed; the Lord is coming. 23 The grace of our Lord Jesus Christ be with you; 24 and my love be with you all in Christ Jesus, Amen.

v. 19. The words 'it is with them I am lodging' do not appear in the Greek or in the best Latin manuscripts.

The Second Epistle of the Blessed Apostle Paul to the Corinthians

Chapter One

FROM PAUL, BY GOD'S will an apostle of Jesus Christ, and Timothy, who is their brother, to the Church of God which is at Corinth and to all the saints in the whole of Achaia; 2 grace and peace be yours from God, our Father, and from the Lord Jesus Christ. 3 Blessed be the God and Father of our Lord Jesus Christ, the merciful Father, the God who gives all encouragement. 4 He it is who comforts us in all our trials; and it is this encouragement we ourselves receive from God which enables us to comfort others, whenever they have trials of their own. 5 The sufferings of Christ, it is true, overflow into our lives; but there is overflowing comfort, too, which Christ brings to us. 6 Have we trials to endure? It all makes for your encouragement, for your salvation. Are we comforted? It is so that you may be comforted. [Are we encouraged? It is for your encouragement, for your salvation.] And the effect of this appears in your willingness to undergo the sufferings we too undergo; 7 making our hopes of you all the more confident; partners of our sufferings, you will be partners of our encouragement too.

v. 6. Neither the text nor the precise bearing of this passage can be established beyond dispute. The words printed in square brackets are probably not genuine; they are absent from the Greek and from the best Latin manuscripts.

v. 8. *It is not known what affliction St. Paul here refers to. 'We despaired of life' in the Latin is 'we were weary of living', but in the Greek 'we were doubtful whether we should live.'*

vv. 12-23. *In I Cor. xvi. 5. St. Paul's plan is to come round by land from Ephesus through Macedonia to Corinth. It seems, however, that he must later have proposed a direct journey across the Aegean Sea from Ephesus to Corinth, with a mere excursion from Corinth into Macedonia. But this visit never took effect. The Corinthians appear to have accused him of inconsistency in altering his plans, and perhaps of cowardice (iv. 1 below). In fact he had delayed his visit, he says, so as to give the Corinthians more time to repent of their disorders.*

v. 22. *This probably refers to the Sacrament of Confirmation, as completing Baptism.*

v. 23. *Some would translate the last words of this verse, as in Rom. xi. 20, 'it is by faith that you are established' (as Christians); but this thought seems irrelevant here.*

8 Make no mistake, brethren, about the trial which has been befalling us in Asia; it was something that overburdened us beyond our strength, so that we despaired of life itself. 9 Indeed, for ourselves we could find no outcome but death; so God would have us learn to trust, not in ourselves, but in him who raises the dead to life. 10 It is he who has preserved us, and is perserving us, from such deadly peril; and we have learned to have confidence that he will preserve us still. 11 Only you, too, must help us with your prayers. So thanks will be given by many on our behalf, and in the name of many persons, for the favour God has shewn to us.

12 It is our boast, made in all good conscience, that we have behaved in the world, and towards you especially, with singleheartedness and sincerity in God's sight, not using human wisdom, but the light of God's grace. 13 And we mean by our letters nothing else than what you read in them, and understand us to mean. I hope that you will come to understand us better, 14 as you do already in some measure; are we not your chief pride, as you are our chief pride, in the day when our Lord Jesus Christ comes? 15 It was with this confidence in you that I had made up my mind to give you a double opportunity of spiritual profit, coming to you first, 16 then passing through Corinth to Macedonia, and so from Macedonia back to you; and you were to put me on my way to Judaea. 17 When I thus made up my mind, do you suppose I did it lightly? Can it be said of me that the plans I form are formed by motives of human prudence, so that it is first Yes, I will, and then, No, I will not, with me? 18 As God is faithful, the message we delivered to you is not one which hesitates between Yes and No. 19 It was Jesus Christ, the Son of God, that I, that Silvanus and Timothy preached to you; and that preaching did not hesitate between Yes and No; in him all is affirmed with certainty. 20 In him all the promises of God become certain; that is why, when we give glory to God, it is through him that we say our Amen. 21 It is God who gives both us and you our certainty in Christ; 22 it is he who has anointed us, just as it is he who has put his seal on us, and given us the foretaste of his Spirit in our hearts.

23 With my soul as the forfeit I call this God to witness that if I did not, after all, visit you at Corinth, it was to give you a fresh chance. (Not that we would domineer over your faith; rather, we would help you to achieve happiness. And indeed, in your faith you stand firm enough.)

332

Chapter Two

N this I was resolved in my own mind, that I would not pay you a second visit on a sad errand. 2 Was I to make you sorry? It meant bringing sorrow on those who are my own best source of comfort. 3 And those were the very terms in which I wrote to you: I would not come, if it meant finding fresh cause for sorrow where I might have expected to find cause for happiness. I felt confidence in you all, I knew that what made me happy would make you happy too. 4 When I wrote to you, I wrote in great anguish and distress of mind, with many tears. I did not wish to bring sorrow on you, only to assure you of the love I bear you, so abundantly. 5 Well, if someone has caused distress, it is not myself that he has distressed but, in some measure, all of you, so that I must not be too hard on him. 6 This punishment inflicted on him by so many of you is punishment enough for the man I speak of, 7 and now you must think rather of shewing him indulgence, and comforting him; you must not let him be overwhelmed by excess of grief. 8 Let me entreat you, then, to give him assurance of your good will. 9 The reason why I wrote to you, after all, was to test your loyalty, by seeing whether you would obey me in full. 10 If you shew indulgence to anybody, so do I too; I myself, wherever I have shewn indulgence, have done so in the person of Christ for your sakes, 11 for fear that Satan should get the advantage over us; we know well enough how resourceful he is.

12 I went to Troas, then, to preach Christ's gospel there, and found a great opportunity open to me in the Lord's service; 13 but still I had no peace of mind, because I had not yet seen my brother Titus; so I took my leave of them all, and pressed on into Macedonia. 14 I give thanks to God, that he is always exhibiting us as the captives in the triumph of Christ Jesus, and through us spreading abroad everywhere, like a perfume, the knowledge of himself. 15 We are Christ's incense offered to God, making manifest both those who are achieving salvation and those who are on the road to ruin; 16 as a deadly fume where it finds death, as a life-giving perfume where it finds life. Who can prove himself worthy of

v. 1. This may mean that St. Paul determined not to pay his second visit (the first being that recorded in Acts xviii. 1) while he had faults to find with the Christians at Corinth. Or it may mean that he determined not to pay a second fault-finding visit; in which case we have no record of the other.

v. 3. St. Paul seems to be quoting here from a letter he had written to the Corinthians, now lost.

vv. 5 and following. It is generally supposed that the unnamed delinquent here alluded to is the person mentioned at the beginning of I Corinthians v. But if another letter had been written since, some other delinquent may have been mentioned in it, of whose offence we have no knowledge. 'So that I must not be too hard on him'; these words are generally translated 'that I may not be a burden to you', but it is hard to see what sense can be attached to this rendering. It seems clear from the context that the apostle is appealing for the remission, in part, of a canonical penalty imposed on the offender by the Corinthian Church.

v. 12. Instead of crossing by sea to Corinth, St. Paul went to Troas, in the North of Asia Minor,

such a calling? 17 We do not, like so many others, adulterate the word of God, we preach it in all its purity, as God gave it to us, standing before God's presence in Christ.

hoping that Titus would bring him news there about the dispositions of the Corinthian Church; and at last, in order to meet him the sooner, he crossed over into Macedonia, so anxious was he to be assured of their loyalty.   v. 14.
Some commentators would translate, 'causing us to triumph', but there is no authority at all for giving such a meaning to the words.

Chapter Three

YOU WILL SAY, PERHAPS, that we are making a fresh attempt to recommend ourselves to your favour. What, do we need letters of recommendation to you, or from you, as some others do? 2 Why, you yourselves are the letter we carry about with us, written in our hearts, for all to recognize and to read. 3 You are an open letter from Christ, promulgated through us; a message written not in ink, but in the spirit of the living God, with human hearts, instead of stone, to carry it. 4 Such, through Christ, is the confidence in which we make our appeal to God. 5 Not that, left to ourselves, we are able to frame any thought as coming from ourselves; all our ability comes from God, 6 since it is he who has enabled us to promulgate his new law to men. It is a spiritual, not a written law; the written law inflicts death, whereas the spiritual law brings life. 7 We know how that sentence of death, engraved in writing upon stone, was promulgated to men in a dazzling cloud, so that the people of Israel could not look Moses in the face, for the brightness of it, although that brightness soon passed away. 8 How much more dazzling, then, must be the brightness in which the spiritual law is promulgated to them! 9 If there is a splendour in the proclamation of our guilt, there must be more splendour yet in the proclamation of our acquittal; 10 and indeed, what once seemed resplendent seems by comparison resplendent no longer, so much does the greater splendour outshine it. 11 What passed away passed in a flash of glory; what remains, remains instead in a blaze of glory.

v. 1. 'A fresh attempt'; St. Paul must have been accused, or must have thought that he was being accused, of dwelling too much on what he had done for the Corinthians.
vv. 5-15. St. Paul compares the position of the Christian missionary, announcing the new law of life, that is, the Gospel, with that of Moses announcing to the Jews the old law, by which sinners are condemned. Moses received the law on tables of stone; the Gospel must be thought of as engraved upon men's hearts. We are told in Ex. xxxiv. 29-35 that Moses' face shone with an unearthly radiance after he had conversed with God on Mount Sinai; for a time, he had to wear a veil, because the Israelites could not bear to look on this brightness. How much more do the faces of Christ's ministers shine with the reflection of his glory! But they do not throw any veil over the glory they have witnessed; they grow in likeness to Christ. It is the

12 Such is the ground of our confidence, and we speak out boldly enough. 13 It is not for us to use veiled language, as Moses veiled his face. He did it, so that the people of Israel might not go on gazing at the features of the old order, which was passing away. 14 But in spite of that, dulness has crept over their senses, and to this day the reading of the old law is muffled with the same veil; no revelation tells them that it has been abrogated in Christ. 15 To this day, I say, when the law of Moses is read out, a veil hangs over their hearts. 16 There must be a turning to the Lord first, and then the veil will be taken away. 17 The Spirit we have been speaking of is the Lord; and where the Lord's spirit is, there is freedom. 18 It is given to us, all alike, to catch the glory of the Lord as in a mirror, with faces unveiled; and so we become transfigured into the same likeness, borrowing glory from that glory, as the spirit of the Lord enables us.

Jews who wear a veil over their faces, listening to the law of Moses sabbath after sabbath and never learning to see the glory of Christ revealed there.

v. 10. 'By comparison'; literally, 'in this part', i.e. this partial manifestation.

vv. 17-18. Many different renderings have been given of these two verses, and it is perhaps impossible for us to ascertain the exact sense in which St. Paul wrote them. It is not certain, in the Greek, whether 'catch' means 'catch sight of', or 'reflect'.

Chapter Four

BEING ENTRUSTED, then, by God's mercy with this ministry, we do not play the coward; 2 we renounce all shamefaced concealment, there must be no crooked ways, no falsifying of God's word; it is by making the truth publicly known that we recommend ourselves to the honest judgement of mankind, as in God's sight. 3 Our gospel is a mystery, yes, but it is only a mystery to those who are on the road to perdition; 4 those whose unbelieving minds have been blinded by the god this world worships, so that the glorious gospel of Christ, God's image, cannot reach them with the rays of its illumination. 5 After all, it is not ourselves we proclaim; we proclaim Jesus Christ as Lord, and ourselves as your servants for Jesus' sake. 6 The same God who bade light shine out of darkness has kindled a light in our hearts, whose

v. 1. St. Paul seems to imply that his opponents accused him of being ashamed of his message, and veiling it in an atmosphere of mystery.

v. 4. 'The god this world worships'; that is, the devil, or Mammon. Some commentators, however, have understood 'the God of this world' as an allusion to Almighty God himself.

shining is to make known his glory as he has revealed it in the features of Jesus Christ.

7 We have a treasure, then, in our keeping, but its shell is of perishable earthenware; it must be God, and not anything in ourselves, that gives it its sovereign power. 8 For ourselves, we are being hampered everywhere, yet still have room to breathe, are hard put to it, but never at a loss; 9 persecution does not leave us unbefriended, nor crushing blows destroy us; 10 we carry about continually in our bodies the dying state of Jesus, so that the living power of Jesus may be manifested in our bodies too. 11 Always we, alive as we are, are being given up to death for Jesus' sake, so that the living power of Jesus may be manifested in this mortal nature of ours. 12 So death makes itself felt in us, and life in you.

v. 13. 'Sharing that same faith'; in the Hebrew, Ps. cxv is continuous with the psalm which precedes it, the last verse of which seems to be a prophecy of the Resurrection.

13 I spoke my mind, says the scripture, with full confidence, and we too speak our minds with full confidence, sharing that same faith, 14 and knowing that he who raised Jesus from the dead will raise us too, and summon us, like you, before him. 15 It is all for your sakes, so that grace made manifold in many lives may increase the sum of gratitude which is offered to God's glory. 16 No, we do not play the coward; though the outward part of our nature is being worn down, our inner life is refreshed from day to day. 17 This light and momentary affliction brings with it a reward multiplied every way, loading us with everlasting glory; 18 if only we will fix our eyes on what is unseen, not on what we can see. What we can see, lasts but for a moment; what is unseen is eternal.

Chapter Five

ONCE this earthly tent-dwelling of ours has come to an end, God, we are sure, has a solid building waiting for us, a dwelling not made with hands, that will last eternally in heaven. 2 And indeed, it is for this that we sigh, longing for the shelter of that home which heaven will give us, 3 if death, when it comes, is to find us sheltered, not defenceless against the winds. 4 Yes, if we tent-dwellers here go sighing and heavy-hearted, it is not because we would be stripped of something; rather, we would clothe ourselves afresh; our mortal

v. 1. There may be an allusion here to the contrast between the tabernacle in the wilderness and the more solidly built temple which after-

nature must be swallowed up in life. 5 For this, nothing else, God was preparing us, when he gave us the foretaste of his Spirit. 6 We take heart, then, continually, since we recognize that our spirits are exiled from the Lord's presence so long as they are at home in the body, 7 with faith, instead of a clear view, to guide our steps. 8 We take heart, I say, and have a mind rather to be exiled from the body, and at home with the Lord; 9 to that end, at home or in exile, our ambition is to win his favour. 10 All of us have a scrutiny to undergo before Christ's judgement-seat, for each to reap what his mortal life has earned, good or ill, acording to his deeds.

11 It is, then, with the fear of the Lord before our minds that we try to win men over by persuasion; God recognizes us for what we are, and so I hope, does your better judgement. 12 No, we are not trying to recommend ourselves to your favour afresh; we are shewing you how to find material for boasting of us, to those who have so much to boast of outwardly, and nothing inwardly. 13 Are these wild words? Then take them as addressed to God. Or sober sense? Then take them as addressed to yourselves. 14 With us, Christ's love is a compelling motive, and this is the conviction we have reached; if one man died on behalf of all, then all thereby became dead men; 15 Christ died for us all, so that being alive should no longer mean living with our own life, but with his life who died for us and has risen again; 16 and therefore, henceforward, we do not think of anybody in a merely human fashion; even if we used to think of Christ in a human fashion, we do so no longer; 17 it follows, in fact, that when a man becomes a new creature in Christ, his old life has disappeared, everything has become new about him. 18 This, as always, is God's doing; it is he who, through Christ, has reconciled us to himself, and allowed us to minister this reconciliation of his to others. 19 Yes, God was in Christ, reconciling the world to himself, establishing in our hearts his message of reconciliation, instead of holding men to account for their sins. 20 We are Christ's ambassadors, then, and God appeals to you through us; we entreat you in Christ's name, make your peace with God. 21 Christ never knew sin, and God made him into sin for us, so that in him we might be turned into the holiness of God.

wards replaced it. Cf. Heb. xi. 9, 10.

v. 11. The precise bearing of this verse is very doubtful; the general sense seems to be that God knows, without any need of persuasion, how sincere the apostle's intentions are, and the Corinthians ought, by this time, to be in the same position.

v. 13. Many interpretations are given of this verse, which reads literally, 'Whether we are out of our senses, it is to God, or whether we are in our right mind, it is to you'.

v. 16. 'We do not think of anybody in a human fashion', literally, 'We do not know anybody according to the flesh'. St. Paul seems to contrast himself here with the persons mentioned in verse 12, who judge everything by outward appearances; for him, all outward considerations of nationality, kinship, etc. disappear in the new unity of the Christian family. It is not easy to suppose that St. Paul knew Christ 'after the flesh' in the sense of knowing him before the Ascension; it is possible, however, that when he says 'we' he is thinking of the other apostles, who had known Christ as a friend and a teacher, some of them as a kinsman.

v. 17. The Greek here may also be rendered, 'When a man is in Christ, he has become a new creature; his old life has disappeared', etc.

Chapter Six

AND now, to further that work, we entreat you not to offer God's grace an ineffectual welcome. 2 (I have answered thy prayer, he says, in a time of pardon, I have brought thee help in a day of salvation. And here is the time of pardon; the day of salvation has come already.) 3 We are careful not to give offence to anybody, lest we should bring discredit on our ministry; 4 as God's ministers, we must do everything to make ourselves acceptable. We have to shew great patience, in times of affliction, of need, of difficulty; 5 under the lash, in prison, in the midst of tumult; when we are tired out, sleepless, and fasting. 6 We have to be pure-minded, enlightened, forgiving and gracious to others; we have to rely on the Holy Spirit, on unaffected love, 7 on the truth of our message, on the power of God. To right and to left we must be armed with innocence, 8 now honoured, now slighted, now traduced, now flattered. They call us deceivers, and we tell the truth; 9 unknown, and we are fully acknowledged; dying men, and see, we live; punished, yes, but not doomed to die; 10 sad men, that rejoice continually; beggars, that bring riches to many; disinherited, and the world is ours.

11 We are speaking freely to you, Corinthians; we throw our hearts wide open to you. 12 It is not our fault, it is the fault of your own affections, that you feel constraint with us. 13 Pay us back in the same coin (I am speaking to you as to my children); open your hearts wide too. 14 You must not consent to be yokefellows with unbelievers. What has innocence to do with lawlessness? What is there in common between light and darkness? 15 What harmony between Christ and Belial? How can a believer throw in his lot with an infidel? 16 How can the temple of God have any commerce with idols? And you are the temple of the living God; God has told us so; I will live and move among them, and be their God, and they shall be my people. 17 Come out, then, from among them, the Lord says to us, separate yourselves from them, and do not even touch what is unclean; then I will make you welcome. 18 I will be your father, and you shall be sons and daughters to me, says the Lord, the Almighty.

v. 2. The first half of this verse is a quotation from Is. xlix. 8. The whole verse is here printed as a parenthesis, because it interrupts the sequence of thought; St. Paul is speaking of the qualifications needed in Christ's ambassadors.

v. 9. 'Acknowledged', probably in the sense of being acknowledged by God as his own. This sense is frequent in the New Testament; cf. I Cor. xiii. 12.

v. 13. 'As to my children', or possibly 'as to children', indicating that he is using schoolroom language to them.

vv. 14–18. These verses, and the first verse of ch. vii, appear to interrupt the sequence of thought; but no doubt there was some special difficulty to which St. Paul alludes here, and we have lost the clue to it. Some think that marriage between Christians and heathens is in question.

v. 16. Lev. xxvi. 12.

v. 17. Is. lii. 11.

v. 18. This quotation does not occur verbally in the Old Testament.

Chapter Seven

UCH are the promises, beloved, that await us. Why then, let us purge ourselves clean from every defilement of flesh and of spirit, achieving the work of our sanctification in the fear of God. 2 Be generous with us; it is not as if any of you could say that we had wronged him, or done him harm, or taken undue advantage of him. 3 I am not finding fault with you when I say this; I have told you before now, we hold you so close in our hearts that nothing in life or in death can part us from you.

4 With what confidence I speak to you, what pride I take in you! I am full of encouragement, nay, I cannot contain myself for happiness, in the midst of all these trials of mine. 5 By the time we had reached Macedonia, our human weakness could find no means of rest; all was conflict without, all was anxiety within. 6 But there is one who never fails to comfort those who are brought low; God gave us comfort, as soon as Titus came. 7 It was not only that he came; he inspired us with that courage he had derived from you. He told us how you longed for my presence, how you grieved over what had happened, how you took my part, till I was more than ever rejoiced. 8 Yes, even if I caused you pain by my letter, I am not sorry for it. Perhaps I was tempted to feel sorry, when I saw how my letter had caused you even momentary pain, 9 but now I am glad; not glad of the pain, but glad of the repentance the pain brought with it. Yours was a supernatural remorse, so that you were not in any way the losers through what we had done. 10 Supernatural remorse leads to an abiding and salutary change of heart, whereas the world's remorse leads to death. 11 See what devotion has been bred in you now by this supernatural remorse; how you disowned the guilt; the indignation you felt, the fear that overcame you; how you missed me, how you took my part, how you righted the wrong done. You have done everything to prove yourselves free from guilt in this matter. 12 So, then, I had written you a letter, and it was neither the wrong-doer nor the injured party that was to be the gainer by it; it was to have the effect of shewing you our devotion to your welfare 13 in God's sight. It was this that brought us comfort; and besides this comfort, we had still greater cause for rejoicing in the joy which Titus felt, with his heart re-

v. 8. Commentators, as before, are divided over the question whether this letter was the First Epistle to the Corinthians, or a later one now lost; and whether the wrong-doer here referred to is the person mentioned in I Cor. v.1 or not.

v. 12. The best Greek manuscripts here read 'your devotion to us' instead of 'our devotion to you'.

freshed by the welcome you all gave him. 14 I had boasted to Titus of the confidence I felt in you, and you did not play me false; no, the boast I had made to Titus proved true, as true as the message which I had delivered to you. 15 He bears a most affectionate memory of you, of the submissiveness you all shewed, of the anxious fear with which you received him. 16 I am rejoiced that I can repose such full confidence in you.

Chapter Eight

 ND now, brethren, we must tell you about the grace which God has lavished upon the churches of Macedonia: 2 how well they have stood the test of distress, how abundantly they have rejoiced over it, how abject is their poverty, and how the crown of all this has been a rich measure of generosity in them. 3 I can testify that of their own accord they undertook to do all they could, and more than they could; 4 they begged us, most urgently, to allow them the privilege of helping to supply the needs of the saints. 5 And their gift went beyond our hopes; they gave their own services to the Lord, which meant, as God willed, to us; 6 so that we were able to ask Titus to visit you again, and finish this gracious task he had begun, as part of his mission. 7 You excel in so much already, in faith, in power of utterance, in knowledge of the truth, in devotion of every kind, in your loving treatment of us; may this gracious excellence be yours too. 8 I say this, not to lay any injunction on you, but only to make sure that your charity rings true by telling you about the eagerness of others. 9 (You do not need to be reminded how gracious our Lord Jesus Christ was; how he impoverished himself for your sakes, when he was so rich, so that you might become rich through his poverty), 10 I am only giving you my advice, then, in this matter; you can claim that as your due, since it was you who led the way, not only in acting, but in proposing to act, as early as last year. 11 It remains for you now to complete your action; readiness of the will must be completed by deeds, as far as your means allow. 12 We value a man's readiness of will according to the means he has, not according to the

vv. 1 and following. St. Paul returns here, as in I Cor. xvi. to the collection he was making in Macedonia and Achaia for the needs of the impoverished church at Jerusalem. It seems likely that in Macedonia (verses 2 and 3) and perhaps also in Achaia (verses 12 and 13) there had been hard times, and the apostle is anxious not to appear as if he were making an unreasonable demand.

v. 2. 'Generosity'; literally 'simplicity', both here and in the following chapter.

vv. 5, 6. The Greek perhaps implies that certain Macedonians offered their own services to St. Paul with the expressed intention of setting Titus free to visit Corinth again.

means he might have, but has not; 13 and there is no intention that others should be relieved at the price of your distress. No, a balance is to be struck, 14 and what you can spare now is to make up for what they want; so that what they can spare may, in its turn, make up for your want, and thus the balance will be redressed. So we read in scripture, 15 He who had gathered much had nothing left over, and he who had gathered little, no lack.

v. 15. Ex. xvi. 18.

16 I thank God for inspiring the heart of Titus, your representative, with the same eagerness. 17 He has accepted our invitation; but indeed, of his own choice he was eager to visit you. 18 And we are sending with him that brother of ours, who has won the praise of all the churches by his proclamation of the gospel; 19 he, too, is the man whom the churches have appointed to be our companion in this gracious ministry of ours, to further God's glory and our own resolve. 20 They were anxious that no suspicion should be aroused against us, with these great sums to handle; 21 it is not only in the Lord's sight, but in the sight of men, that we have to study our behaviour. 22 And, to accompany these, we are sending a brother of whose eagerness we have had good proof, in many ways and upon many occasions; now he is more eager than ever, such is the confidence he feels in you. 23 As for Titus, he is my partner and has shared my work among you; as for these brethren of ours, they are the envoys of the churches, the glory of Christ: 24 give them proof, then, of your charity, and of the good reason we have to be proud of you, for all the churches to see.

v. 16. 'Titus, your representative, with the same eagerness' (as yourselves); others would understand the meaning to be 'Titus with the same eagerness for your welfare' (as myself).

Chapter Nine

And INDEED, TO WRITE and tell you about the collection for the saints would be waste of time; 2 I know well your eagerness, which has made me boast to the Macedonians that Achaia has been ready ever since last year, and this challenge of yours has stirred up others besides yourselves. 3 If I am sending the brethren, it is only for fear that the boast we made of you should prove false in this particular; as I told you, I would have you quite ready; 4 or else, when some of the Macedonians come with me and find you unprepared, we, and you too for that matter, will be put to the blush over this confidence of ours. 5 That is why I have thought it necessary to ask the brethren to visit you first, and see that the free offering you have already promised is prepared beforehand. Only it is to be a free offering, not a grudging tribute. 6 I would remind you of this, He who sows sparingly will reap sparingly; he who sows freely will reap freely too. 7 Each of you should carry out the purpose he has formed in his heart, not with any painful effort; it is the cheerful giver God loves. 8 God has the power to supply you abundantly with every kind of blessing, so that, with all your needs well supplied at all times, you may have something to spare for every work of mercy. 9 So we read, He has spent largely, and given to the poor; his charity lives on for ever. 10 He who puts grain into the sower's hand, and gives us food to eat, will supply you with seed and multiply it, and enrich the harvest of your charity; 11 so that you will have abundant means of every kind for all that generosity which gives proof of our gratitude towards God. 12 The administration, remember, of this public service does more than supply the needs of the saints; it yields, besides a rich harvest of thanksgiving in the name of the Lord. 13 This administration makes men praise God for the spirit of obedience which you shew in confessing the gospel of Christ, and the generosity which you shew in sharing your goods with these and with all men; 14 and they will intercede, too, on your

v. 9. Ps. cxi. 9. The word rendered 'charity' in this and the following verse is literally 'justice'; i.e. compliance with the Law as laid down in Deut. xv. 11 and elsewhere, cf. Matthew vi. 1.

342

THE MOCKING OF CHRIST   JEROME BOSCH
circa 1462-1516

behalf, as the abundant measure of grace which God bestows on you warms their hearts towards you. 15 Thanks be to God for his unutterable bounty to us.

Chapter Ten

AND now, here is Paul, the man who is so diffident when he meets you face to face, and deals so boldly with you at a distance, making an appeal to you by the gentleness and the courtesy of Christ. 2 What I ask is, that you will not force me to deal boldly with you when we meet. I have my own grounds for confidence, and with these I may well be counted a match for those who think we rely on merely human powers. 3 Human indeed we are, but it is in no human strength that we fight our battles. 4 The weapons we fight with are not human weapons; they are divinely powerful, ready to pull down strongholds. Yes, we can pull down the conceits of men, 5 every barrier of pride which sets itself up against the true knowledge of God; we make every mind surrender to Christ's service, 6 and are prepared to punish rebellion from any quarter, once your own submission is complete.

7 Wait and see what happens when we meet. There may be someone who takes credit to himself for being the champion of Christ; if so, let him reflect further that we belong to Christ's cause no less than himself; 8 and indeed, I might boast of the powers I have, powers which the Lord has given me so as to build up your faith, not so as to crush your spirits, and I should not be put in the wrong. 9 It must not be thought that I try to overawe you when I write. 10 His letters, some people say, are powerful and carry weight, but his presence in person lacks dignity, he is but a poor orator. 11 I warn those who speak thus that, when we visit you, our actions will not belie the impression which our letters make when we are at a distance. 12 It is not for us to intrude, or challenge comparison with others who claim credit for themselves; we are content to go by our own measure, to compare ourselves with our own standard of achievement. 13 Yes, we

vv. 1 and following. In spite of the Apostle's general satisfaction with the state of the Church at Corinth, there was evidently a party there still attached to certain teachers who opposed his influence; and the remaining chapters of the epistle shew that he means to combat them with all the power of his apostleship.

v. 6. He wishes to bring as many as possible of his critics to a better mind by reasoning, before he proceeds to punishment.

v. 7. 'What happens when we meet'; literally, 'the things that are face to face', see v. 1 above. Some would translate 'the obvious facts', but this rendering does justice neither to the Greek nor to the context. The Greek may also be rendered 'You think too much of appearances'. 'Being the champion of Christ'; literally 'belonging to Christ', cf. I. Cor. i. 12.

vv. 12 and following. Some Greek manuscripts read 'take credit to themselves, content to take their own measure and compare themselves

with their own stand-
ard of achievement.
But as for us, we
may boast', etc. It
seems clear from this
and the following
verses that St. Paul,
who was careful not
to build on the foun-
dation other men had
laid (Rom. xv. 20),
felt hurt that some
of the Corinthians
should pay more at-
tention to later mis-
sionaries than to him-
self (cf. I Cor. iv.
15).
v. 14. 'Took us all
the way to you'; the
Greek might also
mean, 'made us the
first to reach you'.

may boast, but our boasting will not be disproportionate; it will be in proportion to the province which God has assigned to us, one which reaches as far as you. 14 Nobody can say that we are encroaching, that you lie beyond our orbit; our journeys in preaching Christ's gospel took us all the way to you. 15 Ours, then is no disproportionate boasting, founded on other men's labours; on the contrary, as your faith bears increase, we hope to attain still further vantage-points through you, without going beyond our province, 16 and preach the gospel further afield, without boasting of ready-made conquests in a province that belongs to another. 17 He who boasts, should make his boast in the Lord; 18 it is the man whom God accredits, not the man who takes credit to himself, that proves himself to be true metal.

Chapter Eleven

I F you would only bear with my vanity for a little! Pray be patient with me; 2 after all, my jealousy on your behalf is the jealousy of God himself; I have betrothed you to Christ, so that no other but he should claim you, his bride without spot, 3 and now I am anxious about you. The serpent beguiled Eve with his cunning; what if your minds should be corrupted, and lose that innocence which is yours

v. 4. 'To be patient
with me' as in v. 1;
the more ordinary
rendering is 'to be
patient with him',
but it is difficult to
see how St. Paul
could have written
this, even in irony.

in Christ? 4 Some new-comer preaches to you a different Christ, not the one we preached to you; he brings you a spirit other than the spirit you had from us, a gospel other than the gospel you received; you would do well, then, to be patient with me.

5 I claim to have done no less than the very greatest of the apostles. 6 I may be unexperienced in speaking, but I am not so in my knowledge of the truth; everybody knows what we have been in every way to you. 7 Unless perhaps you think I did wrong to honour you by abasing myself, since I preached God's gospel to you at no charge to yourselves? 8 Why, I impoverished other churches, taking pay from them so as to be at your service. 9 I was penniless when I visited you, but I would not cripple any of you with expenses; the brethren came from Macedonia to relieve my necessities; I would not, and I will not, put any burden on you. 10 As the

truth of Christ lives in me, no one in all the country of Achaia shall silence this boast of mine. 11 Why is that? Because I have no love for you? God knows I have. 12 No, I shall continue to do as I have done, so as to cut away the ground from those who would gladly boast that they are no different from myself. 13 Such men are false apostles, dishonest workmen, that pass for apostles of Christ. 14 And no wonder; Satan himself can pass for an angel of light, 15 and his servants have no difficulty in passing for servants of holiness; but their end will be what their life has deserved.

16 Once more I appeal to you, let none of you think me vain; or, if it must be so, give me a hearing in spite of my vanity, and let me boast a little in my turn. 17 When I boast with such confidence, I am not delivering a message to you from God; it is part of my vanity if you will. 18 If so many others boast of their natural advantages, I must be allowed to boast too. 19 You find it easy to be patient with the vanity of others, you who are so full of good sense. 20 Why, you let other people tyrannize over you, prey upon you, take advantage of you, vaunt their power over you, browbeat you! 21 I say this without taking credit to myself, I say it as if we had had no power to play such a part; yet in fact—here my vanity speaks—I can claim all that others claim. 22 Are they Hebrews? So am I. Are they Israelites? So am I. Are they descended from Abraham? So am I. 23 Are they Christ's servants? These are wild words; I am something more. I have toiled harder, spent longer days in prison, been beaten so cruelly, so often looked death in the face. 24 Five times the Jews scourged me, and spared me but one lash in the forty; 25 three times I was beaten with rods, once I was stoned; I have been shipwrecked three times, I have spent a night and a day as a castaway at sea. 26 What journeys I have undertaken, in danger from rivers, in danger from robbers, in danger from my own people, in danger from the Gentiles; danger in cities, danger in the wilderness, danger in the sea, danger among false brethren! 27 I have met with toil and weariness, so often been sleepless, hungry and thirsty; so often denied myself food, gone cold and naked. 28 And all this, over and above something else which I do not count; I mean the burden I carry every day, my anxious care for all the churches; 29 does anyone feel a scruple? I share it; is anyone's conscience hurt? I am ablaze with indignation. 30 If I must needs boast, I will boast of the things which humiliate me; 31 the God who is Father of our Lord Jesus Christ, blessed be his name for ever, knows that I am telling the

vv. 19, 20. The sense of this passage seems to be, that the Corinthians ought not to complain of St. Paul's vanity, since they did not complain of the unscrupulous treatment they often received from his rivals.

truth. 32 When I was at Damascus, the agent of king Aretas was keeping guard over the city of the Damascenes, intent on seizing me, 33 and to escape from his hands I had to be let down through a window along the wall, in a hamper.

v. 32. Acts ix. 25. Aretas was king of the Nabateans, and there is no reason to think that he ruled in Damascus at the time of St. Paul's conversion. His 'ethnarch' was more probably a representative, a 'consul', as we should call it nowadays.

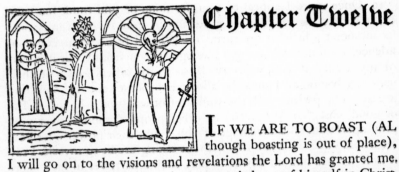

Chapter Twelve

IF WE ARE TO BOAST (ALthough boasting is out of place), I will go on to the visions and revelations the Lord has granted me. 2 There is a man I know who was carried out of himself in Christ, fourteen years since; was his spirit in his body? I cannot tell. Was it apart from his body? I cannot tell; God knows. This man, at least, was carried up into the third heaven. 3 I can only tell you that this man, with his spirit in his body, or with his spirit apart from his body, God knows which, not I, was carried up into Paradise, and heard mysteries which man is not allowed to utter. 4 That is the man about whom I will boast; I will not boast about myself, except to tell you of my humiliations. 5 It would not be vanity, if I had a mind to boast about such a man as that; I should only be telling the truth. But I will spare you the telling of it; I have no mind that anybody should think of me except as he sees me, as he hears me talking to him. 6 And indeed, for fear that these surpassing revelations should make me proud, I was given a sting to distress my outward nature, an angel of Satan sent to rebuff me. 7 Three times it made me entreat the Lord to rid me of it; 8 but he told me, My grace is enough for thee; my strength finds its full scope in thy weakness. 9 More than ever, then, I delight to boast of the weaknesses that humiliate me, so that the strength of Christ may enshrine itself in me. 10 I am well content with these humiliations of mine, with the insults, the hardships, the persecutions,

v. 2. We have no other record of this ecstasy, unless it be that mentioned in Acts xxii. 17.

v. 6. 'A sting to distress my outward nature'; this is often understood as referring to temptations against purity, but some of the earliest Fathers would interpret it rather of those persecutions which were stirred up against the apostle by his fellow countrymen. Other commentators have supposed that St. Paul is speaking of

the times of difficulty I undergo for Christ; when I am weakest, then I am strongest of all.

11 I have given way to vanity; it was you that drove me to it; you ought to have given me credentials, instead of asking for them. No, I have done no less than the very greatest of the apostles, worthless as I am; 12 I have earned the character of apostleship among you, by all the trials I have undergone, by signs and wonders and deeds of miracle. 13 What injustice did I do you, as compared with the other churches, except that to you, of my own choice, I refused to make myself a burden? Forgive me, if I wronged you there. 14 This is the third time I have made preparations for visiting you, and I do not intend to cripple you with expenses: what I claim is yourselves, not anything you can give; it is the parents that should save for their children, not the children for their parents. 15 For my own part, I will gladly spend and be spent on your souls' behalf, though you should love me too little for loving you too well. 16 Ah, you say, that may be; I did not lay any charge on you myself, but I preyed upon you by roundabout means, like the knave I am. 17 What, those envoys I sent you, did I take advantage of you through any of them? 18 I asked Titus to visit you, and there was the brother I sent with him; did Titus take any advantage of you? Did we not all follow the same course, and in the same spirit?

19 You have been telling one another, all this while, that we are defending our conduct to you. Rather, we have been uttering our thoughts as in God's presence, in Christ; yet always, beloved, so as to build up your faith. 20 I have the fear that perhaps, when I reach you, I shall find in you unwelcome hosts, and you in me an unwelcome visitor; that there will be dissension, rivalry, ill humour, factiousness, backbiting, gossip, self-conceit, disharmony. 21 I have the fear that on this new visit God has humiliation in store for me when we meet; that I shall have tears to shed over many of you, sinners of old and still unrepentant, with a tale of impure, adulterous, and wanton living.

some bodily disease or deficiency. If we see here a reference to Num. xxxiii. 55, the second of the explanations given above is to be preferred.

v. 14. This may mean that the apostle had already visited Corinth twice (in which case we have no record in the Acts of his second visit), or it may mean this is the third time the idea of revisiting it has occurred to him during his absence. The language of xiii. 1, below, is somewhat in favour of the former view. See also the note on ii. 1 above.

Chapter Thirteen

THIS will be the third time I have been on my way to see you. Every question, we read, must be settled by the voice of two or of three witnesses. 2 I give you now, still absent, the warning of my second visit; I have told you before, and tell you now, both those who have sinned already and all the rest of you, that I will shew no leniency next time I come. 3 Must you have proof that it is Christ who speaks through me? In him at least you will find no weakness; he still exerts his power among you. 4 Weakness brought him to the cross, but the power of God brought him life; and though it is in our weakness that we are united to him, you will find us too, as he is, alive with God's power. 5 It is your own selves you should be testing, to make sure you are still true to your faith; it is your own selves you must put to the proof. Surely your own conscience will tell you that Christ is alive in you, unless, somehow, you fail at the test; 6 I think you will recognize that we have not failed at ours. 7 When we pray God to keep you from wrong, it is not that we wish to prove successful; our desire is that you should do what is right, even though we seem to have failed. 8 The powers we have are used in support of the truth, not against it; 9 and we are best pleased when we have no power against you, and you are powerful yourselves. That is what we pray for, your perfection. 10 I write this in absence, in the hope that, when I come, I may not have to deal severely with you, in the exercise of that authority which the Lord has given me to build up your faith, not to crush your spirits.

11 Finally, brethren, we wish you all joy. Perfect your lives, listen to the appeal we make, think the same thoughts, keep peace among yourselves; and the God of love and peace will be with you. 12 Greet one another with the kiss of saints. All the saints send you their greeting. 13 The grace of our Lord Jesus Christ, and the love of God, and the imparting of the Holy Spirit be with you all. Amen.

vv. 1 and 2. The former of these verses suggests, though it does not necessarily imply, that St. Paul had visited Corinth twice already. The second, however, seems rather to indicate that the visit which he now proposes to make is only his second visit. Neither view can claim any certain preference; see xii. 14 above. 'Next time I come' may refer to the approaching visit; but the Greek is better understood of some further visit, at an unspecified time, which would have to be made if the delinquents at Corinth should prove 'contumacious. The quotation from Deut. xix. 15 may be intended to suggest that each visit is a 'witness' as to the dispositions of those at Corinth; or it may be simply an intimation that, in judging their disorders, St. Paul will not act on any unsupported evidence.

v. 8. The meaning seems to be, that St. Paul hopes his visit will not be marked by any use of his apostolic authority; it will not be called into exercise, if there are no disorders left to correct.

THE EPISTLE OF THE BLESSED APOSTLE PAUL TO THE GALATIANS

Chapter One

PAUL, AN APOSTLE NOT holding his commission from men, not appointed by man's means, but by Jesus Christ, and God the Father who raised him from the dead, 2 sends his greeting, and greeting from all the brethren who are with him, to the churches of Galatia. 3 Grace and peace be yours from God the Father, and from our Lord Jesus Christ. 4 He it is who has given himself up for our sins, to rescue us from the evil world that surrounds us, according to the will of God, who is our Father; 5 to him be glory for ever and ever, Amen.

6 I am astounded that you should have been so quick to desert one who called you to the grace of Christ, and go over to another gospel; 7 this can only mean, that certain people are causing disquiet among you, in their eagerness to pervert the gospel of Christ. 8 Friends, though it were we ourselves, though it were an angel from heaven that should preach to you a gospel other than the gospel we preached to you, a curse upon him! 9 I repeat now the warning we gave you before it happened, if anyone preaches to you what is contrary to the tradition you received, a curse upon

v. 7. Some commentators would translate here, 'Not a different gospel, no; it is only that certain people are causing disquiet'.

349

him! 10 Do you think it is man's favour, or God's, that I am trying to win now? Shall I be told, now, that I am courting the good will of men? If, after all these years, I were still courting the favour of men, I should not be what I am, the slave of Christ.

11 Let me tell you this, brethren; the gospel I preached to you is not a thing of man's dictation; 12 it was not from man that I inherited or learned it, it came to me by a revelation from Jesus Christ. 13 You have been told how I bore myself in my Jewish days, how I persecuted God's Church beyond measure and tried to destroy it, 14 going further in my zeal as a Jew than many of my own age and race, so fierce a champion was I of the traditions handed down by my forefathers. 15 And then, he who had set me apart from the day of my birth, and called me by his grace, 16 saw fit to make his Son known in me, so that I could preach his gospel among the Gentiles. My first thought was not to hold any consultations with any human creature; 17 I did not go up to Jerusalem to see those who had been apostles longer than myself; no, I went off into Arabia, and when I came back, it was to Damascus. 18 Then, when three years had passed, I did go up to Jerusalem, to visit Peter, and I stayed a fortnight there in his company; 19 But I did not see any of the other apostles, except James, the Lord's brother. 20 Such is my history; as God sees me, I am telling you the plain truth. 21 Afterwards, I travelled into other parts of the world, Syria and Cilicia; 22 and all the time I was not even known by sight to the Christian churches of Judaea; 23 they only knew by hearsay, The man who used to persecute us is now preaching the faith he once tried to destroy, 24 and they praised God for what he had done in me.

v. 18. This may mean three years after St. Paul's return to Damascus, or three years after his conversion. See Acts ix. 26.

CHRIST CARRYING THE CROSS

FLEMISH SCHOOL
late 15th Century

METROPOLITAN MUSEUM, NEW YORK

Chapter Two

THEN, after an interval of fourteen years, once again I went up to Jerusalem with Barnabas, and Titus also accompanied me. 2 I went up in obedience to a revelation, and there I communicated to them (only in private, to men of repute) the gospel I always preach among the Gentiles; was it possible that the course I had taken and was taking was useless? 3 And it is not even true to say that they insisted on my companion Titus, who was a Greek, being circumcised; 4 we were only thinking of those false brethren who had insinuated themselves into our company so as to spy on the liberty which we enjoy in Jesus Christ, meaning to make slaves of us. 5 To these we did not give ground for a moment by way of obedience; we were resolved that the true principles of the gospel should remain undisturbed in your possession. 6 But as for what I owe to those who were of some repute—it matters little to me who or what they were, God makes no distinction between man and man—these men of repute, I say, had nothing to communicate to me. 7 On the contrary, those who were reputed to be the main support of the Church, James and Cephas and John, saw plainly that I was commissioned to preach to the uncircumcised, as Peter was to the circumcised; 8 he whose power had enabled Peter to become the apostle of the circumcised, had enabled me to become the apostle of the Gentiles. 9 And so, recognizing the grace God had given men, they joined their right hands in fellowship with Barnabas and myself; the Gentiles were to be our province, the circumcised theirs. 10 Only we were to remember the poor; which was the very thing I had set myself to do.

11 Afterwards, when Cephas came to Antioch, I opposed him openly; he stood self-condemned. 12 He had been eating with the Gentiles, until we were visited by certain delegates from James; but when these came, he began to draw back and hold himself aloof, overawed by the supporters of circumcision. 13 The rest of the Jews were no less false to their principles; Barnabas himself was carried away by their insincerity. 14 So, when I found that they were not following the true path of the gospel, I said to Cephas in front of them all, Since thou, who art a born Jew, dost follow the Gentile, not the Jewish way of life, by what right dost

v. 1. As before, the fourteen years may be dated either from St. Paul's conversion, or from his return to Damascus. Some commentators, accordingly, would identify this visit with that mentioned in Acts xi. 30; others identify it with that of Acts xv, and suppose that the apostle left the earlier visit unrecorded, through forgetfulness or some other cause.

vv. 3-5. The simplest explanation of these verses is that St. Paul did have Titus circumcised, but not because anybody insisted on it, only so as to avoid giving any scandal to the Judaizing brethren. (Cf. Acts xvi. 3, where the phrase used is exactly the same.) It was not (he adds in verse 5) by way of obedience to any demands from them. as the Galatians had perhaps been told. Other commentators reject this idea as inconsistent with St. Paul's principles, and explain that St. Paul forgot to finish the sentence he began in verse 4.

v. 6. 'Those who were of some repute', perhaps including the apostles, but evidently others too, who are left unnamed.

v. 10. Cf. Acts xi. 30, if that is the occasion referred to.

thou bind the Gentiles to live like Jews? 15 We are Jews by right of nature, we do not come from the guilty stock of the Gentiles; 16 yet we found out that it is through faith in Jesus Christ, not by obeying the law, that a man is justified. We, like anyone else, had to learn to believe in Jesus Christ, so that we might be justified by faith in Christ, not by observance of the law. Observance of the law cannot win acceptance for a single human creature.

17 By putting our hopes of justification in Christ, we took our rank as guilty creatures like the rest. Does that mean that Christ brings us guilt? That is not to be thought of; 18 do I put myself in the wrong, when I destroy and then rebuild? 19 Through the law, my old self has become dead to the law, so that I may live to God; with Christ I hang upon the cross, 20 and yet I am alive; or rather, not I; it is Christ that lives in me. True, I am living, here and now, this mortal life; but my real life is the faith I have in the Son of God, who loved me, and gave himself for me. 21 I do not spurn the grace of God. If we can be justified through the law, then Christ's death was needless.

v. 16. The end of this verse refers to Ps. cxlii. 2.

v. 18. That is, when I deny the doctrine of being justified through the law, but assert instead that of being justified by faith. The more usual interpretation, which makes the sentence a statement, not a question, is explained as meaning: 'It is not by breaking the law that a man becomes a transgressor, but by going back, like Peter, to the old observances he has abandoned'.

Chapter Three

SENSELESS GALATIANS, who is it that has cast a spell on you, that you should refuse your loyalty to the truth, you, before whom Jesus Christ has been exposed to view on his cross? 2 Let me be content with asking you one question, Was it from observance of the law that the Spirit came to you, or from obeying the call of faith? 3 Are you so far out of your right senses? You dedicated your first beginnings to the spirit; and can you now find your completion in outward things? 4 Was it to no purpose that you went through so much? Since it seems it was to no purpose. 5 When God lavishes his Spirit on you and enables you to perform miracles, what is the reason for it? Your observance of the law, or your obedience to the call of faith? 6 Remember how Abraham put his faith in God, and it was reckoned virtue in him. 7 You must recognize, then, that Abraham's real children are the children of his faith. 8 There is a passage in scripture which, long before-hand, brings to Abraham the good news, Through thee all the nations shall be blessed; and that passage looks forward to God's justification of the Gentiles by faith. 9 It is those, then, who take their stand on faith that share the blessing Abraham's faithfulness won. 10 Those who take their stand on observance of the law are all under a curse; Cursed be everyone (we read) who does not per-sist in carrying out all that this book of the law prescribes. 11 And indeed, that the law cannot make a man acceptable to God is clear enough; It is faith, we are told, that brings life to the just man; 12 whereas the law does not depend on faith; no, we are told it is the man who carries out the commandments that will find life in them. 13 From this curse invoked by the law Christ has ransomed us, by himself becoming, for our sakes, an accursed thing; we read that, There is a curse on the man who hangs on a gibbet. 14 Thus, in Christ Jesus, the blessing of Abraham was to be im-parted to the Gentiles, so that we, through faith, might receive the promised gift of the Spirit.

15 Brethren, let me take an argument from common life. A valid legal disposition made by an ordinary human being cannot afterwards be set aside; no one can make fresh provisions in it. 16 The promises you know of were made to Abraham and his offspring; (it does not, by the way, say, To thy descendants, as if it meant a number of people; it says, To thy offspring, in the singu-lar, meaning Christ). 17 And this is my contention; the law, com-ing into being four hundred and thirty years afterwards, cannot un-make the disposition which God made so long ago, and cancel the promise. 18 If our inheritance depends on observing the law, then it is not the inheritance secured to us by promise; that was promised to Abraham as a free gift.

19 What, then, is the purpose of the law? It was brought in to make room for transgression, while we waited for the coming of that posterity, to whom the promise had been made. Its terms were dictated by angels, acting through a spokesman; 20 (a spokesman represents more than one, and there is only one God). 21 Is the law an infringement, then, of God's promises? That is not to be thought of. Doubtless, if a law had been given that was capable of imparting life to us, it would have been for the law to bring

v. 6. Gen. xv. 6.

v. 8. Gen. xii. 3, xviii. 18.

v. 10. Deut. xxvii. 26.

v. 12. Hab. ii. 4, Lev. xviii. 5.

v. 13. Deut. xxi. 23.

v. 15. 'Legal disposi-tion'; the Greek word here used has often the sense of a last will and testament, rarely the sense of a compact between two persons, in the heath-en writers. In the Bible it has often the sense of a com-pact or covenant, rarely the sense of a will (Heb. ix. 16). Here, though St. Paul is referring to the covenant God made with Abraham, he seems to be think-ing, not of contracts, but of binding legal documents in general. 'No one'; that is, no one else; the Law is treated, in pursuance of the metaphor, as if it had been given to Moses by the angels rather than by God himself.

v. 16. Gen. xxii. 18.

v. 19. 'To make room for transgression'; that is, either to dis-courage transgres-sion, or (more prob-ably) to turn our sins into transgres-

sions, make us conscious of them as the breach of a divine law, and therefore of our need for redemption. It was a Jewish tradition that angels gave the law to Moses on Sinai (Acts vii. 53, Heb. ii. 2). 'A spokesman'; literally a mediator or go-between, probably referring to Moses. The mediator who negotiates between two sides in a dispute is so often, at the same time, the spokesman or representative of a body of persons, that the two meanings 'mediator' and 'representative' shade off into one another; (cf. I Kings xvii. 4, where

us justification. 22 But in fact scripture represents us as all under the bondage of sin; it was faith in Jesus Christ that was to impart the promised blessing to all those who believe in him. 23 Until faith came, we were all being kept in bondage to the law, waiting for the faith that was one day to be revealed. 24 So that the law was our tutor, bringing us to Christ, to find in faith our justification. 25 When faith comes, then we are no longer under the rule of a tutor; 26 through faith in Jesus Christ you are all now God's sons. 27 All you who have been baptized in Christ's name have put on the person of Christ; 28 no more Jew or Gentile, no more slave and freeman, no more male and female; you are all one person in Jesus Christ. 29 And if you belong to Christ, then you are indeed Abraham's children; the promised inheritance is yours.

the Hebrew and some of the Greek versions use the word 'mediator' of Goliath, as being the representative or champion of the Philistines). In this passage, it is difficult to find any meaning for verse 20 unless we suppose that the apostle refers to Moses as the spokesman of the angels; God, being a single Agent, would have no need of a spokesman to represent him, and did not employ any spokesman when he made the promises to Abraham. Thus the promises have a higher dignity than the law, as communicated to us directly from God. 'Its terms were dictated'; the same Greek word is used as in verse 15 above.   v. 22. Probably an allusion to Ps. cxli. 2, as quoted in ii. 16 above.   v. 24. 'Our tutor'; the Greek word means a slave who took his master's children to school.   v. 27. 'Have put on the person of Christ'; literally, 'have put on Christ', as in Rom. xiii. 14; here, St. Paul refers to that obliteration of distinctions between man and man which results from our incorporation into Christ.

Chapter Four

v. 3. 'Schoolroom tasks'; the same word is used in Greek of the elements of nature, or of the sun, moon, etc., and some commentators think that this is the sense here; the apostle is reminding the Galatians of the heathen gods they used to serve.

v. 6. The rendering given follows St. Chrysostom; others would translate 'because you are sons'.

ONSIDER this; one who comes into his property while he is still a child has no more liberty than one of the servants, though all the estate is his; 2 he is under the control of guardians and trustees, until he reaches the age prescribed by his father. 3 So it was with us; in those childish days of ours we toiled away at the schoolroom tasks which the world gave us, 4 till the appointed time came. Then God sent out his Son on a mission to us. He took birth from a woman, took birth as a subject of the law, 5 so as to ransom those who were subject to the law, and make us sons by adoption. 6 To prove that you are sons, God has sent out the Spirit of his Son into our hearts, crying out in us, Abba, Father. 7 No longer, then, art thou a slave, thou art a son; and because thou art a son, thou hast the son's right of inheritance. 8 Formerly you had no knowledge of God; you lived as the slaves of deities who were in truth no deities at all. 9 Now you have recognized the true God, or rather, the true God has recognized you. How is it that you are going back to those old schoolroom tasks of yours, so abject, so ineffectual, eager to begin your drudgery all over again? 10 You have begun to observe special days and months, special seasons and years. 11 I am anxious over you; has all the labour I have spent on you been useless?

12 Stand by me; I have taken my stand with you. I appeal to you, brethren. You have never treated me amiss. 13 Why, when I preached the gospel to you in the first instance, it was, you remember, because of outward circumstances which were humiliating to me. 14 Those outward circumstances of mine were a test for you, which you did not meet with contempt or dislike; you welcomed me as God's angel, as Christ Jesus. 15 What has become now of the blessing that once was yours? In those days, I assure you, you would have plucked out your eyes, if you had had the chance, and given them to me. 16 Have I made enemies of you, then, by telling you the truth? 17 Oh, they are jealous over you, but for a dishonourable purpose; their aim is to shut you out from their company, so that you may be jealous of them. 18 Your jealousy should be for the honourable gifts you see in a man of honour; always, not only when I am at your side. 19 My little children, I am in travail over you afresh, until I can see Christ's image formed in you! 20 I wish I were at your side now, and could speak to you in a different tone; I am bewildered at you.

21 Tell me, you who are so eager to have the law for your master, have you never read the law? 22 You will find it written there, that Abraham had two sons; one had a slave for his mother, and one a free woman. 23 The child of the slave was born in the course of nature; the free woman's, by the power of God's promise. 24 All that is an allegory; the two women stand for the two dispensations. Agar stands for the old dispensation, which brings up its children to bondage, the dispensation which comes to us from mount Sinai. 25 Mount Sinai, in Arabia, has the same meaning in the allegory as Jerusalem, the Jerusalem which exists here and now; an enslaved city, whose children are slaves. 26 Whereas our mother is the heavenly Jerusalem, a city of freedom. 27 So it is that we read, Rejoice, thou barren woman that hast never borne child, break out into song and cry aloud, thou that hast never known travail; the deserted one has more children than she whose husband is with her. 28 It is we, brethren, that are children of the promise, as Isaac was. 29 Now, as then, the son who was born in the course of nature persecutes the son whose birth

v. 10. This will refer to the Hebrew sabbaths and other observances, which are here represented as a bondage no lighter than that which was imposed by the rules of heathen worship.

v. 12. That is, abandon the Jewish customs for my sake, as I abandoned them for yours.

v. 13. 'In the first instance'; some commentators think this means 'on the earlier of my two visits'; others would take the phrase generally, holding that this letter was written before the visit mentioned in Acts xv. 'Outward circumstances which were humiliating to me'; literally, 'infirmity of the flesh'. It does not seem likely, however, that illness would have made St. Paul preach to the heathens in Galatia, or that this illness would have been a test for them, or that they would have been tempted by it to despise and dislike him. Many of the Fathers, therefore, understand this phrase of the persecutions which St. Paul suffered at the hands of the Jews; cf. Acts xiii. 45 and following. It is certain that St. Paul speaks of 'the flesh' when he is referring to disappointments and controversies (II Cor. vii. 5), and that 'infirmity' for him can mean any kind of humiliation (II Cor. xi. 30). He also speaks of 'the flesh' in special reference to the Jews, his kinsmen according to the flesh (Rom. xi. 14).

v. 14. 'God's angel'; in the Greek, this might mean, 'God's messenger'. It is perhaps worth noting that when St. Paul healed a cripple at Lystra, the heathen mistook him for Mercury, the messenger of the gods. In the next verse, 'that blessing' perhaps means 'that occasion on which you called me blessed', the Greek word being one especially used in addresses to the pagan gods.

v. 18. The Greek here has 'It is honourable in you to be jealous for what is honourable'; the sense of the words is in any case uncertain. v. 22. Cf. Gen. xvi and xxi. v. 25. Many Greek manuscripts here have 'Agar is mount Sinai in Arabia', perhaps referring to some local name. It is in any case Agar, not Sinai, that is represented as corresponding to the earthly Jerusalem, in the Greek manuscripts. v. 27. Is. liv. 1. v. 30. Gen. xxi. 10.

is a spiritual birth. 30 But what does our passage in scripture say? Rid thyself of the slave and her son; it cannot be that the son of a slave should divide the inheritance with the son of a free woman.

31 You see, then, brethren, that we are sons of the free woman, not of the slave; such is the freedom Christ has won for us.

Chapter Five

TAND fast, and do not let yourselves be caught again in the yoke of slavery. 2 The word of Paul is your warrant for this; if you are for being circumcised, Christ is of no value to you at all. 3 Once again I would warn anyone who is accepting circumcision that he thereby engages himself to keep all the precepts of the law. 4 You who look to the law for your justification have cancelled your bond with Christ, you have forfeited grace. 5 All our hope of justification lies in the spirit; it rests on our faith; 6 once we are in Christ, circumcision means nothing, and the want of it means nothing; the faith that finds its expression in love is all that matters. 7 Till now, you had been shaping your course well; who is it that has come

v. 8. Here, as in i. 6, 'he who called you' refers to Almighty God, not to St. Paul himself.

between you and your loyalty to the truth? 8 Not he who called you; this pressure comes from elsewhere. 9 It takes but a little leaven to leaven the whole batch. 10 I am fully confident in the Lord that you will be of the same mind with me, leaving the disturbers of your peace, be they who they may, to answer for it.

v. 11. It would appear from this verse that the authors of confusion in the Galatian church represented St. Paul himself as recommending circumcision to his Gentile converts. It is difficult to understand how they can have found any colour for such statements, if this letter was written after the deliberations mentioned in Acts xv; cf. Acts xvi. 4.

v. 14. Lev. xix. 18.

11 As for myself, brethren, if it is true that I preach the need of circumcision, why am I persecuted? If I did, the preaching of the cross would no longer give offence. 12 I would rather they should lose their own manhood, these authors of your unrest.

13 Yes, brethren, freedom claimed you when you were called. Only, do not let this freedom give a foothold to corrupt nature; you must be servants still, serving one another in a spirit of charity. 14 After all, the whole of the law is summed up in one phrase, Thou shalt love thy neighbour as thyself; 15 if you are always backbiting and worrying each other, it is to be feared you will wear

each other out in the end. 16 Let me say this; learn to live and move in the spirit; then there is no danger of your giving way to the impulses of corrupt nature. 17 The impulses of nature and the impulses of the spirit are at war with one another; either is clean contrary to the other, and that is why you cannot do all that your will approves. 18 It is by letting the spirit lead you that you free yourselves from the yoke of the law. 19 It is easy to see what effects proceed from corrupt nature; they are such things as adultery, impurity, incontinence, luxury, 20 idolatry, witchcraft, feuds, quarrels, jealousies, outbursts of anger, rivalries, dissensions, factions, 21 spite, murder, drunkenness, and debauchery. I warn you, as I have warned you before, that those who live in such a way will not inherit God's kingdom. 22 Whereas the spirit yields a harvest of love, joy, peace, patience, 23 kindness, generosity, forbearance, gentleness, faith, courtesy, temperateness, purity. No law can touch lives such as these; 24 those who belong to Christ have crucified nature, with all its passions, all its impulses. 25 Since we live by the spirit, let the spirit be our rule of life; 26 we must not indulge vain ambitions, envying one another and provoking one another to envy.

v. 22. The Greek only mentions nine of the Twelve Fruits; viz. the first six, together with gentleness, faith, and temperateness. It is possible that the Latin version has accidentally included, in some cases, two renderings of the same Greek word.

Chapter Six

BRETHREN, IF A MAN IS found guilty of some fault, you, who are spiritually minded, ought to shew a spirit of gentleness in correcting him. Have an eye upon thyself; thou too wilt perhaps encounter temptation. 2 Bear the burden of one another's failings; then you will be fulfilling the law of Christ. 3 The man who thinks he is of some worth, when in truth he is worth nothing at all, is merely deluding himself. 4 Everyone should examine his own conduct; then he will be able to take the measure of his own

v. 2. 'The burden of one another's failings'; this is the meaning preferred by St. Chrysostom and others (cf. the Imitation of Christ, i. 16 and ii. 3). The more usual interpretation of the passage, which understands 'the burdens of one another' to mean the misfor-

worth; no need to compare himself with others. 5 Each of us, then, will have his own load to carry.

6 Your teachers are to have a share in all that their disciples have to bestow. 7 Make no mistake about it; you cannot cheat God. 8 A man will reap what he sows; if nature is his seed-ground, nature will give him a perishable harvest, if his seed-ground is the spirit, it will give him a harvest of eternal life. 9 Let us not be discouraged, then, over our acts of charity; we shall reap when the time comes, if we persevere in them. 10 Let us practise generosity to all, while the opportunity is ours; and above all, to those who are of one family with us in the faith.

11 Here is some bold lettering for you, written in my own hand. 12 Who are they, these people who insist on your being circumcised? They are men, all of them, who are determined to keep up outward appearances, so that the cross of Christ may not bring persecution on them. 13 Why, they do not even observe the law, although they adopt circumcision; they are for having you circumcised, so as to make a display of your outward conformity. 14 God forbid that I should make a display of anything, except the cross of our Lord Jesus Christ, through which the world stands crucified to me, and I to the world. 15 Circumcision means nothing, the want of it means nothing; when a man is in Christ Jesus, there has been a new creation. 16 Peace and pardon to all those who follow this rule, to God's true Israel. 17 Spare me, all of you, any further anxieties; already I bear the scars of the Lord Jesus printed on my body. 18 Brethren, the grace of our Lord Jesus Christ be with your spirit. Amen.

THE EPISTLE OF THE BLESSED APOSTLE PAUL TO THE EPHESIANS

Chapter One

PAUL, BY GOD'S WILL AN apostle of Jesus Christ, to those saints, the faithful in Jesus Christ, who dwell at Ephesus, 2 grace and peace be yours from God, our Father, and from the Lord Jesus Christ. 3 Blessed be that God, that Father of our Lord Jesus Christ, who has blessed us, in Christ, with every spiritual blessing, higher than heaven itself. 4 He has chosen us out, in Christ, before the foundation of the world, to be saints, to be blameless in his sight, for love of him; 5 marking us out beforehand (so his will decreed) to be his adopted children through Jesus Christ. 6 Thus he would manifest the splendour of that grace by which he has taken us into his favour in the person of his beloved Son. 7 It is in him and through his blood that we enjoy redemption, the forgiveness of our sins. So rich is God's grace, 8 that has overflowed upon us in a full stream of wisdom and discernment, 9 to make known to us the hidden purpose of his will. It was his loving design, centred in Christ, 10 to give history its fulfilment by resuming everything in him, all that is in heaven, all that is on earth, summed up in him. 11 In him it was our lot to be called, singled

v. 4. 'For love of him'; or perhaps, 'in his love'.

359

out beforehand to suit his purpose, (for it is he who is at work everywhere, carrying out the designs of his will); 12 we were to manifest his glory, we who were the first to set our hope in Christ; 13 in him you too were called, when you listened to the preaching of the truth, that gospel which is your salvation. In him you too learned to believe, and had the seal set on your faith by the promised gift of the Holy Spirit; 14 a pledge of the inheritance which is ours, to redeem it for us and bring us into possession of it, and so manifest God's glory.

15 Well then, I too play my part; I have been told of your faith in the Lord Jesus, of the love you shew towards all the saints, 16 and I never cease to offer thanks on your behalf, or to remember you in my prayers. 17 So may he who is the God of our Lord Jesus Christ, the Father to whom glory belongs, grant you a spirit of wisdom and insight, to give you fuller knowledge of himself. 18 May your inward eye be enlightened, so that you may understand to what hopes he has called you, how rich in glory is that inheritance of his found among the saints, 19 what surpassing virtue there is in his dealings with us, who believe. Measure it by that mighty exercise of power 20 which he shewed when he raised Christ from the dead, and bade him sit on his right hand above the heavens, 21 high above all princedoms and powers and virtues and dominations, and every name that is known, not in this world only, but in the world to come. 22 He has put everything under his dominion, and made him the head to which the whole Church is joined, 23 so that the Church is his body, the completion of him who everywhere and in all things is complete.

v. 15. Some Greek manuscripts omit the words 'of the love'.

v. 18. It is not certain whether this means that we are God's inheritance (cf. Deut. xxxii. 9) or that God gives us an inheritance, as in v. 14 above. If our inheritance is meant, 'redemption' is perhaps best understood as implying that our inheritance is redeemed for us (cf. Lev. xxv. 25).

v. 22. The Greek here has 'to be the head of the Church above everything else', the Latin, 'to be head over the whole Church'.

v. 23. 'Who . . . is complete'; the Greek verb used here may mean this, or it may mean 'who completes all things in all men (or in all things)'.

Chapter Two

E found you dead men; such were your transgressions, such were the sinful ways 2 you lived in. That was when you followed the fashion of this world, when you owned a prince whose domain is in the lower air, that spirit whose influence is still at work among the unbelievers. 3 We too, all of us, were once of their company; our life was bounded by natural appetites, and we did what corrupt nature or our own calculation would have us do, with God's displeasure for our birthright, like other men. 4 How rich God is in mercy, with what an excess of love he loved us! 5 Our sins had made dead men of us, and he, in giving life to Christ, gave life to us too; it is his grace that has saved you; 6 raised us up too, enthroned us too above the heavens, in Christ Jesus. 7 He would have all future ages see, in that clemency which he shewed us in Christ Jesus, the surpassing richness of his grace. 8 Yes, it was grace that saved you, with faith for its instrument; it did not come from yourselves, it was God's gift, 9 not from any action of yours, or there would be room for pride. 10 No, we are his design; God has created us in Christ Jesus, pledged to such good actions as he has prepared beforehand, to be the employment of our lives.

11 Remember, then, what you once were, the Gentiles, according to all outward reckoning; those who claim an outward circumcision which is man's handiwork call you the uncircumcised. 12 In those days there was no Christ for you; you were outlaws from the commonwealth of Israel, strangers to every covenant, with no promise to hope for, with the world about you, and no God. 13 But now you are in Christ Jesus; now, through the blood of Christ, you have been brought close, you who were once so far away. 14 He is our bond of peace; he has made the two nations one, breaking down the wall that was a barrier between us, 15 the enmity there was between us, in his own mortal nature. He has put an end to the law with its decrees, so as to make peace, remaking the two human creatures as one in himself; 16 both sides, united in a single body, he would reconcile to God through his cross, inflicting death, in his own person, upon the feud. 17 So he came, and his message was of peace for you who were far off, peace for those who were near; 18 far off or near, united in the same

v. 12. Some would divide this verse differently, 'strangers to every dispensation of the promise, with nothing to hope for'.

vv. 13-17. The references to 'peace', 'those who were far off', 'those who were near', are a reminiscence of Is. lvii. 19.

Spirit, we have access through him to the Father. 19 You are no longer exiles, then, or aliens; the saints are your fellow citizens, you belong to God's household. 20 Apostles and prophets are the foundation on which you were built, and the chief corner-stone of it is Jesus Christ himself. 21 In him the whole fabric is bound together, as it grows into a temple, dedicated to the Lord; 22 in him you too are being built in with the rest, so that God may find in you a dwelling-place for his Spirit.

v. 22. 'A dwelling-place for his Spirit'; or perhaps, 'a spiritual dwelling-place'.

Chapter Three

v. 1. This sentence, in the original, has no verb in it; the words 'fall on my knees' have to be supplied from verse 14 below, where the apostle picks up the thread of his sentence again.

v. 3. 'I have been setting out'; in the last two chapters, especially in ii, 11-22.

WITH THIS IN MIND, I fall on my knees; I, Paul, of whom Jesus Christ has made a prisoner for the love of you Gentiles. 2 You will have been told how God planned to give me a special grace for preaching to you; 3 how a revelation taught me the secret I have been setting out briefly here; 4 briefly, yet so as to let you see how well I have mastered this secret of Christ's. 5 It was never made known to any human being in past ages, as it has now been revealed by the Spirit to his holy apostles and prophets, and it is this: 6 that through the gospel preaching the Gentiles are to win the same inheritance, to be made part of the same body, to share the same divine promise, in Christ Jesus. 7 With what grace God gives me (and he gives it in all the effectiveness of his power), I am a minister of that gospel; 8 on me, least as I am of all the saints, he has bestowed this privilege, of making known to the Gentiles the unfathomable riches of Christ, 9 of publishing to the world the plan of this mystery, kept hidden from the beginning of time in the all-creating mind of God. 10 The principalities and powers of heaven are to see, now, made manifest in the Church, the subtlety of God's wisdom; 11 such is his eternal purpose, centred in Christ Jesus our Lord, 12 who gives us all our con-

fidence, bids us come forward, emboldened by our faith in him.
13 Let there be no discouragement, then, over the affliction I
undergo on your behalf; it is an honour done to you.

14 With this in mind, then, I fall on my knees to the Father of
our Lord Jesus Christ, 15 that Father from whom all fatherhood
in heaven and on earth takes its title. 16 May he, out of the rich
treasury of his glory, strengthen you through his spirit with a
power that reaches your innermost being. 17 May Christ find a
dwelling-place, through faith, in your hearts; may your lives be
rooted in love, founded on love. 18 May you and all the saints be
enabled to measure, in all its breadth and length and height and
depth, 19 the love of Christ, to know what passes knowledge.
May you be filled with all the completion God has to give. 20 He
whose power is at work in us is powerful enough, and more than
powerful enough, to carry out his purpose beyond all our hopes
and dreams; 21 may he be glorified in the Church, and in Christ
Jesus, to the last generation of eternity. Amen.

Chapter Four

HERE, THEN, IS ONE
who wears chains in the Lord's
service, pleading with you to live as befits men called to such a
vocation as yours. 2 You must be always humble, always gentle;
patient, too, in bearing with one another's faults, as charity bids;
3 eager to preserve that unity the Spirit gives you, whose bond is
peace. 4 You are one body, with a single Spirit; each of you,
when he was called, called in the same hope; 5 with the same
Lord, the same faith, the same baptism; 6 with the same God, the
same Father, all of us, who is above all beings, pervades all things,
and lives in all of us. 7 But each of us has received his own special
grace, dealt out to him by Christ's gift. 8 (That is why we are

v. 13. 'On your behalf', in the sense that St. Paul has brought persecution on himself by befriending the cause of the Gentiles; cf. Acts xxi. 28.

v. 15. 'All fatherhood'; this can also be rendered, from the Greek, 'every family'.

v. 18. Literally, 'may you, with all the saints, be able to understand what is the breadth, and length, and height, and depth, and to know the love of Christ'.

v. 6. Some of the best Greek manuscripts omit the word 'us' at the end of the sentence; nor does the Greek text make it clear whether the reference in the last three clauses is to men or to things.

v. 8. Ps. lxvii. 19. The Hebrew should more probably be rendered, 'he has received gifts among men'.

vv. 9 and 10. The exact sense of this passage is much disputed. If we understand 'the lower regions of earth' as meaning simply 'this lower earth', St. Paul is saying that our Lord's Ascension presupposes his coming down to earth at his Incarnation. If we understand 'the lower regions of earth' as meaning the grave, or the Limbus Patrum, then St. Paul is saying (verse 9) that the Descent into Hell is presupposed by the Resurrection, after which our Lord gave gifts to men (Mark xvi. 17, John xx. 22); it is only in verse 10 that he refers to the Ascension. Some manuscripts and versions omit the word 'first' in verse 9; if we adopt that reading, a third interpretation becomes possible, namely, that St. Paul speaks of our Lord as going up in his Ascension, and coming down in the Mission of the Holy Ghost at Pentecost.

v. 10. 'To fill creation with his presence'; others would translate 'to bring all things (i.e. prophecies) to fulfilment'.

v. 13. The last clause of this verse is variously interpreted. But the thought seems to be, that as Christ, who is our head, grew up to the perfect age of manhood when Incarnate, so his Church has to grow up to a corresponding perfection of holiness.

v. 15. 'Into a due proportion with Christ'; the Latin here has simply 'in Christ', but it seems probable that St. Paul is continuing his metaphor (taken from nature) of the body which grows up to the scale of its head.

v. 19. 'In despair'; the best Greek manuscripts read 'past all feeling'.

v. 22. 'Wasted its aim on false dreams'; literally 'became cor-

told, He has mounted up on high; he has captured his spoil; he has brought gifts to men. 9 The words, He has gone up, must mean that he had gone down, first, to the lower regions of earth. 10 And he who so went down is no other than he who has gone up, high above all the heavens, to fill creation with his presence.) 11 Some he has appointed to be apostles, others to be prophets, others to be evangelists, or pastors, or teachers. They are to order the lives of the faithful, 12 minister to their needs, build up the frame of Christ's body, 13 until we all realize our common unity through faith in the Son of God, and fuller knowledge of him. So we shall reach perfect manhood, that maturity which is proportioned to the completed growth of Christ; 14 we are no longer to be children, no longer to be like storm-tossed sailors, driven before the wind of each new doctrine that human subtlety, human skill in fabricating lies, may propound. 15 We are to follow the truth, in a spirit of charity, and so grow up, in everything, into a due proportion with Christ, who is our head. 16 On him all the body depends; it is organized and unified by each contact with the source which supplies it; and thus, each limb receiving the active power it needs, it achieves its natural growth, building itself up through charity.

17 This, then, is my message to you; I call upon you in the Lord's name not to live like the Gentiles, who make vain fancies their rule of life. 18 Their minds are clouded with darkness; the hardness of their hearts breeds in them an ignorance, which estranges them from the divine life; 19 and so, in despair, they have given themselves up to incontinence, to selfish habits of impurity. 20 This is not the lesson you have learned in making Christ your study, 21 if you have really listened to him. If true knowledge is to be found in Jesus, you will have learned in his school 22 that you must be quit, now, of the old self whose way of life you remember, the self that wasted its aim on false dreams. 23 There must be a renewal in the inner life of your minds; 24 you must be clothed in the new self, which is created in God's image, justified and sanctified through the truth.

25 Away with falsehood, then; let everyone speak out the truth to his neighbour; membership of the body binds us to one another. 26 Do not let resentment lead you into sin; the sunset must not find you still angry. 27 Do not give the devil his opportunity. 28 The man who was a thief must be a thief no longer; let him work instead, and earn by his own labour the blessings he will be able to share with those who are in need. 29 No base talk must cross your lips; only what will serve to build up the faith, and

bring a grace to those who are listening; 30 do not distress God's holy Spirit, whose seal you bear until the day of your redemption comes. 31 There must be no trace of bitterness among you, of passion, resentment, quarrelling, insulting talk, or spite of any kind; 32 be kind and tender to one another, each of you generous to all, as God in Christ has been generous to you.

rupt according to the appetites of error', a phrase which is variously interpreted.

v. 26. Ps. iv. 5.

v. 29. 'To build up the faith'; some Greek manuscripts read 'to edify others as opportunity arises'.

Chapter Five

AS God's favoured children, you must be like him. Order your lives in charity, upon the model of that charity which Christ shewed to us, when he gave himself up on our behalf, a sacrifice breathing out fragrance as he offered it to God. 3 As for debauchery, and impurity of every kind, and covetousness, there must be no whisper of it among you; it would ill become saints; 4 no indecent behaviour, no ribaldry or smartness in talk; that is not your business, your business is to give thanks to God. 5 This you must know well enough, that nobody can claim a share in Christ's kingdom, God's kingdom, if he is debauched, or impure, or has that love of money which makes a man an idolater. 6 Do not allow anyone to cheat you with empty promises; these are the very things which bring down God's anger on the unbelievers; 7 you do ill to throw in your lot with them. 8 Once you were all darkness; now, in the Lord, you are all daylight. You must live as men native to the light; 9 where the light has its effect, all is goodness, and holiness, and truth; 10 your lives must be the manifestation of God's will. 11 As for the thankless deeds men do in the dark, you must not take any part in them; rather, your conduct must be a rebuke to them; 12 their secret actions are too shameful even to bear speaking of. 13 It is the light that rebukes such things and shews them up for what they are; only light shews up. 14 That is the meaning of the words, Awake, thou that sleepest, and arise from the dead, and Christ shall give thee light.

15 See then, brethren, how carefully you have to tread, not as fools, but as wise men do, 16 hoarding the opportunity that is given you, in evil times like these. 17 No, you cannot afford to be

v. 10. 'To make it clear'; the sense of the verb is 'to prove by experiment', usually in the sense of convincing oneself. The context here suggests that the proof is for the benefit of others, as in I Cor. iii. 13.

v. 13. 'Only light shews up'; the Latin takes the verb in the sense of 'to be manifest', but the Greek allows of rendering it 'to make · (other things) manifest', which is here more

EPHESIANS

suitable to the context. Throughout this passage, St. Paul is explaining that the witness of a Christian life, enlightened by grace, rebukes the wickedness of the surrounding world as inevitably as light reveals darkness.

v. 14. These words do not appear in scripture, and some have thought that St. Paul is quoting from a very early baptismal hymn.

v. 30. The words 'flesh and bone, we belong to him' are omitted by some Greek manuscripts, probably through the carelessness of an early transcriber. They are evidently an inexact quotation from Gen. ii. 23, the next verse being quoted from Gen. ii. 24.

v. 32. The exact bearing of this verse on the argument has been much disputed. It seems probable that the sense is, 'These words, even as they occur in Genesis, convey an important revelation (about the meaning of human love); for us Christians they have a still deeper meaning (since human love illustrates our relation to Christ).'

reckless; you must grasp what the Lord's will is for you. 18 Do not besot yourselves with wine; that leads to ruin. Let your contentment be in the Holy Spirit; 19 your tongues unloosed in psalms and hymns and spiritual music, as you sing and give praise to the Lord in your hearts. 20 Give thanks continually to God, who is our Father, in the name of our Lord Jesus Christ; 21 and, as you stand in awe of Christ, submit to each other's rights. 22 Wives must obey their husbands as they would obey the Lord. 23 The man is the head to which the woman's body is united, just as Christ is the head of the Church, he, the Saviour on whom the safety of his body depends; 24 and women must owe obedience at all points to their husbands, as the Church does to Christ. 25 You who are husbands must shew love to your wives, as Christ shewed love to the Church when he gave himself up on its behalf. 26 He would hallow it, purify it by bathing it in the water to which his word gave life, 27 he would summon it into his own presence, the Church in all its beauty, no stain, no wrinkle, no such disfigurement; it was to be holy, it was to be spotless. 28 And that is how husband ought to love wife, as if she were his own body; in loving his wife, a man is but loving himself. 29 It is unheard of, that a man should bear ill-will to his own flesh and blood; no, he keeps it fed and warmed; and so it is with Christ and his Church; 30 we are limbs of his body; flesh and bone, we belong to him. 31 That is why a man will leave his father and mother and will cling to his wife, and the two will become one flesh. 32 Yes, those words are a high mystery, and I am applying them here to Christ and his Church. 33 Meanwhile, each of you is to love his wife as he would love himself, and the wife is to pay reverence to her husband.

366

THE CRUCIFIXION   HUBERT VAN EYCK

METROPOLITAN MUSEUM, NEW YORK

Chapter Six

Y OU WHO ARE CHIL dren must shew obedience in the Lord to your parents; it is your duty; 2 Honour thy father and thy mother—that is the first commandment which has a promise attached to it, 3 So it shall go well with thee, and thou shalt live long to enjoy the land. 4 You who are fathers, do not rouse your children to resentment; the training, the discipline in which you bring them up must come from the Lord. 5 You who are slaves, give your human masters the obedience you owe to Christ, in anxious fear, single-mindedly; 6 not with that show of service which tries to win human favour, but in the character of Christ's slaves, who do what is God's will with all their heart. 7 Yours must be a slavery of love, not to men, but to the Lord; 8 you know well that each of us, slave or free, will be repaid by the Lord for every task well done. 9 And you who are masters, deal with them accordingly; there is no need to threaten them; you know well enough that you and they have a Master in heaven, who makes no distinction between man and man.

10 I have no more to say, brethren, except this; draw your strength from the Lord, from that mastery which his power supplies. 11 You must wear all the weapons in God's armoury, if you would find strength to resist the cunning of the devil. 12 It is not against flesh and blood that we enter the lists; we have to do with princedoms and powers, with those who have mastery of the world in these dark days, with malign influences in an order higher than ours. 13 Take up all God's armour, then; so you will be able to stand your ground when the evil time comes, and be found still on your feet, when all the task is over. 14 Stand fast, your loins girt with truth, the breastplate of justice fitted on, 15 and your feet shod in readiness to publish the gospel of peace. 16 With all this, take up the shield of faith, with which you will be able to quench all the fire-tipped arrows of your wicked enemy; 17 make the helmet of salvation your own, and the sword of the spirit, God's word. 18 Use every kind of prayer and supplication; pray at all

vv. 14-17. Cf. Is. xi. 5, lix. 17, Wisdom v. 19.

v. 15. 'Readiness to publish the gospel of peace'; other renderings have been suggested here, but it seems most probable that St. Paul, with characteristic independence of his metaphor, is recalling the language of Is. lii. 7.

v. 17. It is not certain whether the clause 'which is God's utterance' refers to the 'sword of the spirit', or whether we should print 'Spirit' with a capital, and understand St. Paul to describe the Holy Spirit as God's utterance. If we take 'the spirit' as meaning 'the spiritual life' in general, it is possible that he is telling the Ephesians to arm themselves with the word (or message) of God, which acts upon the spirit like a sword (cf. Heb. iv. 12). But the sense of interpreters is greatly divided over this passage.

v. 18. Here again it

367

times in the spirit; keep awake to that end with all perseverence; offer your supplication for all the saints. 19 Pray for me too, that I may be given words to speak my mind boldly, in making known the gospel revelation, 20 for which I am an ambassador in chains; that I may have boldness to speak as I ought. 21 If you would know more of my circumstances, my occupations, you may learn all that from Tychicus, my dearly loved brother and faithful servant in the Lord; 22 that is the reason why I have sent him, to let you have news of me, and to bring courage to your hearts. 23 Peace to the brethren, and love joined with faith, from God the Father and our Lord Jesus Christ. 24 Grace be with all those who love our Lord Jesus Christ with an immortal love. Amen.

would be possible to print 'in the Spirit'; if so, 'keep awake to that end' might also be rendered, 'keep watchful in him'.

THE EPISTLE OF THE BLESSED APOSTLE PAUL TO THE PHILIPPIANS

Chapter One

PAUL AND TIMOTHY, the servants of Jesus Christ, to all the saints in Christ Jesus that are at Philippi, with their pastors and deacons; 2 Grace and peace be yours from God who is our Father, and from the Lord Jesus Christ. 3 I give thanks to my God for all my memories of you, 4 happy at all times in all the prayer I offer for all of you; 5 so full a part have you taken in the work of Christ's gospel, from the day when it first reached you till now. 6 Nor am I less confident, that he who has inspired this generosity in you will bring it to perfection, ready for the day when Jesus Christ comes. 7 It is only fitting that I should entertain such hopes for you; you are close to my heart, and I know that you all share my happiness in being a prisoner, and being able to defend and assert the truth of the gospel. 8 God knows how I long for you all, with the tenderness of Jesus Christ himself. 9 And this is my prayer for you; may your love grow richer and richer yet, in the fulness of its knowledge and the depth of its perception, 10 so that you may learn to prize what is of value; may nothing cloud your conscience or hinder your progress till the day when Christ

v. 1. The word here translated 'pastors' is episcopi, that is, bishops. But, here as in Acts xx. 28, it is difficult to see how St. Paul can have been addressing more than one 'bishop' in the modern sense; and it is the opinion of St. Chrysostom that the title is used loosely so as to include the presbyters of Philippi.

v. 3. 'For all my memories of you'; the Greek here might, however, mean 'for all your mindfulness of me'.

v. 6. 'Inspired this generosity in you'; literally 'begun a good work in you', but it seems likely that the work referred to is not God's own operation, but the charitable work of the Philippians *themselves, as shewn by the contribution they had made to St. Paul's own needs (cf. II Cor. viii. 6, where the same verbs are used).*

v. 7. 'You are close to my heart'; the Greek might mean 'I am close to your heart'.

v. 11. 'The full harvest of your justification'; or perhaps, 'a full harvest of holiness'.

v. 13. 'Praetorium'; it is not certain, who were St. Paul's gaolers at Rome, but the word praetorium seems to mean a body of soldiers, or their barracks, not the palace of the Roman Emperor.

comes; 11 may you reap, through Jesus Christ, the full harvest of your justification to God's glory and praise.

12 I hasten to assure you, brethren, that my circumstances here have only had the effect of spreading the gospel further; 13 so widely has my imprisonment become known, in Christ's honour, throughout the praetorium and to all the world beyond. 14 And most of the brethren, deriving fresh confidence in the Lord from my imprisonment, are making bold to preach God's word with more freedom than ever. 15 Some of them, it is true, for no better reason than rivalry or jealousy; but there are others who really proclaim Christ out of goodwill. 16 Some, I mean, are moved by charity, because they recognize that I am here to defend the gospel, 17 others by party spirit, proclaiming Christ from wrong motives, just because they hope to make my chains gall me worse. 18 What matter, so long as either way, for private ends or in all honesty, Christ is proclaimed? Of that I am glad now; yes, and I shall be glad hereafter; 19 I am well assured that this will make for my soul's health, with you to pray for me, and Jesus Christ to supply my needs with his Spirit. 20 This is my earnest longing and my hope, that I shall never be put to the blush; that I shall speak with entire freedom, and so this body of mine will do Christ honour, now as always, in life or in death. 21 For me, life means Christ; death is a prize to be won. 22 But what if living on in this mortal body is the only way to harvest what I have sown? Thus I cannot tell what to choose; 23 I am hemmed in on both sides. I long to have done with it, and be with Christ, a better thing, much more than a better thing; 24 and yet, for your sakes, that I should wait in the body is more urgent still. 25 I am certain of that, and I do not doubt that I shall wait, and wait upon you all, to the happy furtherance of your faith. 26 Yes, you shall be prouder of me than ever in Christ Jesus, when I come once again to visit you.

27 Only, you must play a part worthy of Christ's gospel; whether I come to see you, or only hear about you at a distance, this must be my news of you, that you are standing fast in a common unity of spirit, with the faith of the gospel for your common cause. 28 Shew a bold front at all points to your adversaries; that is the seal of their perdition, of your salvation, and it comes from God; 29 the grace that has been granted you is that of suffering for Christ's sake, not merely believing in him. 30 Your battle is my own battle; you saw how I fought it once, and you have heard how I am fighting it now.

Chapter Two

IF anything is meant by encouragement in Christ, by loving sympathy, by common fellowship in the spirit, by feelings of tenderness and pity, 2 fill up my cup of happiness by thinking with the same mind, cherishing the same bond of charity, soul knit to soul in a common unity of thought. 3 You must never act in a spirit of factiousness, or of ambition; each of you must have the humility to think others better men than himself, 4 and study the welfare of others, not his own. 5 Yours is to be the same mind which Christ Jesus shewed. 6 His nature is, from the first, divine, and yet he did not see, in the rank of Godhead, a prize to be coveted; 7 he dispossessed himself, and took the nature of a slave, fashioned in the likeness of men, and presenting himself to us in human form; 8 and then he lowered his own dignity, accepted an obedience which brought him to death, death on a cross. 9 That is why God has raised him to such a height, given him that name which is greater than any other name; 10 so that everything in heaven and on earth and under the earth must bend the knee before the name of Jesus, 11 and every tongue must confess Jesus Christ as the Lord, dwelling in the glory of God the Father.

v. 6. 'Did not see, in the rank of Godhead, a prize to be coveted'; others would render, 'thought it no usurpation to claim the rank of Godhead'.

v. 11. 'Dwelling in the glory'; the Greek is perhaps more naturally rendered 'to the glory'.

12 Beloved, you have always shewn yourselves obedient; and now that I am at a distance, not less but much more than when I am present, you must work to earn your salvation, in anxious fear. 13 Both the will to do it and the accomplishment of that will are something which God accomplishes in you, to carry out his loving purpose. 14 Do all that lies in you, never complaining, never hesitating, 15 to shew yourselves innocent and single-minded, God's children, bringing no reproach on his name. You live in an age that is twisted out of its true pattern, and among such people you shine out, beacons to the world, 16 upholding the message of life. Thus, when the day of Christ comes, I shall be able to boast of a life not spent in vain, of labours not vainly undergone. 17 Meanwhile, though your faith should prove to be a sacrifice which cannot be duly made without my blood for its drink-offering, I congratulate myself and all of you over that; 18 on your side, you too must congratulate yourselves and me.

19 It is my hope in the Lord Jesus that I shall be sending Timothy

v. 20. 'Who shares my thoughts as he does'; the Greek would also bear the meaning, 'who has a heart like his'.

v. 22. 'You must know'; the Latin represents this as if the apostle were informing the Philippians of something they did not know, but the Greek may equally well imply that it was something they knew already.

to visit you before long; then I shall be able to refresh myself with news of you; 20 I have no one else here who shares my thoughts as he does, no one who will concern himself so unaffectedly with your affairs; 21 one and all have their own interest at heart, not Christ's; 22 his worth is well tried, you must know that he has shared my task of preaching the gospel like a son helping his father. 23 Him, then, I hope to send without delay, when I have had time to see how I stand; 24 and I am persuaded in the Lord that I myself shall be coming to you before long. 25 Meanwhile, here is Epaphroditus, my brother, my companion in so many labours and battles, your own delegate, who has provided for my needs. I felt that I must send him to you, 26 so great was his longing to see you, and his distress that you should have heard about his illness. 27 Ill he certainly was, and in near danger of death; but God had pity on him, and not only on him but on me too; he would not let me have anxiety added to anxiety. 28 So I am hastening to send him back to you; it will be a happiness for you to see him again, and I shall be anxious no longer. 29 Welcome him, then, in the Lord gladly, and do honour to such a man as he is; 30 one who came close to death's door on Christ's errand, risking life itself to do me that kindness, which was all your kindness left to be desired.

Chapter Three

vv. 1, 2. The apostle seems here to embark on a farewell salutation (cf. II Cor. xiii. 11), as if the remaining two chapters of the epistle were an afterthought. It seems to

AND NOW, BRETHREN, joy to you in the Lord. I find no difficulty in always writing the same message to you, and it is your safeguard. 2 Beware of these prowling dogs, beware of their evil practices, of their disfigurement. 3 As for circumcision, it is we who practise it, we who serve God with the spirit, and take pride in Jesus Christ, instead of putting our trust in outward ob-

PHILIPPIANS

servances. 4 Not that I have no outward claims to give me confidence; if others put their trust in outward claims, I can do so with better reason. 5 I was circumcised seven days after I was born; I come from the stock of Israel, from the tribe of Benjamin, Hebrew-speaking as my parents were before me. Over the law, I was a Pharisee; 6 to prove my loyalty, I persecuted the Church of God; in observing what the law commands, I was beyond reproach. 7 And all this, which once stood to my credit, I now write down as loss, for the love of Christ. 8 For that matter, there is nothing I do not write down as loss compared with the high privilege of knowing Christ Jesus, my Lord; for love of him I have lost everything, treat everything else as refuse, if I may have Christ to my credit. 9 In him I would render my account, not claiming any justification that is my own work, given me by the law, but the justification that comes from believing in Jesus Christ, God's gift on condition of our faith. 10 Him I would learn to know, and the virtue of his resurrection, and what it means to share his sufferings, moulded into the pattern of his death, 11 in the hope of achieving resurrection from the dead.

12 Not that I have already won the prize, already reached fulfilment. I only press on, in hope of winning the mastery, as Christ Jesus has won the mastery over me. 13 No, brethren, I do not claim to have the mastery already, but this at least I do; forgetting what I have left behind, intent on what lies before me, I press on with the goal in view, 14 eager for the prize, God's heavenly summons in Christ Jesus. 15 All of us who are fully grounded must be of this mind, and God will make it known to you, if you are of a different mind at present. 16 Meanwhile, let us all be of the same mind, all follow the same rule, according to the progress we have made. 17 Be content, brethren, to follow my example, and mark well those who live by the pattern we have given them; 18 I have told you often, and now tell you again with tears, that there are many whose lives make them the enemies of Christ's cross. 19 Perdition is the end that awaits them, their own hungry bellies are the god they worship, their own shameful doings are their pride; their minds are set on the things of earth; 20 whereas we find our true home in heaven. It is to heaven that we look expectantly for the coming of our Lord Jesus Christ to save us; 21 he will form this humbled body of ours anew, moulding it into the image of his glorified body, so effective is his power to make all things obey him.

be implied here that he had written to the Philippians before, and in doing so had used the curious formula given in verse 2. This becomes more easily intelligible if we suppose that verse 2 was written in autograph (cf. I Cor. xvi. 21, Gal. vi. 11). It warns the Philippians against those who were trying to impose the rite of circumcision on the Gentiles; circumcision, as being a merely outward ceremony, is contemptuously referred to under the name of 'disfigurement', a heathen usage forbidden by the Jewish law (Lev. xxi. 5).

v. 9. 'I would render my account'; literally, 'I would be discovered', cf. I Cor. iv. 2.

v. 12. 'Has won the mastery over me'; this is generally understood as meaning 'taken possession of me', which seems to be the sense of the Latin. The Greek might also be translated 'has overtaken me', in the sense that our Lord has led the way in undergoing death and attaining resurrection.

v. 16. The words 'all be of the same mind' do not appear in the best Greek manuscripts.

373

Chapter Four

HEN, O my brethren, so greatly loved and longed for, all my delight and prize, stand firmly in the Lord, beloved, as I bid you. 2 I call upon thee, Evodia, and I call upon thee, Syntyche, to make common cause in the Lord. 3 Yes, and I ask thee, who sharest the yoke so loyally, to take part with them; they have worked for the gospel at my side, as much as Clement and those other fellow labourers of mine, whose names are recorded in the book of life. 4 Joy to you in the Lord at all times; once again I wish you joy. 5 Give proof to all of your courtesy. The Lord is near. 6 Nothing must make you anxious; in every need make your requests known to God, praying and beseeching him, and giving him thanks as well. 7 So may the peace of God, which surpasses all our thinking, watch over your hearts and minds in Christ Jesus. 8 And now, brethren, all that rings true, all that commands reverence, and all that makes for right; all that is pure, all that is lovely, all that is gracious in the telling; virtue and merit, wherever virtue and merit are found—let this be the argument of your thoughts. 9 The lessons I taught you, the traditions I handed on to you, all you have heard and seen of my way of living—let this be your rule of conduct. Then the God of peace will be with you.

10 It has been a great happiness to me in the Lord that your remembrance of me should have blossomed out afresh. It has flowered late, but then, you had never forgotten me; it was only that you lacked opportunity. 11 I am not thinking of my own want; I have learned by now to be content with my circumstances as they are. 12 I know what it is to be brought low, and what it is to have abundant means; I have been apprenticed to everything, having my fill and going hungry, living in plenty and living in want; 13 nothing is beyond my powers, thanks to the strength God gives me. 14 No, but it was kindness in you to share my hardships in this way. 15 You remember, Philippians, as well as I do, that when I left Macedonia in those early days of gospel preaching, yours was the only church whose sympathy with me meant alms given and received; 16 not once but twice, when I was at Thessalonica, you contributed to my needs. 17 It is not that I set store by your alms; I set store by the rich increase that stands to your credit. 18 I am

v. 3. The 'yokefellow' may possibly have been the husband of Evodia or of Syntyche; but more probably it means either Epaphroditus, who carried the letter, or some leading Christian among the apostle's readers.

v. 5. 'The Lord is near'; this phrase, which does not fit in closely with the context, was perhaps a kind of Christian pass-word, that might be recalled in writing the last lines of a letter, cf. I Cor. xvi. 22.

374

CHRIST ON THE CROSS   ROGER VAN DER WEYDEN
                                                              circa 1400-1464

COURTESY OF THE JOHNSON COLLECTION, PHILADELPHIA

content, more than content; I am fully endowed, ever since Epaphroditus brought me your gift, a sacrifice that breathes out fragrance, winning favour with God. 19 So may he, the God I serve, supply every need of yours; he has treasures of glory laid up in Jesus Christ. 20 Glory to God, who is our Father, for ever and ever, Amen. 21 Greet all the saints in Christ Jesus. 22 The brethren who are with me send you their greeting; greeting, too, from all the saints, especially those who belong to the Emperor's household. 23 The grace of our Lord Jesus Christ be with your spirit, Amen.

THE EPISTLE OF THE BLESSED APOSTLE PAUL TO THE COLOSSIANS

Chapter One

FROM PAUL, BY GOD'S purpose an apostle of Jesus Christ, and Timothy who is their brother, 2 to the saints at Colossae, our brethren who believe in Jesus Christ, 3 grace be yours and peace from God, our Father, and the Lord Jesus Christ. We give thanks to God, the Father of our Lord Jesus Christ, continually in our prayers for you, 4 when we are told of your faith in Jesus Christ, and the love which you shew to all the saints; 5 such hope have you of what awaits you in heaven. Hope was the lesson you learned from that truth-giving message of the Gospel 6 which has reached you, which now bears fruit and thrives in you, as it does all the world over, since the day when you heard of God's grace and recognized it for what it is. 7 Your teacher was Epaphras, for us, a well-loved fellow bondsman, and for you a loyal minister of Jesus Christ; 8 and it is he who has told us of this love which you cherish in the Spirit. 9 So, ever since the news reached us, we have been praying for you in return, unceasingly. Our prayer is, that you may be filled with that closer knowledge of God's will which brings all wisdom and all spiritual insight with

v. 7: 'Fellow bondsman'; that is, probably, in the service of Christ, but the word may imply that Epaphras was sharing, in a manner, the Apostle's imprisonment.

376

it. 10 May you live as befits his servants, waiting continually on his pleasure; may the closer knowledge of God bring you fruitfulness and growth in all good. 11 May you be inspired, as his glorious power can inspire you, with full strength to be patient and to endure; to endure joyfully, 12 thanking God our Father for making us fit to share the light which saints inherit, 13 for rescuing us from the power of darkness, and transferring us to the kingdom of his beloved Son.

14 In the Son of God, in his blood, we find the redemption that sets us free from our sins. 15 He is the true likeness of the God we cannot see; his is that first birth which precedes every act of creation. 16 Yes, in him all created things took their being, heavenly and earthly, visible and invisible; what are thrones and dominions, what are princedoms and powers? They were all created through him and in him; 17 he takes precedence of all, and in him all subsist. 18 He too is that head whose body is the Church; it begins with him, since his was the first birth out of death; thus in every way the primacy was to become his. 19 It was God's good pleasure to let all completeness dwell in him, 20 and through him to win back all things, whether on earth or in heaven, into union with himself, making peace with them through his blood, shed on the cross. 21 You, too, were once estranged from him; your minds were alienated from him by a life of sin; 22 but now he has used Christ's natural body to win you back through his death, and so to bring you into his presence, holy, and spotless, and unreproved. 23 But that means that you must be true to your faith, grounded in it, firmly established in it; nothing must shift you away from the hope you found in the gospel you once listened to. It is a gospel which has been preached to all creation under heaven, and I, Paul, have been brought into its service.

24 Even as I write, I am glad of my sufferings on your behalf, as, in this mortal frame of mine, I help to pay off the debt which the afflictions of Christ leave still to be paid, for the sake of his body, the Church. 25 When I entered its service, I received a commission from God for the benefit of you Gentiles, to complete the preaching of his word among you. 26 This was the secret that had been hidden from all the ages and generations of the past; now, he has revealed it to his saints, 27 wishing to make known the manifold splendour of this secret among the Gentiles—Christ among you, your hope of glory. 28 Him, then, we proclaim, warning every human being and instructing every human being as wisely as we may, so as to exhibit every human being perfect in Christ Jesus.

v. 12. 'Fit', according to the Latin, means 'worthy', but the Greek has rather the sense of 'capable'.

v. 15. 'His is that first birth'; literally, 'he is the first-born of all (or, every) creation'; the rendering given assumes that St. Paul is talking of Christ as God. It is possible that he meant that Christ as Man enjoys primacy over the rest of creation.

v. 16. 'In him', at the end of the verse, should rather be translated 'for him' (literally 'into him') if we follow the Greek.

v. 18. 'His was the first birth out of death'; literally, 'he is the first-born from the dead'. Christ as Man is the Head of a new creation, the Church of the redeemed.

v. 19. 'All completeness'; it is not certain whether we should understand this of the Divine essence, or of a plenitude of graces, or of mankind, and indeed creation as a whole, as mystically identified with Christ.

v. 20. 'With himself' may refer to God the Father, or (like the other pronouns in the sentence) to our Lord.

v. 24. 'The afflictions of Christ' have been understood by some commentators as being those which he suffers in his members, i.e. the Church (cf. Acts ix. 4), and particularly in St. Paul himself. But the Greek verb shews that St. Paul only represents himself as taking a share in the afflictions here referred to; and probably the metaphor is that of a poor man contributing to pay off a sum which a richer man has paid in advance. Thus the obvious meaning is that Christ's sufferings, although fully satisfactory on behalf of our sins, leave us under a debt of honour, as it were, to repay *them by sufferings of our own.*

v. 25. The word 'Gentiles' is not expressed in the Greek or in the Latin, but has been supplied here in order to bring out what is clearly the sense; St. Paul is not thinking of the Colossians in particular, who were not his own converts. 'To complete the preaching', that is, to supplement the teaching of other missionaries, who had gone to the Jews only; cf. Rom. xv. 19. v. 27. The Greek here is usually rendered 'to whom he wished to make known the manifold splendour of this secret among the Gentiles'; but this is to repeat what has already been said in the preceding verse, and the words 'among the Gentiles' have no real force, since the secret (that of the universality of Christ's Church) obviously applied to them, not to anybody else. The same Greek words may also be taken as meaning '(the saints) whom he wished to publish among the Gentiles the manifold splendour of this secret', which seems to give a better sense.

29 It is for this that I labour, for this that I strive so anxiously; and with effect, so effectually does his power manifest itself in me.

Chapter Two

AND indeed, I must let you know what anxiety I feel over you, and the Laodiceans, and those others who have never seen me in person. 2 I would bring courage to their hearts; I would see them well ordered in love, enriched in every way with fuller understanding, so as to penetrate the secret revealed to us by God the Father, and by Jesus Christ, 3 in whom the whole treasury of wisdom and knowledge is stored up. 4 I tell you this, for fear that somebody may lead you astray with high-flown talk. 5 In person, I am far away from you, but I am with you in spirit; and I rejoice to see how well disciplined you are, how firm is your faith in Christ. 6 Go on, then, ordering your lives in Christ Jesus our Lord, according to the tradition you have received of him. 7 You are to be rooted in him, built up on him, your faith established in the teaching you have received, overflowing with gratitude. 8 Take care not to let anyone cheat you with his philosophizings, with empty phantasies drawn from human tradition, from worldly principles; they were never Christ's teaching. 9 In Christ the whole plenitude of Deity is embodied, and dwells in him, 10 and it is in him that you find your completion; he is the fountain head from which all dominion and power proceed. 11 In him you have been circumcised with a circumcision that was not man's handiwork. It was effected, not by despoiling the natural body, but by Christ's circumcision; 12 you, by baptism, have been united with his burial, united, too, with his resurrection, through your faith in that exercise of power by which God raised him from the dead. 13 And in

v. 2. The Greek manuscripts, and many of the Latin, have 'by God, the Father of Jesus Christ.'

v. 7. At the end of this verse, some Latin manuscripts add the words 'in him'; others 'in it' (meaning the faith), which is the sense of the Greek.

v. 8. 'Worldly principles'; cf. note on Gal. iv. 3. Here, as there, some commentators hold that St. Paul is referring to the elements (the sun, moon, stars, etc.) which were worshipped by the heathen; others, with more probability, that he is thinking of Jewish ordinances, like circumcision, as the first rudimentary lessons which mankind took in religion. But the refer-

378

giving life to him, he gave life to you too, when you lay dead in your sins, with nature all uncircumcised in you. 14 He condoned all your sins; cancelled the deed which excluded us, the decree made to our prejudice, swept it out of the way, by nailing it to the cross; 15 and the dominions and powers he robbed of their prey, put them to an open shame, led them away in triumph, through him. 16 So no one must be allowed to take you to task over what you eat or drink, or in the matter of observing feasts, and new moons, and sabbath days; 17 all these were but shadows cast by future events, the reality is found in Christ. 18 You must not allow any one to cheat you by insisting on a false humility which addresses its worship to angels. Such a man takes his stand upon false visions; his is the ill-founded confidence that comes of human speculation. 19 He is not united to that head of ours, on whom all the body depends, supplied and unified by joint and ligament, and so growing up with a growth which is divine. 20 If, by dying with Christ, you have parted company with worldly principles, why do you live by these prescriptions, as if the world were still your element? 21 Prescriptions against touching, or tasting, or handling those creatures which vanish altogether as we enjoy them, all based on the will and the word of men? 22 They will win you, no doubt, the name of philosophers, for being so full of scruple, so submissive, so unsparing of your bodies; but they are all forgotten, when nature asks to be gratified.

ence, both here and in v. 20 below, may be more general.

v. 11. 'By Christ's circumcision'; that is, either the circumcision of our Lord in his infancy, here regarded as mystically efficacious on our behalf, or the spiritual circumcision which he bestows on us by Baptism into his Death. The Greek manuscripts have 'It was effected by the despoiling of the natural body, by the circumcision of Christ'; it is not clear in what sense.

vv. 14 and 15. It is not certain whether the subject here is meant to be God, or Christ himself; the translation given assumes that the former view is right. The 'deed which excluded us' is the ceremonial law of Moses, which now no longer stands as a barrier between Jew and Gentile (cf. Eph. ii. 15). This law was mediated by angels (Gal. iii. 19), and these angels, whom the false teachers at Colossae worship as 'dominions and powers' are here represented as having been relieved of their duty as its custodians, and

deputed to attend, instead, on the triumphal progress of the risen Christ. 'Through him' at the end of v. 15 might (according to the Greek) be translated 'through it', i.e. the Cross. v. 23. It is possible to understand this verse in the Greek quite differently, 'They are in accordance with right reason, when they shew a willing piety, a true humility, a determination not to spare the body; but often the motive is simply to gratify natural vanity.'

Chapter Three

ISEN, then, with Christ, you must lift your thoughts above, where Christ now sits at the right hand of God. 2 You must be heavenly-minded, not earthly-minded; 3 you have undergone death, and your life is hidden away now with Christ in God. 4 Christ is your life, and when he is made manifest, you too will be made manifest in glory with him. 5 You must deaden, then, those passions in you

379

which belong to earth, fornication and impurity, lust and evil desire, and that love of money which is an idolatry. 6 These are what brings down God's vengeance on the unbelievers, 7 and such was your own behaviour, too, while you lived among them. 8 Now it is your turn to have done with it all, resentment, anger, spite, insults, foul-mouthed utterance; 9 and do not tell lies at one another's expense. You must be quit of the old self, and the habits that went with it; 10 you must be clothed in the new self, that is being refitted all the time for closer knowledge, so that the image of the God who created it is its pattern. 11 Here is no more Gentile and Jew, no more circumcised and uncircumcised; no one is barbarian, or Scythian, no one is slave or free man; there is nothing but Christ in any of us. 12 You are God's chosen people, holy and well beloved; the livery you wear must be tender compassion, kindness, humility, gentleness and patience; 13 you must bear with one another's faults, be generous to each other, where somebody has given grounds for complaint; the Lord's generosity to you must be the model of yours. 14 And, to crown all this, charity; that is the bond which makes us perfect. 15 So may the peace of Christ, the very condition of your calling as members of a single body, reign in your hearts. Learn, too, to be grateful. 16 May all the wealth of Christ's inspiration have its shrine among you; now you will have instruction and advice for one another, full of wisdom, now there will be psalms, and hymns, and spiritual music, as you sing with gratitude in your hearts to God. 17 Whatever you are about, in word and action alike, invoke always the name of the Lord Jesus Christ, offering your thanks to God the Father through him.

18 Wives must be submissive to their husbands, as the service of the Lord demands; 19 and you, husbands, treat your wives lovingly, do not grow harsh with them. 20 Children must be obedient to their parents in every way; it is a gracious sign of serving the Lord; 21 and you, parents, must not rouse your children to resentment, or you will break their spirits. 22 You who are slaves, give your human masters full obedience, not with that show of service which tries to win human favour, but single-mindedly, in fear of the Lord. 23 Work at all your tasks with a will, reminding yourselves that you are doing it for the Lord, not for men; 24 and you may be sure that the Lord will give the portion he has allotted you in return. Be slaves with Christ for your Master. 25 Whoever does wrong will be requited for the wrong done; there are no human preferences with God.

v. 9. It is not certain whether St. Paul is thinking here of deceiving people, or of taking away their characters.

v. 16. Some take 'Christ's word' as referring to the gospel; but it seems more likely that the apostle is thinking of Christ as inspiring the utterances of the faithful.

Chapter Four

ND you who are masters, give your slaves just and equitable treatment; you know well enough that you, too, have a Master in heaven.

2 Persevere in prayer, and keep wakeful over it with thankful hearts. 3 Pray, too, for us; ask God to afford us an opening for preaching the revelation of Christ, which is the very cause of my imprisonment, 4 and to give me the right utterance for making it known. 5 Be prudent in your behaviour towards those who are not of your company; it is an opportunity you must eagerly grasp. 6 Your manner of speaking must always be gracious, with an edge of liveliness, ready to give each questioner the right answer. 7 You will hear how things go with me from Tychicus, my dearly loved brother and faithful servant, my fellow bondsman in the Lord; 8 that is the reason why I have sent him, to give me news of you, and to bring courage to your hearts; 9 from Onesimus, too, a brother faithful and well beloved, who is of your own number; they will tell you how things stand here.

10 Greetings to you from my fellow prisoner Aristarchus, and from Mark, the kinsman of Barnabas, about whom you have been given instructions; if he visits you, make him welcome; 11 from Jesus, too, whom they call Justus. These are the only Jews who have helped me to preach God's kingdom; they have been a comfort to me. 12 Your own fellow countryman Epaphras sends you his greeting, a servant of Jesus Christ who ever remembers you anxiously in his prayers, hoping that you will stand firm in the perfect achievement of all that is God's will for you; 13 I can vouch for him as one who is greatly concerned over you, and those others at Laodicea and Hierapolis. 14 Greetings from my beloved Luke, the physician, and from Demas. 15 Greet the brethren at Laodicea, and Nymphas, with the church that is in his household. 16 When this letter has been read out to you, see that it is read out to the Laodicean church too, and that you read the letter they have received at Laodicea. 17 Give this message to Archippus; be careful to fulfil the duty which has been committed to thee in the Lord's service. 18 Here is a greeting for you from Paul in his own hand; do not forget that he is a prisoner. Grace be with you. Amen.

v. 6. 'With an edge of liveliness'; literally, 'seasoned with salt', that being the ancient expression for conversation, etc. which was not dull or insipid.

v. 8. 'To give me news of you'; according to some manuscripts, 'to let you have news of me'.
v. 9. For Onesimus, cf. the letter to Philemon.

v. 11. 'The only Jews'; literally, 'the only persons belonging to the circumcision', but the phrase is evidently not used here, as it is used in Gal. ii. 12, to mean Christians who wished the Gentiles to be circumcised when they joined the Church.

THE FIRST EPISTLE OF THE BLESSED APOSTLE PAUL TO THE THESSALONIANS

Chapter One

PAUL AND SILVANUS and Timothy, to the church assembled at Thessalonica in God the Father and the Lord Jesus Christ, grace and peace be yours. 2 We give thanks to God always for all of you, making mention of you continually in our prayers; 3 such memories we have of your active faith, your unwearied love, and that hope in our Lord Jesus Christ which gives you endurance, in the sight of him who is our God and Father. 4 Brethren, God loves you, and we are sure that he has made choice of you. 5 Our preaching to you did not depend upon mere argument; power was there, and the influence of the Holy Spirit, and an effect of full conviction; you can testify what we were to you and what we did for you. 6 And on your side, you followed our example, the Lord's example. There was great persecution, and yet you welcomed our message, rejoicing in the Holy Spirit; 7 and now you have become a model to all the believers throughout Macedonia and Achaia. 8 Yes, the Lord's message has echoed out from you, and not only in Macedonia and Achaia; your faith in God has overflowed everywhere, so that we do not need to speak a word; 9 our

v. 8. 'Everywhere'; that is, in Thessaly, and perhaps also in Epirus and Illyricum (Rom. xv. 19); in

*continuing his jour-
ney towards 'the
coast', St. Paul may
well have travelled
in those parts before
he reached Athens
(Acts xvii. 15).*
*v. 9. 'Our friends';
in the original sim-
ply 'they', but evi-
dently the Apostle
has some definite per-*

friends themselves tell the story of our journey, and how we first
came among you. They describe how you have turned away from
idolatry to the worship of God, so as to serve a living God, a God
who really exists, 10 and to wait for the appearing of his Son from
heaven, Jesus, whom he raised from the dead, our Saviour from the
vengeance that is to come.

*sons in mind. It seems simplest to suppose that these were the Christians from Macedonia who escorted him on the
journey which finished up at Athens (Acts xvii. 15). It is usually understood to mean 'people' generally in Thessaly, etc.; but it is difficult to see how these persons should have heard the story of St. Paul's earlier travels, or
why they should have been at pains to describe them to St. Paul himself. It is more natural to suppose that it was
friends from Thessalonica, travelling in St. Paul's company, who spread the story of his earlier preaching wherever
they went. Two Thessalonians are St. Paul's travelling companions in Acts xx. 4.*

Chapter Two

*v. 2. 'With great
earnestness'; the
Greek might also
mean, 'amid much
opposition', cf. Acts
xvii. 13.*

YES, BRETHREN, YOU
yourselves can testify that when
we arrived among you, it proved to be no fruitless visit. 2 We had
been ill treated and insulted, as you know, at Philippi, but our God
gave us courage to preach the divine gospel to you with great
earnestness. 3 Our appeal to you was not based on any false or
degraded notions, was not backed by cajolery. 4 We have passed
God's scrutiny, and he has seen fit to entrust us with the work of
preaching; when we speak, it is with this in view; we would earn
God's good opinion, not man's, since it is God who scrutinizes our
hearts. 5 We never used the language of flattery, you will bear us
out in that, nor was it, God knows, an excuse for enriching ourselves; we have never asked for human praise, yours or another's,

*v. 6. 'Made heavy
demands on you';
some think the Greek
means 'claimed im-
portance among you'.
v. 7. 'Innocent as
babes'; this is the
sense of the Latin,
but some of the best
Greek manuscripts
have 'gentle'.*

6 although, as apostles of Christ, we might have made heavy demands on you. 7 No, you found us innocent as babes in your
company; no nursing mother ever cherished her children more;
8 in our great longing for you, we desired nothing better than to
offer you our own lives, as well as God's gospel, so greatly had
we learned to love you. 9 Brethren, you can remember how we
toiled and laboured, all the time we were preaching God's gospel

to you, working day and night so as not to burden you with expense. 10 Both you and God can witness how upright and honest and faultless was our conduct towards you believers; 11 it is within your knowledge that we treated every one of you as a father treats his children, 12 encouraging you, comforting you, imploring you to lead a life worthy of the God who now invites you to the glory of his kingdom. 13 This is why we give thanks to God unceasingly that, when we delivered the divine message to you, you recognized it for what it is, God's message, not man's; it is God, after all, who manifests his power in you that have learned to believe. 14 You took for your model, brethren, the churches of God which are assembled in Judaea in the name of Jesus Christ. You were treated by your own fellow countrymen as those churches were treated by the Jews, 15 the men who killed the Lord Jesus and the prophets, and persecuted us; the men who displease God and shew themselves the enemies of mankind, 16 when they try to hinder us from preaching salvation to the Gentiles. They must always be filling up the measure of their sins, and now it is God's final vengeance that has fallen upon them.

17 Finding ourselves separated from you, brethren, even for a little while, though only in person, not in spirit, we conceived an overwhelming desire to visit you in person, such was our longing for you; 18 and we planned a journey to you, I myself, Paul, more than once; but Satan has put obstacles in our way. 19 What hope or delight have we, what prize to boast of before our Lord Jesus Christ when he comes, if not you? 20 All our pride, all our delight is in you.

Chapter Three

T last we could not bear it any longer, and decided to remain at Athens by ourselves, 2 while we sent our brother Timothy, who exercises God's ministry in preaching the gospel of Christ, to confirm your resolution, and give you the encouragement your faith needed. 3 There must be no wavering amidst these trials; you know well enough that this is our appointed lot. 4 Indeed, when we visited

v. 1. It is doubtful whether this visit to Athens is the same as that mentioned in Acts xvii. 16.

you we told you that trials were to befall us; now you can see for yourselves that it was true. 5 That was my reason for sending him, when I could bear it no longer, to make sure of your faith; it might be that the tempter of souls had been tempting you, and that all our labour would go for nothing. 6 Now that Timothy has come back to us from seeing you, and told us about your faith and love, and the kind remembrance you have of us all the while, longing for our company as we long for yours, 7 your faith has brought us comfort, brethren, amidst all our difficulties and trials. 8 If only you stand firm in the Lord, it brings fresh life to us. 9 What thanks can we return to God for you, to express all the joy we feel in rejoicing over you in the presence of our God, 10 as we pray more than ever, night and day, for the opportunity of seeing you face to face, and making good whatever your faith still lacks? 11 May he himself, our God and our Father, may our Lord Jesus Christ speed us on our journey to you; 12 and as for you, may the Lord give you a rich and an ever richer love for one another and for all men, like ours for you. 13 So, when our Lord Jesus Christ comes with all his saints, may you stand boldly before the presence of God, our Father, in holiness unreproved. Amen.

Chapter Four

AND now, brethren, this is what we ask, this is our appeal to you in the name of the Lord Jesus. We gave you a pattern of how you ought to live so as to please God; live by that pattern, and make more of it than ever. 2 You have not forgotten the warnings we have handed on to you by the command of the Lord Jesus. 3 What God asks of you is that you should sanctify yourselves, and keep clear of fornication. 4 Each of you must learn to control his own body, as something holy and held in honour, 5 not yielding to the promptings of passion, as the heathen do in their ignorance of God. 6 None of you is to be exorbitant, and take advantage of his brother, in his business dealings. For all such wrong-doing God exacts punishment; we have told you so already, in solemn warning. 7 The life to which God has called us is not one of incontinence, it is a

v. 4. 'To control his own body'; literally, 'to take possession of his own vessel'. Some commentators think that the 'vessel' means a wife, and that St. Paul is encouraging the young men at Thessalonica to marry, instead of indulging their passions illicitly.
v. 6. It is probable that the apostle here

life of holiness, 8 and to despise it is to despise, not man, but God, the God who has implanted his Holy Spirit in us. 9 As for love of the brethren, there is no need to send you any message; you have learned for yourselves God's lesson about the charity we ought to shew to one another, 10 or you could not practise it as you do towards all the brethren throughout Macedonia. We would only ask you, brethren, to make more of it than ever. 11 Let it be a point of honour with you to keep calm and to go on looking after your affairs, working with your hands as we bade you; thus your life will win respect from the world around you, and you will not need to depend on others.

12 Make no mistake, brethren, about those who have gone to their rest; you are not to lament over them, as the rest of the world does, with no hope to live by. 13 We believe, after all, that Jesus underwent death and rose again; just so, when Jesus comes back, God will bring back those who have found rest through him. 14 This we can tell you as a message from the Lord himself; those of us who are still left alive to greet the Lord's coming will not reach the goal before those who have gone to their rest. 15 No, the Lord himself will come down from heaven to summon us, with an archangel crying aloud and the trumpet of God sounding; and first of all the dead will rise up, those who died in Christ. 16 Only after that shall we, who are still left alive, be taken up into the clouds, be swept away to meet Christ in the air, and they will bear us company. And so we shall be with the Lord for ever. 17 Tell one another this for your consolation.

goes on to another class of sins, those of fraud; but some think that he is still discussing the same subject, and has the sin of adultery in mind, 'None of you is to commit transgression, and to defraud his brother in this matter'.

v. 11. It seems likely from this verse that some of the Thessalonians, anticipating the immediate return of Christ, were not only giving away their possessions, but ceasing to carry on their ordinary business, for that reason (cf. II Thess. iii. 12). 'To depend on others' might also be translated, 'you will not stand in need of anything'.

v. 14. St. Paul uses the word 'we' here, not as implying that he or any of those to whom he is writing will necessarily be alive to witness the second Coming; he means by 'we' the living, at any given moment of history.

v. 16. This verse gives possibility, though not certainty, to the view that those who are alive at the second Coming will not experience death.

Chapter Five

 HERE is no need, brethren, to write to you about the times and the seasons of all this; 2 you are keeping it clearly in mind, without being told, that the day of the Lord will come like a thief in the night. 3 It is just when men are saying, All quiet, all safe, that doom will fall upon them suddenly, like the pangs that come to a woman in travail, and there will be no escape from it. 4 Whereas you, brethren, are not living in the darkness, for the day to take you by

surprise, like a thief; 5 no, you are all born to the light, born to the day; we do not belong to the night and its darkness. 6 We must not sleep on, then, like the rest of the world, we must watch and keep sober; 7 night is the sleeper's time for sleeping, the drunkard's time for drinking; 8 we must keep sober, like men of the daylight. We must put on our breastplate, the breastplate of faith and love, our helmet, which is the hope of salvation. 9 God has not destined us for vengeance; he means us to win salvation through our Lord Jesus Christ, 10 who has died for our sakes, that we, waking or sleeping, may find life with him. 11 Go on, then, encouraging one another and building up one another's faith.

12 Brethren, we would ask you to pay deference to those who work among you, those who have charge of you in the Lord, and give you directions; 13 make it a rule of charity to hold them in special esteem, in honour of the duty they perform, and maintain unity with them. 14 And, brethren, let us make this appeal to you; warn the vagabonds, encourage the faint-hearted, support the waverers, be patient towards all. 15 See to it that nobody repays injury with injury; you must aim always at what is best, for one another and for all around you. 16 Joy be with you always. 17 Never cease praying. 18 Give thanks upon all occasions; this is what God expects of you all in Christ Jesus. 19 Do not stifle the utterances of the Spirit, 20 do not hold prophecy in low esteem; 21 and yet you must scrutinize it all carefully, retaining only what is good, 22 and rejecting all that has a look of evil about it. 23 So may the God of peace sanctify you wholly, keep spirit and soul and body unimpaired, to greet the coming of our Lord Jesus Christ without reproach. 24 The God who called you is true to his promise; he will not fail you. 25 Brethren, pray for us. 26 Greet all the brethren with the kiss of saints. 27 I adjure you in the Lord's name to see that this letter is read out to all our holy brethren. 28 The grace of our Lord Jesus Christ be with you, Amen.

v. 13. 'Maintain unity with them'; some Greek manuscripts read, 'among yourselves'.

vv. 14, 15. These verses are perhaps particularly directed to the authorities of the church, just mentioned.

vv. 21, 22. These verses probably refer to the utterances of the prophets in the Thessalonian church (cf. I Cor. xiv. 29), but their sense may be more general.

The Second Epistle of the Blessed Apostle Paul to the Thessalonians

Chapter One

PAUL AND SILVANUS and Timothy, to the church assembled at Thessalonica in God our Father, and the Lord Jesus Christ; 2 from God, our Father, and the Lord Jesus Christ, grace be yours and peace. 3 We owe a constant debt of thanksgiving to God, brethren, on your behalf; we have good reason for it, when your faith thrives so well, and your love for one another exceeds all measure; 4 our own boasting, as we visit the churches of God, is of your perseverance and your faith amidst all the persecutions and trials which you have to endure. 5 It will be a proof of the just award God makes, when he finds you worthy of a place in his kingdom, the kingdom for which you are prepared to suffer. 6 Or do you doubt that there is justice with God, to repay with affliction those who afflict you, 7 and you, the afflicted, with that rest which will be ours too? But that is for the day when the Lord Jesus appears from heaven, with angels to proclaim his power; 8 with fire flaming about him, as he pours out vengeance on those who do not acknowledge God, on those who refuse obedience to the gospel of our Lord Jesus Christ. 9 The presence of the Lord,

v. 9. Some commentators would prefer the rendering, 'They will be condemned to eternal punishment, far from the presence of the Lord, and the majesty of his power.'
v. 10. 'Yes, there will be justice when that day comes'; the text has simply 'in that day', but it seems clear that these words are meant to resume the sense of verses 6 and 7 above (verses 6 to 10 forming a single sentence in the original). 'Our witness has reached you Gentiles, and found belief'; literally, in the Greek, 'our witness has been

believed as far as you'. The construction seems to be that of Acts viii. 40, 'Philip was found as far as Azotus', meaning that Philip had reached Azotus before he was heard of again. It is difficult to believe that the conversion of the Thessalonians as such can be referred to in this very general context; more probably we ought to understand 'you' as meaning 'you Gentiles'; cf. Col. i. 25.

and the majesty of his power, will condemn them to eternal punishment, 10 when he comes to shew how glorious he is in his saints, how marvellously he has dealt with all the faithful, that our witness should have reached you Gentiles, and found belief! Yes, there will be justice when that day comes. 11 It is with this in view that we are always praying for you, praying that God may find you worthy of your vocation, and ripen by his influence all your love of well-doing, all the activity of your faith. 12 So may the name of our Lord Jesus Christ be glorified in you, and you glorified in him, through the grace given you by our God and by the Lord Jesus Christ.

Chapter Two

BUT there is one entreaty we would make of you, brethren, as you look forward to the time when our Lord Jesus Christ will come, and gather us in to himself. 2 Do not be terrified out of your senses all at once, and thrown into confusion, by any spiritual utterance, any message or letter purporting to come from us, which suggests that the day of the Lord is close at hand. 3 Do not let anyone find the means of leading you astray. The apostasy must come first; the champion of wickedness must appear first, destined to inherit perdition. 4 This is the rebel who is to lift up his head above every divine name, above all that men hold in reverence, till at last he enthrones himself in God's temple, and proclaims himself as God. 5 Do not you remember my telling you of this, before I left your company? 6 At present there is a power (you know what I mean) which holds him in check, so that he may not shew himself before the time appointed to him; 7 meanwhile, the conspiracy of revolt is already at work; only, he who checks it now will be able to check it, until he is removed from the enemy's path. 8 Then it is that the rebel will shew himself; and the Lord Jesus will destroy him with the breath of his mouth, overwhelming him with the brightness of his presence. 9 He will come, when he comes, with all Satan's influence to aid him; there will be no lack of power, of counterfeit signs and wonders; 10 and his wicked-

v. 1. 'As you look forward to'; the Latin here has 'in the name of', the Greek more probably means 'in connexion with'.

v. 3. There has been much speculation, what person or what influence in his own day St. Paul is here identifying as Antichrist. But it may be observed that he neither expects the Thessalonians to know, nor claims to know himself, anything about the nature of this Rebel who has not yet appeared; all he tells us (in verse 7) is that an influence which makes for evil is already at work in the world; and this does not need to be particularly identified.

v. 4. Dan. xi. 36.

v. 6. The power which holds evil in check and defers the

ness will deceive the souls that are doomed, to punish them for refusing that fellowship in the truth which would have saved them. That is why God is letting loose among them a deceiving influence, so that they give credit to falsehood; 11 he will single out for judgement all those who refused credence to the truth, and took their pleasure in wrong-doing.

12 We must always give thanks in your name, brethren whom the Lord has so favoured. God has picked you out as the first-fruits in the harvest of salvation, by sanctifying your spirits and convincing you of his truth; 13 he has called you, through our preaching, to attain the glory of our Lord Jesus Christ. 14 Stand firm, then, brethren, and hold by the traditions you have learned, in word or in writing, from us. 15 So may our Lord Jesus Christ himself, so may God, our Father, who has shewn such love to us, giving us unfailing comfort and welcome hope through his grace, 16 encourage your hearts, and confirm you in every right habit of action and speech.

appearance of Antichrist may be a human influence or perhaps that of St. Michael or some other angel (cf. Dan. x. 13, 21).

v. 12. 'Picked you out as the first-fruits in the harvest of salvation'; some Greek manuscripts have 'chosen you out for salvation from the beginning'.

Chapter Three

AND now, brethren, let us have your prayers, that the word of the Lord may run its course triumphantly with us, as it does with you; 2 and that we may be preserved from malicious interference; the faith does not reach all hearts. 3 But the Lord keeps faith with us; he will strengthen you, and keep you from all harm. 4 We are sure of you in the Lord, sure that you are doing and will do as we bid you; 5 may the Lord direct you where the love of God and the patience of Christ shew you the way. 6 Only, brethren, we charge you in the name of our Lord Jesus Christ to have nothing to do with any brother who lives a vagabond life, contrary to the tradition which we handed on; 7 you do not need to be reminded how, on our visit, we set you an example to be imitated; we were no vagabonds ourselves. 8 We would not even be indebted to you for our daily bread, we earned it in weariness and toil, working with our hands, night and day, so as not to be a burden to any of you; 9 not that we are obliged to do so, but as a model for your

v. 2. 'The faith does not reach all hearts'; or possibly, 'faith is not to be found in all hearts'.

v. 6. 'Vagabond'; literally 'disorderly', but the context shews that the apostle is referring to those who would not work—probably because they were expecting the second Coming of our Lord to take place immediately; see I Thess. v. 14, and note on I Thess. iv. 11.

own behaviour; you were to follow our example. 10 The charge we gave you on our visit was that the man who refuses to work must be left to starve. 11 And now we are told that there are those among you who live in idleness, neglecting their own business to mind other people's. 12 We charge all such, we appeal to them in the Lord Jesus Christ, to earn their bread by going on calmly with their work. 13 For yourselves, brethren, never weary of doing good. 14 If anybody refuses to listen to what we have said in our letter, he is to be a marked man; avoid his company till he is ashamed of himself, 15 correcting him like a brother, not treating him as an enemy. 16 And may the Lord of peace grant you peace everywhere and at all times; the Lord be with you all. 17 Here is Paul's greeting in his own hand; the signature which is to be found in all my letters; this is my handwriting. 18 The grace of our Lord Jesus Christ be with you all, Amen.

THE FIRST EPISTLE OF THE BLESSED APOSTLE PAUL to TIMOTHY

Chapter One

PAUL, AN APOSTLE OF Jesus Christ by the appointment of God our Saviour, and of Jesus Christ who is our hope, 2 to Timothy, my own son in the faith, grace be thine, and mercy, and peace, from God the Father and from our Lord Jesus Christ, 3 as thou fulfillest the charge I gave thee, when I passed on into Macedonia, to stay behind at Ephesus. There were some who needed to be warned against teaching strange doctrines, 4 against occupying their minds with legends and interminable pedigrees, which breed controversy, instead of building up God's house, as the faith does. 5 The end at which our warning aims is charity, based on purity of heart, on a good conscience and a sincere faith. 6 There are some who have missed this mark, branching off into vain speculations; 7 who now claim to be expounding the law, without understanding the meaning of their own words, or the subject on which they pronounce so positively. 8 The law? It is an excellent thing, where it is applied legitimately; 9 but it must be remembered that the law is not meant for those who live innocent lives. It is meant for the lawless and the refractory; for the

v. 4. The teaching here referred to may, like that prevalent at Colossae, have been akin to the Gnostic heresy. The Gnostics maintained that the creator of the material universe was the last in a long line of angelic beings; and some think that these hierarchies of angels are the 'genealogies' here alluded to. But it is more commonly held that St. Paul is thinking of Jewish speculations, which grafted legends and spurious pedigrees on to the narrative of the Old Testament.

vv. 7-11. These verses suggest that the false

393

teachers at Ephesus concerned themselves with legalistic expositions of the Ten Commandments; Christians ought to live by the law of charity.

godless and the sinner, the unholy and the profane; for those who lay violent hands on father or mother, for murderers, 10 for those who commit fornication or sin against nature, the slave-dealer, the liar, the perjurer. All this and much else is the very opposite of the sound doctrine 11 contained in the gospel I have been entrusted with, that tells us of the blessed God and his glory. 12 How I thank our Lord Jesus Christ, the source of all my strength, for shewing confidence in me by appointing me his minister, 13 me, a blasphemer till then, a persecutor, a man of violence, author of outrage, and yet he had mercy on me, because I was acting in the ignorance of unbelief. 14 The grace of the Lord came upon me in a full tide of faith and love, the love that is in Christ Jesus. 15 How true is that saying, and what a welcome it deserves, that Christ Jesus came into the world to save sinners. I was the worst of all, 16 and yet I was pardoned, so that in me first of all Christ Jesus might give the extreme example of his patience; I was to be the pattern of all those who will ever believe in him, to win eternal life. 17 Honour and glory through endless ages to the king of all the ages, the immortal, the invisible, who alone is God, Amen. 18 This charge, then, I give into thy hands, my son Timothy, remembering how prophecy singled thee out, long ago. Serve, as it bade thee, in this honourable warfare, 19 with faith and a good conscience to aid thee. Some, through refusing this duty, have made shipwreck of the faith, 20 among them, Hymenaeus and Alexander, whom I have made over to Satan, till they are cured of their blasphemy.

v. 20. The reference would seem to be to some not irrevocable form of excommunication; cf. I Cor. v. 5.

Chapter Two

THIS first of all, I ask; that petition, prayer, entreaty and thanksgiving should be offered for all mankind, 2 especially for kings and others in high station, so that we can live a calm and tranquil life, as dutifully and decently as we may. 3 Such prayer is our duty, it is what God, our Saviour, expects of us, 4 since it is his will that all men should be saved, and be led to recognize the truth; 5 there is only one God, and only one mediator between God and men,

vv. 1-7. It is possible that the false teachers at Ephesus, if they were Jews, may have been influenced

Jesus Christ, who is a man, like them, 6 and gave himself as a ransom for them all. At the appointed time, he bore his witness, 7 and of that witness I am the chosen herald, sent as an apostle (I make no false claims, I am only recalling the truth) to be a true and faithful teacher of the Gentiles.

8 It is my wish that prayer should everywhere be offered by the men; they are to lift up hands that are sanctified, free from all anger and dispute. 9 So, too, with the women; they are to dress themselves modestly and with restraint in befitting attire; no plaited hair, no gold ornaments, or pearls, or rich clothes; 10 a virtuous life is the best adornment for women who lay claim to piety. 11 Women are to keep silence, and take their place, with all submissiveness, as learners; 12 a woman shall have no leave from me to teach, and issue commands to her husband; her part is to be silent. 13 It was Adam that was created first, and Eve later, 14 nor was it Adam that went astray; woman was led astray, and was involved in transgression. 15 Yet woman will find her salvation in child-bearing, if she will but remain true to faith and love and holy living.

since the fall of Eve by the obedience of the Blessed Virgin, as is commonly recognized by the Church from St. Irenaeus onwards. 'If she will but remain' is 'if they will but remain' in the Greek; the plural being substituted for the singular to shew that the statement is made about womanhood generally.

by the unpopularity of Roman rule in Judaea, so as to preach disloyalty to the Empire; perhaps, too, they refused to recognize that the gospel was offered to the whole of mankind.

v. 2. 'Decently'; in the Greek 'with dignity', in the Latin 'with holiness' (or perhaps 'chastity').

v. 8. St. Paul is probably teaching here that women are to abstain from offering public prayer, as well as from teaching (in the sense of giving instructions at public worship).

v. 15. The Latin here has 'in the birth of children'; but the text as given in the Greek makes it equally possible to follow Theophylact (as several non-Catholic commentators do), and translate 'in the Child-bearing'. Woman, here considered as a single race, has been re-established

Chapter Three

T is well said, When a man aspires to a bishopric, it is no mean employment that he covets. 2 The man who is to be a bishop, then, must be one with whom no fault can be found; faithful to one wife, sober, discreet, modest, well behaved, hospitable, experienced in teaching, 3 no lover of wine or of brawling, courteous, neither quarrelsome nor grasping. 4 He must be one who is a good head to his own family, and keeps his children in order by winning their full respect; 5 if a man has not learned how to manage his own household, will he know how to govern God's church? 6 He must not be a new convert, or he may be carried away by vanity, and incur Satan's doom. 7 He must bear a good character, too, in the world's

vv. 1-7. It is possible that St. Paul means us to understand these qualifications as applying, not only to the episcopal office, but to that of a priest; he does not mention presbyters in this chapter. Cf. note on Phil. i. 1.

v. 2. 'Faithful to one wife' may mean, but

does not necessarily mean, that in the discipline of the early Church a re-married widower was ineligible for the episcopate.

v. 4. 'By winning their full respect'; in the Greek 'with all dignity'; in the Latin, 'with all holiness' (or perhaps 'chastity').

v. 7. 'The False Accuser' is the name given in Greek to the Devil. Here the sense would seem to be, that a Christian who was an object of suspicion to those outside the Church would bring the Church into discredit, through the scandal which the Devil would attach to his name.

vv. 2 and 11. 'Modest'; in the Greek, 'dignified', in the Latin, 'holy' or 'chaste'.

v. 11. 'The women-folk'; probably meaning the deacon's wife and household. It may, however, imply that women were recognized in the early Church, as they were later, in the character of 'deaconesses', sharing in the charitable work done by the deacons. Cf. Rom. xvi. i, where Phoebe is said to be a 'ministrant' to the church at Cenchrae.   v. 16. This sentence would seem to be connected with what follows, rather than with what goes before. Some think that St. Paul is quoting from an early Christian hymn; cf. Eph. v. 14. The sentence is perhaps best divided into three paradoxes; Christ manifested to the world in his humanity, yet redeeming us through the dignity of his Divine Person; the Resurrection, a sight only witnessed by angels, yet published throughout the world; Christ still making his power felt here below, through the faith of his Church, although he has ascended into heaven.

eyes; or he may fall into disrepute, and become a prey to the False Accuser.

8 Deacons, in the same way, must be men of decent behaviour, men of their word, not given to deep drinking or to money-getting, 9 keeping true, in all sincerity of conscience, to the faith that has been revealed. 10 These, in their turn, must first undergo probation, and only be allowed to serve as deacons if no charge is brought against them. 11 The women-folk, too, should be modest, not fond of slanderous talk; they must be sober, and in every way worthy of trust. 12 The deacon must be faithful to one wife, good at looking after his own family and household. 13 Those who have served well in the diaconate will secure for themselves a sure footing, and great boldness in proclaiming that faith, which is founded on Christ Jesus. 14 So much I tell thee by letter, although I hope to pay thee a visit before long; 15 so that, if I am slow in coming, thou mayest be in no doubt over the conduct that is expected of thee in God's household. By that I mean the Church of the living God, the pillar and foundation upon which the truth rests.

16 No question of it, it is a great mystery we worship. Revelation made in human nature, justification won in the realm of the Spirit; a vision seen by angels, a mystery preached to the Gentiles; Christ in this world, accepted by faith, Christ, on high, taken up into glory.

Chapter Four

WE ARE EXPRESSLY told by inspiration that, in later days, there will be some who abandon the faith, listening to false inspirations, and doctrines taught by the devils. 2 They will be deceived by the pretensions of impostors, whose conscience is hardened as if by a searing-iron. 3 Such teachers bid them abstain from marriage, and from certain kinds of food, although God has made these for the grateful enjoyment of those whom faith has enabled to recognize the truth. 4 All is good that God has made, nothing is to be rejected; only we must be thankful to him when we partake of it, 5 then it is hallowed for our use by God's blessing and the prayer which brings it. 6 Lay down these rules for the brethren, and thou wilt shew thyself a true servant of Jesus Christ, thriving on the principles of that faith whose wholesome doctrine thou hast followed. 7 Leave foolish nursery tales alone, and train thyself, instead, to grow up in holiness. 8 Training of the body avails but little: holiness is all-availing, since it promises well both for this life and for the next; 9 how true is that saying, and what a welcome it deserves! 10 It is for this that we endure toil and reproach, our hope in a living God, who is the Saviour of mankind, and above all of those who believe in him.

11 Such is the charge, such is the doctrine thou art to deliver. 12 Do not let anyone think the less of thee for thy youthfulness; make thyself a model of speech and behaviour for the faithful, all love, all faith, all purity. 13 Reading, preaching, instruction, let these be thy constant care while I am absent. 14 A special grace has been entrusted to thee; prophecy awarded it, and the imposition of the presbyters' hands went with it; do not let it suffer from neglect. 15 Let this be thy study, these thy employments, so that all may see how well thou doest. 16 Two things claim thy attention, thyself and the teaching of the faith; spend thy care on them; so wilt thou and those who listen to thee achieve salvation.

v. 3. 'Certain kinds of food'; either those prohibited by the Jewish law, as in Rom. xiv, or some others (perhaps flesh-meat generally) prohibited by innovating teachers at Ephesus, in the spirit of the later Gnostics.

v. 5. 'God's blessing'; literally 'God's word', which some understand here as meaning 'the words of scripture'; it is doubtful whether St. Paul ever uses the phrase in that sense.

v. 7. For 'foolish' the Greek has 'profane'; it is not clear in what sense.

v. 9. Some commentators think the saying consists of the words given in verse 10.

v. 10. 'Reproach'; many Greek manuscripts read 'struggle'.

v. 14. St. Paul says that the grace was given to St. Timothy 'through prophecy', presumably in the sense that the prophets pointed him out as a suitable person to be made a presbyter, or a bishop (cf. i. 18 above, and Acts xiii. 2). It was, perhaps, through this influence that he was chosen in spite of his youth, on which this chapter seems to lay special emphasis.

v. 16. 'Spend thy care on them'; that is, upon thyself and upon the preaching of the faith, as is indicated by the words which follow.

Chapter Five

v. 3. 'Their due', in-
cluding their main-
tenance by public
alms, according to the
custom of the early
Church (cf. Acts vi.
1). In Hebrew, the
verb 'to honour' some-
times has the sense
of monetary payment
(cf. Eccli. xxxviii. 1,
and note on Matthew
xv. 5).
v. 4. 'She must be
warned'; the Greek
manuscripts, and
many of the Latin,
have 'they must be
warned'. This seems
the more probable
reading, in view of
verse 7.
v. 6. 'Would be alive
and dead both at
once'; literally 'is
dead while she still
lives'. The sense ap-
pears to be, that she
must not attempt to
live a worldly life
and claim, at the
same time, the privi-
leges of widowhood.
v. 9. There is the
same uncertainty here
as in iii. 2 above.
v. 11. This verse is
ordinarily translated
'When they have be-
gun to grow wanton
against Christ', but
this does not trans-
late the Latin, and
is a very doubtful
rendering of the
Greek. St. Paul sure-
ly means, 'When they
have finished living a
luxurious life, upon
the alms of the Chris-
tian community'.
v. 17. 'Considera-
tion' here is the same
word in Greek as
'their dues' in verse
3 above, and is no
doubt used partly in
the same significa-
tion; cf. the verse
which follows.
v. 18. Deut. xxv. 4;
see also Matthew x.
10.

INSTEAD of finding fault, appeal to an older man as if he were thy father, to younger men as thy brothers, 2 to the older women, as mothers, to the younger (but with all modesty) as sisters. 3 Give widows their due, if that name really belongs to them; 4 if a widowed woman is left with children or grandchildren, she must be warned that their own flesh and blood has the first claim on their piety. They must make due returns to those who gave them birth; that is what God asks of them. 5 The woman who is indeed a widow, bereft of all help, will put her trust in God, and spend her time, night and day, upon the prayers and petitions that belong to her state; 6 one who lives in luxury would be alive and dead both at once. 7 Warn them of this, too, or they will bring themselves into disrepute; 8 the man who makes no provision for those nearest him, above all his own family, has contradicted the teaching of the faith, and indeed does worse than the unbelievers do. 9 If a woman is to be put on the list of widows, she must have reached, at least, the age of sixty, and have been faithful to one husband. 10 She must have a name for acts of charity; has she brought up children? Has she been hospitable? Has she washed the feet of the saints? Has she helped those who were in affliction? Has she attached herself to every charitable cause? 11 Have nothing to do with younger widows; they will live at their ease at Christ's expense, and then be for marrying again, 12 thus incurring the guilt of breaking the promise they have made. 13 Meanwhile, they learn habits of idleness as they go from house to house; nor are they merely idle, they gossip and interfere, and say what they have no right to say. 14 So I would have the younger women marry and bear children and have households to manage; they then will give enmity no handle for speaking ill of us. 15 Already there are some who have turned aside, to follow Satan. 16 Meanwhile, if a believer has any widows depending on him, he should undertake their support, leaving the church free to support the widows who are really destitute.

17 Presbyters who have acquitted themselves well of their charge should be awarded double consideration; those especially, who bestow their pains on preaching and instruction: 18 there is a

passage in scripture which tells us not to muzzle the ox while it
is threshing grain, and the labourer has a right to expect his maintenance. 19 Do not take cognizance of any charge made against
a presbyter, unless there are two witnesses or more. 20 Give a
public rebuke to those who are living amiss, and thus put fear into
the rest. 21 I adjure thee in the sight of God and of Jesus Christ,
and the angels he has chosen, to observe these rules without rash
judgement, without yielding to partiality. 22 As for the imposition of hands, do not bestow it inconsiderately, and so share the
blame for the sins of others. Keep thyself clear of fault. 23 (No,
do not confine thyself to water any longer; take a little wine to
relieve thy stomach, 24 and thy frequent attacks of illness.) Some
men have faults that are plain to view, so that they invite question;
with others, discovery follows upon the heels of enquiry; 25 so it
is, too, with their merits; some are plain to view, and where they
are not, they cannot long remain hidden.

Chapter Six

HOSE who are bound to slavery must treat
their masters as entitled to all respect; otherwise God's name and our doctrine will be ill
spoken of. 2 And those whose masters belong
to the faith must not think the less of them,
for being their brethren; they should render
all the better service, when those who benefit by their good will
are believers, worthy of their love. Teach them, and encourage
them, so to act. 3 Is there some rival teacher, who refuses assent
to the sound principles which are the principles of our Lord Jesus
Christ, to the doctrine which accords with holiness? 4 Then it is
because he is puffed up with vanity; knowledge he has none, but an
itch for speculation and controversy. What comes of it? Only
jealousy, quarrelling, recriminations and base suspicions, 5 all such
encounters as must arise between men with corrupted minds who have
lost track of the truth. Religion, they think, will provide them with
a living. 6 And indeed, religion is ample provision for life, though
no more than a bare sufficiency goes with it. 7 Empty-handed we
came into the world, and empty-handed, beyond question, we must

399

together with content-
ment.

leave it; 8 why then, if we have food and clothing to last us out, let us be content with that. 9 Those who would be rich fall into temptation, the devil's trap for them; all those useless and dangerous appetites which sink men into ruin here and perdition hereafter.

v. 10. 'Involving
themselves in' has
rather, in the Greek,
the meaning of 'stab-
bing themselves with'.

10 The love of money is a root from which every kind of evil springs, and there are those who have wandered away from the faith by making it their ambition, involving themselves in a world of sorrows.

11 It is for thee, servant of God, to shun all this; to aim at right living, holiness, and faith, and love, and endurance, and kind forbearance. 12 Fight the good fight of faith, lay thy grasp on eternal life, that life thou wert called to, when thou didst assert the great claim before so many witnesses. 13 I adjure thee before the God who gives life to all things, before Jesus Christ who bore witness to that great claim when he stood before Pontius Pilate, 14 to fulfil thy charge without stain of reproach until the day when our Lord Jesus Christ appears. 15 God will reveal him in due time, the blessed God who alone enjoys dominion; he is King of kings, and Lord of lords; 16 to him alone immortality belongs, his dwelling is in unapproachable light; no human eye has seen or can ever see him; to him be glory and everlasting empire, Amen. 17 Warn those who are rich in this present world not to think highly of themselves, not to repose their hopes in the riches that may fail us, but in the living God, who bestows on us so richly all that we enjoy. 18 Let them do good, enrich their lives with charitable deeds, always ready to give, and to share the common burden, 19 laying down a sure foundation for themselves in time to come, so as to

v. 20. For 'new' the
best Greek manu-
scripts have 'empty'.

have life which is true life within their grasp. 20 It is for thee, Timothy, to keep safe what has been entrusted to thee, avoiding these new, intruding forms of speech, this quibbling knowledge that is knowledge only in name; 21 there are those who profess them, and in professing them have shot wide of the mark which faith sets us. Grace be with thee, Amen.

ῌᴇ SECOND EPISTLE OF THE BLESSED APOSTLE PAUL ᴛᴏ TIMOTHY

Chapter One

Paul, sent as an apostle of Jesus Christ by the will of God, in furtherance of that promise of life which is given us in Christ Jesus, 2 to Timothy, his well beloved son, grace and mercy and peace from God the Father, and from Christ Jesus our Lord. 3 It is with gratitude to that God, whom I worship with a clear conscience in the way my fathers taught me, that I make mention of thee continually, day and night, in my prayer. 4 I keep the memory of thy tears, and long to see thee again, so as to have my fill of joy when I receive fresh proof of thy sincere faith. 5 That faith dwelt in thy grandmother Lois, and in thy mother, Eunice, before thee; I am fully persuaded that it dwells in thee too. 6 That is why I would remind thee to fan the flame of that special grace which God kindled in thee, when my hands were laid upon thee. 7 The spirit he has bestowed on us is not one that shrinks from danger; it is a spirit of action, of love, and of discipline. 8 Do not blush, then, for the witness thou bearest to our Lord, or for me, who am his prisoner; share all the tribulations of the gospel message as God gives thee strength. 9 Has he not saved us, and called us to a vocation of holiness? It was not because of anything we had done; we owe it to his own design, to the grace lavished on us, long ages ago, in Christ Jesus. 10 Now it has come to light, since our Saviour Jesus Christ came to enlighten us; now he has annulled death, now he has shed abroad the rays of life and immortality, through that gospel 11 which I have been appointed to herald, as an apostle and a teacher of the Gentiles. 12 This is what I have to suffer as the result; but I am not put to the blush. He, to whom I have given my confidence, is no stranger to me, and I am fully persuaded that he has the means to keep my pledge safe, until that day comes.

13 With all the faith and love thou hast in Christ Jesus, keep to the pattern of sound doctrine thou hast learned from my lips. 14 By the power of the Holy Spirit who dwells in us, be true to thy high trust. 15 In Asia, as thou knowest, all have treated me coldly, Phigellus and Hermogenes among them. 16 May the Lord grant mercy to the household of Onesiphorus; often enough he revived my spirits. Instead of being ashamed of a prisoner's acquaintance, 17 he sought me out when he was in Rome, and succeeded in finding me. 18 The Lord grant that he may find mercy with his Lord when that day comes; what he did for me in Ephesus I have no need to tell thee.

Chapter Two

AKE strength, my own son, from the grace which dwells in Christ Jesus. 2 Thou hast learned, from many who can witness to it, the doctrine which I hand down; give it into the keeping of men thou canst trust, men who will know how to teach it to others besides themselves. 3 Then, like a good soldier of Christ Jesus, take thy share of hardship. 4 Thou art God's soldier, and the soldier on service, if he would please the captain who enlisted him, will refuse to be entangled in the business of daily life; 5 the athlete will win no crown, if he does not observe the rules of the contest; 6 the first share in the harvest goes to the labourer who has toiled for it. 7 Grasp the sense of what I am saying; the Lord will give thee

quick insight wherever it is needed. 8 Fix thy mind on Jesus
Christ, sprung from the race of David, who has risen from the
dead; that is the gospel I preach, 9 and in its service I suffer hardship like a criminal, yes, even imprisonment; but there is no im-
prisoning the word of God. 10 For its sake I am ready to undergo
anything; for love of the elect, that they, like us, may win salvation in Jesus Christ, and eternal glory with it. 11 It is well said, We
are to share his life, because we have shared his death; 12 if we
endure, we shall reign with him, if we disown him, he in his turn
will disown us. 13 If we play him false, he remains true to his
word; he cannot disown himself.

14 Bring this back to men's thoughts, pleading with them earnestly in the Lord's name; there must be no wordy disputes, such as
can only unsettle the minds of those who are listening. 15 Aim first
at winning God's approval, as a workman who does not need to be
ashamed of his work, one who knows how to handle the claims of
the truth like a master. 16 Keep thy distance from those who are
bringing in a fashion of meaningless talk; they will go far to establish neglect of God, 17 and their influence eats in like a cancer.
Such are Hymenaeus and Philetas, 18 who have missed the true
mark, by contending that the resurrection has come about already,
to the overthrow of the faith in some minds. 19 But God's founda-
tion-stone stands firm, and this is the legend on it, The Lord
acknowledges none but his own; and again, Let everyone who
names the Lord's name keep far from iniquity. 20 A great house,
besides its plate of gold and silver, contains other objects made of
wood and earthenware; those for noble, these for ignoble uses;
21 it is by keeping himself separate from these that a man will
prove the object of his Lord's regard, hallowed, and serviceable,
and fit for all honourable employment. 22 Shun these youthful
ardours I speak of; aim at right living, faith, and hope, and love,
and fellowship with all those who call on the name of the Lord with
a pure heart. 23 Leave these foolish, ill-conceived disputes alone;
be very sure, they breed nothing but quarrels. 24 A servant of the
Lord has no business with quarrelling; he must be kindly towards
all men, persuasive and tolerant, 25 with a gentle hand for correcting those who are obstinate in their errors. It may be that God will
enable them to repent, and acknowledge the truth; 26 so they will
recover their senses, and shake off the snare by which the devil, till
now, has held them prisoners to his will.

v. 8. Cf. Acts xiii.
23 and 35-37.

v. 19. Cf. Matthew
vii. 21-23.

v. 26. The meaning
of the Greek is ob-
scure, and much dis-
puted; the sense of
the Latin is that
given here.

Chapter Three

BE sure of this, that in the world's last age there are perilous times coming. 2 Men will be in love with self, in love with money, boastful, proud, abusive; without reverence for their parents, without gratitude, without scruple, 3 without love, without peace; slanderers, incontinent, strangers to pity and to kindness; 4 treacherous, reckless, full of vain conceit, thinking rather of their pleasures than of God. 5 They will preserve all the outward form of religion, although they have long been strangers to its meaning. From these, too, turn away. 6 They count among their number the men that will make their way into house after house, captivating weak women whose consciences are burdened by sin; 7 women swayed by shifting passions, who are for ever inquiring, yet never attain to recognition of the truth. 8 Moses found rivals in Jannes and Mambres; just so the men I speak of set themselves up in rivalry against the truth, men whose minds are corrupt, whose faith is counterfeit; 9 yet they will come to little, they will soon be detected, like those others, in their rash folly.

vv. 8, 9. Jannes and Mambres (or, according to some manuscripts, Jambres) were the names given by Hebrew tradition to the magicians who withstood Moses by means of enchantments (Ex. vii. 11), and were finally discomfited (Ex. ix. 11).

10 Not such was the schooling, the guidance, thou hadst from me; in firm resolve, in faith, in patience, in love, in endurance; 11 all my persecutions and suffering, such as those which befell me at Antioch, Iconium, and Lystra; what persecutions I underwent! And yet the Lord brought me through them all safely. 12 And indeed, all those who are resolved to live a holy life in Christ Jesus will meet with persecution; 13 while the rogues and the mountebanks go on from bad to worse, at once impostors and dupes. 14 It is for thee to hold fast by the doctrine handed on to thee, the charge committed to thee; thou knowest well, from whom that tradition came; 15 thou canst remember the holy learning thou hast been taught from childhood upwards. This will train thee up for salvation, through the faith which rests in Christ Jesus. 16 Everything in the scripture has been divinely inspired, and has its uses; to instruct us, to expose our errors, to correct our faults, to educate us in holy living; 17 so God's servant will become a master of his craft, and each noble task that comes will find him ready for it.

v. 15. 'Holy learning', including, doubtless, the Old Testament scriptures, but not necessarily confined to them.

404

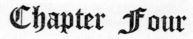

Chapter Four

I ADJURE THEE IN THE sight of God, and of Jesus Christ, who is to be the judge of living and dead, in the name of his coming, and of his kingdom, 2 preach the word, dwelling upon it continually, welcome or unwelcome; bring home wrong-doing, comfort the waverer, rebuke the sinner, with all the patience of a teacher. 3 The time will surely come, when men will grow tired of sound doctrine, always itching to hear something fresh; and so they will provide themselves with a continuous succession of new teachers, as the whim takes them, 4 turning a deaf ear to the truth, bestowing their attention on fables instead. 5 It is for thee to be on the watch, to accept every hardship, to employ thyself in preaching the gospel, and perform every duty of thy office, keeping a sober mind. 6 As for me, my blood already flows in sacrifice; the time has nearly come when I can go free. 7 I have fought the good fight; I have finished the race; I have redeemed my pledge; 8 I look forward to the prize that is waiting for me, the prize I have earned. The Lord, the judge whose award never goes amiss, will grant it to me when that day comes; to me, yes, and all those who have learned to welcome his appearing.

9 Make haste, and come quickly to me. Demas has fallen in love with this present world; he has deserted me, and gone to Thessalonica. 10 Crescens has gone to Galatia, Titus to Dalmatia, 11 and Luke is my only companion. Join company with Mark, and bring him here with thee; he can help me with the exercise of his ministry 12 now that I have sent Tychicus away to Ephesus. 13 When thou comest, bring with thee the cloak which I left in Carpus' hands at Troas; the books, too, and above all the rolls of parchment. 14 I have had much ill usage from Alexander, the coppersmith. As for what he has done, the Lord will judge him for it; 15 only do thou, too, be on thy guard against him; he has been a great enemy to our preaching. 16 At my first trial, no one stood by me; I was deserted by everybody; may it be forgiven them. 17 But the Lord was at my side; he endowed me with

v. 7. 'I have redeemed my pledge', or perhaps 'I have kept the faith', but the context here seems to demand a fresh metaphor; cf. I Tim. vi. 20, II Tim. i. 12.

v. 14. There is no means of determining whether this is the Alexander mentioned in Acts xix. 33.

405

strength, so that through me the preaching of the gospel might attain its full scope, and all the Gentiles might hear it; thus I was brought safely out of the jaws of the lion. 18 Yes, the Lord has preserved me from every assault of evil; he will bring me safely into his heavenly kingdom; glory be to him through endless ages, Amen.

19 My greetings to Prisca and Aquila, and to the household of Onesiphorus. 20 Erastus has stayed on at Corinth; Trophimus fell ill, and I left him behind at Miletus. 21 Make haste, and come to me before winter. Eubulus and Pudens and Linus and Claudia and all the brethren send thee their greeting. 22 The Lord Jesus Christ be with thy spirit. Grace be with you, Amen.

v. 21. According to Eusebius, this is the same Linus who became bishop of Rome after the death of St. Peter.

THE ENTOMBMENT OF CHRIST

FRA ANGELICO
1387-1455

NATIONAL GALLERY OF ART, WASHINGTON, D. C. (KRESS COLLECTION)

THE EPISTLE OF THE BLESSED APOSTLE PAUL TO TITUS

Chapter One

IT IS PAUL WHO WRITES; God's servant, sent out as an apostle of Jesus Christ, with the faith of God's elect for his care; they were to acknowledge that truth which accords with holiness, 2 and fix their hopes on eternal life. It had been promised to us long ages since by the God who cannot fail us; 3 and now, in due time, he has made his meaning clear to us, through the preaching with which God, our Saviour, has seen fit to entrust me. 4 To Titus, my own son in the faith we share, grace and peace from God the Father, and from Christ Jesus our Lord.

5 If I left thee behind me in Crete, it was to put all in order, where order is still needed. It is for thee to appoint presbyters, as I enjoined, in each city, 6 always looking for a man who is beyond reproach, faithful to one wife; one whose children hold the faith, not accused of reckless living, not wanting in obedience. 7 A bishop, after all, since he is the steward of God's house, must needs be beyond reproach. He must not be an obstinate or quarrelsome man, one who drinks deep, or comes to blows, or is grasping over money. 8 He must be hospitable, kindly, discreet, upright, un-

v. 7. St. Paul seems to assume that the qualifications needed by a bishop are those also needed by a presbyter; cf. I Tim. iii. 1-7 and note.

407

worldly and continent. 9 He must hold firmly to the truths which have tradition for their warrant; able, therefore, to encourage sound doctrine, and to shew the wayward their error. 10 There are many rebellious spirits abroad, who talk of their own fantasies and lead men's minds astray; those especially who hold by circumcision; and they must be silenced. 11 They will bring ruin on entire households by false teaching, with an eye to their own base profits. 12 Why, one of themselves, a spokesman of their own, has told us, The men of Crete were ever liars, venomous creatures, all hungry belly and nothing besides; 13 and that is a true account of them. Be strict, then, in taking them to task, so that they may be soundly established in the faith, 14 instead of paying attention to these Jewish fables, these rules laid down for them by human teachers who will not look steadily at the truth. 15 As if anything could be unclean for those who have clean hearts! But for these men, defiled as they are by want of faith, everything is unclean; defilement has entered their very thought, their very consciences. 16 They profess recognition of God, but their practice contradicts it; it is they who are abominable, who are disloyal, who are ill qualified for the practice of any true virtue.

vv. 14-16. The false teachers in Crete are referred to in much the same terms as the false teachers at Ephesus (cf. I Tim. i. 4-11, and note); in Crete, at any rate, they were Jews. They seem to have insisted particularly on the distinction between 'clean' and 'unclean' forms of food; thereby (as St. Paul points out) denying the beneficent intentions of the Creator whom they professed to worship.

Chapter Two

HINE is to be a different message, with sound doctrine for its rule. 2 Teach the older men to be sober, decent, orderly, soundly established in faith, in charity, in patience. 3 The older women, too, must carry themselves as befits a holy calling, not given to slanderous talk or enslaved to drunken habits; teaching others by their good example. 4 From them the younger women must learn orderly behaviour, how to treat their husbands and their children lovingly, 5 how to be discreet, modest, and sober, busy about the house, kindly, submissive to their own husbands; the preaching of God's word must not be brought into disrepute. 6 Encourage the young men, too, to live orderly lives. 7 Let them find in all thou doest the model of a life nobly lived; let them find thee 8 disinterested in thy teaching, worthy of their respect, thy doctrine sound be-

v. 7. 'Disinterested in thy teaching'; literally, in the Latin, 'in teaching, in uprightness', but the

yond all cavil; so that our adversaries may blush to find that they have no opportunity for speaking ill of us. 9 Slaves must be submissive to their own masters, so as to content them in every way; no arguing, 10 no pilfering; they must give good proof of utter fidelity, every action of theirs bringing credit to the teaching which God, our Saviour, has revealed. 11 The grace of God, our Saviour, has dawned on all men alike, 12 schooling us to forgo irreverent thoughts and worldly appetites, and to live, in this present world, a life of order, of justice, and of holiness. 13 We were to look forward, blessed in our hope, to the day when there will be a new dawn of glory, the glory of the great God, the glory of our Saviour Jesus Christ; 14 who gave himself for us, to ransom us from all our guilt, a people set apart for himself, ambitious of noble deeds. 15 Be this thy message, lending all authority to thy encouragement and thy reproof. Let no man lightly esteem thee.

Greek makes it evident that the two words are part of a single thought.

v. 13. We may, with the Greek Fathers, understand St. Paul to have written here 'the glory of our great God and Saviour Jesus Christ'; or we may, by a slightly less natural interpretation of the Greek, render 'the glory of the great God, and of our Saviour Jesus Christ'.

Chapter Three

EMIND them that they have a duty of submissive loyalty to governments and to those in authority, of readiness to undertake any kind of honourable service. 2 They are not to speak injuriously of anyone, or pick quarrels; they must be considerate, and lose no opportunity of shewing courtesy to the world around them. 3 We, after all, were once like the rest of them, reckless, rebellious, the dupes of error; enslaved to a strange medley of desires and appetites, our lives full of meanness and of envy, hateful, and hating one another. 4 Then the kindness of God, our Saviour, dawned on us, his great love for man. 5 He saved us; and it was not thanks to anything we had done for our own justification. In accordance with his own merciful design he saved us with the cleansing power which gives us new birth, and restores our nature through the Holy Spirit, 6 shed on us in abundant measure through our Saviour, Jesus Christ. 7 So, justified by his grace, we were to become heirs, with the hope of eternal life set before us. 8 It is well said, and I would have thee dwell on it, that those who have learned to trust in God should be at pains to find honourable employment. 9 That is their

v. 8. Here, as in I Tim. iv. 9, it is not certain whether the 'true saying' means what has gone before,

TITUS

or what immediately follows. 'Should be at pains to find honourable employment'; the sense might be 'should be champions of all that is good', but verse 14 below points to a more restricted interpretation.

v. 14. The meaning probably is, that Christians should earn an honest living (cf. II Thess. iii. 11), so as to be able to meet extraordinary expenses demanded of the congregation, such as those mentioned in the preceding verse.

duty, and the world will benefit by it. 10 But take no part in vain researches into pedigrees, and controversies that wrangle over points of the law; they are useless folly. 11 Give a heretic one warning, then a second, and after that avoid his company; his is a perverse nature, thou mayest be sure, and his fault has been admitted on his own confession.

12 When I send for thee by Artemas or Tychicus, make haste and come to meet me at Nicopolis; I have decided to spend the winter there. 13 Make careful provision for Zenas, the lawyer, and Apollo on their journey; they must not be left wanting for anything. 14 It would be well if our brethren would learn to find honourable employment, so as to meet what necessity demands of them, instead of having nothing to contribute. 15 All those who are with me send their greeting to you. Greet all those who are our friends in the common faith. The grace of God be with you all, Amen.

THE EPISTLE OF THE BLESSED APOSTLE PAUL to PHILEMON

Chapter One

PAUL, A PRISONER OF Jesus Christ, and Timothy, who is their brother, to the well beloved Philemon, who shares our labours, 2 and to all the church that is in his household, to our dear sister Appia, Archippus, who fights the same battle with ourselves, and the rest; 3 grace and peace be yours from God, our Father, and from the Lord Jesus Christ.

4 I give thanks to my God at all times, remembering thee in my prayers; 5 such accounts I hear of the love and faith thou shewest towards the Lord Jesus and towards all the saints. 6 May thy generosity in the faith be made known, when all your good actions are recognized in Christ Jesus. 7 It has been a happiness and a comfort to me to hear of thy charity, brother, and of the refreshment thou hast brought to the hearts of the saints. 8 And now, though I might well make bold in Christ to prescribe a duty to thee, 9 I prefer to appeal to this charity of thine. Who is it that writes to thee? Paul, an old man now, and in these days the prisoner, too, of Jesus Christ; 10 and I am appealing to thee on behalf of Onesimus, the child of my imprisonment. 11 He did thee

v. 6. This seems to be the sense intended by the Latin; it is, however, based on readings in the Greek which have little support. The Greek, rendered literally, runs: 'May thy sharing in the faith become effective, in the fuller knowledge (or recognition) of all the good that is in us in Christ Jesus'.

v. 9. Some think St. Paul calls himself, not an old man, but 'the ambassador, and now the prisoner too, of Christ Jesus'.

v. 11. The name Onesimus, in Greek, means 'profitable'. There is perhaps a further play upon words in verse 20, below.

an ill service once; now, both to thee and to myself, he can be serviceable, 12 and I am sending him back to thee; make him welcome, for my heart goes with him. 13 I would sooner have kept him here with me, to attend, as thy deputy, on a prisoner of the gospel, 14 but I would do nothing without thy leave; thy generosity should be exercised freely, not from lack of choice. 15 Perhaps, after all, the very purpose of thy losing him for a time was that thou mightest have him always by thee. 16 Do not think of him any longer as a slave; he is something more than a slave, a well loved brother, to me in a special way; much more, then, to thee, now that both nature and Christ make him thy own. 17 As thou dost value thy fellowship with me, make him welcome as thou wouldst myself; 18 if he has wronged thee, or is in thy debt, make me answerable for it. 19 Here is a message in Paul's own hand; I will make it good. Not to remind thee that thou owest me a debt already, thyself. 20 And now, brother, let me claim thy services; give comfort in the Lord to my anxious heart. 21 I write to thee counting on thy obedience, well assured that thou wilt do even more than I ask. 22 Be prepared, meanwhile, to entertain me; I hope, through your prayers, to be restored to you. 23 Greetings to you from Epaphras, my fellow prisoner in Christ Jesus; 24 from Mark, Aristarchus, Demas and Luke, who share my labours. 25 The grace of the Lord Jesus Christ be with your spirit. Amen.

THE EPISTLE OF THE BLESSED APOSTLE PAUL TO THE HEBREWS

Chapter One

IN OLD DAYS, GOD SPOKE to our fathers in many ways and by many means, through the prophets; now at last 2 in these times he has spoken to us, with a Son to speak for him; a Son, whom he has appointed to inherit all things, just as it was through him that he created this world of time; 3 a Son, who is the radiance of his Father's splendour, and the full expression of his being; all creation depends, for its support, on his enabling word. Now, making atonement for our sins, he has taken his place on high, at the right hand of God's majesty, 4 superior to the angels in that measure in which the name he has inherited is more excellent than theirs. 5 Did God ever say to one of the angels, Thou art my Son, I have begotten thee this day? And again, He shall find in me a Father, and I in him a Son? 6 Why, when the time comes for bringing his first-born into the world anew, then, he says, Let all the angels of God worship before him. 7 What does he say of the angels? He will have his angels be like the winds, the servants that wait on him like a flame of fire. 8 And what of the Son? Thy throne, O God, stands firm for ever and ever; the

v. 1. The Greek perhaps implies that God spoke fragmentarily and under various figures.

v. 3. 'His being'; the word we find in the Greek here is hypostasis, which the Latins translated by 'substance', while the Greek theologians used it to mean 'person'.

v. 4. The contrast here instituted between the Divine Word and the holy Angels may have some reference to contemporary errors (cf. Col. ii. 18); but its immediate purpose is to lead up to the beginning of ch. ii, where the new Covenant instituted by Jesus Christ is contrasted with the old Covenant, revealed by angels on

413

sceptre of thy kingship is a rod that rules true. 9 Thou hast been a friend to right, an enemy to wrong; and God, thy own God, has given thee an unction to bring thee pride, as none else of thy fellows. 10 And elsewhere: Lord, thou hast laid the foundations of the earth at its beginning, and the heavens are the work of thy hands. 11 They will perish, but thou wilt remain; they will all be like a cloak that grows threadbare, 12 and thou wilt lay them aside, like a garment, and exchange them for new; but thou art he who never changes, thy years will not come to an end. 13 Did he ever say to one of the angels, Sit on my right hand, while I make thy enemies a footstool under thy feet? 14 What are they, all of them, but spirits apt for service, whom he sends out when the destined heirs of eternal salvation have need of them?

mount Sinai (Acts vii. 53, Gal. iii. 19).
v. 5. Ps. ii. 7, II Kings vii. 14.
v. 6. Some commentators would render 'And again, when the times comes for bringing his first-born into the world. But it is doubtful whether either the Greek or the Latin will bear this meaning, and the general sense of the Fathers is against it. It is not certain whether 'anew' contrasts the Incarnation of our Lord with his activity in Creation (cf. verse 2 above), or his Resurrection with his Incarnation, or his second Coming with his first. The words at the end of the sentence occur in the Septuagint Greek (but not in our present Hebrew text) of Deut. xxxii. 43, with 'sons of God' instead of 'angels'; a similar phrase is found in Ps. xcvi. 7. v. 7. Ps. ciii. 4. The word here used for 'winds' may also be translated 'spirits'. Some think that the meaning of the Psalm is 'who makes the winds (or "spirits") his messengers, and the flame of fire do him service'; but the more generally received interpretation is that given here. vv. 8, 9. Ps. xliv. 7, 8. The Messiah is there addressed, in the person of King Solomon; and some commentators, to avoid the difficulty of the Divine title being used in such a connexion, would render 'God is thy throne', a form of speech which has no parallel elsewhere. Some of the Fathers give the rendering, 'Thy God, O God, has anointed thee'. vv. 10-12. Ps. ci. 26-28. It is not clear why these words should be understood as addressed to the Messiah, unless this was suggested by the use of the word 'Lord' (in the Septuagint Greek, though not in our present Hebrew text). v. 13. Ps. cix. 1.

Chapter Two

MORE firmly, then, than ever must we hold to the truths which have now come to our hearing, and run no risk of drifting away from them. 2 The old law, which only had angels for its spokesmen, was none the less valid; every transgression of it, every refusal to listen to it, incurred just retribution; 3 and what excuse shall we have, if we pay no heed to such a message of salvation as has been given to us? One which was delivered in the first instance by the Lord himself, and has been guaranteed to us by those who heard it from his own lips? 4 One which God himself has attested by signs and portents, manifesting his power so variously, and distributing the gifts of his Holy Spirit wherever he would?

5 We are speaking of a world that is to come; to whom has God entrusted the ordering of that world? Not to angels. 6 We are assured of that, in a passage where the writer says, What is

vv. 6-8. Ps. viii. 5-7.

MOURNING FOR THE DEAD CHRIST

MASTER OF THE VIRGO INTER VIRGINES
active in the last quarter of the 15th Century

METROPOLITAN MUSEUM, NEW YORK

man, that thou shouldst remember him? What is the son of man, that thou shouldst care for him? 7 Man, whom thou hast made a little lower than the angels, whom thou hast crowned with glory and honour, setting him in authority over the works of thy hands? 8 Thou hast made all things subject at his feet. Observe, he has subjected all things to him, left nothing unsubdued. And what do we see now? Not all things subject to him as yet. 9 But we can see this; we can see one who was made a little lower than the angels, I mean Jesus, crowned, now, with glory and honour because of the death he underwent; in God's gracious design he was to taste death, and taste it on behalf of all. 10 God is the last end of all things, the first beginning of all things; and it befitted his majesty that, in summoning all those sons of his to glory, he should crown with suffering the life of that Prince who was to lead them into salvation. 11 The Son who sanctifies and the sons who are sanctified have a common origin, all of them; he is not ashamed, then, to own them as his brethren. 12 I will proclaim thy renown, he says, to my brethren; with the church around me I will praise thee; 13 and elsewhere he says, I will put my trust in him, and then, Here stand I, and the children God has given me. 14 And since these children have a common inheritance of flesh and blood, he too shared that inheritance with them. By his death he would depose the prince of death, that is, the devil; 15 he would deliver those multitudes who lived all the while as slaves, made over to the fear of death. 16 After all, he does not make himself the angels' champion, no sign of that; it is the sons of Abraham that he champions. 17 And so he must needs become altogether like his brethren; he would be a high priest who could feel for us and be our true representative before God, to make atonement for the sins of the people. 18 It is because he himself has been tried by suffering, that he has power to help us in the trials we undergo.

v. 9. Some interpreters would translate differently: 'We can see one who was made a little lower than the angels through the death he underwent, crowned, now, with glory and honour'.

v. 10. 'In summoning'; the Latin appears to mean 'when he had summoned', but this is probably not the sense of the Greek, and indeed it is hard to see how the bestowal of glory on Christians could be represented as earlier in time than the Crucifixion. It seems likely, therefore, that the sense intended by the Latin is, 'since he had decided to summon a multitude of his sons to glory'.

v. 12. Ps. xxi. 23.

v. 13. Is. viii. 17 and 18. 'And then' is expressed by the same word as 'and elsewhere'; but here the apostle seems to be drawing our attention to the connexion of thought between two consecutive verses of Isaias. That confidence with which the prophet inspires his own disciples is regarded as the type of that faith which our Lord communicates to Christian people.

v. 16. 'After all, he does not make himself the angels' champion'; literally, according to the Latin, 'he does not anywhere take the angels', which some have interpreted as meaning, 'he does not take upon himself the nature of angels'; but this interpretation does not accord well with the Greek.

Chapter Three

BRETHREN and saints, you share a heavenly calling. Think, now, of Jesus as the apostle and the high priest of the faith which we profess, 2 and how loyal he was to the God who had so appointed him; just as Moses was loyal in all the management of God's house. 3 In any household, the first honours are reserved for him who founded it; and in that degree, Jesus has a prouder title than Moses. 4 Every household has its founder, and this household of creation was founded by God. 5 Thus the loyalty of Moses in the management of all God's house was the loyalty of a servant; he only bore witness to what was to be revealed later on; 6 whereas Christ's was the loyalty of a Son in a household which is his own. What is that household? We are, if only we will keep unshaken to the end our confidence, and the hope which is our pride.

7 Come, then, the Holy Spirit says, If you hear his voice speaking to you this day, 8 do not harden your hearts, as they were hardened once when you provoked me, and put me to the test in the wilderness. 9 Your fathers put me to the test, made trial of me, and saw what I could do, all those forty years. 10 So I became the enemy of that generation; These, I said, are ever wayward hearts, these have never learned my lessons. 11 And I took an oath in my anger, They shall never attain my rest. 12 Take care, brethren, that there is no heart among you so warped by unbelief as to desert the living God. 13 Each day, while the word To-day has still a meaning, strengthen your own resolution, to make sure that none of you grows hardened; sin has such power to cheat us. 14 We have been given a share in Christ, but only on condition that we keep unshaken to the end the principle by which we are grounded in him. 15 That is the meaning of the words, If you hear his voice speaking to you this day, do not harden your hearts, as they were hardened once when you provoked me; 16 those who provoked him were the people (some, though not all of them) whom Moses had rescued from Egypt. 17 Who was it, during all those forty years, that incurred his enmity? Those who sinned; it was their corpses that lay scattered in the wilderness. 18 To whom did he swear that they should never attain his rest? Those who refused to believe in him. 19 We see, then, the consequences of unbelief; this it was that denied them entrance.

v. 2. 'The God who had so appointed him'; or perhaps, 'the God who had created him', that is, in his human Nature. The reference to Moses is taken from Num. xii. 7.

v. 3. The Greek may also mean, 'greater honours are reserved for him who founded the household, than for the household itself', Moses (as being nothing more than man) being himself a part of God's earthly creation, as a steward is of the household which he governs.

v. 4. 'This household of creation'; literally 'all things', but it seems clear from the context that creation is here regarded as a household, in which Christ rules as the Householder's Son, cf. i. 2 above.

vv. 7-11. Ps. xciv. 8-11. Throughout this passage, the Apostle compares those Christians who lose their hope of heaven by losing their faith, with the first generation of Israelites who came out of Egypt, since these lost their hope of entering Chanaan through want of faith in God.

v. 14. This seems to be the meaning of the Latin; the Greek perhaps means 'keep unshaken to the end our first confidence'.

v. 16. The Greek might also mean, 'Who was it that provoked him? Was it not all those whom Moses had rescued from Egypt?'

Chapter Four

THE PROMISE, THERE
fore, still holds good, that we are
to attain God's rest; what we have to be afraid of, is that there
may be someone among you who will be found to have missed his
chance. 2 The promise has been proclaimed to us, just as it was
to them. The message which came to them did them no good, because it was not met by belief in what they heard, 3 and this rest
is only to be attained by those who, like ourselves, have learned to
believe; that is why he said, I took an oath in my anger, They shall
never attain my rest. God's rest, from what? From labours which
were over and done with, as soon as the world was founded; 4 in
another passage he has said of the sabbath, God rested on the
seventh day from all his labours; 5 and yet in this passage he is
still saying, They shall not attain my rest. 6 It is still left for some,
then, to attain it, and meanwhile, those to whom the message first
came have been excluded by their unbelief. 7 So he fixes another
day, To-day, as he calls it; in the person of David, all those long
years afterwards, he uses the words I have already quoted, If you
hear his voice speaking this day, do not harden your hearts.
8 (Josue cannot have brought them their rest, or God would not
still be talking of a fresh To-day, long afterwards.) 9 You see,
therefore, that God's people have a sabbath of rest still in store for
them; 10 to attain his rest means resting from human labours, as
God did from divine.

11 We must strive eagerly, then, to attain that rest; none of you
must fall away into the same kind of unbelief. 12 God's word to
us is something alive, full of energy; it can penetrate deeper than
any two-edged sword, reaching the very division between soul and
spirit, between joints and marrow, quick to distinguish every
thought and design in our hearts. 13 From him, no creature can
be hidden; everything lies bare, everything is brought face to face
with him, this God to whom we must give our account.

14 Let us hold fast, then, by the faith we profess. We can claim
a great high priest, and one who has passed right up through the
heavens, Jesus, the Son of God. 15 It is not as if our high priest

v. 2. 'In what they heard'; the Greek has, 'In those who heard it'.

v. 3. 'God's rest, from what? From labours which were over and done with'; literally, 'the labours having been accomplished'. There has been much dispute over this sentence which follow; neither their meaning nor their relevance to the context is clear. The translation here given assumes that the apostle's thought is as follows: God himself rested after the Creation, but did not summon any human creatures to share his rest till long afterwards, at the time of the Exodus. That summons having been disregarded, it is not wonderful that he should leave another long interval before repeating it; this time, at the Incarnation.

v. 10. It is possible to take this sentence differently, as referring to Christ; 'He who has attained to God's rest has rested from his labours, as God did from his own'. But it seems doubtful whether this allusion contributes anything to the argument.

v. 12. 'God's word to us'; some have understood this as meaning 'God's Word', that is, Christ.

was incapable of feeling for us in our humiliations; he has been through every trial, fashioned as we are, only sinless. 16 Let us come boldly, then, before the throne of grace, to meet with mercy, and win that grace which will help us in our needs.

Chapter Five

 HE purpose for which any high priest is chosen from among his fellow men, and made a representative of men in their dealings with God, is to offer gifts and sacrifices in expiation of their sins. 2 He is qualified for this by being able to feel for them when they are ignorant and make mistakes, since he, too, is all beset with humiliations, 3 and, for that reason, must needs present sin-offerings for himself, just as he does for the people. 4 His vocation comes from God, as Aaron's did; nobody can take on himself such a privilege as this. 5 So it is with Christ. He did not raise himself to the dignity of the high priesthood; it was God that raised him to it, when he said, Thou art my Son, I have begotten thee this day, 6 and so, elsewhere, Thou art a priest for ever, in the line of Melchisedech. 7 Christ, during his earthly life, offered prayer and entreaty to the God who could save him from death, not without a piercing cry, not without tears; yet with such piety as won him a hearing. 8 Son of God though he was, he learned obedience in the school of suffering, 9 and now, his full achievement reached, he wins eternal salvation for all those who render obedience to him. 10 A high priest in the line of Melchisedech, so God has called him.

11 Of Christ as priest we have much to say, and it is hard to make ourselves understood in the saying of it, now that you have grown so dull of hearing. 12 You should, after all this time, have been teachers yourselves, and instead of that you need to be taught; taught even the first principles on which the oracles of God are based. You have gone back to needing milk, instead of solid food. 13 Those who have milk for their diet can give no account of what holiness means; how should they? They are only infants. 14 Solid food is for the full-grown; for those whose faculties are so trained by exercise that they can distinguish between good and evil.

v. 3. Lev. iv. 3.

v. 5. Ps. ii. 7.

v. 6. Ps. cix. 4.

v. 7. The apostle is no doubt referring to the Agony in Gethsemani, and perhaps also to our Lord's cry from the Cross. Cf. also John xi. 35, 43.
v. 8. See note on Luke ii. 52.

v. 11. 'Of Christ as priest'; literally 'of whom'. Some have understood this as referring simply to Christ, others as referring to Melchisedech (Gen. xiv. 18); but it seems more probable that the word 'whom' includes the whole content of verse 10.

418

Chapter Six

WE MUST LEAVE ON one side then, all discussion of our first lessons in Christ, and pass on to our full growth; no need to lay the foundations all over again, the change of heart which turns away from lifeless observances, the faith which turns towards God, 2 instructions about the different kinds of baptism, about the laying on of hands, about the resurrection of the dead, and our sentence in eternity. 3 Such will be our plan, if God permits it. 4 We can do nothing for those who have received, once for all, their enlightenment, who have tasted the heavenly gift, partaken of the Holy Spirit, 5 known, too, God's word of comfort, and the powers that belong to a future life, 6 and then fallen away. They cannot attain repentance through a second renewal. Would they crucify the Son of God a second time, hold him up to mockery a second time, for their own ends? 7 No, a piece of ground which has drunk in, again and again, the showers which fell upon it, has God's blessing on it, if it yields a crop answering the needs of those who tilled it; 8 if it bears thorns and thistles, it has lost its value; a curse hangs over it, and it will feed the bonfire at last. 9 Beloved, of you we have better confidence, which does not stop short of your salvation, even when we speak to you as we are speaking now. 10 God is not an unjust God, that he should forget all you have done, all the charity you have shewn in his name, you who have ministered, and still minister, to the needs of his saints. 11 But our great longing is, to see you all shewing the same eagerness right up to the end, looking forward to the fulfilment of your hope; 12 listless no more, but followers of all those whose faith and patience are to bring them into possession of the good things promised them.

13 Such was Abraham. God made him a promise, and then took an oath (an oath by himself, since he had no greater name to swear by), 14 in the words, More and more I will bless thee, more and more I will give thee increase; 15 whereupon Abraham waited patiently, and saw the promise fulfilled. 16 Men, since they have

v. 1. 'Lifeless observances'; literally 'lifeless works'. This his often been taken to mean 'sins'; but it probably refers, both here and in ix. 14 below, to those actions in conformity with the law of Moses which are unprofitable to us without faith. So faith without charity is called 'lifeless' by St. James (ii. 26).

v. 2. 'Different forms of baptism'; literally 'baptisms'. It seems likely that the earliest Christian catechists would have had to explain to Jewish converts the difference between our Lord's baptism and that of St. John (cf. Acts xviii. 25).

vv. 4-6. The apostle is not dealing here with the remission of our sins by sacramental penance; he only tells us that baptism cannot be repeated, and therefore the kind of instruction mentioned in verse 2, which was designed for catechumens, would be unsuitable for Jewish Christians, if there are such, who have fallen away from the faith after being fully instructed in it. The enlightenment referred to in verse 4 is almost certainly baptism itself (cf. Eph. v. 14). The 'heavenly gift' may well mean the Holy Eucharist. What is meant by 'knowing' (literally 'tasting') God's utterance has been much discussed; it may refer to the Holy Scriptures, or

419

*to God's word as re-
vealed to the proph-
ets, or simply to
God's influence on
Christian lives. The
suggestion in verse 6
is probably that a
Christian soul could
not receive baptism
a second time unless
Christ were crucified
a second time in its
behalf; but the mean-
ing may be simply, that
the soul which falls
away from the faith
inflicts a fresh Pas-
sion, as it were, on
our Lord himself.*

*v. 14. Gen. xxii. 16,
17.*

something greater than themselves to swear by, will confirm their word by oath, which puts an end to all controversy; 17 and God, in the same way, eager to convince the heirs of the promise that his design was irrevocable, pledged himself by an oath. 18 Two irrevocable assurances, over which there could be no question of God deceiving us, were to bring firm confidence to us poor wanderers, bidding us cling to the hope we have in view, 19 the anchorage of our souls. Sure and immovable, it reaches that inner sanctuary beyond the veil, 20 which Jesus Christ, our escort, has entered already, a high priest, now, eternally with the priesthood of Melchisedech.

*v. 18. 'Wanderers'; this is generally understood as a metaphor taken from those who flee for refuge to a stronghold,
or to the Cities of Refuge mentioned in Numbers, ch. xxxv. But the allusion to an anchor in the next verse would
suggest, rather, the picture of sailors forced by a storm to 'flee landwards' to the nearest possible harbour.*
*v. 19. For the veil which separated the Holy Place from the inner Sanctuary of the Temple, cf. Ex. xxvi. 33, Mat-
thew xxvii. 51.*

Chapter Seven

v. 1. Gen. xiv. 17.

*v. 3. In the narrative
of Genesis, Melchi-
sedech appears on
the scene very sud-
denly, without any
explanation of his
parentage or history.
It seems to be on
this account that the
Apostle regards him
as a type of Christ,
whose priesthood did
not descend to him
by inheritance, and
remains with him in-
stead of having to be
handed on to a suc-
cessor.*

IT was this Melchisedech, king of Salem, and priest of the most high God, who met Abraham and blessed him on his way home, after the defeat of the kings; 2 and to him Abraham gave a tenth of his spoils. Observe, in the first place, that his name means, the king of justice; and further that he is king of Salem, that is, of peace. 3 That is all; no name of father or mother, no pedigree, no date of birth or of death; there he stands, eternally, a priest, the true figure of the Son of God. 4 Consider how great a man was this, to whom the patriarch Abraham himself gave a tenth part of his chosen spoil. 5 The descendants of Levi, when the priesthood is conferred on them, are allowed by the provisions of the law to take tithes from God's people, although these, like themselves, come from the privileged stock of Abraham; after all, they are their brothers; 6 here is one who owns no common descent with them, taking tithes from Abraham himself. He blesses him, too, blesses the man to whom the promises have been made; 7 and it is beyond all question that blessings are only given by what is greater in dignity to what is less. 8 In the one case, the priests who receive tithe are only mortal men; in the other, it is a priest (so the record

tells us) who lives on. 9 And indeed, there is a sense in which we can say that Levi, who receives the tithe, paid tithe himself with Abraham; 10 as the heir of Abraham's body, he was present in the person of his ancestor, when he met Melchisedech.

11 Now, there could be no need for a fresh priest to arise, accredited with Melchisedech's priesthood, not with Aaron's, if the Levitical priesthood had brought fulfilment. And it is on the Levitical priesthood that the law given to God's people is founded. 12 When the priesthood is altered, the law, necessarily, is altered with it. 13 After all, he to whom the prophecy relates belonged to a different tribe, which never produced a man to stand at the altar; 14 our Lord took his origin from Juda, that is certain, and Moses in speaking of this tribe, said nothing about priests. 15 And something further becomes evident, when a fresh priest arises to fulfil the type of Melchisedech, 16 appointed, not to obey the law, with its outward observances, but in the power of an unending life; 17 (Thou art a priest in the line of Melchisedech, God says of him, for ever). 18 The old observance is abrogated now, powerless as it was to help us; 19 the law had nothing in it of final achievement. Instead, a fuller hope has been brought into our lives, enabling us to come close to God. 20 And this time there is a ratification by oath; 21 none was taken when those other priests were appointed, but the new priest is appointed with an oath, when God says to him, The Lord has sworn an irrevocable oath, Thou art a priest for ever; 22 all the more solemn, then, is that covenant for which Jesus has been given us as our surety. 23 Of those other priests there was a succession, since death denied them permanence; 24 whereas Jesus continues for ever, and his priestly office is unchanging; 25 that is why he can give eternal salvation to those who through him make their way to God, he lives on still to make intercession on our behalf. 26 Such was the high priest that suited our need, holy and guiltless and undefiled, not reckoned among us sinners, lifted high above all the heavens; 27 one who has no need to do as those other priests did, offering a twofold sacrifice day by day, first for his own sins, then for those of the people. What he has done he has done once for all; and the offering was himself. 28 The law makes high priests of men, and men are frail; promise and oath, now, have superseded the law; our high priest, now, is that Son who has reached his full achievement for all eternity.

Chapter Eight

v. 2. Some think the 'tabernacle' mentioned here and in ix. 11 below is our Lord's human body (cf. Mark xiv. 58, John ii. 21); others, that it is the Church, either Triumphant (which accords best with ix. 11) or Militant (which accords best with the use of the word 'tabernacle', applying as it does to what is temporary and transient, as in II Cor. v. 4.).

v. 3. 'Must needs have an offering to make'; that is, himself, cf. vii. 27 above. Probably this is what the Apostle means by the pith of his argument (verse 1 above), viz. that Christ has only become our High Priest by dying and triumphing over death. Hence the reference to 'if he were still on earth' in the verse which follows.

v. 5. Ex. xxv. 40.

vv. 8 and following. Jer. xxxi. 31.

ND here we come to the very pith of our argument. This high priest of ours is one who has taken his seat in heaven, on the right hand of that throne where God sits in majesty, 2 ministering, now, in the sanctuary, in that true tabernacle which the Lord, not man, has set up. 3 After all, if it is the very function of a priest to offer gift and sacrifice, he too must needs have an offering to make. 4 Whereas, if he were still on earth, he would be no priest at all; there are priests already, to offer the gifts which the law demands, 5 men who devote their service to the type and the shadow of what has its true being in heaven. (That is why Moses, when he was building the tabernacle, received the warning, Be sure to make everything in accordance with the pattern that was shewn to thee on the mountain). 6 As it is, he has been entrusted with a more honourable ministry, dispenser as he is of a nobler covenant, with nobler promises for its sanction. 7 There would have been no room for this second covenant, if there had been no fault to find with the first. 8 But God, you see, does find fault; this is what he tells them: Behold, says the Lord, a time is coming when I will ratify a new covenant with the people of Israel, and with the people of Juda. 9 It will not be like the covenant which I made with their fathers, on the day when I took them by the hand, to rescue them from Egypt; that they should break my covenant, and I (says the Lord) should abandon them. 10 No, this is the covenant I will grant the people of Israel, the Lord says, when that times comes. I will implant my law in their innermost thoughts, engrave it in their hearts; I will be their God, and they shall be my people. 11 There will be no need for neighbour to teach neighbour, or brother to teach brother, the knowledge of the Lord; all will know me, from the highest to the lowest. 12 I will pardon their wrong-doing; I will not remember their sins any more. 13 In speaking of a new covenant, he has superannuated the old. And before long the superannuated, the antiquated, must needs disappear.

Chapter Nine

HE former covenant, to be sure, had its own ceremonial observances, its own earthly sanctuary. 2 There was an outer tabernacle, which contained the lamp-stand and the table and the loaves set out before God; sanctuary was the name given to this; 3 and then, beyond the second veil, the inner sanctuary, as it is called, 4 with the golden censer, and the ark of the covenant, gilded all round. In the ark rested the golden urn with the manna in it, Aaron's staff that budded, and the tablets on which the covenant was inscribed; 5 above were the Cherubim, heralds of the divine glory, spreading their wings over the throne of mercy. We have no time to treat of these more particularly, 6 but this was the general fashion of it. Into the outer tabernacle the priests made their way at all times, in the performance of their duties; 7 into this other, only the high priest, once a year, and even then not without an offering of blood, for the faults which he and the people had committed unknowingly. 8 The Holy Spirit meant us to see that no way of access to the true sanctuary lay open to us, as long as the former tabernacle maintained its standing. 9 And that allegory still holds good at the present day; here are gifts and sacrifices being offered, which have no power, where conscience is concerned, to bring the worshipper to his full growth; they are but outward observances, connected with food and drink 10 and ceremonial washings on this occasion or that, instituted to hold their own until better times should come. 11 Meanwhile, Christ has taken his place as our high priest, to win us blessings that still lie in the future. He makes use of a greater, a more complete tabernacle, which human hands never fashioned; it does not belong to this order of creation at all. 12 It is his own blood, not the blood of goats and calves, that has enabled him to enter, once for all, into the sanctuary; the ransom he has won lasts for ever. 13 The blood of bulls and goats, the ashes of a heifer sprinkled over men defiled, has power to hallow them for every purpose of outward purification; 14 and shall not the blood of Christ, who offered himself, through the Holy Spirit, as a victim unblemished in God's sight, purify our consciences, and set them free from lifeless observances, to serve the living God? 15 Thus, through his intervention, a new covenant has been be-

vv. 1 and 2. 'Former' and 'outer' are represented by the same word both in the Greek and in the Latin, to contrast (i) the earthly tabernacle with the heavenly and (ii) the outer with the inner court of the earthly tabernacle itself.
v. 4. 'Censer' is the meaning of the Latin; the Greek word should probably be translated 'altar of incense'. Cf. Ex. xvi. 33, Num. xvii. 10. Deut. x. 2.
v. 5. Ex. xxv. 22.

v. 11. 'Blessings that still lie in the future'; some Greek manuscripts have 'blessings already assured'. 'He makes use of a better tabernacle'; that is, his own body (Mark xiv. 58, John ii. 21). Others would understand this 'better tabernacle' as referring to the saints in heaven, and would connect this sentence with the sentence which follows; Christ has passed through the heaven in which the saints have their dwelling, and entered that inner sanctuary which is the presence of God himself.

v. 14. 'Through the Holy Spirit'; the more probable reading in the Greek is, 'through (his) eternal spirit', that is, his human spirit, considered as the vehicle of his Divinity (cf. Rom. i. 3, 4). 'From lifeless observances'; cf. note on vi. 1 above.

vv. 15-17. In Greek, the same word may be used for a covenant between two parties, and for the will by which a man disposes of his property. Here the covenant into which God entered with his people, whether under the Old or under the New Dispensation, is treated as being also a legacy to them.

vv. 19-20. Ex. xxiv. 6-8.

v. 28. 'To drain the cup of a world's sins'; in the Greek 'to take a world's sins upon himself'.

queathed to us; a death must follow, to atone for all our transgressions under the old covenant, and then the destined heirs were to obtain, for ever, their promised inheritance. 16 Where a bequest is concerned, the death of the testator must needs play its part; 17 a will has no force while the testator is alive, and only comes into force with death. 18 Thus the old covenant, too, needed blood for its inauguration. 19 When he had finished reading the provisions of the law to the assembled people, Moses took blood, the blood of calves and goats, took water, and scarlet-dyed wool, and hyssop, sprinkled the book itself, and all the people, 20 and said, This is the blood of the covenant which God has prescribed to you. 21 The tabernacle, too, and all the requisites of worship he sprinkled in the same way with blood; 22 and the law enjoins that blood shall be used in almost every act of purification; unless blood is shed, there can be no remission of sins. 23 And if such purification was needed for what was but a representation of the heavenly world, the heavenly world itself will need sacrifices more availing still. 24 The sanctuary into which Jesus has entered is not one made by human hands, is not some adumbration of the truth; he has entered heaven itself, where he now appears in God's sight on our behalf. 25 Nor does he make a repeated offering of himself, as the high priest, when he enters the sanctuary, makes a yearly offering of the blood that is not his own. 26 If that were so, he must have suffered again and again, ever since the world was created; as it is, he has been revealed once for all, at the moment when history reached its fulfilment, annulling our sin by his sacrifice. 27 Man's destiny is to die once for all; nothing remains after that but judgement; 28 and Christ was offered once for all, to drain the cup of a world's sins; when we see him again, sin will play its part no longer, he will be bringing salvation to those who await his coming.

Chapter Ten

WHAT THE LAW CON tains is only the shadow of those blessings which were still to come, not the full expression of their reality. The same sacrifices are offered year after year without intermission, and still the worshippers can never reach, through the law, their full growth. 2 If they could, must not the offerings have ceased before now? There would be no guilt left to reproach the consciences of those who come to worship; they would have been cleansed once for all. 3 No, what these offerings bring with them, year by year, is only the remembrance of sins; 4 that sins should be taken away by the blood of bulls and goats is impossible. 5 As Christ comes into the world, he says, No sacrifice, no offering was thy demand; thou hast endowed me, instead, with a body. 6 Thou hast not found any pleasure in burnt sacrifices, in sacrifices for sin. 7 See then, I said, I am coming to fulfil what is written of me, where the book lies unrolled; to do thy will, O my God. 8 First he says, Thou didst not demand victim or offering, the burnt sacrifice, the sacrifice for sin, nor hast thou found any pleasure in them; in anything that is, which the law has to offer, 9 and then:—I said, See, my God, I am coming to do thy will. He must clear the ground first, so as to build up afterwards. 10 In accordance with this divine will we have been sanctified by an offering made once for all, the body of Jesus Christ. 11 One high priest after another must stand there, day after day, offering again and again the same sacrifices, which can never take away our sins; 12 whereas he sits for ever at the right hand of God, offering for our sins a sacrifice that is never repeated. 13 He only waits, until all his enemies are made a footstool under his feet; 14 by a single offering he has completed his work, for all time, in those whom he sanctifies. 15 And here the Holy Spirit adds his testimony. He has been saying, 16 This is the covenant I will grant them, the Lord says, when that times comes; I will implant my laws in their hearts, engrave them in their innermost thoughts. And what follows? 17 I will not remember their sins and their transgressions

vv. 5-7. Ps. xxxix. 7-9; where, however, the Hebrew text differs. Our author here follows the Greek Septuagint, which is less obscure than the Hebrew.

v. 12. 'He sits at the right hand of God, atoning for our sins'; in the Greek, 'he has atoned for our sins and taken his seat at the right hand of God'.
v. 13. Ps. cix. 2.
vv. 16, 17. Jer. xxxi. 31-34.

HEBREWS

any more. 18 Where they are so remitted, there is no longer any room for a sin-offering.

19 Why then, brethren, we can enter the sanctuary with confidence through the blood of Christ. 20 He has opened up for us a new, a living approach, by way of the veil, I mean, his mortality. 21 A great priest is ours, who has dominion over God's house. 22 Let us come forward with sincere hearts in the full assurance of the faith, our guilty consciences purified by sprinkling, our bodies washed clean in hallowed water. 23 Do not let us waver in acknowledging the hope we cherish; we have a promise from one who is true to his word. 24 Let us keep one another in mind, always ready with incitements to charity and to acts of piety, 25 not abandoning, as some do, our common assembly, but encouraging one another; all the more, as you see the great day drawing nearer. 26 If we go on sinning wilfully, when once the full knowledge of the truth has been granted to us, we have no further sacrifice for sin to look forward to; 27 nothing but a terrible expectation of judgement, a fire that will eagerly consume the rebellious. 28 Let a man be convicted by two or three witnesses of defying the law of Moses, and he dies, without hope of mercy. 29 What of the man who has trampled the Son of God under foot, who has reckoned the blood of the covenant, that blood which sanctified him, as a thing unclean, mocked at the Spirit that brought him grace? Will not he incur a punishment much more severe? 30 It is one we know well, who has told us, Vengeance is for me, I will repay; and again, The Lord will judge his people. 31 It is a fearful thing to fall into the hands of the living God.

32 Remember those early days, when the light first came to you, and the hard probation of suffering you went through. 33 There were times when you yourselves were publicly exposed to calumny and persecution; there was a time when you took part with those who had the same path to tread. 34 You shewed your sympathy with those who were in bonds; and when you were robbed of your goods you took it cheerfully, as men who knew that a higher, a more lasting good was yours. 35 Do not throw away that confidence of yours, with its rich hope of reward; 36 you still need endurance, if you are to attain the prize God has promised to those who do his will. 37 Only a brief moment, now, before he who is coming will be here; he will not linger on the way. 38 It is faith that brings life to the man whom I accept as justified; if he shrinks back, he shall win no favour with me. 39 Not for us to shrink away, and be lost; it is for us to have faith, and save our souls.

v. 20. 'By way of the veil, I mean, his mortality'; literally, 'through the veil, that is, his flesh'. Some commentators understand this of our Lord's human Nature as such; but it is difficult to see how the Sacred Humanity could be regarded as in any sense an obstacle which has to be removed, as the sense of the passage suggests.
v. 22. 'Sprinkling'; that is, with the precious Blood.

v. 26. 'If we go on sinning'; the tense used in the Greek shews that the Apostle is referring to obstinate sinners, and in particular, no doubt, to those who fall away from the faith.
v. 28. Deut. xvii. 6.

v. 30. Deut. xxxii. 35, 36.

vv. 37, 38. A reminiscence, rather than an exact quotation, of Hab. ii. 3, 4.

426

Chapter Eleven

WHAT IS FAITH? IT IS that which gives substance to our hopes, which convinces us of things we cannot see. 2 It was this that brought credit to the men who went before us. 3 It is faith that lets us understand how the worlds were fashioned by God's word; how it was from things unseen that the things we see took their origin. 4 It was in faith that Abel offered a sacrifice richer than Cain's, and was proved thereby to be justified, since God recognized his offering; through that offering of his he still speaks in death. 5 When Enoch was taken away without the experience of death, when God took him and no more was seen of him, it was because of his faith; that is the account we have of him before he was taken, that he pleased God; 6 and it is impossible to please God without faith. Nobody reaches God's presence until he has learned to believe that God exists, and that he rewards those who try to find him. 7 When Noe received a warning about dangers still unseen, it was faith that made him take alarm, and build an ark to preserve his family. Thus he proved the whole world wrong, and was left heir to the justification which comes through faith. 8 And he to whom the name of Abraham was given shewed faith when he left his home, obediently, for the country which was to be his inheritance; left it without knowing where his journey would take him. 9 Faith taught him to live as a stranger in the land he had been promised for his own, encamping there with Isaac and Jacob, heirs with him of a common hope; 10 looking forward all the while to that city which has true foundations, which is God's design and God's fashioning. 11 It was faith that enabled Sara, barren till then, to conceive offspring, although she was past the age of child-bearing; she believed that God would be faithful to his word. 12 Here is one man, a man for whom life is already over; and from him springs a race whose numbers rival the stars of heaven, or the uncounted grains of sand on the seashore. 13 It was faith they lived by, all of them, and in faith they died; for them, the promises were not fulfilled, but they looked for-

v. 4. Gen. iv. 10.

v. 5. 'Pleased God'; in the Hebrew, 'walked with God', Gen. v. 22.

v. 8. Gen. xii. 1, xvii. 5. 'He to whom the name of Abraham was given'; the Greek should rather be translated, 'Abraham, when he was called.'

427

ward to them and welcomed them at a distance, owning themselves no better than strangers and exiles on earth. 14 Those who talk so make it clear enough, that they have not found their home. 15 Did they regret the country they had left behind? If that were all, they could have found opportunities for going back to it. 16 No, the country of their desires is a better, a heavenly country. God does not disdain to take his title from such names as these; he has a city ready for them to dwell in.

17 Abraham shewed faith, when he was put to the test, by offering up Isaac. He was ready to offer up an only son, this man who had made the promises his own, 18 and received the assurance, It is through Isaac that thy posterity shall be traced. 19 God, he argued, had the power to restore his son even from the dead; and indeed, in a hidden sense, he did so recover him. 20 It was by faith that Isaac, in blessing Jacob and Esau, foretold what was to come; 21 by faith that Jacob, on his death-bed, made reverence to the top of Joseph's staff, as he blessed his two sons in turn; 22 by faith that Joseph, when he, too, came to the end of his life, spoke of the Israelites' escape from Egypt, and gave orders for the removal of his bones. 23 The parents of Moses shewed faith, in making light of the king's edict, and hiding their child away for three months, when they saw what a fine child he was. 24 And Moses shewed faith, when he grew up, by refusing to pass for the son of Pharaoh's daughter. 25 He preferred ill usage, shared with the people of God, to the brief enjoyment of sinful pleasures; 26 all the wealth of Egypt could not so enrich him as the despised lot of God's anointed; he had eyes, you see, for nothing but the promised reward. 27 It was in faith that he left Egypt behind, defying the royal anger, made strong as if by the very sight of him who is invisible; 28 in faith that he performed the paschal rite, and the sprinkling of the blood, to leave Israel untouched by the angel that destroyed the first-born; 29 in faith that they crossed the Red Sea as if it had been dry land, whereas the Egyptians, when they ventured into it, were drowned. 30 Faith pulled down the walls of Jericho, after seven days spent in marching round them; 31 faith saved Rahab, the harlot, from sharing the doom of the disobedient, because she had given the spies a peaceable welcome.

32 What need is there to say more? Time will fail me if I try to go through all the history of Gedeon, of Barac, of Samson, of Jephte, of David and Samuel and the prophets. 33 Theirs was the faith which subdued kingdoms, which served the cause of right,

v. 16. 'To take his title'; that is, to be called 'the God of Abraham and Isaac and Jacob'.

v. 19. Abraham recovered his son from the dead, inasmuch as his life was spared unexpectedly; 'in a hidden sense', because the sacrifice of Isaac was a type of our Lord's Crucifixion.
v. 21. 'Made reverence to the top of Joseph's staff', because the staff was a symbol of the tribe; cf. e.g. Num. i. 49, where 'the tribe of Levi' is literally 'the staff of Levi'.

v. 26. 'Of God's anointed', probably in the sense that Moses was the type of Christ, in being rejected by his people, Ex. ii. 14; but possibly the reference is to the people of Israel, cf. Hab. iii. 13.
v. 27. 'Left Egypt behind'; that is, at the Exodus. Some of the Fathers understand the phrase of Moses' flight in Ex. ii. 15; but it is clear that Moses did fear the king's anger on that occasion.

which made promises come true. 34 They shut the mouths of lions, they quenched raging fire, swords were drawn on them, and they escaped. How strong they became, who till then were weak, what courage they shewed in battle, how they routed invading armies! 35 There were women, too, who recovered their dead children, brought back to life. Others, looking forward to a better resurrection still, would not purchase their freedom on the rack. 36 And others experienced mockery and scourging, chains, too, and imprisonment; 37 they were stoned, they were cut in pieces, they were tortured, they were put to the sword; they wandered about, dressed in sheepskins and goatskins, amidst want, and distress, and ill usage; 38 men whom the world was unworthy to contain, living a hunted life in deserts and on mountain sides, in rock-fastnesses and caverns underground. 39 One and all gave proof of their faith, yet they never saw the promise fulfilled; 40 for us, God had something better in store. We were needed, to make the history of their lives complete.

v. 37. 'Tortured'; literally, 'tested', 'put to the question'.

v. 40. The meaning here seems to be, that the Church of the new covenant is the continuation and the explanation of the Jewish Church which went before it, Christians enjoying here and now the blessings to which the patriarchs looked forward.

Chapter Twelve

W HY THEN, SINCE WE are watched from above by such a cloud of witnesses, let us rid ourselves of all that weighs us down, of the sinful habit that clings so closely, and run, with all endurance, the race for which we are entered. 2 Let us fix our eyes on Jesus, the origin and the crown of all faith, who, to win his prize of blessedness, endured the cross and made light of its shame, Jesus, who now sits on the right of God's throne. 3 Take your standard from him, from his endurance, from the enmity the wicked bore him, and you will not grow faint, you will not find yours souls unmanned. 4 Your protest, your battle against sin, has not yet called for bloodshed; 5 yet you have lost sight, already,

vv. 5, 6. Prov. iii. 11 and 12.

of those words of comfort in which God addresses you as his sons;
My son, do not undervalue the correction which the Lord sends
thee, do not be unmanned when he reproves thy faults. 6 It is
where he loves that he bestows correction; there is no recognition
for any child of his, without chastisement. 7 Be patient, then,
while correction lasts; God is treating you as his children. Was
there ever a son whom his father did not correct? 8 No, correction
is the common lot of all; you must be bastards, not true sons, if
you are left without it. 9 We have known what it was to accept
correction from earthly fathers, and with reverence; shall we not
submit, far more willingly, to the Father of a world of spirits, and
draw life from him? 10 They, after all, only corrected us for a
short while, at their own caprice; he does it for our good, to give
us a share in that holiness which is his. 11 For the time being, all
correction is painful rather than pleasant; but afterwards, when it
has done its work of discipline, it yields a harvest of good dispositions, to our great peace. 12 Come then, stiffen the sinews of
drooping hand, and flagging knee, 13 and plant your footprints in
a straight track, so that the man who goes lame may not stumble
out of the path, but regain strength instead. 14 Your aim must be
peace with all men, and that holiness without which no one will
ever see God. 15 Take good care that none of you is false to God's
grace, that no poisonous shoot is allowed to spring up, and con-
taminate many of you by its influence. 16 None of you must be
guilty of fornication, none of you earthly-minded, as Esau was,
when he sold his birthright for a single dish of food; 17 afterwards,
you may be sure, he was eager enough to have the blessing allotted
to him, but no, he was rejected. He pleaded for it in tears, but no
second chance was given him.

18 What is the scene, now, of your approach to God? It is no
longer a mountain that can be discerned by touch; no longer
burning fire, and whirlwind, and darkness, and storm. 19 No
trumpet sounds; no utterance comes from that voice, which made
those who listened to it pray that they might hear no more,
20 (daunted by the command, that if even a beast touched the
mountain it should die by stoning. 21 Moses said, in terror at the
sight, I am overcome with fear and trembling). 22 The scene of
your approach now is mount Sion, is the heavenly Jerusalem, city
of the living God; here are gathered thousands upon thousands of
angels, 23 here is the assembly of those first-born sons whose names
are written in heaven, here is God sitting in judgement on all men,
here are the spirits of just men, now made perfect; 24 here is

v. 15. Deut. xxix. 18.

v. 16. Gen. xxvii. 34.

v. 17. 'No second chance'; literally, 'no room for repentance'. This seems to have been an idiom of Roman law, meaning an opportunity to reconsider one's decision; in this case, the decision of Esau to sell his birthright.

vv. 18-20. Ex. xix. 12-19, xx. 18, 19.

v. 21. Cf. Deut. ix. 19; where, however, a different occasion is referred to.

430

THE HOLY WOMEN AT THE SEPULCHRE   SCHOOL OF MANTEGNA
                                            around 1500

NATIONAL GALLERY, LONDON

Jesus, the spokesman of the new covenant, and the sprinkling of his blood, which has better things to say than Abel's had. 25 Beware of excusing yourselves from listening to him who is speaking to you. There was no escape for those others, who tried to excuse themselves when God uttered his warnings on earth; still less for us, if we turn away when he speaks from heaven. 26 His voice, even then, made the earth rock; now, he has announced to us that it shall happen again, only once; he will shake earth and heaven too. 27 Only once again; that means that what is shaken, this created universe, will be removed; only the things which cannot be shaken are to stand firm. 28 The kingdom we have inherited is one which cannot be shaken; in gratitude for this, let us worship God as he would have us worship him, in awe and reverence; 29 no doubt of it, our God is a consuming fire.

v. 26. Aggaeus ii. 7.

v. 28. 'In gratitude for this, let us worship'; this may also mean, 'We have grace given us, to worship'.
v. 29. Deut. iv. 24.

Chapter Thirteen

ET brotherly love be firmly established among you; and do not forget to shew hospitality; in doing this, men have before now entertained angels unawares. 3 Remember those who are in prison, as if you were prisoners too; those who endure suffering, since you have mortal bodies of your own. 4 Marriage, in every way, must be held in honour, and the marriage-bed kept free from stain; over fornication and adultery, God will call us to account. 5 The love of money should not dwell in your thoughts; be content with what you have. God himself has told us, I will never forsake thee, never abandon thee; 6 so that we can say with confidence, The Lord is my champion; I will not be afraid of what man can do to me.

7 Do not forget those who have had charge of you, and preached God's word to you; contemplate the happy issue of the life they lived, and imitate their faith. 8 What Jesus Christ was yesterday, and is to-day, he remains for ever. 9 Do not be carried aside from your course by a maze of new doctrines; what gives true strength to a man's heart is gratitude, not observances in the matter of food, which never yet proved useful to those who followed them. 10 We have an altar of our own, and it is not those who carry out the

v. 5. Deut. xxxi. 6.

v. 6. Ps. cxvii. 6.

v. 7. 'The happy issue of the life they lived'; literally, 'the outgoing of their behaviour'. This is usually understood of their deaths (cf. Wisdom ii. 17); but it seems more likely that the Apostle refers to the results (cf. I Cor. x. 13) of the holy life lived by the earliest Christian missionaries, in the establishment of the faith.

v. 8. This verse seems to point forward to what follows; since the Christ we worship is the same in every age, there can be no room for new doctrines in the Church.

v. 9. 'What gives true strength to a man's heart is gratitude, not observances in the matter of food'; literally, 'it is good that the heart should be made firm with thankfulness (or, with grace), not with foods'. There is perhaps a reference to Ps. ciii. 15. Some commentators would understand the 'foods' in question to be the sacrificial meat eaten by the worshipper under the old Covenant.

vv. 10-13. These reflections are doubtless meant to console the Jewish Christians, in case any of them should regret being cut off from their ancestral worship. The 'altar' is understood by some commentators of the Holy Sacrifice, by others of the Cross, by others of Christ himself.

v. 20. 'That great shepherd, whose flock was bought with the blood of the eternal covenant'; literally, 'that great shepherd of the flock in the blood of the eternal covenant'. According to some, these last seven words should be taken with the main verb, 'raised from the dead'.

v. 21. Here, as in I

worship of the tabernacle that are qualified to eat its sacrifices. 11 When the high priest takes the blood of beasts with him into the sanctuary, as an offering for sin, the bodies of those beasts have to be burned away from the camp; 12 and thus it was that Jesus, when he would sanctify the people through his own blood, suffered beyond the city gate. 13 Let us, too, go out to him away from the camp, bearing the ignominy he bore; 14 we have an everlasting city, but not here; our goal is the city that is one day to be. 15 It is through him, then, that we must offer to God a continual sacrifice of praise, the tribute of lips that give thanks to his name. 16 Meanwhile, you must remember to do good to others and give alms; God takes pleasure in such sacrifice as this.

17 Obey those who have charge of you, and yield to their will; they are keeping unwearied watch over your souls, because they know they will have an account to give. Make it a grateful task for them: it is your own loss if they find it a laborious effort. 18 Pray for us; we trust we have a clear conscience, and the will to be honourable in all our dealings. 19 And I make this request the more earnestly, in the hope of being restored to you the sooner. 20 May God, the author of peace, who has raised our Lord Jesus Christ from the dead, that great shepherd, whose flock was bought with the blood of an eternal covenant, 21 grant you every capacity for good, to do his will. May he carry out in you the design he sees best, through Jesus Christ, to whom glory belongs throughout all ages, Amen. 22 I entreat you, brethren, bear patiently with all these words of warning; it is but a brief letter I am sending you. 23 You must know that our brother Timothy has been set at liberty; if he comes soon, I will bring him with me when I visit you. Greet all those who are in authority, and all the saints. 24 The brethren from Italy send you their greetings. 25 Grace be with you all, Amen.

Pet. iv. 11, it is not clear whether 'to whom' refers to 'God' or to 'Christ'. v. 22. It is difficult to believe that the Apostle refers to the whole of these thirteen chapters as a short letter. Perhaps we should understand that he is referring only to the immediate context, verses 18 to 25, as his 'letter' (in the sense that these alone bring a personal message from him), and distinguishing it from the lengthy 'words of warning', which have had to be read with patience. v. 24. 'The brethren from Italy', as an English phrase, would suggest that the Apostle was not writing from Rome. But he may well have been writing from Rome, since the same words, according to classical usage, might mean 'the brethren in Italy send their greetings from there'.

The UNIVERSAL EPISTLE OF THE BLESSED APOSTLE JAMES

Chapter One

James, a servant of God and of our Lord Jesus Christ, sends greeting to the members of the twelve tribes scattered throughout the world. 2 Consider yourselves happy indeed, my brethren, when you encounter trials of every sort, 3 as men who know well enough that the testing of their faith breeds endurance. 4 Endurance must do its work thoroughly, if you are to be men full-grown in every part, nothing lacking in you. 5 Is there one of you who still lacks wisdom? God gives to all, freely and ungrudgingly; so let him ask God for it, and the gift will come. 6 (Only it must be in faith that he asks, he must not hesitate; one who hesitates is like a wave out at sea, driven to and fro by the wind; 7 such a man must not hope to win any gift from the Lord. 8 No, a man who is in two minds will find no rest wherever he goes.) 9 Is one of the brethren in humble circumstances? Let him be proud of it; it exalts him, whereas the rich man takes pride in what in truth abases him. 10 (The rich man will pass by like the bloom on the grass; 11 the sun gets up, and the scorching wind with it, which dries up the grass, till the bloom on it falls,

v. 10. 'Whereas the rich man takes pride in what in truth abases him'; others would interpret, 'Let

433

the rich (Christian) take pride in his abasement', that is, in bearing reproach for the sake of his religion; but this does not seem to fit the context so well.

v. 13. 'God may threaten us with evil'; this seems to be the only possible meaning of the Latin, if the text here is correct. The sense of the Greek is, 'God is unversed in evil', or perhaps 'is not tempted by evil'; others would render it, 'does not tempt men to evil'.

and all its fair show dies away; so the rich man, with his enterprises, will disappear.)

12 Blessed is he who endures under trials. When he has proved his worth, he will win that crown of life, which God has promised to those who love him. 13 Nobody, when he finds himself tempted, should say, I am being tempted by God. God may threaten us with evil, but he does not himself tempt anyone. 14 No, when a man is tempted, it is always because he is being drawn away by the lure of his own passions. 15 When that has come about, passion conceives and gives birth to sin; and when sin has reached its full growth, it breeds death. 16 Beloved brethren, do not deceive yourselves over this. 17 Whatever gifts are worth having, whatever endowments are perfect of their kind, these come to us from above; they are sent down by the Father of all that gives light, with whom there can be no change, no swerving from his course; 18 and it was his will to give us birth, through his true word, meaning us to be the first-fruits, as it were, of all his creation. 19 You know this, my beloved brethren, well enough. It is for us men to be ready listeners, slow to speak our minds, slow to take offence; 20 man's anger does not bear the fruit that is acceptable to God. 21 Rid yourselves, then, of all defilement, of all the ill will that remains in you; be patient, and cherish that word implanted in you which can bring salvation to your souls.

v. 23. 'The face he was born with'; some understand this as meaning 'the face which belongs to his perishable body'.

22 Only you must be honest with yourselves; you are to live by the word, not content merely to listen to it. 23 One who listens to the word without living by it is like a man who sees, in a mirror, the face he was born with; 24 he looks at himself, and away he goes, never giving another thought to the man he saw there. 25 Whereas one who gazes into that perfect law, which is the law of freedom, and dwells on the sight of it, does not forget its message; he finds something to do, and does it, and his doing of it wins him a blessing. 26 If anyone deludes himself by thinking he is serving God, when he has not learned to control his tongue, the service he gives is vain. 27 If he is to offer service pure and unblemished in the sight of God, who is our Father, he must take care of orphans and widows in their need, and keep himself untainted by the world.

Chapter Two

BRETHREN, you believe that all glory belongs to our Lord Jesus Christ; do not combine this faith of yours with flattery of human greatness. 2 Suppose that a man comes into your place of meeting in fine clothes, wearing a gold ring; suppose that a poor man comes in at the same time, ill clad. 3 Will you pay attention to the well-dressed man, and bid him take some place of honour; will you tell the poor man, Stand where thou art, or sit on the ground at my footstool? 4 If so, are you not introducing divisions into your company? Have you not shewn partiality in your judgement? 5 Listen to me, my dear brethren; has not God chosen the men who are poor in the world's eyes to be rich in faith, to be heirs of that kingdom which he has promised to those who love him? 6 And here are you putting the poor man to shame. Is it not the rich who use their power to oppress you? Are not they the very men who drag you into court, 7 the very men who speak evil of that honoured name, by which you are called? 8 True, you do well to observe, in their regard, the royal law you find in the words of scripture, Thou shalt love thy neighbour as thyself. 9 But if you flatter the great, you incur guilt; the law finds you out in a transgression. 10 And the man who has failed in one point, though he has kept the rest of the law, is liable to all its penalties: 11 he who forbids adultery has forbidden murder as well. The murderer, though he be no adulterer, has yet transgressed the law. 12 You must speak and act like men already on their trial before a law of freedom. 13 The merciless will be judged mercilessly; mercy gives its judgment an honourable welcome.

14 Of what use is it, my brethren, if a man claims to have faith, and has no deeds to shew for it? Can faith save him then? 15 Here is a brother, here is a sister, going naked, left without the means to secure their daily food; 16 if one of you says to them, Go in peace, warm yourselves and take your fill, without providing for their bodily needs, of what use is it? 17 Thus faith, if it has no deeds to shew for itself, has lost its own principle of life. 18 We shall be inclined to say to him, Thou hast faith, but I have deeds to shew. Shew me this faith of thine without any deeds to prove it, and I am prepared, by my deeds, to prove my own faith. 19 Thou

v. 12. 'Men already on their trial'; in the Greek, 'men who are to be tried'.

v. 13. 'Mercy gives its judgement an honourable welcome'; literally, 'mercy exalts judgement'. This appears to be the sense of the Latin text, which is perhaps due to an error of copying. The sense of the Greek is, 'Mercy can boast over (its) judgement'.

v. 18. 'We shall be inclined to say'; the phrase here used commonly introduces an objection, 'But someone will say'. But such a render-

435

ing would not fit the present context.

believest that there is only one God; that is well enough, but then, so do the devils, and the devils shrink from him in terror. 20 Rash soul, wouldst thou be assured that faith without deeds to shew has no life in it? 21 Think of our father Abraham; was it not by his deeds that he found approval, when he offered his son Isaac on the altar? 22 See how his faith conspired with deeds done, and through those deeds his faith was realized. 23 Thus he confirmed

v. 23. Gen. xv. 6.

the words of scripture, which tell us, Abraham put his faith in God, and it was reckoned virtue in him, and he earned the title of God's friend. 24 You see, then, that it takes deeds as well as faith if a man is to be justified. 25 Or again, how did Rahab, the harlot, win

v. 25. Josue ii. 1-16.

God's approval? Was it not by her deeds, when she harboured the spies and sent them home by a different way? 26 Body separated from spirit is a dead body, and faith separated from good deeds is a dead faith.

Chapter Three

O not be too eager, brethren, to impart instruction to others; be sure that, if we do, we shall be called to account all the more strictly. 2 We are betrayed, all of us, into many faults; and a man who is not betrayed into faults of the tongue must be a man perfect at every point, who knows how to curb his whole body. 3 Just so we can make horses obey us, and turn their whole bodies this way and that, by putting a curb in their mouths. 4 Or look at ships; how huge they are, how boisterous are the winds that drive them along! And yet a tiny rudder will turn them this way and that, as the

v. 6. 'The proper element in which all that is harmful lives'; literally, 'iniquity's world'. Some think that these words should be attached to the foregoing sentence. 'This mortal sphere of ours'; literally, 'the circle of our birth (or, becoming)'; probably the phrase means simply 'the world'.

captain's purpose will have it. 5 Just so, the tongue is a tiny part of our body, and yet what power it can boast! How small a spark it takes to set fire to a vast forest! 6 And that is what the tongue is, a fire. Among the organs of our nature, the tongue has its place as the proper element in which all that is harmful lives. It infects the whole body, and sets fire to this mortal sphere of ours, catching fire itself from hell. 7 Mankind can tame, and has long since

v. 7. 'And all else'; in the Greek, 'and of fishes'.

learned to tame, every kind of beast and bird, of creeping things and all else; 8 but no human being has ever found out how to tame the tongue; a pest that is never allayed, all deadly poison. 9 We use it to bless God who is our Father; we use it to curse our fellow men, that were made in God's image; 10 blessing and cursing come from the same mouth. My brethren, there is no reason in this. 11 Does the fountain gush out fresh and salt water from the same outlet? 12 What, my brethren, can a fig-tree yield olives, or a vine figs? No more easily will brackish water yield fresh.

13 Does any of you lay claim to wisdom or learning? Then let him give proof of his quality by setting a good example, living peaceably as a wise man should. 14 As long as you find bitter jealousy and thoughts of rivalry in your hearts, let us have none of this boasting that perverts the truth; 15 such wisdom as yours does not come from above, it belongs to earth and to nature, and is fit only for devils. 16 Where there is jealousy, where there is rivalry, there you will find disorder and every kind of defect. 17 Whereas the wisdom which does come from above is marked chiefly indeed by its purity, but also by its peacefulness; it is courteous and ready to be convinced, always taking the better part; it carries mercy with it, and a harvest of all that is good; it is un-censorious, and without affectation. 18 Peace is the seed-ground of holiness, and those who make peace will win its harvest.

Chapter Four

WHAT LEADS TO WAR, what leads to quarrelling among you? I will tell you what leads to them; the appetites which infest your mortal bodies. 2 Your desires go unfulfilled, so you fall to murdering; you set your heart on something, and cannot have your will, so there is quarrelling and fighting. Why cannot you have your will? Because you do not pray for it, 3 or you pray, and what you ask for is denied you, because you ask for it with ill intent; you would squander it on your appetites. 4 Wantons, have you never been told that the world's friendship means enmity with God, and the man who would have the world for his friend makes himself God's enemy? 5 Do you think scripture means nothing when it tells you that the Spirit which dwells in you loves with a jealous love? 6 No, the grace he gives us is something better still; and so he tells us, God flouts the scornful, and gives the humble man his grace. 7 Be God's true subjects, then; stand firm against the devil, and he will run away from you, 8 come close to God, and he will come close to you. You that are sinners must wash your hands clean, you that are in two minds must purify the intention of your hearts. 9 Bring yourselves low with mourning and weeping, turn your laughter into sadness, your joy into downcast looks; 10 humble yourselves before the Lord, and he will exalt you.

11 Brethren, do not disparage one another. In disparaging one of his brethren, in passing judgement on him, a man disparages the law, passes judgement on the law; and in passing judgement on the law thou art setting thyself up to be its censor, instead of obeying it. 12 There is only one Lawgiver, only one Judge, he who has power to destroy and to set free. 13 Who art thou, to sit in judgement on thy neighbour?

See how you go about saying, To-day, or to-morrow, we will make our way to such and such a town, spend a year there, and make profit by trading, 14 when you have no means of telling what the morrow will bring. 15 What is your life but a wisp of smoke, which shews for a moment and then must vanish into nothing? You ought to be saying, We will do this or that if it is the Lord's will, and if life is granted us. 16 As it is, your self-conceit makes boasters of you; all such boastfulness is an evil thing. 17 Yes, if a man has the power to do good, it is sinful in him to leave it undone.

v. 5. Literally, this verse runs, 'Or do you think that the passage in scripture means nothing when it says, The Spirit which dwells in you (in the Greek, which God has sent to dwell in you) longs after you even to envy?' The whole phrase cannot be found in the Old Testament; the notion that God is a jealous God frequently occurs, e.g. Ex. xx. 5. The Hebrew language does not distinguish between envy and jealousy.

v. 6. 'The grace he gives us is something better still'; literally, 'He gives a greater grace', perhaps by way of contrast with the earthly subjects of petition mentioned in v. 3 above. The quotation is from Prov. iii. 34.

v. 17. It is difficult to see how this fits into the context, unless we suppose that the whole passage from iv. 13 to v. 6 is directed against the rich, who are here accused of neglecting the great opportunities they have for doing good.

JESUS APPEARS TO MARY MAGDALENE   SCHOOL OF MANTEGNA
around 1500

NATIONAL GALLERY, LONDON

Chapter Five

COME, YOU MEN OF riches, bemoan yourselves and cry aloud over the miseries that are to overtake you. 2 Corruption has fallen on your riches; all the fine clothes are left moth-eaten, 3 and the gold and silver have long lain rusting. That rust will bear witness against you, will bite into your flesh like flame. These are the last days given you, and you have spent them in heaping up a store of retribution. 4 You have kept back the pay of the workmen who reaped your lands, and it is there to cry out against you; the Lord of hosts has listened to their complaint. 5 You have feasted here on earth, you have comforted your hearts with luxuries on this day that dooms you to slaughter. 6 You have condemned and murdered the innocent man, while he offered no resistance.

7 Wait, then, brethren, in patience for the Lord's coming. See how the farmer looks forward to the coveted returns of his land, yet waits patiently for the early and the late rains to fall before they can be brought in. 8 You too must wait patiently, and take courage; the Lord's coming is close at hand. 9 Brethren, do not bring complaints against one another; if you do, you will be judged, and the judge is already standing at your doors. 10 If you would learn by example, brethren, how to work on and wait patiently in evil times, think of the prophets who spoke in the Lord's name. 11 See how we congratulate those who have shewn endurance. You have heard of Job's endurance; and you have read, in that story, how kind and merciful the Lord is in rewarding us. 12 But above all, my brethren, do not bind yourselves by any oath, by heaven, by earth, or by any oath at all. Let your word be Yes for Yes, and No for No; if not, you will be judged for it.

13 Is one of you unhappy? Let him fall to prayer. Is one of you cheerful? For him, a psalm. 14 Is one of you sick? Let him send for the presbyters of the church, and let them pray over him, anointing him with oil in the Lord's name. 15 Prayer offered in faith will restore the sick man, and the Lord will give him relief;

v. 3. 'Heaping up a store of retribution'; in the Greek, 'heaping up treasure'.

v. 6. 'The innocent man'; this might also be translated 'the Just One', and understood as a reference to our Lord; cf. Acts iii. 14, vii. 52, Wisdom ii. 12-20.
v. 7. In Palestine, the rains of early autumn and late spring are especially important to the crops.

v. 11. 'How kind and merciful the Lord is in rewarding us'; literally, 'the fulfilment of the Lord, how kind and merciful he is'. Cf. Rom. vi. 21, I Pet. i. 9.
v. 12. Cf. Matthew v. 33. It seems probable that St. James had some special reason for warning the Jewish Christians against taking oaths, perhaps because he was afraid of their taking part in unlawful conspiracies.
v. 15. 'Give him re-

lief'; in the Greek,
'raise him up'.

v. 17. II Kings xvii.
1, xviii. 41.

v. 20. That is, prob-
ably, his own sins;
cf. 1 Peter iv. 8.

if he is guilty of sins, they will be pardoned. 16 Confess your sins to one another, and pray for one another, for the healing of your souls. When a just man prays fervently, there is great virtue in his prayer. 17 Elias was only a mortal man like ourselves, and when he prayed and prayed that it might not rain on the land, there was no rain for three years and six months; 18 then he prayed anew, and rain fell from heaven, and so the land yielded its harvest.

19 My brethren, if one of you strays from the truth, and a man succeeds in bringing him back, 20 let him be sure of this; to bring back erring feet into the right path means saving a soul from death, means throwing a veil over a multitude of sins.

THE FIRST EPISTLE OF THE BLESSED APOSTLE PETER

Chapter One

PETER, AN APOSTLE OF Jesus Christ, to the elect who dwell as foreigners up and down Pontus, Galatia, Cappadocia, Asia, and Bithynia, 2 chosen in the foreknowledge of God the Father, to be sanctified by the Spirit, to give their allegiance to Jesus Christ and be sprinkled with his blood; grace and peace be yours abundantly. 3 Blessed be that God, that Father of our Lord Jesus Christ, who in his great mercy has begotten us anew, making hope live in us through the resurrection of Jesus Christ from the dead. 4 We are to share an inheritance that is incorruptible, inviolable, unfading. It is stored up for you in heaven, 5 and meanwhile, through your faith, the power of God affords you safe conduct till you reach it, this salvation which is waiting to be disclosed at the end of time. 6 Then you will be triumphant. What if you have trials of many sorts to sadden your hearts in this brief interval? That must needs happen, 7 so that you may give proof of your faith, a much more precious thing than the gold we test by fire; proof which will bring you praise, and glory, and honour when Jesus Christ is revealed. 8 You never saw him, but you

v. 6. 'You will be triumphant'; both here and at the end of verse 8 the Latin gives the verbs in the future tense; the Greek, somewhat obscurely, has the present tense, 'You are triumphing'.

v. 8. The words 'you

441

believe in him, and' are not found in the Greek.

learned to love him; you may not see him even now, but you believe in him; and, if you continue to believe in him, how you will triumph! How ineffable your joy will be, and how sublime, 9 when you reap the fruit of that faith of yours, the salvation of your souls! 10 Salvation was the aim and quest of the prophets, and the grace of which they prophesied has been reserved for you. 11 The Spirit of Christ was in them, making known to them the sufferings which Christ's cause brings with it, and the glory that crowns them; when was it to be, and how was the time of it to be recognized? 12 It was revealed to them that their errand was not to their own age, it was to you. And now the angels can satisfy their eager gaze; the Holy Spirit has been sent from heaven, and your evangelists have made the whole mystery plain, to you instead.

v. 13. 'Rid your minds, then, of every encumbrance'; literally, 'gird up the loins of your mind', cf. Luke xii. 35.

13 Rid your minds, then, of every encumbrance, keep full mastery of your senses, and set your hopes on the gracious gift that is offered you when Jesus Christ appears. 14 Obedience should be native to you now; you must not retain the mould of your former untutored appetites. 15 No, it is a holy God who has called you, and you too must be holy in all the ordering of your lives;

v. 16. Lev. xi. 44.

16 You must be holy, the scripture says, because I am holy. 17 You appeal to God as your Father; yes, but he judges each man impartially by what he has done; look anxiously, then, to the ordering of your lives while your stay on earth lasts. 18 What was the ransom that freed you from the vain observances of ancestral tradition? You know well enough that it was not paid in earthly currency, silver or gold; 19 it was paid in the precious blood of Christ; no lamb was ever so pure, so spotless a victim. 20 Before the beginning of the world, God had foreknown him, but it was only in these last days that he was revealed, for your sakes; 21 through him you have learned to be faithful to God, who raised him from the dead and endowed him with glory; your faith and your hope are to be centred in God. 22 Purify your souls with

v. 22. 'Purify your souls with the discipline of charity'; the Greek has, 'Now that you have purified your souls by obedience to the truth'.

v. 23. The Greek might also be translated 'through the word of God which lives and lasts for ever'.

the discipline of charity, and give constant proof of your affection for each other, loving unaffectedly as brethren should, 23 since you have all been born anew with an immortal, imperishable birth, through the word of God who lives and abides for ever. 24 Yes, all mortal things are like grass, and all their glory like the bloom of grass; the grass withers, and its bloom falls, 25 but the word of the Lord lasts for ever. And this word is nothing other than the gospel which has been preached to you.

v. 24. Is. xl. 6-8.

442

Chapter Two

YOU MUST PUT ASIDE, then, every trace of ill will and deceitfulness, your affectations, the grudges you bore, and all the slanderous talk; 2 you are children new-born, and all your craving must be for the soul's pure milk, that will nurture you into salvation, 3 once you have tasted, as you have surely tasted, the goodness of the Lord. 4 Draw near to him; he is the living antitype of that stone which men rejected, which God has chosen and prized; 5 you too must be built up on him, stones that live and breathe, into a spiritual fabric; you must be a holy priesthood, to offer up that spiritual sacrifice which God accepts through Jesus Christ. 6 So you will find in scripture the words, Behold, I am setting down in Sion a corner-stone, chosen out and precious; those who believe in him will not be disappointed. 7 Prized, then, by you, the believers, he is something other to those who refuse belief; the stone which the builders rejected has become the chief stone at the corner, 8 a stone to trip men's feet, a boulder they stumble against. They stumble over God's word, and refuse it belief; it is their destiny. 9 Not so you; you are a chosen race, a royal priesthood, a consecrated nation, a people God means to have for himself; it is yours to proclaim the exploits of the God who has called you out of darkness into his marvellous light. 10 Time was when you were not a people at all, now you are God's people; once you were unpitied, and now his pity is yours.

11 Beloved, I call upon you to be like strangers and exiles, to resist those natural appetites which besiege the soul. 12 Your life amidst the Gentiles must be beyond reproach; decried as malefactors, you must let them see, from your honourable behaviour, what you are; they will praise God for you, when his time comes to have mercy on them. 13 For love of the Lord, then, bow to every kind of human authority; to the king, who enjoys the chief power, 14 and to the magistrates who hold his commission to punish criminals and encourage honest men. 15 To silence, by honest living, the ignorant chatter of fools; that is what God expects of you.

v. 2. 'The soul's pure milk'; some would render the Greek here, 'the pure milk of the word'.
v. 3. Ps. xxxiii. 9.

v. 6. Is. xxviii. 16; see note on Rom. ix. 33.

v. 7. Ps. cxvii. 22. 'Prized, then, by you, the believers'; according to some commentators, this should be 'The honour, then, belongs to you, the believers'.

v. 10. Osee ii. 23, 24.

v. 12. 'To have mercy on them'; literally, 'to visit them', but the sense here is probably that which the verb has in Luke i. 68.

16 Free men, but the liberty you enjoy is not to be made a pretext for wrong-doing; it is to be used in God's service. 17 Give all men their due; to the brethren, your love; to God, your reverence; to the king, due honour.

18 You who are slaves must be submissive to your masters, and shew all respect, not only to those who are kind and considerate, but to those who are hard to please. 19 It does a man credit when he bears undeserved ill treatment with the thought of God in his heart. 20 If you do wrong and are punished for it, your patience is nothing to boast of; it is the patience of the innocent sufferer that wins credit in God's sight. 21 Indeed, you are engaged to this by the call of Christ; he suffered for our sakes, and left you his own example; you were to follow in his footsteps. 22 He did no wrong, no treachery was found on his lips; 23 he was ill spoken of, and spoke no evil in return, suffered, and did not threaten vengeance, gave himself up into the hands of injustice. 24 So, on the cross, his own body took the weight of our sins; we were to become dead to our sins, and live for holiness; it was his wounds that healed you. 25 Till then, you had been like sheep going astray; now, you have been brought back to him, your shepherd, who keeps watch over your souls.

v. 22. Is. liii. 9.

v. 23. 'Of injustice'; the Greek here has, 'of a just judge', that is, his heavenly Father.

v. 24. Is. liii. 4, 5.

v. 25. 'The shepherd who keeps watch'; literally 'the shepherd and overseer (or bishop) of your souls'.

Chapter Three

YOU, TOO, WHO ARE wives must be submissive to your husbands. Some of these still refuse credence to the word; it is for their wives to win them over, not by word but by example; 2 by the modesty and reverence they observe in your demeanour. 3 Your beauty must lie, not in braided hair, not in gold trinkets, not in the dress you wear, 4 but in the hidden features of your hearts, in a possession you can never lose, that of a calm and tranquil spirit; to God's eyes, beyond price. 5 It was thus that the holy women of old time adorned themselves, those women who had such trust in God, and paid their husbands such respect. 6 Think how obedient Sara was to Abraham, how she called him her lord; if you would prove yourselves her children, live honestly, and let no anxious thoughts disturb you. 7 You, too, who are husbands must use marriage considerately, paying homage to woman's sex as weaker than your own. The grace of eternal life belongs to both, and your prayers must not suffer interruption.

8 In a word, think the same thoughts, all of you, and share the same feelings; be lovers of the brethren. I would see you tender-hearted, modest, and humble, 9 not repaying injury with injury, or hard words with hard words, but blessing those who curse you. This God's call demands of you, and you will inherit a blessing in your turn. 10 Yes, long life and prosperous days, who would have these for the asking? My counsel is, keep thy tongue clear of harm, and thy lips free from every treacherous word. 11 Neglect the call of evil, and rather do good; let peace be all thy quest and aim. 12 On the upright, the Lord's eye ever looks favourably; his ears are open to their pleading. Perilous is his frown for the wrongdoers. 13 And who is to do you wrong, if only what is good inspires your ambitions? 14 If, after all, you should have to suffer in the cause of right, yours is a blessed lot. Do not be afraid or disturbed at their threats; 15 enthrone Christ as Lord in your hearts. If anyone asks you to give an account of the hope which you cherish, be ready at all times to answer for it, 16 but courteously and with due reverence. What matters is that you should have a clear conscience; so the defamers of your holy life in Christ will be disappointed in their calumny. 17 It may be God's will that we should suffer for doing right; better that, than for doing wrong. 18 It was thus that Christ died as a ransom, paid once for all, on behalf of our sins, he the innocent for us the guilty, so as to present us in God's sight. In his mortal nature he was done to death, but endowed with fresh life in his spirit, 19 and it was in his spirit that he went and preached to the spirits who lay in prison. 20 Long before, they had refused belief, hoping that God would be patient with them, in the days of Noe. That ark which Noe was then building, in which a few souls, eight in all, found refuge as they passed through the waves, 21 was a type of the baptism which saves us now. Our baptism is not a putting away of outward defilement; it is the test which assures us of a good conscience before God, through the resurrection of Jesus Christ.

v. 7. Cf. I Cor. vii. 5.

vv. 10-12. Ps. xxxiii. 13 sqq.

vv. 19-20. It is certain that this passage represents the holy patriarchs as living in a place of detention, neither heaven nor hell, till our Lord came (cf. Matthew xxvii. 52, 53). It is not clear why the Apostle concentrates his attention on the contemporaries of Noe, or how those who had refused be-

445

22 He sits, now, at the right hand of God, annihilating death, to make us heirs of eternal life; he has taken his journey to heaven, with all the angels and powers and princedoms made subject under his feet.

lief attained salvation afterwards; it seems best to suppose that they were incredulous while the ark was being built, and repented when it was too late to escape the Deluge. 'Hoping that God would be patient with them'; in the Greek, apparently, 'while God's patience waited for them'. 'As they passed through the waves'; some would translate 'by means of water', but this does not apply to the story in Genesis; Christian baptism typifies passing through the waters of death (cf. I Cor. x. 2). v. 21. 'The test which assures us of a good conscience'; the Greek might also mean 'the petition for a good conscience'. v. 22. The words 'annihilating (literally, swallowing up) death, to make us heirs of eternal life' are not found in the Greek manuscripts.

Chapter Four

CHRIST'S mortal nature, then, has been crucified, and you must arm yourselves with the same intention; he whose mortal nature has been crucified is quit, now, of sin. **2** The rest of your mortal life must be ordered by God's will, not by human appetites. **3** Time enough has been spent already in doing what the heathen would have you do, following a course of incontinence, passion, drunkenness, reveling, carousal, and shameful idolatry. **4** They are surprised that you do not rush headlong into the same welter of debauch, and call you ill names accordingly; **5** they will have to answer for it before him who is all in readiness to pass sentence on the living and the dead. **6** That is why dead men, too, had the gospel message brought to them; though their mortal natures had paid the penalty in men's eyes, in the sight of God their spirits were to live on.

7 The end of all things is close at hand; live wisely, and keep your senses awake to greet the hours of prayer. **8** Above all things, preserve constant charity among yourselves; charity draws the veil over a multitude of sins. **9** Make one another free of what is yours ungrudgingly, **10** sharing with all whatever gift each of you has received, as befits the stewards of a God so rich in graces. **11** One of you preaches, let him remember that it is God's message he is uttering; another distributes relief, let him remember that it is God who supplies him the opportunity; that so, in all you do, God may be glorified through Jesus Christ; to him be the glory and the power through endless ages, Amen.

12 Do not be surprised, beloved, that this fiery ordeal should have befallen you, to test your quality; there is nothing strange in

v. 1. 'Christ's mortal nature has been crucified . . . he whose mortal nature has been crucified'; literally, 'Christ has suffered as far as the flesh is concerned . . . he who has suffered as far as the flesh is concerned'. It is difficult to see in what sense 'he who has suffered is quit of sin', unless suffering here means death. Probably the apostle refers to baptism as mystical association with Christ's death; cf. the very similar passage in Rom. vi. 3-7. It is possible, however, that physical death is alluded to in both parts of the sentence. v. 6. 'Though their mortal natures had paid the penalty in men's eyes, in the sight of God their spirits were to live on'; literally, 'that they might be judged according to men in the flesh, but live according to God in the spirit'. This much-disputed passage probably refers us back to iii. 19 and 20 above; there were

446

what is happening to you. 13 Rather rejoice, when you share in some measure the sufferings of Christ; so joy will be yours, and triumph, when his glory is revealed. 14 Your lot will be a blessed one, if you are reproached for the name of Christ; it means that the virtue of God's honour and glory and power, it means that his own Spirit, is resting upon you. 15 Let it not be said that any of you underwent punishment for murder, or theft, or slander, or infringing other men's rights; 16 but, if a man is punished for being a Christian, he has no need to be ashamed of it; let him bear that name, and give glory to God. 17 The time is ripe for judgement to begin, and to begin with God's own household; and if our turn comes first, what will be its issue for those who refuse credence to God's message? 18 If the just man wins salvation only with difficulty, what will be the plight of the godless, of the sinner? 19 Why then, let those who suffer in fulfilment of God's will commend their souls, all innocent, into his hands; he created them, and he will not fail them.

souls who, through incredulity, incurred the outward penalty of temporal death at the time of the Deluge, and nevertheless, through contrition, were reserved for spiritual life, which was brought to them by Christ after his Passion. This illustrated why God 'judges the dead' (verse 5); physical death is only a temporary penalty, and their eternal destiny had still to be settled.
v. 8. Prov. x. 12; cf. James v. 20; the sense may be that charity 'hides away, obliterates in its effects', the sin of another; but more probably the doctrine here is that of Luke vii. 47.
v. 9. 'Make one another free of what is yours'; literally 'be hospitable to one another', but it seems

necessary to take the words in this more general sense, in order to connect them with the two verses which follow.
v. 11. Cf. note on Heb. xiii. 21.   v. 14. The text here is uncertain; some manuscripts omit the words 'honour' and 'power'; some add, after the word 'Spirit', the words 'blasphemed by others, but honoured by you'.
v. 15. For 'slander', the Greek has 'wrong-doing'. The word which follows means, literally, 'one who looks after business which is not his own'; it is possible that political agitators are referred to.

Chapter Five

AND NOW I HAVE A charge to give to the presbyters in your company; I, who am a presbyter like themselves, I, who bear witness of Christ's sufferings, I, who have my part in that glory which will one day be revealed. 2 Be shepherds to the flock God has given you. Carry out your charge as God would have it done, cordially, not like drudges, generously, not in the hope of sordid gain; 3 not tyrannizing, each in his own sphere, but setting an example, as best you may, to the flock. 4 So, when the Prince

v. 3. The words 'as best you may', literally 'from the heart',

PETER I

of shepherds makes himself known, your prize will be that crown of glory which cannot fade. 5 And you, who are young, must defer to these, your seniors. Deference to one another is the livery you must all wear; God thwarts the proud, and keeps his grace for the humble.

6 Bow down, then, before the strong hand of God; he will raise you up, when his time comes to deliver you. 7 Throw back on him the burden of all your anxiety; he is concerned for you. 8 Be sober, and watch well; the devil, who is your enemy, goes about roaring like a lion, to find his prey, 9 but you, grounded in the faith, must face him boldly; you know well enough that the brotherhood you belong to pays, all the world over, the same tribute of suffering. 10 And God, the giver of all grace, who has called us to enjoy, after a little suffering, his eternal glory in Christ Jesus, will himself give you mastery, and steadiness, and strength. 11 To him be glory and power through endless ages, Amen.

12 I count on Silvanus as a faithful brother; and through him I have written you these brief lines of encouragement; to assure you that the grace in which you are so firmly established is the true grace of God. 13 The church here in Babylon, united with you by God's election, sends you her greeting; so does my son, Mark. 14 Greet one another with the kiss of fellowship. Grace be to all of you, friends in Christ Jesus. Amen.

are not found in the Greek.
v. 6. Cf. note on ii. 12 above.
v. 7. Ps. liv. 23.
v. 9. The Greek here should perhaps be rendered, 'you know how to pay the same tribute of suffering as your brethren, all the world over'. The idea of 'tribute' is probably suggested by the Greek verb used, though it is not rendered in the Latin.
v. 10. Some commentators would make the words 'after a little suffering' follow on the words 'will himself give you'.
v. 12. Silvanus is probably the companion of St. Paul (I Thess. i. 1).
v. 13. The word 'church' is not expressed, but is evidently meant to be understood, in the Greek. There can be little doubt that Babylon means Rome; cf. Apoc. xvii. 5. The Mark here mentioned is doubtless the Evangelist, whom a very early tradition describes as the 'interpreter' of St. Peter.
v. 14. For 'grace' the Greek has 'peace'.

448

ᚱᚻe SECOND EPISTLE OF THE BLESSED APOSTLE PETER

Chapter One

SIMON PETER, A SERV
ant and apostle of Jesus Christ, to
those who share with us the common privilege of faith, justified
as we are by our God and Saviour Jesus Christ, 2 grace and peace
be yours abundantly, as you gain fuller knowledge of God, and of
Christ Jesus our Lord. 3 See how all the gifts that make for life
and holiness in us belong to his divine power; come to us through
fuller knowledge of him, whose own glory and sovereignty have
drawn us to himself! 4 Through him God has bestowed on us
high and treasured promises; you are to share the divine nature,
with the world's corruption, the world's passions, left behind.
5 And you too have to contribute every effort on your own part,
crowning your faith with virtue, and virtue with enlightenment,
6 and enlightenment with continence, and continence with endurance, and endurance with holiness, 7 and holiness with brotherly love, and brotherly love with charity. 8 Such gifts, when
they are yours in full measure, will make you quick and successful
pupils, reaching ever closer knowledge of our Lord Jesus Christ;
9 he who lacks them is no better than a blind man feeling his way

*v. 1. 'Our God and
Saviour Jesus Christ';
others would render,
'our God, and the
Saviour Jesus Christ',
but this seems a less
accurate rendering of
the Greek.*

*v. 3. For 'See how
all the gifts that
make for life and
holiness in us belong
to his divine power',
the Greek has 'Since
his divine power has
given us all that
makes for life and
holiness'. Most of the
Latin manuscripts
have, apparently, 'See
how all things belong
to his divine power,
which has been given
to us to make for life
and holiness'.*

*v. 4. 'Through him';
the Greek has,
'through them'.*

about; his old sins have been purged away, and he has forgotten it. 10 Bestir yourselves then, brethren, ever more eagerly, to ratify God's calling and choice of you by a life well lived; if you do this, you will make no false step, 11 and it will be no grudging entrance that is afforded to you into the kingdom of our Lord and Saviour Jesus Christ.

12 I shall never fail, then, to go on reminding you of this, although you know it well, and are firmly grounded in a truth that is present to your minds. 13 I hold it my duty to keep the memory awake in you, while I am still in this brief dwelling-place; 14 I am assured, by what our Lord Jesus Christ has made known to me, that I must fold my tent before long. 15 And I will see to it that, when I am gone, you shall always be able to remember what I have been saying. 16 We were not crediting fables of man's invention, when we preached to you about the power of our Lord Jesus Christ, and about his coming; we had been eyewitnesses of his exaltation. 17 Such honour, such glory was bestowed on him by God the Father, that a voice came to him out of the splendour which dazzles human eyes; This, it said, is my beloved Son, in whom I am well pleased; to him, then, listen. 18 We, his companions on the holy mountain, heard that voice coming from heaven, 19 and now the word of the prophets gives us more confidence than ever. It is with good reason that you are paying so much attention to that word; it will go on shining, like a lamp in some darkened room, until the dawn breaks, and the day-star rises in your hearts. 20 Yet always you must remember this, that no prophecy in scripture is the subject of private interpretation. 21 It was never man's impulse, after all, that gave us prophecy; men gave it utterance, but they were men whom God had sanctified, carried away, as they spoke, by the Holy Spirit.

v. 15. This verse seems to suggest that the apostle intended to put his doctrine on record in some other way, independently of his epistle.

v. 17. See Matthew xvii. 5, and parallels.

v. 19. 'The word of the prophets gives us more confidence than ever', since it has been ratified by the Transfiguration; or perhaps 'The word of the prophets gives us even more confidence' (than the Transfiguration), since it rests on admitted facts, not on an experience which might be called in question by the incredulous.

Chapter Two

THERE WERE FALSE prophets, too, among God's people. So, among you, there will be false teachers, covertly introducing pernicious ways of thought, and denying the Master who redeemed them, to their own speedy undoing. 2 Many will embrace their wanton creeds, and bring the way of truth into disrepute, 3 trading on your credulity with lying stories for their own ends. Long since, the warrant for their doom is in full vigour; destruction is on the watch for them. 4 God did not spare the angels who fell into sin; he thrust them down to hell, chained them there in the abyss, to await their sentence in torment. 5 Nor did he spare the world he had first made; he brought a flood on that world of wickedness, preserving Noe, who had borne witness to holiness, and only seven others with him. 6 The cities of Sodom and Gomorrha, too, he punished with utter ruin, turning them to ashes, for an example to the godless of a later time. 7 Yet he saved Lot, an innocent man who was overborne by the violence and the wantonness of his wicked neighbours; 8 eye and ear could testify to his innocence, although he lived among men whose lawless doings, day after day, wrung that blameless heart. 9 The Lord does not find it difficult to save his true worshippers from their trials, while the wrongdoers must await the day of judgement, marked down for torment; 10 those especially, who follow the defiling appetites of their corrupt nature, and make light of authority. So bold are they, so obstinate, that they are not afraid to bring in new and blasphemous ways of thought, 11 whereas angels, with a strength and a capacity far above theirs, do not bring on themselves any charge so abominable.

12 Such men, like dumb creatures that are born to be trapped and destroyed, sneer at what they cannot understand, and will soon perish in their own corruption; 13 they will have the reward their wickedness has deserved. To live in luxury while the day lasts is all their pleasure; what a stain they are, what a disfigurement, when they revel in the luxury of their own banquets, as they fare

v. 4. 'Chained them there in the abyss'; the Greek means, literally, 'in ropes' (or perhaps, in pits) of darkness'. The Latin has simply 'in ropes of hell'.

v. 8. This appears to be the meaning of the Latin (cf. Job xxix. 11); or the sense may be, 'he was innocent in spite of all that he heard and saw'. The Greek of the whole sentence is different: 'that innocent man, living in their company, fretted (or perhaps, gave proof of) his innocent soul over the lawless doings of which the sound and sight came to him, day after day'.

v. 10. The word 'authority', according to some, should be understood of the holy Angels (cf. Eph. i. 21, Col. i. 16, where the same word has been translated 'powers') according to others, of God himself. But it may equally well refer to earthly authorities. 'Bring in new and blasphemous ways of thought'; the Greek has 'insult august names', as in Jude, verse 8.

v. 11. 'Do not bring on themselves any charge so abominable'; this appears to be the sense of the Latin; the Greek has, 'do not bring against them (it is not clear, against whom) a derogatory sentence before the Lord'; cf. Jude, verse 9.

v. 13. 'While the day lasts'; literally, 'in the day', either in the sense of daylight, or as referring to the shortness of life (cf. Wisdom ii. 1-8). The latter part of the sentence probably refers to those common meals at which Christians met for social intercourse (cf. Jude, verse 12); if so, it seems clear that the false teachers here in question were rich men who brought their own victuals and did not share them with their poorer neighbours (cf. I Cor. xi. 21).

v. 16. Num. xxii. 28.

v. 18. 'Those who have had but a short respite from false teaching'; literally, 'those who have barely (in some Greek manuscripts, have genuinely) escaped from those who walk in error'.

v. 22. Cf. Prov. xxvi. 11; it does not appear, however, that St. Peter is quoting scripture, and it may be that there was a current saw of this kind. There is no reference in the Book of Proverbs, to the sow wallowing in the mire.

sumptuously at your side! 14 Their eyes feast on adultery, insatiable of sin; and they know how to win wavering souls to their purpose, so skilled is all their accursed brood at gaining its own ends. 15 They have gone far astray, leaving the true path, and following the path of Balaam the son of Bosor, the man who was content to take pay in the cause of wrong, 16 and was rebuked for his perversity, when the dumb beast spoke with a human voice, to bring a prophet to his senses. 17 They are wells with no water in them, clouds driven before the storm; the lot that awaits them is darkness and gloom. 18 Using fine phrases that have no meaning, they bait their hook with the wanton appetites of sense, to catch those who have had but a short respite from false teaching. 19 What do they offer them? Liberty. And all the time they themselves are enslaved to worldly corruption; whatever influence gets the better of a man, becomes his master. 20 That they should have been rescued, by acknowledging our Lord and Saviour Jesus Christ, from the world's pollution, and then been entangled and overpowered by it a second time, means that their last state is worse than the first. 21 Better for them, never to have found their way to justification, than to have found it, and then turned their backs on the holy law once handed down to them. 22 What has happened to them proves the truth of the proverb, The dog is back at his own vomit again. Wash the sow, and you find her wallowing in the mire.

Chapter Three

THIS IS MY SECOND LETter to you, beloved; I write such letters as a reminder, to awaken in you your clear sense of the truth. 2 Do not forget those predictions of the holy prophets which I mentioned to you, or the charge which our Lord and

v. 2. The Greek has, 'Do not forget what has been foretold by

Saviour laid on your apostles. 3 Remember always that in the last *the holy prophets, or the charge . . . etc.'.* days mocking deceivers must needs come, following the rule of their own appetites, 4 who will ask, What has become of the promise that he would appear? Ever since the fathers went to their rest, all is as it was from the foundation of the world. 5 They are fain to forget how, long ago, heaven stood there, and an earth which God's word had made with water for its origin, water for its frame; 6 and those were the very means by which the world, as it then was, came to perish, overwhelmed by water. 7 That same word keeps heaven and earth, as they now are, stored up, ready to feed the fire on the day when the godless will be judged, and perish. 8 But one thing, beloved, you must keep in mind, that *v. 8. Cf. Ps. lxxxix. 4.* with the Lord a day counts as a thousand years, and a thousand years count as a day. 9 The Lord is not being dilatory over his promise, as some think; he is only giving you more time, because his will is that all of you should attain repentance, not that some should be lost. 10 But the day of the Lord is coming, and when it comes, it will be upon you like a thief. The heavens will vanish in a whirlwind, the elements will be scorched up and dissolve, earth, and all earth's achievements, will burn away.

11 All so transitory; and what men you ought to be! How unworldly in your life, how reverent towards God, 12 as you wait, and wait eagerly, for the day of the Lord to come, for the heavens to shrivel up in fire, and the elements to melt in its heat! 13 And meanwhile, we have new heavens and a new earth to look forward to, the dwelling-place of holiness; that is what he has promised. 14 Beloved, since these expectations are yours, do everything to make sure that he shall find you innocent, undefiled, at peace. 15 If *v. 15. If the letter referred to has been preserved, it may perhaps be I Thessalonians. But as St. Peter's second epistle bears no particular address, we can have no certainty on the point.* our Lord stays his hand, count it part of his mercy. Our beloved brother Paul, with the wisdom God has granted him, has written you a letter, 16 in which, as in all his letters, he talks of this. (Though indeed there are passages in them difficult to understand, and these, like the rest of scripture, are twisted into a wrong sense by ignorant and restless minds, to their own undoing.) 17 For yourselves, beloved, be warned in time; do not be carried away by their rash errors, and lose the firm foothold you have won; 18 grow up in grace, and in the knowledge of our Lord and Saviour Jesus Christ. To him be glory, now and for all eternity. Amen.

THE FIRST EPISTLE OF THE BLESSED APOSTLE John

Chapter One

OUR MESSAGE CON cerns that Word, who is life; what he was from the first, what we have heard about him, what our own eyes have seen of him; what it was that met our gaze, and the touch of our hands. 2 Yes, life dawned; and it is as eye-witnesses that we give you news of that life, that eternal life, which ever abode with the Father and has dawned, now, on us. 3 This message about what we have seen and heard we pass on to you, so that you too may share in our fellowship. What is it, this fellowship of ours? Fellowship with the Father, and with his Son Jesus Christ. 4 And if we are writing to you now, it is so that joy may be yours in full measure. 5 What, then, is this message we have heard from him, and are passing on to you? That God is light, and no darkness can find any place in him; 6 if we claim fellowship with him, when all the while we live and move in darkness, it is a lie; our whole life is an untruth. 7 God dwells in light; if we too live and move in light, there is fellowship between us, and the blood of his Son Jesus Christ washes us clean from all sin. 8 Sin is with us; if we deny that, we are cheating ourselves; it means that

v. 1. That 'the Word' here is used in a personal sense would seem clear from a comparison of this passage with St. John's Gospel, i. 1-4.

v. 7; 'There is fellowship between us' may refer to fellowship between man and man, but the context suggests man's fellowship with God (verse 3 above).

455

truth does not dwell in us. 9 No, it is when we confess our sins that he forgives us our sins, ever true to his word, ever dealing right with us, and all our wrong-doing is purged away. 10 If we deny that we have sinned, it means that we are treating him as a liar; it means that his word does not dwell in our hearts.

Chapter Two

ITTLE children, the purpose of this letter is to keep you clear of sin. Meanwhile, if any of us does fall into sin, we have an advocate to plead our cause before the Father in the Just One, Jesus Christ. 2 He, in his own person, is the atonement made for our sins, and not only for ours, but for the sins of the whole world. 3 Have we attained the knowledge of God? The test is, whether we keep his commandments; 4 the man who claims knowledge of him without keeping his commandments is a liar; truth does not dwell in such a man as that. 5 No, if a man keeps true to God's word, then it is certain that the love of God has reached its full stature in him; that is what tells us that we are dwelling in God. 6 One who claims to dwell in him must needs live and move as he lived and moved. 7 Beloved, I am not sending you a new commandment; it is an old commandment, which you were given from the very first; what was the message to which you listened long ago but this same commandment, now grown old? 8 And yet it is a new commandment I am sending you, now that it is verified in him and you; the darkness has passed away now, and true light shines instead. 9 He who claims enlightenment, and all the while hates his brother, is in darkness still. 10 It is the man who loves his brother that lives in light; no fear of stumbling haunts him. 11 The man who hates his brother is in the dark, guides his steps in the dark without being able to tell where he is going; darkness has fallen, and blinded his eyes.

vv. 12-14. 'I call you children'; literally, 'I write to you, children', and so throughout. It is possible to read these phrases as if St. John was ad-

12 I call you little children; have not your sins been forgiven in his name? 13 I call you fathers; have you not knowledge of one who was from the first? I call you young men; have you not gained victory over the evil one? 14 I call you sons; you have learned to

recognize the Father. I call you young men; you are strong, with God's word dwelling in you always; you have gained your victory over the evil one. 15 Do not bestow your love on the world, and what the world has to offer; the lover of this world has no love of the Father in him. 16 What does the world offer? Only gratification of corrupt nature, gratification of the eye, the empty pomp of living; these things take their being from the world, not from the Father. 17 The world and its gratifications pass away; the man who does God's will outlives them, for ever.

18 My sons, this is the last age of time. You have been told that Antichrist must needs come; and even now, to prove to us that it is the last age of time, many Antichrists have appeared. 19 They came of our company, but they never belonged to our company; if they had belonged to it, they would have persevered at our side. As it is, they were destined to prove that there are some who are no true companions of ours. 20 With you, it is otherwise; the Holy One has anointed you, and now nothing is hidden from you, 21 so that I am not writing to you as to men from whom the truth is hidden. Rather, I am appealing to your knowledge of it; the truth, after all, cannot give birth to a lie. 22 To whom do we give the lie, if not to him who tells us that Jesus is not the Christ? Such a man is Antichrist, disowning as he does both the Father and the Son. 23 To disown the Son is to have no claim to the Father; it is by acknowledging the Son that we lay claim to the Father too. 24 Enough for you, that the message which was first brought you should dwell in you. 25 If that first message dwells in you, you too will dwell in the Son, and in the Father. 26 He himself has made us a promise, the promise of eternal life. So much I have written about those who are trying to mislead you. 27 Meanwhile, the influence of his anointing lives on in you, so that you have no need of teaching; no lesson his influence gives you can be a lie, they are all true. Follow those lessons, and dwell in him. 28 Yes, little children, dwell in him, so that when he appears we may greet him confidently, instead of being ashamed at his presence. 29 You are sure that God deals rightly with us; be sure, then, that whoever does right is born of him.

dressing, in turn, three or four different classes in the Christian community, divided according to their ages. But it seems unlikely that he should have addressed himself to children; or that he should have no message at all for women.

v. 14. After the words 'recognize the Father', the clause used above, 'I call you fathers; have you not knowledge of one who was from the first?' is repeated, according to the Greek manuscripts.

Chapter Three

EE how God has shewn his love towards us; that we should be counted as his sons, should be his sons. If the world does not recognize us, that is because it never recognized him. 2 Beloved, we are sons of God even now, and what we shall be hereafter, has not been made known as yet. But we know that when he comes we shall be like him; we shall see him, then, as he is. 3 Now, a man who rests these hopes in God lives a life of holiness; God, too, is holy.

4 The man who commits sin, violates order; sin of its nature is disorder. 5 You know well enough that when God revealed himself, it was to take away our sins; there is no sinfulness in him, 6 and no one can dwell in him and be a sinner. The sinner must be one who has failed to see him, failed to recognize him. 7 Little children, do not allow anybody to mislead you; the man who lives right is the man who is right with God; God, too, is right in all his dealings. 8 The man who lives sinfully takes his character from the devil; the devil was a sinner from the first. If the Son of God was revealed to us, it was so that he might undo what the devil had done, 9 and if a man is born of God, he does not live sinfully, he is true to his parentage; he cannot be a sinner, if he is born of God.

v. 9. 'He is true to his parentage'; literally, 'the seed of God persists in him', that is, being a child of God he inherits a strain proper to his ancestry.

10 This, then, is how God's children and the devil's children are known apart. A man cannot trace his origin from God if he does not live right, if he does not love his brethren. 11 To love one another; that, from the first, was the charge given to you; 12 you were not to be like Cain, who took his character from the evil one, and murdered his brother. Why did he murder him? Because his own life was evil, and his brother's life was acceptable to God. 13 No, brethren, do not be surprised that the world should hate you. 14 Remember that we have changed over from death to life, in loving the brethren as we do; whereas, if a man is without love, he holds fast by death. 15 A man cannot hate his brother without being a murderer, and you may be sure that no murderer has eternal life dwelling in him. 16 God has proved his love to us by laying down his life for our sakes; we too must be ready to lay down our lives for the sake of our brethren. 17 And now, suppose that a

man has the worldly goods he needs, and sees his brother go in want; if he steels his heart against his brother, how can we say that the love of God dwells in him? 18 My little children, let us shew our love by the true test of action, not by taking phrases on our lips. 19 That proves to us that we take our character from the truth, and we shall be able to satisfy our consciences before God; 20 if our consciences condemn us, it is because God is above conscience, and nothing is hidden from him. 21 Beloved, if conscience does not condemn us, we can appear boldly before God, 22 and he will grant all our requests, since we are keeping his commandments, and living as he would see us live. 23 What he commands is, that we should have faith in the name of his Son Jesus Christ, and at his command should love one another. 24 When a man keeps his commandments, it means that he is dwelling in God, and God in him. This is our proof that he is really dwelling in us, through the gift of his Spirit.

v. 20. This seems to be the most probable rendering of a verse whose meaning has been much disputed.

v. 24. Or the last sentence may be connected with what follows, and rendered, 'What assures us that he is really dwelling in us is the gift of his Spirit.'

Chapter Four

NOT all prophetic spirits, brethren, deserve your credence; you must put them to the test, to see whether they come from God. Many false prophets have made their appearance in the world. 2 This is the test by which God's Spirit is to be recognized; every spirit which acknowledges Jesus Christ as having come to us in human flesh has God for its author; 3 and no spirit which would disunite Jesus comes from God. This is the power of Antichrist, whose coming you have been told to expect; now you must know that he is here in the world already. 4 You, little children, who take your origin from God, have gained the mastery over it; there is a stronger power at work in you, than in the world. 5 Those others, belonging to the world, speak the world's language, and the world listens to them; 6 we belong to God, and a man must have knowledge of God if he is to listen to us; if he does not belong to God, he does not listen to us at all. That is the test by which we distinguish the true Spirit from the false spirit. 7 Beloved, let us love one another;

v. 3. 'Which would disunite Jesus'; apparently in the sense that it would deny the identity of the human Jesus with the divine Christ; but the phrase might have a more general sense of 'destroying' Jesus. This reading goes back to the Fathers of the second century; our present Greek manuscripts have simply 'which does not acknowledge Jesus'.

love springs from God; no one can love without being born of God, and knowing God. 8 How can the man who has no love have any knowledge of God, since God is love?

9 What has revealed the love of God, where we are concerned, is that he has sent his only-begotten Son into the world, so that we might have life through him. 10 That love resides, not in our shewing any love for God, but in his shewing love for us first, when he sent out his Son to be an atonement for our sins. 11 Beloved, if God has shewn such love to us, we too must love one another. 12 No man has ever seen God; but if we love another, then we have God dwelling in us, and the love of God has reached its full growth in our lives. 13 This is our proof that we are dwelling in him, and he in us; he has given us a share of his own Spirit. 14 We apostles have seen for ourselves, and can testify, that God sent out his Son to be the redeemer of the world; 15 and where a man acknowledges that Jesus is the Son of God, God dwells in him, and he in God; 16 we have learned to recognize the love God has in our regard, to recognize it, and to make it our belief. God is love; he who dwells in love dwells in God, and God in him. 17 That our life in the world should be like his, means that his love has had its way with us to the full, so that we can meet the day of judgement with confidence. 18 Love has no room for fear; and indeed, love drives out fear when it is perfect love, since fear only serves for correction. The man who is still afraid has not yet reached the full measure of love. 19 Yes, we must love God; he gave us his love first. 20 If a man boasts of loving God, while he hates his own brother, he is a liar. He has seen his brother, and has no love for him; what love can he have for the God he has never seen? 21 No, this is the divine command that has been given us; the man who loves God must be one who loves his brother as well.

v. 13. 'This is our proof'; it is not certain whether this refers to what has gone before, or to what immediately follows; perhaps to both.
v. 14. 'We apostles'; the word 'apostles' does not appear in the text, but has been supplied for the sake of clearness in reading, since this is evidently what is meant.
v. 18. 'Since fear only serves for correction'; literally, 'since fear has chastisement'. Others would interpret this as meaning 'because fear is painful', or 'because fear involves the prospect of punishment'; but it is doubtful whether the language of the Greek justifies either rendering.
v. 19. 'We must love God'; in the Greek, 'we love God', in the Latin, 'let us love God'.

Chapter Five

EVERYONE WHO BE
lieves that Jesus is the Christ is a
child of God, and to love the parent is to love his child. 2 If we
love God, and keep his commandments, we can be sure of loving
God's children. 3 Loving God means keeping his commandments,
and these commandments of his are not a burden to us. 4 Whatever takes its origin from God must needs triumph over the world;
our faith, that is the triumphant principle which triumphs over the
world. 5 He alone triumphs over the world, who believes that
Jesus is the Son of God. 6 He it is, Jesus Christ, whose coming has
been made known to us by water and blood; water and blood as
well, not water only; and we have the Spirit's witness that Christ
is the truth. 7 Thus we have a threefold warrant in heaven, the
Father, the Word, and the Holy Ghost, three who are yet one;
8 and we have a threefold warrant on earth, the Spirit, the water,
and the blood, three witnesses that conspire in one. 9 We are
ready to trust human authority; is not divine authority higher still?
And we have that higher divine authority for this; God has borne
witness to his own Son. 10 The man who believes in the Son of
God has this divine attestation in his heart; the man who does not
believe in the Son treats God as a liar; although God himself has
borne witness to his Son, he has refused to believe in it. 11 And
what is the truth so attested? That God has given us eternal life,
and that this life is to be found in his Son. 12 To keep hold of the
Son is to have life; he is lifeless, who has no hold of the Son of God.
13 There is my message to you; be sure that you have eternal life;
go on believing in the name of the Son of God.

14 Such familiar confidence we have in him, that we believe he
listens to us whenever we make any request of him in accordance
with his will. 15 We are sure that he listens to all our requests, sure
that the requests we make of him are granted. 16 If a man knows
his brother to be guilty, yet not of such a sin as brings death with
it, he should pray for him; and, at his request, life will be granted
to the brother who is sinning, yet not fatally. There is a sin which

v. 6. 'That Christ is
the truth'; the Greek
has 'that (or, be-
cause) the Spirit is
the truth'. It is not
clear what mystical
significance St. John
attached to the Spirit,
the water, and the
blood, here and in v.
8; he may, perhaps,
have had the Sacra-
ments of Baptism,
Confirmation, and
the Holy Eucharist
in mind. In John i.
33 water and the
Spirit are closely as-
sociated, water and
blood in John xix.
34; in both these
passages the idea of
human testimony is
prominent.
v. 7. This verse does
not occur in any
good Greek manu-
script. But the Latin
manuscripts may have
preserved the true
text.
v. 8. 'Conspire in
one'; literally, in the
Latin, 'are one', in
the Greek 'form one'.
v. 16. For 'if a man
knows', the Greek
has, 'if a man sees'.
Commentators are
much disagreed as to
the nature of the sin
which brings death
with it. It has often
been identified as
final impenitence, but
the context seems to
demand an action,
rather than a state
of mind. Since St.
John is warning us,
all through his epis-
tle, against the dan-
ger of apostasy from
Christ, he may be
distinguishing here
between various de-
grees of culpability
in sinners of that
kind (cf. Jude, verses
22, 23). He does not
explicitly say that
'fatal' sin is irremis-

461

sible, only that we
are not bound to
pray for one who
shews so little evi-
dence of good dispo-
sitions; cf. II John,
verse 10.

v. 19. 'Of evil'; or
perhaps 'of the evil
one'.

v. 20. It is not certain
whether the word 'he'
refers to the word
'God' or to the word
'Son'.

kills; it is not over this that I bid him fall to prayer. 17 Sin may be wrong-doing of any kind; not all sin is fatal. 18 The man who has been born of God, we may be sure, keeps clear of sin; that divine origin protects him, and the evil one cannot touch him. 19 And we can be sure that we are God's children, though the whole world about us lies in the power of evil. 20 We can be sure, too, that the Son of God has come to us, and has given us a sense of truth; we were to recognize the true God, and to live in his true Son. He is true God, and eternal life. 21 Beware, little children, of false gods.

The SECOND EPISTLE OF THE BLESSED Apostle John

 the presbyter, send greeting to that sovereign lady whom God has chosen; and to those children of hers who are my friends in the truth, loved, not by me only, but by all those who have recognized the truth, 2 for love of that truth which dwells in us, and will be our companion for ever. 3 God the Father, and Jesus Christ, the Son of the Father, send you grace, mercy and peace in a spirit of truth and love. 4 It has given me great happiness, in meeting some of thy children, to find that they followed the way of truth, obeying the command that came to us from the Father. 5 And now, sovereign lady, I have a request to make of thee. It is no new command that my letter brings, only the command we were given from the first; let us all love one another. 6 Love means keeping his commandments; love is itself the commandment which our earliest lessons bade us follow. 7 Many false teachers have appeared in the world, who will not acknowledge that Jesus Christ has come in human flesh; here is the deceiver you were warned against, here is Antichrist. 8 Be on your guard, or you will lose all you have earned, instead of receiving your wages in full. 9 The man who goes back, who is not true to Christ's teaching, loses hold of God; the man who is true to that teaching, keeps hold both of the Father and of the Son. 10 If you are visited by one who does not bring this teaching with him, you must not receive him in your houses, or bid him welcome; 11 to bid him welcome is to share the guilt of his doings. 12 I might add to this letter, but I have thought it best not

v. 1. *If, as is probable, the word 'presbyter' (or senior) referred in the first instance to those who were 'foundation members' of a given church (cf. Acts xx. 17, 18), it is easy to see why St. John should describe himself as 'the senior' (in relation to the Church at large) at a time when he was the only Apostle left. The 'lady' whom he addresses is no doubt a local church; the notion that a person is addressed (some think, by a proper name, Kyria) does not accord well with the use of the plural in verses 8-12.*

v. 8. *'All you have earned'; some Greek manuscripts have 'all the result of our labours'.*

v. 9. *'The man who goes back'; other manuscripts of the Latin have 'the man who goes on in front', which corresponds better with the Greek. The sense may be (if that is the true reading), 'the man who tries to go beyond' the fixed deposit of faith, perhaps by adopting a Docetic view of our Lord's Incarnation.*

463

to entrust my message to paper and ink; I hope to visit you, and
convey it by word of mouth, to give you happiness in full measure.
13 The children of thy sister, God's chosen, send thee greeting.

ᴛhe Chird Epistle of the Blessed Apostle John

GREETINGS FROM THE presbyter to Gaius, his most dear friend in the truth. 2 Beloved, my prayer is that all goes well with thee, and that thou art in health; with thy soul, all goes well. 3 What happiness it gave me, when the brethren who came here bore witness of thy loyalty to the truth, the loyalty thou shewest in all thy dealings! 4 I have no greater cause for thankfulness, than when I hear that my children are following the way of truth. 5 Beloved, thou art playing a faithful man's part in shewing such kindness to the brethren, even when they are strangers to thee. 6 They have borne public witness before the church of thy charity, and thou wilt do well to set them forward on their journey in such a manner as befits God's service; 7 it was undertaken for love of his name, the heathen contributed nothing to it. 8 Yes, it is our duty to help on the cause of truth by giving welcome to such men as these. 9 I might have sent this message to the church at large, were it not that Diotrephes, ever eager to take a leading part among them, refuses to acknowledge us. 10 If I should pay you a visit, be sure I will tax him with his ill conduct. He maligns us with his foolish

v. 1. See note on II John, verse 1.

v. 7. 'Of his name'; the Greek has, 'of the Name', as in Acts v. 41, where the name of Jesus Christ is clearly meant.

465

gossip; is not that enough for him, without refusing to acknowledge our brethren, and putting restraint on those who would, by expelling them from the church? 11 Beloved, choose the right pattern, not the wrong, to imitate. He who does right is a child of God; the wrongdoer has caught no glimpse of him. 12 Demetrius is one whom all speak well of, and the truth itself is his warrant; we, too, commend him, and thou knowest that our commendation is true. 13 I have much to tell thee, but I have no mind to convey the message with paper and ink; 14 I hope to see thee before long, and we will converse by word of mouth. Peace be with thee. Thy friends here greet thee. Give our friends, each of them by name, our greeting.

The UNIVERSAL EPISTLE OF THE BLESSED APOSTLE JUDE

JUDE, A SERVANT OF Jesus Christ, and brother of James, to those who have met with loving-kindness from God the Father, those whom he has set apart for Jesus Christ, and called them, 2 mercy and peace and love be yours, in full measure. 3 Beloved, as one who is ever ready to write to you about that salvation which is your common concern, I am compelled to send you this letter of warning; you have a battle to fight over the faith that was handed down, once for all, to the saints. 4 Godless men, long since destined thus to incur condemnation, have found their way secretly into your company, and are perverting the life of grace our God has bestowed on us into a life of wantonness; they even deny Jesus Christ, our one Lord and Master. 5 Learn one lesson, and you know all. Let me remind you, how the Saviour who had rescued his people from Egypt went on to destroy those who had proved unfaithful. 6 The angels, too, who left the place assigned to them, instead of keeping their due order, he has imprisoned in eternal darkness, to await their judgement when the great day comes. 7 So with Sodom and Gomorrha and the cities round them, which

v. 5. 'The Saviour'; the name 'Jesus' is here used, apparently, to designate the God who brought Israel out of Egypt. Some Greek manuscripts have 'the Lord'.

467

fell into the same debauchery as their neighbours and pursued unnatural lust; they bear, for our warning, their sentence of eternal
fire. 8 And so it is with these as it was with those others; they
pollute nature, they defy authority, they insult august names.
9 (And yet, when the archangel Michael held debate with the
devil, in their dispute over the body of Moses, he did not venture
to accuse him insultingly; he was content to say, May the Lord
rebuke thee.)

10 Such men sneer at the things they cannot understand; like
the brute beasts they derive knowledge only from their senses, and
it serves to corrupt them. 11 Woe betide them, they have followed
in the path of Cain; greed, that led Balaam astray, has been their
ruin; they have taken part in the fatal rebellion of Core. 12 What
defilement there is in their banquets, as they fare sumptuously at
your side, shepherds that feed themselves without scruple! They
are clouds with no water in them, driven before the winds, autumn
trees that bear no fruit, given over anew to death, plucked up by
the roots; 13 they are fierce waves of the sea, with shame for their
crests, wandering stars, with eternal darkness and storm awaiting
them. 14 Of these, among others, Henoch was speaking, Adam's
descendant in the seventh degree, when he prophesied, Behold,
the Lord came with his saints in their thousands, 15 to carry out
his sentence on all men, and to convict the godless. Godless and
sinners, with how many ungodly acts they have defied God, with
how many rebellious words have they blasphemed him! 16 Such
men go about whispering and complaining, and live by the rule of
their own appetites; meanwhile, their mouths are ready with fine
phrases, to flatter the great when it serves their ends.

17 But as for you, beloved, keep in mind the warnings given you
long since by the apostles of our Lord Jesus Christ; 18 how they
told you, that mocking spirits must needs appear in the last age,
who would make their own ungodly appetites into a rule of life.
19 Such are the men who now keep themselves apart; animal
natures, without the life of the Spirit. 20 It is for you, beloved,
to make your most holy faith the foundation of your lives, and
to go on praying in the power of the Holy Spirit; 21 to maintain
yourselves in the love of God, and wait for the mercy of our Lord
Jesus Christ, with eternal life for your goal. 22 To some you
must give a hearing, and confute them; 23 others you must pluck
out of the fire, and rescue them; others again you can only pity,
while you shun them; even the outward fringe of what the flesh
has defiled must be hateful to you. 24 There is one who can keep

you clear of fault, and enable you to stand in the presence of his glory, triumphant and unreproved, when our Lord Jesus Christ comes; 25 to him, who alone is God, to him, who gives us salvation through Jesus Christ our Lord, glory and majesty and power and domination are due, before time was, and now, and for all ages. Amen.

ward fringe of what the flesh has defiled'; literally, 'the garment defiled by the flesh'.

v. 24. The words 'when our Lord Jesus Christ comes' are not in our Greek text.

469

THE ASCENSION OF CHRIST   SCHOOL OF AMIENS
around 1480

COURTESY OF THE ART INSTITUTE OF CHICAGO

the APOCALYPSE of the BLESSED Apostle John

Chapter One

THIS IS A REVELATION from Jesus Christ, which God has allowed him to make known to his servants, of things which must soon find their due accomplishment. And he has sent his angel to disclose the pattern of it to his servant John, 2 one who bore witness for God's word, and for the truth concerning Jesus Christ, as his own eyes had seen it. 3 A blessing on him who reads this, and on all who listen to these words of prophecy, and keep true to their message; the time is close at hand.

4 Thus John writes to the seven churches in Asia, Grace and peace be yours, from him who is, and ever was, and is still to come, and from the seven spirits that stand before his throne; 5 and from Jesus Christ, the faithful witness, first-born of the risen dead, who rules over all earthly kings. He has proved his love for us, by washing us clean from our sins in his own blood, 6 and made us a royal race of priests, to serve God, his Father; glory and power be his through endless ages, Amen. 7 Behold, he comes with clouds about him, seen by every eye, seen by those who wounded him, and he shall bring lamentation to all the tribes of earth. So it

v. 2. 'One who bore witness for God's word' others would understand this as meaning 'the man who has now borne record of God's word', and as referring to the Apocalypse itself. But a comparison of i. 9, vi. 9, and xx. 4 below suggests that the verb here means bearing witness to God's word in face of persecution (cf. I Tim. vi. 13); in which case the apostle is identifying himself as an eye-witness of the gospel story and a confessor for the faith.
v. 7. Cf. Zech. xii. 10, John xix. 37.

471

must be, Amen. 8 I am Alpha, I am Omega, the beginning of all things and their end, says the Lord God; he who is, and ever was, and is still to come, the Almighty.

9 I, John, your brother, who share your ill usage, your royal dignity, and your endurance in Christ Jesus, was set down on the island called Patmos, for love of God's word and of the truth concerning Jesus. 10 And there, on the Lord's day, I fell into a trance, and heard behind me a voice, loud as the call of a trumpet, 11 which said, Write down all thou seest in a book, and send it to the seven churches in Asia, to Ephesus, and Smyrna, and Pergamum, and Thyatira, and Sardis, and Philadelphia, and Laodicea. 12 So I turned, to see what voice it was that was speaking to me. And as I

v. 13. Orichalc, an unidentified metal of the ancient world.

turned, I saw seven golden candlesticks, 13 and in the midst of these seven golden candlesticks one who seemed like a son of man, clothed in a long garment, with a golden girdle about his breast. 14 The hair on his head was like wool snow-white, and his eyes like flaming fire, 15 his feet like orichalc melted in the crucible, and his voice like the sound of water in deep flood. 16 In his right hand were seven stars; from his mouth came a sword sharpened at both its edges; and his face was like the sun when it shines at its

v. 17. Cf. Is. xliv. 6, Matthew xiv. 27.

full strength. 17 At the sight of him, I fell down at his feet like a dead man; and he, laying his right hand on me, spoke thus: Do not be afraid; I am before all, I am at the end of all, 18 and I live. I, who underwent death, am alive, as thou seest, to endless ages, and I hold the keys of death and hell. 19 Write down thy vision of what now is, and what must befall hereafter. 20 As for the

v. 20. This may refer to the angel guardians of the churches, but more probably to their bishops.

meaning of the seven stars which thou hast seen in my right hand, and the seven golden candlesticks, the seven stars are the angels of the seven churches thou knowest, and the candlesticks, seven in number, are the seven churches.

Chapter Two

To THE ANGEL OF THE church at Ephesus write thus: A message to thee from him who bears the seven stars in his right hand, and walks amidst the seven golden candlesticks: 2 I know of all thy doings, all thy toil and endurance; how little patience thou hast with wickedness, how thou hast made trial of such as usurp the name of apostle, and found them false. 3 Yes, thou endurest, and all thou hast borne for the love of my name has not made thee despair. 4 Yet there is one charge I make against thee; of losing the charity that was thine at first. 5 Remember the height from which thou hast fallen, and repent, and go back to the old ways; or else I will come to visit thee, and, when I find thee still unrepentant, will remove thy candlestick from its place. 6 Yet this is in thy favour, thou dost abhor the ways of the Nicolaitans, as I, too abhor them. 7 Listen, you that have ears, to the message the Spirit has for the churches. Who wins the victory? I will give him fruit from the tree of life, which grows in the Paradise of my God.

v. 6. There is a tradition that this sect was founded by Nicolaus the deacon (Acts vi. 5) but this is uncertain. They seem to have been antinomian in doctrine.

8 And to the angel of the church at Smyrna write thus: A message to thee from him, who is before all and at the end of all, who underwent death and now is alive: 9 I know how sorely tried thou art, how stricken with poverty (yet, all the while, so rich); how thy name is traduced by men who claim to be Jews (though they are no true Jews; they are rather the chosen people of Satan). 10 Do not be afraid of the suffering thou art to undergo. Before long, the devil will throw some of you into prison, to have your faith tested there, and for ten days you shall be in sore distress. Keep faith with me to the point of death, and I will crown thee with life. 11 Listen, you that have ears, to the message the Spirit has for the churches. Who wins the victory? The second death shall have no power to hurt him.

12 And to the angel of the church at Pergamum write thus: A message to thee from him whose sword is sharpened at both its edges: 13 I know well in what a place thou dwellest, a place where Satan sits enthroned. And yet thou art true to my name, and hast not

473

disowned thy faith in me. Such in former times was Antipas, who bore me faithful witness, and was put to death in Satan's dwelling-place, your city. 14 Yet here and there I have fault to find with thee; thou hast followers there of the school of Balaam. It was Balaam who taught Balac how to lay a trap for the people of Israel, when they ate what was sacrificed to idols and fell into fornication; 15 and thou, too, hast followers of the Nicolaitan school. 16 Do thou, in thy turn, repent; or I will quickly come to visit thee, and fight against them with the sword of my mouth. 17 Listen, you that have ears, to the message the Spirit has for the churches. Who wins the victory? I will feed him with the hidden manna, and give him a white stone, on which stone a new name is written, known to him only who receives it.

18 And to the angel of the church at Thyatira write thus: A message to thee from the Son of God, who has eyes like flaming fire, and feet like orichalc: 19 I know of all thy doings, thy faith, thy love, thy generosity, thy endurance, how in these last days thou art more active than at first. 20 Yet here and there I have fault to find with thee; thou allowest the woman Jezabel, who claims the gift of prophecy, to mislead my servants with her teaching, so that they fall into fornication, and eat what is offered to idols. 21 I have given her time for repentance, but she will not mend her harlot's ways. 22 I have a bed ready to lay her in; and those who commit adultery with her will be in sore straits, if they do not repent of their wrong-doing. 23 And her children I will kill out-right, so that all the churches may know me for one who probes the innermost heart, and will repay each of you what his deeds have earned. But I say to you, 24 those others in Thyatira who do not follow this teaching, who have never learned the deep mysteries (as they are called) which Satan offers; I have no fresh burden to lay upon you; 25 keep hold of what is in your grasp already, until I come. 26 Who wins the victory? Who will do my bidding to the last? I will give him authority over the nations; 27 to herd them like sheep with a crook of iron, breaking them in pieces like earthenware; 28 the same authority which I myself hold from my Father. And the Star of morning shall be his. 29 Listen, you that have ears, to the message the Spirit has for the churches.

Chapter Three

AND TO THE CHURCH'S angel at Sardis write thus: A message to thee from him who bears the seven spirits of God, and the seven stars. I know of all thy doings, how thou dost pass for a living man, and all the while art a corpse. 2 Rouse thyself, and rally whatever else still lives, but lives at the point of death. There are tasks my God expects of thee, and I find them unfulfilled. 3 Remember how the gift, how the message came to thee; hold it fast, and repent. If thou failest in thy watch, I will come upon thee like a thief; thou shalt never know the hour of my coming to thee. 4 Yet here and there in Sardis thou canst claim souls which have kept their garments undefiled, and these shall bear me company, clothed in white; it is their due. 5 Who wins the victory? So shall he be clothed, in white garments; his name I will never blot out of the book of life, his name I will acknowledge before my Father and his angels. 6 Listen, you that have ears, to the message the Spirit has for the churches.

7 And to the angel of the church at Philadelphia write thus: A message to thee from him, who is all holiness and truth; who bears the key of David, so that none may shut when he opens, none open when he shuts: 8 I know of thy doings, and see, I have set before thee an open door, there is no shutting it. I know how little thy strength is, and yet thou hast been true to my message, and hast not denied my name. 9 Before long, I will give thee for thy own some of Satan's chosen people, the men who falsely claim to be Jews when they are none; before long, I will make them come to thee, doing reverence at thy feet, and acknowledging the love I have shewn for thee. 10 Thou hast kept true to my lesson of endurance, and I will keep thee safe from the hour of trial which is soon to fall upon the whole world, for the testing of all who dwell on the earth. 11 Patience, I am coming soon; hold what is in thy grasp, so that none may rob thee of thy crown. 12 Who wins the victory? I will make him a pillar in the temple of my God, never to leave it again. I will write on him the name of my God, and the

name of the city my God has built, that new Jerusalem which my God is even now sending down from heaven, and my own new name. 13 Listen, you that have ears, to the message the Spirit has for the churches.

14 And to the angel of the church at Laodicea write thus: A message to thee from the Truth, the faithful and unerring witness, the source from which God's creation began: 15 I know of thy doings, and find thee neither cold nor hot; cold or hot, I would thou wert one or the other. 16 Being what thou art, lukewarm, neither cold nor hot, thou wilt make me vomit thee out of my mouth. 17 I am rich, you sayest, I have come into my own; nothing, now, is wanting to me. And all the while, if thou didst but know it, it is thou who art wretched, thou who art to be pitied. Thou art a beggar, blind and naked; 18 and my counsel to thee is, to come and buy from me what thou needest; gold, proved in the fire, to make thee rich, and white garments, to clothe thee, and cover up the nakedness which dishonours thee; rub salve, too, upon thy eyes, to restore them sight. 19 It is those I love that I correct and chasten; kindle thy generosity, and repent. 20 See where I stand at the door, knocking; if anyone listens to my voice and opens the door, I will come in to visit him, and take·my supper with him, and he shall sup with me. 21 Who wins the victory? I will let him share my throne with me; I too have won the victory, and now I sit sharing my Father's throne. 22 Listen, you that have ears, to the message the Spirit has for the churches.

Chapter Four

THEN A VISION CAME to me; I saw a door in heaven, standing open. And the same voice, which I had heard speaking to me before, loud as the call of a trumpet, said to me, Come up to my side, and I will shew thee what must find, after this, its due accomplishment. 2 And all at once I was in a trance, and saw where a throne stood in heaven, and one sat there enthroned. 3 He who sat there bore the semblance of a jewel, jasper or sardius, and there was a rainbow about the throne, like a vision of emerald. 4 Round it were twenty-four seats, and on these sat twenty-four elders, clothed in white garments, with crowns of gold on their heads. 5 Lightnings came out from the throne, and mutterings, and thunders, and before it burned seven lamps, which are the seven spirits of God; 6 facing it was a whole sea of glass, like crystal. And in the midst, where the throne was, round the throne itself, were four living figures, that had eyes everywhere to see before them and behind them. 7 The first figure was that of a lion, the second that of an ox, the third had a man's look, and the fourth was that of an eagle in flight. 8 Each of the four figures had six wings, with eyes everywhere looking outwards and inwards; day and night they cried unceasingly, Holy, holy, holy is the Lord God, the Almighty, who ever was, and is, and is still to come. 9 And as often as these figures gave glory and honour and blessing to him who sat on the throne, who lives for ever and ever; 10 the twenty-four elders fell down in worship before him who sat on the throne, who lives for ever and ever, and threw down their crowns before the throne, crying out, 11 Thou, our Lord God, claimest as thy due glory and honour and power; by thee all things were created; nothing ever was, nothing was ever created, but in obedience to thy will.

v. 4. The word 'elders' here may also be translated 'presbyters'.

vv. 5-10. All the verbs in these sentences, except one, are in past tenses, according to our version. The Greek, and some manuscripts of the Latin, give the present tense in vv. 5-8, the future in vv. 9 and 10.

v. 6. Cf. Ezech. i. 5-11. These figures were identified by some of the earliest Christian writers as representing the four Evangelists.

Chapter Five

ND now I saw that he who sat on the throne carried in his right hand a scroll. The inside of the page and the outside were both written on, and it was sealed with seven seals. 2 And I saw an angel of sovereign strength, who was crying in a loud voice, Who claims the right to open the book, and break the seals on it? 3 But there was no one in heaven, or on earth, or under the earth, who could open the scroll and have sight of it. 4 I was all in tears, that none should be found worthy to open the scroll or have sight of it; 5 until one

of the elders said to me, No need for tears; here is one who has gained the right to open the book, by breaking its seven seals, the Lion that comes from the tribe of Juda, from the stock of David. 6 Then I saw, in the midst, where the throne was, amid the twenty-four elders, a Lamb standing upright, yet slain (as I thought) in sacrifice. He had seven horns, and seven eyes, which are the seven spirits of God, that go out to do his bidding everywhere on earth. 7 He now came, and took the scroll from the right hand of him who sat on the throne, 8 and when he disclosed it, the four living figures and the twenty-four elders fell down in the Lamb's presence. Each bore a harp, and they had golden bowls full of incense, the prayers of the saints. 9 And now it was a new hymn they sang, Thou, Lord, art worthy to take up the book and break the seals that are on it. Thou wast slain in sacrifice; out of every tribe, every language, every people, every nation thou hast ransomed us with thy blood and given us to God. 10 Thou hast made us a royal race of priests, to serve God; we shall reign as kings over the earth. 11 Then I heard, in my vision, the voices of a multitude of angels, standing on every side of the throne, where the living figures and the elders were, in thousands of thousands, 12 and crying aloud, Power and Godhead, wisdom and strength, honour and glory and blessing are his by right, the Lamb that was slain. 13 And every creature in heaven and on earth, and under the earth, and on the sea, and all that is in it, I heard crying out together, Blessing and honour and glory and power, through endless ages, to him who sits on the throne, and to the Lamb. 14 Then the four living figures said, Amen; and the twenty-four elders fell prostrate, worshipping him who lives for ever and ever.

v. 8. 'Disclosed'; it is not clear in what sense. The Greek manuscripts have 'took it up'.

vv. 9, 10. Some of the Greek manuscripts have 'them' and 'they' instead of 'us' and 'we'.

v. 11. The Greek has, 'in ten thousands of ten thousands, and thousands of thousands'.

v. 12. 'Godhead'; the Greek here has 'riches', and it seems likely that the Latin version arose from a faulty reading.

v. 13. 'And on the sea, and all that is in it'; this is perhaps the best account to give of the Latin text here, but it is curious that 'on' and 'in' should be rendered by the same preposition in Latin. The Greek text seems to be 'every creature in heaven and on earth, and under the earth, and on the sea, and all that is in them'; it is hard to see that the last six words add anything to the sense.

v. 14. The last seven words of this verse are of doubtful authority in the Greek, and are missing in some Latin manuscripts.

THE DESCENT OF THE HOLY GHOST

SCHOOL OF AMIENS
around 1480

COURTESY OF THE ART INSTITUTE OF CHICAGO

Chapter Six

Then, in my vision, the Lamb broke open one of the seven seals, and with that I heard one of the four living figures say, in a voice like thunder, Come and look. 2 So I looked, and saw there a white horse, whose rider carried a bow; a crown was given him, and he rode out victorious, and to win victory. 3 And when he broke the second seal, I heard the second figure say, Come and look; 4 and a second horse came out, fiery-red, whose rider was empowered to take away all peace from the world, bidding men slay one another; and a great sword was given to him. 5 And when he broke the third seal, I heard the third figure say, Come and look; so I looked, and saw there a black horse, whose rider carried in his hand a pair of scales; 6 I thought, too, I heard a voice that came from where the living figures were. A silver piece, it said, for a quart of wheat, a silver piece for three quarts of barley; but do the wine and the oil no hurt. 7 And when he broke the fourth seal, I heard the voice of the fourth living figure say, Come and look. 8 So I looked, and saw there a cream-white horse; its rider was called Death, and Hell went at his bridle-rein; he was allowed to have his way with all the four quarters of the world, killing men by the sword, by famine, by plague, and through wild beasts that roam the earth. 9 And when he broke the fifth seal, I saw there, beneath the altar, the souls of all who had been slain for love of God's word and of the truth they held, 10 crying out with a loud voice, Sovereign Lord, the holy, the true, how long now before thou wilt sit in judgement, and exact vengeance for our blood from all those who dwell on earth? 11 Whereupon a white robe was given to each of them, and they were bidden to take their rest a little while longer, until their number had been made up by those others, their brethren and fellow servants, who were to die as they had died. 12 Then, in my vision, he broke the sixth seal; and with that there was a great earthquake, and the sun grew dark as sackcloth, and the whole moon blood-red; 13 the stars of heaven fell to earth, like unripe fruit shaken from a fig-tree, when a high wind

v. 1. 'Come and look'; most of the Greek manuscripts, here and in the parallel passages lower down, have simply, 'Come'.

v. 6. These are famine prices, at which a labourer would have to spend the whole of his day's wages to provide bread for himself alone.

rocks it; 14 the sky folded up like a scroll, and disappeared; no mountain, no island, but was removed from its place. 15 The kings of the world with their noblemen and their captains, men of wealth and of strength, all alike, slaves and free men, took shelter in caves and rock-fastnesses among the hills. 16 Fall on us, they said to the hills and the rocks, and hide us from the presence of him who sits on the throne, and from the vengeance of the Lamb. 17 Which of us can stand his ground, now that the great day, the day of their vengeance, has come?

v. 17. 'Their vengeance'; the Greek manuscripts have 'his vengeance'.

Chapter Seven

AND NOW I SAW FOUR angels, standing at the world's four corners, and holding back the four winds of the world, so that no wind should blow on land or sea, or upon any of the trees. 2 And I saw a second angel coming up from the east, with the seal of the living God. And he cried out with a loud voice to the four angels who were empowered to lay waste land and sea; 3 Do not lay waste land or sea or wood, until we have put a seal on the foreheads of those who serve our God. 4 Then I heard the count of those who were sealed, a hundred and forty-four thousand of them, taken from every tribe of the sons of Israel. 5 Twelve thousand were sealed from the tribe of Juda, twelve thousand from the tribe of Ruben, twelve thousand from the tribe of Gad; 6 twelve thousand from the tribe of Aser, twelve thousand from the tribe of Nephthali, twelve thousand from the tribe of Manasse; 7 twelve thousand from the tribe of Simeon, twelve thousand from the tribe of Levi, twelve thousand from the tribe of Issachar; 8 twelve thousand from the tribe of Zabulon, twelve thousand from the tribe of Joseph, twelve thousand from the tribe of Benjamin. 9 And then I saw a great multitude, past all counting, taken from all

vv. 4-8. The list makes no mention of Dan; St. Irenaeus and other authors think that this was because Antichrist was expected to come from that tribe.

nations and tribes and peoples and languages. These stood before the throne in the Lamb's presence, clothed in white robes, with palm-branches in their hands, 10 and cried with a loud voice, To our God, who sits on the throne, and to the Lamb, all saving power belongs. 11 And all the angels that were standing round the throne, round the elders and the living figures, fell prostrate before the throne and paid God worship; 12 Amen, they cried, blessing and glory and wisdom and thanksgiving and honour and power and strength belong to our God through endless ages, Amen. 13 And now one of the elders turned to me, and asked, Who are they, and whence do they come, these who are robed in white? 14 My Lord, said I, thou canst tell me. These, he said, have come here out of the great affliction; they have washed their robes white in the blood of the Lamb. 15 And now they stand before God's throne, serving him day and night in his temple; the presence of him who sits on the throne shall overshadow them. 16 They will not be hungry or thirsty any more; no sun, no noonday heat, shall fall across their path. 17 The Lamb, who dwells where the throne is, will be their shepherd, leading them out to the springs whose water is life; and God will wipe away every tear from their eyes.

Chapter Eight

THEN HE BROKE OPEN the seventh seal; and, for about half an hour, there was silence in heaven.

2 And now I saw seven trumpets given to the seven angels who stand in God's presence. 3 There was another angel that came and took his stand at the altar, with a censer of gold; and incense was given him in plenty, so that he could make an offering on the golden altar before the throne, out of the prayers said by all the saints. 4 So, from the angel's hand, the smoke of the incense went

v. 3. 'Make an offering . . . out of the prayers'; in the Greek, 'put it upon the prayers', which are thus represented as live coals in the angel's thurible.

v. 4. 'Kindled by', literally 'from'; the

up in God's presence, kindled by the saints' prayer. 5 Then the angel took his censer, filled it up with firebrands from the altar, and threw it down on to the earth; thunder followed, and mutterings, and lightning, and a great earthquake. 6 And now the seven angels with the seven trumpets made ready to sound them. 7 When the first sounded, there was a storm of hail and fire, mingled with blood, that fell on the earth, burning up a third part of earth, burning up a third of the trees, burning up all the green grass on it. 8 And when the second angel sounded, it was as if a great mountain, all in flames, fell into the sea, turning a third part of the sea into blood, 9 and killing a third of all the creatures that live in the sea, and wrecking a third of the ships. 10 And when the third angel sounded, a great star fell from heaven, burning like a torch, fell upon a third part of the rivers, and on the springs of water. 11 The name of this star is Wormwood; and it changed a third of the water into wormwood, till many died of drinking the water, so bitter had it become. 12 And when the fourth angel sounded, a third of the sun and a third of the moon and a third of the stars were smitten with darkness, so that the day must go without light for a third of its length, and the night too. 13 And I heard, in my vision, words spoken by an eagle that flew across the middle part of heaven, crying aloud, Woe, woe, woe to all that dwell on earth, when those other calls are sounded by the three angels whose trumpets have yet to sound.

Chapter Nine

ND when the fifth angel sounded, I saw where a star had fallen from heaven to earth. 2 This star was entrusted with the key of that shaft which leads to the abyss. 3 So it opened the shaft which leads to the abyss, and smoke rose from the shaft as smoke rises from a great furnace, till the smoke rising from the shaft darkened both the sun and the air. 4 And out of the smoke a swarm of locusts spread over the world, endowed with such power for mischief as scorpions have on earth; they were not to injure the grass on the land, the green things that grew there, or the trees; they were to attack men, such men as did not bear God's mark on their foreheads. 5 These they had no power to kill, only to inflict pain on them during a space of five months; such pain as a man feels when he has been stung by a scorpion. 6 (When those days come, men will be looking for the means of death, and there will be no finding it; longing to die, and death will always give them the slip.) 7 The semblance of these locusts was that of horses caparisoned for war; on their heads they wore a kind of circlet that shone like gold, and their faces were like human faces; 8 they had hair like women's hair, and teeth like lions' teeth. 9 They wore breastplates that might have been of iron, and the noise of their wings was like the noise of chariots, drawn at full speed by many horses into battle. 10 It was their tails and the stings in their tails that made them like scorpions, and with these they were empowered to do men hurt for a space of five months. And they fought under a king; 11 their king was the angel of the abyss, whose name in Hebrew is Abaddon, in Greek Apollyon, that is, in Latin, the Exterminator. 12 Of the three woes that were pronounced, one is now past; the two others are still to come.

v. 11. The Latin equivalent is not given here by the Greek manuscripts.

13 And when the sixth angel sounded, I heard a voice that came from the four corners of the golden altar which stands in the presence of God. 14 It said to the sixth angel, as he stood there with his trumpet, Release the four angels who are imprisoned by the great river, the river Euphrates. 15 So these were released, four angels who were waiting for the year, the month, the day, the hour, when they were to destroy a third part of mankind. 16 And the muster of the armies that followed them on horseback (for I heard their muster called) was twenty thousand armies of ten thousand. 17 This is what I saw in my vision of the horses and of their riders; the riders had breastplates of fiery-red, and blue, and brimstone yellow, and the horses' heads seemed like the heads of lions, with fire and smoke and brimstone coming out of their mouths. 18 This fire, this smoke, this brimstone that came out of their mouths were three plagues, from which a third part of mankind perished. 19 The power these horses have to do mischief lies in their mouths and in their tails; their tails are like serpents, with serpents' heads, and they use them to do hurt. 20 The rest of mankind, that did not perish by these plagues, would not turn away from the things their own hands had fashioned; still worshipped evil spirits, false gods of gold and silver and brass and stone and wood, that can neither see, nor hear, nor move. 21 Nor would they repent of the murders, the sorceries, the fornications, and the thefts which they committed.

Chapter Ten

AND now I saw a second angel of sovereign strength coming down from heaven, with a cloud for his vesture, and a rainbow about his head; with a face bright as the sun, and legs like pillars of fire. 2 He carried in his hand an open book. Setting his right foot on the sea, and his left on the dry land, 3 he cried with a loud voice, like the roaring of a lion; and as he cried, the seven thunders of heaven made their voices heard. 4 And I, when the seven thunders had finished their utterance, was making as if to write it down, when I heard a voice say from heaven, Do not write down the message of the seven thunders, keep it sealed. 5 Then that angel, whom I had already seen with his feet on the sea and on the dry land, lifted up his right hand towards heaven, 6 and swore on oath by him who lives through endless ages, who made heaven and all that is in heaven, earth and all that is on earth, the sea and all that is in the sea. He swore that there should be no more waiting; 7 when the time came for the seventh angel to make himself heard, as he stood ready to sound his trumpet, God's secret design, made known by his servants the prophets, would be accomplished. 8 Then once more I heard the voice speaking to me from heaven, thus: Go and take the open book from the hand of that angel, whose feet are on the sea and on the dry land. 9 So I went to the angel, bidding him give me the book. Take it, he said, and eat it; it will turn thy belly sour, though in thy mouth it be as sweet as honey. 10 So I took the book from the angel's hand and ate it; it was sweet as honey in my mouth, but my belly turned sour once I had eaten it. 11 Then he said to me, Thou art to make a fresh prophecy, which concerns many peoples, many races, many languages, and many kings.

v. 6. 'No more wait-ing'; literally, 'no more time', in which sense many commen-tators have under-stood the passage.

484

Chapter Eleven

HEN I was given a reed, shaped like a wand, and word came to me, Up, and measure God's temple, and the altar, and reckon up those who worship in it. 2 But leave out of thy reckoning the court which is outside the temple; do not measure that, because it has been made over to the Gentiles, who will tread the holy city under foot for the space of forty-two months. 3 Meanwhile I will give the power of prophecy to my two witnesses; for twelve hundred and sixty days they shall prophesy, dressed in sackcloth; 4 these are the two olive-trees, the two candlesticks thou knowest of, that stand before him who is Lord of the earth. 5 Does anyone try to hurt them? Fire will come out from their mouths and devour such enemies of theirs; that will be the end of all who try to do them hurt. 6 These two have it in their power to shut the doors of heaven, and let no rain fall during the days of their ministry; they can turn the waters into blood, and smite the earth with any other plague, whenever they will. 7 Then, when they have borne me witness to the full, the beast which comes up out of the abyss will make war on them, and defeat and kill them. 8 Their bodies will lie in the open street, in that great city which is called Sodom or Egypt in the language of prophecy; there, too, their Lord was crucified. 9 For three days and a half, men of every tribe and people and language and race will gaze at their bodies, those bodies to which they refuse burial; 10 and all who dwell on earth will triumph over them, and take their ease, and send presents to one another; such a torment were these two prophets to all that dwell on the earth. 11 Then, after three and a half days, by God's gift the breath of life entered into them, and they rose to their feet, while great dread fell on all who watched them. 12 Then they heard a loud voice from heaven, Come up to my side; and, while their enemies watched them, they went up, amid the clouds, to heaven. 13 At that hour there was a great earthquake, which overthrew a tenth of the city; the count of those who were killed by the earthquake was seven thousand, and the rest were filled with dread, and acknowledged the glory of God in heaven. 14 So the second of the three woes that were pronounced is past, and the third will come speedily.

15 Then the seventh angel sounded, and with that, a great cry

vv. 2, 3. The forty-two months, or twelve hundred and sixty days, represent three and a half years. These, with the three and a half days of v. 11, recall the 'time, times, and half a time' of Dan. xii. 7 (cf. xii. 14 below).

v. 4. Cf. Zech. iv. 3 and following.

v. 6. Cf. James v. 17, Ex. vii. 20.

v. 11. The language of prophecy is here exchanged for that of narrative, the apostle being so absorbed by his vision that he feels plunged, as it were, into the events he is describing.

was raised in heaven, The dominion of the world has passed to the Lord of us all, and to Christ his anointed; he shall reign for ever and ever, Amen. 16 And the twenty-four elders who sit enthroned in God's presence fell prostrate, worshipping God and crying out, 17 Lord God Almighty, who art, and ever wast, and art still to come, we give thee thanks for assuming that high sovereignty which belongs to thee, and beginning thy reign. 18 The heathen have vented their rage upon us, but now the day of thy retribution has come; the time when thou wilt judge the dead, rewarding thy servants, prophets and holy men and all who fear thy name, little or great, and destroying the corrupters of the world. 19 After this, God's heavenly temple was thrown open, and the ark of the covenant was plain to view, standing in his temple; and there were lightnings, and mutterings, and an earthquake, and a great storm of hail.

Chapter Twelve

AND NOW, IN HEAVEN, a great portent appeared; a woman that wore the sun for her mantle, with the moon under her feet, and a crown of twelve stars about her head. 2 She had a child in her womb, and was crying out as she travailed, in great pain of her delivery. 3 Then a second portent appeared in heaven; a great dragon was there, fiery-red, with seven heads and ten horns, and on each of the seven heads a royal diadem; 4 his tail dragged down a third part of the stars in heaven, and flung them to earth. And he stood fronting the woman who was in childbirth, ready to swallow up the child as soon as she bore it. 5 She bore a son, the son who is to herd the nations like sheep with a crook of iron; and this child of hers was caught up to God, right up to his throne, 6 while the mother fled into the wilderness, where God had prepared a place of refuge for her, and there, for twelve hundred and sixty days, she is to be kept safe.

7 Fierce war broke out in heaven, where Michael and his angels fought against the dragon. The dragon and his angels fought on their part, 8 but could not win the day, or stand their ground in heaven any longer; 9 the great dragon, serpent of the primal age, was flung down to earth; he whom we call the devil, or Satan, the whole world's seducer, flung down to earth, and his angels with him. 10 Then I heard a voice crying aloud in heaven, The time has come; now we are saved and made strong, our God reigns, and power belongs to Christ, his anointed; the accuser of our brethren is overthrown. Day and night he stood accusing them in God's presence; 11 but because of the Lamb's blood and because of the truth to which they bore witness, they triumphed over him, holding their lives cheap till death overtook them. 12 Rejoice over it, heaven, and all you that dwell in heaven; but woe to you, earth and sea, now that the devil has come down upon you, full of malice, because he knows how brief is the time given him. 13 So the dragon, finding himself cast down to earth, went in pursuit of the woman, the boy's mother; 14 but the woman was given two wings, such as the great eagle has, to speed her flight into the wilderness, to her place of refuge, where for a year, and two years, and half a year she will be kept hidden from the serpent's view. 15 Thereupon the serpent sent a flood of water out of his mouth in pursuit of the woman, to carry her away on its tide; 16 but earth came to the woman's rescue. The earth gaped wide, and swallowed up this flood which the dragon had sent out of his mouth. 17 So, in his spite against the woman, the dragon went elsewhere to make war on the rest of her children, the men who keep God's commandments, and hold fast to the truth concerning Jesus. 18 And he stood there waiting on the sea beach.

v. 14. Literally, 'a time, times, and half a time' (but cf. verse 6 above), the mystical reckoning of Daniel's vision (vii. 25).

v. 18. Some manuscripts read 'I stood' for 'he stood'.

Chapter Thirteen

AND OUT OF THE SEA, in my vision, a beast came up to land, with ten horns and seven heads, and on each of its ten horns a royal diadem; and the names it bore on its heads were names of blasphemy. 2 This beast which I saw was like a leopard, but it had bear's feet and a lion's mouth. To it the dragon gave the strength that was his, and great dominion. 3 One of its heads, it seemed, had been mortally wounded, but this deadly wound had been healed. And now the whole world went after the beast in admiration, 4 falling down and praising the dragon for giving the beast all this dominion; praising the beast too. Who is a match for the beast? they asked; Who is fit to make war upon him? 5 And he was given power of speech, to boast and to blaspheme with, and freedom to work his will for a space of forty-two months. 6 So he began to utter blasphemy against God, blasphemy against his name, against his dwelling-place and all those who dwell in heaven. 7 He was allowed, too, to levy war on the saints, and to triumph over them. The dominion given to him extended over all tribes and peoples and languages and races; 8 all the dwellers on earth fell down in adoration of him, except those whose names the Lamb has written down in his book of life, the Lamb slain in sacrifice ever since the world was made. 9 Listen to this, you that have ears to hear with. 10 The captor will go into captivity; he who slays with the sword must himself be slain with the sword. Such good ground have the saints for their endurance, and for their faithfulness.

11 Then, from the land itself, I saw another beast come up; it had two horns like a lamb's horns, but it roared like a dragon. 12 And it stood in the presence of the former beast, to carry out all that it was empowered to do, bidding the world and all its inhabitants worship the former beast, that beast whose deadly wound was healed. 13 Such wonders could it accomplish, that it brought down fire, before men's eyes, from heaven to earth; 14 and by these wonders, which it was enabled to do in its master's presence, it deluded the inhabitants of the world, bidding those who

vv. 8-14. The Greek here (except in v. 11) gives the verbs in the present or future, not in the past tense.

v. 10. The reading here is uncertain, both in the Greek and in the Latin. It is probable that the first clause means, 'He who is marked out for captivity, must go into captivity', and possible that the following clause means, 'and he who is marked out for death, must go to his death'; cf. Jer. xv. 2. In that case, the sense is that Christians must submit to persecution without resistance; and the last part of the sentence should be rendered, 'Such are the

488

dwell in it set up an image to that beast which was smitten with the sword, and lived. 15 Further, it was able to put life into that beast's image, so that even the beast's image uttered speech; and if anyone refused to worship the image of the beast, it had him put to death. 16 All alike, little and great, rich and poor, free men and slaves, must receive a mark from him on their right hands, or on their foreheads, 17 and none might buy or sell, unless he carried this mark, which was the beast's name, or the number that stands for his name. 18 Here is room for discernment; let the reader, if he has the skill, cast up the sum of the figures in the beast's name, after our human fashion, and the number will be six hundred and sixty-six.

endurance and the faithfulness which belong to the saints.'

v. 18. Both in Greek and in Hebrew, the letters of the alphabet are used for numerical figures. In Greek, the letters of Latinus, in Hebrew, the letters of Nero Caesar, would add up to the required sum, but these identifications are uncertain.

Chapter Fourteen

HEN I looked, and saw where the Lamb stood on mount Sion, amidst a company of a hundred and forty-four thousand, with his name, and his Father's name, written on their foreheads. 2 And I heard a sound from heaven, louder than water in full flood, or heavy thunder. This sound which I heard seemed to come from harpers, playing on their harps, 3 as they sang a new song, there before the throne, and the living figures, and the elders. It was a song none else might learn to sing but the hundred and forty-four thousand that came ransomed from the earth. 4 These have kept their virginity undefiled by the touch of woman; these are the Lamb's attendants, wherever he goes; these have been ransomed for God and the Lamb as the first-fruits of mankind. 5 Falsehood was not found on their lips; they stand there untainted before the throne of God.

6 I saw, too, another angel flying in mid-heaven, carrying with him a final gospel to preach to all those who dwell on the earth, to every race and tribe and language and people. 7 Fear the Lord, he cried aloud, and give him the praise; the hour of his judgement has come. Fall down before him who made heaven and earth, and the sea, and the springs of water. 8 A second angel followed, who cried out, Babylon, great Babylon has fallen; she who made all the nations drunk with the maddening wine of her fornication. 9 And

v. 6. 'Final'; literally 'eternal'. It is not clear why the 'gospel' preached by the angel is so described; but the context suggests that it is the last call to repentance which will be offered to men this side of eternity.

these were followed by a third angel, who cried aloud, Whoever worships the beast and his image, or wears the beast's mark on forehead or hand, 10 he too shall drink; but the wine he shall drink is God's anger, untempered wine poured out in the cup of his vengeance. Fire and brimstone shall be his torment, in the presence of the holy angels, in the presence of the Lamb. 11 The smoke of their torment goes up for ever and ever; day and night no rest is theirs, who worshipped the beast and his image, who bore the mark of his name. 12 This is the test which the saints endured, keeping true to God's commandment, and the faith of Jesus. 13 I heard a voice, too, from heaven, Write thus: Blessed are the dead who die in the Lord. Yes, for ever henceforward, the Spirit says; they are to have rest from their labours; but the deeds they did in life go with them now.

14 Then, in my vision, a white cloud appeared; and on this cloud sat one who seemed like a son of man, with a crown of gold on 15 his head, and a sharp sickle in his hand. And now, from the temple, came another angel, crying out to him who sat on the cloud, Put in thy sickle, and reap; the crop of earth is dry, and the time has come to reap it. 16 So he who sat on the cloud put in his sickle, and earth's harvest was reaped. 17 Then another angel came from the heavenly temple; he too had a sharp sickle. 18 And from the altar came another angel, the same that had power over the fire on it, and cried aloud to the angel with the sharp sickle, Put in thy sharp sickle, and gather the grapes from earth's vineyard; its clusters are ripe. 19 So the angel put in his sickle over the earth, and gathered in earth's vintage, which he threw into the great wine-press of God's anger; 20 and when the wine-press was trodden out, away from the city, blood came from the wine-press, and reached as high as a horse's bridle, sixteen hundred furlongs off.

Chapter Fifteen

HIS was another great portent I saw in heaven, and a strange one; seven angels, the bearers of seven plagues, those last plagues by which the vengeance of God is finally achieved. 2 I saw, too, what might have been a sea of glass, tinged with fire. And by this sea of glass the victors were standing, safe now from the beast, and his image, and the mark of his name, with harps of God's fashioning. 3 Theirs is the song of God's servant Moses, theirs is the song of the Lamb. Lord God almighty, they cry, the deeds thou doest are great and wonderful; King of all the ages, thy ways are just and true. 4 Lord, who alone art holy, who shall refuse reverence and glory to thy name? All the nations shall come and fall down before thee, now that thy just retribution has been made known. 5 Then, as I looked, the tabernacle that bears record in heaven opened its inner shrine, 6 and the seven angels who bear the seven plagues came out of the shrine, clad in pure white linen, with golden girdles at their breasts. 7 And one of the four living figures gave to these seven angels seven golden cups, filled with the vengeance of God, who lives for ever and ever. 8 Meanwhile, God's majesty and power filled the whole shrine with smoke, so that none could enter the shrine until the plagues borne by the seven angels had run their course.

v. 3. 'The song of Moses' refers presumably to Ex. xv. It is not clear whether 'the song of the Lamb' is a song inspired by the Lamb, or one which had the Lamb for its theme; in the latter case, it refers perhaps to verse 12 above. For 'king of the ages' some of the best Greek manuscripts have 'king of the nations'.

Chapter Sixteen

HEN I heard a loud voice coming from the shrine, that said to the seven angels, Go and pour out the seven cups of God's vengeance on the earth. 2 The first angel went on his errand, pouring out his cup on to the earth; whereupon an ulcer broke out, malignant and troublesome, upon all the men who bore the beast's mark, and worshipped his image. 3 And the second angel poured out his cup over the sea, where it turned into blood, as if murder had been

491

done there, till every living creature in the sea was dead. 4 And the third poured out his cup over the rivers and the springs of water, where it turned into blood. 5 Then I heard the angel of the waters cry out, Holy thou art, O Lord, and wast ever holy, and this is a just award of thine, 6 blood to drink for those who have shed the blood of thy saints and prophets; it is their due. 7 I heard another, too, saying from the altar, Yes, the judgements thou dost pronounce, Lord God almighty, are true and just. 8 The fourth angel poured out his cup over the sun, which thereupon was given power to afflict mankind with burning heat; 9 and in the great heat which burned them, men blasphemed the name of God, who disposes of these plagues, instead of repenting, and giving praise to him. 10 And the fifth angel poured out his cup where the beast's throne was; and with that, all the beast's kingdom was turned into darkness, in which men sat biting their tongues for pain, 11 finding cause to blaspheme the God of heaven in their pains and their ulcers, instead of finding cause for repentance in their ill deeds. 12 And the sixth angel poured out his cup over the great river Euphrates, whose waters dried up, to make a passage for the kings that march from the East.

13 Then, in my vision, three unclean spirits appeared in the form of frogs; one from the mouth of the dragon, one from the mouth of the beast, and one from the mouth of his false prophet. 14 These are devilish spirits that can do miracles, and find access to all the kings of the world, bidding them meet in battle when the great day comes, the day of almighty God. 15 (Behold, I come as the thief comes; blessed is he that keeps watch, and is ready clad, so that he has no need to go naked, and be ashamed in men's sight.) 16 The place where they are bidden to meet is the place called in Hebrew, Armagedon.

17 And the seventh angel poured out his cup over the air. Then a loud voice came out of the shrine, a voice which cried from the throne, It is over; 18 and there were lightnings and mutterings and thunder, and a violent earthquake; since man came into the world there was never an earthquake so great and so violent as this. 19 The great city broke in three pieces, while the cities of the heathen came down in ruins. And God did not forget to minister a draught of his wine, his avenging anger, to Babylon, the great city. 20 Gone were all the islands, and the mountains were no more to be seen. 21 And hailstones as big as a talent-weight fell upon mankind out of heaven, till men cursed God for his plague of hail, so great it was, and so grievous.

v. 7. 'I heard another, too, saying from the altar'; in the Greek, I heard, too, the altar saying'.

v. 13. 'The false prophet'; that is, apparently, the second Beasts (xiii. 11).

v. 15. This verse is a parenthesis, which insists upon the suddenness of God's visitations; cf. Matthew xxiv. 18, II Cor. v. 3.
v. 16. The Latin here has 'he will gather them'; in the Greek, 'they gathered them'.

v. 19. 'The great city' may be Jerusalem (xi. 8); but some commentators understand a double reference in this verse to Babylon, that is, Rome.

492

Chapter Seventeen

AND NOW ONE OF THE angels that bear the seven cups came and spoke to me. Come with me, he said, and I will shew thee how judgement is pronounced on the great harlot, that sits by the meeting-place of many rivers. 2 The kings of the world have committed fornication with her; all the dwellers on earth have been drunk with the wine of her dalliance. 3 Then, in a trance, he carried me off into the wilderness, where I saw a woman riding on a scarlet beast, scrawled over with names of blasphemy; it had seven heads, and ten horns. 4 The woman went clad in purple and scarlet, all hung about with gold and jewels and pearls, and held a golden cup in her hand, full to the brim with those abominations of hers, with the lewdness of her harlot's ways. 5 There was a title written over her forehead, The mystic Babylon, great mother-city of all harlots, and all that is abominable on earth. 6 I saw this woman drunk with the blood of saints, the blood of those who bore witness to Jesus; and I was filled with great wonder at the sight. 7 But the angel said to me, Why dost thou find cause for wonder? I will disclose to thee the mystery of this woman, and of the beast she rides, with its seven heads and ten horns. 8 The beast thou sawest is that which lived once, and now is dead; soon it must rise from the abyss, and find its way to utter destruction. The sight of this beast which lived once, and now is dead, will strike awe into every dweller on earth, except those whose names have been written, before the world was, in the book of life. 9 Here is need for a discerning mind. These seven heads are seven hills; upon these the woman sits enthroned. They are also seven kings; 10 of these, five have fallen already, one is reigning now; the last has not come yet, but when he does, his reign will be a short one. 11 And the beast which lived once and now is dead must be reckoned as the eighth, yet it is one of the seven; now it is to find its way to utter destruction. 12 And the ten horns which thou sawest are ten kings, who have not yet received their royal title, but are to enjoy such power as kings have, for one hour, in succession to the beast. 13 All of them have a

vv. 8-11. It has been conjectured that the seven kings are the emperors Augustus, Tiberius, Gaius, Claudius, Nero, Vespasian, and Titus (Galba, Otho, and Vitellius being regarded as usurpers). There seems to have been a popular legend that Nero was not really dead, or perhaps would come to life again; he would thus be one of the seven and yet, as reincarnate, count as an eighth. If this interpretation is right, the present passage seems to allude to the short reign of Titus as the seventh king, and to identify his successor, Domitian, as a reincarnation of Nero, whose persecuting policy he revived.

v. 12. 'In succession

493

---

single policy; they surrender to the beast the power and the dominion which is theirs. 14 And they will fight against the Lamb, but the Lamb will have the mastery of them; he is Lord of all lords, King of all kings; whoever is called, is chosen, is faithful, will take his part. 15 Then he told me, These waters in thy vision, at whose meeting the harlot sits enthroned, are all her peoples, nations, and languages. 16 And the ten horns, which the beast had in thy vision, will become the harlot's enemies; they will lay her waste, and strip her quite bare, eat her flesh away, and then burn down what is left of her. 17 God has put it into their hearts to carry out his design, and to give their dominion over to the beast, so that at last all the words of God may be fulfilled. 18 And as for the woman of thy vision, she is that great city that bears rule over the rulers of the earth.

to the beast'; the Greek has 'together with the beast'.

v. 16. 'The ten horns, which the beast had in thy vision'; the Greek has, 'the ten horns in thy vision, together with the beast'.

Chapter Eighteen

AFTER this I saw another angel, entrusted with great power, come down from heaven; earth shone with the glory of his presence. 2 And he cried aloud, Babylon, great Babylon is fallen; she has become the abode of devils, the stronghold of all unclean spirits, the eyrie of all birds that are unclean and hateful to man. 3 The whole world has drunk the maddening wine of her fornication; the kings of the earth have lived in dalliance with her, and its merchants have grown rich through her reckless pleasures. 4 And now I heard another voice from heaven say, Come out of her, my people, that you may not be involved in her guilt, nor share the plagues that fall upon her. 5 Her guilt mounts up to heaven; the Lord has kept her sins in remembrance. 6 Deal with her as she has dealt with you; repay her twice over for all she has done amiss; brew double measure for her in the cup she has brewed for others; 7 requite her with anguish and sorrow for all her pride and luxury. She tells herself, Here I sit enthroned like a queen; widowhood is not for me, I shall never know what it is to mourn; 8 and all her plagues shall come upon her in one day, death and mourning and famine, and she will be burned to the ground; such power has the God who is her judge.

v. 6. 'As she has dealt with you'; in the Greek, 'as she has dealt with others'. If the sentence be understood in this way, it is best to regard it as addressed to the angels in heaven, not to the martyrs.

THE LAST JUDGEMENT

HUBERT VAN EYCK

METROPOLITAN MUSEUM, NEW YORK

9 How they will weep over her and beat their breasts, those kings of the earth who once lived in dalliance and took their pleasures with her, as they see the smoke rise where she burns! 10 Standing at a distance, for fear of sharing her punishment, they will cry out, Alas, Babylon the great, alas, Babylon the strong, in one brief hour judgement has come upon thee! 11 And all the merchants of the world will weep and mourn over her; who will buy their merchandise now? 12 Their cargoes of gold and silver, of precious stone and pearl, of lawn and purple, of silk and scarlet; all the citrus wood, the work in ivory and precious stone and brass and iron and marble; 13 cinnamon and balm, perfume and myrrh and incense, wine and oil and wheat and fine flour, cattle and sheep and horses and chariots, and men's bodies, and men's souls. 14 It is gone from thee, the harvest thy soul longed for; all that gaiety and glory is lost to thee, and shall never be seen any more. 15 The merchants that grew rich from such traffic will stand at a distance from her, for fear of sharing her punishment, weeping and mourning; 16 Alas, they will say, alas for the great city, that went clad in lawn and purple and scarlet, all hung about with gold and jewels and pearls; 17 in one brief hour all that wealth has vanished. The sea-captains, too, and all that sail between ports, the mariners and all who make their living from the sea, stood at a distance, 18 crying out, as they saw the smoke rise where she was burning, What city can compare with this great city? 19 They poured dust on their heads, and cried aloud, weeping and mourning, Alas, alas for the great city, whose magnificence brought wealth to all that had ships at sea; in one brief hour she is laid waste. 20 Triumph, heaven, over her fall, triumph, you saints in heaven, apostles and prophets; God has avenged you on her.

21 And now an angel, of sovereign strength, lifted up a stone like a great mill-stone and cast it into the sea, crying out, So, with one crash of ruin, will Babylon fall, the great city, and there will be no trace of her any more. 22 Never again will men listen there to the music of harper and of minstrel, of flute-player and trumpeter; never again will the craftsmen of all those crafts be found in thee, never again the grinding of a mill heard in thee; 23 never again the light of lamps shining, never again the voice of bridegroom and of bride. Once the great men of the earth were thy purveyors; once thy sorceries bewitched the world. 24 The blood of prophet and saint lay at her doors; the blood of all that were ever slain on the earth.

v. 13. The word 'balm' is omitted, probably by an error of printing, in the Clementine edition of the Vulgate.

v. 17. 'Between ports'; literally, 'to a place', according to the Greek. Some Latin manuscripts have 'to the lake', apparently through the misreading of a single letter.

Chapter Nineteen

AFTER this I heard, as it seemed, the voices of countless multitudes crying out in heaven, Alleluia; salvation and glory and power belong to our God; 2 his sentence is ever true and just, and now he has given sentence against the great harlot, who poisoned the earth with her harlot's ways; now he has called her to account for the blood of his servants. 3 And again they cried, Alleluia, the smoke of her burning goes up everlastingly. 4 Then the twenty-four elders and the four living figures fell down and worshipped God, where he sits enthroned, crying, Amen, Alleluia. 5 And a voice came from the throne, which said, Praise our God, all you that are his servants, and all you that fear him, little and great alike; 6 whereupon I heard, as it seemed, the noise of a great multitude, like the noise of water in flood, or the noise of deep thunder, as they cried out, Alleluia, the Lord our God, the Almighty, has claimed his kingdom; 7 let us rejoice and triumph and give him the praise; the time has come for the wedding-feast of the Lamb. His bride has clothed herself in readiness for it; 8 hers it is to wear linen of shining white; the merits of the saints are her linen.

9 And now the angel said to me, Write thus: Blessed are those who are bidden to the Lamb's wedding-feast. All this is true, he said; it is God's own utterance. 10 Thereupon I fell at his feet, to worship him. But he said, Never that; keep thy worship for God; I am only thy fellow servant, one of those brethren of thine who hold fast the truth concerning Jesus. It is the truth concerning Jesus that inspires all prophecy.

11 Then, in my vision, heaven opened, and I saw a white horse appear. Its rider bore for his title, the Faithful, the True; he judges and goes to battle in the cause of right. 12 His eyes were like flaming fire, and on his brow were many royal diadems; the name written there is one that only he knows. 13 He went clad in a garment deep dyed with blood, and the name by which he is called is the Word of God; 14 the armies of heaven followed him, mounted on white horses, and clad in linen, white and clean. 15 From his mouth came a two-edged sword, ready to smite the nations; he will herd them like sheep with a crook of iron. He treads out for them the wine-press, whose wine is the avenging

v. 3. It is not certain that the words 'the smoke of her burning goes up everlastingly' are represented as part of the triumph-song.

v. 8. 'The merits'; literally, 'the things which justify them'.

v. 10. St. Augustine thinks that St. John mistook the Angel (cf. xvii. 1 above) for Christ himself; but the ground on which the Angel refuses his worship seems to be that St. John, too, was a prophet. Some think that the passage is a warning against the worship of Angels mentioned in Col. ii. 18.

v. 15. Ps. ii. 9, Is. lxiii. 3.

anger of almighty God. 16 And this title is written on his cloak, over his thigh, The King of kings, and the Lord of lords.

17 And I saw an angel standing in the sun's orb, who cried aloud to all the birds that hovered in mid-air, Come and gather at God's great feast, 18 where you shall eat the flesh of kings, the flesh of captains, the flesh of the strong, the flesh of horses and their riders, the flesh of all mankind, free men and slaves, the little and the great. 19 And then I saw the beast and the kings of the earth muster their armies, to join battle with the rider on the white horse and the army which followed him. 20 The beast was made prisoner, and with it the false prophet that did miracles in its presence, deluding all those who bore the beast's mark and worshipped its image; and both were thrown alive into the fiery lake that burns with brimstone. 21 All the rest were slain by the sword of that horseman, the sword that comes from his mouth; and all the birds feasted on the carrion, and had their fill.

Chapter Twenty

I SAW, TOO, AN ANGEL come down from heaven, with the key of the abyss in his hand, and a great chain. 2 He made prisoner of the dragon, serpent of the primal age, whom we call the devil, or Satan, and put him in bonds for a thousand years, 3 thrusting him down to the abyss and locking him in there, and setting a seal over him. He was not to delude the world any more until the thousand years were over; then, for a short time, he is to be released. 4 Then I saw thrones prepared for those to whom judgement was committed; I saw the souls of all those who went to execution for love of the truth concerning Jesus, and of God's word, and all who would not worship the beast, or its image, or bear its mark on their foreheads and their hands. These were endowed with life, and

vv. 2-7. This passage gave rise to the error of the Millenarians, who held (as some Jewish authors held) that Christ would reign on earth, in visible triumph, for the period of a thousand years, between the Second Coming and the Final Judgement. Catholic expositors identify the thousand years with an indefinite but prolonged period between the Resurrection and the Second Coming in Judgement (which

497

reigned as kings with Christ for a thousand years; 5 but the rest of the dead remained lifeless while the thousand years lasted. Such is the first resurrection. 6 Blessed and holy is his lot who has a share in this first resurrection; over such a second death has no power, they will be priests of God, priests of Christ; all those thousand years they will reign with him. 7 Then, when the thousand years are over, Satan will be let loose from his prison, and will go out to seduce the nations that live at the four corners of the earth—that is the meaning of Gog and Magog—and muster them for battle, countless as the sand by the sea.

8 They came up across the whole breadth of the earth, and beleaguered the encampment of the saints, and the beloved city. 9 But God sent fire from heaven to consume them, and the devil, their seducer, was thrown into the lake of fire and brimstone, where, like himself, the beast 10 and the false prophet will be tormented day and night eternally.

11 And now I saw a great throne, all white, and one sitting on it, at whose glance earth and heaven vanished, and were found no more. 12 Before this throne, in my vision, the dead must come, great and little alike; and the books were opened. Another book, too, was opened, the book of life. And the dead were judged by their deeds, as the books recorded them. 13 The sea, too, gave up the dead that lay there, and death and hell gave up the dead they imprisoned, and each man was judged according to his deeds, 14 while death and hell were thrown into the lake of fire. This is the second death; 15 everyone must be thrown into this lake of fire, unless his name was found written in the book of life.

Chapter Twenty=one

Then I saw a new heaven, and a new earth. The old heaven, the old earth had vanished, and there was no more sea. 2 And I, John, saw in my vision that holy city which is the new Jerusalem, being sent down by God from heaven, all clothed in readiness, like a bride who has adorned herself to meet her husband. 3 I heard, too, a voice which cried aloud from the throne, Here is God's tabernacle pitched among men; he will dwell with them, and they will be his own people, and he will be among them, their own God. 4 He will wipe away every tear from their eyes, and there will be no more death, or mourning, or cries of distress, no more sorrow; those old things have passed away. 5 And he who sat on the throne said, Behold, I make all things new. (These words I was bidden write down, words most sure and true.) 6 And he said to me, It is over. I am Alpha, I am Omega, the beginning of all things and their end; those who are thirsty shall drink—it is my free gift—out of the spring whose water is life. 7 Who wins the victory? He shall have his share in this; I will be his God, and he shall be my son. 8 But not the cowards, not those who refuse belief, not those whose lives are abominable; not the murderers, the fornicators, the sorcerers, the idolaters, not those who are false in any of their dealings. Their lot awaits them in the lake that burns with fire and brimstone, and it is the second death.

9 And now an angel came and spoke to me, one of those seven who bear the seven cups charged with the seven last plagues. Come with me, he said, and I will shew thee that bride, whose bridegroom is the Lamb. 10 And he carried me off in a trance to a great mountain, high up, and there shewed me the holy city Jerusalem, as it came down, sent by God, from heaven, 11 clothed in God's glory. The light that shone over it was bright as any precious stone, as the jasper when it is most like crystal; 12 and a great wall was raised high all round it, with twelve gates, and twelve angels at the gates, and the names of the twelve tribes of Israel carved on the lintels; 13 three gates on the east, three on the north, three on the

v. 5. 'These words I was bidden write down'; literally, 'He says to me, Write it down'. It is not clear whether this direction was given by the Voice from the throne, or by the Angel mentioned in xvii. 1 (who is clearly the speaker in xix. 9, although the word 'angel' does not occur in the original).

v. 16. 'Are every-
where equal', not, pre-
sumably, equal to one
another, which would
make the city nearly
1500 miles high,
whereas the next
verse gives the height
of the wall as 144
cubits. More prob-
ably the meaning is
that the height of the
city was uniform at
every point, as its
length and its breadth
were.

south, three on the west. 14 The city wall, too, had twelve foundation stones; and these, too, bore names, those of the Lamb's twelve
apostles. 15 The angel who was speaking to me had a rod of gold
for a rule, to measure the city, and its gates, and its wall. 16 The
city lies foursquare, the same in its length as in its breadth, and
when he measured it with his rod, he counted twelve thousand
furlongs. Length and breadth and height are everywhere equal.
17 And when he measured its wall, he counted a hundred and
forty-four cubits, reckoned by the measure of a man, that is, of an
angel. 18 The fashioning of its wall was of jasper, but the city
itself was pure gold, that seemed to have the purity of glass. 19 And
the foundations of the city wall were worked in every kind of
precious stone. The first foundation was a jasper, the second a
sapphire, the third a chalcedony, the fourth an emerald; 20 the
fifth a sardonyx, the sixth a sardius, the seventh a chrysolite, the
eighth a beryl; the ninth a topaz, the tenth a chrysoprase, the
eleventh a jacynth, the twelfth an amethyst. 21 And the twelve
gates were twelve single pearls, one pearl for each gate; and the
street of the city was of pure gold, that seemed like transparent
glass. 22 I saw no temple in it; its temple is the Lord God Almighty,
its temple is the Lamb. 23 Nor had the city any need of sun or
moon to shew in it; the glory of God shone there, and the Lamb
gave it light. 24 The nations will live and move in its radiance;
the kings of the earth will bring it their tribute of praise and
honour. 25 All day the gates will never be shut (there will be no
night there), 26 as the nations flock into it with their honour and
their praise. 27 Nothing that is unclean, no source of corruption
or deceit can ever hope to find its way in; there is no entrance but
for those whose names are written in the Lamb's book of life.

Chapter Twenty=two

HE SHEWED ME, TOO, A river, whose waters give life; it flows, clear as crystal, from the throne of God, from the throne of the Lamb. 2 On either side of the river, midway along the city street, grows the tree that gives life, bearing its fruit twelvefold, one yield for each month. And the leaves of this tree bring health to all the nations. 3 No longer can there be any profanation in that city; God's throne (which is the Lamb's throne) will be there, with his servants to worship him, 4 and to see his face, his name written on their foreheads. 5 There will be no more night, no more need of light from lamp or sun; the Lord God will shed his light on them, and they will reign for ever and ever.

6 Then the angel said to me, These words are sure and true. The Lord God who inspires his prophets has sent his angel to tell his servants what must soon find its due accomplishment. 7 Patience, I am coming soon. Blessed is he who holds fast the words prophecy this book contains. 8 All this I, John, heard and saw, till, hearing and seeing it, I fell down as if to worship at the feet of the angel who revealed it to me. 9 But he said, Never that; I am only a fellow servant of thine, and of thy brother prophets, and of all who hold fast the words which this book contains. Keep thy worship for God.

10 Then the command came to me, Do not seal up the words of prophecy that are contained in this book; the time is close at hand. 11 Meanwhile, the wrongdoer must persist in his deeds of wrong, the corrupt in his corruption, the just man in winning his justification, the holy in his life of holiness. 12 Patience, I am coming soon; and with me comes the award I make, repaying each man according to the life he has lived.

13 I am Alpha, I am Omega, I am before all, I am at the end of all, the beginning of all things and their end. 14 Blessed are those who wash their garments in the blood of the Lamb; so they will have access to the tree which gives life, and find their way through the gates into the city. 15 No room there for prowling dogs, for sorcerers and wantons and murderers and idolaters, for anyone who

v. 2. It is likely enough that the trees are represented as bearing twelve different kinds of fruit, but St. John's language does not make this certain.

v. 6. 'The angel said to me'; literally, 'he said to me'.

v. 9. See note on xix. 10 above.

v. 10. 'The command came to me'; literally, 'he said to me'. The context seems to indicate that our Lord is here the speaker, not the angel, as in verse 6.

v. 14. Some Greek manuscripts have 'those who carry out his commandments', instead of 'those who wash their garments'. The words 'in the blood of the Lamb' are not given in the

501

Greek, or in most
Latin manuscripts.

v. 19. For 'the book
of life', the Greek
(followed by many
Latin manuscripts)
has 'the tree of life';
our text probably
arises from a mis-
take in the Latin.

v. 20. The words
'Be it so' represent
'Amen' in the Greek,
which is attached by
some commentators
to the sentence which
goes before it.

v. 21. The best read-
ing in the Greek here
is 'with the saints',
or 'with all the saints',
not 'with you all':
many of the Greek
manuscripts omit the
word 'Amen'.

loves falsehood and lives in it. 16 I, Jesus, have sent my angel to give you the assurance of this in your churches; I, the root, I, the offspring of David's race, I, the bright star that brings in the day. 17 The Spirit and my bride bid me come; let everyone who hears this read out say, Come. Come, you who are thirsty, take, you who will, the water of life; it is my free gift.

18 To all who hear the words of prophecy this book contains, give this warning. If anyone adds to them, God will add to his punishment the plagues which this book threatens; 19 and if any-one cancels a word in this book of prophecy, God will cancel his share in the book of life, in the holy city, in all that this book promises. 20 And he who gives this warning says, Indeed I am coming soon. Be it so, then; come, Lord Jesus.

21 May the grace of our Lord Jesus Christ be with you all. Amen.

Linea Christi
Dauid secūdus rex Isrl'
Anno mūi. 40 85.

Roboam · 420 5.

Abya · 4222.

Asa · 422 5.

Josaphat

Joram

Uzias

chabab Prim̄ūamō

Salomon Rex

Joakthan

mas · 3º Abolon

Achas

Ezechias

Manasses